ISBN 978-1-4675-7211-8

F … CONTENTS

BOOK ORDERING:

See last page - Send to Lew White, or

TORAH INSTITUTE
PO Box 436044
LOUISVILLE, KY 40253-6044

www.fossilizedcustoms.com
www.torahzone.net

WHAT IS THIS BOOK ABOUT?

Primarily, it's about our "walk", which explains the footprint on the cover. Everyone has questions, and they want to know if they have it right, or not. This book is intended to address the unanswered questions that lurk in the back of many people's minds. It exposes the lies, and reveals the truth. The origins of popular customs have been a life-long study of mine, and revealing them to others in a way that *makes sense* is my main goal here. To most, the information presented here will be new and ***shocking***. Please realize that anything in this study can be easily verified, and I encourage you to do some research on your own ~ in this way, you will have **facts** that you can believe, rather than just mysterious traditions. Try to be objective, and not "filter" the **facts** through what you've chosen to **believe**, or a denominational bias. No one alive is responsible for having woven together the Pagan designs we are embedded in, and even those who did it I do not judge. As with any audience, there are those who will read this that are my superior in knowledge. But, the plan of our Creator is so simple, that being wise in certain specialized disciplines may be of little use. A small child can understand the secret that is locked in the Scriptures, but when the meaning is distorted, comprehension suffers. There are dozens of excuses for maintaining the status quo, but once the truth is available to the average person, hiding behind lies invented by men long-dead is useless. The distortions of the Truth came about because Paganism became **mixed** into it, and the "**bride**" (wife of the Creator) was attacked, along with the **Covenant** (a marriage covenant). Religion shouldn't be about killing people who are different. The Inquisition burned and tortured millions of people to death for having just come in contact with a ***little*** truth. Now let's allow the facts to expose the Greco-Roman roots, or "Replacement Theology". The true roots of our faith are HEBREW - and are based on **TORAH**. The Messiah is the *Mediator* of the re-newal of the Covenant, which is the *Torah written in our heart*. If we turn to the left, or turn to the right, we must listen to the voice of our Teacher, who says,

"This is the way, walk in it."

11th EDITION

WRITTEN FROM A NATSARIM ISRAELITE PERSPECTIVE

A Restoration of Our ***Israelite Roots***

Engrafting into Israel

"Even the stork in the sky knows her appointed times. And a turtledove, and a swallow, and a thrush observe the time of their coming ~ but My people do not know the ordinance of Yahuah."

- Jeremiah (Yirme Yahu) 8:7. (The people had stopped observing the appointed times (moedim), and had begun to observe the festivals of the Gentiles ~ read chapters 7—10 of Yerme Yahu).

"Seek Yahuah, all you humble of the land, you who do what He commands. Seek righteousness, seek humility; perhaps you will be sheltered on the day of Yahuah's anger." Zephaniah (Zefan Yah) 2:3.

A REFERENCE TO THE "NEW COVENANT"*:

"I will give you a new heart and put a new spirit in you; I will remove from you your heart of stone and give you a heart of flesh. And I will put My Spirit in you, and move you to follow My decrees and be careful to keep My Laws." - Ezek. 36:26,27.

HYPOTHESIS: Due to compromise, syncretism, ignorance, confusion, and the intentional deceit of humanity by fallen spatial beings, mythological Pagan designs were assimilated into the lives of most every person on Earth. Unwittingly, humanity has embraced ancient Babylonian customs rooted in *sun worship.*

The customs were *re-invented* so as to have different meanings, yet behind them remain the cunning ruses of an ancient spatial being, who seeks to be worshipped by means of trickery, perpetrated upon everyone alive. There is *so much* Paganism active in cultures today, there can be no doubt that it was deceitfully placed into our traditions, then through fraud and disguise, obscured with new meanings. This ***camouflaged Paganism*** pollutes and rots the spiritual condition of all mankind, yet a little flock has always held on to the true faith delivered to those set apart. Here in the last days, the final message is now going out to the ends of the Earth. This book is written from the perspective that there is a Creator, as well as a spiritual enemy loose on Earth; and that the Scriptures of the Hebrew prophets are all true.

Hopefully, this book will lift some of humanity out of the dense fog of history, and awaken people who are dreaming, as they walk into a new dawn of living — with an eternal perspective. Love, the most powerful force in the universe, will save your life.

*OR ***RENEWED COVENANT***, *REFRESHED COVENANT*
HEBREW: ***BRITH CHADASHA***

Fossilized Customs

THE PAGAN SOURCES OF POPULAR CUSTOMS

ARE YOU READY TO GO TO THE NEXT LEVEL?

"He who answers before listening ~ that is his folly and his shame." Prov. 18:13.

In this book, you will discover the true origins of many cherished customs. They come from Babylonian sun worship, cleverly "inculturated" into Christianity over many centuries of darkness.

Wreaths, branches, boughs, and trees had been used by Pagans as emblems of fertility, used to decorate during the winter solstice, thought of as the "re-birth" of the sun. In their mythology, Nimrod had died and become the sun, worshipped as Baal (the **LORD**), Marduk, Mithras, Ahura Mazda, Gott, Aton, and Dagon. Later, the tree became the Cananites' image of **ASHERAH**, and *carried into the nations by the 10 lost tribes of Israel - the Samaritans.*

WHAT IS THIS TREE, *REALLY?*
DO RESEARCH, AND YOU'LL FIND OUT!

SMELL SOMETHING FUNNY, HONEY?

YOU WANTED THE TRUTH, SO HERE IT IS. THIS IS NOT FICTION.

YOU'LL *WISH* THIS WAS ONLY A BOOK

PAGAN CUSTOMS BECAME DISGUISED LONG AGO, AS MESSIANIC BELIEF DEVELOPED AMONG ANCIENT SUN-WORSHIPPING PEOPLES. THE PAGANS WERE ABSORBED, ALONG WITH THEIR RELIGIOUS MANNERISMS. A BLEND OF THE TRUTH MIXED WITH ABOMINATIONS OCCURRED. PAGAN CELEBRATIONS WERE ADOPTED TO REPLACE THE SCRIPTURAL OBSERVANCES. WITH EYES WIDE SHUT, BILLIONS ENTRUST THEIR ETERNITY TO MEN WHO EXPLOIT THEM, MASQUERADING AS MESSENGERS OF LIGHT.

This book is dedicated to Rabbi OWYAZ ha Mashiach of Nazareth, our High Priest, Sovereign Ruler, and Image of the Invisible Elohim; the Maker of heaven and Earth. Also to the goal of helping as many as possible be enabled to understand the message of the Kingdom, so they will be spared the awesome catastrophism ahead.

"Repent, for the Reign of Heaven draws near!"

~ WARNING ~

PREPARE YOURSELF FOR A SHOCK

YOUR HEART WILL BREAK WHEN YOU LEARN THE TRUTH

11th Edition, 2013 CE

Lew White

CHANGING THE WORDS OF OUR CREATOR RESULTS IN WHAT HE CALLS WORMWOOD

AMOS 5:7

Lew is a graduate of the University of Louisville, and has always been an avid student of history, culture, art, biology, cosmology, and has pursued a balanced, realistic understanding of Who the Creator of Heaven and Earth is, and what He expects of His Children, the human race.

The facts need to expose the **strongholds**.

There will always be those who will say,

"My mind is made up; don't confuse me with the facts."

For the rest, prepare to be challenged and set free by the Truth.

FOREWARD - LOOK UP THE WORD "GOD" IN A GOOD ENCYCLOPEDIA

THE FIRST THING that will go through your mind when you see the **fire** consume people around you will be something like, *"why didn't I do more to reach them with the Truth, so this may not have happened to them?"* (See 2Pet.3:7, Zech. 14, Mt. 3:12).

This is what Yahuah Shabuoth says: "In those days, ten men from all languages and nations will take firm hold of one Yahudi by the hem* of his robe and say, 'Let us go with you, because we have heard that Elohim is with you.'" Zec. 8:23	***"Brothers, children of Abraham, and you Elohim-fearing Gentiles, it is to us that this message of salvation has been sent."*** Acts 13:26 (The word "**GOD**" was used by ***translators*** in place of the Hebrew word "Elohim", meaning mighty one.) In this book, you will discover what other changes were made.

At first glance, this book might enrage the average person. By reading a little, you will begin to understand the Truth ~ that what we see in the traditions practiced by Christianity were originally pagan designs. We will show how they admit this is so. We will look at the Scriptures to see if this is valid behavior. If you have ever prayed for Truth, or if you are diligently seeking it, you may find this very helpful. We inherited the habits we have from people of long ago, so no one alive is responsible.

"Most people, sometime in their lives, stumble across truth. Most jump up, brush themselves off, and hurry on about their business as if nothing had happened."— Sir Winston Churchill.

To better understand things, this book will restore names and other words to the more accurate 'sound' of their originals. Letters, in any language, are symbols for sounds. Over the centuries, ***translating*** the Scriptures from Hebrew into Greek, then Latin, German, and English, led to some loss of meaning. This partly explains why people have difficulty understanding what the Scriptures are saying.

The idea of **translating** is to find the best word in your language that expresses the meaning of the original word. We say "hello", while a Hawaiian uses "aloha" for both "hello" and "good-bye". Similarly, "shalom" is used to say "peace", and is used as a greeting, or to signal departing. Many times an original Hebrew word is ***transliterated*** ~ which means the **sounds** of the original word are carried over using the letters of the new language. This is commonly done when there is no word in the new language that expresses the same idea. Hebrew is the inspired language. This is also the way we correctly "sound-off" or pronounce the names of people.

The Greek alphabet is incapable of transliterating the sound of the Messiah's Name, but the English alphabet is. Israel's former PM, **Benjamin NatanYahu**, has a Hebrew name that was properly ***transliterated*** in the English language. In his own ears, he can hear his name perfectly pronounced by people of any language! His name also has a meaning, but it would be improper to "translate" his name, or anyone's, just because someone of another language uses it. *Your* name retains the same **sound** out of the mouth of people of *any* language. If you make a friend with someone from Taiwan, they will do their best to pronounce your name as closely as they can to accurately address you as you are accustomed to hearing it. Distortions of people's names have occurred, and we will attempt to restore them to their closest originals in this book. "Noah" was really "Noach", having a "K" sound at the end of it. His son's name, "Shem", means "name". Noach may have named him this as a reminder of the Name of the Creator, which you will discover in this book. The word "Semites" is derived from Shem's descendants, the people who bear the Creator's Name, as referred to at Daniel 9:19. The "SH" sound was lost because Greek has no such sound; so, the more correct word is "Shemites". We inherited little errors here and there. Wouldn't it be great to be able to hear how the Mashiach's Name really sounded? If you can accept it, we will attempt to explain how that can be done.

TRUTH and LIES

Let's imagine you are 1000 feet in the air, standing on the high steel framework of a new skyscraper under construction. You are supported by each of the steel girders below you, and the massive concrete foundation resting on the bedrock of the Earth. Your primary interest at this point is your safety. The girders below must each be riveted well to one another; because if even ONE is just jammed in with no rivets, the whole structure could fall at any moment! Any girder with no rivets is like a lie, because you put your trust in it as if it were the truth. The only way to know if each girder is "true" is to closely examine each one. To ***appear*** to be a part of the structure is not enough in itself, because you place your trust in every girder below you believing they are "true". So, this book will shake and inspect some frameworks.

* THIS "HEM" REFERS TO THE **TSITSITH**, WORN BY YAHUSHA AND OBSERVANT ISRAELITES - Num. 15, Dt. 22

If you are on a framework built up on **100%** TRUTH, then you are safe. If this book can show you the "girders" that have no rivets, exposing the deceptions as the lies they really are, then you would be wise to re-evaluate remaining where you are.

"For with much wisdom comes much sorrow; the more knowledge, the more grief."
Eccl. 1:18 This book is to inform you and make you wise, and when you become aware, ***you will mourn.*** It would be senseless to defend a building which you knew had girders with no rivets. And it would be extremely hazardous to remain there. In fact, you would warn anyone who even went near it. Why? Because of LOVE. Your concern for others can become even greater than self-preservation. Lies are poison, but Truth is like fire; it tests the purity of metals, and refines them.

In the writings of Daniel 2, a metal image of a man is used to illustrate the kingdoms of the Earth ***over time.*** The purity of the metals and their successive devaluation over time is significant. First, the "head" (beginning) of gold represents the first "kingdom" on Earth, **Babylon**. It's man-made, ruled by men. Following, is the chest and arms of silver, belly of bronze, legs of iron, and feet composed of a ***mixture*** of iron and clay. The clay is sometimes thought of as people ruling themselves, as we understand in a democracy. That may be, but remember that the whole image, from head-to-toe, is man's attempt to rule himself. ***All*** of these kingdoms will perish, and man will not rule himself; the whole point is that our Creator is coming to restore the Earth. It is not our task to "fix" man's kingdom, or fight it, change it, argue about its economics, or struggle with it. Conquering, overpowering, killing, dividing, controlling - these are not things we do, but they are the things which men ruling themselves do. Lies have become mixed into civil government as well as moral government (Church, pulpit), yet trusted in as Truth. So, we are "called-out" of the kingdoms of men altogether. If we remain ignorant, we will be found participating in a process of traditions that date all the way back to Babylon, the head or beginning. A Rabbi from Natsarith came to deliver the message of the Kingdom: ***"Repent! For the Reign*** (Kingdom) ***of Yahuah draws near!"*** "Repent" means ***turn back****, turn around, or return.* The Rabbi was saying *"shub"* in His Hebrew tongue, not the Latin word, *repent.* Today, we ask *"What is your religion?"* The word ***"re-ligion"*** is also Latin; *"Re"* means "go back", start again, return. *"Ligare"* is the second part, meaning *"bind",* related to the word "ligament", which binds our bones together. So it would appear that even the Latin word "re-ligion" carries the idea that something became *unfastened!* It was man and his Creator. By tradition, lies have become mixed with Truth, and we will uncover, expose, or reveal to you some of the things we inherited from Babylon. ***They have become "fossilized" into our customs.*** You may not be able to comprehend and digest everything immediately, because there will be great emotional trauma resulting from what you are about to learn. Just hold on to the knowledge that the Truth will suffer no harm at all from the exposing of the lies. It is important to remain humble, continuing to learn. You can recognize a tree by its fruit. The fruit you should bear (show) is **love, joy, peace, patience, kindness, goodness, faithfulness, gentleness, and self-control.** This is the character of our Creator, and His children that walk (live, perform, work) in His teachings, His Commandments of love. They go against no law.

The real reason you have this information is because you have been called-out of the man-made kingdoms. What this book contains is not original, but is based on Scripture and many others' research work. Truth is more than entertaining facts - the search for Truth is what "science" and reality is. To know Truth is far from "believing" in a theory. The fact that the Messiah rose from the dead is the evidence that what we believe (His Word) is Truth. He is the first "re-born" from the dead, and the "first-fruits" of a great harvest to come. Since He spoke of Adam, Noach, Mosheh, Daniel, and the creation of the universe, then it happened the way the Writings explain it. The word "Scripture" is Latin, *scriptum,* meaning *hand-writing*).

ETYMOLOGY is the study of word origins. The word itself come from 2 Greek words, ***etumo*** (truth, true) + ***logos*** (word). So it means "true-word". Being a student of etymology makes you an *etymologist*. The ideal is to seek the origin of words all the way back to the confusion of tongues at Babel. If the whole world was originally speaking one language, what was it? Since the Creator had conversations with Adam and many others before the Flood, all His children spoke His language, rather than Him adapting to theirs. The Creator has been with us all through history, and all the prophets spoke and wrote in His language. Etymology can be thought of as an archaeological tool! The Hebrew word **EMET** means *"truth",* then later became the Greek word ETUMO. EMET is the root of another Hebrew word, EMUNAH, which means *faithfulness,* *steadfastness,* and *fidelity.* Emunah is most commonly translated to the English word FAITH. ***"The tsedek*** (righteous) ***shall <u>live</u> by his emunah.*** (faith)***"*** Hab. 2:4

THIS BOOK'S PURPOSE is to expose the origins of everyday beliefs, customs, and rituals that have become camouflaged in new meanings. Common activities performed today have passed down from ancient Pagan cultures, and are often claimed to be "secular", yet are perfectly preserved religious witchcraft, or nature worship (i.e., Halloween/ Samhain/Saween). Mythological Paganism, superstition, belief in MAJIK, and ignorance were tolerated over the past 19+ centuries in order for our political and religious ancestors to maintain control with a minimum of effort. The true model all mankind is supposed to live by was abandoned and outlawed. Our modern traditions could easily have been based on what is true, but instead Pagan syncretisms were used to fuse together error and truth - poisoning the clean waters we wish to educate our children with. This fusion of lies and truth overwhelmed our ancestors, so we have inherited the lies and profane patterns. Secret brotherhoods have passed much of this knowledge down through the centuries, never allowing the common people access to it, because it would cause disruption and a loss of their control. These "illuminated" men, the Adepts, would often speak to one another in Latin, (*Italic,* meaning *hidden*), to keep their secrets safe. Because Latin is a "dead" language, the meaning of words doesn't undergo change. It will become apparent that this Earth is ruled by man-made domains, focused into 3 main groups: Ecclesiastical, Political, and Mercantile. Presently, these are under the control of a fallen spatial being called Satan, who oversees many masquerading "angels of light". There is so much Pagan design in the cultures of the world, that it is utterly amazing that it could have gone on for so long without more men standing up to it. This book is written in obedience to Ephesians 5:6-11.

<u>ANTI-LAW TEACHERS</u> vs. dying to sin . . . . .

DO WE NEED TO OBEY THE COMMANDMENTS?

WHAT WOULD SATAN TELL YOU?

IF YOU GET THIS ANSWER INCORRECT, YOU'RE DOOMED.

> *"Satan himself masquerades as a messenger of light . . . His servants also masquerade as servants of righteousness . . ."*

The political machine is used to "exterminate" whatever threatens the authority of the religious establishment. The Mashiach could have *"fixed their wagon"* when He was being beaten to a bloody mess, but He didn't raise a finger. Reading the Writings (Scripture) by "laity" was ***banned*** in 1229 CE, because it would be readily seen that the "system" was off-course.

(CE means *Christian Era,* or *Common Era**).

"The understanding of this <u>message</u> will bring sheer terror" ~ so wrote a prophet called "Isaiah" (really *Yesha Yahu*) at 28:19. The **message: ***"Repent! For the Reign of 𐤉𐤄𐤅𐤄 draws near!"*** While the **Torah** of the Creator was taught, the vineyard (mankind) was green (growing) and fruitful (peaceful) because the ***living waters*** provided life to the soil. The Torah, or Commanded Teachings, produce peace. By removing the living waters, the vineyard becomes "dry", withers, and the dead branches will be burned up. A "**key**" of knowledge has been withheld from the people: the Personal Name of the Creator! When the Bridegroom returns, those unwise "virgins" who think they will have a place in the household of Yahuah, will be turned away; having had *insufficient* ***light*** to find their way. The "apostles" knew their way, and you can too. It's narrow, straight, and very easy to follow the path, because *it's written down in the best-selling textbook in the history of the world:* Scripture! Men have struggled to corrupt it, ignore it, and *trick people out of obeying what it says.* The first woman was told by the father of lies, *"You shall certainly not die"* (for ignoring Yahuah's Word). The liar is now leading millions to "just believe", and disobey the Torah ~ they say, "it's not even for you!" And, it's working like a dream. WWJD? (What Would J-sus Do) ~ well, the ***Rabbi*** would definitely still *obey the Torah*; after all, He is the law-giver! (The term **"rabbi"** means *my teacher*, and is ***transliterated*** 17 times in the Messianic Writings. It was used many *more* times, because whenever you see the word "teacher" or "master", the original word was most likely *rabbi*). This Hebrew word is not found in the TaNaKh. Learning from <u>drunken</u> (men in a stupor who don't understand) <u>merchants</u> (men who fleece the sheep), the message of the Reign of Yahuah sounds like ***"do and do, rule on rule, a little here, a little there"***. The message is "sealed" to them, because they have not received a love for the **Truth** (they have not received a <u>love</u> for the **Torah**, Wisdom). ***"For you this whole vision is nothing but words sealed in a scroll"*** Is. 29:11. ***"These people come near to Me with their mouth and honor me with their lips, but their hearts are far from me. Their worship of me IS MADE UP ONLY OF RULES TAUGHT BY MEN"***

***C.E. - CAN ALSO MEAN "COMMON ERROR"**

****The "message" (BESORAH) of the Kingdom is the <u>Torah</u>, what we "turn back" to.**

Is. 29:13.
Now, lets find out which parts are "man-made" and not a part of the Eternal Kingdom.

"You will not see Me again, until you say, 'baruch haba bashem 𐤄𐤅𐤄𐤉'" Mt. 23:39 / Ps. 118:26. — Natsarim are saying it again! Remember, Paul was a "ringleader of the ***sect of the Natsarim***", not the "sect of Christianity" (see Acts. 24:5). WE ARE ENGRAFTED INTO ISRAEL; Ephesians 2:8-13, Romans 11.

CONSTANTINE

HOW THEY INVENTED YOUR WORLD

Doctrines of Demons

THE OBJECTIVE of the enemy of your soul is to keep you from the truth, and waste your time so you'll die without it. He must distract you, or lead you to think other "smarter" or "educated" men have it all figured, and all you have to do is get dunked, go to a Sun-day assembly, and pay, pay, pay. Arise, shine, for your light has come!
Soon, you will know more than your denomination's preacher about what Scripture teaches.

CAMOUFLAGED PAGANISM

"Doctrine" means *teaching.* It's a Latin word, related to "document" (written instruction) and "doctor", meaning "teacher". We have all been trained or *programmed* from birth with various traditions, rituals, and customs; all paganism is targeted at children. How we keep track of ***time*** is a world-wide type of programming. Here we will look into how we came to be trained to think of and organize time ~ in our *days, months,* and *years.*

One of the first things we do when we awake each day is check the **time**. Originally, the **hours** of daylight were measured using a **sundial**, and the shadow of the sun marked off 12 "hours" until it set. The marked hours on the dial pass more quickly in the winter months, and slower in the summer months. The variance in the length of an hour is less important than knowing where you are in time relative to the whole day, so this system worked fine. There was no "daylight-saving-time" trick to deal with! However crazy the sundial seems to us, the gaining and losing of an hour is at least as weird. There were always 12 hours in every "daytime". "Noon", Latin *nones* (9), was the 9th hour after sunrise, or 3 p.m. in the ancient world.

Each day of the week was originally referred to by a **number**. The 7th day also had a name: *Shabbat*, meaning *rest.* Yes, even Adam and Chuwah, the first man and woman, observed the 7-day week. (There is no one named "Eve" in the Hebrew; this name was embraced to appease pagans because one of the names for their *Earth Mother* was "Eve" The name *Chuwah* is derived from the Hebrew word ***chai***, meaning "life" ~ thus her name means *mother of the living.* The ending *–ah* renders it feminine, similar to the ending in *Sarah*. *Sar* means prince, or ruler; *Sarah* means *princess*). If you check your "calendar", you will notice the days of the week have been given **names**. The names were taken from among Pagan peoples who honored their deities by ***calling the days by the names of their idols.***

SUN-DAY (day 1)
From Latin, *dies Solis*, the *Day-of-the-Sun.* Since Babylon was established, Pagans have worshipped the **Sun**. Here's a few of the names they've used: Baal, Bel, Shamash, Moloch, Ahura-Mazda, Dagon, Sol, Marduk, Mithras, Krishna, Amon-Ra, Aton, Woden (Odin, Adonis), Zeus, Deus, and the Druid / Teutonic "**God**". You may recall that the Pharaoh and the Caesar (Khazar/Czar) were worshipped as the sun. This began with the first king, **Nimrod**, discussed later. This pattern of worshipping the sun, moon, planets, and stars permeated the Babylonians, Persians, Chaldeans, Egyptians, Greeks, Romans, Celts, Mayans, Aztecs, and Indians. They were turned-over to worship the heavens (Acts 7:42). *The governments were the religion.* If they were "good" Pagans, at death they would be transported to the skies (Heaven) to live with their deities. This was called *Nirvana, Shambala,* or *Elysian Fields.* The Roman Consul/Emperor **Constantine I** gave us the term ***Sun-Day***, which referred to *Sol Invictus Mithras* (the unconquerable sun, Mithras). In 321 CE he decreed under the penalty of death that all artisans, merchants, and people of his Empire cease work on the *Venerable Day of the Sun*, to honor Mithras. This was a Universal Edict, and is still enforced in our western culture with our "blue laws". (Interestingly, the **government phone numbers** are printed on *blue pages* in our US phone books). It was a weekly ritual of sun-worshippers to assemble at dawn on this day to greet the sun at its rising. A great pillar, or sun-ray *obelisk* was the solar religion's primitive high place, condemned by Scripture as a "pillar of jealousy" ~ secretly interpreted as a male fertility symbol. Various tower designs such as steeples, pagodas, turrets, ziggurats, minarets, spires,

BAAL IS DEFINED AS "LORD", SO THE "LORD'S DAY" TRULY IS SATAN'S SABBATH - A DAY NOT BLESSED AS WAS YAHUAH'S SABBATH, THE SEVENTH DAY OF EACH WEEK obelisks, and pyramids have served Pagans well. The Temple did not have a high place, nor do synagogues. "Sacred pillars" were to be demolished - Yahuah hates them. These Pagan "high places" would receive the first hallowed rays of dawn. At this point, ***bells*** were rung by hand, as in a shaker-grid, and large ones were struck with oak logs swung horizontally. Gongs struck with hammers were especially fun for the Oriental Pagan, but they also used the familiar bell shape too. In the book, The Conquest of Peru, Prescott is an eye-witness to blatant sun-worship:

"The Inca would assemble at dawn eagerly. They watched the coming of the deity, and no sooner did his first yellow rays strike the turrets, than a shout of gratulation broke forth from the assembled multitude, the wild tunes from barbaric instruments swelled louder and louder as his bright orb shone in full splendor on his votaries."

The Romans considered anyone who did not worship the sun to be an atheist and a traitor, since Caesar was the sun enthroned in a man. Foreign beliefs found some tolerance in the Edict of Milan, 313 CE. Religion, politics, and sports were all different facets of the same thing. More discussion on Sun-Day will follow later.

MON-DAY

(day 2)

The *Day-of-the-Moon.* To the Romans, *lunae dies.*

The Old English term was *monan daeg,* as translated from Latin, where ***mona*** means *moon. Mona Lisa* means "**moon lily**". We get our word ***month*** (*moonth*) from *mona*, the 29.5 day orbital cycle, but this 2nd weekday is named what it is *because it has been dubbed the **moon's day***. The moon was identified with Artemis* (Diana), and in some cults the sun and moon were the 'eyes of heaven'. Artemis* is depicted with the crescent moon beneath her feet as if riding in a boat ~ exactly as you will see Miryam (Mary) in Roman Catholic illustrations. The Astral King, the sun, and his sister the moon, were the dominant figures that shaped the astro-biological mind. The futility of honoring Pagan deities resulted because their foolish hearts were darkened, because they did not honor or give thanks to the Creator, though His invisible attributes are clearly seen.

TUES-DAY (day 3)

Tyr's Day: "day of Tiu". Teutonic Druid-Celtic idol.

SIGN OF WODEN ⇦

Unable to help themselves, the population of the Angles and Saxons were kept under control by various Druid priest cults. Like any other Pagan religion, the population lived in fear and ignorance, while the **parasite** fed off of them and kept them brain-washed. The Druids still worship the sun at Stonehenge every Summer Solstice.

Tyr, or Tiu, was the Norse deity of **war,** considered the son of Odin (Woden). The French call this day ***Mardi*** (Mar's Day), after Mars, the Roman's deity of war! ***Mardi Gras*** is the French name meaning "fat Tuesday", still bearing the name of the Roman deity. This festival falls the day before *Ash Wednesday*, the beginning of *Lent*, both to be discussed later.

WEDNES-DAY (day 4)

Well, *DUH* ~ as expected by now, it's another Pagan idol's name! An elder in Iceland couldn't stand it anymore, and changed the days back to numbers for that island several hundred years ago. By saying it's "Wednesday"(Woden, Odin), we are declaring it to be *Woden's Day*. Considered highly skilled in magic (majik), this Celtic deity was, to the Teutonic Pagan, the husband of Freya, or *Frigga.* The Romans honored *Mercury* on this day, calling it *Mercurii dies*(Mercury's Day). This mid-week evening was highly regarded as a night of majik ~ the Druids met to hold hands in a **circle**, chant, enchant, cast spells, and do it while surrounding a **burning cross**, the symbol of Woden (Odin). Some believe the Celtic crux is a Pagan majik symbol, the *Trifolium clover leaf* representing *Woden, Frigga, and Thor.* Other Druid trinities included *Esus, Teutates, & Taranus.* Anglo-Saxon xenophobia (*fear of foreigners*) and Druid customs are seen today in the modern *Ku Klux Klan.* They still call their leaders *wizards* and use the Celtic term "clan", a traditional social unit in Scot Land. The word comes from the Greek *kuklos,* meaning "**circle**". A very secretive society, it rose up mainly in the South (US) after the civil war, to reassert "white supremacy" by terroristic methods. The Druids were *very* nationalistic, so it was difficult for Rome to conquer them. The only way "Christianity" could win them over was to *absorb* their culture. This is called *inculturation.* "Syncretisms" — the attempt to reconcile or combine differing beliefs in philosophy or religion by uniting them — mixes of two or more behaviors together, re-inventing the meaning "on the surface". Is this the real reason some Christians

****ARTEMIS** IS THE OLD DEITY **ASHERAH**, A PHOENICIAN CONSORT OF **BAAL** - A DEAL-BREAKER WITH YAHUAH*

THOR

FRIGGA:

SATYR:

meet together on this night? Catholics have always had a "novena" session on this night. **CHRISTIANOS** is the source word for **CRETIN**.
A dictionary defines Cretin* (kret'n) as *"a fool; and idiot.* [French ***cretin***, idiot, from Swiss French, *crestin,* CHRISTIAN". Sorry, *look it up yourself.* We will have a look at the word "Christian" as a translation of *Mashian* (a follower of any generic "messiah"/mashiach) a bit later. For now, let it be enough to say that the sect which was established by the true *Mashiach* was called ***Natsarim****. But most hang their hat on one text, or never question a translator's choices. Well, did you know that the word "Christian / Christians" is only used a total of 3 times in all of Scripture, and it is only in the Greek ***translation***? Woden's emblem was the Celtic Crux, a cross with the **circle** (the sun). No wonder we see so many pictures of crosses with the sun nimbus behind it, and sunsets in Christian art — not to mention the "halos" of yellow around the heads of "Jesus" and the "saints". This will be shown to be a world-wide Pagan influence; Buddha, Krishna, Ahura-Mazda, and Jupiter are only a few.
(*Now often called "NAZARENES")

THURS-DAY (day 5)

The Celtic *Thor's Day;* the deity of thunder and son of Woden and Freya. The same as *Taranus,* Thor was associated with thunder; the Dutch *donder,* or Germanic *donner* (one of Santa's reindeer!). The Romans honored *Jupiter* on this day, which was originally ***IU-PITAR***, meaning *Jovis-father.* "Jove" corresponds to *Zeus.* The altar of Zeus, used at every Olympic game, is lit by a torch. The altar is shaped like a "T". Thor's emblem was the hammer, secretly interpreted as the letter "T", harkening back to *Tammuz* (Babylonian *Duzu*), the son of Nimrod and Semiramis. "Zeus" was pronounced "DZEUS".

FRI-DAY (day 6)

Old English, *Frigedaeg,* this was Frey Day or Frigga Day. Frigga was the wife of Woden. The fertility concept associated with this day is very ancient. The Greeks honored ***Aphrodite*** on this day, and the Romans venerated *Venus* (Astarte). This day was the Egyptian's day of ***Isis***, depicted with the symbol of the fish on her head. The fish symbol pre-dates the Egyptians, coming from the Phoenician/Philistine cult of Dagon (Jdg. 16:23, 1Sa. 5:2). "Dag" is Hebrew for *fish,* and the Latin is *Pisces.* It was chosen by Pagans because a female fish lays hundreds, sometimes thousands, of eggs ~ a symbol of fertility. The Romans believed *Venus* (Astarte) came from the sky in a huge egg (not a saucer). We'll go into more detail when we study the Great Mother, Queen of Heaven (Asherah). Frigga's emblems were also mistletoe and the FISH, hence it is seen today that Roman Catholics ***inculturated*** this into avoiding red meat on this day, replacing it with fish: the "fish fry" (even the word "fry" is describing a young fish). The Great Mother (Magna Mater) was universally represented by the fish emblem. The Greek word ***ichthys*** (ikhthus) spelled iota (Ι), chi (Χ), theta (Θ), upsilon (Υ), sigma (Σ) — spells **"ICHTHYS"** ("fish"). ΙΧΘΥΣ doesn't mean "Christ", but ***fish***. With considerable craft, the fish has become a Christian symbol, due to a Greek anagram designed to utilize the Greek ICHTHYS, **Ιησουζ – Χριστοζ – θεου – Υιοζ – Σωτηρ** (**I**esous **C**hristos **Th**eou **H**uios **S**oter). *Not to worry*, it's only a man-made tradition—too bad it just spells "**fish**". The real "sign" of the Mashiach isn't a crux or a fish, but a "lampstand" (menorah) Rev. 1&2. The Hebrew "menorah" has 7 lamps, and represents His body, the **7 assemblies**, through which flows the "living water" (lamp oil, the laws which give light to the world). At Rev. 2:5 he said He would remove their ***menorah*** if they didn't repent (stop breaking Commandments). Have you noticed any menorahs in any Christian homes or meeting houses? Soon, you'll learn why — He never threatened to remove any *fish.*

SATUR-DAY (day 7)

This was the Greco-Roman *Day of Saturn.*
Saturn was the Romans' deity of agriculture, corresponding to the Greeks' deity *Cronus.* This day was dedicated to *Saturnus*, as was the big party at the end of the Roman year at the Solstice, *Saturnalia.* Satur Day was also called *Sater Day*, and is unmistakenly linked to other Greco-Roman mythology. The *SATYR,* a goat-legged half-man with horns and pointed ears, was believed to be a drunken, lecherous demon with an abnormal sexual appetite. The 7th day and the festival of

*CRETAN; IN SUNKRETIZEIN, TO UNITE IN THE MANNER OF THE CRETAN CITIES — CRETANS WERE ALSO KNOWN AS LIARS—TITUS 1:12

"Satyrnalia" was modeled perfectly after the satyr profile; mischievousness, drunkenness, and orgiastic revelry. As you consider the wild week-ends enjoyed today by dating couples and party animals with their "mojo" drives, it's clear nothing has changed.

Here's a big foundational girder with no rivets, installed by Constantine in the Roman year 321 CE. This 7th day, the <u>commemoration</u> of <u>Creation</u> in which we honor the Creator *AS* the Creator is a "Temple in time" from sunset "Frey Day" to sunset "Satyr Day" ~ changed to his "Sun-Day" under penalty of death, by only the authority of a man! All theologians and scholars admit there is no Scriptural basis for this change, but it was done by the authority of "the Church". ***Sabbath*** is the "sign" of the Everlasting Covenant, indicating who ***<u>we</u>*** worship, but most refuse the Covenant. This day which was set-apart (dedicated) at Creation to be a day of complete rest from work has been "superseded" by traditions that served to unite Pagans with the Natsarim sect. Constantine's historian, *Eusebius,* records the Emperor's edict: *"All things what so ever that is was duty to do on the* ***Sabbath****, these* ***WE*** *have transferred to the Lord's Day".* He also recorded Constantine's infuriated words, *"The cursed wretches who killed our Lord . . .* (the Italian Romans executed Him, Constantine's people) . . . *We will have NOTHING in common with the hostile rabble of the Yahudim* ("Jews")". Remember, the Romans executed our Natsarim Rabbi for *sedition*, or the claim that He was a king ~ Caesar ruled as a religious king.

***<u>A WORD ABOUT TIME</u>* ~**

Since Creation, just under 6000 years have been completed. Given the distances in *light years* that we can see into the heavens (outer space), many have fixed the age of the universe at almost 20 billion years. To look at Adam 5 minutes after he was created, they might estimate him to be 20 years old too. The trees with fruit on them were brought into being fully developed. The animals, created the day after the plants, needed the oxygen from the plants, that's possibly why the animals came second. Relativity has been at work also since the beginning. When Yahuah created the quasars and galaxies of stars, He **brought** their light to shine upon the Earth ~ that's what it says. That's why it's called *super*-natural. He created space-time. You just have to keep in mind just how *awesome* the true Creator is, instead of trying to figure out the whole scheme without factoring Him in.

The **real** moons and years are based on the signs and seasons, and measured in packages of years called *Jubilees* (Yob-hel), numbering 50 years each. However, the reprobate Pagan mind interpreted the sun, moon, stars, and changing seasons based on ***SEX***. That's what is at the root of all Paganism! Plant and animal sex is a created thing, but the fallen state of man caused him to worship it, and established Pagan religion based on its processes, as we will see. All of history was recorded by the "winners" — usually the tyrants. So, it is only natural that their process of measuring time be what we use today. The original pattern of Roman **time-keeping** established by the authority of Julius Caesar in 46 BCE is still with us (There were only **10 months** in a Roman year). Our Roman 'moonths' totally disregard the real new moons. The proclaiming of the new month settled into when Caesar **announced** it, and this act was called Caesar's *calends,* Latin for *proclaim.* Originally, the first Roman month was March. After you have read this a number of times, you may begin to see this Pagan process of keeping **time** is a kind of ***MARK*** on us.

<u>ROMAN TIME</u>: THE MONTHS

<u>**MARCH**</u> (1st month):

Named for the war deity ***Mars.***

When the weather began to show signs of warming, the Roman armies would '*march*' out to war. Marching is what armies have done ever since, to conquer in the power of the deity "Mars".

<u>**APRIL**</u> (2nd month): The month of Venus, also called *Aprilis,* from Etruscan *Apru,* from Greek *Aphro,* a short form of *Aphrodite,* the Greek fertility deity. This was the primary month of the Great Mother Earth, known by many names. The Earth Mother was "fertilized" or impregnated on a Sun-Day after the Vernal (Venus) Equinox (when the length of days and nights are equal). This Sun-Day was called "Easter". Prior to this, the Pagan priests imposed a "fast" from sexual relations. We get the term **LENT** from the Germanic word *lengten*, which refers to the *lengthening* of the days as winter turns to spring. The first day of this fast, the mark of Tammuz was placed on the foreheads of the worshippers, the ancient "TAU" (see page 204 palaeo-Hebrew). The 40th day prior to "Easter" was always a "Woden's Day", giving us the term *Ash Wednesday.* Nine months ***after*** the Earth Mother was impregnated at "Easter" (a gestation period), the SUN was "re-born" at the winter solstice, December 25th, further explained under "December".

<u>**MAY**</u> (3rd month): This month was named after the Italic fertility deity ***MAIA***.

<u>**JUNE**</u> (4th month): This was the month dedicated to ***JUNO***, an important Roman female deity, the wife and sister of Jupiter, identified with the Greeks' Hera. "Father's Day" was always in this month, and on a Sun-Day, because the sun was the Pagans' father. He was in his strength at the summer solstice, so you will notice this is still practiced.

**** A "SYNAGOGUE" IS AN ASSEMBLY, OR QAHAL, NOT A BUILDING***

<u>JULY</u> (5th month): This month was dedicated to Julius Caesar, the first emperor. He was honored as a deity, son of the sun.

<u>AUGUST</u> (6th month): This word is Latin meaning venerable, magnificent, awesome. Gaius Octavius took the name "Augustus Caesar" after becoming Emperor, and had his name used for this month. He did this to honor himself, as Julius had done before.

<u>SEPTEMBER</u> (7th month): This is the Latin word for the number "7" ~ ***septem***. Now things will begin to make sense a little, but hang on!

<u>OCTOBER</u> (8th month): This is the Latin word ***octo-ber***, "eighth month", from *OCTO,* meaning "eight".

<u>NOVEMBER</u> (9 month): This month was *Novembris*, from the Latin word ***novem***, meaning "nine".

<u>DECEMBER</u> (10th month): Latin *Decembris*, from the number ***decem***, ten. We get the word *decimal* from the Latin also.

All these months are shifted by ***two*** now, as you know. Even though we are saying "December", the Latin for "10", we number it the ***12th moon***. Rather than correcting this, we just keep it up. Not only that, but the whole beginning point is based on the "re-birth" of the sun! According to the Writings (Scripture), we are to begin our counting of the moons in what is called "spring", as the sun nears the equatorial region. The Creator has spoken, but man's kingdoms ignore Him. Speaking to the converts at Galatia, Paul mentions ***"You are observing special days and months and seasons and years!"*** Gal. 4:10. The Galatians were once Pagan, enslaved in the weak, miserable principles, turning back to that which was based in what was their heathen, Babylonian mythology (you must read this in context, because your footnotes will lead you to think Paul was speaking about Sabbaths, and the way the Creator established our "watch" in the skies). He said, ***"Let there be lights in the expanse of the sky to separate the day from the night, and let them serve as signs to mark seasons and days and years . . ."*** Gen. 1:14. It is written, ***"This month is to be for you the first month, the first month of your year"*** Ex. 12:2. He had to tell them, because they had been captive as slaves for over 400 years, and were now "called-out".

<u>JANUARY</u> & <u>FEBRUARY</u> With only 10 months in the Roman year, the seasons were appearing later and later every year! Julius Caesar began hearing many complaints, so he appointed an Alexandrian astrologer named ***Sosigenes*** to devise the needed corrections. Sosigenes added the 2 months of ***January*** and ***February*** to the year 46 BCE, and it was called the *year of confusion.* He even set up the cycle of *leap years*, which added a day to the month of February every 4 years. January is named for a domestic deity, ***Janus***, who was the ruler of "beginnings", and protected doorways, gates, and arches. You will recall processions through great "arches" when ancient kings would march their armies in triumphant display? February was named for the female idol ***Februa***. The authority to proclaim new moons, and change the system, resided with the Caesar; his seat of power ruled, and he was the *priest of Janus.* The Roman title, *Pontifex Maximus* is Etruscan, bestowed on Caesar as the Pagan head of the Pontifical College of Priests of Janus: the ***Cardinals***. "Cardinal" is Latin (*cardo*) meaning *hinge*. They assisted the priest of Janus in opening "the door" to the Elysian Fields, the Pagan "Heaven".

"Pontifex Maximus" means *highest priest* in Etruscan, so Caesar was the gateway to the after-life for a Roman Pagan. Julius Caesar's calendar is called the *Julian Calendar.* We now have the *Gregorian Calendar* because the title "Pontifex Maximus" was <u>inherited</u> by the Roman Catholic popes. The authority of Caesar was transferred to this bishop, the Roman Catholic pope! He also kept his "cardinals". This "Bishop of Rome" also uses Caesar's title, "*papa*" (pope), a Mithraic title. In 1582, "pope" Gregory implemented a 10-day adjustment to the calendar designed by Sosigenes, by *wiping out 10 days for that year.* This was obeyed by the "papal states", but the rest of the western world remained on the former timetable. It was not until the time of Benjamin Franklin that the rest of society came into line with Rome. Up to then, landowners thought they would lose 10 days' rents, but Franklin convinced them they would actually be receiving their rents 10 days *sooner* by obliging the pope; and so now we have the ***Gregorian Calendar***. This same pope authorized what is known as *Gregorian Chant*. These "chants" stem directly from Pagan monks' hymns, originally called *Orphic Hymns*, or the *Hymns of Orpheus.* He simply "sanctified " the Pagan hymns.

<u>NIMROD YEARS</u>

The Pagan priests were astrologers who closely monitored the positions of the sun, moon, 5 of the planets, and constellations of stars. These were the physical deities they worshipped, and they modeled time over their year based on **sex**. They knew the path of the sun "crossed" the celestial

THE DEIFICATION OF NIMROD, THE BUILDER OF BABYLON AND NINEVEH (LATER THE CAPITAL OF ASSYRIA), IS EXPRESSED IN MASONIC ICONOLOGY LIKE THE GREAT SEAL AT RIGHT.

THE GREAT SEAL

***TEQUFAH** (circuit. cycle) - when the sun reaches the equatorial region, plants respond bringing forth leaf buds, signaling that a cycle has begun—See Mt 24:32. Any cycle, i.e., a gestation

ATHENA

EASTER

♀♂

ISHTAR WITH LILIES

WREATH-CIRCLES WERE SYMBOLS OF THE WOMB OF THE DEITY, USED AT THE WINTER SOLSTICE

FLEUR-DE-LIS:

equator at the Vernal and Autumnal Equinoxes, producing equal days and nights at those events. So, who's "**Nimrod**"? He was the first king on the Earth, the grandson of Ham (see Gen. 10). His secular name is suspected to be Sargon I, and he built Babylon and Nineveh. It was possibly Nimrod who built the *Tower of Babel*, a ziggurat made of bricks; the ruins exist still. Nimrod was a ***tyrant***, and that is what his name means! He was a *"mighty hunter before Yahuah"*. The word "before" means "against" in the Hebrew if you check a concordance. Nimrod turned the people against the truth, and began the worship of the sky luminaries. Children were sacrificed in exchange for prosperity. He wore a headpiece with a "horn" in front as ruler, a symbol of power and authority. In fact, all crowns that are modeled with "horns" are based on this design. The marauding heathens of Ghengis Khan and the Vikings of the Norse wore horned hats and helmets in their wars. Nimrod's idolatry and ruthlessness caused his uncle, Shem, to destroy him, cutting his body into parts and distributing them around the kingdom. It is said Nimrod took his mother, **Semiramis** as a wife. At his death, his wife/mother consoled the people of Sumer by saying she carried Nimrod's child, and named him Tammuz. Nimrod, she explained, had gone into the heavens and was now the sun! So, the sun was the "father", and the Earth was now the "mother". Semiramis was, in effect, a deity representing the Earth. "Ish" is Hebrew for "man", and she was worshipped as "Ishtar". Babylonian pillars—obelisks– represented the generative powers of the male, and were simultaneously images of the phallus, Nimrod, and a sun-ray! Fertility rituals such as "May Pole" dances are still seen today. "Ishtar" is the same word we have today in "Easter", which superseded Passover. It's Nimrod's mother, also known around the world as **Asherah**, Astoreth, Ishtar, Eostre, Astarte, Maia, Gaia, Diana, Ninurta, Nana, Ceres, Ostara, Austron, Isis / Nut (the sky), Aphrodite, Venus, Indrani, Devaki, Tanit, Cybele, Artemis, **Athena** (pictured), and many others. The Canaanites called their shrines to the Earth Mother "**Asherim**".

<u>**EASTER**</u> (Jezebel brought this into Israel).

This word has been adopted from Pagans as an attempt to "inculturate" by syncretism a behavior that is absolutely an abomination. If you recognise "Halloween" for what it is, then this will be no different after you learn the truth. Easter was already one of the two biggest celebrations observed by Pagans, long before Christianity came along. It is my belief that when this is exposed, it will fulfill the prophecies of Revelation 18. Go read it now. Babylon is still with us, but it is going to fall. Easter was celebrated by the Assyrians, the Phoenicians, and the Philistines (Goliath, no doubt, had an *Easter basket*). You should look up "Easter" in a Webster's Dictionary, and do further research in other sources! This festival involved the *"Rites of Spring"* near the Equinox of Venus, when Pagans believed the Earth Mother was ***impregnated by the sun***. They engaged in ritual sex acts, and used symbols of fertility like eggs, rabbits, and "hot cross buns". The Babylonian symbol for the "female" was, and is, <u>a circle with a crux beneath</u>. The round cakes were baked for the "Queen of Heaven" (Regina Coeli), and "Great Mother" (Magna Mater), with the "**cross**" symbol <u>indicating the female</u>. The cross also indicated the Equinox, when the Earth's orbit "**crossed**" the celestial equator. Hold on now, because everything will be just fine. Stop and go read Jeremiah 44 right now. You'll see "**Asherah**" was this same Earth Mother, called the **Queen of Heaven**, which Israel committed sexual idolatry with*.

To ensure a prosperous growing season, Pagans rolled eggs decorated with bright colors of Spring on their fields, hoping to imbue fertility. These eggs were then hidden from "evil spirits" in rabbits' nests, another symbol of fertility. "Easter" is the ***name*** of the Babylonian "Mother of Harlots", Rev. 17, and her image stands as the sungoddess "Lady Liberty" in New York Harbor. This Colossus statue even has the "tower" headpiece, as seen worn by Artemis. The 7 horns or sunrays should be a strong indication of her true identity. Her emblem is the flower of the lily, seen illustrated with her on this page. An American society, the *Easter Seals Society,* uses the *fleur-de-lis* (French, *flower of the lily*) as their logo, and they have no religious affiliations whatsoever. Most "churches" decorate with the lilies on "Easter morning". Instead of inheriting the truth, they inherited Babylon! If we only study history as people, places, and dates without comprehending "why" things occurred as they did, then everything is unorganized. It's a junkpile. When you assemble it correctly, it all fits together perfectly, clarify-

****JEZEBEL LED NORTHERN ISRAEL INTO THIS PHOENICIAN/CANAANITE IDOLATRY WITH BAAL AND ASHERAH—SEE REV. 2:18-29***

ing the path we walk on. "Satan" ***disguises*** "himself" — "he" is quite often "female". We know "he" was behind Nimrod, as Moloch, Baal, Mithras, and so on; but "he" is also Ishtar. Sun-Day is "his" diversion; it's a lie. I refer to "Easter Sun-Day" as "**Beaster Sun-Day**". We don't have to wait for a "beast", it's here right now. The patterns and appointments found in the Writings are the ones that are snubbed, excused, and ignored you will notice.

But you say, *"The word 'Easter' is in my King James Version".* Translations are not "inspired", and errors exist by the tens of thousands in many translations! The word in the Greek that underlies the word "Easter" in the KJV is ***pascha***, and it means *Passover*, from the Hebrew word "Pesach". All scholars admit that this is an error in translation, and it only appears ONCE, at Acts 12:4. Luke, who wrote almost 40% of the Mashian writings (NT), didn't put it there as "Easter". The KJV is the ***only one*** with this error, since translators corrected it in all others! There was a previous English translation made by the Catholic priest John Wycliffe during the 14th century. He lived from 1320-1384, and his bones were burned in effigy for this unauthorized English work. He never used the word "Church", but the word "congregation" for the word *ecclesia.* Before the KJV, no one had ever used the word "Church", and soon you'll learn why.

Pagan religions through time paralleled each other, carrying the Sun, Earth Mother, and child model from Babylon to Media Persia, Phoenicia, Egypt, Greece, Rome, and Celts. The Medes cooked the mythology into "Zoroastrianism", producing the magician priests called "Magi". They worshipped Ahura, Haoma, and Ohrmazd as their trinity. (We'll survey them all under "Trinities" later). The Greeks' "Zeus" was their sun deity, whose mother is sometimes seen with a head-piece very much like "Lady Liberty" depicting the rays of the sun. Take another look at "Athena" and "Ishtar" on the previous page; those heads are indications that we are seeing the same person. The Britannica Encyclopedia (1934) states: "**EASTER** (es'ter). Ostara, or Eastre, was the goddess of Spring in the religion of the ancient Angles and Saxons. Every April a festival was celebrated in her honor. With the beginnings of Christianity, the old gods were put aside. From then on the festival was celebrated in honor of the resurrection of Christ, **but was still known as Easter after the old goddess."**

In contrast, the Creator says:

"Break down their altars, smash their sacred stones and burn their Asherah* (Easter) ***poles in the fire; cut down the idols of their gods and WIPE OUT THEIR NAMES from those places. YOU MUST NOT WORSHIP 𐤉𐤄𐤅𐤄 YOUR ELOHIM IN THEIR WAY."*** Dt. 12. OK, that's pretty clear. But what happened? The hypothesis of this book states on the outset that as the Pagans were absorbed into Chrisianity, it was the policy to accept everything they were accustomed to celebrating also. Let's hear it directly from the Catholic organization itself; the Catholic Cardinal John Henry Newman's book, ***The Essay on the Development of Christian Doctrine***, published in 1878, states in chapter 8: *"The rulers of the Church from early times were prepared, should the occasion arise, to adopt, to imitate, or to sanctify the existing rites and customs of the population, as well as the philosophy of the educated class. The use of temples and those dedicated to particular saints, and ornamented on occasion with* ***branches*** *of* ***trees*** (wreaths)*, incense, lamps, candles, votive offerings on recovering from illnesses, holy water, holy days and seasons* (the entire Church calendar)*, use of calendars, processions, blessings on the fields, sacerdotal vestments, the ring in marriage, chants, the Kyrie Eleison —* ***are all of Pagan origin, and sanctified by adoption into the Church."*** There you have it. But, you may ask, *"If Easter was a Pagan festival celebrating the impregnation of 'Mother Earth', how did it get mixed up with Christianity?"* Christianity's "Pagan Connection" started with one man more than any other. In 325 CE, the Roman Emperor ***Constantine I*** convened what is now called the ***Nicene Council***, gathering 220 elders (bishops) together, in order to unify basic doctrines (teachings), and establish common practices. This "universalizing" produced the ***Roman Catholic Church*** (RCC). The Latin word "Catholic" means *universal.* There was no "Catholic" on planet Earth prior to this Council. The only Council mentioned in the Writings conducted by the first Natsarim is mentioned at Acts 15, the purpose of which was to determine how to accommodate ***Gentile converts*** who were turning to the true Creator. The only topic: circumcision ~ and since immersion in the Name and receiving the Spirit into your heart is our "circumcision", it was decided that physical circumcision was not necessary (this is a very important beginning text to be understood by all adult male Gentiles!). Constantine's Council sought to institute new tolerances for Pagan patterns, and outlaw the patterns that the Savior lived by and taught ~ he had already proclaimed "Sun-Day" as a day of rest

*** ASHERIM IS OFTEN TRANSLATED "GROVES"**

dedicated to the sun (321 CE), and now it came time to "syncretize" more Paganism. By not "repenting" and turning away from elementary foolishness, it was simpler to just "absorb" the behavior. Political and religious ***CONTROL*** is a *slippery* thing; so by keeping the Pagan rituals in place, control was maintained with a minimum of effort! "Truth" was twisted by the "spin doctors" so the opposite of truth became our custom. Rather than make 99% of the people conform to a totally new behavior, it was easier to just exterminate the 1%, and put a Scriptural "spin" on the Pagan customs. This is what overwhelmed all our ancestors, *being taught these things as young children.* Paganism has always been highly skilled at wrapping dissimilar things together, making things appear one way on the surface, and making the loosely understood things shrouded in what they call the "mysteries of the faith".

In order to blend practices into universal (Catholic) behavior, the real Shabbat (Sabbath) was outlawed, along with Passover and other annual "Jewish" observances. This was a prophecy revealed to Daniel. In the prophecy, four "beasts" or kingdoms would arise, which are clearly (1) Babylon, (2) Media-Persia, (3) Greece, and (4) Rome. At Dani'el 7:25, the 4th beast is clearly described:

"The fourth beast is a fourth kingdom that will appear on Earth (Rome). ***It will be different from all the other kingdoms and will devour the whole Earth, trampling it down and crushing it. The ten horns are ten kings who will come from this kingdom*** (Caesars/Khasars/Kaisers/Czars ~ Julius Caesar up to Constantine). ***After them another king will arise, different from the earlier ones*** (Constantine "fused" the sun worshippers with the Natsarim writings, and was not of the family name "Caesar"); ***he will subdue three kings. He will speak against the Most High, and oppress His saints*** (qodeshim, those set-apart, especially the Hebrew people), ***and try to change the set-times* and law".*** Scripture is a pattern for our living in peace, guiding us with its "LAW". The *changing* of the "set times" (or seasonal appointments decreed at Deut. 16 and Lev. 23) were wiped-out and replaced with Pagan observances, imposed by Constantine.

Instead of PEACE, we have inherited WAR. The coveting (desiring) of power, land, and wealth is ravaging the whole Earth, and this picture illustrates one of the tiny victims of war. The fruit of the Spirit (when the Torah is lived by) produces love, joy, peace, patience, kindness, goodness, faithfulness, gentleness, and self-control. Aggression produces poverty and death. At Constantine's ***Nicene Council***, he put such fear in some of the visiting elders, that encyclopedias state that many *ran for their lives* when they heard the things being discussed! The *Edict of Milan* had already outlawed synagogues, but Constantine's Council boldly outlawed the ***Torah***, fulfilling the prophecy of Daniel 7:25. Everything that we know went wrong long ago, and it became a powerful institutionalized "beast", just as the Writings called it. If there were just a few little traces that were Pagan, that would be error; but let's investigate further, so we can decide whether or not the steel framework on which we stand has any rivets in *any* of its girders.

There is not ONE encyclopedic article that does not bring Constantine's so-called "conversion" to "Christianity" into question. Yet, a couple of billion people today are following his edicts. He founded Catholicism, and there is no dispute about that. The 95 issues that Martin Luder (called "Luther") nailed to the door put the Reformation into full blown splendor, beginning with "indulgences" being **sold** to shorten one's stay in "Purgatory". The seeds of this "Reformation" began with John Wycliffe's unauthorized translation of the Messianic Writings (NT) into English. This is not intended to make Catholicism into a "whipping boy", but let's just stop and think for a moment. Does the Creator's religion, or the one that everyone believes was founded by our Good Shepherd have any popes? No? How about "monks"? Or nuns? Well, ***Pagans have all of these things, and always have.*** The "Dalai Lama" means "highest monk". Has someone "monked around" with a few things? **Nuns** were Pagan temple prostitutes, covering themselves to keep from being recognized; or "Vestal virgins" who kept watch over the "sacred fires". In Zoroastrian ritual, men did this. They wore black, being

Master Yoda: a demon

DALAI LAMA:
"HIGHEST MONK"
376 MILLION FOLLOWERS
OBJECTIVE: OBLIVION

NOTICE THE "BALD PLACES" ON THE HEADS OF THESE PAGAN PRIESTS, PROHIBITED AT LEV. 19

****set-times** HEBREW TERM, ZEMAN (SEASONAL TIMES) OR "MOED'IM", THE APPOINTED TIMES GIVEN AT LEV. 23, DT. 16* called ***"dark ones"*** because their robes became soiled easily with the soot and ashes of keeping the "sacred fires" going. These fires were used to sacrifice human lives. **Monks** also wear red ceremonial robes, symbolic of the fire of the sun. Israel had *no one dressed in black or red* ~ the priests wore *white linen*. Try to picture Rabbi 𐤏𐤔𐤅𐤄𐤉 wearing black. There were no shaven-headed monks, because such "trimming" was specifically forbidden by the Creator at Lev. 19, most likely ***because*** the Pagans did it. It doesn't take a rocket scientist to figure it out, but people wear black today to funerals because the pagans often burned their dead on raised platforms. The smoke and ashes soiled their garments, so ashes became a symbol of mourning. You see corpse burning occasionally in movies. The new *Star Wars* movie ends with a scene where they burn one of their fallen comrades, and Luke Skywalker burned his dead father in a previous episode. The dead were burned because Pagans believed that burying them would "defile" the Earth. Fire, water, winds, and the Earth were sacred to the Pagans. Cremation is very popular still. "Holy water" is an echo of the Pagan belief that water is sacred. Since the Roman "papa", monks, nuns, wearing black, shaving heads into "tonsure" cuts, burning the dead, playing with "holy" water, "Sun-Day", and Easter are not in the Writings, then it's pretty obvious we don't need them. However, if they originated in Pagan worship, then what creature can you think of who masquerades as a messenger of "righteousness" caused mankind to embrace them? The definition of "science" is interesting, when you consider what we're exposing here: "***Sci-ence** (si'ens): n.* **1.** *Learning or study concerned with demonstratable truths."*

Science is the *"search for truth", based on the Latin* ***scire****, "to know".* To ignore "the truth" and continue to follow lies would be unthinkable; but even if people never find out the truth, they still participate in *"pseudo-science"* (false knowledge, untruth) if they stay in error. Pretty much the lower floors supporting Christianity as practiced today have been taken away. But, now we are going to pause, and deal with the ***REAL*** Name of the Creator. This is foundational material in a better building. It is not guile, so you will not be "beguiled". Don't overlook His Name!

"The art of being wise is the art of knowing what to overlook" ~ William James. (Bad advice).

"The first to present his case seems right, till another comes forward and questions him." Prov. 18:17 (Good advice).

HAS YOUR PREACHER EXPLAINED AWAY THE TRUE NAME FOR YOU YET? *"The Name of 𐤉𐤄𐤅𐤄 is a strong tower; the righteous run to it and are safe."* Prov. 18:10

Covenant Name:

The <u>Sinai</u> <u>Autograph</u>

The truth is right beneath a false façade. Once again, *to maintain control*, and keep everyone from having to change anything, we have inherited the long-standing custom of only using "generic" terms and devices to refer to the true Creator. Non-specific, general terms were employed to conceal the personal names of Pagan deities, and only the "initiated" would know them. Secret societies still have special hand signs and passwords, and they control their membership with strict hierarchical designs. Examples are the Rosicrucians, Masons, Illuminati, Knights Templars, etc.,. The expressions we are familiar with, like "GOD", "LORD", "Almighty", "Eternal" or even the "Creator" as I've been using up to now in this book have all been used in the past to refer to Pagan deities; NONE of them, except one, was ever a name. Everyone who defends the use of these expressions uses the excuse that we are speaking "English", and these terms we are familiar with are "translations". No, these words are not even originally English. The term "GOD" was never used to refer to the true Creator, until Christianity went into the Norse areas in the 6th century CE. The original Hebrew term which underlies the word "GOD" in our English translation is either **EL, ELOI, ELOAH,** or **ELOHIM**. This word *means* "one of strengths, or awesome one, the root being **alef-lamed*.** This is describing a Being of tremendous power. The Pagans' deities never became angry, or pleased, because they simply aren't there. Even these Hebrew terms are only expressions for "what" the true Creator *is*, but not used as His personal Name. But He has one, and ***ONLY ONE***. <u>Adjectives</u> attached to His Name cause people to think He has more than one, but really there is just one; and you can prove it from a good dictionary or encyclopedia. Look up ***YAHWEH***. It is only an <u>attempt</u> to "sound" the Name using English letters, and *originally* comes from **four palaeo-Hebrew letters;** yod-hay-uau-hay

𐤉𐤄𐤅𐤄 (Check your NIV or KJV preface)

"PALEO" or *palaeo* means "ancient". The letters are written from right-to-left in this original script. It is called ***Hebrew***, derived from one of Shem's descendants, whose name was **EBER** (Gen. 10). A few generations later, **ABRAM** was born, the son of Terah, one of **Eber's** descendants. When Abram's nephew **LOT** was carried off by invading armies, the text says ***"one who had escaped came and informed Abram the <u>Hebrew</u>"*** (Gen. 14:13). Hebrew is called the *Lashon Qodesh*, or set-apart tongue.

CANNIBAL: LITERALLY FROM KOHAN + BAAL, OR "PRIEST OF BAAL". PAGAN PRIESTS WOULD PARTAKE OF THE DEAD BODY

IS THE NAME OF THE CREATOR LOST?

Encyclopedias state that the proper personal Name of the Most High began to be suppressed by the true worshippers, the children of Israel, because of their dispersion among Pagans. For their failure to honor the Law to let the land rest, and release debts every 7 years, 𐤄𐤅𐤄𐤉 allowed them to be carried off to Babylon for 70 years, beginning in 586 BCE. Daniel's lifetime encompassed this "Babylonian Captivity". The Babylonians knew they were called "Yahudim", bearing the Name of "**YAH**", their Elohim. To ridicule them, these Pagans began to call them *Yahoo's.* Hearing the Name blasphemed (treated commonly) on the lips of Pagans was so offensive, the Name was avoided completely. Over time, it became *an offense worthy of death by stoning* for pronouncing the Name aloud, except by a Kohen (priest). This is why Shaul (Paul) was sent out to arrest the early Natsarim, because this "**Key** of Knowledge" was being used by them openly. At Acts 9:21, Luke records that Paul was converted, and teaching in the synagogues of Damascus. There they began saying, ***"Is this not he who in Yerushalayim destroyed those who <u>called</u> on this Name . . . ?"*** Then it goes on to describe how they plotted to <u>stone</u> Paul; but he slipped away. Indeed Paul was beaten with rods and stoned for the Name, but didn't die that way. (see 2Co 11:25)

Stephen's death (Acts 7) occurred because he uttered the Name, causing the Sanhedrin to cover their ears, screaming "blasphemy!"; and then they stoned him to death. This is also why the other sects, the Pharisees and Sadducees, picked up stones to try to kill the Savior. Carefully reading 3 Jn. 1:7, Jn. 5:43, 17:6, 17:26, and Acts 4:7, 4:12 & 4:17, will give insight to the problem of using the Name. The followers' immersion into the <u>Name</u> and the "placing of hands on them" certainly involved using the Name. The "priestly blessing" involved placing hands on the head, and saying:

"𐤄𐤅𐤄𐤉 bless you and keep you;
𐤄𐤅𐤄𐤉 make His Face shine upon you and show favor to you;
𐤄𐤅𐤄𐤉 lift up His countenance upon you, and give you peace.
So, they will put My Name on the Israelites, and I will bless them." Numbers 6:22-27.

This is the way He wrote it at Sinai, with His own finger: 𐤄𐤅𐤄𐤉. The 4 letters are called the <u>*Tetragram*</u>, or <u>**Tetragrammaton**</u>, the Greek word meaning "*four letters".* The Hebrew letters individually you'll find on the back cover: YOD, HAY, UAU, HAY. Some of the *transliterations* for these four letters have been J e H o' V a H, J a H, J a H'- V e H, Y a H' W e H, IAOUE, Y a H u' W a H, Y a H o' W a H, Y a H u' W a H, Y a H u' eH, Y a H u' aH, I A U E, Y a H V e, and others. (**hovah** means *wicked* in modern Hebrew).

First, we must eliminate blatant errors. Even a rather shallow encyclopedia will explain the error of "Jehovah". The Tetragram YHUH is changed to JHVH, and the vowels of another word, *adonai*, are stuffed into the spaces. This happened because Christian translators' ignorance of Hebrew failed to alert them that the "vowel points" placed beneath the Name were to "cue" the reader *NOT to pronounce it, but say "Adonai" <u>instead</u>.* (The man who gave us the hybrid word "Jehovah" was Petrus Galatinus). <u>**You can easily find that the letter "J" didn't even exist on the planet until about 1520 CE.**</u> The letter is less than 500 years old! " J " came from the letter YOD in Hebrew, and was brought into the Greek with the letter "IOTA", or our letter " I " since they had no " Y ". Gradually, customs developed that put a <u>tail</u> on the letter I when it began a sentence, or was used as the first letter of a proper name. There is no " J " or " V " in Hebrew. The V has a W sound in European languages. The letter UAU in Hebrew is commonly the sound of *"OO"* as you hear in *hallel<u>u</u>-Yah.* It has the same sound in *NatanYah<u>u</u>*. Even the new letter, W, is named *double—U* (UU), giving us the symbol of the European double V, W. The importance of doing our best to be accurate concerning the Name of Yahuah cannot be overstated. You may have already become convinced of one special way of writing it, but remember He only wrote it as 𐤄𐤅𐤄𐤉. Later, after the Babylonian Captivity, it became ה ו ה י. The first translation into Greek by the Sanhedrin during the 2nd century BCE is called *The Septuagint,* and in its original, the Name was always preserved in its original palaeo-Hebrew, 𐤄𐤅𐤄𐤉. I prefer to call Him YAHUEH or YAHU'AH (ya-HOO'-ah), but I will write it as 𐤄𐤅𐤄𐤉. Clement of Alexandria wrote that it can be transliterated in the Greek as **IAOUE**, but the original is better.

Because the Name was not to be blasphemed by improper use, it became the custom to NEVER use it. They could not **destroy** it in any way, and <u>that's why they buried the worn-out scrolls in jars at the Dead Sea</u>. Yet, they DID destroy it by not speaking it, and this violates the 3rd Commandment. (The letter "**W**" has only existed since the 13th century, and is <u>not</u> a Hebrew letter).

To "destroy"* (SHOAH) *the Name means to <u>not</u> <u>use</u> it, substituting it with another word. We must not cast or send His Name to ruin.

"The ax is already at the root of the trees, and every tree that does not produce good fruit will be cut down and thrown into the fire." Matt 3:10

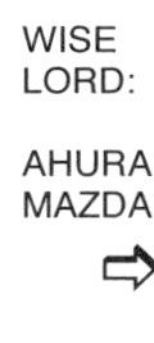

AHURA-MAZDA

Who Is "The LORD"?

You may already be familiar with some of the "Hebrew" forms like *Y'shua* and *Yeshua.* Footnotes say it means *"the **LORD** is our salvation".* If your translation has a preface, it may explain that the translators *"adopted the device"* of using the capital letters "LORD" in place of the Name of 𐤉𐤄𐤅𐤄 because it has become the "tradition". Please look up **BAAL** in a good dictionary; you will discover it means "LORD". To appease Pagans, and not use the proper Name, the generic term "LORD" was adopted. Pagans often veiled the proper names of their deities. The Romans worshipped "SOL" by the names "Deus" (a variant of Zeus), and "Domini" (Latin for "LORD"). "D" and "Z" were interchanged sounds, often heard as a "DZ" sound. The Pagan prophet Zarathustra (Zoroastrianism) called the sun ***Ahura Mazda***. "Ahura" means "**LORD**" in Old Persian, and "**Mazda**" means "wise" — so it means ***Wise LORD***. They were referring to ***Mithras***. In the time of Daniel, the ruler of Babylon, *Darius*, worshipped Ahura Mazda. **"Ormazd"** is the contraction. Pictured above wielding the power of the sun as a fire weapon, the bird could be a Nazi logo or even the original model for the US Presidential Seal. The anthromorphic symbol used was an eagle, but they worshipped FIRE in fire temples. Fire was sacred, associated with the sun. The torch held by the Statue of Liberty, and the Olympic Games torch relate directly to this. Pagans used eagles on gold balls to illustrate the sun being carried across the sky. The priests of Ahura Mazda were *Magians* (magi, magicians; Greek "magus"). Simon Magus (Acts 8) was a magician, and for attempting to "buy" the abilities he witnessed in the Natsarim, we now have the word "simony". In India, the sun is called "LORD KRISHNA". We have inherited the term "LORD" from these Magians, carried through other religions like *Manichaeanism.* Augustine, one of the "Church fathers", was previously a Manichaean; a sun-worshipper.

THE NAME ABOVE *ALL NAMES*

If you study the Writings of the *Brith Chadasha* (Renewed Covenant), you will notice that the Mashiach is called ***RABBI*** and ***RABBONI*** *(my teacher)* by the people who addressed Him. *(There is only ONE Rabbi, and we are not to be called such* ~ Mt. 23:8). His Name was given to Yusef (called "Joseph") by the messenger Gabriel because He would **deliver** His people from their sins. The Hebrew root for "deliver" is yaSHA, while the Greek term is SOTER, and the Latin is SALVARE. So, why do we see the word ***Jesus*** written in our English translations? "Jesus" isn't a Hebrew name, and has no meaning in Hebrew. It isn't a translation either, because it is supposed to mean 𐤉𐤄𐤅𐤄 *our Deliverer.* He came in His Father's Name, YAH. You hear the Name of the Father when you say *hallelu* ***Yah*** (praise you Yah). You should be hearing the Father's Name in Mashiach's Name also. Encyclopedias agree that the Mashiach has the same name as "Joshua". At Acts 7:45 and Hebrews 4:8, where both the names "Jesus" and "Joshua" are written in Greek, the letters in the Greek are the same for both names : ***IESOUS*** (Ιησουζ). The Hebrew Name "Joshua" is really Yahusha. Mosheh changed Husha's name to Yahusha*. It is seen written in the interlinears as יהושע in "modern" Hebrew, which Mosheh himself couldn't read. It was originally written in palaeo-Hebrew as: 𐤉𐤄𐤅𐤔𐤏. This later changed letter shapes during the Babylonian Captivity to the "modern" Hebrew.

Our traditions were shaped by people attempting to smooth-over differences. By avoiding the real Name, and using "devices" and generic terms, no one would be offended; but we violate the 3rd Commandment! (You will not find even one instance in the Writings where anyone referred to 𐤉𐤄𐤅𐤄 as "HaShem", The Name). The monks couldn't "monk" with all the Torah Scrolls held by the Yahudim, but they could "monk" with the Greek. For 2 centuries, the Natsarim held a copy of the memoir of Mattit Yahu (Matthew's real name), penned in the original Hebrew. A copy of it was discovered in the *Dead Sea Scrolls*. I wonder if that was what the document was that made the pope faint when he saw it several decades back. As a transliteration of the above palaeo-Hebrew Name, people have used Y'shua, Yeshua, Yasua, Yehoshua, Yahushua, and Yahusha. I prefer ya-HOO'-sha, but I will print it as it was originally written, 𐤉𐤄𐤅𐤔𐤏. For one thing, *Mosheh could read it:* **YOD-HAY-UAU-SHIN-AYIN.**

Daniel could read it too, as well as King Da'ud (remember, no "**V**"). Why am I so "hung-up" on the *old* Hebrew? It's the **inspired** script. Remember at Daniel 5, there was a feast for 1000 nobles in Babylon, and King Belshazzar took out the Temple utensils his father had plundered from the Yahudim? Emerging from ***thin air*** near the

***HUSHA - HAY-UAU-SHIN-AYIN; SEE NUM 3:16; OSHEA, HOSHEA, HOSEA, ARE #1954, CHANGED TO JOSHUA, #3091**

lampstand (the **menorah**?) where Belshazzar was sitting, a **HAND** wrote these words in the plaster of the wall:

𐤌𐤍𐤀 𐤌𐤍𐤀 𐤕𐤒𐤋 𐤅𐤐𐤓𐤎𐤉𐤍

It was NOT written in *modern* Hebrew. During the Babylonian Captivity, the Hebrew letters became altered, and only the older educated Hebrews would recall the original letters shapes. 𐤉𐤄𐤅𐤄 chose to write in His own "hand", uncorrupted by human whims and designs. When no one could be found to even read the letters themselves, Belshazzar's mother recommended that Daniel (by now an elderly man) be summoned. He could read it. The words transliterated were *mene mene tekel uparsin* (measure, measure, weighed, divided). That night Belshazzar was killed, and his kingdom was taken over by Cyrus the Mede. The kingdom of the "head of gold" had just passed into the chest and arms of silver! The original script is part of what is being restored in the world today; and with it, the rock of truth in the real Name. Peter quoted the prophet Yah el (Joel) when he said ***"And everyone who calls on the Name of 𐤉𐤄𐤅𐤄 will be saved"*** Acts 2:21. The inspired script is our foundation, and I simply stopped making excuses that it can be ignored. It will change everything. Acts 4:12 states ***"there is no other name under heaven*** (the skies) ***given among men by which we must be saved".*** The Name is the hidden treasure! At Yesha Yahu (Isaiah) 33:6, this is clear: ***"The fear*** (respect) ***of 𐤉𐤄𐤅𐤄 is the key to this treasure".***

Mashiach's Name *Altered?*

So, what does the name "JESUS" mean? The beginning part in Greek, Iη (IE), is the sound "Yeh" which is a *"hail"* . It's not "Yah", because it was changed! Now, we're left with the "SUS" part. It may be significant, so I should tell you that the word we sometimes see in the Latin, *"YESU"* (yeh' zoo) has been traced to a Hebrew word meaning "a curse be upon". A good book to check out is the Dictionary of Christian Lore and Legend by J. C. J. Metford. One source has this to say:

"*It is known that the Greek name endings of sus, seus, and sous (which are phonetic pronunciatations for Zeus) were attached by the Greeks to names and geographical areas as a means to give honor to their supreme deity, Zeus. Examples are Parnassus, a sacred mountain in Greece; the Greek deity of wine and son of Zeus, Dionysus; the Greek hero of the Trojan War was Odysseus, and the Greek deity of healing was Ieusus (which is a variant spelling of Iesous or the Latin Iesus / Jesus). They also changed the names of the prophets EliYahu (whose name means 'my mighty one is Yah') and Elyesha (whose name means 'my mighty one saves'), to 'Elias' and 'Eliseus' (which means 'my mighty one is Zeus'). This was done so often that it later was the basis for their rules of written grammar which followed the common or vernacular spoken language.*"

There are plenty of other Greek words that end with 'sus'; like the city of *Tarsus* (meaning '*sweat of Zeus*'), and *Pegasus.* How can we explain the Spanish "Hey-Zeus"? Even the name 'Yosef' was corrupted to 'Joseph', then Guiseppe; but they didn't tack the name 'Zeus' on it. As a syncretism, the Greeks *had* to hear 'Zeus' in the Mashiach's name! If you stop 50 people walking out of a "Church service" and ask them what the name of the Creator of the Universe is, you will usually hear them respond with GOD, The LORD, or *"JESUS".* The fact is, the word "Jesus" has no meaning in Hebrew, and the closest Hebrew word to the Greek "sus" is ***soos**, meaning HORSE.* So, "**he-sus**" literally means "the horse". The adversary (ha satan) has altered much more as you will learn later on in this book. Let's look at our English word, "**GOD**". It's not a name, as the Writings say there are "many gods". Also, you should know that there is no difference if the letters are capitalized or not, because there are no different-sized letters at all in Hebrew. "Small" letters began with the Greek alef-bet (yes, we even get our word ***alpha-bet*** from the first two Hebrew letters, but use the later Greek letter names!).

This is what the Encylopedia Americana (1945 Edition) says under the topic "GOD":

"**GOD** *(god) Common Teutonic word for personal object of religious worship, formerly applicable to super-human beings of heathen myth; on conversion of Teutonic races to Christianity, term was applied to Supreme Being."* ***NO! IT CAN'T BE TRUE! But it is true.***

This shocked me the first time I read it. Most of my research was done without anyone telling me these little details, I just looked things up. I could hardly stand it. I felt betrayed and deceived. Further research revealed that these Teutonic 'Druids' called the sun Gud, Gudh, **Goth**, or 'GOTT'. In some countries, they still call the sun "GOTT". Druidic mythology says Woden rides an 8-legged horse, Sleipnir, in ***Gotland***. Look up "Valhalla".

Notice the term *GOTH*, used in *Visigoths* (western goths) and *Ostragoths* (eastern goths—see the term 'Ostra'?). "Ostra" refers to the "east" where the sun rises, and is a variant of Easter or Ishtar / Astarte). Woden is pictured in some books riding his 8-legged steed in *GOTLAND.* ***Gotland*** is the equivalent to ***Mount Olympus***, where Zeus lived in their mythology. So, we've inherited the custom of calling 𐤉𐤄𐤅𐤄 "GOTT", and His Son 𐤉𐤄𐤅𐤔𐤏 "YEH-ZEUS". The Rabbi's Name is ravaged, and we call the Father by a Pagan name originally used for the proper name of their sun-deity. And just for fun, they have us calling Him "LORD" which means "**BAAL**" in Hebrew! What next? Everyone who calls upon the name of GOTT or BAAL will not be saved. You have to prove all things. Rabbi 𐤉𐤄𐤅𐤔𐤏 revealed His Father's Name to his *talmidim* (students, disciples). A "disciple" is a *student of a discipline.* "John" was originally *Yahuchanon* (gift of Yah), corrupted to *Jonathon,* then *Johann,* and finally just "John". At Yahuchanon 17:6, Rabbi says: ***"I have revealed*** (uncovered) ***Your Name to those whom You gave me out of the world."***

After *Hebel* (Abel) was killed by *Qayin* (Cain), and Seth was born to Adam and Chuwah, Gen. 4:26 says: ***"At that time, men began to call on the Name of 𐤉𐤄𐤅𐤄".*** *Now Read Is. 43:10-13.*

One Shabbat, Rabbi 𐤉𐤄𐤅𐤔𐤏 healed a man (see Yahuchanon 5), and the ruling Yahudim sought to kill Him for breaking Shabbat, and calling 𐤉𐤄𐤅𐤄 His Father. At 5:43, He says, ***"I have come in my Father's Name . . ."*** Not only in His Father's "authority", but literally in His Name: Yah. As He was entering Yerushaliyim (12:13) He was greeted by throngs of followers shouting ***"Hushanu"*** the Syraic Aramiac Hebrew word "save us" (Ps. 118:25). They also cried out the Hebrew words from Psalm 118:26, ***"Baruch haba baShem 𐤉𐤄𐤅𐤄"*** meaning *"Blessed is he who comes in the Name of 𐤉𐤄𐤅𐤄"*. This vocalization of the Name of 𐤉𐤄𐤅𐤄 caused some of the Pharisees in the crowd to yell out *"Rabbi, rebuke your talmidim!"* (Luke 19:39). Rabbi 𐤉𐤄𐤔𐤅𐤏 was spreading the Name of the Father all around — revealing the true Name of the Father to all the world! Ha Satan had stolen it away, and it was being restored! Since ha Satan is still in the world, he rules over mankind religiously to deceive, and has once again destroyed the use of the true Name. "Ha Shatan" is the original sound of the Hebrew words "the adversary". When 𐤉𐤄𐤅𐤔𐤏 told Cephas (Peter) ***"get behind me shatan"*** He was simply calling Cephas His *adversary* in accomplishing His mission! Cephas wasn't "possessed". Natsarim are now re-appearing on the Earth to proclaim the Name of 𐤉𐤄𐤅𐤄, just before Rabbi 𐤉𐤄𐤅𐤔𐤏 returns, with the message of the kingdom of 𐤉𐤄𐤅𐤄:

"Repent - for the Kingdom of 𐤉𐤄𐤅𐤄 draws near." Matt. 4:17. Mark 1:15 records these very words of Mashiach's as the "Gospel"; ***"The Kingdom of 𐤉𐤄𐤅𐤄 draws near. Repent and believe the good news!".**** That "good news" or report would be what we are to teach the nations to obey: TORAH. ***YOUR MISSION - SHOULD YOU CHOOSE TO ACCEPT IT:***

THE GREAT COMMISSION:

"Therefore go and make disciples of all nations, baptizing them in the Name of the Father and of the Son and of the Ruach haQodesh, and teaching them to obey everything I have commanded you. And surely I am with you always, to the very end of the age." *Matt 28:19-20*

As Natsarim Yisraelites, we are ***each*** *commanded to act on this! Who Yahusha was speaking to in the above is most relevant. He was speaking to Torah-observant Israelites, his privately-taught students. They were not Christians. Any "Gentile" that engrafts into Israel also observes the same Torah / Covenant as any other Israelite; the followers of Yahusha simply have it inscribed upon their hearts!*

When the true message or "Gospel" is proclaimed anywhere in the world, an important "sign of authenticity" will accompany it: the woman who came to 𐤉𐤄𐤅𐤔𐤏 with an alabaster jar of very expensive perfume will also be told, in memory of her. (see Mt. 26:7-13). This must be one of those "real" messages, because I just made mention of her. As I illustrated earlier, Shaul (Paul) was sent out at first by the Sanhedrin to arrest the early Natsarim for openly using the Name, citing how Stephen was stoned as Shaul held the outer cloaks of the killers (he admitted this at Acts 22:19,20). At Acts 4, Cephas and Yahuchanon had been arrested by the Sanhedrin. The elders of Israel were so steeped in the tradition of not saying the Name aloud, they conferred among themselves saying ***"But to stop this thing from spreading any further among the people*** (the Name)***, we must warn these men to speak no longer to anyone in this Name."*** Acts 4:17. The Name 𐤉𐤄𐤅𐤔𐤏 contains the Name of 𐤉𐤄𐤅𐤄. Acts 4:7 begins their examination. Brought before the elders, Cephas and Yahuchanon are asked ***" By what power or by what name did you do this?".*** This was to entrap them into saying the Name aloud, as they had Stephen. Cephas said it was by the Name of 𐤉𐤄𐤅𐤔𐤏 ha Mashiach of Nazareth that a man had been healed of being crippled at beyond the age of 40. When they were released, they returned to the other Natsarim, addressing 𐤉𐤄𐤅𐤄 by Name at verse 24, after which the Earth shook. His Name is authority over disease, daemons, and a strong tower of refuge!

A CONSPIRACY TO CONCEAL THE NAME

We've surveyed only a few examples of how the real Name became veiled or concealed. If it is not known, how can we "call" (Hebrew *qara*) on it and so be delivered as Yah el and Cephas said we must? 𐤉𐤄𐤅𐤄 says ***"My people will know My Name"***. The prophet Yerme Yahu (Jeremiah ~ note the ending ***-iah*** in many prophets names?) declared at 23:27:

****good news*** - In Hebrew, "**BESORAH**", meaning "message"

"They think the dreams they tell one another (made-up words, substitutions) ***will make My people forget My Name, just as their fathers forgot My Name through BAAL*** (LORD)***"***. Lying teachers of the people were misleading them, and their teachings were just being "dreamed-up". That's what "spin-doctors" do. This was during the time the Name was first being avoided, and they were substituting the term "Adonai" (Heb. *MY LORD*). The Babylonians were worshipping the sun with the name "Baal", meaning "LORD", and were concealing the deity's real name from even their people. It was ***DAGAN***, which later was ***DAGON*** to the Philistines and Phoenicians. You can read about the half-fish, half-man image that kept falling down when the Philistines put the Ark of 𐤉𐤄𐤅𐤄 in the temple of Dagon in 1 Sam. Chaps. 4 & 5. The Ark itself was called by the Name of 𐤉𐤄𐤅𐤄 (2 Sam. 6:1,2). The English word "LORD" isn't even a name of any kind. It comes from the Celtic term *hlaf-weard*, meaning *keeper of the loaf.* "Monking" with the texts have led to not only doctrinal *"slants"*, but also mutilations and maskings of original words. Some have even said, *"If the King James version was good enough for the Apostles, then it's good enough for me!"* This version contains one of the best opportunities to see what was added, because the words the translators *added* are printed in *italics* ~ but what was changed and omitted they didn't tell us. It was authorized by the Queen, not King James (1611). Translations are ***not inspired*** as the original prophets were who wrote the words of 𐤉𐤄𐤅𐤄 in Hebrew. Scholars admit that *"of the 5000 Greek manuscripts which contain all or part of the New Testament, every one of these hand-written copies differs from every other one."* These scholars confess that *"There is not one sentence in the NT in which the manuscript tradition is wholly uniform";* this is due to *"variants put in them deliberately",* and *"careless handling of the text",* or *"many created for theological or dogmatic reasons".* The Greek text itself was being *"constantly interpreted and re-interpreted by each succeeding generation".* In constrast, the consistency of the Hebrew *"Old Testament"* text which was copied with a reverent fear by the scribes remains without discrepancy in its many copies. They would not change even one LETTER. Since the discovery of the Dead Sea Scrolls, the myth that the "NT" was inspired in the Greek language has been exploding.

DEAD SEA SCROLLS

In 1947, a young Bedouin shepherd boy was in the northwestern area of the Dead Sea, chasing after one of his clever animals. The animal scrambled into a cave hole. The boy couldn't easily get to him, so he threw some rocks in to spook him out. The boy heard a loud crashing sound, like a large jar breaking! He entered the cave, now called "cave 1", and discovered many jars with lids containing old scrolls. He took one to an antiquities dealer in town, and it turned out to be an ancient scroll written in Hebrew! Of course he sold it, and the dealer wanted to know where he found it. The rest is modern history. What you will usually not hear is WHY the scrolls were there. As scrolls of "Scripture" were used in the Temple or synagogues, they would wear-out eventually, and were carefully copied by scribes. They would not discard or destroy the worn out copy profanely, but bury it respectfully. WHY? Because *these worn scrolls contained the personal Name* of 𐤉𐤄𐤅𐤄 *written* on them. Every worn scroll was placed in a jar with a lid, and buried. Now the scrolls are either in the Rockefeller Museum, or the Shrine of the Book, both in Yerushaliyim. Every one of them has the Name on them. Since it is used 6,823 times, ~ more than any other word, you would think the "scholars" would bring it the recognition it deserves! But, you will often find these men are "sectarian", or even unbelievers that happen to be familiar with ancient languages. Just look up the word "LORD" in any concordance. The scrolls that did not contain the Name are absent, such as the scroll we call "Esther". (The scroll of "Esther" has the Name in "acrostic" 4 times, but it is concealed from Pagan eyes). The scrolls of Enoch, Baruch, Jubilees (Yob-hel), and all the others we call "Old Testament" are present. The Shrine of the Book building is designed like a huge jar lid, like the kind the scrolls were found in. This is a good place to bring up another oddity. What do the Scrolls call themselves? We use the traditional term "Scriptures", which is a Latin-rooted word, from *scriptum* meaning *hand-writing.* The most common term heard is "**Bible**".

BIBLE

The word "Bible" is not found anywhere in the text of the Writings themselves! This is a traditional term given to the inspired words by mankind. The term has been used for so long, people have come to accept it readily.

𐤉𐤄𐤅𐤔𐤏 never used the word "Bible", nor did any Natsari after Him. No prophet uttered the word. And, it's not a translation for what the Writings call themselves either. At Luke 24:44 you will be given insight into what our Prophet of prophets called the Writings themselves. The term was (as He said it): *Torah* (Law), *Nebi'im* (prophets), and *Kethubim* (writings, beginning with Psalms). This is shortened to the one-word **T**a**N**a**K**h, an acronym. We use the words "scuba" and "laser" as acronyms (**S**elf **C**ontained **U**nderwater **B**reathing **A**pparatus). A "scroll" is the Hebrew word "megillah". The Bereans examined the "scrolls", which we now call "books". In fact, the Greek word "biblia" means the same idea. But, you know that "books" are just that; books. Of course everyone knows what "scrolls" the Bereans were examing. They weren't consulting the Egyptian Book of the Dead, or an operating guide to some computer hardware. Shaul, imprisoned (2 Tim. 4:13), requests his cloak for warmth, and his scrolls, especially the "parchments". Hey, that looks like they were using a different term than we do today ~ but where am I going with this? First, let's reflect on an important but overlooked item. We attempt to worship the same Awesome, Mighty, Jealous, and Everlasting 𐤉𐤄𐤅𐤄 that Mosheh did, Who states

"I 𐤉𐤄𐤅𐤄 do not change" Mal. 3:6.

This is what He says at Ex. 23:13:

"Be careful to do everything I have said to you. Do not invoke the names of other elohim; DO NOT LET THEM BE HEARD ON YOUR LIPS." (See also Ps. 16:4). Today, we assume we can ignore a little thing like that, and call the days of the week by Roman and Norse deities, even calling the planets by ancient idols' names. If we love Him, we will do whatever pleases Him. He watches us, to see if there is any who understand. He is big enough to hold the universe together, and knows where every hair is on your head. He knows if you care, too. He knows your dreams, and your thoughts. No created being can know what He knows.

The Origin of the Word "Bible"

This word was originally Phoenician, then passed into Greek, then Latin. It means "books" in Greek, and is only on the cover and commentary text of what we call our "Bibles". It became ***the name of a Phoenician port* city** that exported papyrus; so, scrolls, or what we would call "books" came to be called by the name of this port, a city called: ***BYBLOS***. Don't let the "Y" fool you! There is no "Y" in Greek. This port was about 50 miles north of Sidon, and you'll see it on your maps in your "Bible". The reason the city was named "BYBLOS" is because the Phoenicians worshipped a *fertility deity* named **BYBLIA***, and her temple was there! See the "etymology" now? Calling the Words of 𐤉𐤄𐤅𐤄 by the name of "BYBLOS" / Bible is yet another trick foiled upon us by men, *long dead.* And you can bet it was on purpose. Who would be cunning enough to pull this off? A spatial being bent against us getting at the Truth, ha shatan, Diablos. Those in ignorance are not held accountable, except for what they know. Designs have been made to entrap everyone in a dragnet of false worship, having no basis in The **T**a**N**a**K**h, or Brit Chadasha. Shaul wept for what he knew would happen, and Yahuchanon wrote the Revelation of 𐤉𐤄𐤅𐤔𐤏 which clearly illustrated to him how Babylon would fill the Earth, and collapse on the "Day of 𐤉𐤄𐤅𐤄". He searches for any who understand. Without wisdom, His **Torah**, it cannot be understood.

"In the past, He let all nations go their own way, yet He did not leave Himself without Testimony . . . " Acts 14:16,17.

"In the past, Elohim overlooked such ignorance, but now He commands all people everywhere to repent. For He has set a day when He will judge the world with justice by the man whom He has appointed. He has given proof of this to all men by raising Him from the dead." Acts 17:30,31.

"And this message of the Kingdom shall be preached in the whole world, as a Testimony to the nations, and then the end will come." Mt. 24:14.

WHAT IS "WORSHIP"?

The word "worship" is two words, *worth-ship.* It simply means the outward showing of respect and esteem to a higher authority. The key elements necessary are fear and humility, and ultimately **LOVE**. Fear is not used in the sense of terror, but rather respect for another's awesome power and authority. The Hebrew concept basically has always been termed **obeisance**, or the status of a servant who obeys his master. The word "obey" comes from the Hebrew word OBED, or servant; the prophet "Obadiah" means *servant of Yah.* The generosity and Fatherhood of 𐤉𐤄𐤅𐤄 demands His creatures to return praise and recognition. He has feelings; wrath, humor, compassion, and desires a relationship with each of us. How would you feel if your pet ignored you, and even bit your hand whenever you came into its space? But He considers us His children! Rabbi 𐤉𐤄𐤅𐤔𐤏 even calls us "brothers" (and sisters). The Writings of the TaNaKh and Brit Chadasah show His love for us by providing the rules for living in peace, and it is the perfect "book" of law. It is a "light" for us to "walk" in, and without it we stumble in "darkness". He has literally created us to be a part of His **family**. Worship is something we perform, and is seen as obedience. In the hands of men, this "worship" has become perverted, and we serve another entity, deceived by diversion tactics. Worship is not something we do only one day each week, but everyday; by adopting the pattern of living we see in the 10 Commandments. These are the ***living waters***, and the "food" which 𐤉𐤄𐤅𐤔𐤏 desired Cephas (Kepha, Shimon Peter) to "feed" His sheep. Today, the sheep are being "fleeced", and are feeding the predators, or wolves, who parasitically plunder them and lead

****** *BYBLIA WAS ANOTHER NAME FOR ASHERAH, ALSO KNOWN AS ARTEMIS IN EPHESUS***

them away from obeying יהוה. The parable about the "hirelings" who work in the vineyard while the Owner is away shows us that they want the "business" to be their own (Mt. 21:33-45). This whole planet is the vineyard. יהוה "dwells" in His Temple, His *people*, who make up the "living stones". יהושע threw the merchants out of the man-made Temple, who had turned it into a den of thieves. Instead of being a place of worship and learning, it had become defiled because tradition had turned **worship** into a **business**. Today's "clergy" has become what the Temple priests and scribes had been in Temple times, yet they don't seem to be aware of it. They are plundering the flock, and usurping the promises without *obeying the Covenant*. One cannot claim to be ***Israel***, *yet not observe the Covenant*.

LEGALISM or ***ILLEGALISM?***

Obeying specific "Commandments" with the thinking that this somehow "**earns**" salvation, or a place in the coming Kingdom, has been called "legalism". This grew out of the Reformation, when the teaching of the Protestant sects based their doctrine of salvation on the work of יהושע and His atoning death. We **are** "saved" by "grace", and grace alone. Yahuchanon 3:16-21 needs to be studied carefully; one should not stop reading at verse 16:

"For יהוה so loved the world that He gave His one and only Son, that whoever believes in Him shall not perish but have eternal life. For יהוה did not send His Son into the world to condemn the world, but to save the world through Him. Who ever believes in Him is not condemned, but whoever does not believe stands condemned already because he has not believed in the Name of יהוה's one and only Son. <u>This is the verdict</u>: Light has come into the world, but men loved darkness instead of Light because their deeds were evil. Everyone who does evil hates the Light, and will not come into the Light for fear that his <u>deeds will be exposed</u>. But whoever <u>lives by the Truth</u> comes into the Light, so that it may be <u>seen</u> plainly that what he has done has been done in יהוה." Obedience is <u>evidence</u> of salvation.

What is "Light", and "Truth"? Proverbs 6:23 defines "Light" as the **Torah**. The word that underlies "teaching" is Torah. The "Truth" is the "Word" of יהוה, Yahuchanon 17:17. Once again, the "Word" is the Torah, made into flesh in יהושע; as if the Commandments, the personality of יהוה, became a man and lived a perfect life without transgressing His own teachings. He gave us the "Keys" to the Kingdom: **TORAH**, which produces LOVE. What is love?

"Love is patient, love is kind. It does not envy, it does not boast, it is not proud. It is not rude, it is not self-seeking. It is not easily angered, it keeps no record of wrongs. Love does not delight in evil, but rejoices with the Truth. It always protects, always trusts, always hopes, always perseveres. Love never fails." 1 Cor. 13. The fruit of the Spirit, and the fruit of the Torah, produces: **love, joy, peace, patience, kindness, goodness, faithfulness, gentleness,** and **self-control.** ***"Folly is joy to him who lacks sense, but a man of righteousness walks straight."*** Pr. 15:21. Something that is "legal" is right. The word is based on "logic", and involves "reasoning". The opposite of legalism is *illegalism,* and that is what <u>separates</u> us from our Creator. You will recognize a tree by its fruit. The 10 Commandments produce this fruit. Although the Torah is a gift and model for living, *we cannot obey it in our flesh* ~ we need something more: the Renewed Covenant! What is that? When people read Galatians and other texts, they misunderstand what is being spoken of as "the Law"*. There is the **MORAL** law that *<u>defines</u>* "sin", and there is the **CEREMONIAL** law, that *<u>atoned</u>* for "sin". A life lived ignoring the MORAL law ~ with murder, theft, adultery, idolatry, etc., is doomed to the second death in the Lake of Fire. But hardly anyone would call it "legalism" if they obeyed certain moral laws. The CEREMONIAL law made atonement, but it could not rescue permanently, because it involved animal deaths, in place of the individual dying for the sins. The ceremonial law that cannot "save" pointed the way to the permanent solution: the death of the perfect sacrifice, יהושע. The blood of the Renewed Covenant covers us permanently, ending the *ceremonial* law. It is the hatred of the law of "sin and death" that were ordinances against us, nailed to the wood. It was not the MORAL law that was "done away", but the CEREMONIAL law. How then, can we obey the MORAL laws? This is where the Renewed Covenant comes into play! The Old Covenant was the blood of animals ~ the New is the blood of יהושע. It is our belief in the Resurrection, and the reality of it, that we have eternal life. We receive the Spirit of יהושע when we confess with our mouth and believe in our heart that He was raised from the dead. He comes into us, and WRITES the moral law (Torah) on our hearts and minds, enabling us to LOVE the Commandments! You will not live a life ignoring them, because this "change" inside you causes you to agree with the moral laws. The "Law of Liberty" is our freedom ~ not to sin, but rather our freedom *<u>from</u>* sin; sinning **against** the <u>moral</u> laws (and we don't have to sacrifice animals). Mashiach יהושע really does ***save*** His people *from* sin, as His Name says! The deciding factor is: do you ***LOVE*** the Commandments? ***"If you love Me,***

****LAW: THE GREEK WORD "NOMOS" IS USED TO REFER TO TORAH; HOWEVER CAN ALSO BE RULE OR PRINCIPLE***

you will obey what I command." Yn. 14:15. When you can say ***"I love the Torah"***, He has "circumcised" your heart. Even Daniel, Dawid, YeshaYahu, Mosheh, Adam, etc., who lived by the moral law could not obtain eternal life by it; but because 𐤉𐤄𐤅𐤔𐤏 resurrected, these captives were delivered from the ceremonial law that was against them. Stop and read Psalm 1, and Psalm 119. ***"Oh, how I love your Torah! I meditate on it all day long. Your Commands make me wiser than my enemies . . ."*** Ps. 119:97,98.

And, my friend, *THAT* is what "grace" is! It is the gift of 𐤉𐤄𐤅𐤄 to receive a LOVE for the Truth.

"For it is by grace you have been saved, through faith (emunah)***, and this not from yourselves, it is the gift of 𐤉𐤄𐤅𐤄—not by works***(ceremonial offerings)***, so that no one can boast. For we are 𐤉𐤄𐤅𐤄's workmanship, created in Mashiach 𐤉𐤄𐤅𐤔𐤏 to do good works, which 𐤉𐤄𐤅𐤄 prepared in advance for us to do."*** (Those "good works" prepared in advance are the Torah.) Eph. 2:8-10. This has stood in doctrinal opposition to "James" (Ya'akob) 2:17-20, who after explaining that lawbreakers (non-legalists) will be judged, says: ***". . . Faith, by itself, if it is not accompanied by works, is dead. But someone will say, 'You have faith; I have works'. Show me your faith without deeds, and I will show you my faith by what I do. You believe there is one Elohim; Good! Even the demons believe that — and shudder. You foolish man, do you want evidence that faith without deeds is useless?"*** What he is saying is, obedience is not the thing that saves us, but when we are seen obeying the Torah, it is evidence of our salvation. There is only forgiveness of sins against Torah if there is *repentance*, the turning away from sin, and living by the Torah. Martin Luther was used to spearhead the understanding, but there was more to comprehend. The complete understanding became cut short, no doubt because the adversary saw how close to the Truth people were getting. He began his ***INQUISITION***, murdering over 83 million people over a 600-year period. The junk-pile of history should now begin to form a picture for you, if we are assembling it correctly. Love is the key! You ***obey*** your Earthly father as a child, partly out of fear; but as you mature you begin to obey because you love your father, and do not want to let him down. Our Father says, ***"Love Me, and keep My Commandments."*** We show Him we love Him when we ***obey***. It's not "legalism", it's LOVE.

And that is what worship is.

TITHING: ***"Religion that 𐤉𐤄𐤅𐤄 our Father accepts as pure and faultless is this:***

To look after orphans and widows in their distress, and to keep oneself from being polluted by the world." Ya'akob 1:27.

"There were no needy persons among them. For from time-to-time, those who owned lands or houses sold them, brought the money from the sales and put it at the apostles' feet, and it was distributed to anyone as he had need." Acts 4:34,35.

Tithing is the area exploited by the predators (wolves), which 2 Pet. 2 calls "false teachers". They are engaged in religion, and teach it. They would establish a precedent of plundering the flock, and introduce destructive heresies (lies) with cunning seduction. ***"Many will follow their shameful ways and will bring the Way of Truth*** (Torah) ***into disrepute. In their greed, these teachers will exploit you with stories they have made up."*** You must read the whole context. He even goes on to say ***"It would have been better for them not to have known the Way of Righteousness*** (Torah) ***than to have known it and then to turn their backs on the sacred command that was passed on to them. Of them the proverbs are true: 'A dog returns to its vomit', and 'A pig that is washed goes back to her wallowing in the mud'."*** One of the "stories they have made up" is that we must "tithe" to spread the "Gospel", and to provide a comfortable setting (a building) in which to study and help others worship and come to salvation. This is programming. "Tithe" is mentioned at Lev. 27:30, Num. 18:26, Deut. 12:17, & 14:22. ***HEY*** ~ isn't that "OLD Testament"? That it's called, but it will never pass away. Altogether, tithing is referred to 16 times in Scripture, and is the ***"ma'aser"***, or a 10th of the increase used for 3 purposes. It consists of food only, as you will quickly discover. Clearly, Malachi 1:7 and 3:10 show this. Preachers will select their own "parts" of the texts in order to make the listener believe that money is to be collected and "put at the apostles' feet" to support *them* in their GOD's work. 𐤉𐤄𐤅𐤄's message is *repent,* not pay. The tithe supported (fed) the Lewites, poor, fatherless, foreigners, and widows. Shaul, at 1 Cor. 1-4, & 16:1, is also talking about food, to be taken back to Yerushaliyim to those in need. There was a famine, and gold coins cannot be eaten. If a teacher of Torah is traveling and one of us has him stay at our home for a time, he is able to eat from our table. "You must not muzzle the ox" while it is turning the grindstone, but let it eat the fruits of what it is grinding, for sustenance. *The ox doesn't cart off a percentage!* The Lewites were not able to own land, but performed the tedious ceremonial law requirements we just discussed. They had to eat, as well as their families. If a preacher tells you he is entitled to 10% of your income, and everyone else's income (numbering 100's or even 1000's of people), remind him that he is not a Lewite. A Lewite had to be a descendant of Lewi, a strict bloodline of priests. Also, the ceremonial law, and the need to support those Lewites who implemented it, is no more. These *predators* are not the poor, through some physical defect. They are not children without a father to support them. They are not foreigners fleeing a famine or war, or widows in their old age with no husband. They must work! I do, and Shaul did, even though he traveled about.

ELDERS MEETING (Acts 20:13-38)

Shaul called a meeting of the elders in Ephesus (a Pagan town, note the name-ending). He was in a rush to get to Yerushaliyim by the day of Shabuoth (called Pentecost), and knew he would never again see these brothers in his flesh. ***"Now I know that none of you among whom I have gone about preaching the Kingdom will ever see me again."*** He passionately pleaded with them, and then mentioned the coming in of savage "**wolves**" among them:

"Keep watch over yourselves and all the flock of which the Ruach ha Qodesh (set-apart Spirit) ***has made you overseers*** (elders, bishops)***. Be shepherds of the assembly of 𐤉𐤄𐤅𐤄, which He bought with His own blood. I know, that after I leave, SAVAGE WOLVES will come in among you and will not spare the flock. Even from your own number*** (that group of men) ***men will arise and distort the Truth in order to draw away disciples after them. So be on your guard! Remember that for 3 years I never stopped warning each of you night and day with tears. Now, I commit you to 𐤉𐤄𐤅𐤄 and to the Word*** (Torah) ***of His lovingkindness*** (chasid)***, which can build you up and give you an inheritance among all those who are set-apart*** (Qodeshim, saints)***. I have not coveted anyone's silver or gold or clothing. You yourselves know that these hands of mine have supplied my own needs and the needs of my companions. In everything I did, I showed you that by this kind of hard work WE must help the weak, remembering the words the Rabbi 𐤉𐤄𐤅𐤔𐤏 Himself said, 'IT IS MORE BLESSED TO GIVE THAN TO RECEIVE'.***

Who was Shaul talking to? Elders! What did he know some of them would eventually begin to do? He knew it would turn into a **business**, and even mentioned the "wolves" I referenced from 2 Pet. 2. There can be no mistake here, because this is a 2nd witness in the Writings to what we see happening around the world today ~ he even quoted 𐤉𐤄𐤅𐤔𐤏's words about "receiving", and this quote is never taken in context. Instead, it's turned around and used *to plunder the flock!* The "merchants" are also mentioned in the book called Revelation (Apocalypse, *uncovering*). These merchants have drunk the maddening wine (*teachings*) of Babylon, taught heresies like Easter / Ishtar, Sun-day, and other Nimrod nonsense, and grown RICH from having done so.

This knowledge, when made known, will rock Babylon to its roots. THIS is the "rebellion" Shaul prophesied to occur at 2 Thess. 2:3! This is the exposing of the *Man of Lawlessness*. Study this thoroughly, because your eyes are being opened. All that has to happen is for a billion people to stop paying these men, and it all comes down. The message is FREE. Now knowing this, how much money will you have spared yourself, and be enabled to help desperate relatives and friends? I certainly don't want any of your earnings, nor do I need your "last will and testament" to leave money to print these books. They will be supported by those who buy the truth, and sell it not. The printing and mailing costs will be covered by each book. Reading 1 Tim. 5:7-9 shows your first duty is to your own relatives, to lessen the burden on the assembly of supporting widows. At 6:5, men of corrupt minds think that religion is a means to financial gain. (Read the context).

The "merchants" use Acts 4:32-36 to trick the listener into believing that money is to be collected and "put at the apostles' feet" to support *THEM* in the Creator's work. If you stop right now and read this in its full context, you will see that this "programming" is completely wrong. The support was distributed among the needy among them, and no one was in want. This is just one area where "inoculating" or "vaccinating" the masses of people against the correct behavior is done. It's almost like everyone is under hypnosis. These merchants are businessmen. To steer you away from obeying Commandments, they will say "*We now have liberty in Christ*", or "*We now live in the Age of Grace*". But, they sure want a lot of your money! It is interesting that Rabbi 𐤉𐤄𐤅𐤔𐤏 threw some merchants out of His Father's House ~ He must not like money being involved in spiritual matters. He also once said, ***"Give to Caesar what is Caesar's, and to Elohim what is Elohim's".*** The government wants your money, and 𐤉𐤄𐤅𐤄 wants your **obedience**. When the veil in the Temple was torn from top to bottom, it signaled the end of the ceremonial law; but the moral law that *defines* "sin" is still here, and always will be. To steal, kill, adulterate, or covet was a sin 10 years **before** He died for sin; and they were still sinful 10 years **afterward** as well. If we are free from the Torah, then human sacrifice (or murder) would not be sinful. The goal of Torah is love. We have to have love for our neighbor, so the suffering poor, fatherless children, widows, and foreigners fleeing wars are everyone's concern. Paul (Shaul) wrote that believing Gentiles must support the needy Yahudim: ***"For if the Gentiles have shared in the Yahudim's spiritual blessings, they owe it to the Yahudim to share with them their material blessings."*** ~ Rom. 15:27. This is quite a contrast to what Martin Luther wrote three years before he died; *"For the glory of GOD and His Church, Jews' synagogues and holy books should be burned and covered over with soil, and Jewish homes should be likewise destroyed".* His writings were used by Nazi war criminals in their defense at Nuremberg. Giving to the poor is the highest form of tithing, yet "spreading the Gospel" is never associated with a tithe in the Scriptures ~ it's just programmed into peoples' heads that way. Luther knew that "indulgences" were just a big fund-raiser, and that their spiritual benefits amounted to nothing. When 𐤉𐤄𐤅𐤔𐤏 told the rich young man to give his wealth to the poor, He clearly didn't want any for Himself, nor did He say to give any to the Lewites. A Gentile convert to Yahudaism (Acts 10) who feared 𐤉𐤄𐤅𐤄 and studied Torah at the synagogue is another interesting case. He was Cornelius, a Roman centurion, who sent ***3 servants*** to go find Peter, and the text says he always gave generously to those in need. A messenger (*malak, angel*) was sent from 𐤉𐤄𐤅𐤄 and appeared to him saying, ***"Your prayers and GIFTS TO THE POOR have come up as a memorial offering before Elohim."*** Acts 10:1-5. This is where the ***3 sheets*** filled with unclean animals appear to our sleepy Peter, to ***prepare him*** to go with the ***3 Gentile men*** who were about to appear at his house gate ~ something he would not have done otherwise! The vision of the 3 sheets of unclean animals wasn't about food, but about Gentiles. One use of the tithe is commanded to be for YOU to bring to the place He has established His Name (Yerushaliyim) and EAT IT before Him. If it is too far and or too much to travel with, He says to sell the food or animals, and put the money in your hand ~ and then come and *buy food, strong drink, or whatever warms your heart,* and eat it rejoicingly before Him, sharing what you have with those who have little. The "merchants" must be thrown out of the Temple again; and WE are that Temple. The time has come now that true worshippers in the Truth worship from where they are, not in Yerushaliyim, as 𐤉𐤄𐤅𐤔𐤏 explained to the woman at the well. But, we will see the New Yerushaliyim when He returns, and be with Him! Now for the **MAN OF LAWLESSNESS:**

"For the secret power of <u>lawlessness</u> is already at work; but the one who now holds it back will continue to do so till he is taken out of the way. And then the lawless one will be revealed (uncovered), ***whom Rabbi 𐤉𐤄𐤅𐤔𐤏 will overthrow with the breath of His mouth and destroy by the splendor of His coming. The coming of the lawless one will be in accordance with the work of Shatan displayed in all kinds of counterfeit miracles, signs and wonders, and in every sort of evil that deceives those who are perishing. They perish because they refused to love the Truth and so be saved. For this reason 𐤉𐤄𐤅𐤄 sends them a powerful delusion so that they will believe the lie and so that all will be condemned who have not believed the Truth but have delighted in lawlessness."*** 2Th. 2:7-12. Who are these people who would "delight" in lawlessness, and refuse the Truth? Well, the Truth is Torah, what they call the Law, and they teach that it has been "done away", nailed to the crux. Then, by their definition, there is no criteria to define what a "sin" is, because if there is no law, then there is no way to sin against it (Romans 4:15). Yet, it says at 1 Yn. 3:4:

" Everyone who sins breaks the Torah; in fact, <u>sin is Torahlessness</u>". By stealth, the "seed" (the Word of 𐤉𐤄𐤅𐤄) was stolen away by the "birds", or trampled under the feet of men, as the parable says (Luke 8:5-15). You see, the words in the Writings we read as *Light, Truth, Word, Voice, Wisdom, Living Water, Commands, the Way, Seed, Life, etc.,* are all metaphors for the TORAH, or teachings of 𐤉𐤄𐤅𐤄. ***"'These people honor Me with their lips, but their hearts are far from Me. They worship Me in vain; <u>their teachings are but rules taught by men'.</u> You have let go of the commands of 𐤉𐤄𐤅𐤄 and are holding on to the traditions of men. You have a fine way of setting aside the Commands of 𐤉𐤄𐤅𐤄 in order to observe your own traditions!*** Mark 7:6-9, Yesha Yahu 29:13.

Do traditions we see in the practices of religion have any basis in the Writings? Can Paul make new Commandments, or annul the Torah of Yahuah? Can you find "Sun-day" or a "worship service" on Sun-day in the Writings? Is there any mention that the Shabbat was changed to the first day of the week? Tithing is certainly the work of the predators; and the poor, fatherless, and widows simply take a backseat. Legalism is some sort of *heresy* in the minds and words of most, yet 𐤉𐤄𐤅𐤔𐤏 said: ***"Do not think that I have come to abolish the Law*** (Torah) ***or the Prophets*** (Nebi'im)***; I have not come to abolish them but to fulfill*** (fill-full) ***them. I tell you the truth, <u>until heaven</u>*** <u>(skies)</u> ***<u>and Earth disappear, not the smallest letter</u>*** <u>(yod)</u>***<u>, not the least stroke of a pen, will by any means disappear from the Torah until everything is accomplished.</u> Anyone who breaks one of the least of these Commandments, and teaches others to do the***

same, will be called least in the kingdom of 𐤉𐤄𐤅𐤄, but whoever practices and teaches these Commandments will be called great in the kingdom of 𐤉𐤄𐤅𐤄. For I tell you that unless your righteousness surpasses that of the Pharisees and the teachers of the Torah, you will certainly not enter the kingdom of 𐤉𐤄𐤅𐤄." Mt. 5:17-20. These words sound very much like we should be knowing and acting on the 10 Commandments, as well as all the Moral teachings that the Torah has, which builds us up and protects us. A rich young man asked Rabbi 𐤉𐤄𐤅𐤔𐤏: ***"'Tob Rab*** (Good Teacher)***, what must I do to inherit eternal life?'"*** (Mark 10:17-27) Rabbi replied, ***"You know the Commandments: 'You do not murder, you do not commit adultery, you do not steal, you do not give false testimony, do not defraud, honor your father and mother . . .'"***

As I mentioned, without the Torah to live by, AND the gift of receiving a LOVE for them, you are not under the "New Covenant", and have not received the Spirit of 𐤉𐤄𐤅𐤔𐤏; so the wrath of 𐤉𐤄𐤅𐤄 abides on your head. Acts 5:32 says, ***"We are witnesses to these things, and so is the Ruach ha Qodesh*** (set-apart Spirit, *Yahusha*)***, whom 𐤉𐤄𐤅𐤄 has given to those WHO OBEY HIM."*** The "man of lawlessness" should be easy for you to identify. His office is the "Vicar" (substitute), also known as "Holy Father". His powers extend to any human being who is deceived, and seeks to deceive others, with the heresy that the Torah is no longer in force. Moral law has been **changed** in their thinking. This beast also has a "mark" (Sun-day), which you will find fulfills Dan. 7:25, the "change" of the Torah. The "Covenant Sign" of the 7th-day Shabbat, and the annual appointments, were annulled by this beast. Yet, Mashiach clearly warned us not to think that He had come to abolish or alter the slightest stroke of a pen, until the skies and Earth disappear. That's my whole world, because if I look up, there's the sky; if I look down, there's the Earth. Two witnesses again. He called them as witnesses to the **presence** of the Torah, as He had when He gave the Torah to the children of Yisrael: (see Deut. 30:19, 31:28) ***"This day, I call heaven and Earth as witnesses against you that I have set before you life, and death; blessings, and curses. Now choose life, so that you and your children may live and that you may love 𐤉𐤄𐤅𐤄 your Elohim, listen to His voice, and hold fast to Him."*** And, these two witnesses are still in existence, so the Torah we live by is still in force. And, it is our life. At Mt. 4, 𐤉𐤄𐤅𐤔𐤏 uses "the sword" or Word (Torah) to resist Shatan: ***"It is written, 'Man does not live on bread only, but on every word that comes from the mouth of 𐤉𐤄𐤅𐤄'".*** The "Bread of Life", is what 𐤉𐤄𐤅𐤔𐤏 is, the Living Word made flesh; the Torah became a living, breathing Person ~ the image of the invisible Elohim, 𐤉𐤄𐤅𐤄. The Father is in Him, and spoke to us. His body is a new creation now, never to die; and we will have such a body. Our new body will be our "house" or "tent" that will clothe our spirit, leaving behind the clay vessel we now inhabit that must die. It is appointed for man ONCE to die, and after this, the judgment; He will say **"Well *DONE, good and faithful servant"*,** not "*well believed"*. What will He say to the people who have never responded to His call, or were deceived by the Babylonian Mother of Harlots (and her daughters)? At Mt. 7:15-23, after explaining that false teachers would be inwardly ferocious wolves, Rabbi tells us we can tell a good tree from a bad tree by their fruit. Then He says, ***"Not everyone who says to me 'Adonai, Adonai', will enter the Kingdom of 𐤉𐤄𐤅𐤄, but only he who does the will of My Father who is in heaven. Many will say to Me on that day, 'Adonai, Adonai, did we not prophesy in your Name, and in your Name drive out demons and perform many miracles*** (great works)***?' Then I will tell them plainly, 'I never knew you. Away from me, you who practice lawlessness'".***

You can also look at what He is ***NOT*** saying. He **never** suggests that those who do their very best to obey Torah are to face a charge of "legalism". Shatan's messengers steer you away from Torah, but appear as messengers of righteousness. These also are the ones who look oddly at you when you bring up the real Name of the Creator. Let's face it; the translators carried over the name for the Yerushaliyim garbage pit (gehenna) very accurately, but couldn't do the same for the Name above every name. There is much to learn from footnotes, but you will notice they steer you away from believing you should obey the "laws" that please our Father. Without Torah, the whole world is filled with violence, as in the days of Noach.

ROSARIES

The prayer beads which monks and nuns wear, and are sold to the "laity" in Catholicism, came into their system around CE 1090, about the same time "indulgences" and celibacy were embraced. Prayer beads originated with Pagans, and are very common among Buddhists and Muslims. The Rudraksha beads of the Buddhists have 108 beads, and are sometimes "seeds". The Muslims use 99 sacred stones on their rosaries, and Catholics have 59. During the time that the lands of Spain and Portugal were controlled by the Islamic "Moors", a city was established called "Fatima", named after one of Muhammad's daughters. The

KEEP YOUR EYE ON EAGLE SYMBOLS, LIKE THE ONE CARVED IN THE UPPER RIGHT OF THIS PHOTOGRAPH.
THE SPREADING WINGS WILL EVENTUALLY TAKE ON A SYMBOLIC MEANING.
IT IS THE IMAGE OF THE BEAST!

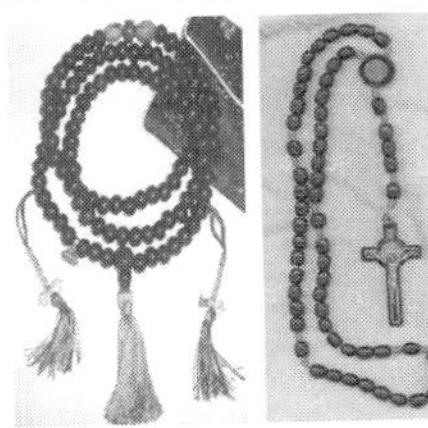

Upper left: Buddhist prayer beads, then Catholic, and the Islamic style. This "rosary" entered Catholicism in 1090 CE, about the same time they introduced "indulgences" and "celibacy".
Nicolaitanes promote their teachings through "strongholds" of all types.

story is that three Catholic children met an apparition of "Mary" in Fatima, and this "Mary" gave one of them the prayer beads, to pray to her with. Mary worship had started in CE 431, and kept growing more and more over the centuries. "Mary" is in the news quite often still, popping up in people's houses, or in the clouds. Catholics rally to see her. It is an odd thing, but Muslims also pray to "Mary", because Muhammad married a Roman Catholic nun named Kadijah, and learned to venerate Mary from her. They only pray to "Allah" and "Mary", yet they don't pray to Muhammad. Both Muhammad and Mary are dead and rotting in the ground.

Pagans' "repetitive" prayers are condemned by Rabbi OWYƎZ, since He said at Mt. 6:7: ***"And when you pray, do not keep on babbling like Pagans, for they think they will be heard because of their many words. Do not be like them, for your Father knows what you need before you ask Him."*** Also, Dt. 18 and Yesha Yahu (Is.) 8 forbid prayer to any entity other than ƎYƎZ. Contacting the dead is absolutely forbidden. Intercessory prayer may be done by living saints for other saints, but prayers **TO** the dead are an abomination. Any contact with "spirits" is a grievous transgression, and is demonic.

ISLAM .... ***IT'S LIKE THE 7TH CENTURY ALL THE TIME***

BABYLONIAN WORSHIP Above we see a Nimrod-influenced ruler ringing a hand-bell. In the upper right, you can see the eagle-sun representing Mithras, the Wise Lord Ahura-Mazda.
Note the "tower" head piece he is wearing. The deity Baal is also pictured at the top of the relief.

The Arabs are the children of Abraham by the Egyptian Hagar, who lived apart from the tribes of Israel, and *became Pagans*. They worshipped *hundreds* of deities. The big black "box" now called the **Ka'aba** (Arabic for "cube") was filled with images of their deities, one of which was called "Allah" - a ***moon deity***. Asherah was also a moon deity of the Canaanites, and Jericho was a major seat of her followers. So, ***Asherah*** and ***Allah*** *are the same deity.* Muhammad declared "Allah" to be the "greatest" (of the deities). The ***moon symbol*** is prominent in this religion. "Islam" means *submission.* Muhammad was born among the Pagan Arabs, his family being overseers of the Ka'aba, inside which hundreds of idols were worshipped by Pagans who made pilgrimages to Mecca. They would "*circumambulate*" the cubical building, just as the Hindus circumambulate their stupas. (They walk in a *circle* around the object they worship). In his youth, Muhammad converted to Yahudaism. He was eventually ejected by the synagogue *because of his violence*.

IF ISLAM IS A PEACEFUL RELIGION, WHY DOES THE WORD *HAMAS* MEAN *"VIOLENCE"*?

He later sought to convert his misguided people from their Paganism, but had to flee for his life from Mecca to his birthplace in Medina in CE 622, because the Arabs were dedicated to their idols. This "flight", or *hejira*, is the beginning point in the Islamic calendar. When he was in his mid 20's, he organized a large band of followers, and attacked the Pagan hierarchy in Mecca, and destroyed the idols in the Ka'aba, replacing them with oil lamps. The Ka'aba and its environment had to be re-invented to mask its former use. A large black meteor rock is believed to be a gift from an angel to their father Abraham, and the Ka'aba is considered to be the "holiest" place on Earth today by Muslims. "Muslim" means *one who submits*, and is based on the same word as Islam. He married an older woman in her 40's, Kadijah, who was a Roman Catholic nun. It is believed by many that she had been sent to him by the Vatican, who taught him from the Scrolls of the TaNaKh. In these scrolls, there is a "transposition" of the names **Isaac** and **Ishmael**, indicating that "the Covenant" was really with the firstborn son of Abraham, Ishmael. This may have been with the purpose of causing the Ishmaelites to eventually rise up and re-capture the land of Israel from the Persians. After the slaughter, Rome would make her move, which history shows she did, <u>in the Crusades</u>. The "sign" of the land Covenant is circumcision, which the Pagan Arabs did not practice. The Muslims embraced praying to "Mary" because of Muhammad's wife's dedication to her. They consider Rabbi 𐤉𐤄𐤅𐤔𐤏 to be a prophet, but they pray to His dead mother! The "sacred" writings of Islam are called the Koran (or Quran, from the Hebrew word ***qara***, for "proclaim"). Their use of the word "Allah" is known to them as meaning *the god*, and seems to be from the word *elah*, which in Hebrew means *mighty one;* <u>but it is not a name</u>. Muhammad instituted Islam's "Sabbath" as one day before the 7th day, or what is called "Friday". The Ishmaelites and Israelites are both Hebrews, and are brothers, yet they fight over the land given to Abraham. The problem is really their difference of religion. The Romans re-named the land "Palestine", a Latinism for "Philistia", the land of the old Philistines, who came there as settlers. They were another wandering "sea people".

When we see the Arabs referring to themselves as "Palestinians", they are calling themselves "Philistines", as if their claim to the land pre-dates the "Jews" because of this. Yet, Genesis 21:34 states ***"Abraham sojourned in the land of the Philistines many days."*** Obviously, Abraham wasn't a Philistine, so neither Isaac or Ishmael, his sons, were either! Ishmael was half Egyptian, because Hagar was Egyptian. The Ishmaelites lived in ***Arabia***, hence their name

BANNER OF THE HOLY ROMAN EMPIRE

"Arabs". Arab means "dark" or *darkening*, referring to their darker skin. They were the merchants who bought Yoseph who was carried off to Egypt and sold to Potiphar, Pharaoh's captain of the guard (Gen. 39:1). When all of these things are objectively presented to a Muslim, they become very confused. They face Mecca when they pray. When they rise up in their "jihad" (holy war), they are sometimes heard chanting *"first the Saturday people, then the Sunday people!".* The name "Ishmael" means *Elohim hears.* The descendants of Ishmael have lived in hostility to all their brothers (Gen. 25:18). The name "Ishmael" was given by 𐤉𐤄𐤅𐤄 to the boy of Hagar, since she had fled Sarah for being mistreated (Gen. 16), and He told her that Ishmael's hand would be against everyone, and would live in hostility toward all his brothers. There is nothing worse than a religious fanatic. They are taught that if they die in *jihad*, they will be instantly taken into "paradise" and given dozens of dark-eyed women as wives. They actually can't wait to die; they strap explosives to themselves, put their children in the line of fire when they instigate skirmishes, and generally seek to kill everyone who will not submit to their "Allah". The objective of Islam is control of the whole Earth, and the extermination of the "unbelievers". They control the Temple Mount in Yerushalayim, so the focus remains being hostile to their brothers, even though no one is meddling with their "holiest" place in Mecca.

Now, notice the similarity of the above ***image of the beast*** with the one on page 17. It represents THE SUN, Mithras. It is the original flag of the **HOLY ROMAN EMPIRE.**

The above flag was modeled after the old *Roman Empire flag*, and came into use during the 800's under Charlemagne. Most Pagan nations' flags utilize a "beast" of one sort or another, and the **eagle** is as old as Zoroastrianism ~ being a symbol of Ahura Mazda, or Mithras. The Pagan priests, "Magi", wore an eagle over their chests. Many cultures have used and still use this old Pagan BEAST image.

The Egyptians, Romans, Germans, Americans, and others cherished this image of the sun, the **great Mithras eagle** ~ an eagle is a *vulture* (see encyclopedia).

Christmas
"CHRIST'S MASS"
BREAKING THE TRUTH BARRIER

A Christian minister once responded to a letter I sent him, admitting that there are many traditions within Christianity that were ***originally Pagan***, but he said they are only in the "background" now. Yes, they certainly are, buried under new meanings, reinterpreted to obscure them! The Arabs did it with their Ka'aba, and we can *see that*; but when it's something WE want to do, we go into denial. This minister also said that since we don't intend to be worshipping the sun now, that it's all OK. When a person chooses to believe in something, their heart follows after it. Even if it's a lie, or a fantasy, it matters not to them. Prov. 19:2 says, ***"It is not good to have zeal without knowledge, nor be hasty and miss the way. A man's own folly ruins his life, yet his heart rages against 𐤉𐤄𐤅𐤄."*** Many believe that "Christmas" is in the Writings, with the stable, manger, star of Bethlehem, shepherds, and Magi visitation. Also, everyone is programmed to celebrate birthdays, so why not celebrate the birth of the most important Person ever born? Please bear with this carefully.

BIRTHDAYS

The popular celebration of one's annual birth-day is acknowledged to be, by all authorities on ancient customs, a Pagan ritual from Babylon. The Babylonians served the sun, moon, planets, and constellations, a Gentile practice condemned by 𐤉𐤄𐤅𐤄. ***"Do not learn the ways of the Gentiles, and do not be alarmed by the signs of shamayim** (heavens, skies, outer space) **although the Gentiles are alarmed by them."*** Yerme Yahu 10.

Birthdays are mentioned in Scripture a total of 3 times: when Yusef was in prison in Egypt ~ Gen. 40:20, Iyob (Job) 1:4,5, and Herod's birthday when Yahuchanon the immerser (John the Baptist) was beheaded, Mt. 14:6. In the situation described in Iyob 1, Iyob sacrificed an animal because he was aware of his children's idolatry, for which they all died when the house they celebrated in collapsed on them in a violent wind storm. ***"His sons used to go and hold a feast in the house of each one on his day . . ."*** (the NIV eliminated this phrasing, but you can clearly see it in the *KJV, NAV, NAS,* and others). The baker was hanged on the Pharaoh's birthday, and the Lewite Yahuchanon (our Savior's cousin) was beheaded on Herod's birthday.

THE BIRTHDAY RITUAL

IS HE NIMROD?
SORCERY?
Merry Mithras!

Merry Mithras!

LET'S PUT SATAN BACK INTO MITHRAS, AND KEEP YAHUSHA OUT OF IT . . . . .

The ritual of the cake, candles, wish, and presents serve to give thanks to sky luminaries for allowing the birthday celebrant to reach the annual cycle of their birth. The cake was baked for the ***Queen of Heaven*** **(Asherah)**. It was decorated, and monogrammed with the celebrant's name. The candles symbolized the sacred fire, carefully numbered for each annual cycle completed. The prayer chant and all the ritual procedures are carefully preserved, and it is a religious occasion. Witches regard the day of one's birth the most significant event in a person's life. Astrologers base everything on it. If the celebrant can blow-out all the candles, then a secret wish made to a GENIE (or JUNO if the person is female) will be granted. The birthday itself was a time of great superstition to a Pagan, so they were surrounded by their friends and relatives for protection. In the Greek culture, it was believed that personal abilities and talents were bestowed on an individual by being "inhabited" (possessed) by one or more demons, called *MUSES*. A person's "genius" was the gift of the Genie, thought of as the overseer of the Muses. The Muses were 9 female deities believed to endow skills in speech, art, science, memory, scholastics, agility, and *music* ~ a word derived from the 'MUSES" (9 daughters of Zeus & Mnemosyne). The names of these 9 Muses were *Clio, Euterpe, Thalia, Melpomene,* Terpsichore, *Erato, Polymnia, Urania, and Calliope.* You may recognize some of their names as having become part of our language, like "Uranus". They are the Greek deities of the ***Arts*** and ***Sciences***, giving us the word ***museum***, a showplace of Art and Science. The fairy tale Sleeping Beauty directly refers to the gifts and benefits bestowed by the Muses, since the Muses were known as Fairies in the Germanic and Gaelic cultures. The "***Three Fates***" were a triad of female deities also known as the *Three Graces*, or *Three Charities*. In the Greek and Roman mythologies, they ruled the lives of men, and determined the ***length*** of a person's life. *"Clotho"* spun the "thread of life", "*Lachesis"* determined its length, and "*Atropos"* cut it. This is the type of idolatry that Shaul was correcting the

Galatians and Ephesians for observing, since they were falling back into these patterns instead of exposing them and excluding them from their lives. He told them that they had lived as Pagans and been in darkness, but now were called-out from such ignorance. This "programming" in these practices became absorbed, and people are either ignorant of them, or too weak to break free of them. Their spiritual leaders aren't going to tell them, because they are hypnotized as well. The reason the Writings don't make much sense to people is because they are not aware, and don't recognize their own behavior as being Pagan. Everything has been pushed into the "background" so well, their eyes are "blinded" to the real truth. Astrology, an ancient Babylonian process of worship, was used to determine the "***sign***" under which a person was born. Everything that happened to a person was determined by "the stars". The position of the sun, moon, planets, and stars at the time of one's birth produced a personal "horoscope", used since ancient times by witches, palmistry experts, fortune tellers, diviners, sorceresses, tarot card readers, magicians, soothsayers, and others who dabble in the "OCCULT". The word "occult" means *hidden*. Such "divination" is idolatry: ***"Do not practice divination or sorcery"*** and ***Do not turn to mediums or seek out spiritists"*** Lev. 19, Dt. 18:14. Ex. 22:18 says we are not to allow a sorceress to live. ***"Let your astrologers come forward, those stargazers who make predictions moon by moon, let them save you from what is coming upon you . . ."*** Yesha Yahu 47:13. These practices from Babylon are tightly woven into our cultural tapestry.

When the people of 𐤉𐤄𐤅𐤄 mixed Gentile religious practices into their lives, He brought the punishments forth that He had promised would come upon them at Dt. 28, and Dt. 30. The severe punishments for idolatry documented in the TaNaKh are to serve as *examples* for us (1 Cor. 10:5-7). ***"This calls for patient endurance on the part of the qodeshim*** (saints, called-out ones) ***who obey 𐤉𐤄𐤅𐤄's Commandments and remain faithful to 𐤉𐤄𐤅𐤔𐤏".*** Rev. 14:12. The Sovereign 𐤉𐤄𐤅𐤔𐤏 commands us from the skies, to come out of Babylon: ***"Come out of her, My people, so that you will not share in her sins, so that you will not receive any of her plagues, for her sins are piled up to shamayim, and 𐤉𐤄𐤅𐤄 has remembered her crimes."*** Rev. 18:4,5. The great "dragnet" is the calendar we use based on the solstices. Witches have used it since Babylon. Shatan, by stealth, has this planet worshipping him by diversion. By the process you are about to see explained in the following pages, it will be evident to you that everything is designed (although in the background) according to the plans of Shatan. He is behind the sun-worship customs: ***"How you have fallen from heaven, O morning star, son of the dawn! You have been cast down to the Earth, you who once laid low the nations! You said in your heart, 'I will ascend to heaven; I will raise my throne above the stars of Elohim; I will sit enthroned on the mount of assembly, on the utmost heights of the sacred mountain. I will ascend above the tops of the clouds; I will make myself like the Most High."*** Yesha Yahu 14:12-14. Shatan will be exposed as the source of sun worship! If it is in the "background", then it's still there.

"Christmas" is really 2 words: *Christos* (Greek), and *missa* (Latin). *Christos* means "anointed", and *missa* means "depart". Both of these words were inherited from Pagans. The Mashiach was never called "Christ" in His own tongue (language). The "anointing" in the Pagan mind was performed by a physician, who carried a wooden box with various ointments in jars. The medical symbol "Rx" is derived from 2 Greek letters, *rho* (ρ) and *chi* (X). These are the first two letters in the Greek word *Christos* spelled χριστοζ ~ anointed. The sick were anointed for healing, and the letters rho and chi were used as a "logo" for the physician's trade ~ hung up as a sign designed to appear as an EYE (the "eye in the sky"). It was the Egyptian "Eye of Horus", which the Greeks had adopted. Medical students learn this history of the RX symbol in their study of pharmaceuticals. At this point, let me remark that the Mashiach never authorized or invented a new "religion", but rather was upset because of changes already made. He said "repent" ~ turn back. This is what makes all this so bizarre. The word Christos is cognate with the Hindi *Krista*, the sun deity of Hindus. It means *shining one*. The Latin word *Lucifer* means *light bringer*. ***Kris*** means ***shining***. The Hebrew "*Mashiach*" means anointed one, but refers to Him as Sovereign or King, as Samuel anointed Dawid. The "oil" (lamp oil) symbolized the power of LIGHT, or wisdom of Torah, poured on the head (reasoning organ) so that the king would rule wisely in the Commandments. The Torah is "a lamp", and a "light". But, you can still see the way the original word was avoided, and Shatan's "shining" was adopted instead. The word Christmas means *"anointed-depart"*, and is seen abbreviated in "X—mas". The "X" stands for Christos. Let me just say this: *"If men originated any word or*

P = RO X = CHI
FIRST 2 LETTERS IN "CHRISTOS"
THIS WAS THE GREEK SYMBOL
FOR MEDICINE;
ANOINTING OILS MADE FROM
PLANTS.

idea, then be suspicious of it." Is nothing sacred? The word "sacred" is Latin, *sakra*, and is used in place of the Hebrew word *qodesh,* meaning *set-apart.* Sakra itself traces back to an *Indo-*European language, "Sanskrit", and turns out to be a Vedic form of an India sun deity, "Indra". It came into Old Persian, and in one of its 12 forms is "Sakra". Another form is Mitra, or the Persian/ Roman "Mithras". OK, then is nothing ***qodesh****?* Yes! The Name of 𐤉𐤄𐤅𐤄 is set-apart, which is in the Name 𐤉𐤄𐤅𐤔𐤏. The Word, or *Torah* (Commandments) is qodesh. The *Temple Mount* ~ which He calls His set-apart mountain forever, where He has placed His Name is qodesh. And finally, *His people*, called *Yahudim*, who bear His Name are qodesh. Pretty much everything else is rock, dirt, metal, water, air, and such. The day we call *Shabbat* is set-apart in time, as a memorial of creation, and is in the Torah. The teachings of Torah are a solid "Rock" on which to build, because they will never change, nor can any man bend them. They were made "straight" by 𐤉𐤄𐤅𐤄.

Missa, Latin for *depart,* was the last word spoken at a Catholic *"Mass"*, and so the word for the liturgical procedure ***seems*** to be from that. It was tacked-on to the word "Christ" because the Mass ritual on December 25th was called *Christ's Mass*. But, even the "Mass" existed before Catholicism. It was what the Pagan priests of Mithraism and Mandaeanism called their *Mass of the Dead*, which was a ghastly "sacra-mental" ritual of animal and human sacrifice ~ on an indoor "altar", with the Pagan worshippers assembled in two rows of benches with a center aisle. The Pagan priest would be at one end of the room, mumbling obscurely, leading the service to Mithras. At the spring equinox, new "initiates" into the mysteries of the cult were "baptized" (sprinkled) in blood, under a bull being hacked to death. This was the time which the Earth's orbit "crossed" the celestial equator. These sun-worshippers interpreted this as "*Mithras* ***<u>slaying the bull</u>*** " ~ the sun had "crossed" over the celestial equator, overcoming the "bull", which they called the constellation of ***Taurus*** (Latin for "bull"). Every "Mass" is truly a Black Mass. The Pagan mind "mixed" this up with the Passover Seder known as "the Last Supper", and *POOF! The 'magic' became our Sun-Day* ***morning*** "supper". You have just broken the *Truth Barrier,* as I call it. The word *abracadabra* was used during the Mithraic mystery Mass, when they *transubstantiated* a sun-shaped disc of bread into the sun, and ate it. You can find this out by digging it up in a library or the Internet. The Catholic priest is believed to be endowed with the power to **transubstantiate** any bread into *Yahusha* simply by saying the words, *HOC EST CORPUS MEUM*, "THIS IS MY BODY". This produced the phrase, ***hocus-pocus***, a euphemism for any type of sleight-of-hand. The Mandaeans also had *"7 sacraments"*, among which were *Holy Matrimony, the "Eucharist" sun-disc bread wafer, "Confession", Holy Orders, and the Mass of the Dead itself.* They were sun-worshippers, from which a "Church Father", Augustine, had come from. There was never an ***indoor*** altar in the ceremonial law of 𐤉𐤄𐤅𐤄, and now there is no need for any altar. Our Rabbi had to die but once, and He said *"It is finished".* The RCC (*Roman Catholic Church*) hasn't gotten the message. Catholicism calls the Mass a "**<u>bloodless</u> sacrifice**", offering the "miraculous" transformed bread into the body of 𐤉𐤄𐤅𐤔𐤏 to the Father over and over. But, Heb. 9:22 says ***"<u>without</u> the shedding of blood there is no forgiveness."*** At Heb. 9:28, it says ***"Mashiach was sacrificed ONCE, to take away the sins of many people."*** (see Heb. 10:12 also). He cannot be sacrificed over again! There was no such term as "Christmas" until the 9th century. Going back to the 6th century, there was a time when our "years" were not even reckoned as we think of them today.

Imagine it is the year 525 CE. No one at that time knew it was "525" though; here's why: There was a real man named ***Dionysus Exiguus.*** Mr. Exiguus was a pretty Pagan guy, but he didn't know it. He was a "monk", and lived in a part of the world called Scythia, an ancient region of Asia, north of the Black Sea. Remember, "monks" are unknown to the Writings, as are nuns, popes, and cardinals. But, Mr. Exiguus had no idea he was toiling as a monk for absolutely no reason at all, other than ignorance. During his time, and for over 1000 years after him, the city of Rome was venerated above every other place on Earth, even Yerushalayim. The greatest "pilgrimage" a person could make was to the city of Rome. Finally, the opportunity came for Mr. Exiguus to make his journey to this city of his dreams. Upon arriving, he witnessed things that disgusted his devout sensibilities. The people were drunken, orgies were in full swing; ivy, ribbons, wreaths, garbage, and madness seemed to be everywhere. He was exasperated at the spectacle. What did he witness? He saw the authentic, raw and abominable Pagan festival of the winter solstice: ***Saturnalia*** (also called Paganalia, the **nativity of the sun**). The ivy was considered the "sacred plant" of

WOMB-WREATH

NATIVITY SYMBOL

FERTILITY SYMBOLS DECORATED TEMPLES AND HOMES OF PAGANS DURING SATURNALIA. BELIEVERS BEGAN TO USE THEM TO DIVERT ATTENTION AND BLEND IN - BUT IT IS CONDEMNED BY YAHUAH.

Saturn, so this custom has become an important feature of the "nativity" all over the Earth. It was an ancient belief that the winter sun was slowly dying, because it was seen rising further and further to the south each morning. "Sol-stice" means *sun-stop.* By December 25th, the ancient world's solstice, it could be recognized as beginning to return northward, and was said to be "reborn". It marked the time for a celebration that lasted for days. Carved idols were exchanged (dolls), people hung wreaths on their doors, or wore them around their necks (an echo of the symbol of Nimrod, the branch of a tree, twisted into a circle, symbolic of the shape of the sun, and the annual cycle). Hawaiians use a "lai", a circle of brightly colored flowers as a "sacred" religious emblem of protection and friendship. This "rebirth" of the sun came 9 months (a gestation cycle) after "Easter", when the Earth Mother was impregnated by the sun at the "crossing" of the Vernal (Venusian) equinox, when Mithras (the sun) "slayed the bull" (the constellation of Taurus), and the sun moved into the next constellation ~ bringing on warmer weather. If all of this sounds complicated and wild, that's why it was called the "sacred mysteries". The Writings call it *"folly".* Folly is the religion of fools, and if what they were doing was foolishness, falsehood, lies, and of no profit, then the Writings explain why people will say: ***"To you the nations will come from the ends of the Earth and say, 'Our fathers have inherited nothing but falsehood, futility, and things of no profit'"*** (Yerme Yahu 16:19). ***"We have made a lie our refuge, and falsehood our hiding place"*** (Yesha Yahu 28:15). This is why what you are reading will cause what the prophet says ***"The understanding of this message will bring sheer terror"*** (28:19). The "world" which the Writings speak of which we are to be set-apart (qodesh) from is the "broad road" of tradition we see everywhere, based on folly. We are called-out of the ignorance, and repent of observing "Easter", birthdays, Christmas, Halloween, Sun-day, the Nimrod based year cycle, and so on. But, we don't show "hatred" for people who are still trapped in them, but love. Nimrod, Constantine, Exiguus, and many others ***rule the world from the grave*** when practices they established are still observed by people today.

A.D. & B.C.

Under the topic "calendar", your encyclopedia will no doubt mention Dionysus Exiguus. When he became upset by what he saw being practiced when he visited Rome, Mr. Exiguus believed the beginning of the "year" was January 1st, as most do today, but we'll explain why that is under ***Nimrod*** when his truth barrier gets broken. Mr. Exiguus knew that the Pagan festival of Saturnalia, the re-birth of the sun at the winter solstice, had to go. So, he proposed to simply change the reason for observing the time. All the customs, the date, and symbols remained in place, but he camouflaged the behavior by declaring it to be observed as the **BIRTHDAY of OWYAZ**. . . . NOT THE SUN. To better "anchor" the idea, he estimated that the actual birth of OWYAZ had been **525 YEARS** prior to his visit. He imagined that the end of the Roman/Babylonian year of His birth was "YEAR ZERO", making that year our Rabbi's ***525th birthday***. He further declared it be the 525th *year of our Lord. "year"* is the Latin word *anno,* and *"our Lord"* is the Latin word *domini.* This produced his main contribution to our present numbering of years. Now, we have embraced his estimate world-wide, and have recorded all history since his time with references to what *year of our Lord* (A.D.) anything happened. There had never been anyone thinking it was the year "524", because this idea had not yet been established. He referenced everything that happened before the birth as before Christ, giving us the term "B.C.". Since the time of Exiguus, scholars have refined the accuracy of his estimate. It turns out that he was ***5 years off***, and should have determined that year as 530 A.D. You will see this when you look at any "timeline" in the study versions of the Writings ~ the scholars print the birth of OWYAZ as 4 B.C. to 6 B.C. That's really very funny, because that means we entered the 21st century back in "1996 A.D.", roughly. But, no one recognizes it; and besides, it's just a made-up date invented by a man anyway. The real truth is, our Rabbi was not born on December 25th, but during the fall. It has been carefully calculated that, based on the exact time when Zechariah's duties in the Temple occurred (Luke 1), and the visitation Miryam made to his wife Elizabeth, that Miryam gave birth to the Prince of Peace during "Tabernacles", an annual observance given at Lev. 23, and Dt. 16. He literally "tabernacled" among men, didn't He? The years are all wrong, as well as when they are supposed to start. But, even if the world insists on this system, let's look at more nonsense. For years, the media has "brain-washed" the public into believing that the year "2000" is the beginning of the 21st century. A broadcaster remarked, *"This will be the last World Series Game* (US baseball) *of the millennium".* He said this in 1999! The *"20th"* century began on January 1st, 1901, and the Centennial Year 2000 cannot be called the beginning of the 21st century at all. If you can count, consider 2000 pennies. There are 100 pennies in a dollar; and 2000 pennies in 20 dollars. To think that you begin your 21st dollar at your 2000th penny is just bad mathematics. The 19th century included the year 1900. Scholars are not deceived by this, and history will record this blunder. I point this out only to show how easily the masses can be led with blatant errors.

The Satanists and Wiccans know more about the concealed origins of Christian traditions, and often laugh behind their backs. One said:

"The Nazarene Barbarian Church (the one in the hands of the barbarians) *stole the tradition of the Folk* (Pagan people); *what it could not absorb was turned into their own perverse fantasies"* (signed *Cernunnos*><*Satan*). I believe evil is real, and the errors that were absorbed are an outward sign of rebellion against 𐤉𐤄𐤅𐤄. It is also true that a deceiver (liar) is in our midst, and has planted his seeds (teachings). ***"The great dragon was hurled down ~ that ancient serpent called the devil, or Shatan, <u>who leads the whole world astray</u>"***. (Rev. 12:9). Mr. Exiguus was devout, sincere, and had great zeal, but was deceived and lacked knowledge. Teachers have said that it would not be a good idea to change the calendar to the correct year because *"it would just confuse the children"*. Who is the real "kook": the one who ignores the truth and wallows in fantasy, or the one who exposes the illusions for what they really are? Inventing man-made methods of worshipping 𐤉𐤄𐤅𐤄 are not new, and He has given several specific commands forbidding His people from worshipping in Pagan designs, or "adding" anything to His observances. During the Exodus from Egypt, the children of Israel imitated the Pagan Egyptians when they fabricated the Apis (golden calf). It had never been their intention to offend Him, but they constructed an altar and were going to sacrifice to Him on it the following day. But, they "mixed" an Egyptian custom <u>they were accustomed to</u> into worshipping Him. This "calf" had a sun-disc between its horns. It was also the time of year in the spring when a "calf" or BULL image was an important Pagan item. Remember, the sun was in the "constellation of Taurus" (the bull). If something is Pagan, even if put into "the background" with camouflage, then we should be VERY AFRAID of mixing it into our worship of Him. He doesn't change.

Shaul (Paul) wrote to the Ephesians, people who had been previously Pagans, but converted to walk in the Truth (Torah). He warned them in the following texts, and these are the texts which I am responding to in obedience to warn you also:

"For of this you can be sure: no immoral, impure or greedy person ~ such a man is an idolator ~ has any inheritance in the Kingdom of Mashiach and of Elohim. Let no one deceive you with empty words, for because of such things Elohim's wrath comes on those who are disobedient. Therefore do not be partakers with them. For you were once dark-

ness, but now you are Light in the (Rabbi)***. Live as children of Light (For the fruit of the Light consists in all goodness, righteousness and Truth) and FIND OUT what pleases the*** (Rabbi)***. Have nothing to do with the fruitless deeds of darkness, <u>BUT RATHER, EXPOSE THEM</u>. For it is shameful even to mention what the disobedient do in secret. But everything exposed by the Light becomes visible, for it is Light that makes everything visible. This is why it is said: 'Wake up, O sleeper, rise from the dead, and Mashiach will shine on you.' BE CAREFUL HOW YOU LIVE ~ not as unwise but as wise, making the most of every opportunity, because the days are evil."*** (Eph. 5:5-16).

We must prove all things, to see if they are being done according to the "Word" (Torah). "Light" is Torah, and "darkness" is lawlessness. Ephesians 6 discusses the *armor of Elohim.* We must buckle on the belt of *Truth* (Torah). We must be steadfast, or possess the shield of ***emunah*** (faithfulness); we must shod our feet (our walk) in ***peace*** (Torah); put on the breastplate of ***righteousness*** (Torah); take the helmet of ***salvation*** (Torah); and **wield the Sword of the Spirit, *which is the Word of Elohim*** (Torah). This enables us to be able to stand on solid ground in the struggle against the lies sown by the rulers, powers, and spiritual forces of this darkened world. Lies, deceptions, and excuses are the storms and winds that blow against the "house" we have built ~ that skyscraper with missing rivets, or the one with rivets. The foundation, the Torah, is not shifting sand. As it is written, so we walk in it. The wise man will build on it as his foundation! The flesh must be disciplined by *practice* in walking in the Light of <u>Torah</u> (Heb. 5:14). This is so that when lawlessness approaches, we will be steadfast. What a rabbi teaches his students is Torah; so also our Rabbi. A rabbi "binds" and "loosens". If a student goes to ask, *"What does Torah teach about this . . . "*, any rabbi will answer according to his knowledge and skills learned from **Torah**. If Torah prohibits it, then the action is "bound". If Torah permits it, then it is "loosed". Without Torah, a minister, pastor, or teacher is "blind"; and when the blind lead the blind, both will fall into a pit. 𐤉𐤄𐤅𐤔𐤏 gave eyesight to us, so we would not be blind. Paganism defiles us.

𐤉𐤄𐤅𐤔𐤏 gave us the "Keys" to the Kingdom, the Torah written on our <u>hearts</u>. He left us the authority to "bind" and "loose". I do not "bind" anything alone, but with the Spirit of 𐤉𐤄𐤅𐤔𐤏, we Natsarim around the world can bind and loose, and we have bound the items being exposed in this book. We expose them as counterfeit worship. For this, we will suffer, and though we come in peace, some will be killed for it. The merchants have too much to lose. We see that "the Mass" in Christ's Mass (Christmas) is really a song-and-dance operation that has been used for well over 1000 years to take up collections of wealth. Christmas itself is about 4000 years old - if one traces the tradition back far enough. This assembling" on Sun-day has carried over into the Protestant assemblies. They carried-over the collections, the indoor "altar" relic of the Mandaean Mass, Sunday, steeples, the Roman Calendar with all of the "festivals" dressed up in their bright and shiny clothing to disguise Pagan folly. But they left the images of people behind; but this did not keep them from adopting the sign of the "cross", which entered with Constantine. And, then some if not most absorbed the sacramental dispensation of "grace" to some large degree. The weekly plundering of the flock cannot be justified in the Writings at all. There is no "law" ***requiring*** anyone to attend a weekly assembly either, but Catholicism instituted a Sun-day attendance ordinance which made it a "mortal sin" if one missed it. We are not to forsake the "assembling of ourselves", but this is speaking of the 3 annual ***appointed times*** (Passover, Shabuoth, and Sukkot / Tabernacles), not a ***weekly*** regulation. Even some of these are only binding on males 20 years old or over. Synagogues are places to study the Torah, Prophets, and Writings to educate people, proselytes as well. The Mashiach's real "religion" (way, walk) is "Torah". "Yahudaism" means the worship of Yah, but Rabbincal Judaism ADDS the Talmud. Many are shocked to learn He is a Rabbi; but it is even more disturbing to realize He is not even a Christian. He never practiced ~ nor does He now ~ *anything* that Christianity practices. He is not a Catholic, Baptist, Pentecostal, Mormon, or Presbyterian; but He is a Rabbi, of the sect of the Natsarim. The fact that He is about to return and rule the Earth is not a common message you hear, yet we are told to comfort one another with this knowledge, as we see the day approaching (1 Thess. 4:18). At His return, those who died awaiting Him whose names are written in the Scroll of Life (the one with the 7 seals) will be resurrected. Then, we who are alive will be changed; so fast, it will be like the wink of your eyelids, 1 Cor. 15:52. The rest will be caught by surprise. This will be when the elements will be burned, 2 Pet. 3:7.

You already realize that Santa Claus is not in the Writings, but how did this character get mixed into the stew? A character which has many faces to many people, this enigmatic illusion inspires all ages. Ancient Shamanic cave drawings, Pagan Germanic deities, places of cold and heat alike ~ all have this faceless and nameless one in common since long before history was recorded. Or at least the knowledge extends over the sight-horizon of our knowledge about the past. **WHO** he is was passed down to us from a story from the early Norsemen. That is only true of the English world, because other language groups have a shared cultural memory or such a character as our Santa Claus also. You only get the latest "echo" of what the character was, because the last major change in him happened within the last 70 years ~ one generation, or span of an average life. At adulthood, when it is realized that it's all fiction, most continue to lie to their children, and the cycle continues.

The whole objective of Nimrod worship, and the character of Santa Claus, seems to be intended to divert our worship away from Father 𐤉𐤄𐤅𐤄. Even the cycle of Easter and Christmas itself is the adversary's design, so it's really SATANISM in disguise. When a person turns away from these things, other cultural pressures are brought into play, and the name "Scrooge" is often applied to them. As you read this book, it is "sweet" because you are getting your curiosity for the Truth satisfied; but as you "digest" it, it turns your stomach sour, doesn't it? Read Revelation 10:7-11. Most of mankind is worshipping Nimrod still, but they don't know it. Incredible effort is expended by most everyone to conform to the adversary's hidden agendas, but they don't see it happening. The whole world is deceived.

There is a war going on against the Truth. The vast majority believe that in the beginning, there was nothing; ***then, it exploded***. Rain weathered rocks, and in solution developed into the building blocks of life, and eventually became biophysicists, who believe they came from a rock. The second largest rock-carving in the world, Mt. Rushmore in the Black Hills of South Dakota, depicts the faces of George Washington, Thomas Jefferson, Theodore Roosevelt, and Abraham Lincoln (each about 18 meters high). If you ask one of the evolutionists if they think the universe could ever randomly create such a formation by itself, over ANY period of time, they will logically admit it to be impossible. Yet, they believe the universe COULD randomly create the actual men depicted on the rock! The adversary wants people to believe there is no Designer, and this helps him because he can go about manipulating us, because most believe he doesn't exist either.

It is a possibility that the memory of the "character" of Santa Claus may lead all the way back to Nimrod, the king of Babylon, Nineveh, and all of Sumer. We sure have received plenty of the other “baggage” from Babylon, and it all seems to be closely related. If the historical time of man could be thought of as an expanding shoreline, the Pagan baggage and the Santa-is-Nimrod idea could be something “washing ashore” together from some ancient, single source. The word “Santa” contains all the letters of the word Satan, perhaps as a little personal joke of his. And the letters are only one off from being in perfect order. If he is dangling that, and we don't believe there's a connection, then we might not get the other one he's “dangling” to see if we'll notice it; SUN-DAY.

THE MAGI

“Magi” was the term used for the Pagan priests of Mithras, and they were ***“magi-cians”,*** who used fire and eagles as representations of their deity. These are Shatanic designs. Ancient Pagans gave us the worship of Fire, “religious” discs, haloes, or circles, wreaths, (*boughs, branches*), domes with an “oculus” in the top, bells, towers/steeples; candle-altars in front of statues; holy water, wearing *black*, indoor altars shaped like a flat autopsy table; the idea of dead people's bones being a “relic” that contains powers; tea leaves (scapulas); the dates of Easter/Ishtar and Christmas/Saturnalia being exactly the same; “Easter” being the authentic name for the Pagan event itself; Sun-day; Lent (lengten); Valentine's Day; Halloween; Father's Day, Mother's Day, the ring in marriage; rolling eggs on the grass, or fields; monks; prayer-beads like the Buddhist monks use (also inherited by a separate path to the Pagan Arabs before they converted to Islam); Princes on flying carpets and flying Santas; gurus, popes, “fathers”, Asherah poles, obelisks, colossus images of dead men; crosses of candles . . . *(PUFF . . . PUFF), It sounds like some wild* ***VOODOO*** *doesn't it? That's exactly what it is.*

Let's see if we can establish a difference between the relative advantage of having the Santa myth in our lives, ***or*** spinning a dead chicken by its neck over our heads. *You go first.* OK, you've imagined that; which of the two gains you the greater advantages? If you're truthful with yourself, they gain you the very same results ~ ***nothing*****;** in the here and now, as well as in the eternal perspective. (Keep your eye on the Torah, and you'll see it is turning out to be a better ***foundation*** and house than any other structure around. Names, beliefs, customs, and teachings all dissolve as *shifting sand* on the beach of history, but the Torah stands like a ROCK.) Let's pause and look at some of the time-traveling luggage we see “washed up” on history's beach. The Magi who visited the young Mashiach OWYƎZ came when He was about 2 years old, not the night of His birth. They spoke to

MYSTERY BABYLON CAN BE SEEN ALL AROUND OUR WORLD

Herod first, and he carefully examined them to learn exactly when the star had appeared. The Magi were probably Mandaeans, sun-worshippers, and were watching for this star because they were descendants of the Babylonians, who had preserved copies of Daniel's writings, and probably other prophets' as well. The reason the Magi paid close attention was because Daniel was quite a famous and important figure among the Babylonian “wise men”, and his interpretation of ***Nebuchadnezzar's dream*** had saved the lives of all of their ancestors. They were what we would call *wizards*, and may have been “keepers of the flame” ~ the sacred fire. Remember that these men were also the primary reason the “clergy” wears black today ~ they played with ashes a lot of the time. They were mumblers who interpreted the “mysteries”. No doubt “Nostradamus” had a lot in common with them; he gazed into a fire when writing his quatrains. They engaged in “Magi-c”. This logically led to the medieval attempt to “trans-mutate” metal, like iron into gold. The gifts these Magi brought were gold (a gift for a king), frankincense (a gift for a priest), and myrrh (a burial ointment used to glue the wrappings of the body). But, these costly gifts also provided for the flight and stay in Egypt, since Yusef, Miryam, and the Prince of Peace left that very night, being warned by Gabriel of Herod's design to kill the Child. Speaking of “child” ~ any child can show you which day is the 7th day of the week on a calendar. How is it that we adults find it so difficult to rest on the proper day? At Luke 18:17, OW-YƎZ said, ***“whoever does not receive the Kingdom of ƎYƎZ like a child shall not enter it.”*** We tend to “read through” the printed text of the Writings, looking for deeper meanings. From Kabbalism, there are 4 “levels” of meaning that certain sects “puffed-up” the Writings with, like leavening expands bread. We are warned to beware of the “leavening” (inflated teachings) of the scribes and Pharisees. These men and others like Kabbalists, “interpreted” Torah on these 4 levels: *PASHAT* (the literal meaning of the words), *REHMEZ* (the simple secondary meaning), *DROSH* (an exotic derivative going “out on a limb”, straining the meaning severely), and *SOOD* (let's hope we aren't responsible for this interpretation level!). Anyway, if we “strain” to see past what Torah literally says, this might cause us to

THE “SANTA” CHARACTER HAS DIVERSE NAMES, AND VARIES FROM CULTURE TO CULTURE.

overlook it. Straining out a gnat, we could swallow a camel as we drink the milk of Torah. Or, we could find that as we correct another on a small detail, we have overlooked a huge "log" in our own ability to see with clarity what Torah says. So, receive the Words of Torah as if you were a child listening to its father.

The remark which 𐤉𐤄𐤅𐤔𐤏 made must have really been insulting to the puffed-up "interpreters" who heard Him. The Pharisees' Kabbalism had "leavened" or puffed-up their self-image, and added much. *Yahusha* was clearly saying that a child was superior to them in comprehension.

NIMROD STUFF & THE "SANTA" DISQUISE

We've heard all the nice stuff; but what entanglements do we have with a man who supposedly flies horned beasts through the air at night? Is it about sorcery? He wears a wizard cap. The red costume is recent, but it's the ancient color of fire. Its our cultural color for danger. The costume is trimmed in sheepskins. He descends into a fire pit at midnight ~ the hearth is directly linked to the idolatry of the Romans. The fire was sacred to them, and its place was the center of the Pagan worship of their deities. Our mythology of him comes to us through Angle-Land (Eng-land), and that traces to Holland, and Germany, and back to Turkey. One version involves a 3rd-century story about a "Saint Nicholas"; it had no mention of "elves", chimneys, flying reindeer, or supernatural feats. The "Christmas tree" isn't mentioned in the story. Christianity had made no in-roads into the northern areas of Angle Land, Hol Land, Scot Land, Fin Land, and Eire Land, until well into the 5th century. If anyone named "Nicholas" existed in Holland during the 3rd century, he was a Pagan who obeyed his Druid priests. In the **8th century**, a man named ***Boniface*** encountered these Druid-led people of the north, and sought to convert them. He saw them bringing oak trees into their homes at the winter solstice, decorating them with gold balls representing testicles (note picture on page 3). The word "Dru-id" means "oak-wise", because oak trees were sacred to them. This comes from Babylon. At the death of Nimrod, the wife/mother Semiramis taught the young Tammuz to go into the groves *(Asherim, forests)* and place a gift on a tree at the winter solstice. This was an offering to his father, Nimrod, who was now the sun. The custom of tying a "yellow ribbon" around an *oak tree* represents a ***prayer*** to the sun. The oak tree was sacred to Odin*. At this point, branches of trees came to symbolize Nimrod also, so decorating Pagan temples and homes with holly, boughs, and wreaths was the custom. The wreaths are branches twisted into circles, so the branches would be associated with the sun, but were also representations of a WOMB and associated birth canal. Remember, it is the "nativity of the sun". Ezekiel 8:14-18 shows how the women in Yerushalayim were "**weeping for Tammuz**", and the Lewite priests (25 men) were facing the rising sun and putting a "branch" to their nose. These customs were called a detestable thing.

"Do not learn the ways of the Gentiles, and do not be terrified by the signs (zodiac) ***of the skies, although the Gentiles are terrified by them; for the CUSTOMS of the Gentiles are DELUSION; they cut a tree from the forest, the work of a cutting tool, they DECORATE it with silver and gold; they fasten it with nails and with hammers."*** Yirme Yahu 10:2-4.

A Benedictine monk effectively influenced the Druids in 722 CE to adopt a slight variation on the **Asherah tree.** When Boniface saw the people of the Druids bringing ***oak trees*** into their homes, he ***diverted*** them to consider the ***evergreen tree*** instead, and used it to teach them about eternal life. He never taught them that the tree or the wreath was a detestable thing, set-apart for destruction (along with anyone who would bring it into their home - Deut. 7:26). People of other regions used date palms. Scholars call it "syncretism" when a religious or philosophical behavior is united or combined with another behavior. ***It is a conscious attempt to DISGUISE one of them in the camouflage of the other by re-inventing a new meaning, and believing in it.*** Moloch is lurking nearby at Christmas, so maybe he really is Santa Claus too! The Christmas tree ~ whether an oak, evergreen, or palm, points back to Babylon and Nimrod. Even further also, because it was in the GARDEN that we first find that TREES are involved in determining whether mankind would sin or not. Shatan is a usurper, liar, and imitates closely many things - and imitation is the highest form of flattery. Shatan is still using trees to whisper lies to us. When I go out to stores at the end of the Roman year, I walk by many of these displays, knowing the trees are Asherim, and the wreaths are fertility symbols.

We'll cover more details about the Christmas tree and wreath custom shortly.

If there really was a real person named Nicholas, and it's not all just a legend, he sure went through some changes. The oldest account of his existence is vague, and of relatively recent origin. His location places him among the Germanic Dutch, but as I mentioned, these people were not yet Christians. The date and location for him makes it an ***anachronism*** (the time is "against" it being true). In the 3rd century, the people of the north were ***barbarians*** (meaning "bearded Aryans"). They were Druids who burned their enemies and criminals in wicker cages over fires, threw wealth into lakes to water idols (like we still

ODIN & WODEN ARE CELTIC FORMS THAT CAME FROM THE HEBREW "ADON", WHICH BECAME THE EGYPTIAN ATON

see people do in fountains), burned children as offerings to the sun, and placed jack-o-lanterns outside their homes lit by candles made from the fat of their own children. If they weren't Pagans, nobody was! So, the legendary Nicholas couldn't have been there at that time. Another major problem is this: they claim Nicholas was a "bishop" (presbyter, elder). Yet, at his death on December 6th, he had only reached the ripe old age of 17. "Bishop" means *elder,* from the Greek word *presbus,* "old man". I'm not leaning heavily in favor of believing the tale with all these conflicting facts. The RCC honors him as a "saint". How did we get from ***Nicholas*** to ***Santa Claus***? In the late Middle Ages, the Germanic Dutch who told the story of Nicholas to English listeners spoke in a very *pronounced accent.* When they said "*Saint Nicholas",* it came out sounding like this:

" ***SAINTNI - CHOLAS*** "

The English hearers of this took it down at first as *"Santy Claus"*, and it took the more Spanish form *"Santa"* later on. You will sometimes see the form "Santy" in old books from earlier in the 20th century.

Irish Potato Blight

The Irish (*of Eire Land*) had grown very dependant upon the potato during the 18th and 19th centuries. The potato was a transplant to Eire Land from Columbia, South America. In 1846, a **fungus** destroyed the crops, causing widespread famine in Eire Land. Vast numbers of people died, and the decline of the population was catastrophic ~ so much so, that the only hope of escape from death was emigration. It was precisely at this point that most Irish came to the United States, fleeing the Great Famine. What they brought to the United States for the first time was **Catholicism**, since many of the earlier colonizers had fled here from the religious persecution of Catholic and Anglican intolerance. These Irish Catholics had the rich cultural background of Druidism, which they had blended together with Roman Catholicism. Their belief in ***elves***, banshees, leprechauns, fairies, luck, and all sorts of Celtic Magic came with them. They brought their pumpkin ritual seen as "Halloween", which had been a Druid festival honoring ***Samhain***, their deity of the dead. They also brought their "Christmas tree" tradition, along with Christmas, which had been outlawed as Pagan in many colonies. The Catholics in South America have assimilated the cultural background of the Aztecs. Other Catholics from around the world would **not** recognize many things they do ~ and so it is with them in many other parts of the world. Whatever the Pagans were doing **before** became inter-mixed with the Roman Catholic façade, forming a kind of "crust," **masking the Paganism**. The Haitian VooDoo of Cajun Catholics has produced a spicy "mix" of Pagan and Catholic tradition down in Louisiana, where the alligators grow so mean. There were no pumpkins on peoples porches, or Christmas trees in America until that **fungus** drove the Irish people to flee their homeland and migrate to North America.

CHILDREN WERE OFFERED TO THE MOABITE IDOL
MOLOCH.
INFANTS WERE PLACED INTO HIS ARMS AND AS THE ARMS LIFTED TO THE MOUTH, THE INFANT DROPPED INTO THE "LAP" WHICH WAS A LITERAL FURNACE

Things, ~ *like Paganism* ~ ***go better with Coke.*** In the late 1800's, a pharmacist put some cocaine in a sweetened, bubbling cola beverage, and named it *Coca~Cola.* **Coca-Cola** was invented by Dr. John Pemberton, an Atlanta pharmacist.

By the 1930's, it was a major business, and had its own advertising department, strategists, and artists. One of the artists, *Rosenblum*, decided to attempt something new. The Dutch/Irish character called *"Santy Claus"* was beginning to get a lot of attention, so he set his mind on aligning the *Coca~Cola* product with him.

In Rosenblum's time, ***Santy*** Claus didn't look like he does now. The original character was an Irish transplant, coming from people who had based their beliefs on Druid magic, and **ELVES**. The 19th century poem <u>*The Night Before Christmas*</u> had catapulted our Christmas Elf into the spotlight, because the character was so appealing. Rosenblum used his artistic imagination to change Santy Claus into what we think he looks like today. ***Before, Santa was no more that 2 feet tall, skinny, and wore green.*** He had a long white beard, and for all practical purposes he was a *leprechaun / elf* creature with magical powers to grant wishes, watch you without being seen, and so on. He could also do you harm. The alignment with the hearth is another Pagan syncretism, right down to the stockings hung by the chimney with care. To make this night-visitor charming, and more human, Rosenblum made him a full-sized man, jolly and plump, to better assume the distinctive shape of the Coke bottle. He also used the appealing red and white **product colors** to clothe Santa in. The drooping wizard hat was a must. The final art work was combined with a marketing message to encourage customers to leave a bottle of Coke near the hearth when he visits at midnight, Christmas Eve. Now you know why little children say, *"But how can Santa fit down our chimney, isn't he too big?"* Yes, he is now, but they tell the children that Santa has magical powers. When he was less than 2 feet tall, he could fit into many such tight squeezes. The moral implications of telling an outright lie to your own children also has an effect on them later in life. It perpetuates the lie for generations down the line, and cripples them for life regarding believing in things they cannot see ~ such as an unseen Creator. Lying to them about Santa certainly isn't going to help them believe. Who is the father of lies? If you put up a tree, hang stockings by the fireplace, and exchange gifts this coming Roman December, watch for the mistletoe. It's poisonous, and a Pagan spell surrounds its ritual use too. It is just a parasite to a tree, but the custom of hanging it up and collecting kisses comes from Druidism. The name "Saint Nicholas" may coincidently relate to Rev. 2:15, and the reference to "Nicolaitans". The messenger to the assembly at Pergamum was to carry a warning about the teachings of "Balaam" that they embraced. ***"Likewise you also have those who hold to the teaching of the NICOLAITANS. Repent therefore!"*** It has been said that these were a sect of religious teachers who "***lorded over the laity***" ~ which is what "Nicolaitan" means. I smell Nimrod all over this, don't you? I don't get the impression that OW – YƎZ likes us to mix up our worship of Him with Pagan designs, or wants us to have any contact with it. Light and darkness cannot be mixed. Now, consider how the Christmas tree is mixed up in all of this.

ASHERAH

THE CHRISTMAS TREE CONNECTION
BAAL & ASHERAH:
THE SUN KING & HIS CONSORT

Asherah *is known in Scripture as the "Queen of Heaven", and is called* ***"Artemis"*** *by the Ephesians in the book of Acts (chapter 19). The word "Asherah" is found at least 40 times in the* ***T****a****N****a****K****h*, and refers to a wooden object, used in the worship of a* ***consort*** *of BAAL. The* ***image of Asherah*** *was* ***a tree*** *used by the Pagan Canaanites and Sidonians. One of these Pagan Sidonians was "Jezebel", who married Ahab, king of northern Israel (Samaritan king). Northern Israel*

Holly
A plant "sacred" to the Roman deity Saturn. Decking the halls with boughs of holly marks us for destruction.

was in apostasy, being led into rebellion by their leadership, and violated the Covenant of Yahuah. They added an 11th Commandment:
"You shall worship Yahuah your Elohim in Mount Gerizim" Note that this is one of the topics of the conversation between *Yahusha* and the Samaritan women at the well at Jn. 4.

The northern tribes began to worship the "Baals" (Baalim), consisting of Baal and Asherah, influenced by king Ahab's Sidonian wife, Jezebel. Such tree worship was put under the ban, yet the 10 northern tribes failed to carefully guard Yahuah's Commandments, or Declarations. Asherah became the deal-breaker, and the northern tribes were taken away into the nations - they remain so now, after 2700+ years.

When northern Israel was dispersed into the nations by the Assyrians in 722 BCE, ***they carried this "tree" custom with them****. The lost tribes of dispersed Israel have preserved one of their most cherished Pagan customs among them:* ***the Christmas tree, or Asherah.***

If you were brought up with this custom, then you are most likely descended from these northern tribes, even if only "doctrinally". You were taught to practice an ancient Phoenician form of idolatry, and never knew it.

Asherah was the "Queen of Heaven" (see Jer. chaps. 7 & 44). Now, read specifically how the Creator feels about it:

Deut 7:26: ***" Do not bring a detestable thing into your house or YOU, like IT, will be set apart for destruction. Utterly abhor and detest it, for it is set apart for destruction."***

Yahuah distinctly warned Israel to not erect an Asherah next to His altar, nor bring a "detestable

T*a****N****a****K****h: **T**orah, **N**ebi'im (Prophets), **K**ethubim (Writings)*

LEARNING THE WAYS OF THE HEATHEN

Canaanite / Phoenician religious traditions exploded into the world when northern Israel was expelled from the land 2700 years ago. The wreath is the "womb", and the tree is the "phallus". The customs of the nations are altogether worthless, and their objects of worship are accursed things. No amount of time will ever clean them from their defiled past, even if ***people*** *are ignorant of that past.*

BAAL & ASHERAH

SUN WREATH &
IMAGE OF JEALOUSY

thing" into our house. Even though YOU may not remember what it represented long ago, Yahuah hasn't forgotten at all. He does not change.

As some have said, the Asherah is a deal-breaker with Yahuah - He won't stand for it. He dispersed the northern tribes of Israel into the nations, and they have lived as Pagans for 2700+ years. They left Yahuah's Covenant, but they have held fast to the Asherim (plural of Asherah).

"ASHER" is a Hebrew term meaning "happy", and is a word used as a proper noun, the father of the tribe of Asher (alef-shin-resh). This term was modified, and became the word "ASHERAH", a proper name used by Pagans for the female consort of Baal (Celtic Bel). Baal/Asherah worship is clearly seen during the time of "Elijah" (ElYahu), when 450 prophets of Baal and 400 prophets of Asherah assembled at Mt. Carmel, and ElYahu (Elijah) challenged them to decide whether **Yahuah** is Elohim, or **Baal** (and his consort, **Asherah**).

A sister asked the following questions regarding Asherim:

1. What is an Asherah?

Answer: The adversary misled mankind with various fertility rites, and receives "worship" through these rites. Yahuah doesn't provide us with the details of the heathen rites, but we know generally from Scripture they performed their rituals in forests or "***groves***".

The word ***"Asherim"*** is often translated as "groves". He mentions how the Israelites would bring "Asherim" and put them near His Hekal (Temple), behavior which we see inherited as the "Christmas Tree". The trees most likely used were ***date palms***. Modern witchcraft and Satanism in general follow most closely to the worship of ***Asherah***. The name is most likely directly related to Ishtar, and ***Artemis***, worshipped by modern day witches as well as the ancient ***Ephesians*** (Acts 19:28). Stumps of trees found in groves were also used as the altars of Asherah, which may be directly related to the fallen Nimrod, cut down by Shem (as tradition informs us).

2. What does she look like?
3. Where can I find pictures of her?
4. Why is it so difficult to do research on an Asherah?

Answer: Images of Asherah vary, but you can see one photo of an image of this deity at http://www.teenwitch.com/DEITY/CANAAN/ASHERAH.HTM (if this page still exists).

Yahuah has not wanted His people to study this demonic worship, yet it persists today. The most insidious part is right out in the open, and not "occult" (hidden) at all: ***the Christmas tree object!*** A more secretive side is also growing in popularity. In fact, it is the most popular fad among teens and young adults today. The reason it is not very easy to learn about is mostly because it is ***"occult"*** (hidden); it has been so since the patterns of worshipping the adversary went "underground" after the execution of Nimrod. They had once practiced their rebellion openly, but then withdrew into secrecy to ***hide*** their worship behind symbolism, which could only be interpreted correctly by those initiated in the occult. One dominant pattern found in occultic behavior is the ***matrilinear*** (mother-goddess) ideal. Rebellion against Yahuah is accentuated by this matrilinear focus, as opposed to the patrilinear - so we see ***the moon*** being used to represent the female astrologically.

Although the original concept of Asherim worship has remained hidden from the general public, I feel that the acceptance of the solstice tree is drawn directly from the Pagan worship, transformed for public consumption. The Asherim were considered altars in themselves also, where animals and humans were ritually sacrificed at the Equinoxes and Solstices. This altar could take the form of a tree stump, with the trunk snapped-off, leaving jagged spike-like splinters. The Christmas tree phenomenon is also a type of altar, where gifts and offerings are placed. (***Easter*** is a word derived from Ishtar, Astoreth, and Astarte. Tree worship is the most prominent feature, however the serpent gets involved also. It seems that the adversary has the tree and the serpent seared into "his" mind indelibly. A serpent around a stump is one of the symbols we find used in ancient Pagan religions. The ***Tree of Life*** (ets ha'chayim) and the ***Tree of the knowledge of good and evil*** may be the sources this fallen being is borrowing from in the design of the false worship. But we know it is forbidden to worship Yahuah in any false or perverted manner. Rebellion is as the sin of witchcraft, and we certainly know that any involvement with Asherim ***is witchcraft***. Some have even suggested that the symbol of "the cross" may have been a style of **Asherah pole** used by certain Pagans, and that it was brought into the mixed worship of Christianity. Some styles of Asherim have crux-like and ankh-like shapes. Certainly, the Christmas tree is considered a "Christian" symbol, yet the common culture has no idea how it actually relates to anything associated with Yahuah, or "Santa Claus" for that matter! No one can explain what the Christmas tree has to do with Santa Claus either, it's all developed very rapidly in western culture. It's like a Cajun GUMBO, where every possible Pagan item has been thrown together into a big, stinky stew (or cup) of abominations. The Harlot teaches them to her subjects, keeping them in a drunken stupor by making them all drink from her cup every week, on Sun-day.

Eph 5:5-14:
"For of this you can be sure: No immoral, impure or greedy person-such a man is an idolater -has any inheritance in the kingdom of (Mashiach) ***and of*** (Elohim)***. Let no one deceive you with empty words, for because of such things*** (Eloah's) ***wrath comes on those who are disobedient. Therefore do not be partners with them. For you were once darkness, but now you are light in the*** (Master)***. Live as children of light*** (for the fruit of the light consists in all goodness, righteousness and truth) ***and find out what pleases the*** (Master)***. Have nothing to do with the fruitless deeds of darkness, but rather expose them. For it is shameful even to mention what the disobedient do in secret . But everything exposed by the light becomes visible, for it is light that makes everything visible."***

BAAL & ASHERAH HAD A "SHOWDOWN" WITH YAHUAH, REMEMBER?

1 Kings 18:16-21:
So Obadiah went to meet Ahab and told him, and Ahab went to meet Elijah. When he saw Elijah, he said to him, "Is that you, you troubler of Israel?"
"I have not made trouble for Israel," Elijah replied. "But you and your father's family have. You have abandoned Yahuah's commands and have followed the Baals. Now summon the people from all over Israel to meet me on Mount Carmel. And bring the four hundred and fifty prophets of Baal and the four hundred prophets of Asherah, who eat at Jezebel's table."
So Ahab sent word throughout all Israel and assembled the prophets on Mount Carmel. Elijah went before the people and said,
"How long will you waver between two opinions? If Yahuah is Elohim, follow Him; but if Baal is Elohim, follow him."

WREATH, ORNAMENTS, Etc.,.

*The round wreath symbolized the sun, and at the same time the "**womb**", both thought of as symbols of fertility to Pagans. The sun was "male", but "his" symbol was that of the female. The vertical tree was decorated with male symbols of fertility, testes (balls), yet was the image of the "female", connecting the heavens to the Earth. This consort of Baal was worshipped as **Asherah**, Astarte, Artemis, Athena, Isis, Gaia, Nana, Austron, Ostara, Eastre, Easter, Aphrodite, Eostre, Astoreth, Ishtar, Diana, Ninurta, Cres, Nut, Venus, Indrani, Devaki, Tanit, and others. This "tree" was named Asherah in the Hebrew Scriptures, **and her worship continued as we see recorded in the book of Acts, chapter 19.** She is **still** worshipped today by Wiccans, and other Earth Mother cults. The Vernal Equinox pointed to the impregnation of this Earth Mother, and the Winter Solstice pointed to the birth of Baal, the sun, showing the human gestation cycle of nine months. To the Pagan, the cycle of yearly observances had great influence over them. Their festivities were all about fortune, fertility, and sex. See Shaul's words above.*

Paul knew about Pagan customs:

Gal 4:8-11
"Formerly, when you did not know Yahuah, you were slaves to those who by nature are not elohim. But now that you know Yahuah- or rather are known by Yahuah- how is it that you are turning back to those weak and miserable principles? Do you wish to be enslaved by them all over again? You are observing special days and months and seasons and years! I fear for you, that somehow I have wasted my efforts on you."

*The round ornaments represented the testes as mentioned, and have also come to be known as **"witch balls"**. Fertility symbols abound in nature worship; throwing rice at weddings in ancient cultures represented semen. It would be interesting to see what a "theologian" might use as an excuse for all this, wouldn't it?*

*YirmeYahu was the "Professor" to the **northern tribes**, known as the "**house of Israel**". They had fallen into idolatry with the worship of **Asherah**, so as you read the following, realize that Yahuah was warning the tribes in Samaria about a specific thing they were doing:*

Jer/YirmeYahu 10:1-5:
Hear what Yahuah says to you, O house of Israel. This is what Yahuah says:
"Do not learn the ways of the nations or be terrified by signs in the sky, though the nations are terrified by them. For the customs of the peoples are worthless; they cut a tree out of the forest, and a craftsman shapes it with his chisel. They adorn it with silver and gold; they fasten it with hammer and nails so it will not totter. Like a scarecrow in a melon patch, their idols cannot speak; they must be carried because they cannot walk. Do not fear them; they can do no harm, nor can they do any good." Jezebel taught them about Asherah.

Deut 12:29-32: ***"Yahuah your Elohim will cut off before you the nations you are about to***

invade and dispossess. But when you have driven them out and settled in their land, and after they have been destroyed before you, be careful not to be ensnared by inquiring about their elohim, saying, "How do these nations serve their elohim? We will do the same." You must not worship Yahuah your Elohim in their way, because in worshiping their elohim, they do all kinds of detestable things Yahuah hates. They even burn their sons and daughters in the fire as sacrifices to their elohim."

Deut 16:21-22: ***"Do not set up any wooden Asherah pole beside the altar you build to Yahuah your Elohim, and do not erect a sacred stone, for these Yahuah your Elohim hates."*** Asherah poles are a deal-breaker with Yahuah. *Learn NOT the ways of the heathen, and do not bring a detestable thing into your home!*
Deut 7:26: ***"Do not bring a detestable thing into your house or you, like it, will be set apart for destruction. Utterly abhor and detest it, for it is set apart for destruction."***

THE INITIATED KNOW THE SECRETS

The *tree*, and the ***ornaments*** on the Asherah tree, have specific meanings to them. The tree is a "phallus", the male reproductive member. The little balls are testicles, and the "tinsel" represents the semen of the deity being worshipped. During the late middle ages, the little balls were interpreted by Christians to be "witch balls", borrowed from witchcraft, to attract, then *capture "evil" spirits*. ***Where, exactly, did Yahuah tell us to do <u>that</u>?*** The wreath was used to represent the male deity, the sun, yet was the "womb" symbol. So, the *male* deity's symbol incorporated the *feminine* features, while the female's sign incorporated the masculine features. Similarly, a "witch" is seen utilizing the male characteristics of the pointed hat and broomstick - both male features.
These "figures" were clear to the initiated, but to the uninitiated they meant nothing. Now, the secrets are being shouted from the rooftops, eh? Christians went *deeper* and ***deeper*** into apostasy as they ADOPTED the Pagan customs from those around them.
The green ivy and holly were common symbols of "Saturn", the Roman deity. Early believers thought that if they decorated ***their*** homes with these trappings, they would *appear* to be conforming to the Pagan culture around them, as everyone was observing ***Saturnalia***. Thus they would "blend-in", appear to be a part of the culture, and they would suffer less persecution. As time passed, the custom became part of their own family traditions, *and you will see the **wreaths** and **Asherim trees** in their assemblies and homes today.* Now, those of us that don't "join-in" with the celebration are considered to be freaks, or "Scrooges", saying bah! Humbug! Is it humbug? Now, many centuries later, the doctrinal offspring of those who might have otherwise been persecuted for ***avoiding*** these Pagan traditions, believe that we who do not adopt them are in a "cult".
It's not them, but Father Yahuah that we would wish to not offend. We know His heart, and He has called us to obey His Voice:
"Come out of her My people" (Rev. 18).

The word "PAGAN" comes from the Latin word, ***pagus***, referring to a person that was from the "rural" hinterlands. The more educated, erudite, urban-dwellers viewed those who were "pagus" as superstitious, illiterate imbeciles because they had quaint beliefs about reality, especially the unseen, spiritual world. As the darkness of the world without the Torah of Yahuah increased, those who professed themselves to be wise had become fools. "Pagan" became a label for anything that was outside the accepted religious practices of those in the majority who practiced the universalized state religion, which after Constantine was termed "Catholic", the Roman word for "universal".

As you see them decorating with the boughs, wreaths, trees, and holly, you might help them to repent of this behavior by explaining what these things actually are, loaning them a copy of this book. They can then look these facts up to see if they are really true, or not. The trappings themselves are set apart for destruction, *and those who decorate with them are set apart for destruction as well.* All of it together is **witchcraft,** and blatant

IMAGES OF ASHERAH (ASTARTE, DIANA)

WITCH HAT MEANING: A SYMBOL OF ASTARTE WAS THE "CONE OF POWER"

Ezek 37:23
"They shall no more defile themselves with their idols, nor with their disgusting matters, nor with any of their transgressions. And I shall save them from all their dwelling places in which they have sinned, and I shall cleanse them. And they shall be My people, and I be their Elohim."

idolatry. People living in the "mind of the flesh" only "see" with their own hearts, minds, and desires of their flesh. Once they receive a glimpse of how the Pagan customs appear through the eyes of Yahuah, they will grieve over their former blindness. Until they consider His Will, they are blind to His point-of-view, and are perishing and don't even know it.

People imagine "sin" lurking in men's hearts over many issues. Some even believe that celebrating ***Hanukkah*** *might be "adding" to Torah, and therefore is sinful. In all of Scripture, Hanukkah is mentioned once (if one ignores Maccabees I & II), at* ***Yn. 10:22****. So, Hanukkah* **is** found *in Scripture, yet "Christmas" is not. If a person shuns Christmas, and begins to celebrate Hanukkah, it will, more often than not, have consequences for them. Relatives and friends will shun or persecute them for it, thinking they have become influenced by radical ideas. Christmas has been celebrated for 5000 years by Pagans, it simply has a new name and application. The Romans used "womb-wreaths" at Saturnalia, so what could these possibly have to do with Yahuah's people?*

An Awakening After 2730 Years?

"Ephraim" was sown among the Gentiles in **722 BCE.** Ephraim is referred to as the "lost tribes" of Israel, the "house of Israel", and Samaritans (being from Samaria). Ephraim was the dominant tribe, the one tribe that received the blessing of the first-born. Ephraim is also sometimes called "Joseph" (Yusef). Here in the extreme last days, *the descendants of the northern tribes* are living in the billions among the Gentiles, *as* Gentiles. They were carried away for their idolatry with ***Baal—Asherah***, a corruption brought into their customs by Jezebel, a Sidonian wife of Ahab, king of ***northern*** Israel. When Yahuah lifts the penalty on them, a great awakening is to occur prior to *Yahusha*'s Return, and as Jer. 31:6 says:

"There will be a day when watchmen (Natsarim) ***cry out on the hills of Ephraim, 'Come, let us go up to Zion, to Yahuah our Elohim.'"***

Remember that Paul was called the "ringleader" of the sect of the ***Natsarim***, not the "ringleader" of the ***Christians***, the Greek word we have been led to accept; the followers of *Yahusha* called themselves Natsarim, ***watchmen***, or *branches*. Since "Ephraim" cannot be confused together with the Yahudim (Jews), the text is clearly declaring a sweeping movement among "former Gentiles", an awakening and return to the Torah, the Covenant.

Consider now what *Yahusha* described concerning the extreme last days. Matt. 24 relates to the *End of Days*, and the fulfillment of the times of the Gentiles. During this analysis, remember that Ephraim was the son of Yosef, and Yosef was told that he would become fruitful, his numbers would be ***multiplied***, and he would become a ***"community of peoples"***, Gen. 48:4. Remember, the descendants of Yosef are not "Jews", but rather Yahuah refers to the northern tribes by the term "Ephraim". *Yahusha* had said that He was only sent to the "lost sheep of the ***house of Israel***" (Mt. 15:24), and these are the northern tribes that were dispersed. At Mt. 24, Yahusha begins by describing how the massive stones will be leveled, and this happened about 40 years later, in 70 CE - but then He moves on to describe more calamity that follows. Ultimately He describes how a ***great tribulation*** will occur which exceeding anything that has been seen since Creation. He declares that if the days of this tribulation were not shortened, then NO FLESH would survive at all. But, for the sake of the ***Elect*** (those qodeshim observing His Torah) *who are still on Earth enduring to the end,* He would shorten the days. So, what He is indicating here is obviously the extreme end times, just prior to His return - which are the days we now live in. In the midst of this, ***He orders us to pray that our flight will not be in winter or on a Sabbath day.*** So, the Sabbath is ***still in force*** in the extreme last days, not changed as most have been taught. But there is more to understand here. The ***lost sheep*** scattered in 722 BCE are to come to their senses after ***2730 years***, so that's why there are books like this suddenly being written! (Read YeshaYahu 11*). The prophecy at Ez. 4:4,5 concerning the exile of the lost sheep of the house of Israel (Samaritans driven into the nations in 722 BCE) shows us that ***390 years*** was the original prescribed penalty for their Baal/Asherah worship. Having not repented after 390 years in captivity, the ***northern tribes then had to endure the seven-fold increase of the 390-year*** penalty (see Lev. 26:27,28).

This means that 7 x 390 years from **722 BCE** (2730 years), Israel's punishment will be lifted, and a remnant of ***Ephraim will cry out to return to the Torah.*** (see YirmeYahu 31). About when is this cry to take place? They've been living among the Gentiles with their ***Asherim*** (Christmas trees) for **2730** years as of ***the Roman year 2008, and have begun to cry out***. We are praying that our flight will not be in winter or on a Sabbath as Yahusha told us to do, because of the hardship it will cause the weak among us. The flight will be caused by a great Distress that is apparently planet-wide, and may include nuclear fallout:

Matt 24:15-27 ***"So when you see standing in the set-apart place 'the abomination that causes desolation,' spoken of through the prophet Daniel - let the reader understand - then let those who are in Yahudah flee to the mountains. Let no one on the roof of his house go***

****AT YESHAYAHU 11, EPHRAIM & YAHUDAH COME TOGETHER AGAIN INTO 'ONE' - THROUGH THE COVENANT***

down to take anything out of the house. Let no one in the field go back to get his cloak. How dreadful it will be in those days for pregnant women and nursing mothers! Pray that your flight will not take place in winter or on the Sabbath. For then there will be great distress, unequaled from the beginning of the world until now-and never to be equaled again. If those days had not been cut short, no one would survive, but for the sake of the elect those days will be shortened. At that time if anyone says to you, 'Look, here is the Mashiach!' or, 'There he is!' do not believe it. For false Mashiachim and false prophets will appear and perform great signs and miracles to deceive even the elect-if that were possible. See, I have told you ahead of time.

"So if anyone tells you, 'There he is, out in the desert,' do not go out; or, 'Here he is, in the inner rooms,' do not believe it. For as lightning that comes from the east is visible even in the west, so will be the coming of the Son of Man." Jezebel taught us about ASHERAH:

He warns us to ***"Come out of Her"*** at Rev. 18, but the Great Harlot Jezebel's *teachings* are also specifically referred to as *"sexual immorality"* at Rev 2:18-3:1:

"To the messenger of the assembly in Thyatira write:

These are the words of the Son of Yahuah, whose eyes are like blazing fire and whose feet are like burnished bronze. I know your deeds, your love and faith, your service and perseverance, and that you are now doing more than you did at first.

Nevertheless, I have this against you: You tolerate that woman Jezebel, who calls herself a prophetess. By her <u>teaching</u> she misleads my servants into <u>sexual</u> immorality and the eating of food sacrificed to idols. I have given her <u>time</u> to repent of her immorality, but she is unwilling (390 years?). ***So I will cast her on a bed of suffering, and I will make those who commit adultery with her suffer intensely, unless they repent of her ways. I will strike her children dead. Then all the assemblies will know that I am he who searches hearts and minds, and I will repay each of you according to your <u>deeds</u>*** (such as bringing an accursed *thing* into your house). ***Now I say to the rest of you in Thyatira, to you who do not hold to her <u>teaching</u> and have not learned Satan's so-called deep <u>secrets</u> (I will not impose any other burden on you).*** (Satan's Deep secrets, like womb-wreaths, phallus-trees, and the ornaments of the Asherim - all Jezebel's teachings).

Only hold on to what you have until I come.

To him who <u>overcomes</u> and does <u>My</u> will to the end, I will give authority over the nations - 'He will rule them with an iron scepter; he will dash them to pieces like pottery' - just as I have received authority from my Father. I will also give him the morning star. He who has an ear, let him hear what the Spirit says to the assemblies." The Olive tree is blossoming now.

The remnant of the lost tribes are now awakening.

The Cry of the Natsarim

Yahuah will restore us to His Torah and from Captivity in the nations for 2730 years:

Ps 80: ***Hear us, O Shepherd of Israel, You who lead Yosef like a flock; You who sit enthroned between the cherubim, shine forth before Ephraim, Benjamin and Manasseh. Awaken your might; come and save us.***

<u>Restore</u> us, O Elohim; make Your Face shine upon us, that we may be saved.

O Yahuah El Shaddai, how long will your anger smolder against the prayers of your people? You have fed them with the bread of tears; You have made them drink tears by the bowlful. You have made us a source of contention to our neighbors, and our enemies mock us.

<u>Restore</u> us, O El Shaddai; make Your Face shine upon us, that we may be saved.

You brought a vine out of Egypt; you drove out the nations and planted it. You cleared the ground for it, and it took root and filled the land. The mountains were covered with its shade, the mighty cedars with its branches. It sent out its boughs to the Sea, its shoots as far as the River.

Why have You broken down its walls so that all who pass by pick its grapes? Boars (beasts, men without Torah) ***from the forest ravage it and the creatures of the field feed on it. Return to us, O El Shaddai! Look down from heaven and see! Watch over this vine, the root your right hand has planted, the son you have raised up for yourself.***

Your vine is cut down, it is burned with fire; at Your rebuke Your people perish. Let your hand rest on the Man at your Right Hand, the Son of Man you have raised up for yourself. Then we will not turn away from You; revive us, and we will call on Your Name.

<u>Restore</u> us, Yahuah El Shaddai; make Your Face shine upon us, that we may be saved."

To our brother, **Yahudah,** we say, ***"I am Yosef!"*** Like Yosef, we can also tell our brothers:

"But Elohim sent me ahead of you to preserve for you a remnant on earth and to save your lives by a great deliverance." Gen 45:7

GOOD SEEDS OR BAD SEEDS?

YAHUSHA'S YOKE: WHAT IT MEANS - We have no power to change others, but we have the choice to imitate our Creator, and He will, in turn, see our behavior and help us to endure and conform to his will, His light YOKE. This is the "yoke" He has given to us. A "yoke" (Hebrew word, OLE) in the Hebraic sense is a **set of teachings** (as from a teacher). Our "Rabbi" (exalted One) said His "yoke" (set of teachings) is gentle and light: Mat 11:28-30: **" 'Come to Me, all you who labour and are burdened, and I shall give you rest. Take My yoke upon you and learn from Me, for I am meek and humble in heart, and you shall find rest for your beings. For My yoke is gentle and My burden is light.' "**

Many of you have seen the *humor* in referring to "seminaries" as *"cemeteries".* You will be shocked to learn what the word ***seminary**** actually means after you read a little about the metaphorical use of the term *"seed"* in Scripture.

What are the ***seeds*** that Yahuah has sown?

What are the ***seeds*** sown by an enemy?

Can they be identified?

The instructions (Torah, Commandments) of Yahuah ***are the good seeds*** which ***He*** has planted.

Added, changed, or omitted instructions are the "bad seed".

Mankind is the diverse kinds of "soil" they are planted in. We must discern which kind of seed we live by, and who planted it.

Those who accept the seed, and allow it to grow in them, become less "soil" and more the "fruit" of that which is planted. As time passes, more and more fruit is seen, just as we see soil becoming the vegetation that grows in it. Yahusha once went to a fig tree to look for its fruit, but it had none, so He caused it to wither (Mt. 21:19). So, even if one has "good seed", if they don't produce the fruit that is expected of them, He will reject them.

"Bad seed" sown by an enemy of Yahuah are ***unintended instructions*** that "choke-out" the good teachings (Torah) which Yahuah originally intended. We recognize which "seed" was sown by observing the "fruit" that has developed in a person. If you compare today's religious culture and its traditions with Yahuah's instructions for us in His Word, it is apparent that there is a huge difference in the two. We are not taught by traditional "religious leaders" to walk in the Torah of Yahuah, but rather we are taught to walk in the *inherited traditions* passed down from Gentile, Greco-Roman Pagan customs which became mixed into the good seed. If you think otherwise, just ask a Christian minister what he thinks about observing the true, authentic Sabbath as a day of rest, and ignoring "Sun-day" entirely. Then, you will begin to see the "fruit" of the "bad seed", and how it seeks to "choke-out" the good seed that is trying to grow in the same field. Who planted the seed helps reveal which is "good" and which is "bad" even before we see the fruit. We either obey the Words of Yahuah, or we obey men; it's always our own choice. If we eat from the forbidden fruit we will bear bad fruit and pass on bad seed (instructions) to others. The parables reveal hidden secrets of the reign of Yahuah, and the following excerpts use "seed" to illustrate how to discern what we should listen to and live by.

The Parable of the Sower

"That same day (Yahusha) went out of the house and sat by the lake. Such large crowds gathered around Him that He got into a boat and sat in it, while all the people stood on the shore. Then He told them many things in parables, saying:

"A farmer went out to sow his **seed**. As he was scattering the **seed**, some fell along the path, and the birds came and ate it up. Some fell on rocky places, where it did not have much soil. It sprang up quickly, because the soil was shallow. But when the sun came up, the plants were scorched, and they withered because they had no root. Other **seed** fell among thorns, which grew up and *choked the plants.* Still other **seed** fell on good soil, where it produced a crop—a hundred, sixty or thirty times what was sown. He who has ears, let him hear."

The disciples came to Him and asked, *"Why do you speak to the people in parables?"*

He replied, "The knowledge of the ***secrets of the kingdom of heaven*** has been given to you, but not to them. Whoever has will be given more, and he will have an abundance. Whoever does not have, even what he has will be taken from him. ***This is why I speak to them in parables:*** 'Though seeing, they do not see; though hearing, they do not hear or understand.' In them is fulfilled the prophecy of Isaiah: 'You will be ever hearing but never understanding, you will be ever seeing but never perceiving. For this people's heart has become calloused; they hardly hear with their ears, and they have closed their eyes. Otherwise they might see with their eyes, hear with their ears, understand with their hearts and turn, and I would heal them.' But blessed are your eyes because they see, and your ears because they hear. For I tell you the truth, many prophets and righteous men longed to see what you see but did not see it, and to hear what you hear but did not hear it.

Seed = Word, the *Torah of Yahuah:*
"Listen then to what the parable of the Sower means: When anyone hears the message (besorah, gospel) about the kingdom and does not understand it, the evil one comes and snatches away *what was sown in his heart.* This is the **seed** sown along the path. The one who received the **seed** that fell on rocky places is the man who hears the **Word** and at once receives it with joy. ***But since he has no root, he lasts only a short time. When trouble or persecution comes because of the Word*, he quickly falls away. The one who received the seed that fell among the thorns is the man who hears the Word, but the worries of this life and the deceitfulness of wealth choke it, making it unfruitful. But the one who received the seed that fell on good soil is the man who hears the Word and understands it. He produces a crop, yielding a hundred, sixty or thirty times what was sown." "This is the meaning of the parable: The seed is the Word*** (Torah) **of** (Yahuah). ***Those along the path are the ones who hear, and then the devil comes and takes away the Word from their hearts, so that they may not believe and be saved. Those on the rock are the ones who receive the Word with joy when they hear it, but they have no root. They believe for a while, but in the time of testing they fall away. The seed that fell among thorns stands for those who hear, but as they go on their way they are choked by life's worries, riches and pleasures, and they do not mature. But the seed on good soil stands for those with a noble and good heart, who hear*** (and obey) ***the Word, retain it, and by persevering produce a crop."*** Luke 8:11-15 (Yahusha defined the "seed" to be the "Word", Yahuah's Torah - fruit means offspring).

The Parable of the Weeds

"(Yahusha) told them another parable: "The kingdom of heaven is like a man who sowed good seed in his field. But while everyone was sleeping, His enemy came and sowed weeds among the wheat, and went away. When the wheat sprouted and formed heads, then the weeds also appeared. The Owner's servants came to Him and said, 'Sir, didn't You sow good seed in your field? Where then did the weeds come from?'
" 'An enemy did this,' He replied. The servants asked Him, 'Do You want us to go and pull them up?'
"'No,' He answered, 'because while you are pulling the weeds, you may root up the wheat with them. Let both grow together until the harvest. At that time I will tell the harvesters: First collect the weeds and tie them in bundles to be burned; then gather the wheat and bring it into My barn.' " (This is to say that the first to be "raptured" away will be the lawless, the weeds!)

The Parable of the Mustard Seed

"What is the (Reign) of (Yahuah) like? What shall I compare it to? It is like a mustard seed, which a man took and planted in his garden. It grew and became a tree, and the birds of the air perched in **its branches." Luke 13:18-19 (The small mustard seed indicates that the teachings begin in what appears to be a very weak, humble condition - but one day they will grow to fill the whole Earth and dominate all other seeds. The Torah will do that!).**

The Parable of the Yeast
He told them still another parable: "The kingdom of heaven is like yeast that a woman took and mixed into a large amount of flour until it worked all through the dough." (The Torah will do that).

(Yahusha) spoke all these things to the crowd in parables; He did not say anything to them without using a parable. So was fulfilled what was spoken through the prophet: "I will open my mouth in parables, I will utter things hidden since the creation of the world."

The Parable of the Weeds Explained

"Then He left the crowd and went into the house. His disciples came to Him and said, "Explain to us the parable of the weeds in the field."
He answered, "The one who sowed the good seed is the Son of Man. The field is the world, and the good seed stands for the sons of the kingdom. The weeds are the sons of the evil one, and the enemy who sows them is the devil. The harvest is the end of the age, and the harvesters are angels.
"As the weeds are pulled up and burned in the fire, so it will be at the end of the age. The Son of Man will send out his angels, and they will weed out of his kingdom everything that causes sin and all who do evil. They will throw them into the fiery furnace, where there will be weeping and gnashing of teeth. Then the righteous will shine like the sun in the kingdom of their Father. He who has ears, let him hear."

The Parables of the Hidden Treasure and the Pearl: ***"The kingdom of heaven is like treasure hidden in a field. When a man found it, he hid it again, and then in his joy went and sold all he had and bought that field.***

"Again, the kingdom of heaven is like a merchant looking for fine pearls. When he found

**WORD: THE HEBREW TERM IS DEBAR, AND THE "TEN WORDS" ARE CALLED ESERET HA'DEBARIM*

one of great value, he went away and sold everything he had and bought it."

The Parable of the Net

"Once again, the kingdom of heaven is like a net that was let down into the lake and caught all kinds of fish. When it was full, the fishermen pulled it up on the shore. Then they sat down and collected the good fish in baskets, but threw the bad away. This is how it will be at the end of the age. The angels will come and separate the wicked from the righteous and throw them into the fiery furnace, where there will be weeping and gnashing of teeth. "Have you understood all these things?" (Yahusha) ***asked. "Yes," they replied.***
He said to them, "Therefore every teacher of the law (Torah of Yahuah) ***who has been instructed about the kingdom of heaven*** (Torah of Yahuah) ***is like the owner of a house who brings out of his storeroom new treasures as well as old."***

***Seminary:** Now it's time to look at the word "**seminary**". In some of the larger communities in Europe during the 1500's, the Catholic bishops realized how uneducated their priests were. In order to educate them better and bring more uniformity and control to the organization, they called the priests to attend lessons, taught by the bishops, in "Cathedral schools". Many diverse subjects were added as time passed, and the broader selection of instructed subjects caused the term "university" to become applied to the schools.
Another term was applied to those "universities" of religious learning:

SEMINARY: definition: ***A special school providing education in theology, religious history, etc., primarily to prepare students for the priesthood, ministry, or rabbinate.*** Now, look at the etymology of the word:
[Middle English, ***seed plot***, from Latin seminarium, from seminarius, of ***seed***, from semen, semin, ***seed***.]

The **good seeds** and **bad seeds** are mixed together in these "seed plots", and allowed to grow - but the bad seeds quickly choke-out the good seed, as we see the teachings of these seminaries teach their "replacement theology" and scream "legalism" and "Judaizer" when anyone wishes to live according to the good seed, the Torah of Yahuah. Knowing that the "bad seeds" are sown by the devil, who has been behind the seminaries and their teachings (seeds)? The bad seeds are: ***lies, omissions, and alterations.***

HOW THINGS CHANGED FOR ME

When I was 34 in 1984 CE, my son Michael was about 3. I worked all the time, but one night I had the chance to see him to bed and read to him. On the far side of the darkened room was a small, glowing ***tree*** which had been decorated and placed there by a friend and my wife. He asked, ***"Dad, what is that?".*** Puzzled for a few moments, I told him *"I don't really know, son, but I'll find out - and I'll tell you one day."* I told him I didn't think it would be good, whatever it was. This was the beginning of what became 15+ years of research, eventually to become this book you're now reading. I promised my son that I would never lie to him, but tell him the straight truth, always. That same night I told him that people would try to teach him about "Santa Claus", but that they were all lies. I wanted him to believe me when I told him the truth.
And he does; he's now 27 years old (2008),
And FC is in its 8th edition.

JUDGING OTHERS

As an interlude, let me remind you that as I write this information, I am not condemning or criticizing PEOPLE, but rather exposing the **facts** about why we see them performing the Pagan "format". They were set up; it had me in it's grips, and I am just as easily overwhelmed as anyone. The Torah provides us the Light to enable us to **see** what we're doing, right or wrong. We must NOT look down on others, call them fools, or feel superior because we have the eyesight to see. They may be "blind", at the moment, but now you have the responsibility to tell them the truth. It must be done in a gentle, loving way, otherwise they will be repelled. We must help them to see we do not judge **them**, but rather the customs they have embraced since childhood. The Torah does the judging: ***"For the Word*** (Torah) ***of 𐤉𐤄𐤅𐤄 is living and active. Sharper than any double-edged sword, it PENETRATES even to dividing soul and spirit, joints and marrow; IT JUDGES THE THOUGHTS AND ATTITUDES OF THE HEART. Nothing in all creation is hidden from 𐤉𐤄𐤅𐤄's sight. Everything is uncovered and laid bare before the eyes of Him, to Whom we must give account."*** Heb. 4:12,13. I am sure some of you have read that, yet the meaning was beyond you. It sounded profound. But now, you can read ANY of the Writings, and comprehend, because His ***Name*** has unlocked the secret. ***"He who scorns instruction will pay for it, but he who respects a command is rewarded. The teaching of the wise is a fountain of life, turning a man from the snares of death."*** Prov. 13:13,14. The Torah is Wisdom (note the feminine -ending as in *Sarah*). If we "rank" ourselves above

THE TERROR CONTINUES!

others because of their impairments, lack of knowledge, education, race, or poverty, we show <u>contempt for their maker</u>. (Prov. 14:31). 𐤉𐤄𐤅𐤄 says He HATES certain things: **haughty eyes, a lying tongue, hands that shed innocent blood, a heart that devises wicked schemes, feet that are quick to rush into evil, a false witness who pours out lies, and a man who stirs up dissension among brothers.** Prov. 6:16-19. He also says at Mal. 2:16, ***"<u>I HATE DIVORCE</u>".*** Let's not go there, OK? Patch up those differences. When a sack of mud (ourselves) becomes angry and filled with pride, we are not very fun to be around. Identify your real enemy! It's not your spouse, but the powers of evil in this world. 𐤉𐤄𐤅𐤄 seeks righteous offspring, and divorce is not the way to accomplish that. The adversary "divides" and conquers. A kingdom, or marriage, divided against itself, cannot stand.

Now you know a little more about potatoes than you may have before, and how relatively quickly "Santa Claus" rose up and launched into everyone's lives because of the lack of those potatoes. The Germanic term, *"**Kris Kringle**"* means "Christ Child" - you can see the word "kris" (shining) is right there in the forefront. "Kringle" is a mangling of the word ***kindl***, and is the root for "<u>kindergarten</u>". The vagueness of who this "shining child" really is should cause you to be suspicious. No doubt it is Nimrod "re-born". Nicholas, Nicolaitans, and Nimrod all begin with the same letter, so maybe it is a loose thread pointing to the origin. The Pagan's "shining child" was the re-born sun at the winter solstice. Did you know that "St. Nick" is a popular euphemism for "satan"? One preacher on a radio program once commented that if you removed all the Pagan components from Christianity, there would be absolutely NOTHING LEFT to do. *It would vaporize*.

THE DRUIDS

The Terror Continues !!!

The word *Germani* originally was the name for a Celtic tribe of Druids, and now is the name of a country, Germany. The Norsemen, such as Vikings, Picts, and even King Arthur were Pagans. The wizard/sorcerer Druid dude *"Merlin"* certainly wasn't trying to convert Camelot to Christianity. The Hollywood versions of history are often *anachronistic* (going against the timeframe). Life for a Pagan under the Druids was like a nightmare. Parents had to endure risking their children's lives because the Druids demanded sacrifices. Children were made to stand in a large **circle** with marker stones, with a tall oak pole at the center. At sunrise, the shadow of the pole would fall upon a single child. This child was tied-up and burned alive on a "***bone-fire***" (now bonfire), and the charred bones were buried under the stone marker. Given the 2 solstices and 2 Equinoxes, this stone circle with the oak pole shadows produce a familiar symbol: the "peace" sign. This is one of the religious symbols of the Druids, dating back at least 2200 years. The term "**Yule Log**" means "child log". The Celts have name prefixes like "Mc" and "Mac", which both mean *son of,* which indicated a person was the *son of Donald,* or *son of Kensey*. An "O" prefix meant *grandson of.* Another Celtic/Aryan prefix that indicated a person was an illegitimate child was "*Fitz*". It was common, and when they called someone "Fitz", they were calling them "bastard". The prefix "VON" or VAN (as in Von Meter or Van Halen) also means "son of".

HALLOWEEN

(Source material from YNCA,).

The two Celtic words *Hallowed Evening* came from ***All Hallowed's Ev'n***, and now we call it "Halloween". This is now even more popular than Easter, and rivals Christmas. The roots of this festival come to us from Druid demon worship. Witches were said to fly brooms over the crops to "teach" them how to grow. It was a fertility myth. When the first Roman Catholic missionaries encountered these Druids, they met stubborn resistance because the inhabitants of Angle Land, Sweden, Neder Land, northern Germany, Fin Land, and Eire Land were very nationalistic. The ritual we embrace as Halloween was originally called the Feast of the Dead, ***Samhain*** (pronounced *Sa-ween*), and was on November 1st. These pre-Christian Druids had the barbarians doing ghastly things. It was a dreaded occasion, since it was thought that time stood still, and the souls of the dead walked the land. Gifts, especially food, were left outside for these roaming ghosts, with the hope that no harm would come to the households. The Druids chose certain children to be burned alive on "bone-fires", as offerings to the sun. Parents tied yellow ribbons around oak trees as prayers to the sun to have their children spared. The fat left over from the child was fashioned into a candle, and placed into a carved-out pumpkin, or a hollowed out vegetable with a "round" (sun-shaped) design. The victim was called *Jack-of-the-lantern.* Prisoners and unliked people were burned alive in wicker cages shaped in the form of animals, hung from trees. All of this was ultimately to pay homage to the sun, *Woden,* or *Odin.* As you now know, this Druid deity gives us our name for the 4th day of the week: *Woden's Day.*

FROM SAMHAIN TO ALL SAINTS

Without forcing the Pagans to drop their practices but accept Christianity, the RCC merely made allowances to accommodate the barbarians, and called it *"acculturation"*. They *"sanctified"* the Pagan rituals by absorbing and camouflaging them. In the 7th century, the *Pantheon* at Rome was extracted from the barbarians, and made into a *"cathedral"* (Greek, *kathedra,* meaning *seat, or throne*). "Pan Theon" means *All Gods.* They renamed it the ***Church of the Blessed Virgin and ALL MARTYRS.*** Thus, it changed from the worship of *"All Gods"* (Pantheon) to the center for honoring *"All Saints"*. The day chosen to honor all the "hallowed" saints was first observed on the evening of May 13, and was known as *All Hallows Festival.* This festival was officially authorized in 835 CE by pope Gregory IV after it was moved to November 1st, to *coincide* with the festival of *Samhain.* It began on the evening of October 31st, which was called *All Halloweds Eve. "Saints"* in Hebrew is the word *"QODESHIM"* based on the word *qodesh*, meaning set-apart. A "qodeshi" is a living person, and they don't need the RCC to "canonize" them after they die to be a "saint". "Qodesh" has been translated to the word *"holy"* and *"hallowed"* which really means *"haloed"*. Pagans used yellow nimbuses and floating gold "hoops" in stone carvings, paintings, and stain-glassed windows, as well as statues ~ to identify their deities and founders as being inhabited by the sun. When you see a "halo" about the head of someone in real life, it's probably ball lightning. But, in any case, get away from them! The translation "Holy Spirit" comes from the original Hebrew ***ruach ha qodesh***, the set-apart Spirit. *"Ruach"* is the Hebrew word for *wind*, and it is the presence of the helper, 𐤉𐤄𐤅𐤔𐤏 in Spirit. He is not a Haloed Spook, and after His resurrection distinctly said He was not a ghost. He first sent His RUACH to the Natsarim gathered in the Temple on the 50th day from the count from the day after Shabbat to the day after the 7th Shabbat, now called "Pente-cost" (Greek for *count fifty*). This was the annual appointed time (Lev. 23, Dt. 16) which commemorated the *giving of the Torah at Sinai.* It is really called *Shabuoth,* meaning *weeks.* The Torah was written on the <u>hearts</u> of the Natsarim, fulfilling the prophesied "New Covenant" (Yirme Yahu 31, Heb. 8:10).

MYTHOLOGY

A thesaurus will tell you that mythology is the study of fictional traditions, fables, or imaginary stories which sometimes originate from prehistoric times. To keep the Natsarim from being deceived, our old Pharisee / Natsari brother Shaul wrote an important letter to his younger pupil Timothy. In the letter, he told Timothy that things were going to be really depraved later on. ***"I give you this charge*** (order, command)***: <u>Preach the Word</u>*** (Torah)***. Be prepared IN SEASON, and out of SEASON*** ("in season" means during the <u>appointed times</u> declared for assemblies at Lev. 23 & Dt. 16, which were *"done away"* by Constantine, fulfilling Dan. 7:25)***. Correct, rebuke, and encourage ~ with great patience and careful instruction. <u>For the time will come when men will not put up with sound doctrine</u>*** (teaching)***. Instead, to suit their own desires, they will gather around them a great number of teachers to say what their itching ears want to hear. They will turn their ears away from the Truth*** (Torah) ***and turn aside to MYTHS."*** (Read all of 2 Timothy, especially chapters 3 & 4).

HEAVEN ~ and the myth of going there.

The word "heaven" stands in place of the original inspired Hebrew word *SHAMAYIM.* This means the skies, or even our modern term *outer space*. It was also used as a customary substitution for the Name of 𐤉𐤄𐤅𐤄 ~ perhaps to keep from offending Yahudim who considered it "profaning" or "blaspheming" the Name to utter it aloud. All the family of beings created by 𐤉𐤄𐤅𐤄 are named by the Name of 𐤉𐤄𐤅𐤄. He has set His Name upon those He has "called-out" from

WHY POSTING THE 10 COMMANDMENTS IS A PROBLEM FOR THEM:

THE 4TH COMMANDMENT, BEING OUR DAY OF REST AS A COMMEMORATION OF YAHUAH'S REST AFTER 6 DAYS OF CREATION, CONFLICTS WITH THE GOVERNMENT'S RELIGION THAT TEACHES THE UNIVERSE <u>CREATED ITSELF</u>.

"FOR IN 6 DAYS *<u>YAHUAH</u>* MADE THE HEAVENS AND THE EARTH, THE SEA, AND ALL THAT IS IN THEM, BUT HE RESTED ON THE SEVENTH DAY — THEREFORE YAHUAH BLESSED THE SABBATH DAY AND MADE IT QODESH."

SHEMOTH/EX. 20:11 HE <u>BLESSED</u> IT

(BLESSED— HEBREW: BARUCH;

MEANS COMMENDED, SET APART AS SPECIAL).

THEY NEVER COME OUT AND DISCUSS THE CORE PROBLEM AT ALL; THAT BEING THE CONFLICT IT CAUSES WITH **<u>EVOLUTION</u>.**

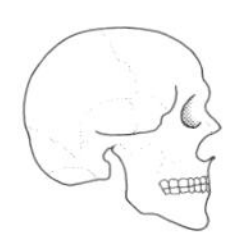

Babylonian practices, and given them the Family Name, "Yahudim". Israel's wife Leah named her 4th child *Yahudah*, meaning *"worshipper of Yah"*. Daniel 9:19 shows also how His people bear His Name. "Yahudah" was corrupted to "Judah", then "Jude", and for the last several hundred years the word "JEW" has come into use. I guess you'll have to answer "yes" if anyone asks you if you are a "JEW". But, will anyone *"go to Heaven"* when they die, or in the resurrection? You will only find the idea of ***"the Kingdom of Heaven"*** written in the Writings, and this is really referring to the *world-to-come,* the "Reign / Kingdom of 𐤉𐤄𐤅𐤄". He fills the Universe, but says His Throne will be in the New Yerushalayim. Yerushalayim means *foundation of peace*. "UR" or "IR" means "city", so it also means ***city of peace***. The site was at first inhabited by Pagans, and was called "Yebus". They were moon worshippers, but all the Pagans knew about the TRUE creator 𐤉𐤄𐤅𐤄. They simply chose to have fun in their own way. The occupants of Yericho knew that the people of 𐤉𐤄𐤅𐤄 were coming, and their deities wouldn't be able to help them.

The "New Yerushalayim" will be coming down from the skies, and the meek will inherit the Earth. There is not even a hint in the Writings that anyone will be going to anywhere in the skies. We will be "caught up" and gathered to be with 𐤉𐤄𐤅𐤔𐤏 ~ but we will not be living anywhere in the sky. Even the dead will be raised, but if they are already "in heaven" with Him, then why are they only then being gathered to Him? They will "sleep" until He returns. Yerushalayim will be a ***city of peace****, but it will receive a new Name: "𐤉𐤄𐤅𐤄 Shammah" (Yahuah is there). The Earth will be restored, and those who obey the living water that flows from the city (Torah) will enter it. The Kingdom of outer space will be established on Earth among men, with the Throne of the Creator here. The High Priest (Kohen Gadol) ~ a "Jewish" (Yahudi) Rabbi, will be seated on the Throne. So, the dead saints (qodeshim), and the Natsarim who follow 𐤉𐤄𐤅𐤔𐤏, will be ***here on Earth*** clothed in immortality.

"Most of us ask for advice when we already know the answer, but we want a different one."
Ivern Ball

WHAT HAPPENS WHEN YOU DIE?

Pagans always believed they would go into the skies to live with their deities. Wizards and magicians have struggled to defeat death, but failed. The Egyptians went to great lengths to ensure that the dead were provided for, and did so according to their "Book of the Dead". Houdini promised to escape and return to the world, but hasn't. A young boy named Eutycus (Acts 20:9) fell and

died, a young girl was raised up from her deathbed (Mark 5), and Lazarus was called out of his tomb after several days (Yn. 11). Where did their spirits go? Nowhere! Their spirits were there, but their flesh was unable to walk again under the sun without <u>supernatural</u> help from their creator. El Yahu (Elijah) was used (1 Kings 17:22) to restore the life to a widow's son by the power of 𐤉𐤄𐤅𐤄. Those people died twice! The new creation that we will be will not be flesh like we have now, but like the spiritual body Rabbi 𐤉𐤄𐤅𐤔𐤏 has ~ He is the foremost, first born of a new thing that 𐤉𐤄𐤅𐤄 is doing. You shouldn't, but if your body is turned to ashes and spread over the ocean, the

THE EAGLE: THE SYMBOL OF THE SUN-SPIRIT; LATIN: *AQUILA.* HEBREW: *NESHER. LOOK IT UP IN A GOOD RESOURCE, AND YOU WILL DISCOVER IT IS A MEMBER OF THE VULTURE FAMILY, AND A BIRD OF PREY.*

RULED BY THE LOWLIEST

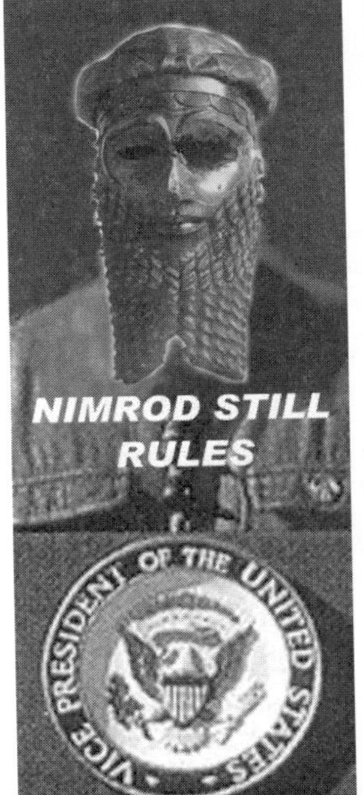

NOTE THE EAGLE EMBLEM; SAME OLD EMBLEM OF MITHRAS.
IT JUST DOESN'T SEEM TO EVER GO AWAY, DOES IT?

"IN ORDER THAT THE LIVING MAY KNOW THAT THE MOST HIGH IS RULER OVER THE REALM OF MANKIND, AND BESTOWS IT ON WHOM HE WISHES, AND SETS OVER IT THE LOWLIEST OF MEN."
DANIEL 4:17

YERUSHALAYIM MEANS <u>CITY</u> OF <u>PEACE</u> - UR SHALOM, OR IR SHALOM (not YAHrushalayim)

Creator 𐤉𐤄𐤅𐤄 will still bring you back.

The parable of the 10 virgins explains that as they waited for the Bridegroom, they all fell "asleep". This means their bodies died. When the "midnight cry" is uttered, "Come out to meet Him", five raise in imperishable spiritual bodies. When we die, we fall asleep. No matter how much time passes, it will be as if we are re-awakening immediately when we are re-born, clothed with immortality. It will seem like no time passed at all. Your spirit doesn't occupy any space at all. A neurologist once said that the human brain is such a sensitive and well designed thing, that it could be operated by a "ghost". It is, in fact, an instrument that we are all equipped with that represents the most sophisticated machine that exists in the universe. Our "life" ~ the nephesh, or breath of life, keeps our body alive, as any animal. We have a spiritual component, created a little inferior to the malakim (angels, messengers, watchers). It cannot be destroyed, except by 𐤉𐤄𐤅𐤄. At Luke 12:5, 𐤉𐤄𐤅𐤔𐤏 told us not to fear those who kill the body, but rather He who can destroy the "real" you in the "lake of fire" (yam esh). You don't want to get thrown into His garbage can. That's the point, and this points us to the Torah. You cannot inherit eternal life without it, and you cannot obey without the New Covenant ~ having 𐤉𐤄𐤅𐤔𐤏 come in and write Torah on your heart. You cannot receive Him, and not receive the love for His Torah. ***"Multitudes who sleep in the dust of the Earth will awake; some to everlasting life, others to shame and everlasting contempt. Those who are WISE will shine like the brightness of the skies, and <u>those who lead many to righteousness</u>, like the stars for ever and ever."*** (Dan. 12:1-4). This means they will endure like the stars, unchanging. If they were already in a place called "heaven", then they wouldn't be "asleep", or coming from heaven, would they? So, if your "pastor" tells you your dead family members are "in heaven with the LORD", kindly remind him what the Writings say. If you really want to stand out, wear white to funerals.

"Let us hear the conclusion of the whole matter; Fear 𐤉𐤄𐤅𐤄 <u>and keep His Commandments</u> for this is the duty of man." Eccl. 12:13.

The dead know nothing of what goes on in the world after they are gone, but their spirit sleeps. ***"If there is a natural body, there is also a spiritual body."*** 1 Cor. 15:44. Reading 1 Cor. 15:12 forward will help you see that after the natural body dies, it will be raised later as a spiritual body, and that flesh and blood <u>cannot inherit</u> the kingdom of 𐤉𐤄𐤅𐤄. Some teach that a belief in an "immortal soul" is heresy, and a myth that comes from Paganism. It is more important to note what Pagans taught about the "spirits" of the dead being transported to "heaven". That is the heresy that has been accepted. If when we die our life goes to oblivion, then we are no different than a dead dog. It is the reality of the resurrection of 𐤉𐤄𐤅𐤔𐤏 that we are alive in our spirit. Our spirit is living because of His life in us, so that He may be all in all. At the time the dirt is being thrown on us, we have His seed in us, and He will "clothe" us in a new spiritual body at the resurrection of the saints. This is not heresy; but ignorance of 𐤉𐤄𐤅𐤄 is shameful. Everyone who believes and is immersed in His Name will be saved.

I'M NOT INFALLIBLE. Just for the record, let me say that I'm learning ~ I haven't nearly arrived at "all truth", and some things I'm saying in this book you <u>must</u> <u>verify</u>. If you hang on to truth as being found in verifiable "footnotes", merely citing other men's words, then you need to realize that if the source is just another man, it should be highly suspect. The facts in this book can easily be verified in home or school dictionaries and encyclopedias, and most easily on the Internet. More detailed research will require specialized tools like Hebrew lexicons or the original Hebrew texts. You will only be convinced by personal research, and you <u>should</u> question basic statements, no matter what their source is, including this one. If I have a personal opinion about a topic, I'll try to be sure to mention is only my opinion ~ and you are welcome to have a different opinion. But, opinions are best when founded on a great deal of evidence.

Things like evolution are opinions, often "decided" on with very little personal research. If "nature" experimented to develop an eyeball, where are all the experiments?

The "evolution" of Paganism into Christianity (by men) is on display in this book, but the "evolving" of monkeys into people is not. While we're discussing it, the theory of evolution really comes apart when the fossil record is examined from the standpoint that much of the paleontology is really only proving that the **Great Flood** actually occurred. The "layers" of animals show that the larger, more mobile creatures fought to survive the flood better than the smaller, less mobile ones. The smaller critters are naturally on the <u>bottom</u> layers, being the first to get washed away. Often, the so-called "layers" spanning hundreds of thousands of years (ha-ha) will have an upside-down tree, roots-up, penetrating the "layers" for several meters. Also, isn't it interesting that the ancient world had millions of species of plants and animals, and this **total** quantity of species has been continuing to decline in number over time? No new species are appearing now, and what is here has *always* been here from the fossil record after their kinds. If evolution were true, then there should be MORE species as time progresses, not less and less! Every year, thousands of species become extinct, and **no** new ones are ever seen emerging. At this rate, it won't be long before no species exist, and this doesn't follow the "evolutionary" model very well, now does it? An evolutionist will say that it takes many tens of thousands of years to witness an emerging specie, but it seems that it doesn't take very long to witness the demise of *thousands* of species. They will say these are nature's "experiments"; but again, the total *number* of species is *dwindling*, not getting larger. Where are all those "experiments" of nature attempting to make a functioning eyeball? They all appear "abruptly" - functioning perfectly and appear to be designed for their purpose. If "nature" ever attempted to "develop" an eyeball, we'd surely find millions of its failed attempts in the fossil record. If something doesn't make sense, then you should suspect that something is wrong. What makes sense is the original quality and quantity of species were designed and created, and are slowly becoming extinct over time. This is what we in fact see occurring.

In the "fossilization" of ***human customs***, former Paganism transformed in meaning, and *turned into something else while retaining the imprint of its former pattern perfectly.* Ancient Nimrod-Babylonian customs *adapted* because they were already ***socially accepted***, and "Christmas" is only the surface crust on the old winter ***solstice festival***. "Sun-Day" is another adaptation, as is Easter and Halloween. Nimrod turned into Santa (Satan?). How much of the "smoke-screen" we accept is based on how much we want to conform to the "world" around us.

The "4th beast" is Rome, and from this beast a "little horn" appears, which is Anti-Messiah. The serpent gives him power over the secular rulers. The beast itself is the government, but the little horn is the source of pure evil and deception.

The Roman Beast

Caesar, Pope, Maitreya, &
THE FOURTH BEAST SYSTEM, ROME

Daniel recorded this about the little horn:

"He will be successful until the time of wrath is completed, for what has been determined must take place." ~ DAN. 11:36

Historians say that Constantine was not of the royal family of Caesars, and Daniel 11:21 refers to such a person. Beginning in the record of Daniel chapter 10, an un-named Being visits him, and His dissertation continues to the end of Daniel's writings. You may be able to guess Who this was. He described many things, including the destruction of the Temple in 70 CE (11:31). At Dan. 11:28-30, an **EVIL KINGDOM** is described that vents its fury against the "Qodesh Covenant" (the Torah, or

SCANDINAVIAN SOLSTICE FESTIVAL AROUND BONFIRE WITH CRUX-POLE

CIRCLE (KUKLUX) KLAN SERVICE TO FIRE CRUX, SYMBOL OF WODEN

marriage covenant between 𐤉𐤄𐤅𐤄 and His bride, Yisrael). Obviously, this effort was led by Shatan. Any effort brought **against the Covenant** is led by the same. Daniel records the words of the Being, which seem to refer to the "sealed message" called the Gospel:

"Go your way, Daniel, because the words are <u>closed up</u> and <u>sealed</u> until the time of the end. Many will be purified, made spotless and refined, but the wicked will continue to be wicked. None of the wicked will understand, but those who are wise will understand." 12:9,10. This "Being" is described by Daniel (10:5,6), and is identical to the One described by Yahuchanon at Rev. 1:12-16. Of course it was the same Person, 𐤉𐤄𐤅𐤔𐤏. Yahuchanon writes that the reason he was imprisoned on Patmos was because of the **"Word of 𐤉𐤄𐤅𐤄"** (the Torah, Covenant), and the **"Testimony of 𐤉𐤄𐤅𐤔𐤏"** (the message, "*Repent, for the Reign of 𐤉𐤄𐤅𐤄 draws near*") - 1:9. One of the biggest stumbling blocks for those who observe "Sun-day" as the "LORD's Day" is Revelation 1:10. ***"I was in the Spirit on the LORD's Day . . . ."*** The term "LORD's Day" is only found **ONCE** in all of the Writings, and it refers to the ***Day of*** 𐤉𐤄𐤅𐤄, or the great <u>day of wrath</u> ~ which is the FOCUS of the whole 22 chapters; the vision, or Revelation. Yahuchanon wasn't concerned with <u>which day</u> of the week it was, nor can we imagine he was thinking "Sun-day" was anything other than Baal's Day in his time. Of course "Baal's Day" was the LORD's Day, because *Baal means LORD.* The ***Time of Wrath*** will bring a complete end to man ruling himself, and this Earth will be ruled by the Torah:

"In the last days, the mountain of 𐤉𐤄𐤅𐤄's Temple will be established as chief among the mountains; it will be raised above the hills, and peoples will stream to it. Many nations will come and say, 'Come let us go up to the mountain of 𐤉𐤄𐤅𐤄, to the house of the Elohim of Ya'akob. He will teach us His ways, so that we may walk in His paths. THE TORAH WILL GO OUT FROM TSIYON, THE WORD OF 𐤉𐤄𐤅𐤄 FROM YERUSHALAYIM." Micah 4. These words match perfectly with Revelation 22, describing the "Water of Life", or *living water* (Torah, the Covenant). The "Roman Beast" is set against the Covenant, having altered it by **changing** the day of rest which gives honor to 𐤉𐤄𐤅𐤄 for **creation**, as well as the 2nd Commandment which forbids images in our worship. The 7th-day Shabbath is the "sign" of the Eternal Covenant. The idolatry is glaring, and unmistakable. The 4 beasts described in Daniel 7 are all there will be, and the 4th one will endure until the ***"Time of Wrath is completed"***, Dan. 11:36. Daniel 7:23—25 describes this 4th beast, which will attack the saints and alter the "set times and law":

"He will speak against the Most High (say his "authority" can change the Covenant) ***and oppress His saints and <u>try to change the set times</u>*** (annual appointments) ***<u>and the Torah</u>."***

This was done by Constantine in 321 CE and 325 CE, and ratified by the Roman Council of Laodicea. The 4th Beast enforced the "Sun-day" law under penalty of death, and called the faithful Shabbath-keepers ***"Judaizers"***, and pursued "the woman" (𐤉𐤄𐤅𐤄's wife, bride). Shatan's "wrath" against the marriage <u>Covenant</u>, and the <u>BRIDE</u> who obeys it, has never relented. You see and hear about the struggle on the news constantly. The right to post the 10 Commandments in public view on public property has been a controversy for many years. Which "list" to post is an undiscussed part of the controversy, because Catholics have a different list in their <u>minds</u> than they have in their own translation of the Writings. Also, how can you have a "Sun-day" day of rest when the Commandments say it's the 7th day? How can you misuse the Name of 𐤉𐤄𐤅𐤄, when it is not used? Misusing it is one thing; but to *never use His Name at all* is also shaming Him. Certainly snarling "GOD", "LORD" or "JESUS" (being Pagan deities) brings no misuse of the Name of the Maker of Heaven and Earth. The Covenant, and the Bride of the Covenant, are the real target in the war between the sons of Light and darkness:

"Then from his mouth the serpent spewed water like a river, to overtake the woman and sweep her away with the torrent. But the Earth helped the woman by opening its mouth and swallowing the river that the dragon had spewed out of his mouth." Rev. 12:15,16—read the context. This means the wife of 𐤉𐤄𐤅𐤄 fled to safety, and distance provided it. ***"Then the dragon was enraged at the woman, and went off to make war against the rest of her offspring ~ THOSE WHO OBEY THE COMMANDMENTS, AND HOLD TO THE TESTIMONY OF 𐤉𐤄𐤅𐤔𐤏."*** 12:17.

If one can "change" the Torah, then it is not a Rock, but shifting sand. This makes a weak foundation on which to build. The Torah is called the "Word", and the "Word" became flesh, and dwelled with us for a time, showing us perfection. If we build on it, we will not be shaken or carried away by winds of other teachings. What 𐤉𐤄𐤅𐤄 has made straight, no man can bend or change! Persecution "for righteousness' sake" is written in the pages of history. When 𐤉𐤄𐤅𐤄 said, ***"Everyone is TO STAY WHERE HE IS ON THE SEVENTH DAY; NO ONE IS TO GO OUT"***, He meant what He said (Ex. 16:29). This idea of not traveling any considerable distance is supported by Luke at Acts 1:12:

"Then they returned to Yerushalayim from the hill called the Mount of Olives, A SHABBATH DAY's WALK FROM THE CITY." If there was some change, Luke would have not mentioned it, or said what ***USED TO BE*** a Shabbath Day's walk, would he not? He wrote the record many **years** after the resurrection and ascension. If you have ever walked 1,000 cubits (a man's elbow to his fingertips), you know it's a considerable journey. I'm GLAD I don't have to do such a thing on Shabbath. If people in the early times wished to go to a synagogue to hear the Torah, it wasn't nearly as far as we might think. Settlements, and even cities were only a few acres. Today, we have the increase in knowledge (literacy), as well as printing, so anyone who wants to read the Torah can do so with ease. Torah is a family centered practice, but we should gather when we have the opportunity. We can't ignore one teaching in order to try to obey another, just because we desire it. Interestingly, if a person rests on the 7th day, other people have no problem guessing their "religion", because this "sign" of the Covenant reveals Who they worship and obey. My best "family" day is Shabbath.

The Beast instituted an ordinance that required everyone to attend "Mass" on the 1st day of each week, without one single verse in the Writings to support either the 1st day as set-apart, or a required gathering. My "gathering" or "convocating" is with my wife and children, who I am to teach **diligently** the Words of the Covenant. If I work six days (a part of the Commandment), then there is only Shabbath left to **diligently** teach them. And because it is such a wonderful family time, they will always love and cherish it, and strive to make it their "custom" as well. This is not evil, although some find it different from their habits. It was our Rabbi's custom, as well as Shaul's, to go to the synagogue ~ surely not far away! Why? To teach, and because that's where the Scrolls were.

THE DEVELOPMENT OF THE DECEPTION

The dragon, who wages war against the Covenant and Bride of Mashiach, controls the "kingdoms" presently. He institutionalized the power of his religion, and centralized the implementation of his plan in the seat of the most powerful empire, ROME.

ROMAN HISTORY

Pagans worshipped the sun, and used fire, the hearth, wreaths, circles, pillars, bells, and many other items seen today as relics of their rituals. Some of the early Roman beliefs came from the Etruscans, Greeks, Egyptians, Persians, and of course Babylonians. The central foundation of Roman nationalism began at Roma, the original name of the city and language of the proto-empire. The mythology of the Romans taught that the empire began with two orphaned boys named Romulus and Remus, who were nurtured by a she-wolf. Their importance to the early Romans was observed by a national day of "purification", associated with the "wolf" (Latin *lupis*) that preserved their lives. Each year on their February 15, a purification festival was held which was called "Lupercalia", or wolf festival. 2 youths (who represented Romulus and Remus) ran around the city in the nude, laughing and whipping around strips of wolf skins, dipped in blood. Unmarried girls exposed their posteriors to be lashed with these bloody wolf hides, supposedly to imbue fertility. As part of the ritual, every eligible girl's name was collected and placed in a large "vat" or jar, and all the young men would "draw" a name from it. This gives us the phrase "luck of the draw". Whatever name a young man would draw out, that girl would be his consort in the festival. This was a very solemn religious process. "Lupercalia" was changed into "**Valentine's Day**" and moved to the 14th after being "Christianized". Instead of having nothing to do with the idolatry, it was simply altered slightly and adapted to the new "universal" religion. This is where we inherit the custom of "Valentine's Cards", and HEART SHAPED symbols. The shape of the heart is an IVY LEAF, the symbol of Bacchus, the male deity of wine and love (orgiastic). He corresponds to Nimrod and Tammuz, and also the archer, Saggitarius or "Cupid". Another name for him is Orion, the hunter. The arrow penetrating the "heart" symbol represented mating. Bacchus is seen in art wearing a wreath of ivy leaves on his head during his mating rituals. So, even the familiar "heart" symbol comes from Pagan Rome, and echoes their idolatry, as the symbol of Bacchus.

***"St. Peter's Basilica"* ~ built on an ancient Etruscan cemetery; VATICANUS MONS. Note the Dome, chariot wheel, and obelisk of Caligula as its axel - elements we see in Washington DC**

Rome is established on seven "hills", and each

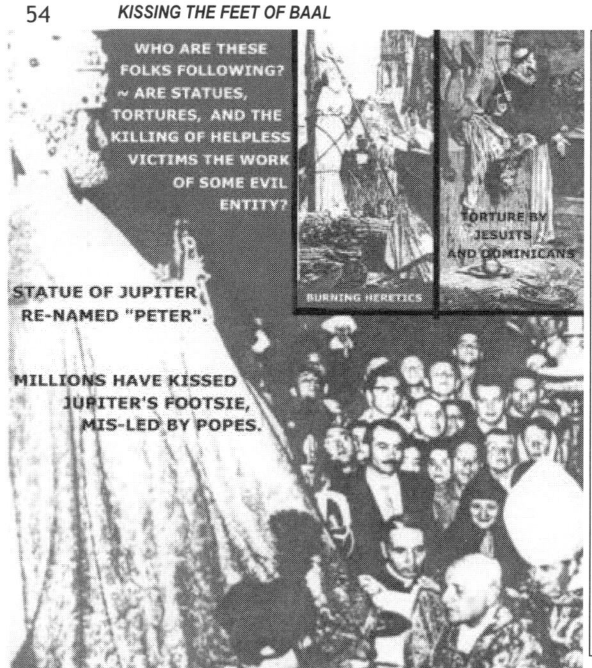

WHO ARE THESE
FOLKS FOLLOWING?
~ ARE STATUES,
TORTURES, AND THE
KILLING OF HELPLESS
VICTIMS THE WORK
OF SOME EVIL
ENTITY?
TORTURE BY
JESUITS
AND DOMINICANS
BURNING HERETICS
STATUE OF JUPITER
RE-NAMED "PETER".
MILLIONS HAVE KISSED
JUPITER'S FOOTSIE,
MIS-LED BY POPES.

IDOLATRY IN PICTURES

The authentic Roman statue of Jupiter, and the ancient custom of kissing the feet of the image.
1 Kings 19:18:
"Yet I reserve seven thousand in Israel — all whose knees have not bowed down to Baal and all whose mouths have not kissed him."

TORTURE by MONKS

The "fruit" of the tree will indicate whether the tree is a good tree or a bad tree. The secret, evil activities of the RCC have been the norm, not the exception. The information here may be the only warning some will ever have. History has been recorded from the viewpoint of deluded men.

was originally named by the Etruscans. There were settlements on six of these, but the seventh hill was a boggy, swampy place, where the soil was loose. The Etruscans buried their dead there for centuries. Because the graves were shallow, dogs would often go there to dig up and feed on the dead bodies! The Etruscans named this hill **VATICANUS**, meaning *habitation of dogs.* Later, a Roman ruler named Caligula drained this site, and held enormously popular "carnivals" (Latin for *flesh raising*). Caligula was a devotee of Bacchus, and held orgies and drunken parties on a regular basis. The obelisk of Caligula stands today in the center of the chariot wheel design in front of St. Peter's Cathedral (previous page). The Vatican stands on the same hill where the Etruscans buried their dead, so it is an enormous graveyard. The tunnels beneath the Vatican have entire walls made of human bones in certain places.

STATUE OF JUPITER

See the pope in the picture above, puckering-up to kiss the toes of the statue? This very image was made by the Romans, and was their **Jupiter** colossus. It was adopted and **re-named** "Peter", as they will explain to you if you take a tour of the Cathedral. On certain occasions, it is dressed-up in rich robes and crowned as you see it here, and kissed by throngs of Catholic devotees. The toes are worn smooth from the millions of Catholics and previous Romans who have kissed the statue's foot over the centuries. In the days of El Yahu (Elijah), multitudes are said to have *bowed* to Baal, and *kissed him.* Pagan temples often had a colossus idol inside. The "Lincoln Memorial" in Washington is such a colossus, and the inscription on the wall states the place is a "temple". Under the 3-tier miter crown of the image the pope is about to kiss, the statue of Jupiter/Peter has a round "halo", placed there by the sun-worshipping Romans. To associate images with the sun, statues, paintings, and reliefs often had round golden nimbuses or hoops encircling their heads. ***"It is not good to have zeal without knowledge, nor to be hasty and miss the way."*** Pr. 19:2. If a Natsari like Paul (Shaul) were to see this place, he would be traumatized by the spectacle.

PAGAN CLASH

As goes the family, so goes the nation. The fall of Rome had several causes, but all scholars agree that it was fundamentally caused by the deterioration of the family unit. The old phrase, "all roads lead to Rome" was quite true, and it was because of the efficient and extensive road system that the Roman Empire could conquer, control, and trade so effectively. Their quasi-Persian religion, called "Mithraism" was spread over vast distances, but its center was Rome. During the time of Constantine, a more tolerant policy was adopted toward "foreign" religions, as long as everything could be "fused" under one "universal" doctrinal format. With the newly arriving Natsarim faith, there was a clash between it and Mithraism, and the Pagan rule of Diocletian was perhaps the bloodiest one of all. As a young boy, Constantine had witnessed this clash. As a man, he embraced a policy much different from his predecessors, and tried to appease all sides. His Nicene Council established Easter's universal celebration, and blended essential Pagan customs with Natsarim overtones.

THE BEAST'S DEADLY WOUND

During Constantine's rule, he set up a new center for the Empire at what he called "Constantinople", now re-named Istanbul in Turkey. Since this action abandoned the historical center of the Empire at Rome, it accelerated the collapse of the Empire. The well-established "circulatory system" of Roman roads were now useless. Rome fell into ruin, and attackers from the north reduced it to rubble. It became little more than a squatter's camp. By moving the "capital" or "head" of the Empire, Constantine had inadvertently ripped the "head" off the Roman Empire (the head was separated from the heart, the road system). He had also managed to blend the solar religion of Mithraism with belief in the Natsari Mashiach, which he confused with the sun. Mithras and "Christ" were one and the same to him. The following is an overview of Mithraic doctrine.

THE ROMAN RELIGION:
MITHRAISM

Understanding Constantine, Mithraism, and the fertile Pagan background environment of the Romans will help explain many beliefs and practices seen today. Mithraism is about the worship of the sun, which was titled *Mithras Solis Invictus* (Mithras, the unconquered sun). The "mysteries" of this religion were revealed only to the initiates, who were predominantly soldiers of the Roman army. They spread this religion all over the civilized world by way of the good Roman roads. Mithraism was ***the primary religion of the Roman Empire from BCE 222 through the 4th century CE.*** It was the chief rival of "Christianity", which history shows compromised radically in order to convert pagans into "believers". By the 4th century CE, the sect of Yahudaism called the ***N'tzarim*** no longer existed openly, and gnostic clones of it had sprung up and began to compete with Mithraism for dominance. One historian said, *"The entire European continent and New World would be Mithraic today, if Christianity hadn't come along."* Other historians have put it another way: *"Christianity didn't conquer Mithraic Paganism. Mithraism blended in, and CHANGED NAMES."* The doctrines, feast dates, rituals, accouterments, and organizational structure have scarcely changed at all. The religion of Mithraism itself was the result of a merger of the astrology of the Chaldean priests of Marduk (Baal) with the Indo-Iranian priests of Mithras. The sun-idol, Mithras, is mentioned in the 'sacred writings' of both cults; the *Avesta* and the *Vedas*. The sun-idol is called *"THE LORD"* in both. The Hindu *Krishna* is called *THE LORD*, as you will recall the syncretistic lyrics in the song, *My Sweet Lord* by George Harrison, where vocalists chant *hare Krishna* interchangeably with *hallelu Yah.* All the while, the song blends the concepts under the impersonal, indefinite, and vague title, "LORD".

MITHRAIC DOCTRINE

1. The center of the Mithraic sun-cult was at Rome.
2. The leader of the ritual service was titled ***pater***, Latin for *father* ~ inherited by the priestcraft of Catholicism (against Mt. 23:9), and they wore cruxes as amulets, with costumes of black, having NEHRU collars, originating from the Indo-Iranian roots.
3. There was a ***Pater-Patratus*** over the paters; a *papa,* or ***pope***.
4. The hierarchy initiates below *pater* were called *brothers*.
5. The cult was for *men only*.
6. The cult had the Trinity: ***Mithras, Rashnu,*** and ***Vohu Manah*** ~ 3 'persons', but yet 'one'.
7. ***Sun-day*** was kept hallowed in honor of Mithras, the sun, called *Mithras Solis Invictus*. This has produced our popular name for the first day of the week, *Sunday*. The pattern of resting on Sun-day comes to us directly through what is called the ***Blue Laws***, enforced first throughout the Roman Empire, then through the western traditions into our "New World". The edict was initiated by Constantine I, forbidding officials, artisans, or merchants from engaging in any work on the ***Sun-Day***, to give honor to the sun, ***Mithras***.
8. There were 5 levels within the hierarchy.
9. ***December 25*** was observed as ***Mithras' Birthday***, called *"Natalis Invictus"*, the re-birth of the winter sun, unconquered.
10. Initiates had to undergo a ritual sprinkling (affusion, which involved being under a bull, or *Taurus*, which being cut to death allowed the initiate to become saturated. The custom of bloody ***bullfights*** seen in Spain hearken back to this cult. The custom of performing Christian "baptisms" in the spring at Eastertime will take on greater meaning as you learn the following information).
11. Special value was attributed to the moral

virtues of religion, truthfulness, purity, and generosity.

12. Mithraists would enter "paradise" (a Persian word itself, also called *Eleusian Fields, Nirvana, and Nether World*) by the ***Three Steps:***
    A. The Good Thought.
    B. The Good Word.
    C. The Good Deed.
13. The cult supported the ***divine right of kings*** (including Emperor worship).
14. The ***pater*** (father) stood at one end of an oblong room, performing mysterious blood rituals; there was an indoor "altar" at his end, on which a victim (Latin, "host") was sacrificed. They had a sun-shaped wafer disc like the Egyptians, and the assembly knelt, sat, and stood in unison.

It was during this time of the "clash" when Christianity and Mithraism merged, that Jerome translated the Greek Writings of the "New Testament" into Latin (391-403). His real name was Eusibius Heirymonius Sophronius. He took the Greek word ***STAUROS*** (beam, stake, pole) and carried it over to the Latin word ***CRUX***. This was an important shift in the meaning of the original word. The Hebrew term was "NAS", used for the word "POLE" that the serpent was lifted up on. To a Mithraist, the CRUX had a significant religious meaning. It could be represented as an "X" or a vertical line crossed horizontally. In the spring, when the Mithraists sacrificed a Taurus (bull), the sun was "CROSSING" the celestial equator, and was in the zodiac sign of the Taurus. ("Zodiac" actually means *animal* figures, related to the word "zoo"). These rabid Pagans "allegorized" or interpreted this as the sun (Mithras) *overcoming the bull, "crossing"* the celestial equator, so the cross was their most cherished religious symbol. The cross symbols of many different Pagan cults from around the world is what scholars call *"the symbol of the sun, par excellance".* The words we have inherited from "Jerome's" Latin translation include *cross, crucifixion, and crosier.* So, "cross" is a Latinism. In one of it's Babylonian forms, it was a tilted crux, with an arrow point at the high end, representing Nimrod standing on the tower shooting his hunter arrow at the skies. It was a bow and arrow. He may have even done this, shooting at the constellation Taurus. This is the link with the "Golden Calf". We still call the center of an archery target "the bull's eye". The sign of the "cross" was a Pagan sign of "overcoming". The Babylonian constellation "Orion" the Hunter (Archer) represents Nimrod of Babylon. Pagans practiced Astromancy, Pyromancy, Necromancy, and other occult forms of divination, and the cross was intimately linked to their rituals ~ and still is. A "Black Mass" uses the cross, and was practiced long before Christianity existed. Let's keep our spiritual priorities intact as we move along, and see if the Mark of the Beast can be linked in any way to Sun-day, the sun itself in Pagan worship, and the Pagan's **symbol** of the sun.

Since the Earth Mother was thought to be "fertilized" in the spring (Ishtar, or Easter), the Babylonian symbol for "woman" was also a cross, with the sun circle above it (the sun did the "fertilizing"). If you research Constantine, you will learn he had a vision of the sun with a "cross" beneath it, the same symbol used for "female" today in biology, a type of "ankh". The circle is also interpreted as the sun, and "circuses" like the ones held by Caligula were occultic religious displays, involving animals of the Zodiac, and three "rings". The Olympic Games today use 5 rings as a logo, representing the 5 original planetary deities worshipped in Babylon. In fact, it is still the custom to carry a torch lit by the "sacred fire" altar on Mount Olympus to the site of the games. Where the games are held, an altar dedicated to Zeus is lighted with this torch, so all the nations and athletes who participate are unknowingly worshipping Zeus. That's why this book is titled "Fossilized Customs", to open your eyes so that you can ***see them***. The whole world follows after the "Beast", through the ***fossilized customs***. So, you can see there are many ways we can be found practicing a lie, and having a "mark" or outward sign of following this beast. **Human traditions** may appear innocent, but if you can easily trace their origins to ancient Paganism, they are abominations.

ODD THING: People who are Christians today don't usually ever think of their "Jesus" as being a Yahudi, nor do they realize He is the Rabbi, and was called such by many in the Brit Chadasha. Yet they also use the "excuse" that the TaNaKh (O.T.) was mainly written to "Jews" and by "Jews" for "Jews", so Commandments like observing Shabbaths or making a distinction between the "clean" and "unclean" are now irrelevant for them. Quoting verses from the TaNaKh will often be met with a response like, *"but that's Old Testament".* Likewise, unbelieving Yahudim will not acknowledge the Brit Chadasha either. Can you imagine Shaul or Peter standing there quoting a passage from the TaNaKh, and being told *"but that's Old Testament"*?

CHRISTIANITY'S PAGAN CONNECTION

Constantine is the connection which bonded Paganism to the belief in the Yahudi Mashiach. Excused as "inculturation", Paganism poisoned the message of repentance beyond all recognition. If you study any aspect of the growth of Christendom, you will only encounter one bloodbath after another. If you go in search of the worst persecu-

FACT: The word "JESUS" first appeared in the KJV. The Geneva translation had no letter "J".

tion of Christians by Pagans, you will find that it was a picnic in the park compared to what Christians did over many centuries to non-Christians, and even to one another in various struggles for dominance. Constantine made Christianity the Roman State religion, but its form was far from anything known to the first Natsarim. Constantine had to MERGE the multitudes of Pagans—who were mostly his own soldiers—with the Natsari faith, in order to control his vast empire. This reconciliation, or merger of the Natsari faith with Mithraism, produced what we see today as "Christianity". He made the "cross" the primary symbol of this new merger, thus rallying the Pagans around its emotional meaning. The main issue at his Nicene Council in 325 CE centered on the date of "EASTER", again the most important point in the Pagan mind when the sun "crossed" the Zodiac at Taurus. Constantine confused Mithras and "Christ" together, borrowing from the Pagan background of sun-worship for every interpretation. Many of the Pastors in Christendom ***know*** these things, but never bring them up. Most don't care, it's just a job. A few are afraid that bringing it up will unravel their world. You will notice that if you privately discuss these things with a pastor, he will pluck two or three verses from Shaul's letters, then turn to stone ~ not wanting to pursue the real truth. He really doesn't want to get to the bottom of it, because it will expose everything he teaches and lives by as being a lie.

The secular population live in their own dream world as well. Some are idealists, blissfully going through life getting the weather reports and sports scores. There are many distractions to occupy yourself with, but very few people can get **real** information, or put it into a meaningful form.

The Roman Beast's most powerful tool is the calendar, as I called it the great "dragnet". When people are made aware that old Babylonian "rhythms" are being kept in the annual cycles of Sun-day, Christmas, Easter, and Halloween, it sometimes endears these rituals to them even more. The "Eastern" religions have become fascinating to many westerners, and they search for hidden secrets in them ~ and call it "New Age". One recent movement of a New Age cult has been the embracing of the Statue of Liberty as an idol. They place lilies near a plaque which displays a prayer to her as the Earth Mother. This enormous colossus is an image of the Babylonian goddess of the dawn, the Earth Mother. The "liberty" she offers the people of Earth is liberty from the Creator's pattern for living: ***"Why do the nations conspire and the peoples plot in vain? The kings of the Earth take their stand and the rulers gather together against ᴲYᴲZ and against his Anointed One. 'Let us break their chains' they say, and throw off their fetters."*** This is from Psalm 2, and sums up how people seek to be "free" to choose their own way to happiness. Queen Semiramis remains their image, although she was a witch. The image was a gift to America from the French people, a larger replica of a statue of the sungoddess on a bridge in France. The global "secret societies" linked to the Illuminati know all about this, and they just make sure the common people are manipulated to carry out their agendas. They refer to their armed forces as "cannon fodder", and actually use wars to make more money, and keep populations under their control. The love of money drives the evil. But, remember, we are not called to change any of this; but endure to the end in peace with all men. We love our enemies, they kill them.

Constantine adopted the insignia called the "**labarum**", a cross with a wreath above it with the Greek letters *CHI* and *RHO* inside it. He had it displayed on the shields of his soldiers, as the "Christian" emblem to go forth to conquer in. Later, the "Crusades" were launched with the marauding murderers wearing large red cruxes emblazoned on their chests. The word "Crusade" refers to this crux. The errors overwhelm the world because they and it are in great darkness. Rabbi OWYᴲZ came to teach the world, but it has not received His teachings. Therefore, when the time comes, it will be punished, convicted of its crimes against Him, and the obedient children of the Father will inherit it. **The saying goes that a wise man pointed at the moon. *The idiot only looked at the finger.*** Considering the processes and outcomes of Christianity over the last 1600 years, it would appear that early on, the whole point was lost. Constantine's government tried to "**fix**" a perceived problem, and wound up making it worse. It's a sad commentary, but governments haven't changed much in that respect.

The idiot didn't get the "point", he only looked at the finger doing the pointing.

(Dogma from the Catholic Encyclopedia)

ROMAN CHURCH TIMELINE

DATE	***DOGMA***
CE 300	"Baptism" by immersion changed to affusion (sprinkle).
CE 300	Prayers to the dead. (Against Deut. 18:11 & Yesha Yahu 8:19).
CE 310	Making the "sign" of the CROSS.
CE 325	Anathema (death) decreed to anyone who adds or changes the creed of faith of Nice. (See years 1545 & 1560).
CE 370	Council of Laodicea rejects Apocrypha, calls Sabbath observers "Judaizers", worthy of death.
CE 375	Veneration of angels and dead saints.

KNIGHTS TEMPLAR
KNIGHTS OF COLUMBUS
PRIORI OF SION
OPUS DEI
INQUISITION
ALUMBRADOS
JESUITS
ILLUMINATI

The ones who control the ***MONEY*** *CONTROL THE WORLD.*

THINGS CAN REALLY PILE UP

CE 394	***The Sacrament of the Mass:*** *Missa Recitata,* Low Mass, priest + 1 *Missa Cantata*, Sung Mass, " + 1 *Missa Solemnis,* High Mass, " + 2 *Missa Pontificalis,* Bishop + " + ?
CE 431	The worship of Miryam (Mary).
CE 431	Miryam "Queen of Heaven" (against Yirme Yahu 7:18, 44:17, 44:25).
CE 431	Miryam "ever virgin" (against Mt. 1:25, Mk. 6:3, Yn. 2:2-4).
CE 431	Miryam "Mediatrix" (against 1 Tim. 2:5, Yn. 11:28).
CE 500	Priestcraft began to dress in "priestly garb".
CE 526	Sacrament of "Extreme Unction".
CE 593	Doctrine of "Purgatory" ~ by Gregory (against Yn. 5:24, 1Yn. 1:7-9, 2:1,2, Romans 8:1).
CE 600	Latin language only language permitted for prayer (against 1 Cor. 14:9).
CE 709	Kissing the feet of pope is ordered (against Acts 10:25,26, Rev. 19:10, 22:8,9).
CE 750	Temporal Power of pope declared (against Mt. 4:8,9, 20:25,26, Yn. 18:38).
CE 754	Council of Constantinople ordered removal of all images and abolition of image worship.
CE 785	Miryam "co-redemptrix" (against Acts 4:12, Ps. 146:5, Yisraelites/ Hebrews 7:25).
CE 788	Miryam "worship" (against Romans 1:25, Yesha Yahu 42:8, Mk. 3:21).
CE 788	Worship of cross, relics, and im ages re-authorized (against Ex. 20:4, Dt. 27:15, Ps. 115:4-8).
CE 850	Fabrication and use of "holy water".
CE 890	Veneration of St. Yosef, husband of Miryam.
CE 965	Baptism of the bells ~ ceremony of actually "baptizing" bells to ward off demons and to call the elect to vespers when blessed bells are rung.
CE 995	Canonization of dead saints (against Romans 1:7, 1 Cor. 1:2).
CE 998	Fasting on "**Fri-days**" & during "**Lent**" (against Mt. 15:11, 1 Cor. 10:25, 1 Tim. 4:1-8).
CE 1079	Celibacy of priesthood/priestcraft declared (married priests ordered to cast off wives, against 1 Tim. 3:2-5, 3:12, Mt. 8:14,15).

CE 1090 Institution of **rosary prayer beads**, or "chaplet" (against Mt. 6:7, Dt. 18:10,11 Yesha Yahu 8:19 ~ also, Budhism, Shinto, and Islam practice prayer bead counting).

CE 1190 **Sale of indulgences** (against Eph. 2:8-10). For those of you who don't know, this was a practice of people actually paying the clergy money to have punishment time taken off from burning in "Purgatory" after their death. They probably weren't swimming in their own gene pool to be swindled so easily, but they were just kept uneducated.

CE 1215 Dogma of **"trans-substantiation"** declared (against Luke 22:19,20, Mk. 13:21, Yn. 6:35, Mt. 24:23-28, 1 Cor. 11:26 ~ this was truly a case of the idiot looking at the finger!).

CE 1215 Confession of sins to priest ordered (against Ps. 51:1-10, Luke 7:48 & 15:21, 1 Yn. 1:8,9).

CE 1220 **Adoration of the wafer "host"** (matzah adoration! Against Yn. 4:24).

CE 1229 **Scriptures forbidden to "laymen"** (against Yn. 5:39, 8:31, 2 Tim. 3:15-17).

CE 1265 Miryam's **house moved** by angel to Lorento Italy. (as fishy as this smells, I don't think they violated Torah, <u>unless they were lying ~ what do you think</u>?).

CE 1287 **Scapular protection** decreed (brown cloth talisman with picture of virgin packed with tea leaves proclaimed to contain supernatural powers or "virtues" to protect wearer. Sure, like Miryam and "St. Christopher" are omni-present, and can speak and hear you. They're DEAD, Jim).

CE 1414 "Chalice" forbidden to laity at "communion" (a radical distortion of the Passover Seder, the annual remembrance of OWYƎZ's death).

CE 1439 Dogma of **seven sacraments** (against Mt. 28:19,20, & 26:26-28).

CE 1439 **Purgatory** declared valid dogma (against Mt. 25:46, Luke 23:43).

CE 1508 Miryam "Mother of GOD" (against Mt. 12:46-50, Lk. 8:19-21, Acts 1:14).

CE 1545 **Church tradition equal to Scripture** (against Mt. 15:6, Mk. 7:7-13, Col. 2:8 ~ also ***adds*** all of above and many other dogma to Council of Nice!).

CE 1560 Creed of pope Pius IV decreed (against Gal. 1:8).

CE 1580 Pope declared to be **"LORD GOD"** (that ought to just about be enough to get some people roasted).

CE 1593 "Ave Maria" adopted.

CE 1710 **Stuffed donkey** in Verona, Italy, at Church of the Madonna of the Organs, *decreed to be the actual animal Rabbi Yahusha ha Mashiach entered Yerushaliyim on*. (This is "the idiot" looking at the finger again. When I first heard about it, I couldn't stop laughing for about 10 minutes.)

CE 1854 **Immaculate Conception** of Virgin Miryam (against Romans 3:23, & 5:12, Ps. 51:5, Yerme Yahu 17:9).

CE 1864 Miryam "sinless" (against Luke 1:46,47, Romans 3:10-19, & 23).

CE 1870 **Papal infallability** decreed (against 2 Thess. 2:2-12, Rev. 17:1-9, 13:5-8, 18).

CE 1907 All sciences condemned.

CE 1922 Pope declared to be "Jesus Christ".

CE 1930 All public schools condemned.

CE 1950 Declaration of the bodily assumption of the Virgin Miryam into Heaven.

The dogma of "**trans-substantiation**" that popped-up in **1215** caused many people to lose their lives. The idiot was looking really closely at the finger, because when our Rabbi said "***This is My Body***"*, and "***This is My Blood***", He was picturing what was soon to be. The matzah is pierced and bruised, and the blood of the grape is red. These emblems are to remind us once every year at Passover, OF HIS DEATH. First of all, this remembrance isn't done every day, or every week. Second, the "metaphor" for "eating" and "drinking" His Body and Blood was mistaken to be ***literal*** by several Pagan rulers, so they killed as many of these "believers" as they could find, *because they thought there was some sort of cannibalism involved*. The believers being killed didn't even understand ***why*** they were being killed! But the "believers" were led astray also by their enchanters, thinking the "priests" had some supernatural ability to call out certain Latin words, wave items in the air, and by some superior powers in them LITERALLY CHANGE BREAD AND WINE INTO THE ACTUAL LIVING BODY OF THE MASHIACH. Rabbi meant that He would be ***IN US*** <u>like</u> the food we eat, not ***BE*** the food we eat. The New Covenant is receiving the Spirit of

****CATHOLIC PRIESTS SAY "HOC EST CORPUS MEUM" , LATIN FOR "THIS IS MY BODY" - HOW ODD***

FASCISTS SALUTE THEIR CAESAR IN ROME IN 1938

THE ROMAN SALUTE

OWY∃Z, where He writes His Covenant Torah on our hearts, and we walk in the Commandments obediently. Our mind of the "flesh" no longer controls us, He does. We don't receive Him by eating bread. The bread we eat at Passover is to **remember His death** by, at **that** time of year (Passover). People need to stop looking at the finger. Millions are entranced, and can't wake up from this bad dream! No one has explained it to them, because no one "gets it" in the circles they find themselves in. The pope himself doesn't understand. But I pray he will learn, and then teach everyone who is Catholic what they need to comprehend. It's still a huge "mystery" to most Protestants too ~ many have an indoor "altar" left over from the Catholic "bloodless sacrifice of the Mass". But, remember ~ without the shedding of **blood**, there is **no remission** of sins. Throw out the "altar", tear down the "steeple", and start over again is my advice to pastors. Tell the congregation ***THEY ARE THE TEMPLE*** ~ if the Mashiach dwells in them. If He does not, they are not His!

NATSARIM - not "Nazi"

"There will be a day when WATCHMEN cry out on the hills of Ephraim . . ." ~ this is from 31:6 of Yerme Yahu (Jeremiah), and in the same chapter as the prophesied New Covenant. The word "watchmen" is *NATSARIM*. Those today who "see" are announcing that the world is off course, and out-of-bounds.

THE BEAST'S DEADLY WOUND: HEALED

After Constantine's action of moving the head of the Roman Empire to Constantinople, the Empire faded into what is called the Byzantine Empire. Rome was in ruins, wounded to death. By the 6th century CE, the bishop at Rome was regarded more highly than any other by reputation, simply because the name "Rome" was a profoundly stirring one. During the 7th century, the bishop of Rome took on the Mithraic title, "pope", or papa. The title "Pontifex Maximus"* was also bestowed on him, the Caesar's title. ("Caesar" is also spelled Czar and Khasar). By the end of the 8th century, Rome was resurrected back to life in the leadership office of the "pope", and in the year 800 this bishop crowned King Charlemagne the "Defender of the Faith", and announced the beginning of ***The Holy Roman Empire***, or ***First "Reich"***. This remained intact for 1000 years. The pages of history record the evil "fruit" of death and destruction of this empire. The **symbol** of Caesar's authority can be seen on the front of a US coin, the dime, or 10-cent piece. It is a bundle of reeds, wrapped in red leather strapping, called a **FASCIS**, from which we derive the term *fascist.* Caesar's throne had this symbol under the armrests on the left and right. It symbolized complete unity, and the power to control and punish all opponents to magistrates and Caesar's universal authority. (Thomas Jefferson designed US currency).

The men in the picture above include Adolf Hitler, Mussolini, and Hitler's inner circle of fascist henchmen. Who would Hitler himself salute with the old Roman soldier's salute? These fascists marched with a swastika crux inside a golden wreath modeled after the old Roman style banners in their military parades. The word "Reich" means "realm", and the First Reich was the "Holy Roman Empire", as your dictionary will explain. This "3rd Reich" was planned to last 1000 years, like the 1st one. Shatan was unleashing his "Final Solution" on the Earth, establishing Catholicism, with Hitler as the "Defender of the Faith".

CONCORDATS

Individual nations signed a "Concordat" with the Vatican, a written arrangement which officially recognized only Catholicism as the national religion. All other religions were banned, and severely persecuted by the power of the state which signed the Concordat. "Concordat" means the state was in accord, or agreement, with the Vatican. To a citizen in such a Catholic nation, their ultimate authority was the pope, then the leader of their nation, local civil authorities, teachers, and parents. The pope wielded both "temporal" and "spiritual" authority over the citizens, which is the secret behind the "hand-sign" of two fingers you often see in religious art, and lifted in the air by the pope as he "blesses" his votaries. Germany and Italy had a Concordat with the Vatican.

[The US Constitution stands in the way of ever having a Concordat with the Vatican, since it safeguards complete freedom to practice one's

****PONTIFEX MAXIMUS*** MEANS "BRIDGE-BUILDER", BUT REFERS TO THE "HIGHEST PRIEST". IT WAS USED AS THE PAGAN TITLE FOR THE ***PRIEST OF JANUS***; THE PRIEST WAS ***CAESAR***, THE HEAD OF THE **CURIA**, OVER 30 YEARS BEFORE YAHUSHA WAS BORN. HOW COULD ANYONE CLAIM THIS TITLE AND BE A FOLLOWER OF YAHUSHA AT THE SAME TIME?

religion; the state cannot restrict religious practice in any way under the US Constitution. The Constitution controls the **government**, not the free citizens.]

At the end of World War 2, thousands of Nazi fascists fled to Brazil, the world's densest concentration of Catholics. War criminals are still hiding there in their old age. The pope visited this country in 1999. He was born in Poland, and his real name isn't "John Paul II", but Karol Wojtyla. As a young Catholic man, he worked for a large chemical firm which manufactured the deadly gas which the Nazi fascists used to kill 6 million Yahudim men, women, and children. Leaving the chemical firm, he became a Catholic priest, and in a surprisingly short time became a Cardinal. The hidden history of this man is well-documented. He was in attendance at the signing of the Concordat with Germany as a "prelate", and has been much closer to the "action" than most ever get. If you would like to get more acquainted with just how close Hitler was to the pope, Pius XI, find the new book "Hitler's Pope" at a bookstore.

CRUSADES

They were called "crusades" because the rampaging murderers wore a large red "crux" on their chest. They were sent off by various popes, to re-capture the "holy land" from "the infidels". Killing, raping, looting, and burning libraries in their path, these 13 "divine campaigns" defy description. They flung the civilized world into the dark ages, and made no small contribution to the spread of the Black Death. Sure, fleas on rats carried the Plague, but 25% of the continent perished in part because the fleas were being carried by these travelers as well. [Several organized secret societies were spawned within Catholicism during this time period, which you can independently research: Curia, The **Society of Jesus**, (Jesuit Order, founded by Ignatius de Loyola), **Jesuit General** (the "Black Pope", the real power behind the pope), **Alumbrados**, **Opus Dei**, **Knights Templar**, and **Ecole Biblique**.]

(The following was received by internet in CE 1986, from an anonymous source):

ILLUMINATI

In recent years, there have been hushed whispers about the secret society called the "illuminati", and their conspiracy to control the world. The Order of the Illuminati was founded May 1, 1776 by Dr. Adam Weishaupt. Born a Yahudi, he converted to Roman Catholicism and became a professor of Canon law at the University of Ingolstadt in Bavaria. He became Jesuit priest, and then formed his own secret organization. The secret order began with 5 members, and each had a secret name. Weishaupt was "Spartacus", and his chief assistant, Herr Von Zwack, took the name "Cato". Weishaupt hoped to attract the German Freemasons, but was unsuccessful. Finally a few prominent citizens joined in Munich, to receive the mysterious title, "Areopagite".

3 CLASSES ~ In 1779, Weishaupt divided his secret organization into 3 classes: **Novice, Minerval, and Illuminatied Minerval** ("Minerva" is the Pagan name for the "Mother of the Sun", from <u>The Mystic Hymns of Orpheus</u>—the hymns which are the basis of "Gregorian Chant"). Each candidate had to swear an oath to secrecy plus unconditional obedience to Weishaupt. One feature of their society was a most unusual system of "mutual espionage". Every member spied on every other member. When the Novice was promoted to the Minerval stage, a solemn initiation ceremony was performed. In a dimly lit room, the identities of other members of the society were revealed to him, up to and including the Minerval grade, but not the upper grades. By the time he reached the

IDENITFYING ROME AS THE 4TH BEAST CAN BE DONE BY THE ROMAN NUMERAL SYSTEM.

Rev 13 tells us the "man" (of sin) will come <u>from</u> this beast (Rome). The original SIX letters of the Roman numbering system were

D — 500
C — 100
L — 50
X — 10
V — 5
I — 1

DO THE MATH IF YOU CAN

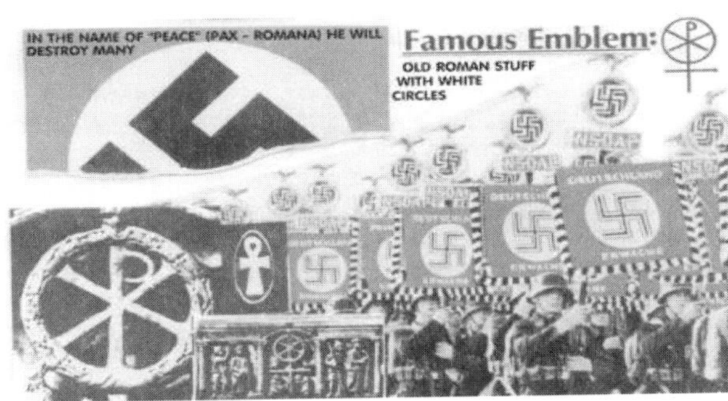

Here is the wisdom!
He who has understanding, let him calculate the number (NUMERAL) ***of the <u>beast</u>,***
for it is the number of a man,
and his number is 666."

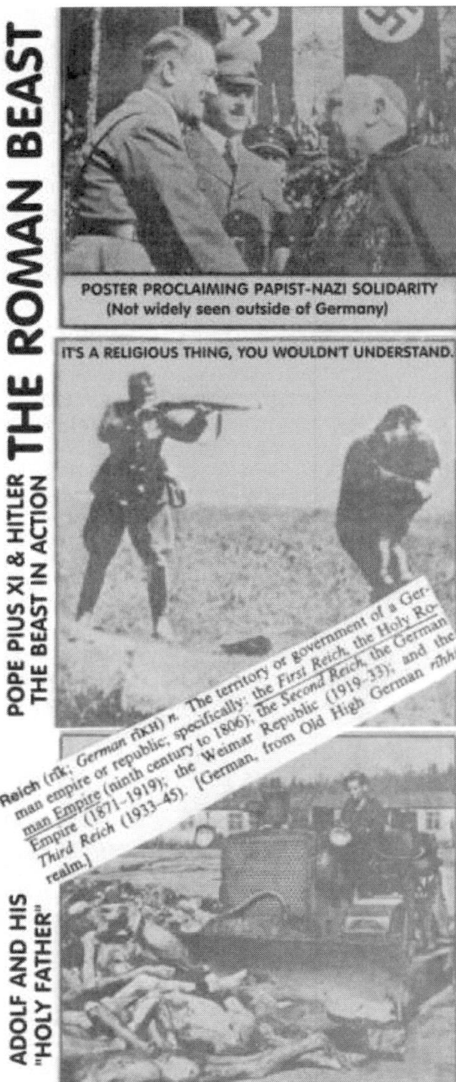

THE ROMAN BEAST
POPE PIUS XI & HITLER
THE BEAST IN ACTION
POSTER PROCLAIMING PAPIST-NAZI SOLIDARITY
(Not widely seen outside of Germany)
IT'S A RELIGIOUS THING, YOU WOULDN'T UNDERSTAND.
ADOLF AND HIS
"HOLY FATHER"

Reich (rīk; *German* rīkн) *n.* The territory or government of a German empire or republic; specifically: *the First Reich*, the Holy Roman Empire (ninth century to 1806); *the Second Reich*, the German Empire (1871–1919); the Weimar Republic (1919–33); and the *Third Reich* (1933–45). [German, from Old High German *rīhhi*, realm.]

grade of Illuminated Minerval, he learned the ultimate aims of the Order:

THE ABOLITION OF: *all governments, inheritance, private enterprise, patriotism, religion, the family unit, and the creation of* ***A NEW WORLD ORDER***. (Fascism had much the same objectives, since the leader was the "Father", and there was no room for any other allegiance). The ***United Nations*** is the **NWO**.

Weishaupt wrote to his chief assistant "Cato": *"The most admirable thing of it all is, that great Protestant and reformed theologians who belong to our order really believe they see in it the true and genuine mind of the Christian religion. Oh, man! What can not you be brought to believe?"* Weishaupt knew how to lure the unsuspecting, and at one time wrote:

"These people swell our numbers and fill our treasury; get busy and make these people nibble at our bait . . . But do not tell them our secrets. They must be made to believe that the low degree that they have reached is the highest."

Weishaupt gradually infiltrated the Freemasons. On July 16, 1782 at the Congress of Wilhelmsbad, an alliance between Illuminism and Freemasonry was finally sealed. On that day the leading secret societies were infiltrated, and to some degree, ***united***, numbering more than 3 million members. Eventually, the Bavarian government banned both the Illuminati and Freemasonry on March 2, 1785. Weishaupt was forced to leave the country. The Bavarian government heard 4 leading members of the Illuminati testify before a court of inquiry, exposing the Luciferic nature of its aims. A vast array of documents were found in the Illuminati headquarters. The Bavarian government published them, to warn all other .countries of Europe. The name of the document was: The Original Writings of the Order and Sect of the Illuminati. ("Lucifer" is a Latin word based on lucia, "light", and means *"light—bringer"*. The word Illuminati means "*holder of the light*). By the time the document was published, 15 lodges of the Order of the Illuminati had been established in the 13 American colonies. There was a lodge in Virginia that was identified with Thomas Jefferson. In 1797, Professor John Robison published Proofs of a Conspiracy, in which he warned the world of Illuminati infiltration into Masonic Lodges. (Perhaps there is a connection between the American Revolution and the Illuminati?).

Dr. Adam Weishaupt, the Illuminati founder, adopted the familiar ***All Seeing Eye*** symbol when he first set up operations in Bavaria. This symbol is found on the back of the $1.00 US bill. The Roman numerals at the base refer to 1776, the date he founded the Illuminati ~ and it conveniently corresponds to the year of the US Declaration of Independence. This "eye" symbolized a "big brother", and the mutual spying system of the domain. The Latin words above and below the eye on the dollar bill in translation mean *"Announcing the Birth of a New World Order".* The All Seeing Eye is seen in the meditation room at the United Nations building in New York City. The "Great Seal" was designed under the authority of Thomas Jefferson and John Adams (both Freemasons), and Benjamin Franklin (a member of another secret society, the Rosicrucians).

(Masons revere Nimrod, the eye above, as their founder)

After Adam Weishaupt died, an Italian revolutionary leader became the director of the Illuminati: **Giuseppe Mazzini**, who held the position from 1834 to 1872. "Mazzini" gives the first letter to the acronym, **M.A.F.I.A:**

Italian word	*English meaning*
Mazzini	Mazzini
Autorizza	Authorizes
Furti	Thefts
Incindi	Arsons
Avvelemanti	Poisonings

This "Mafia" acronym developed in about 1859. The organization was previously called "Camorra" since 1800, and was an Italian criminal society. This information is supplied in the 1945 Encyclopedia Americana. Shortly after Mazzini took control, an obscure intellectual joined a branch organization called "The League of the Just". His name was Karl Heinrich **Marx**. Marx denounced the Messianic Judaism of his parents, and embraced atheism, studied at the Universtiy of Bonn and Berlin, and wrote the book Das Kapital, laying the foundation of the communist movement (set against private enterprise and property ownership). In 1847 Marx wrote the Communist Manifesto, which was basically a rehash of the writings of Adam Weishaupt. At this time, Mazzini selected Albert Pike to head the Illuminati activities in the US. Pike was an admirer of the Secret Hebrew Cult of Cabala (Qabbalism). Mazzini, in a letter dated January 22, 1870, wrote to Pike:

"We must create a Super Rite, which will remain unknown to which we will call those Masons of high degree whom we shall select. With regard to our brothers in Masonry, these men must be pledged to the strictest secrecy. Through this supreme rite, we will govern all Freemasonry which will become the one international center, the more powerful because its direction will be unknown."

This letter was published in the book, Occult Theocracy, by Lady Queensborough, pgs. 208, 209. Supreme councils were formed in Charleston, South Carolina (US), in Rome, and in Berlin. Known secretly as "Palladism", it is the cult of Satan in the inner shrines of a secret ritual to surpass all other secret rituals. On July 14, 1889, Pike issued this statement to the 23 Supreme Councils of the world:

"That which we must say to the CROWD is: 'We worship a god, but it is the god that one adores without superstition.' To YOU sovereign Grand Inspectors General, we say this, that you may repeat it to the brethren of the 32nd, 31st, and 30th degrees: 'The Masonic Religion should be, by all of us initiates of the high degrees, maintained in the purity of the Luciferian doctrine. If Lucifer were not god, would Adonay (Yahusha) *calumniate him? . . . Yes, Lucifer is GOD . . .'"*

~ *General Albert Pike, 33rd degree*

(Quoted from The Freemason, the organ of English Freemasonry, 19th January 1935).

In 1871, Giuseppe Mazzini issued a remarkable letter in which he graphically outlined plans for **3 world wars**. Until recently, this letter was on display in the British Museum Library in London. Pike aided in making this plan known in the US. It was a blue-print for 3 wars. Called ***The Mazzini-Pike Plan***, its ultimate goal was eventual ***world domination***. The letter outlined three relatively simple strategies. It called for communism, fascism, and the struggle for the Mid-East to foment three global wars and at least two major revolutions. WW1 was to destroy the Czarist government of Russia, and replace it with militant atheism. WW2 would begin by manipulating Great Britain and Germany to achieve a global war, which was done almost single-handedly by Adolf Hitler. WW3 of the Mazzini-Pike blue-print called for the firing up of the controversy between the Israeli and Moslem world. They hoped that the "Zionists" and the Moslems would destroy one another, and bring the rest of the world into a final conflict. The "Great Battle" would usher in a complete social, political, and economic chaos. To fill the void created by the "Great Battle" would come a world government, headed by the Illuminati. In Illuminati doctrine, "Lucifer" is "GOD", and

ADAM WEISHAUPT WAS A JESUIT UNTIL THEY WERE OUTLAWED IN 1773. HE THEN EMERGED WITH A NEW ORDER, THE ILLUMINATI IN 1776. THEY ARE THE "MEN IN BLACK", THE MILITIA OF THE PAPACY.

THE GREAT SEAL

RESEARCH "AGENDA 21"

this seal is that of the ***Jesuit-Illuminati***, promoted through the highest levels of Masonry. The eye is the "Light", the seething power of Lucifer. It also refers to the ***unknown superior***, which is the Superior General of the Jesuits, or "Black Pope". As of 2009, his name is Adolfo Nicolas Pachon.

Satanism is heresy.

— END OF INTERNET DATA —

(If you research a man named Ignatius de Loyola, you will find he founded *The Alumbrados*, which eventually became *The Inquisition*).

I don't wish to turn this book into a critique on politics, but the world is controlled presently by ha Shatan, and you can see that the conflicts around the world are ROOTED in religious differences caused by his "divide-and-conquer" methods, and driven by greed. [Here in the US, Norman Thomas ran for President in 1936 on the Socialist ticket, and stated: *"The American people will never knowingly adopt Socialism, but under the name of Liberalism, they will adopt every fragment of the Socialist program, and America will be a Socialist nation without ever knowing how it happened."*] The word "NAZI" is short for *National Socialist Party*. The objective of fascism and National Socialism is government control of business, religion, the family, and the economy. Look up the definitions for "fascism" and "Nazi" in a dictionary, and you will be amazed that they are identical to the aims of the socialism we find ourselves surrounded by. Where is the "Illuminati" today? Let's find out.

THE ILLUMINATI AND THE COUNCIL ON FOREIGN RELATIONS (excerpt) by Myron Fagan:

"Now then, this satanic plot was launched back in the 1760's when it first came into existence under the name 'Illuminati'. This Illuminati was organized by one Adam Weishaupt, born a Jew, who was converted to Catholicism and became a Catholic priest, and then, at the behest of the then newly-organized House of Rothschild, defected and organized the Illuminati. Naturally, the Rothschilds financed that operation and every war since then, beginning with the French Revolution, and has been promoted by the Illuminati operating under various names and guises. I say under various names and guises because after the Illuminati was exposed and became notorious, Weishaupt and his co-conspirators began to operate under various other names. In the United States, immediately after World War 1, they set up what they called the "Council on Foreign Relations", commonly referred to as the **CFR,** and this CFR is actually the Illuminati in the United States and its hierarchy."

So, watch the behavior of the **UN*** and the **World Bank**. *Food control* is one of their objectives. This is brought about by undermining foreign governments, using Jesuit priests under "deep cover" to create religious conflicts. The Vietnam war was fought over religion. The president of South Vietnam (Diem) was a Catholic, and was persecuting his Buddhist subjects. North Vietnam was Buddhist, and sought to come to the aid of their Buddhist brothers. You'll recall headlines with images of Buddhist monks in South Vietnam burning themselves in front of their pagodas to attract the world's attention! Religious bickering is causing civil unrest in Northern Ireland, the Balkans, India, Africa, and Indonesia. They "plant" the seeds of unrest, then come in with their "international peace keepers", and on the surface appear to be "the good guys". But, the soldiers who work to restore the peace are what they internally call "cannon fodder". All the while, they develop and test new deadlier weapons at secret facilities like Area 51, and encircle the globe with nuclear submarines. They have weapons in orbit, which can target individual persons, or shoot down planes which carry the people they wish to eliminate. Mysterious crashes for unexplained reasons occur all the time; but if you check the record of those who were on board the planes, you will find people of prominent influence every time. Planes which suddenly explode for no reason, or crash into the sea like John Kennedy Jr's did, might not be the "accidents" they appear to be. I became aware of this possibility several years ago when I heard about a plane going down that had the US Air Force Procurement officer on board. The Illuminati controls political leaders with money and sex, as you see these two issues swarm around them constantly. But, we must live in peace, and trust that all these wars, conspiracies, storms, earthquakes, firestorms, and other record-breaking natural disasters are signs that the end is near for Shatan. Where ever you see eagles or "obelisks", Shatan cannot be far away.

THE SEAL OF MASONRY

The "fraternal club" of masonry is for men only, but they started a women's chapter for the wives, called the "Eastern Star". Masonry is a very old craft, really. It didn't involve all the convoluted "secrets" it has today, but only had one objective: BUILDING. Yes, the men who designed and built all the ancient and modern temples and government buildings were **stone masons**. They took on apprentices, or students, who eventually became journeymen, and finally master craftsmen. They had to learn how to lay foundations, measure, and cut stone. The graduates of schools wear a flat square-topped hat, which is really a "mortar board", attached to the round hat of "Hermes", an idol of the Greeks, which scholars wore as a badge of learning. (This "beanie" hat was imposed on the Hellenized Yahudim, and now "Jews" wear them when they attend synagogue).

The "seal" of modern masonry has a compass open above a square, which are two tools used in the geometry of their craft, with a capital letter "G" in the center. The letter is "interpreted" to stand for "GOD", and Christians who join see it this way.

****THE CFR ESTABLISHED THE UN AFTER THE LEAGUE OF NATIONS FAILED; IT'S A FOREIGN POWER ON U.S. SOIL.***

Some see it as standing for "Great Architect". It really stands for the Greek word "gnostic", which means "knowledge" ~ the knowledge of the craft. But it also stands for "GUILD". During the Middle Ages, stonemasonry formed into organized groups of men called "guilds", which were pre-cursors of unions. The building trades were monopolized by the guilds. Their most cherished item was their apron, which they wore when laying stones. Without this apron, they could not work, and it became their "badge" of approval, or "righteousness". The emblem of each guild was displayed on the apron. **THE GREAT ARCHITECT**

Originally, Masonry was a trade, but after Adam Weishaupt, people with no building skills were accepted into the organizations, and advanced in grade as they acquired knowledge carefully "fed" to them over time. Hideous blood oaths, some involving murder, are sworn to maintain control and secrecy. In the original guilds, mathematical formulas were held as secrets (πr2, 2πr, 4πr3, etc.) but Masonry today doesn't involve architecture anymore. To be a Mason, a man has to believe in a deity who is referred to as "the Great Architect", who they must invoke for blessings and protection. Salvation is taught by Masonry to have many roads, and all religions are believed to lead to the "Great Architect". They meet in what are called "Masonic Temples", and call their leaders "Worshipful Masters".

Knowledge is power, and the skills of a master stonemason enabled him to rise above a common person. He knew the formulas and ratios necessary to construct great buildings. Naturally, you wouldn't want everyone to control such "secret" information, if your trade could be more secure by withholding it. Today, with engineering schools teaching the detailed formulas for architecture, chemistry, and electronics, the old "guilds" have no secrets anymore. But, the gullible members of today's Masonry are led to believe they will achieve some secret knowledge if they remain members.

PENTAGRAMS Masonry uses the five-pointed star as one of its "secret" symbols, and it is used by the women's organization, which is called "the Eastern Star". Christians see it as an evil sign, especially when it is displayed point-down, because they understand Satanists use it to worship "Baal". It is said to outline the features of a goat head, which represents a Pagan deity called "Baphomet". Many of these ancient names are two or three deities' names joined together. Masons call on "Jabulon", which is supposed to represent "Jehovah", "Baal", and "On" (the "On" part is an Egyptian deity).

In reality, the pentagram is an ancient building tool, a geometric figure which contains what is called "the golden section", or "golden mean". This is a repeating mean RATIO. It was used like a ruler in the ancient world in building design. It is **61.25%** of any given length. It is the division of a length, such that the smaller part is to the greater as the greater is to the whole. Pentagrams' lines intersect one another at these key places. It is much used as a "key" or **proportion** in design. The main measurements in many arches, bridges, and buildings have used this "golden mean" since early times. Artists, architects, sculptors, and engineers frequently use the **golden mean** in industrial design. This proportion is found in all living things; the rate of curve in the nautilus, the placement of the eyes on the head, the location of the heart in man relative to his height, the knees, the elbows in the arm span, etc.,. Beauty is determined by how close to the golden mean one's features approach! It was discovered by the Greek mathematician Euclid II in the mid 5th century BCE, and later used by the Pythagoreans as a sign of salvation and secrecy. The Italian mathematician Luca Pacioli called it *divina proportione* (divine proportion), and Johannes Kepler (d. 1630) called it *sectio divina* (divine section).

Since we know that the proportions found in the pentagram are used by the true Creator, 𐤉𐤄𐤅𐤄, there is no need to fear the symbol. If Pagans adopted it, then they only show their ignorance by not knowing its true origin. Pagans also adopted the "serpent on the pole" as the sign for healing! Originally, the bronze serpent "Nehushtan" (2 Kings 18:4, Num. 21:8, John 3:14) was a sign to be looked upon, and those bitten by a snake were healed. But, the serpent on the "staff" became a Greek sign of a healing deity, Aesculapius, a symbol embraced by the medical sciences, and called a "caduceus". The "Seal" of those who worship the True Creator is the Name: 𐤉𐤄𐤅𐤄.

Paul exhorts us: ***"Examine yourselves TO SEE WHETHER YOU ARE IN THE FAITH; TEST YOURSELVES."*** ~ 2 Cor. 13:5. If you have the Spirit of 𐤉𐤄𐤅𐤔𐤏, you pass the test. When you are able to **closely examine** the trappings and observances you are programmed to follow in Christendom, you will discover unsettling truths. This book is written for those who have wished to learn the truth, and want to progress to the next level. The practices like Christmas, Easter, Sunday, steeples, holy water, the wearing of black by "clergy", wreaths, trees, etc., are all customs "fossilized" from Paganism. The meanings behind them have been put "out of focus", to keep the masses from discovering how they are camouflaged counterfeits. Look closely at them, their true origins become clear.

Here's a practical example of how to see the

"fine print" that often gets people into trouble for not reading it: (It's a ***"pin-hole lens"***)

Take your first finger, and put your thumb below the "crease" of the first knuckle, making a tiny "pin-hole" to look through right up close to your eye. Now, find some really small print that you find difficult to read, like on a cassette or CD. Hold the print in good lighting about 5 to 6 inches away from your eye, and look through the "pin-hole" you make with your first finger and thumb, very close to your eye. You will discover you can read a word very clearly through this pin-hole, and by opening the pin-hole too much, the small print will become blurred.

The pin-hole you make becomes the lens, or primary focal point; your eye lens is taken out of the picture. Now, it is just the fine print focused through the pin-hole, onto your retina in the back of your eye. The reason you can "focus" better on fine print in a bright light is because your iris closes to make a smaller "hole", but this thumb-and-finger "pin-hole" makes a much more powerful lens than your iris can make.

The physics of this practical example should also apply to the close scrutiny we give to what's behind our customs. Look closely, and test everything. Just because the origins are "out-of-focus" doesn't mean you can't look closely enough to see them clearly. Christendom has "blurred" quite a few things, wouldn't you say? Remember that we fight NOT AGAINST FLESH AND BLOOD, but against **spiritual forces** of evil. Rabbi 𐤉𐤄𐤅𐤔𐤏 was not hateful or mean-spirited when He spoke with Pilate, even when He knew this man would pronounce His death-sentence. Surely we can be patient with those who disagree with us. The Church of Rome, and her daughters, are the "beast" upon which rides **Mystery Babylon**. This Roman Beast is the 4th and last beast prophesied at Daniel 7, and will be successful ***"until the time of wrath is completed"*** Dan. 11:36.

"This calls for wisdom. The seven heads are seven hills on which the woman sits." ~ Rev. 17:9. Rome was founded on 7 hills. It is often referred to as *the seven hills of Rome.* ***"Mystery Babylon, the Great Mother of Prostitutes and of the Abominations of the Earth."*** This "title" is written on her forehead, so says Rev. 17:5. What is her name, or how can we identify her? Her name is the same as it was in ancient Babylon:

ISHTAR - ASHERAH

As we have already covered, this name became Astoreth, Asherah, Astarte, Eostre, Eastre, and she is now embraced (or blurred) in the festival called ***Easter.*** Find ***Easter***, and you find ***her***. She's a bit *fossilized*, but nonetheless still around. The "beast" is here, and has been here for many centuries. If you are waiting for a "beast", then you will miss it, because it has been here deceiving ~ even the very elect ~ since it's deadly wound was healed, since the bishop of Rome became Pontifex Maximus. You will know them by their fruits. If you can honestly say that Rome isn't the beast, in the face of the wars she's waged, the Inquisition, the Crusades, the Roman Catholic Hitler, Concordats, Pogroms, and the bloody "convert-or-die" policy from Constantine onward, then many men before me have been wrong. If, on the other hand, Rome is not masquerading but is in fact doing the deeds of the Father, 𐤉𐤄𐤅𐤄, would she be capable of such evil fruit? No, she is doing the work of her father ha Shatan. 𐤉𐤄𐤅𐤄 would not "change" His Shabbath to the Pagan Sun-day, nor use the Earth Mother's name for a celebration of His Son's resurrection, or re-invent by deception the Pagan festival for the rebirth of the sun, and call it His Son's birthday. He would not promote "Halloween", called such because it was *"all Halloweds' Eve'n,* the night before *All Saints' Day,* a re-invented Druid feast of the dead. 𐤉𐤄𐤅𐤄 would not continue to "sacrifice" His beloved Son over and over in a ghastly "mass" ritual ~ but ha Shatan would. 𐤉𐤄𐤅𐤄 would not have us "praying" to anyone but Himself in His Son's Name, but Shatan guides the Church of Rome to pray to Miryam, and many other so-called dead "saints" for blessings, protection, guidance, and intercession. I can go on and on. But, if there is the chance that these things are being misunderstood, perhaps the pope would like to **discuss** some of these issues with myself or any other Natsari, then let it *be televised worldwide in the City of Yerushalayim.* We'll bring 𐤉𐤄𐤅𐤔𐤏 with us.

Opposite, some Egyptian "priests" are honoring an image of the sun that looks very familiar. The priests in the picture below are also offering to an image that is sun-like. The Roman Catholic "Monstrance" in the picture at the above right looks quite a bit like these other images. There is no such item mentioned in the Scriptures, so they must have borrowed it from the Pagans.

(Many share this opinion).

See the "Monstrance" on the following page. Catholicism has taught that these display the actual "presence" of the literal body of Mashiach. Millions were killed for denying it was. Yet, Rabbi 𐤉𐤄𐤅𐤔𐤏 told us:

"At that time, if anyone says to you, 'Look, here is the Mashiach!' or 'There He is!', do not believe it . . . So, if anyone tells you 'There He is, out in the desert', do not go out; or, 'Here He is, in the inner rooms', do not believe it." ~ Mt. 24:23 - 26.

RELIGION HAS BEEN THE "DISNEY WORLD"

OF MANY CENTURIES, DISPLAYING WONDROUS SIGNS AND MARVELS, WHILE PILFERING THE IGNORANT.

A funny quote:
"Isn't Disney World a ***people trap****, operated by a mouse?"* ~ Steven Wright

A famous quote: *"That which you find hateful to yourself, do that not unto your neighbor."*
~ Hillel, 1st century Pharisee

Many Christians are *awaiting* a one-world "government" they call the "beast" system.

The text doesn't say there will ***suddenly*** be a "beast" government ruling the whole world prior to 𐤉𐤄𐤅𐤔𐤏's return, but rather it says,

"The whole world was astonished (overwhelmed) ***and followed the beast . . . All inhabitants of the Earth will worship the beast . . ."*** Rev. 13. This is not just a government, but a religious system ~ people are not legislated to worship this beast, they are tricked into it through *tradition, the establishment.* The intoxicating "wine" is the Roman calendar, sacraments, and all the "teachings" held in the golden cup of the whore of Babylon.

The beast doesn't appear suddenly; we were all born riding it, and it is still galloping and exploding across the planet. We have to get off of it.

HERE'S A FOSSILIZED CUSTOM FOR YOU:
The average person would expect that medical professionals would be fairly bright people. Taking an oath is a serious affair, and Yahusha told us not to do it.
A contemporary with Herodotus composed the following which is still in use.

HIPPOCRATIC OATH
(Or Oath of Hippocrates)

"I SWEAR by Apollo the physician and Æsculapius, and Health, and All-heal, and all the gods and goddesses, that, according to my ability and judgment,
I will keep this Oath . . ."

That's the opening part, swearing to Pagan deities; but among some of the more decent contents of the oath we read words that cut against the grain of the elitists who seek to reduce global population:

"I will give no deadly medicine to any one if asked, nor suggest any such counsel; and in like manner I will not give to a woman a pessary to produce abortion. With purity and with holiness I will pass my life and practice my Art."

Egyptian Sun Worship

GOD OF MANY NAMES Shatan conceals his identity, and uses many names — while 𐤉𐤄𐤅𐤄 only needs one. Shatan is not omnipresent, and uses a network to gather information. Among his names like Baal, Molech, and Woden, he also uses the "female" forms like Ishtar, Frigga, Venus, or Aphrodite. Masons revere Nimrod, whose eye it is at the top of the pyramid on the back of the US $1 bill.

Monstrance

IN GOD WE TRUST takes on new meaning when one discovers Shatan, the "shining one", is the "**GOD** of this world". He uses the "reins" of old customs to rule us. So, it is really not Nimrod ruling us from the grave!

IF A CATHOLIC WERE TO STUDY THIS PICTURE OF SUN WORSHIP IN PERU, THEY MAY BEGIN TO COMPREHEND THE PAGAN ORIGIN OF THE PRACTICES THAT BECAME MIXED INTO THEIR CUSTOMS LONG AGO - STARTING WITH MARCION, THE CHURCH FATHERS, AND CONSTANTINE. IT'S MORE ABOUT THE WORSHIP OF BAAL AND ASHERAH THAN ANYTHING ELSE. CAN YOU SEE THE TREE NEXT TO THE ALTAR?

INTERMISSION

In view of the fact that some readers may be developing facial twitches, shuffling walk, smacking lips, neck-jerking, twisting movements, or other assorted characteristics, let's try to calm down. Let's evaluate what all this means.

Where does all this information we are gathering place us in the grand scheme? What "religion" or **way** (halak) of living does all of this point to? Since the "broad road" can be exposed as diverse "sects" traced to individual men who came out of one or another sect themselves, let's just look past them all, and only look at the One Who walked out of His tomb. What is His religion? It was, and still is, the ***Torah of Yahuah***. Not only is He a **Rabbi**, but also the High Priest, and our Bridegroom. **One** of the reasons He died was to end the marriage vow of the previous Covenant, which ended in His divorcing Yisrael for harlotry (idolatry). He discusses this divorce, before the New Covenant happened, at **Yesha Yahu 50**. At Yerme Yahu 3, "faithless Yisrael" (His wife) was given a "certificate of divorce" ~ when the ***northern house of Israel*** was carried into captivity by the Assyrians in **722 BCE**. Later, in 586 BCE, the house of Yahudah was likewise carried into captivity by the Babylonians. Their captivity ended with 10% of the people returning after 70 years. The northern tribes were warned to repent at Ez. 4, and would have spent 390 years in captivity for their idolatry with the Asherim trees. They didn't, so the *sevenfold penalty* kicked-in (Lev. 26), and their captivity has lasted ***2730 years***. 722 BCE to 2008 CE. The Prodigal Son is turning back to the Torah, and the Olive tree is blossoming. The Husband pleaded, "Return to Me, and I will return to you." Remember, before a wife can re-marry, **her Husband must die!** In latter times, these times, we finally understand. He has taken the SAME Covenant people (His bride), and those He had sown into the Gentiles that were natural branches broken off long ago, and made a renewed COVENANT with His bride. Hebrews chapters 8 & 9 help explain this. Yes, Elohim died, and remained so for 3 days and 3 nights. The bride is now free to re-marry, because the former Husband died, ending the former marriage Covenant. It's not a new bride, nor a new Husband; yet ***He*** died, ending the older Covenant. By making the renewed Covenant in His own blood, our Maker calls-out His bride, and **writes the Covenant on their HEARTS**, not stone. The blood of bulls and lambs did not change their hearts to obey, but in the power of the resurrection, 𐤉𐤄𐤅𐤔𐤏's Spirit comes into us, enabling selected ones to repent, be immersed, and become a new creation as children of 𐤉𐤄𐤅𐤄.

NAZARENES (better, "NATSARIM")

Natsarim means "watchmen", and "branches". The word found for "watchmen" at Jer. 31 is the word ***Natsarim***. See also Acts 24:5 - Shaul was not a ringleader of the sect of the Christians, but rather the Natsarim. Our faith does not have a Greek name - our **walk** is the Torah of Yahuah.

Some form of "handle" is commonly used for different groups, so that others will know what "bunch" or "compartment" to put them in. There are thousands of sectarian groups; Roman Catholic, Eastern Orthodox Catholic, Quakers, Shakers, Baptists, Mennonites, Amish, Pentecostals, Church of GOD, Christian Church, Mormons, Jehovah Witnesses, 7th Day Adventists, and so on. Each views all the rest as having serious doctrinal errors. Yet, the Mashiach is nothing even close to any of them. Now, we come to the "Natsarim". We are not "organized" as a financial corporation. There's only a Spiritual "Head", and we are all members of His Body, with diverse gifts. We are all so different, we would not recognize each other necessarily by anything but how we live, or sometimes our tsitsith, or tassels.

MESSIANICS

This is another "handle", sometimes commonly understood to be descendants of Abraham who believe in the Messiahship of Rabbi 𐤉𐤄𐤅𐤔𐤏. All Nazarenes (Natsarim) are Messianics, but not all Messianics are Natsarim. Sure, many ***former*** Gentiles are Natsarim, and Messianics. Some "Messianics" are really practicing Christianity (Constantine's invention), but using *Hebrew terms and symbols*. The "elect" can even be deceived, as it was prophesied. Many of them have NO CLUE of the message of the Reign of 𐤉𐤄𐤅𐤄, nor know what the renewed COVENANT is. If you can read this book and still not know what these are, then I've failed miserably. I am a Natsari, and a Messianic. I am also a "Yahudi", or ***worshipper***

of Yah. My son, Adam, attended a school where he was often made fun of by Christians, because the other children had no idea what a Natsari Israelite is. Their "handle" is a ***Greek term***, and they are taught by their parents, teachers, and community at large to celebrate Christmas, Easter, Halloween (some of them), and keep Sun-day as their "day of worship". We worship by obeying, every day. What about "tithing"? Our giving is as the Writings require; and part of this is explained at 1 Tim. 5. At 5:16, the assembly of believers not only helps support the needs of "elders" (those who are aged), but widows (and their children, the fatherless). It even says that the assembly should not be "burdened" with legitimate widows, ***if she has a family that can help instead*** (5:16). In fact, it says at 5:8: ***"If anyone does not provide for his RELATIVES, and especially for his immediate family, he has denied the faith and is WORSE THAN AN UNBELIEVER."*** Elders, who need to eat also, are worthy of "double honor" if they direct the affairs of the assembly well. I'm in full-time ministry, and only should receive from those who are in the office of "giving", as were the wealthy women that supported Yahusha in His work (Luke 8). It certainly doesn't mean the "elders" receive the WHOLE TITHE, nor is it for "spreading the Gospel". YOU are the letter; YOU spread the message of the Reign of ƎYƎZ. We elders are here to teach, encourage, and guide, so many of you can become elders. The word "elder" in Hebrew is ZAKAN, and is the same word for "beard", with only a vowel sound changed. It came into the Greek using the word "PRESBUS", the root of "Presbyterian". It then took another turn in the word "BISHOP". We're just brothers with a responsibility, we're not any more important! Shaul considered Timothy an elder, and told him not to be hasty in the laying on of hands. Armed with knowledge, anyone can objectively see that most have wandered from the faith. The stubborn and ignorant cannot repent, until they are changed inside, spiritually.

Instead of unity in the Body of Mashiach, what we have is "compartmentalism"; each claiming to be following OWYƎZ, but actually each "compartment" follows a man who founded their "denomination". They don't actually come out and say "I am of Herbert Armstrong", or "I am of John Smyth", but that's still the result of it. C.E. Tozer noted that if 100 pianos are tuned to the same tuning fork, then they are tuned together perfectly. If each of us "tunes" himself to Rabbi OWYƎZ, then we are automatically in unity! That's one of the reasons I'm using the palaeo-Hebrew when I write the Name; men have "monked" with things, ***but the original cannot be denied by any honest scholar***.

FLESH: A BODY OF DEATH!

As you know, we are approximately 83% water, and 17% dust. We are the sum total of what we eat; plant life, or animals who ate the plant life. What are plants made of? Dirt, and water! As we age, our cells divide about once every 7 years. When they do, they lose information each time. In our DNA molecules, there are **"telomeres"** at each end, which the DNA uses as a building platform to begin assembling another cell when the time comes. Each time a new DNA strand is assembled, roughly every 7 years, a "telomere" is lost. They act as "counters", *counting down to the point when there are no more*, and the cell cannot divide, because there are no more telomeres! We're all gonna DIE! Inside this body of death, we have our spiritual body, which doesn't age. Sometimes, more often these days, people develop clusters of *rapidly reproducing cells* called **cancer**. As our cells divide, *sometimes a molecule is plugged in where it should not be*, but still "fits". This is a mis-reading, and cellular information is lost. So, cancerous cells are more "stupid", and are not as stable as normal cells. We can eat what we think is good food, but since the farmlands have been depleted of vital nutrients over the many decades of overuse, vitamins and minerals that should be there in our food just aren't there anymore. You should eat some seaweed, and wheat grass tablets; cows eat mainly grass, so how can this supplement hurt? The land is supposed to lie "fallow" for one year in every 7.

Normally, when a cell goes "foul", our body issues an order *telling it to self-destruct.* Because cancer is a **mutated**, stupid cell, it doesn't understand this command. Normally, cells have "receptors" on their outer cell walls which convey this message to self-destruct when they are detected by our body to have problems. The outer cell wall of cancer cells lack the ability to "hear" the message to self-destruct, because they are ***mutants***. Medical science uses "cell poison" (Latin: cytoxin) to attempt to destroy these mutants. But, it also kills normal cells indiscriminately, attacking the immune system, arterial walls, bone marrow, hair follicles, fingernails, and sensitive cells in the eyes. Cancer can be caused by a variety of types of **damage to DNA:** electromagnetic "ionization", where strong magnetic fields can snatch-away an electron from one of the DNA molecules; radiation, such as being bombarded by or ingesting radioactive elements, or being subjected to cosmic rays, X-rays, or even solar radiation! Chemical abrasion can easily occur to DNA as well, as with nicotine or alcohol. . . And, simple trauma, or ripping away the DNA in tearing cuts and wounds can cause a cell to mutate.

NEW RESEARCH ON CANCER: CHECK INTO "DCA" - which activates a critical mitochondrial enzyme. **ALSO LOOK UP VITAMIN B17**

IF YOU HAVE CANCER

Find a health food store, and buy a "tea" called **FLOR-ESSENCE**. Get it fast, and use it. It is a detoxifier, and puts a strain on cancerous cells. Waiting too long, or trying it after the point-of-no-return (like after the chemo-therapy has destroyed your ability to recover), makes it useless. Not using it after being told about it doesn't help either. Every **hour** counts. For some reason, the mutant cells respond to it, and the "message" to self-destruct begins to work. Cancerous tentacles recede, and the "tumors" shrink away. Skin cancers fade away to nothing. **IF** it's used as directed, as **EARLY** as possible, you will absolutely not believe what 3 to 6 months will do. Find it on the internet. I sell it mail-order, and have used it for skin cancer (caused by the sun) personally. You cannot even tell the cancer was ever there.

During the Roman year 2006, I developed a new spot on my nose, and treated it with Flor-Essence Tea*, and Cansema, a black salve. We carry the Flor-Essence Tea, but you'll need to locate the black salve on the Internet. So far, the spot has been reduced to a small scar, and it has stopped feeling like it did before. I could feel the spot growing, but Yahuah has healed it using the herbs He has provided for healing, like cedar oil.

ANTIBIOTICS AND ANTISEPTICS

To better care for this body of death we live in, we should strive for proper nutrition, exercise, safety, and proper hygiene. Back in the late 1800's, a doctor named Joseph Lister revolutionized surgery with his study of antiseptics. Better than 50% of those patients who underwent surgery died of infections, *caused by the surgery.* Joseph Lister succeeded in popularizing the idea of hand-washing before surgery, and in the use of antiseptics, such as alcohol. Cinnamon is an antiseptic too. Today, the mouthwash ***Listerine*** bears his name. If you would like to have the use of your teeth for most or all of your life, ***pre-rinse*** with a mouthful of Listerine full strength, then brush your teeth with a good anti-plaque toothpaste. Then, rinse well. **Always** brush your teeth each night before bed, after breakfast, and especially immediately following candies, desserts, and gooey foods. Tooth decay occurs within the first 15 minutes of eating sweets, and progresses rapidly. Soft drinks will cause you to lose every tooth in your head. "Diet" soft drinks with sugar substitutes contain a nerve toxin in their ingredient **aspartame**, which when it reaches 86 degrees, releases methanol. It is linked to neurological damage, birth defects of every description, and seizures. The phenylalanine in aspartame breaks down the seizure threshold; and its depletesserotonin causes manic depression, panic attacks, rage, and violence. The mysterious "Gulf War Syndrome" was no doubt caused by the thousands of pallets of diet drinks sitting for weeks in 120-degree Arabian heat. Our own bodies are 98.6 degrees, well above the required 86 degrees that chemically changes the aspartame! Men from the Gulf War came home, and produced children with no arms, brain damage, and they themselves had "shaking", seizure-like symptoms for months. Now you know why you can't "cook" with sugar substitutes ~ it becomes chemically altered by heat. It only seems sweet until it gets past our tongue ~ but it's deadly. Over 20 years ago, it was suspected to cause long-term memory damage. If you are on the internet, search for "aspartame disease". You don't have to believe me, the evidence is overwhelming!

MAD COW'S DISEASE

This deadly disease is caused by a molecular "crystal" which replicates itself much like rock candy does in a glass of sugar solution. It goes after the **nervous system** in animals and humans. Only this crystal is not sugar; it's a **non-living** crystalline molecule (It's an epidemic of a fatal brain disease called bovine spongiform encephalopathy, or BSE). Animals which are only fed **plants** don't get it. But, the cattle industry "supplements" the diet of the vegetarian animals (cattle) with food pellets manufactured from the waste products of **other animals' bodies**. This molecular crystal cannot be "cooked-out" because it is not alive. Eating "kosher" meats makes no difference we've learned, because the diet of the animals doesn't matter to the orthodox rabbis (we checked). Pigs are out of the question; not only are they declared "unclean" to consume, but they will eat anything. (We'll look at Mark 7 and Acts 10, to see if we really can eat pigs). You are what you eat.

[Something tells me you may not be relaxing during this intermission, but bracing even more!]

CURE FOR VIRUSES

Dr. Madeleine Mumcuoglu, doing research at the Hebrew University ~ Hadassah Medical center in Jerusalem, has found the answer to the influenza virus, and the common cold. It is a syrup derived from the plant *Sambucus Nigra*, better known as the black elderberry (she calls it **Sambucol**). The man who discovered **interferon**, Dr. Jean Lindenman, was the supervisor at the virology lab when Madeleine was looking for a topic for her doctorial research. He suggested elderberries; *"They have possibilities"*, he said, *"In any case, I've got 10 kilos of them in my deep-freeze".* As viruses cannot replicate themselves outside of living cells, they have to **invade** cells to survive. *"If you can stop them from invading cells, you've defeated the disease",* she said. She tested the black elderberry proteins against the Influenza B virus first, and

***FLOR-ESSENCE TEA: ORDERING DETAILS IN BACK OF THIS BOOK, OR ON-LINE AT TORAHZONE.NET**

discovered that *"they actually prevent the virus from invading the cell".* The influenza virus invades cells by **puncturing** the cell wall with the tiny spikes of hemaglutinin that cover its surface. The active ingredient in the elderberry disarms the spikes, binds to them, thus stopping them from piercing the cell membrane. *"This was the first discovery",* says Dr. Mumcuoglu. *"Next, we found evidence that elderberry proteins fight the influenza virus in another way, too. The viral spikes are covered with the enzyme,* ***neuraminidase****, which helps break down the cell wall. The elderberry inhibits the action of the enzyme. My guess is, that we'll find that elderberry acts against viruses in other ways, as well."* Clinical trials have proven that this 'healthfood product' actually works, and requires no medical approval because it is not a drug! For example, in a study of patients with influenza, half were given four doses daily of **Sambucol** (the name given to the product), and half were given a placebo. Within 24 hours, the symptoms of 20% of the **Sambucol** patients had significantly improved (fever, cough, muscle pain). After the second day, 735 declared themselves ***cured***. Among the placebo group, only 16% were improved after two days, and it took most of them six more days to feel well again. **Sambucol** is no more than a 'health food' officially, but interest is snow-balling all over the world. In Hadassah's virology lab, it has been seen to inhibit the AIDS virus, and encouraging results are being seen now against the herpes and Epstein-Barr viruses. You can probably find this product in any good health food store; we stock it in lozenge form for if you need it for $12.95 per bottle. I spent almost two years trying to get in touch with the suppliers when it first came out, so that people would have access to it. A friend of mine came down with chicken pox (as an adult, it could have been fatal or severely damaging to him) ~ and he was covered from head-to-toe with sores. Two days later, after taking **Sambucol***, he was not only completely well, but had no signs of the sores. Another case involved a mother who had been suffering from a flu for three months. She was getting worse in spite of antibiotics and the best in medical care, and was about to be put in the hospital. She talked to my wife Phyllis, and began taking **Sambucol** immediately. She was well in two days. How much money and suffering can be saved from not treating "symptoms"? Think of the lives to be saved, especially the fragile elderly ~ time lost from work, and so on. I've lost two close friends in their 70's over the years before this product was available, who both caught a flu and perished within 2 weeks from it. Once you've tried this product, you'll wonder why it isn't on the cover of every magazine. Why hasn't Madaleine won a Nobel Prize? If you think about it, the answer will come to you: it upsets too many money-making endeavors, exactly like this book does.

We've discussed how cancer is caused by abrasions and damage at the cellular level. Nicotine and estrogen-substitutes cause cancer. ("**Estro-gen**" is named after "Easter", the Babylonian **Ishtar**). Proto-cancer cells are in all of us. From now on, we can only expect the incidences of cancer to increase; currently ***2 out of every 5 people will develop cancer*** sometime during their lifetime. That's 40% of everybody, and only about half of those will survive the traditional **therapy**. I've watched them die, that's why I'm telling you. Avoid cheese, or at least treat it like you would chocolate, because it clogs your arteries and intestines, making the absorption of nutrients greatly reduced. Also, clots break free and block blood-flow to the heart or brain. Buy a jug of cranberry juice every month, and force yourself to drink it. It cleans your system out.

Now, for a bit of more calming news. During this relaxing intermission, it's nice to be able to go outside and breathe in some fresh air, and gaze up into the peaceful universe above us. While we're doing this, let's consider the 5th planet, called "Jupiter".

JUPITER STAR

Jupiter -- 5th planet, named for Roman idol meaning "Zeus-father" (IU-PITAR). NOTE: It's a pagan name, folks, forbidden by Ex. 23:13, Ps. 16:4. This giant ball of mostly hydrogen has always been intriguing to scientists, since it would have been the **second star** in our system if it had only a slightly larger bit of mass. It has the same general composition as our sun. With only a little more mass, the core temperature would be sufficient to cause *a fusion effect*; the nuclear reactions of the hydrogen cycle -- to ignite the star! For all practical purposes, it *is* an **un-ignited star**. This is the premise of the movie 2010 (the sequel to 2001 A Space Odyssey). This movie was based upon a real possibility, however.

In the real world, a controversial book called *Behold a Pale Horse* by Milton William Cooper has revealed many unsettling government secrets, and has quite an extensive historical perspective of events world-wide. Since the last edition of this book was printed, Bill Cooper was executed under strange circumstances. Like the book you are reading, Bill's book was based upon facts. He discussed the spacecraft *Galileo* which was sent to orbit the 5th planet, and how its decaying orbit was expected to deliver its payload into the dense inner regions of the planet sometime about De-

***SAMBUCOL IS AVAILABLE AT HEALTHFOOD STORES, OR FROM OUR WEB SITE: TORAHZONE.NET**

cember 1999. Bill's book goes on to say that the dangerous ***power plant*** on board the Galileo generated from a nuclear source: 49.7 pounds of weapons-grade **PLUTONIUM**. It has since fallen into the planet, yet has not ignited the hydrogen atmosphere. The pressures it ***may yet*** encounter in the deep, hot regions of the planet could simulate the conditions created by an implosion detonator. There is no worse place in our solar system for such a set of circumstances to exist, since the possibility of igniting the planet into a sun is still very real. Just how long it would burn is unknown, because sustaining the nuclear reactions is linked to the stability of the hydrogen cycle in the core. But, it could explode so violently that it actually destroys the planet, causing a chain-reaction that turns the planet into a huge hydrogen bomb, or a dim star. The plutonium is encased in ceramic chips to keep it from going 'critical' under normal conditions, and it is undergoing fission to generate the heat necessary for electrical production for on-board systems. But, if the ceramic chips are subjected to intense heat and pressure, they will **melt** -- and they could take their time to do it. It could sink into the liquid planet, drifting into hotter and hotter regions. It could take years, or even decades to explode, or maybe nothing will ever happen. There is also the **asteroid belt** to consider (between the 4th & 5th planets); if the star ignites, the explosive action would disrupt millions of chunks from this belt, sending them right at us, and distributing them into the entire inner solar system! That would be '**stars**' falling from the sky, burning as they enter our atmosphere, and impacting on our planet! The asteroid belt may have been put there for this very purpose, as the waters of the FLOOD were. Planets do not emit energy, as a star does. Yet, the 5th planet is radiating twice as much infra-red (heat) as it receives from the sun! Something is *already* happening inside it -- scientists estimate that only several hundred miles down, the metallic hydrogen is liquid, and is thousands of degrees. The core could be tens of thousands of degrees, or hotter. The Earth is one "**AU**" (astronomical unit) from its center to the center of our sun. The 5th planet is about 5.2 AU from the sun, making it 4 AU from Earth at its closest position. Double stars are more common than our system's single sun, and it appears that we could be responsible for igniting the giant gas bag. The additional radiant heat from a second star in our system would completely melt the Northern and Southern polar ice of Earth, flooding the lower elevations and coasts -- many islands would be no more (another prophetic occurrence). Then we really would have to "flee to the mountains", high ground! When you take it all in together, with the added situation of the asteroid belt to pelt us, the final days of distress were created beforehand to fulfill their purpose; like the frogs, flies, locusts etc., that plagued ancient Egypt! Being children of light (Torah), we will understand these things, while many others' hearts will fail from fear of the things coming upon the Earth.

If and **when** any of this happens, this Earth will be in distress. "And the fourth *angel* poured out his bowl upon the sun, and it was given to it to scorch men with fire. And men were scorched with fierce heat; and they blasphemed the name of Elohim who has the power over these plagues, and they did not repent so as to give Him esteem." - Rev. 16:8,9. There is no indication which 'sun' is being referred to! People will "blaspheme" His Name (not use it), thus not giving Him esteem. The saints will be on Earth during the Tribulation, counter to the Christian Rapture Myth, and it will be the 'weeds' who will be taken first. The 144,000 are being sealed with the Name in their foreheads right now: the palaeo-Hebrew four letters 𐤄𐤅𐤄𐤉 (Yod-Hay-Uau-Hay).

According to the book, scientists have already chosen the name for the new star: *LUCIFER*, which means *light-bringer* in Latin.

Our Natsari Rabbi, 𐤏𐤔𐤅𐤄𐤉, told us of a prominent sign or signal that He is coming: ***"But pray that your flight may not be in winter, or on a Shabbath; for then there will be a great tribulation, such as has not occurred since the beginning of the world until now, nor ever shall. And unless those days had been cut short, no life would have been saved; but for the sake of the elect, those days shall be cut short."*** -- Matt. 24:20-22. As a prelude to the final days of the 'times of the Gentiles', a world-wide message is to go forth, called the 'Gospel' or message of the Kingdom: **"Repent! For the Reign of 𐤄𐤅𐤄𐤉 draws near".**

This report was the same message spoken by Yahusha's cousin called 'John the Baptist'. 'John' just prepared the way for it, and the One Who will be our Ruler one day soon. The whole Earth will be in distress. **And then, the end will come.**

(You might have guessed, but "John" wasn't a "Baptist", but rather a *Torah-observant Levite priest.* Being a priest, they didn't stone him when he said the Name ~ it was only a problem for non-priests. But, no one else was ever saying it, and many probably didn't even know he *was* saying it, not realizing what it was). I certainly wasn't called by Yahuah to obfuscate His Name, or tell you to ignore His Torah - yet many false teachers do exactly that.

Pictured above, study carefully the stone carving of Mithras as a lion standing on a "sphere" with

MITHRAS SLAYING THE BULL

a cross on it, and again as a man figure slaying a bull. The stars, sun, moon, and other figures are highly significant if we are to properly understand how mankind has been deceived and manipulated in the past.

Plato wrote that the universe was created in the shape of an **X**, being the intersection of the celestial equator with the axis of the **Zodiac** (constellations of "living animals", since "zoo" and "zodiac" are related words). Could this "X" be the image of the beast? To the above right, we have a Pagan altar piece depicting Mithras slaying the bull, or overcoming the constellation of Taurus the bull. This is reverently cared for in the Vatican museum. Mithras, the sun deity, is shown in the act of *tauroctony,* slaying the bull. This act showed Mithras to be the supreme power in the universe, able to move the spring equinox out of the Age of Taurus (really caused by the precession of the Earth ~ a wobble). In this photo, the zodiac animals are represented along with the sun and moon (upper corners); the bull is Taurus, the dog is Canis Minor, the snake is Hydra, the raven is Corvus, the scorpion is Scorpio, and the stars around Mithras' head are thought to be planets, but could also be the Pleiades, or seven sisters. The lion motif represents the constellation of Leo, the lion. The universe is illustrated as a sphere with the cross on its surface, depicted above with Mithras standing on it as its supreme ruler with a lion's head. Atlas is seen holding this same sphere with the intersecting axis on its surface.

CHURCH FATHERS ABANDONED THEM

The "church fathers" were former Pagans, and they allegorized (and interpreted) much of the Scriptures through their Pagan lens.

They absolutely hated the Yahudim, and all that reminded them of them, such as the Covenant, or "Law" as they interpreted it.

Eusebius, in AD 324, wrote, ***"We have transferred the duties of the Sabbath to Sunday."***

Who are the "we"? The Roman State religion.

The "apostles" didn't have the authority to change the Torah, and we know they never hinted at such an idea of altering the Covenant.

Just three years before, in 321, **Constantine** made the first law to keep the ***"Venerable day of the sun***."

In Translation from Latin, the Edict of Constantine says:

"Let all the judges and townspeople and the occupations of all trades rest upon the venerable day of the sun. But let those who are situated in the country, freely and at full liberty attend to the business of agriculture. Because it often happens that no other day is so fit for the sowing of corn or the planting of vines, lest the critical moment being let slip, men should lose the commodities of heaven. Given this 7th day of March, Crispus and Constantine being consuls each of them for the second time."

YAHUAH'S TORAH ABOUT CLEAN & UNCLEAN FOOD WAS ABANDONED, AND THEY USED ACTS 10 TO DO IT. ALSO, THEY ADDED WORDS AT MARK 7, TO MAKE PEOPLE BELIEVE YAHUSHA MADE "ALL FOOD CLEAN" - SEE THE ITALICIZED WORDS IN THE KJV. PIGS SIMPLY ARE NOT FOOD; UNCLEAN ANIMALS WERE NEVER GIVEN AS FOOD.

PETER'S VISION, ACTS 10

Eusebius firmly believed that the church had replaced the Jews (replacement theology) and had become the new Israel. Early church fathers such as Origen, Eusebius, Justin Martyr, Ignatius Bishop of Antioch, John Chrysotom, Augustine, etc, were ***anti-Semites***. They changed the Sabbath, and eliminated the "High Sabbaths" given to Israel at Lev. 23. The Hebrew word for festival is "chag". Although many a "mo'ed" is also a "chag", this is by no means always the case. Elohim legislated these Appointed Times to be just that; a time that He has appointed for us to draw near to Him to serve Him, to worship Him. In 3 Mosheh 23 *(Lev. 23),* we find these Appointed Times listed. The very first and most important one is the weekly **Shabbat**, of course. The weekly Shabbat, as well as the yearly Shabbat, the Day of Atonement *(Yom Kippur),* are "mo'edim", but they are not festivals. The other Appointed Times in 3 Mosheh 23 are also called "festivals". If we turn our attention to these "Festivals of 𐤉𐤄𐤅𐤄", we naturally ask two questions: What is their significance, and secondly, why were they done away with by the Church? Before we discuss this, please note that the seven festivals are grouped in three groups:

1. The festivals of the first moon, Abib,
2. The Festival of Weeks (Shabuoth)
3. The festivals of the seventh moon.

THEIR SIGNIFICANCE They were instituted "as a law forever", as we repeatedly read. In the first Scriptural month, Abib, we find the **PASSOVER** Pesach, also called Unleavened Bread. *(These are 2 separate things. One is an observance at twilight on the 14th, while Unleavened Bread begins the next evening ~ but some will differ on this).* Certainly having been fulfilled in the Messiah, our Passover Lamb slaughtered for us (1Cor. 5:7) ~ why insist that we still keep it? *(While the firstborn died in Egypt on the Passover, the blood on the doorposts pre-figured the Firstborn Son of 𐤉𐤄𐤅𐤄 dying to cover our Torah-breaking).* The Passover was instituted forever, but as *(Rabbi)* Yahusha fulfilled it, His Body and His Blood took the place of the Passover lamb and its blood. Therefore we still observe the Passover, but with its Messianic emblems, the unleavened bread and the cup of the vine. Suffice it to say, the apostles kept on observing Unleavened Bread *(Matzah)* (Acts 12:3 and 20:6), and *(Rabbi)* Yahusha also promised that He will again drink of the fruit of the vine when the Reign of Elohim is physically set up, here on Earth (Mt. 26:29). *(The 1st and 7th days of Matsah are "rest days" from work. The 7th day is traditionally believed to be the day that Yisrael crossed the yam suph, or Sea of Reeds. The mightiest army on Earth perished that day, and Egypt has not recovered from it and the 10 plagues even to this day).*

The second group actually consists only of

SHABUOTH ~ The Festival of Weeks

(Called "Pentecost", Greek for "count-fifty", 7 weeks from a count of Shabbats from Passover). Traditionally this is thought to commemorate the giving of the Torah on Mt. Sinai. *(This is the event recorded at Acts 2, and saw the fulfullment of the promise of the New Covenant given at Yerme Yahu 31, where the Torah given at Sinai was written on the **hearts** of the 120 Nazarenes assembled in the upper room at the Temple. If they had not been observing this, they would not have received the Ruach ha Qodesh. Constantine redesigned its determination at the first Council of Catholicism, at Nicea in 325 CE, and involved the Vernal Equinox in setting it. He also set up the policy that if ever "Easter" and Passover occurred on the same day, "Easter" would be observed the following "Sun-day", so as not to have anything "in common with the hostile rabble of the Yahudim.")* When the taught-ones were assembled on Shabuoth, as we read in Acts 2, the Set-apart Spirit was poured out on them. Nevertheless, they simply kept on keeping Shabuoth year by year, e.g. Acts 20:16 and 1Cor. 16:8.

The third group, those of the seventh Scriptural month, are most interesting, because they have never been fulfilled. The Appointed Times of the seventh month consist of **Trumpets** *(or shofar/ ram's horn blowing, called Yom Teruah),* **Day of Atonement** *(Yom Kippur),* **Festival of Booths** *(Sukkot, or Tabernacles),* and the **Last Great Day**. Interestingly, the Festival of Booths also has the name "Festival of Ingathering".

In Col. 2:16,17, we read that these festivals, new moons, and Shabbats ***"are a shadow of what is to come"***. Notice, it is not past tense "were". No, it is present tense, "are". Some years ago, the editor of Midnight Cry, a well-known prophetic magazine, said; "The Church has been robbed of its festivals." He then went on and elaborated on the great prophetic significance of the festivals of the seventh moon in particular. What do these Appointed Times of the seventh moon foreshadow? By the way, we all know that the weekly Shabbat is a shadow of the seventh millennium, yet to come. Nevertheless, we still keep the Shabbat for it is the sign of the Eternal Covenant (Exodus 31:13-17 and Ezekiel 20:12-20).

TRUMPETS ~ **Yom Teruah**

This is generally interpreted as being a shadow of the Last Trumpet—1Cor. 15:52, Mt. 24:31, 1Thess. 4:16, Rev. 11:15—heralding the Second Coming of Messiah and the establishment of the Reign of Elohim here on Earth! *(This is also called Rosh Hashanah, and is the 1st day of the seventh moon).*

DAY OF ATONEMENT ~ **Yom Kippur**

Yahusha has certainly atoned for us as individuals when He died in our stead. However, as a nation, Yisrael is still awaiting its national atonement. Yisrael is still to be reconciled to Elohim, through Yahusha, the Sovereign of the Yahudim, the Shepherd of Yisrael. *(This is the 10th day of the 7th moon, called "the Fast" at Acts 27:9).*

FESTIVAL OF BOOTHS ~ **Sukkot**

This is a shadow of Elohim setting up His Booth as the New Yerushalayim comes from heaven. *(Outer Space, Shamayim, or skies. Dwelling in tents ourselves for 7 days, we are reminded of the wilderness experience of Yisrael, but more importantly the spiritual teaching that we are sojourners in these bodies of flesh, and we will move into a "permanent" or immortal "house" when we put on incorruption).* Let us read Rev. 21:3; ***"See, the Booth of Elohim is with men, and He shall dwell with them and be their Elohim."*** But, in spite of Him dwelling among His people, the Festival of Booths continues to be observed ~ read all of ZekarYah 14! Even those who are left from the Gentiles *(goyim, v. 16),* after Yahuah had fought against all the Gentiles who came up to fight against Yerushalayim (vv. 2,3), shall be compelled to worship Yahuah and to observe the Festival of Booths (vv. 16-18).

THE LAST GREAT DAY

This is a shadow of what Yahusha will do in the Last Day, as we read of its fulfillment in Rev. 7:17, 21:6, and 22:1,2. As Messiah was observing the Festival of Booths in Yoch. 7, we read in Yoch. 7:37-39 how He will give us to drink from the fountain of the river of life, sometimes called the fountain of living waters. Already this has had a *partial* fulfillment in the lives of the True Believers, but the final consummation of the prophetic promise is still future! *(Get ready for* ***Y6K****).*

The seventh Scriptural month is the time when the ingathering from the threshing-floor and the winepress has been completed (read Deut. 16:13). This ingathering includes those truly converted Gentiles who joined themselves to Yahuah (Yesha Yahu 14:1, 56:6-8, ZekarYah 2:11), ***"even all the Gentiles on whom My Name has been called"*** (Acts 15:17).

Why did the Church do away with these festivals? The answer is given to us at Daniel 7:25 ~ the little horn (generally interpreted as Rome, but could be Islam as well) ***"intends to change Appointed Times and Law."*** This is exactly what took place when the Roman Church was set up to lay waste the True Worship, to trample underfoot that which is set-apart. The Festivals of Yahuah were done away with and they continued with their old Gentile customs and festivals ~ Christmas, Easter, Sunday, etc.,. *(Let's not forget the Pagan underpinnings of Halloween, Valentine's Day, Lent, and the "feasts" dedicated to particular "saints" that were all re-interpreted Pagan days).*

Chris Koster sent me this explanation of the High Sabbaths just a year before he died.

Brother Chris fell asleep in the Spring of 1993 CE. Wilhelm Wolfaard and myself are carrying on the work of ***ISR*** (Institute for Scripture Research), which is listed in the back, under *Resources.*

Note: *Chris died from cancer.* Everyone needs to be taking the very BEST vitamins and minerals . . . This gives your cells the right stuff so they can divide without "errors" from free radicals. Remember your ***VITAMINS, VITAMINS, VITAMINS!***

THE WORD, "GOSPEL"

The word "Gospel" is Old English. It's really 2 words crammed together: ***GOD*** + ***SPEL***. We have

OUR RABBI DECLARES,

FOLLOW ME!

Isa 30:21:

"Whether you turn to the right or to the left, your ears will hear a voice behind you, saying, 'This is the way; walk in it.'"

Yahuah BLESSED the SEVENTH day.

When Yahuah blesses something, it stays blessed.

WE WALK ON THE EARTH ONLY A SHORT TIME. SCRIPTURE WARNS US, MORE THAN ANYTHING ELSE, TO BEWARE OF FALSE TEACHINGS AND DECEPTIONS.

OUR "WALK" IS A PERSONAL CHOICE FOR EACH OF US.

IF WE FOLLOW MEN, AND THE HUMAN TRADITIONS, WE WILL BE OVERCOME BY THEM AND PUT OUR TRUST IN THEM. IF WE OVERCOME THE TRADITIONS, AND WALK AS YAHUSHA WALKED, WE WILL SUFFER PERSECUTION FOR RIGHTEOUSNESS' SAKE; BUT WE MUST DO IT OUT OF LOVE FOR YAHUSHA. WE WILL BE PERSECUTED FOR OUR LOVE FOR TORAH.

A TIMELINE TO CONSIDER

"But do not forget this one thing, dear friends; with 𐤉𐤄𐤅𐤄 a day is like a thousand years, and a thousand years are like a day . . . But the Day of 𐤉𐤄𐤅𐤄 will come like a thief. The heavens will disappear with a roar; the elements will be destroyed by fire, and the Earth and everything in it will be laid bare . . . But in keeping with His promise we are looking forward to a new heaven and a new Earth, the home of righteousness." 2Pet. 3:8-13. Life's lessons are repeated until you learn them, and ignoring them will only cause you to go through old lessons again and again.

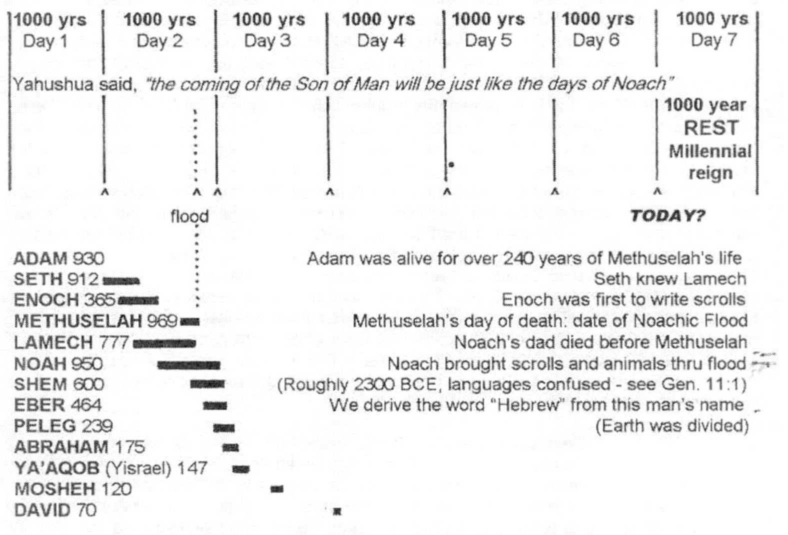

FOSSILIZE THIS: *The custom of "ribbon cutting" when opening a new venture is a ceremonial event usually presided over by a leader, such as a governor or mayor. The ribbon represents the **HYMEN**, a ribbon-like membrane named after the Greek deity of love and marriage, **HUMEN**. In ancient cultures, the first to have sexual relations with a new bride was the leader, so the "honor" of cutting the "ribbon" when a new business or venture is begun is often bestowed upon the highest government official in the area. The ribbon was usually RED, symbolizing the blood when a virgin is "deflowered".*
Are you at all still skeptical that Pagan worship really is based upon sexual themes?

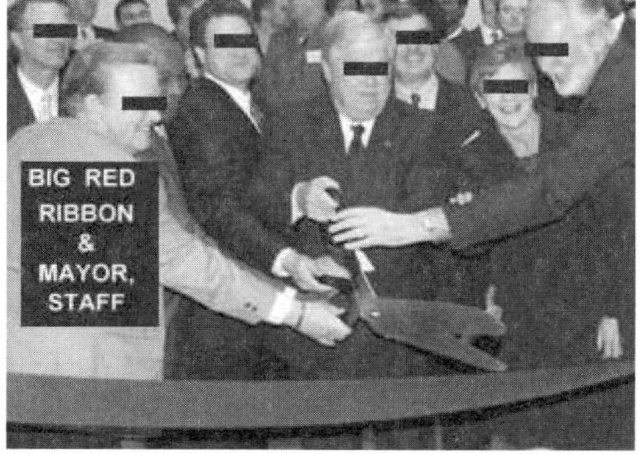

VERY FEW OF THE PEOPLE THAT ENGAGE IN THESE CEREMONIES HAVE ANY IDEA WHAT THEY ARE ACTUALLY DOING. BUT A FEW DO!

"Surely our fathers have inherited lies, vanity, and things wherein there is no profit."

YirmeYahu
(Jer) *16:19*

already seen that the Teutonic Celts worshipped the sun with the word "GOD", and it was a proper name. It was used because it was already a familiar word to them, coming from the Greeks' translation. The Greeks used ***THEOS*** instead of "Elohim", because they were already familiar with their old word also. The Greeks called Zeus "*Theos*", and their letter "theta" Θ was originally a circle with a dot in the center, representing the sun running across the sky. They called all their deities by the title "Theos". Some scholars believe that using "GOD" and "THEOS" to refer to 𐤉𐤄𐤅𐤄 is the prophesied *abomination of desolation.* Pillars of Jealousy (steeples), Sun-day, calling 𐤉𐤄𐤅𐤔𐤏 "Yeh-Zeus", Easter, and more yet to be exposed follow in that line of thought.

The second part of the word "Gospel", ***SPEL***, is also Celtic in origin. It means incantation, speech, spiel, news, message, or report. It is the "spell" spoken to others.

In 1948 CE, A. W. Tozer wrote the following words, underscoring how we can become swept up in mindless devotion by imitating others:

"Christian literature, to be accepted and approved by the evangelical leaders of our times, must follow very closely the same train of thought, a kind of 'party line' from which it is scarcely safe to depart. A half-century of this in America has made us smug and content. We imitate each other with slavish devotion and our most strenuous efforts are put forth to try to say the same thing that everyone around us is saying."

The true "Gospel" is virtually unknown by most people on Earth today, yet "collections" to "spread" the "Gospel" are being donated to men who don't know what it is. It's all wasted, because like cancer researchers, they stumble in great darkness. The original followers of 𐤉𐤄𐤅𐤔𐤏 carried its free message, but it died out (on the surface) with the last of the Nazarenes and Ebionites before the 4th century. The Writings reveal that it is a ***SECRET***, and a mystery, and will one day be revealed just before the end of men's kingdoms. It is directed only for the understanding of those whose names are written in the Scroll of Life, sealed with 7 seals. These are the ***BRIDE*** of Mashiach. The wedding ***betrothal*** occurred at Sinai, when the children of Israel listened to the Voice of the Groom, and agreed to obey Him. Other "sheep" not of this fold (Gentiles) will also take the Name of the Groom. We'll discuss this in greater detail here. The word "Gospel" is one of many words we have inherited from dead translators that has taken on a kind of life of its own. Even encyclopedias admit that it is a bit "fuzzy". Scholars accept the term, but both what it is, and how the term came into use, are not clearly understood. The word's meaning and use is the result of our imitating each other for centuries, or our attempting to say the same thing everyone around us is saying. People who want to defend the altered names and other words they are conditioned to use by imitation sometimes will say, *"Well, I speak **English**, and not some **foreign language**."* English is like a wide river with many other languages flowing into it. "Gospel" is Celtic. "Evangelical" is Greek (from *euangelion,* meaning *message, or report*). It became the Latin word *evangelium.* You can see the word *angel* in both, which simply means *messenger.* "Epistle" is Greek for *letter.* Many words we think of as English are really *Celtic, Latin, Greek, French, Hebrew, or aboriginal tongues* spoken by the natives of an area prior to English settlers. Rivers, states, and countries are often named by "foreign" terms. They're not "English", but our familiarity with them causes us to believe they are.

When Rabbi 𐤉𐤄𐤅𐤔𐤏 was in the synagogue (Lk. 4) and read from the TaNaKh, He read aloud in Hebrew the words of Yesha Yahu 61. He told them that this prophecy had been fulfilled in their ears! He announced the fulfullment of the prophecy of the awaited Mashiach, as His listeners comprehended. He proclaimed the *"acceptable year of 𐤉𐤄𐤅𐤄"*, known as the year of *Jubilee* (every 50th year, native-born Yahudim are to be freed, and land is to be returned to the heirs according to their tribes). He was also proclaiming the *"Gospel"*: the announcement that the ***"Reign of 𐤉𐤄𐤅𐤄"*** had come into their midst. If you read all of Yesha Yahu 61 & 62 (as He probably did), you'll discover that it promises the day when the ***"Bridegroom"*** will rejoice over His ***BRIDE***. At Mt. 11:5 where this passage of Yesha Yahu is being quoted, the word "Gospel" appears in our *translation* from the original Hebrew word ***BASAR*** (𐤁𐤔𐤓 or ר ש ב), meaning *tidings, message, report, or news.* ***You must know what the message is, to carry it to others. The Hebrew word for "Gospel" is BESORAH. It is ultimately the TORAH, which Yahusha instructed us to "GO and teach all nations" - thus ISRAEL is increased, as a "Covenant people". Gentiles who engraft through the Torah, BECOME fellow Israelites*** (see Eph. 2:8-13).

THE REIGN OF 𐤉𐤄𐤅𐤄

(*Otherwise known as the "Kingdom of GOD"*)

How do we know it's a **secret**? At Mark 4:11,12: ***"And when He was alone, those about Him, with the 12, asked Him about the parable. And He said to them, 'To you it has been given to know the SECRET of the REIGN OF 𐤉𐤄𐤅𐤄, but to those who are outside, all are done in parables, so that seeing they see but do not perceive, and hearing they hear but do not understand, lest they should turn*** (repent) ***and their sins be forgiven them'".*** (He was quoting Yesha Yahu 6:9). The "secret" or "mystery" is really the "Gospel" itself. At Romans 16:25:

"Now to Him who is able to establish you according to my (GOSPEL, BESORAH) ***and the preaching of 𐤉𐤄𐤅𐤔𐤏 ha Mashiach, according to the revelation of the MYSTERY which has been kept SECRET for long ages past . . ."***

So, the *"GOSPEL"* isn't something new, but was first spoken to ***Abraham*** (see Gal. 3:8, Gen. 12:3). Abraham was *called-out* from among Pagans and Gentile practices, and was ultimately to become a blessing to the Gentiles because of his *"fidelity"* (faithfulness, *emunah*). Paul had to sternly warn the Gentiles who had converted at Galatia, and to those at Ephesus (4:17,18) he said: ***"This I say therefore, and affirm together with 𐤉𐤄𐤅𐤄, that YOU NO LONGER WALK AS THE GENTILES WALK, in the futility of their thinking, being darkened in their understanding, excluded from the Life of 𐤉𐤄𐤅𐤄, BECAUSE OF THE IGNORANCE THAT IS IN THEM, because of the hardness of their heart."***

They were just overwhelmed by the Pagan patterns of everyday living. When Paul stood before the Greek idolators in Athens, he stood as Yonah had in Nineveh:

"Therefore having overlooked the times of ignorance, 𐤉𐤄𐤅𐤄 is now declaring to men that all everywhere should REPENT, because He has fixed a day in which He will judge the world in righteousness through a Man whom He has appointed, having furnished PROOF to all men by raising Him from the dead." Acts 17.

The Reign of 𐤉𐤄𐤅𐤄 will be to most like a trap springing shut, and catch the majority by complete surprise. They are in a Roman system, ignorant of the annual observances they are taught are "Jewish". Weekly Shabbat, Passover, Shabuoth (Pente-cost), Yom Teruah, Yom Kippur, and Sukkot (Tabernacles) all picture the redemption of 𐤉𐤄𐤅𐤄's Bride, but they are kept from the knowledge of the plan, and what to watch for. (For those unaware, Paul used to be "Shaul").

Paul explains it is a mystery to the Ephesians at 6:19: ***"and pray on my behalf, that utterance may be given to me in the opening of my mouth, to make known with boldness the MYSTERY of the (GOSPEL) . . ."*** (see also Eph. 3:3-9). In Col. 1, Paul states his goal is ***"That I might fully carry out the preaching of the Word of 𐤉𐤄𐤅𐤄, the MYSTERY of which has been hidden from the past ages and generations, but has now been manifested in His qodeshim*** (set-apart ones, saints) ***TO WHOM 𐤉𐤄𐤅𐤄 willed to make known what is the riches of the esteem of this SECRET among the Gentiles*** (the Torah written on your hearts) ***which is: MASHIACH IN YOU, the expectancy of esteem, Whom we announce, WARNING every man and TEACHING every man in all WISDOM*** (Torah, Commandments)***, in order to present every man perfect in Mashiach 𐤉𐤄𐤅𐤔𐤏 . . ."***

Shaul's reference to <u>Mashiach in you</u> indicates that the believer is *ENABLED* to *LOVE* the Torah, and thus obey it (𐤉𐤄𐤅𐤄's Word), because His "seed" (the Commandments) came into the Nazarenes literally, fulfilling Yerme Yahu 31, implementing the *New Covenant:*

"'But this is the Covenant which I will make with the house of Yisrael after those days', declares 𐤉𐤄𐤅𐤄, 'I will put my Torah within them, and on their HEART I will write it . . .'"

This prophecy is quoted at Heb. 10:16, and 2Cor. 3:3, and it first occurred at "Pente-cost" (the commanded convocation called "Shabuoth", which commemorates the ***giving of Torah at Sinai***).

Paul is quoted very often by today's preachers when they need to justify their "freedom" <u>from</u> the Commandments, making "sin" more of a state of the heart than a tangible, definable thing. Sin is definable, because 1 Yahuchanon 3:4 says:

"Everyone who sins breaks the Torah; in fact SIN IS TORAHLESSNESS." (anti-nomia, *lawlessness*). 𐤉𐤄𐤅𐤔𐤏 came to *destroy the devil's work* in us, and Yahuchanon goes on at 3:9 saying: ***"No one who is born of 𐤉𐤄𐤅𐤄 will continue to sin, because 𐤉𐤄𐤅𐤄's seed remains in him; he cannot go on sinning, because he has been born of 𐤉𐤄𐤅𐤄. <u>This is how we know who the children of 𐤉𐤄𐤅𐤄 are and who the children of the devil are: Anyone who does not do what is right is not a child of 𐤉𐤄𐤅𐤄; nor is anyone who does not love his brother.</u>"***

2Pet. 3:15,16 discusses how this lawlessness was being propagated by ***DISTORTIONS OF PAUL'S WRITINGS***:

"Our beloved brother Paul wrote to you according to the wisdom given him, as also in all his letters, speaking in them concerning these matters, IN WHICH SOME ARE HARD TO UNDERSTAND, WHICH THOSE WHO ARE UNTAUGHT AND UNSTABLE TWIST, as they do also the other Writings, to their own destruction. Therefore, dear friends, since you already know this, BE ON YOUR GUARD so

that you may not be carried away by THE ERROR OF LAWLESS MEN and fall from your secure position." The "merchants" draw away your attention to the fact that Peter is calling Shaul's words "Scripture", but they cause you to overlook the serious warning of Peter ***talking about the very men you are listening to!*** Paul is always the one they quote to "prove" the Torah is no longer in force, yet here is Peter warning us of "falling" for that lie. (Paul is speaking of the "ceremonial" law coming to an end). The "Message", called the "Gospel", is very simple. The Writings are very clear about what it is, but listening with "lawless" ears, it is ***veiled*** to those who are perishing:

"'The time has come, He said. '<u>The Kingdom of</u> <u>𐤉𐤄𐤅𐤄</u> is near. <u>Repent</u> and believe the good news'". Mark 1:15.

"The Torah and Nebi'im (Law, or *Teachings*, and prophets) ***were proclaimed through Yahuchanon. Since that time, the good news of the <u>Reign of 𐤉𐤄𐤅𐤄 is being preached</u>, and everyone is forcing his way into it. It is easier for heaven and Earth to disappear than for the least stroke of a pen to drop out of the Torah."*** (Luke 16:16,17). What "Gospel/good news" have you been taught all your life? Commonly, it involves not being condemned for disobedience to the Torah. This is partly true, but it overlooks what the resurrection means to us, and what receiving 𐤉𐤄𐤅𐤔𐤏 accomplishes, by His writing His Torah on our hearts! Shaul said to the Galatians, who were falling back into their old Pagan customs:

"But even though we, or a messenger from the skies brings a message ("Gospel") ***to you besides what we announced to you, LET HIM BE ACCURSED."*** - Gal. 1:8.

THE REAL MEANING

The *real* **"Gospel"** (message) is not the popular one. It is ***"Repent, for the Reign of 𐤉𐤄𐤅𐤄 draws near."*** Mt. 3:2, 4:17, Luke 16:16, Mark 1:15, Acts 8:12, etc.,. In fact, **ALL THE PARABLES** describe it in great detail. The message of the Reign of 𐤉𐤄𐤅𐤄 is the subject matter of the parables, which veil its meaning from those not called. (Many are called, few chosen).

"I will open My mouth in a parable; I will utter dark sayings of old which we have heard and known, and our fathers have told us." Ps. 78. You can praise the Living 𐤉𐤄𐤅𐤄 till you drop; but if you will not ***obey*** Him, your prayers and praise are an abomination, Pr. 15:8,9, 28:9, Yesha Yahu 1:15.

At 2Cor.4:3, Shaul states that he does not distort the "Word of 𐤉𐤄𐤅𐤄", and says: ***"Even if our (Gospel) is veiled, it is veiled to <u>THOSE WHO ARE PERISHING</u>. The elohim*** (Shatan) ***of this age has blinded the minds of unbelievers, so they cannot see the Light of the (Gospel) of the esteem of Mashiach, Who is the Image of 𐤉𐤄𐤅𐤄."*** At 2Cor. 2:15-17, Shaul speaks also of those perishing, and says something that might really open your eyes:

"Unlike so many, WE DO NOT PEDDLE THE WORD OF 𐤉𐤄𐤅𐤄 FOR PROFIT."

The "WE" would be the ones called the *Nazarenes,* who follow the Lamb where He leads us, into Truth.

The "Gospel", or *glad tidings,* announcing that all men everywhere should REPENT (turn from sin, and obey Torah), is our commission:

"And these good tidings of the Kingdom shall be preached in the whole world for a testimony to all the nations; and then shall the end come." Mt. 24:14.

(Those who are perishing do not understand the message, and they are being plundered by false teachers who are profiting from the faith).

The **first thing** a person must do is be <u>convicted of their sin against the Torah.</u> Hearing first that their "sins are covered" doesn't emphasize repentance from sin, it sounds like they can live in their mind of the flesh, "believing".

Where is it written, that we will be punished for attempting to obey the Torah? Your enemy wants you to ignore the Torah, just as he tricked the first woman. If we think she goofed over such a simple thing, then we should look at how we find ourselves in the very same situation. Shatan is a liar, and has many people following his masquerading messengers of lawlessness. "Legalism" and the accompanying criticisms cannot be found in the Writings anywhere. The merchant messengers will tell you "*rest any day you like, just try to do it about every 7 days"*. They still "program" you to come to a Sun-day morning assembly, so you will be able to feel good about contributing to their wonderful "work". They are the "priests of Baal" (the LORD), wearing black. "The LORD's Day", Baal's Day, is Sun-day. Start obeying the 7th day Shabbat, and <u>watch what they say to you.</u> It's the sign of the Eternal Covenant, which we will see details of later. I picked the 7th day Shabbat to rest, and do it without fail. I'm "marked" now, with a mark called the Sign of the Eternal Covenant Ez. 20:12, Yesha Yahu 56:4-8, Ex. 31:12-17, Gen. 2:2, Heb. 4.

THE EVERLASTING COVENANT

The Everlasting Covenant establishes a new *relationship* between 𐤉𐤄𐤅𐤄 and mankind. It's the relationship of a ***Husband*** and His ***wife***. It's metaphoric, or a figure of speech that draws an analogy. Like a marriage, there are two processes involved: ***betrothal*** and ***consummation***. 50 days after leaving Egypt, representing the bondage of sin, the children of Yisrael (the chosen wife of the promise) were at Mount Sinai. This was the first "Shabuoth", now called "Pentecost". The elements found in the Everlasting Covenant correspond to Yahudim wedding traditions. 𐤉𐤄𐤅𐤄 refers to Yisrael as His "wife", because He has engaged in a formal betrothal. Sinai was this betrothal, and two written copies of the Torah (teachings, written in stone on front & back) were the marriage "ketuba". One for the Husband, and one for the wife. These were placed into a special container, called ***The Ark of the Covenant***. The Husband chose His wife, Yisrael, to care for, provide for, and protect. The wife agreed to ***obey***, ***forsaking all others***. *Two witnesses* were called forth to hear the Covenant: *shamayim* (heavens, skies), and *Eretz* (Earth). They are the witnesses to the wife making her vows: ***"All the words which 𐤉𐤄𐤅𐤄 has spoken we will do."*** Ex. 24:3. At this point, the 70 elders of **Yisrael** (the Sanhedrin of the time) ate and drank with the Husband, Bridegroom, Creator, and Sovereign. The "wife" provided her contribution to the marriage covenant, a type of property brought by a bride to her husband at a marriage: the gold, silver, bronze, fabrics, oils, and precious stones for the construction of the ark and dwelling of the Husband among them. The terms of this formal covenant (the written wedding agreement, or *ketuba*), were burned into stone with the finger of 𐤉𐤄𐤅𐤄. The ***NAME*** of the Husband was taken by His wife; and so they (we) are called: ***YAHUDIM***. This was corrupted to *Judah*, by translators, then *Jude*, and for the last several hundred years, it has been *Jew*. 𐤉𐤄𐤅𐤄 speaks of His Covenant without ceasing, reminding His wife of the marriage. ***"For your Maker is your Husband ~ 𐤉𐤄𐤅𐤄 Shaddai is His Name"*** (Read all of Yesha Yahu 54, 55 & 56). Being in the Covenant, we are ISRAEL.

GENTILES ALSO CALLED TO JOIN ISRAEL

"Blessed is the man who does this, the man who holds it fast; who KEEPS THE SHABBATH without defiling it, and keeps his hand from doing any evil. LET NO FOREIGNER who has bound himself to 𐤉𐤄𐤅𐤄 say, '𐤉𐤄𐤅𐤄 will surely exclude me from His people'. And let not any eunuch complain, 'I am only a dry tree'. For this is what 𐤉𐤄𐤅𐤄 says: "To the eunuchs who keep my Shabbaths, who choose what pleases Me and hold fast to my covenant ~ to them I will give within My Temple and its walls a memorial and a name better than sons and daughters; I will give them an everlasting name that will not be cut off. And FOREIGNERS who bind themselves to 𐤉𐤄𐤅𐤄 to serve Him, to love the Name of 𐤉𐤄𐤅𐤄 and to worship Him, ALL WHO KEEP THE SHABBATH without defiling it and who hold fast to My Covenant, these I will bring to My qodesh mountain and give them joy in My house of prayer . . . . For My house will be called a house of prayer for all nations.'" Yesha Yahu 56:2-7.

All of the "converts" underwent an immersion, called now a "baptism", which is a logical progression for us to turn to now. Any body of water can be used; the Hebrew term is "MIKVA". Traditionally, a mikva is a place to wash away "uncleanness", as a woman would bath after her monthly cycle before having contact with her husband. Likewise, our "Husband" doesn't wish contact with us until we have washed away our past sins (ignoring Torah). Our immersion is an outward sign of our commitment to obey from that point on, and the New Covenant promises the Spirit (our "helper") which writes the Torah (Covenant, marriage vows to obey) on our hearts. This pledge identifies us with His Name, His burial, and His resurrection from the dead. At 1Peter 3:18-22, Cephas (Peter) states that the 8 persons on the ark were also *saved through water*,and that water symbolizes our immersion that now saves us. Those who came through the water fleeing Pharaoh came through the sea, along with "foreigners". All were saved through water. Immersion is our outward sign of a good conscience toward 𐤉𐤄𐤅𐤄, and now represents our "circumcision", Col. 2:11,12:

"In Him you were also circumcised, in the putting off of the sinful nature, not with a circumcision done by the hands of men, but with the circumcision done by Mashiach, having been buried with Him in (baptism) and raised with Him through your faith in the power of 𐤉𐤄𐤅𐤄 Who raised Him from the dead." Obviously, not comprehending this at the time of one's immersion means it was not anything but a fraud, and probably wasn't in the correct Name! An infant cannot possibly be considered capable of knowing what is happening. Immersion is an act of your own personal will; You covenant with 𐤉𐤄𐤅𐤔𐤏 - and become an Israelite.

LAYING ON OF THE HANDS

You can immerse yourself, but it is my advice to find an elder if possible to attend. After immersion, you should seek to have an elder's hands laid upon your head, reciting the priestly blessing which places the Name of 𐤉𐤄𐤅𐤄 on you (Numbers 6:22-27). At this point, you may bring others to the water, and lay hands on them. The students (disciples) of Rabbi 𐤉𐤄𐤅𐤔𐤏 did this, but *He immersed no one* ~ it is our duty to make converts and immerse them into His Name. At the time of the laying on of hands, you will receive a greater "measure" of יהושע's Spirit, or gifts; not that the man touching your head has any "power" of his own, but rather by your obedience, our Beloved יהושע witnesses your actions; and brings you an increase in His power. Do you feel driven to the water now? This knowledge is free, and the "Kingdom" of יהוה is not a thing to "go" to, because it is in our hearts, unseen. We are the set-apart (qodesh) "Temple", not a building dedicated to the financial plundering of the lost. I was immersed in a creek here in Louisville, with only my 8-year-old son present, when I was 39 years old. I had been immersed as a baby, and by a Christian minister a couple of years before, but I called on Yahusha when he said "Jesus". He looked pretty shocked when I said it. But, I did it again myself in the creek, because I felt disturbed over the other situation. The Blood of the Lamb covers our sins, but we inherit eternal life by the resurrection of יהושע ~ which is what our immersion pictures. Although my son and I were the only people present at the creek, I felt the presence of יהוה, and other beings in His presence who witnessed my immersion. You will also, when you obey, and undertake this "circumcision". Romans chaps. 7 & 8 are a must-read! Read the whole context without a "lawless mind". The secret is unlocked for you. Shaul explains the whole struggle with "sin", and how we, with the Spirit, delight in יהוה's Torah in our inner being. The "law" is spiritual; but while we remain in an unspiritual condition, it produces death. The "law" was created to produce LIFE, but can only do so if we become spirit-minded by having Mashiach in us, destroying our sinful, lawless nature. ***"Those who live according to the sinful nature have their minds set on what that nature desires; but those who live in accordance with the Spirit have their minds set on what the Spirit desires. The mind of sinful man is death, but the mind controlled by the Spirit is life and peace; the sinful mind is hostile to יהוה. IT DOES NOT SUBMIT TO יהוה's TORAH, NOR CAN IT DO SO. Those controlled by the sinful nature cannot please יהוה. You, however, are controlled NOT by the sinful nature, but by the Spirit, IF THE SPIRIT OF יהוה LIVES IN YOU. And if anyone does not have the Spirit of Mashiach, he does not belong to Mashiach."*** Rom. 8:5-9. Please read Romans chapters 7 & 8. You will be confronted by many people in the future who struggle to understand what Shaul really means. Men attend B-ble colleges, seminaries, and spend their entire lives without being able to "crack" the secret, nor can it be done ~ unless your mind gives up, and you ask יהושע for the TRUTH. As I said on page 4 of this book, you must have asked Him for the TRUTH, because now you have it. I asked, and I received. "The Truth Is Out There" ~ but now it can be **IN** you. You have just found the treasure of eternal life, if you will only pick it up and put it on! That is what the ("Gospel") message of the Reign of יהוה is, and the 1st part of the secret:

REPENT. ***FOR THE REIGN OF יהוה DRAWS NEAR.*** This means He reigns in our hearts and minds, and we obey Him because we love the Covenant (the marriage vows, the 10 Commandments). We show our love for Him by our faithfulness. We change, they don't. The "change" in the "law" between the Old Covenant and the New concerned the ceremonial animal sacrifices, which were imperfect, and could not justify us permanently.

The New Covenant: This is the 2nd part of the secret. It was "cut" in the Blood of the Lamb of יהוה, when ONE sacrifice put an end to atoning for lawbreaking. Having become convicted of our sinfulness, we "turn" or repent to the Torah. Our belief in Him as our substitution, convinces us of our sinfulness and need for a debt payer. However, we cannot be perfect, because of our mind of the flesh. This is where the New Covenant brings us eternal life. Showing our repentance to the marriage vows by obedience, we go to the water in full submission to our Husband, and wash clean spiritually. We actually "die" to sin. We are then "raised" with Him, and He comes into us ~ you will feel Him, it is like a "wind" grabbing you from the inside, filling you. You will feel something change in your will, and have a new clarity of mind. Your flesh will no longer rule your mind, but your spirit will rule your flesh. By His resurrection, we have eternal life also. We are atoned for by His death; but we are SAVED by His LIFE, the resurrection from the dead. This is the complete Truth, and it is absolutely free. You don't have to pay for it, by going to a steeple for decades giving a man 10% of your money, because he doesn't even know it.

As you continue to learn, you will see that Christianity is a man-made religion, and absolutely nothing like the faith (religion) that was delivered to the saints. The Nazarenes existed for centuries before a "Christianity" did.

The **Covenant *is*** the 10 Commandments, Dt. 4:13. If you read Galatians chaps. 4 & 5, you will see that "Sinai" represents the slave woman. The slave woman is fleshly, carnal, and non-spiritual. But the "free" (spiritual) woman represents those

THE 10 COMMANDMENTS - TORAH

CALLED THE "DECALOGUE", DECA (TEN), LOGUE (WORDS), Ex. 20:1-17 **ESERET** (TEN) HA'**DABARIM** (WORDS)

1. I AM 𐤉𐤄𐤅𐤄 YOUR ELOHIM. HAVE NO OTHER BEFORE MY FACE.

[NO FOREIGN NAMES, RITUALS, CUSTOMS OF PAGANS]

2. YOU DO NOT BOW TO IMAGES.

3. YOU DO NOT CAST THE NAME OF 𐤉𐤄𐤅𐤄 YOUR ELOHIM TO RUIN.

["SHOAH" = RUIN - WE ARE NOT TO *DESTROY* HIS NAME]

4. REMEMBER SHABBATH, TO KEEP IT QODESH.

[SIGN OF EVERLASTING COVENANT OF LOVE, EX. 31:13, EZ. 20:16-20. CHANGED (DAN. 7:25) BY CONSTANTINE TO HIS "DAY OF THE SUN" IN 321 CE FOR CHRISTIANS, CHANGED BY MUHAMMAD TO 6TH DAY, CIRCA 622 CE. SHABBATH ACKNOWLEDGES 𐤉𐤄𐤅𐤄 AS **CREATOR**, HEB. 4. IN THE WORLD BEFORE SIN CAME, AND REMAINS FOR ALL ETERNITY, IS. 66:23, PS. 119:152, EX. 31:13.

5. YOU RESPECT YOUR FATHER AND YOUR MOTHER.

6. YOU DO NOT MURDER.

7. YOU DO NOT BREAK WEDLOCK.

8. YOU DO NOT STEAL.

9. YOU DO NOT BEAR FALSE WITNESS AGAINST YOUR NEIGHBOR.

10. YOU DO NOT COVET YOUR NEIGHBOR'S HOUSE, WIFE, SERVANTS, OX, ASS, OR ANYTHING THAT BELONGS TO YOUR NEIGHBOR.

THESE ARE TO BE DILIGENTLY TAUGHT TO YOUR CHILDREN, AND POSTED ON THE DOORPOSTS OF YOUR HOME. (Dt. 6).

NOTE: Roman Catholicism eliminated the 2nd (so as to continue the Pagan behavior of bowing and kneeling before images), and split the 10th Commandment into two, so as to maintain 10. They briefly outlawed images during the 8th century, but after 34 years without them, reverted back by wiping out the dogma. (At the Council of Constantinople in 754, image worship and images were abolished. In 788, worship of the cross, relics (dead bones), and images were re-authorized. Source: *The Catholic Encyclopedia*

When Rabbi 𐤉𐤄𐤅𐤔𐤏 warned us that *"a little leaven* (yeast) *leavens the whole lump* (bread dough), He meant that a "little" error will spread and corrupt the entire group, if it is ignored. "A rotten apple spoils the whole barrel". Constantine "spoiled" the true day of rest, and turned it into his "Baal's Day", Sun-day. He brought in the Pagan festival of "Easter" to obliterate Passover. If you were Shatan, wouldn't you "possess" the man with the most power, and divert things? Where do you think Shatan is today? It's easy to figure out.

born of the Spirit, having the Covenant written on their hearts, not stone. The "law" that could **not justify** us was the ceremonial law of animal sacrifices (Heb. 10:1-4), but the Renewed Covenant is able to justify us, being in the Blood of the Lamb of 𐤉𐤄𐤅𐤄 (one sacrifice for sins, Heb. 10:12). The 10 Commandments are called the "**Covenant of Love**" (1Kings 8:23, 2Chr. 6:14, Ne. 1:5). Look over the list of them at the left; is there **ONE** that is not good? If your inner being AGREES with them, then you are being called! When you can say **"I *LOVE* *these teachings*"** ~ you have crossed-over into a Spirit-led realm, controlled by the Spirit of 𐤉𐤄𐤅𐤔𐤏 ~ and you will not sin against them, because they are now your personality, as they are His. ***"If we deliberately keep on sinning after we have received the knowledge of the truth, no sacrifice for sins is left, but only a fearful expectation of judgment and of raging fire that will consume the enemies of Elohim. "*** (Heb. 10:26, 27). These Commandments are your marriage vows. You change; **they don't!**

HOW DO GENTILES BEGIN?

THE ANSWER IS AT ACTS 15. At the Yerushaliyim Council, the issue of fleshly circumcision (the sign of the land covenant) was debated, and called "a yoke that neither we nor our fathers have been able to bear". Peter told them of how he learned that no man is "unclean" (the 3 sheets, Acts 10). He saw that "unclean animals" alluded to **MEN**, not food, as he explained at Acts 11.

When Gentiles heard the **message**, Peter said their hearts were purified by belief, and **they received the gift of the Spirit**, and were immersed (spiritual circumcision). Then "James" (Ya'akob) decided the beginning steps for Gentiles:

"It is my judgment, therefore, that we should not make it difficult for the Gentiles who are turning to Elohim (no fleshly circumcision). ***Instead we should write to them, telling them to :***

(1) ***abstain from food polluted by idols, from*** **(2)** ***sexual immorality, and from*** **(3)** ***the meat of strangled animals and from*** **(4)** ***blood. For Mosheh*** (Moses, the Torah) ***has been preached in every city from the earliest times and is read in the synagogues on every Shabbath."*** (Acts 15:19-21). Because few could read and write (being illiterate), and because scrolls were not widely available, the converts needed to attend the readings of the Torah, Prophets, and Writings at synagogues (houses of study) in order to **learn**

more. The Natsarim remained a part of the wider group of Yahudim, and even many "synagogue rulers" were Natsarim. The main disruption of this "oneness" was caused by the Romans (a "war" conducted by Shatan), when they destroyed the Temple in 70 CE, and again crushed the Yahudim 60 years later. Shatan managed to kill millions of us, and dispersed us into the surrounding regions. Because our Rabbi had warned us beforehand that when we saw armies surrounding the city to "flee to the mountains", the Natsarim were "shunned" because they **did not stay and fight**. Without the Temple and the ceremonial sacrificial system, "rabbinical" Yahudaism developed among the dispersed Yahudim. Shatan pursued "the woman" (𐤉𐤄𐤅𐤄's bride, wife): ***"Then the dragon was enraged at the woman and went off to make war against the rest of her offspring ~ THOSE WHO OBEY 𐤉𐤄𐤅𐤄's COMMANDMENTS AND HOLD TO THE TESTIMONY OF 𐤉𐤄𐤅𐤔𐤏."*** (Rev. 12—read it all). What is the "TESTIMONY" of 𐤉𐤄𐤅𐤔𐤏? It is: ***"Repent ~ for the Reign of 𐤉𐤄𐤅𐤄 draws near".*** We are engaged in a war, and wear the Torah as our armor. We are the meek. Our sword is the Word of 𐤉𐤄𐤅𐤄, His Torah. The true elders who serve our Rabbi do not plunder the flock, but serve and feed the flock. You can recognize us by our "fruits" ~ whether or not we **keep** and **teach others** the Commandments. Read all of 1 Yahuchanon carefully. We also carry the true "message". We have been saved by "grace", the unmerited lovingkindness of the GIFT of the Spirit of 𐤉𐤄𐤅𐤔𐤏, <u>Who has written His Torah on our hearts and minds</u>. Now, having the ability to LOVE the Commandments, we do not sin against them. We are led by the Spirit (the spiritual seed), not the flesh (Hagar, the mind of the "flesh"). The Commandments are spiritual, but the mind of the flesh wars against them. How do we show our love for 𐤉𐤄𐤅𐤄? We obey His Torah, teachings, Covenant of Love! We are the "wise virgins" who await our Bridegroom, having the "oil" (Torah) that lights our way. If you have been raised in, or converted to Christianity, you should by now be starting to see the "rotten" decay that Paganism brought into the barrel of apples long ago. The Torah (teachings) is the "Rock" that the wise man will build his house on. You need no other "rabbi", or the approval of any man, to convert to the religion of 𐤉𐤄𐤅𐤔𐤏. We do not beg for money, but work ourselves. The love of money is the root of all kinds of evil. The wisdom of Torah is more precious than gold or rubies! It must not be "sold". The New Covenant makes you an heir of the promises, and you will be included at the Wedding Supper of the Bridegroom, not locked outside. It doesn't matter how much you pay your pastor to spread the message of the Reign; you must do it **yourself!** His **Name** and the **Covenant** is the "buried treasure", so apply your whole heart and mind to remain steadfast. You can trust your Husband to be faithful, and He will say, "well done, good and faithful servant". If He gives you 5 pieces of "**silver**" (wisdom, knowledge, understanding), and you return to him 5 **additional** pieces at His return (you have invested and helped **others convert**), you will be greatly rewarded. Your money cannot help. People who misunderstand the parables, or are tricked by their pastors, not only are blocked from the **Covenant**, but they are also plundered. The reason so many men can peddle the Word of 𐤉𐤄𐤅𐤄 for profit is because <u>the message is veiled</u>. The harvest is great, because there are billions alive **right now** who need to hear the <u>true message</u> of the Reign of 𐤉𐤄𐤅𐤄. The harvest of the Earth is coming very soon, probably **within** the generation (70 years) of the re-gathering to Yisrael (1948 CE). But no man knows the day or hour of His coming; we will know the "season" however. First, you must be **immersed**, calling upon the Name of 𐤉𐤄𐤅𐤔𐤏 for the forgiveness of your past uncleanness (sins), then walk in the Truth (Torah, the Covenant). You will know you are 𐤉𐤄𐤅𐤄's Bride.

THE "ONENESS" OF MARRIAGE

The "message" (gospel) of the Reign of 𐤉𐤄𐤅𐤄 is **LINKED** to the idea of a marriage covenant, and begins with 𐤉𐤄𐤅𐤄's CALL. If we agree to His COVENANT (the 10 Commandments), then we love Him and obey Him as a Husband is to be obeyed. He loves, provides for, and protects us as a wife. The immersion into the waters (called baptism now) removes our "uncleanness", and we are then enabled to become ONE with our Maker. He only seeks the love of a faithful bride, and He is not bashful about telling us He is JEALOUS. He calls us out from **ancient Paganism** which pollutes His bride. This is why the prophet Hosea was told to make a prostitute his bride, to illustrate how we make 𐤉𐤄𐤅𐤄 feel. At our resurrection, He will inhabit us fully. It is most important that we be **immersed** in His **NAME**, then **sealed** in His **NAME** with the laying on of hands. A faithful wife is an obedient wife, who obeys out of LOVE. It's a <u>Covenant of Love</u>.

Ha shatan attacks marriages of all kinds.

PAGANISM EXPOSED

It's very important that we consider the impact that Constantine had on our accepted customs, **because he acted as a "lens" which filtered-out the (Jewish) roots of the faith.** The habits of the western Pagan Gentiles like Sun-day, Easter,

Saturnalia, Samhain, towers, and many familiar symbols were carried along and blended into the Nazarene faith as a matter of state policy. OW-YꟻZ's death and resurrection occurred at the time of **Passover**. Since the Gentiles of the western localities were in the habit of their Earth Mother fertilization festival, Easter, they continued to keep it in a new perspective when they converted to Christianity. The eggs and rabbits, rolling eggs on the fields, egg "hunts", etc., should be more than enough evidence to show this. The early Nazarenes who were less inclined to "inculturate" the Paganism were disturbed as they witnessed the Gentiles' changes. Since they continued to observe the **Passover**, it meant even more to them than ever before. OWYꟻZ had revealed the mystery that Passover had foreshadowed. We know there was a controversy concerning the alterations made by Constantine when he set up "Sun-day", and "Easter", replacing the Covenant Commandments. In Eusebius' ***Ecclesiastical History***, there is the record of the following letter written by an **elder**, **Polycrates**, to Victor of the Church of Rome:

"We, therefore, observe the genuine day; neither adding thereto nor taking therefrom. For in Asia great lights have fallen asleep, which shall rise again in the day of the (Rabbi's) ***appearing, in which He will come with esteem from Shamayim, and will raise up all the saints; Philip, one of the twelve apostles, who sleeps in Hierapolis, and his two aged virgin daughters. His other daughter, also, who having lived under the influence of the Ruach ha Qodesh, now likewise rests in Ephesus. Moreover, Yahuchanon, who rested on the bosom of our*** (Rabbi)***; who also was a priest, and bore the sacerdotal plate, both a martyr and a teacher. He is buried in Ephesus; also Polycarp of Smyrna, both elder and martyr of Eumenia, who is buried at Smyrna. Why should I mention Sagaris, elder and martyr, who rests at Laodicea? Moreover, the blessed Papirius; and Melito, the eunuch, whose walk and conversation was altogether under the influence of the Ruach ha Qodesh, who now rests at Sardis, awaiting the episcopate from Shamayim, when he shall rise from the dead. ALL THESE OBSERVED THE 14TH DAY OF THE PASSOVER ACCORDING TO THE WORD, DEVIATING IN NO RESPECT, BUT FOLLOWING THE RULE OF FAITH. Moreover, I, Polycrates, who am the least of all of you, according to the tradition of my relatives, some of whom I have followed. For there were seven, my relatives elders, and I am the eighth; and my relatives always observed the day when the people threw away the leaven."***

There it is, friends. An elder who saw the changes, and wrote to another elder who was being carried away by "winds" of doctrine. He mentioned the throwing away of the leaven for the 7 days of the Feast of Unleavened bread (Matsah), as Shaul also mentioned at 1 Cor. 5:7-10. Shaul even said ***"Let us therefore celebrate the Feast"***, speaking of **Matsah**. Remember how Shaul said he wept and pleaded with the elders for years (Acts 20), knowing that these things would come after he was gone. The assemblies were turning aside to "myths". The heretics have distorted the true walk to suit themselves, and created a powerful hierarchy which has killed tens of millions, and is still in place causing human catastrophes. The current "times of the Gentiles" will not be set right by human means, but will be obliterated by our returning Mashiach, as a roaring lion from space, as lightning from one end of the sky to the other. You have to be a "saint" while you are alive, if you expect to enter the New Yerushaliyim in the resurrection. There is no religion in the Writings that requires us to meet together on Sun-day morning, or observe "Easter", or "Christmas". To follow "leaders" who are blind, you will fall into a pit. Many trust their own hearts, saying *"I believe in my own way"*, or *"I worship the Creator in my own personal way"*. They do what seems right in **their own eyes**. ***"You are NOT to do as we do here today, everyone as he sees fit . . ."*** Dt. 12:8.

Following your own heart, you will be deceived also: ***"The heart is crooked above all, and desperately sick ~ who shall know it?"*** Yerme Yahu 17:9.

At 18:12, the prophet wrote that the people said to themselves, ***"It's no use. We will continue with our own plans; each of us will follow the stubbornness of his evil heart."*** People find comfort in cliches like *"When in Rome, do as the Romans do."* Is this what our Rabbi taught us to do? ***"And the fire shall prove the work of each one, what sort it is. If anyone's work remains, which he has built on, he shall receive a reward. If anyone's work is burned, he shall suffer loss, but he himself shall be saved, but as though through fire."*** 1 Cor. 3:13-15. The prophesied "**apostasy**", or falling away from the Torah, has happened. Be warned.

"Blessed are those doing His Commands, so that the authority shall be theirs unto the tree of life and to enter through the gates into the city. Outside are the dogs, those who practice magic arts, the sexually immoral, the murderers, the idolaters and EVERYONE WHO LOVES AND PRACTICES FALSEHOOD." Rev. 22:14,15.

"It would have been better for them not to have known the way of righteousness, than to have known it and then to turn their backs on the

qodesh command that was passed on to them. Of them the proverbs are true: 'A dog returns to its vomit', and 'A sow that is washed goes back to her wallowing in the mud'." 2Pet. 2:21,22. "Dogs" is the term used for Gentiles without any hope (see Mt. 7:6, and 15:26). The 'vomit' a dog returns to is his old Pagan ways.

The "Last Supper" was at the beginning of the 14th of Abib, and was the memorial meal of Yahusha's day of death. He said ***"Go and make preparations for us to eat the Passover"*** (Luke 22:8), and ***"I have eagerly desired to eat this Passover with you before I suffer.*** (Notice that He said He desired to eat "this Passover" before I suffer?) ***For I tell you, I will not eat it AGAIN until it finds fulfillment in the Kingdom of 𐤉𐤄𐤅𐤄."*** (Luke 22:15,16). This reinforces John 19:31, which states it was the Day of Preparation since the next day was a **special** (annual) Shabbat, beginning at sunset. There is no "lamb" mentioned, but our Rabbi is the Lamb. ***"It was the Day of Preparation of Passover Week, about the sixth hour"*** (John 19:14), being what we would call "noon" when Pilate sentenced Yahusha. Luke records that it was about the sixth hour that darkness came over the whole land until the 9th hour (3 p.m., Luke 23:44). This agrees with Mark 15:33, but Mark 15:25 says it was the 3rd hour when they hung Yahusha up on the tree. These variations could have been made by copyists, since no two sentences in the Greek manuscripts are uniform among the many copies; or different forms of time-keeping were being used. There is the Roman method that begins at midnight, and the Hebrew method that begins at sunrise, and others that begin at different "watches" of the night. What is important to realize is that it was the 14th day of Abib that Yahusha was sentenced and shed His precious blood on the tree for us. The Lamb was to be slain on the 14th, and Yahusha certainly was slain at exactly the right time. "Pesach" is a memorial at several levels; the first-born was slain in Egypt, and Yahuah's First-Born was slain for us at Golgatha; Israel was redeemed from slavery and captivity in Egypt, and with Yahusha's death we were redeemed from our sins. During this week of Pesach, Yahusha resurrected, becoming the "First-fruits" offering before Yahuah. All of these combine to form a picture of redemption, or rather a "shadow" of things to come for the body of Messiah. The body of Messiah is Israel, and the outward signs of His redemption are **Pesach**, the **Sabbath**, and the **circumcision of our hearts.**

Although there is a chance of 14% that an annual Shabbat can coincide with a weekly Shabbat, both kinds have a "Preparation Day". Mark also records ***"It was Preparation Day"*** (15:42). As most understand it, this day of preparation was the day *before* the 1st Day of Matsah, the 7 days of Unleavened Bread, which was (and is) also generally called "Pesach". We notice at John 18:28, where our Rabbi is being brought to Pilate from Caiaphas: ***"By now it was early morning, and TO AVOID CEREMONIAL UNCLEANNESS, the Jews*** (Sadducees) ***did not enter the palace; THEY WANTED TO BE ABLE TO EAT THE PASSOVER".*** The "Last Supper" may have been just a meal, and Rabbi Yahusha didn't "eat" the Passover, but He may have meant that He looked forward to eating with His talmidim **before** He suffered at this most special Passover season.

I have come to observe a memorial meal at the beginning of the 14th of Abib at twilight, the same day our Rabbi was executed. Passover is best observed as the 15th begins. Lev. 23:5,6 says: ***"𐤉𐤄𐤅𐤄's Passover begins AT TWILIGHT on the fourteenth day of the first month. On the fifteenth day of that month 𐤉𐤄𐤅𐤄's Feast of Unleavened Bread begins; for seven days you must eat bread made without yeast."*** Passover, the slaying of the first-born, the plundering of the Egyptians, and the exodus all occurred on the "same day" - see Ex. 12. "Twilight" is just after sunset, between sunset and darkness. Today, we find many people learning the "Hebrew roots" of the faith by looking closely at the doctrinal descendants of the ***Pharisees*** - the ultra-orthodox who adhere to the Torah and the Talmud, or Rabbinical Judaism. The doctrinal descendants of the ***Sadducees*** would most closely be the Karaites. As I continue to study Scripture, I notice many things are done correctly yet not well understood by these groups, while other things are not observed exactly as Scripture dictates. The distortions are caused by fallible men, so each of us should study the original Hebrew texts carefully to learn how to straighten-out what is bent out of shape.

THE LAST SUPPER

Most people have come to understand the final meal of the talmudim (disciples, students) and our Rabbi 𐤉𐤄𐤅𐤔𐤏 the night before He died was

Do you see a face or 3 little raccoons?
I drew this from a photo I saw on a book of animals, and added the rest to make it appear as a face. The line is an adaptation from a Simon & Garfunkle song.

MEN SEE WHAT THEY WANT TO SEE, AND DISREGARD THE REST.

something new. Catholicism has taught it to be the model for what they call the "consecration" and "offertory" of the "mass". They instituted this annual observance of "Passover" into a **weekly** "morning" observance. The Mithraists were already holding a Sun-day morning service to worship the sun deity, and used a flat disc of bread. The moment the Pagan priest would lift it into the air to receive the sun's rays, it became "transformed" with the word "***abracadabra***". The Roman "priest" says "hoc est corpus meum", (Latin, *this is my body*), which later became ridiculed by the words ***hocus-pocus*** (meaning trickery). These words are now used to refer to superstitious nonsense. Catholics actually believe the bread "transubstantiates" into the actual presence of the body and blood of Mashiach when the priest says hoc est corpus meum, and by eating it, they would possess the powers of the deity. The Egyptians laid the round wafers out in the sunlight at their "consecration". To a Nazarene, these rituals are an abomination, and the wafer is a "death cookie".

PASSOVER OBSERVANCE

Many of you will differ with me, and that's fine, but it is my opinion that the "Last Supper" was what our Rabbi said it was: ***"I have eagerly desired to eat this Passover with you before I suffer."*** Luke 22:15. There is confusion on this. It is possible that this was what was called a *teaching seder*, as rabbis would commonly hold a seder the evening before the actual Passover, so the students could be with their families as required for the real Passover. We just don't really know. But, how Christendom has NO Passover is what is amazing, but now some are beginning to.

The "Last Supper" was not a "Mass", but a very familiar observance. The students of Rabbi 𐤉𐤄𐤅𐤔𐤏 were talking about it for days before it came. The word "seder" means ***order***. The primary objective is to remove all "***chametz***" or leavened bread from our homes (no doubt an inherited activity we now call "spring cleaning"). It has been said that it took Leonardo De Vinci almost **20 years** to paint this famous picture, known as

THE LAST SUPPER:

The actual word for "Passover" is ***PESACH***. If something is "Kosher" (appropriate, approved) for Pesach, then it doesn't contain yeast or anything that makes it "rise". This is to remind us of the hasty departure from the bondage of Egypt (Mitzraim) by the mighty hand of 𐤉𐤄𐤅𐤄. It is always observed in the evening (darkening) at the 14th of the 1st month of the year, determined by the arrival of the first moon in the spring. This pictures the beginning of the redemption plan for 𐤉𐤄𐤅𐤔𐤏's bride, since He is the "first-fruits" of the Reign of 𐤉𐤄𐤅𐤄, our "wave offering". Other neglected observances will be discussed in sequence. This "wave offering" occurred after the most significant event in the history of mankind: The resurrection from the dead of Rabbi 𐤉𐤄𐤅𐤔𐤏. The "first-born" from the dead, of what will be a great **harvest** of mankind, was like grain, cut-down; then, upon resurrecting, was "waving". He is literally the first to be "born" of the spirit, because He doesn't have a body like we do any more; He's something completely NEW. We receive a small "seed" of this rebirth upon being immersed, but while we are still in our flesh, we are not yet "born of the spirit" in the complete way we will be. We are, however, re-born in a spiritual way, even while we are in our flesh. We must be born of water, at our immersion, and later, raised as spatial beings like 𐤉𐤄𐤅𐤔𐤏 is. ***"Dear friends, now we are children of 𐤉𐤄𐤅𐤄, and what we will be has not yet been made known. But we know that when He appears, WE WILL BE LIKE HIM, for we shall see Him as He is."*** ~ 1 Yn. 3:2. This painting of the Last Supper is widely recognized, and most think it is linked in some way to what they do on "Sun-day" morning. Not true. "**Supper**" and "**morning**" are oxymoronic. When Rabbi said, ***"Do this in remembrance of Me"*** (Luke 22:19), He was referring to the observance of Pesach. **Once** every year, we are to remember Him and His ***death***, as our Passover

The lamb was slain on the 14th, and the following evening (the 15) Yahuah went through the land of Egypt slaying the firstborn in the houses of those without the blood on their doors.

ISRAEL PLUNDERED THE EGYPTIANS ON THE 15TH, AS THEY AROSE IN THE NIGHT URGING THEM TO DEPART. YAHUSHA ESTABLISHED A REMEMBRANCE AT THE BEGINNING OF THE 14TH, AND DIED ON THE 14TH AS OUR PASSOVER. HE REDEEMED ISRAEL PERMANENTLY BY HIS BLOOD. ONE DAY, THOSE WITHOUT A PASSOVER WILL RECEIVE JUDGMENT ON THE "DAY OF JUDGMENT", JUST AS THE EGYPTIANS DID. YAHUSHA HIMSELF IS OUR PASSOVER LAMB, AND STILL BEARS THE WOUNDS.

Lamb. The unleavened bread, known as "MATSAH", reminds any observant Yahudi of our Lamb. If you look at one of these flat, square pieces of cracker-like bread, it is **PIERCED** and **BRUISED**. During the annual cycle of reading the TaNaKh in synagogues, Yesha Yahu 53 is skipped. This is no accident! ***"But He was PIERCED for our transgressions, He was BRUISED for our iniquities; the punishment that brought us peace was upon Him, and by His wounds, we are healed."*** v. 5.

With no "Passover", how is it that Catholicism and her daughters have a "Passover Lamb"? Sounds like some serious mental acrobatics, or folly is afoot. Whose transgressions did He die for? His bride's! The penalty for her idolatry (harlotry) was death. (The bride's name is "Daughter of Tsiyon" but her new name will be **HEPHZIBAH** (*My delight is in her,* 62:4.)

A little entertaining background concerning Leonardo's portrait of *The Last Supper* gives perspective to what a life **without Torah** is like. It is said that as Leonardo began his painting, he studied the text of the Writings for who was present, and he imagined their appearance. Naturally he had to search for subjects to pose for each person in the portrait. He **began** by looking for the most "angelic" and pure features he could find for the face of our Rabbi. After a thorough search, he finally found a young boy with the face of **absolute innocence**. Leonardo kindly asked the boy if he would pose for him, and compensated him for his time. Over the years, Leonardo carefully selected models to pose for each of the men. This took almost 20 years. Finally, he was down to the last man in the painting, known as "Judas" (really *Yahudah*). He spent months searching for the perfect model, but there just didn't seem to be anyone who looked evil enough for this modeling job. At long last, he discovered a man who had sunken as low as any man had ever gone. He was in a tavern, drunk, and had lines of pain and sin in his face that reflected the kind of life he had lived. Leonardo knew at once he had to get him to pose. Offering the man compensation, Leonardo had him pose for the most famous betrayer in the world. As Leonardo busily arranged his model, and was mixing his paints, the man spoke to him saying, *"You know me."* Leonardo was sure he had never been around *anyone* who was like this man, and replied, *"Oh no, I'm sure you're mistaken, I've never laid eyes on you."* The man, sure of himself, replied saying, *"Oh yes, sir, it was me,* ***when I was very young****, who posed for this portrait. I was the* ***first****, you said."* Hearing this, Leonardo put his hands to his face, and wept over the young boy he had crossed paths with so long ago.

Each of us have people we cross paths with, who need something from us. We either help them, ignore them, or push them down lower. I work in a store that for over the past 20 years has had a wide mixture of people coming into it. Most everyone who comes in is "searching" for something to embrace; or fulfill a need or emptiness within them. With your daily contacts, neighbors, co-workers, clients, etc., there are many who are looking for guidance which you can inspire them with. One of my missions in life is to dispel error, and replace it with Truth.

Concerning this Passover Seder known as ***The Last Supper***, there was a Medieval superstition that arose, based on error. Most have become convinced (hypnotized) into the thinking that 𐤉𐤄𐤅𐤔𐤏 was executed on a "**Fri-Day**", the Day of Preparation for the weekly Shabbath, and resurrected at SUNRISE on "**Sun-Day**". This is not anything like what the memoirs reveal to us. This is just a traditional misinterpretation, propagated by Rome. In fact, there is no phrase "*last supper*" in the Writings, but only this "Passover" which our Rabbi said He had looked forward to observing **before** He suffered, and He had observed it every year of His life. He also said he would observe it again, drinking again the fruit of the vine, in His Father's Kingdom/Reign. Shatan de-railed the train, folks. The only "sign" (like "tongues", a sign for unbelievers, 1 Cor. 14:22) to prove that 𐤉𐤄𐤅𐤔𐤏 is the Mashiach was the "sign of Yonah". As Yonah was 3 days and 3 nights in the belly of the fish, so 𐤉𐤄𐤅𐤔𐤏 was **3 days** and **3 nights** in the tomb. The year 𐤉𐤄𐤅𐤔𐤏 was executed, he observed Passover on what Pagans today would call a "Tues-Day" evening at twilight. Later that night He was arrested, and by the 3rd hour of the next day (our 9 a.m.), Rabbi 𐤉𐤄𐤅𐤔𐤏 was being pierced. At the 6th hour (our "noon"), darkness fell on the land until the 9th hour. With a loud cry, 𐤉𐤄𐤅𐤔𐤏 breathed His last, and the 60-foot-high curtain in the Temple was ripped from top-to-bottom, as a man tears his robes in grief. Because the meal we call the "Last Supper" was, according to some, a Passover observance, some observe it at the *beginning* of the 14th day of the moon, at the "darkening" between sunset and night (twilight). There is some controversy about this, and you should study all sides thoroughly. However, the "superstition" I mentioned that developed, from the Christian ignorance of what "Preparation Day" we are dealing with, gave rise to what is called **"FRI-DAY THE 13TH".** "Preparation Day" indeed includes every sixth day of the week. Six of the seven "annual appointments" are movable, one of which is the **1st Day of Matsah**, or *Unleavened Bread*, and also have preparation days. Obviously there are not **3**

DAYS AND 3 NIGHTS between "Fri-Day" night at sunset and "Sun-Day" morning. Shatan's "spin-doctors" twisted it for us, to "bend" things toward a "Sun-day" morning "supper". That's not just quaint, it's goofy. Because the entire Christian world has been "programmed" to believe that the annual observance of the day of our Rabbi's **death** is somehow linked to the days of the week, and not Passover (a movable appointment), **"FRI-DAY"** just before "EASTER" is *celebrated* as "Good Friday". OUCH! Good? In a selfish way, yes, for us; but it is the day on which Shatan pierced our beloved OWYAZ. (Only it wasn't a "Fri-Day"). In fact, if you asked Shatan what was the most significant thing he's ever accomplished, nothing else could compare to it. It fulfilled the prophecy at Gen. 3:15. The "myth" that it was a "Fri-Day", and not the preparation day for the High Shabbath of "Matsah" (Yn. 19:31) is part of the superstition of "Fri-Day the 13th". The "13" represents the fact that there were **13 MEN** present at the meal the previous evening. The 13th day of each Roman month has no connection with the real moon, nor the number of men present at the meal. Not only that, but what day the resurrection occurred has *nothing to do with what DAY is the Shabbath, our day of rest.* It's hard to understand how such obvious "smoke and mirrors" masked so much of the truth, and could be propagated by so many scholars over so many centuries. Shatan successfully blinded the eyes of populations with his "teachers", and desolated the correct pattern of observances. The "head" (Shatan) of this fiendish scheme controlled Constantine I, and the office of the papacy, BECAUSE HE RULES THIS WORLD.

CHRISTIANITY'S PAGAN CONNECTION

THE TRICK: APOSTASY

It's the same old trick: the **LIE** that "we don't really have to OBEY". The FALSE "Gospel" is what most understand, woven into their minds by the "merchants" who masquerade as messengers of righteousness. It's partly true, but it leaves out the core of the New Covenant, "***Mashiach IN* you**". Here's how they usually teach it: "*You don't have to obey, your sinning is atoned for. Besides, NO ONE can possibly obey the Commandments perfectly. J-sus obeyed them FOR us, and died to atone for all our sins, past, present, and future. You cannot out-sin the grace of G-d. When the Father looks at us, He only sees the righteousness of His Son*". So, just *believing* on this "Gospel" message makes a person extremely grateful to their J-sus, and they think they will show him how grateful they are by going to "Church" every Sun-day. This is a false, COUNTERFEIT, and incomplete message, and they don't know the True Mashiach. The soul that sins will die (Ezek. 18). The New Covenant is having ***Mashiach in us***, allowing us to love and ***agree*** with the Torah; we no longer live in the "mind of the flesh". Catholicism taught for centuries that this "Mashiach in you" was achieved by receiving "communion", a man-made "sacrament" they associated with the symbols of bread and wine at the Passover seder the night before He was put to death. It's true that the emblems represented what the New Covenant pictures, but it's only a model for what was to literally take place when He came into them with power, as He does when we accept the TRUE message of salvation. The Protestant sects carried this out of the Mother, leaving behind the belief in the bread and wine *trans-substantiating* (changing into His literal Body by the mystical "powers" endowed in the "priest"). Never learning that they are empowered to obey by having the Ruach ha Qodesh (the set-apart Spirit of OWYAZ) in them, they keep coming back week after week. They want to learn more, but never do. The tragic thing is, Shatan has turned this into a world-wide business, and his messengers go to the bank thinking "The Lord" is blessing them. Remember, a liar tells part truth, but withholds important information.

Do we go on sinning, that "grace" may abound? ***"Shall we go on sinning so that grace may increase? By no means! We died to sin*** (at our immersion)***; how can we live in it any longer?"*** Romans 6:1,2. ***"Shall we sin*** (break and ignore Commandments) ***because we are not under law but under grace? By no means! Don't you know, that when you offer yourselves to someone to obey him as slaves, you are slaves to the one whom you OBEY ~ whether you are slaves to sin, which leads to death, or to OBEDIENCE, which leads to righteousness?"*** v. 15,16.

If you carefully read Romans 6, 7, and 8, you will eventually see that Shaul is looking at the Torah from 2 perspectives; the mind of the flesh, and **the mind controlled by the Spirit**. Since the "law" is spiritual, our inner being must be controlled by the Spirit of OWYAZ in order to live by it. Shaul says ***"For in my inner being, I delight in*** AYAZ's ***Torah"*** Rom. 7:22. He also makes it clear that without the Spirit to change us, we are doomed:

"For if you live according to the sinful nature, YOU WILL DIE." Rom. 8:13.

PILLARS OF JEALOUSY

Ezekiel saw Paganism mixing into the worship of AYAZ. ***"Then He said to me, 'son of man,***

look toward the north'. So I looked, and in the entrance north of the gate of the altar I saw this pillar of jealousy." Ezek. 8:5.

"HIGH PLACES" which harken back to the tower of Babel, are ziggurats, obelisks, pyramids, poles, pagodas, spires, stupas, and a whole array of sky-pointing structures. Try to find a steeple in the worship of Yahuah in the Writings. All Pagan temples utilized a tower, and bells or gongs to summon the sun-worshippers. Hand-held bells were also used in their worship, sometimes made in rows which they would shake like rattles. In the worship of Circe, altar bells were rung periodically during the "services", inherited by Roman Catholicism and their "Mass".

One of the oldest relics of Pagan worship is the pillar of jealousy called an **OBELISK**. *Any ancient Pagan would recognize one.* They were interpreted to be a ray of the sun, but also the image of male generative power, the ***phallus***. Pagans also stood stones up in circles, and prayed within the area they defined. Most of the time the stones were only a few inches tall, but Stonehenge was one exception. In the time of Daniel, in Babylon, Nebuchadnezzar constructed an image ninety feet high, and nine feet wide, and this obelisk was to be bowed to when the "national anthem" sounded (Dan. 3). If you were able to ask Shadrach, Meshach, and Abednego if they would accompany you to most Christian places of worship, what do you think they would have to say about the big "steeple" near the entrance? I'd wager they wouldn't go near the place. You can even see obelisk shapes in the building designs, signs, and window shapes of many of these buildings. They are also very partial to "circles", which related to the sun in Pagan temple design. Some Christian congregations have torn down the steeples of their meeting places, after learning of the origin of these "high places".

CHURCH

Circe, a Greek deity who turned men into pigs, is the origin from which springs our English word **KIRCHE**, producing the word "Church". In the very first English translation of the Brit Chadasha (New Covenant Writings), a Catholic priest named John Wycliffe used the word **"congregation"** for the Greek word *ecclesia* (ek-la-*SEE*-a), not "Church". It really means ***called-out ones.*** These are those who have submitted to immersion in His Name, and repented of sin. The Hebrew word is ***QAHAL***, the congregation of Yisrael. We get our English word "call" from *qahal.* There is no covenant with "Christians", only Yisrael, and foreigners must engraft into Yisrael to partake of the Covenant:

"Therefore, remember that formerly you who are Gentiles by birth and called 'uncircumcised' . . . . At that time you were

SUN PILLARS AND OTHER HIGH PLACES ARE OLD IMAGES THAT THE PAGANS INTERPRETED AS SEXUAL OBJECTS. THEY ARE EXPRESSLY FORBIDDEN BY YAHUAH, YET THE MASSES ACCEPT THEM READILY BECAUSE THEY ARE KEPT IN IGNORANCE BY THE ELITE, OR "ENLIGHTENED ONES", THE ADEPTS. THE OBELISK AND PYRAMID ARE AMONG THE OLDEST

separate from Mashiach, excluded from citizenship in Yisrael and foreigners to the covenants of promise, without hope and without יהוה in the world. But now, in Mashiach יהושע you who once were far away have been brought near through the blood of Mashiach. For He Himself is our peace, Who has made the two ONE, and has destroyed the barrier, the dividing wall of hostility, by abolishing in His flesh the law with its commandments and regulations." Eph. 2:11-15.

"Consequently, you are no longer foreigners and aliens, but FELLOW CITIZENS with יהוה's people, and members of יהוה's household, built on the foundation of the apostles and prophets, with Mashiach יהושע Himself as the chief cornerstone." - 2:19,20.

The "law with its commandments and regulations" referred to here are what the ceremonial law required for atonement and cleansing, they don't refer to what defines sin. Shaul cannot make laws, nor annul them. Not eating blood (Acts 15), or disregarding Shabbath (Heb. 4), or murder (Ex. 20) etc., are still "Commandments" in force. "Foreigners" are no longer foreigners if they observe the Torah, and can now call themselves Yisrael, if they are immersed in His Name and live in the Covenant. If they don't "engraft", they are outside the Covenant promises, and Shatan knows it!

"The way of peace they do not know . . ." YeshaYahu 59:8. ***"Truth has stumbled in the streets, honesty cannot enter. Truth is nowhere to be found, and whoever shuns evil becomes a prey."*** 59:14,15. The "Truth" and "way of peace" is the Torah, the Word. The invitation to the "feast" shown in the parables represents the Shabbats of יהוה. At Yesha Yahu 58:11-13, once again we see the Torah is what is called the "ancient ruins", and those who obey are like a well-watered garden (see also Ps. 1). ***"You will be called Repairer of Broken walls, Restorer of Streets with Dwellings ~ if you keep your feet from breaking the Sabbath, and from***

doing as you please on My Qodesh Day; if you call the Sabbath a delight, and 𐤉𐤄𐤅𐤄'***s Qodesh Day honorable."***

"I GAVE THEM MY SABBATHS"

"Also, I gave them My Sabbaths as a sign between us, so they would know that I 𐤉𐤄𐤅𐤄 ***made them qodesh."***

You may want to read all of Ezekiel chapter 20. We've learned that a mere man was responsible for instituting the change from the 7th day to the 1st day of each week, and the "Sun-day Sabbath" has been the "Christian Sabbath" ever since. Let's just take a brief overview of the Sabbath, and determine if there is one, and if so what "choice" we should make in observing it.

MASTER OF THE SABBATH

Please take this only as from a lover of the Commandment, not as any condemnation or personal criticism, bearing in mind, "He who answers before listening ~ it is to his folly and shame" (Pr. 18:13). I was once in denial and rebellion against Gentiles needing to follow the 4th Commandment, but I listened to all of what Scripture says, not men, or Constantine's establishment of "Sun-day" as the new Christian day of rest. Hebrews 4 has been "allegorized" to mean our "rest" in Mashiach, but really the whole section deals with the disobedient, and mentions the "Gospel". **The message of repentance is of no value to the lost**, and it says ***"He has spoken about the seventh day in these words: 'And on the seventh day Elohim rested from all His work'."*** At v.9: ***"There remains, then, a Sabbath-rest for the people of Elohim; for anyone who enters Elohim's rest also rests from his own work, JUST AS ELOHIM DID FROM HIS. Let us, therefore, make every effort to enter that rest, so that no one will fall by following their example of DISOBEDIENCE. For the Word of Elohim (Torah) is living, and active. Sharper than any double-edged sword, it penetrates even to dividing soul and spirit, joints and marrow; it judges the thoughts and attitudes of the heart . . ."*** With the New Covenant, we receive the Torah written on our hearts, and His "Word" is the Torah. If the Sabbath is for only Hebrews, not Gentiles, then why would Gentiles be punished for not observing the Feast of Tabernacles after Yahusha's return, cited at Zech. 14? Also, there is no difference now between a Hebrew and a Gentile, **as a follower of Mashiach**. The Replacement Theology has lulled us into thinking Gentiles (or the "Church") are now "Israel", but it is rather these wild olive tree branches **grafted into** the original olive tree, Israel (Rom. 11). This is far more than a "Pharisaical" issue. There is no "Covenant" in Scripture with "Christians", only Yisrael!

BINDING OURSELVES TO Yahuah

At Is. 66, in the Millennial Reign: ***"FROM ONE SABBATH TO ANOTHER, ALL MANKIND will come and bow down before Me, says Yahuah. And they will go out and look upon the DEAD BODIES of those who rebelled against Me".*** (Is 56): ***"Blessed is the man who does this, the man who holds it fast: who keeps the Sabbath without desecrating it . . . . "Let no foreigner who has bound himself to Yahuah say, 'Yahuah will surely exclude me from His people'. . . . .To the eunuchs who keep My Sabbaths, who choose what pleases me and hold fast to My Covenant ~ to them I will give within My Temple and its walls a memorial and a name BETTER THAN SONS AND DAUGHTERS . . . . AND FOREIGNERS WHO BIND THEMSELVES TO Yahuah, to serve Him, to LOVE THE NAME OF Yahuah and to worship Him, ALL WHO KEEP THE SABBATH WITHOUT DESECRATING IT, and HOLD FAST TO MY COVENANT, these I will bring to My holy mountain and give them joy in My house of prayer . . . . for My house of prayer will be called a house of prayer for ALL NATIONS."***

JERUSALEM COUNCIL CONCERNING GENTILES

After deciding that fleshly circumcision is not a requirement, the Gentiles who BEAR THE NAME are told to begin by abstaining from idolatry, sexual immorality, FOOD STRANGLED, AND BLOOD. ***"For Mosheh*** (the Torah) ***has been preached in every city from the earliest times, AND IS READ IN THE SYNAGOGUES EVERY SABBATH."*** The Nazarenes studied next to the other sects in the places where the Scrolls were read, until after the destruction of Yerushaliyim, then were shunned for having fled the city instead of defending it, as they were obeying what Rabbi Yahusha had warned them of. Many of the synagogue rulers were believers in the Mashiach! At Acts 1, Luke records ***"Then they returned to Yerushaliyim from the hill called the Mount of Olives, A SABBATH DAY'S WALK from the city."*** Even the "day of Pentecost", called Shabuoth (weeks), is an annual Sabbath ~ one of **seven**, and is the **memorial of the receiving of Torah at Sinai** (the Nazarenes received it in their hearts, circumcised by Mashiach on that day, fulfilling the prophecy at Yerme Yahu 31). Paul even states that we should "keep the feast", speaking of the **7 days of unleavened bread**, at 1 Cor. 5:8. "The Fast", or **Yom Kippur**, is referred to at Acts 27:9, because the weather was turning bad because of the lateness in the year. I completely understand the turmoil this causes in your mind; I remember it well. I endured it when I had to weigh all the evidence, but I received Him; and the Sabbath, and all His Commandments fill me with extreme joy. Will Yahuah punish you for resting on Sabbath, or is it really the "bad seed" (teachings) of ha Shatan that inoculates most people from repenting? It is only Israel, Yahuah's obedient Bride, who will enter the gates into the city. There is no gate named "the Church", or "Christianity" ~ only gates bearing the names of the 12 tribes of Israel. When Scripture says "Israel", it is not just speaking of the Yahudim — they are **one** of the tribes — Israel is all 12 tribes.

THE DRAGON RECOGNIZES SABBATH-KEEPERS BY THEIR OBEDIENCE

"Then the dragon was enraged at the woman (the Bride) and went off to make war against the rest of her offspring ~ those WHO OBEY ELOHIM'S COMMANDMENTS, and hold to the TESTIMONY OF YAHUSHA (which is: 'repent - for the Reign of Yahuah draws near'.)**."** The 4th Commandment tells us all to **remember the Sabbath**, and it's the 7th day of every week. As a regular observer of Sabbath, I stay home and rest, and study with my wife and children. Obedience is worship. Can we "obey Elohim's Commandments", and not have His Sign of the Covenant, His Sabbath? If Rabbi Yahusha is **"Master of the Sabbath"**, and it was made for man, will ignoring it bring us closer to Him in our walk? If the 4th Commandment is only for "Jews" to obey, then the Creator has 2 different sets of rules ~ or, an enemy has sown weeds among the wheat! The parables are "dark sayings" that only the Bride will understand, and Proverbs 9 even refers to the 7 annual appointments: ***"Wisdom*** (Torah) ***has built her house; she has hewn out its seven pillars."*** From Passover through Tabernacles and the Last Great Day, there are "7 pillars" or high Sabbaths. These outline the redemption plan of Yahuah's Bride. The parable about the "Great Banquet" (Luke 14:16-24) illustrates how many are just not interested in coming to the appointed observances of 𐤉𐤄𐤅𐤄.

As you can readily see, there is no "break" between what is meant by the "Sabbath" in the **T**a**N**a**K** and Brit Chadasha, as many would lead you to believe. If you'd really like to learn how this rift occurred, you can look up a man named **Marcion** in a good encyclopedia, or go to a library. He was a heretic, who taught that we need to completely disregard the "Old Testament". However all scholars realize that the New Covenant authors consistently used the "Old" as their foundation, and never taught the changes we see today. Gentiles must enter into the Covenant.

HOW TO BEGIN (and become an Israelite)

If you are not immersed, you are a Gentile. You may have a little knowledge already, but you should re-ground yourself by starting with Acts 15. Then do as it says, and study the writings of Mosheh, the Torah (Ten Commandments). Read all of Exodus 20, Lev. 19, Lev. 23, then Deut. 16, understanding that you are about to enter into a Covenant with your Creator, 𐤉𐤄𐤅𐤄. *When you know and understand* ***how you are to live***, you must be *immersed* in water as your '***circumcision***'. Your 'Husband' doesn't wish to dwell in the vessel of your body before you have washed, and this immersion signifies the death of your mind of the flesh, the washing away of your sins by ***your trust*** in Rabbi 𐤉𐤄𐤅𐤔𐤏's death which covers your sins against Torah, and the resurrection life of 𐤉𐤄𐤅𐤔𐤏, so you will receive His Spirit, and WANT to obey the Torah.

1. Pronounce your belief, "I believe Rabbi 𐤉𐤄𐤅𐤔𐤏 (Yahusha) of Natsarith is the Mashiach, and that He raised from the dead 3 days and 3 nights after His execution for my past sins."
2. "𐤉𐤄𐤅𐤔𐤏 *please deliver me."*
3. Going under the water, think of your mind of the flesh "dying", no longer controlling your actions against Torah. Your sins are left behind you, lifted from you, and you are now a "new creature". The old nature dies.
4. Coming up, you have committed to the Covenant: to obey 𐤉𐤄𐤅𐤔𐤏, hold to His Testimony, and you will show Him you love Him by observing the Torah. Having obeyed Him, you will now receive the promise of the New Covenant: **His Spirit**, which will write His Commandments on your heart and mind, **enabling you to love them and obey them**. *You are no longer Gentile.*

This is the way you give yourself to the Bridegroom. As a woman will bath after her period of uncleanness before contact with her husband, so we wash away our uncleanness (past sins), and ***COVENANT*** to obey our Husband. We are His virgin bride! The unrepentant and the very young cannot be immersed, because they have not been convicted of their sinfulness. Next, you are ready to receive "gifts", that which you are to use to serve the body. This is received by an elder laying hands upon you and reciting the priestly blessing (Num. 6:22-27). At Acts 9:17, Shaul had the hands of Ananias placed upon him <u>before</u> immersion. You can receive your "anointing" without an elder, but eventually you should submit to the laying on of the hands when you encounter an elder. The "power" comes from 𐤉𐤄𐤅𐤔𐤏, not the brother; the Ruach ha Qodesh is given to those who obey Him (Acts 5:32). As I said, the MYSTERY of the Kingdom that we all hope to be partakers of is revealed in <u>all the parables</u>. One of the most misunderstood parables speaks about how יהושע will "go away on a journey", and entrusts His property to His servants. At Mattit Yahu 25:14-46, the parable of the "talents", our Rabbi illustrates Himself as a man who went away for a long time, and returned to see what his servants had done with the various "talents" He had left them in charge of. According to their abilities, each servant was given 5, 2, or 1 talent each. The "talents" represent the number of Torah-observant people, and the objective was to produce more by the time the Master returned to "settle accounts". (It's not about "money", but PEOPLE). If we go through life without "investing" in others the Word of Life, but rather "bury" the "talent", we produce no growth in those around us, and we are as a dead branch ourselves.

TEN MINAS The "talents" are one illustration, and at Luke 19:11-27, a similar parable is given. Again, ***"A man of noble birth went to a distant country to have himself appointed king, and then to return."*** Before leaving, this man gave ten (the 10 virgins?) of his servants a mina each, and told them to put the "money" to work, until he returned. While he was away, the servants "invested" such that one gained 10 more, another 5; but one of them just wrapped up his mina and hid it. In other words, one gained 10 converts, another 5, and the other NONE. While he was away, the man heard that the "subjects" he had left (all the people of the Earth) proclaimed ***"We don't want this man to be OUR king."*** Upon his return, the new King of the Universe proclaimed, ***"But those enemies of mine who did not want me to be king over them ~ bring them here and kill them in front of me."*** That's exactly what will happen to the "weeds" when He returns as a roaring Lion. You had better get busy, my friend, because the servant who hid his "mina" lost his "mina", and was not found to be worthy of his Ruler any longer. If we are not spreading the "seed" (Torah, and the message of the Kingdom), then we have not understood that it is US, not the preachers, who must be actively engaged in reaching those around us. ***"Unless you repent, you too will all likewise perish."*** Luke 13:3. Why people will perish is clearly explained at 2Thess. 2. The return of our Sovereign יהושע ha Mashiach will not come until ***the rebellion*** occurs, and the ***man of lawlessness*** is revealed. The rebellion is the Nazarene sect, exposing the lie; the whole world is in the power of lawlessness, and religious merchants have taught lawlessness for centuries. We rebel against the lie, and the work of Shatan ***"displayed in all kinds of counterfeit miracles, signs and wonders, and in every sort of evil that deceives those who are perishing. They perish because they refused to love the Truth, and so be saved. For this reason, יהוה sends them a powerful delusion, so that they will believe the LIE, and so that all will be condemned who have not believed the Truth, but have delighted in lawlessness."*** The "lie" is clearly lawlessness, and it is everywhere taught that "legalism" is evil. How amazing, because this is the *strong delusion.* The "delusion" is taught by twisting Paul's writings, EVERYTIME! Peter warned us of those who use Paul's writings to support their error: ***"Just as our dear brother Paul also wrote to you with the wisdom that יהוה gave him; he writes the same way in all his letters, speaking in them of these matters. His letters contain some things that are hard to understand, which ignorant and unstable people DISTORT, as they do the other Writings, to their own destruction. Therefore, dear friends, since you already know this, BE ON YOUR GUARD, so that you may not be carried away by the error of lawless men, and fall from your secure position."*** ~ 2Pet. 3:15-17.

At Luke 8:11,12, the parable of the Sower, the Torah is sown by the Master of the harvest: ***"The seed is the Word of יהוה."*** The adversary, Shatan, steals the Word from people's hearts, so they will not believe and obey, and so be saved. Shatan's messengers are disguised, masquerading as messengers of righteousness. Be careful how you listen! We must produce a crop, by spreading the true seed, not the seed of weeds. Psalm 119:152 says, ***"Long ago, I learned from your statutes that you established them to last FOREVER."*** 119:160 says ***"All your words are TRUE; ALL your righteous LAWS ARE ETERNAL."*** With David, we who love the Torah say, ***"Streams of tears flow from my eyes, for your LAW is NOT obeyed."*** 119:136. He's not talking about the CEREMONIAL LAW, but the MORAL LAW. That's why Paul is not properly understood. Paul cannot make new rules, and certainly cannot annul any of the 10 Commandments that define sin.

History was "revised" over and over, making it appear that "Christianity" was "founded" by יהושע. But, in truth, He founded the sect of the Nazarenes, and these remained in the true faith. Acts 24:5 tells us that Paul was a "ringleader of the sect of the Natsarim", not a ringleader of the sect of the Christians. The Greek is a translation. Pursued by the "dragon", this "woman" (the Natsarim, citizens of Israel) had to endure many severe trials.

TURNING THE WORLD UPSIDE DOWN

(*How They Used To Get "Stoned" In The Old Days*)

THEY USED THE NAME ALOUD!

The Book of Acts (the book of "Action") records how the early students of 𐤉𐤄𐤅𐤔𐤏 "turned the world upside down". Put yourself in that life-setting. The **Name** of the Creator had been concealed from the common people for centuries, since the Babylonian Captivity. Learning this truth, everyone was **astounded**, and a natural curiosity swirled among everyone. When Peter stood up and addressed the crowds at Acts 2, he quoted Yah El 2 (Joel) and told them to be immersed into the Name. Today, just before the end of the "times of the Gentiles", the world is being turned upside down once again by the growing knowledge of the Name, which has been concealed for many centuries by the religious merchants. Like today, it was the **Name** of the Creator that caused the religious establishment to be turned on its head.

NAME OR NO-NAME? People are quick to label others with "handles". Christians in general are called by a Greek term, having no idea that the term was used by Pagans first, as worshippers of Serapis, or that it is cognate with "cretin" (see your dictionary). They hang their hat on one translated verse from the Scriptures (Acts 11:26), while scholars know they were called **Nazarenes**, as a sect within Judaism.

Many today are apprehensive of groups that use the Hebrew personal Name of the Creator, calling them "sacred name" groups. These who would criticize those who use the Hebrew Name should remember our Rabbi's prayer at John 17, where He said He had revealed the Name to them, and that they be kept as one by the power of the Father's Name. Now, I'm going to initiate a new "handle" ~ the "NO-NAMERS". The **no-namers** use traditional terms in place of the Name, as most prefaces of the Scriptures will acknowledge. The words "GOD" and "LORD" are used as traditional replacements for the Name, a regrettable situation considering John 17. In review, the Encyclopedia Americana has this to say about the word "GOD":

GOD (god, gawd) A common Teutonic word for personal object of religious worship, formerly applicable to superhuman beings of heathen myth; on conversion of Teutonic races to Christianity, term was applied to Supreme Being, and to Persons of Trinity."

Swell. So, what does this mean ~ are we calling on the Creator with a word originally used by Pagans, to avoid the "ethnic" Name for the Creator? Look up the word "BAAL" in Webster's. It is defined as "LORD". Belial is a form of BAAL, and is another term for Satan. What's going on?

The over-looked issue here is this: at the time our Savior came, Whose Name is Yahusha, the Name was concealed, and any who spoke it aloud could be stoned to death for saying it. He said He revealed it to those given to Him out of the world, and that we be kept as ONE (in unity) by it. Are we in unity? He criticized the Pharisees for withholding the "Key of Knowledge" (Luke 11:52), and what they withheld was the Name! Why did they constantly want to stone Yahusha? He kept saying the Name. At Luke 19:38, the crowds were crying out a verse from Psalm 118:26 which contained the Name, and the Pharisees told Yahusha to rebuke them ~ because they were using the Name. Why were the disciples called to stand before the Sanhedrin? The Name! Why was Stephen **stoned** (Acts 7)? When he said the Name, they screamed and put their hands over their ears, and killed him. Yahusha Himself was condemned because He spoke the Name before the Sanhedrin, which caused the High Priest to tear his clothes, saying, "He has spoken blasphemy!" Blasphemy only involves one thing: **the Name**. Why was Paul on his way to Damascus to arrest Nazarenes? To carry them back to the Sanhedrin to see if they would say the Name and be similarly condemned to death. Why were the Dead Sea Scrolls buried in the first place? Because worn-out scrolls were treated with respect and buried in jars instead of being profanely burned or discarded, because they had the Name written on them. The book of "Esther" isn't among them, because the Name is not written anywhere in the text. Even at Acts 2, Peter quoted Joel 2:32, emphasizing the importance of calling on the Name ~ and then to be immersed calling on it. No-namers insist it is of no importance, and don't use it in their immersions. Falsehood and futility is what the prophet Jeremiah says the Gentiles have inherited: ***"Yahuah . . . To you the nations will come from the ends of the Earth and say, 'our fathers have inherited nothing but falsehood, futility, and things of no profit' . . . This time I will make them know My power and My might; and they shall know that My Name is Yahuah."*** -16:19-21.

If you are afraid of being lonely, don't try to be right. -Jules Renard, writer (1864-1910)

At Romans 10:14, after quoting Joel 2:32, Paul asks, ***"How then shall they call upon Him in Whom they have not believed? And how shall they believe in Him Whom they have not HEARD?"*** They don't know, or call, on His Name. "***HALLELU-YAH*** " means *"praise Yah".* It's easily seen that monks and translators **sterilized** the Scriptures by removing the Name from the texts, especially when you look at Acts 7 and the stoning of Stephen, or even read your preface. Taken as a whole, the main controversy in the New Testament seems to be the Name issue, and the announcing of the Kingdom of Yahuah. Yahusha's own Name contains the Name. Revelation 7 and 14 connect together, because the "seal" in the foreheads (minds) of the 144,000 is this Name of the Father. Taking His Name "in vain" means to bring it to nothing, missing it, or wiping it out. The "Sinai Autograph" of the original Name Yahuah written by His own hand was in what is called palaeo-Hebrew. All the prophets wrote it in this script. The oral traditions forbade its utterance.

SHAUL HAD NATSARIM KILLED,
FOR PRONOUNCING THE NAME!

The Yahudim were hoping for the Mashiach to come, and Rabbi 𐤉𐤄𐤅𐤔𐤏 was not going around telling anyone He was ~ but rather kept that an inside secret. The only thing He did that caused the law teachers and priests to pick up stones to kill Him was what they called "blasphemy". It was against *their* law to say the Name of 𐤉𐤄𐤅𐤄 ~ and the penalty was death. This is not usually mentioned by the merchant preachers, because people would naturally start to search it out, and the "Key of knowledge" would be widespread. The Name of 𐤉𐤄𐤅𐤔𐤏 contains the Name of the Father, so even His Name was part of the problem for them. The name "Yeshua" means *salvation,* and was a rather common name at the time; however "Yahusha" means *Yah is our salvation*, and had the Name being clearly heard by all. (See "TALMUD" below).

Paul explains how he fought against those who were found in the synagogues that proclaimed 𐤉𐤄𐤅𐤔𐤏. At Acts 26:9-11, Paul explains:

"I truly thought with myself that I ought to do many things contrary to the Name of the Mashiach of Nazareth. And this I also did in Yerushalayim: and I both shut up many of the saints in prisons, having received authority from the chief priests, and WHEN THEY WERE PUT TO DEATH I GAVE MY VOTE AGAINST THEM. And punishing them constantly in the synagogues, I STROVE TO MAKE THEM BLASPHEME; and being exceedingly mad against them, I persecuted them even to foreign cities." They weren't being killed for any other reason than that they were going against the "law" of pronouncing the Name. After "Shaul" was knocked-down on his way to Damascus, and encountered the risen 𐤉𐤄𐤅𐤔𐤏, he began to pronounce the Name, and did what he had watched others die for! This is no small side-line issue, but is really central to what the entire Brit Chadasha reveals to us. After Shaul was immersed by Ananias, (who was himself very afraid at first when he learned he was to be visited by the infamous Shaul), he took the name of "Paulos". The name "Shaul" and his reputation was terrifying to the Nazarenes, and you can well understand why. For some time, Nazarenes were still afraid and distrustful of Paul: ***" . . . Is not this he that in Yerushalayim made havoc of them that called on this Name? And has he come here for the intention that he might bring them bound before the chief priests,"*** (Acts 9:15,16).

Yes, pronouncing the Name was a REALLY big deal. Paul was nabbed by the Yahudim of Achaia, and they wanted him dead so much that they rushed him to the Roman proconsul Gallio. Gallio, no doubt a Pagan, must have thought they were crazy when he heard the reason they were so murderously enraged, and he said:

"If indeed it was an act of injustice or reckless evil, O Yahudim, according to REASON I would bear with you; BUT if it be a question concerning a WORD, or NAMES, and that law which is among YOU, see you to it, for I will be no judge of THESE things." (Acts 18:14,15). Paul had to be locked up to protect him. He claims he was stoned on one occasion for pronouncing the Name. Men had sworn oaths to see Paul dead before they would eat again. Paul had to hide, and sneak out of the city in a basket. How many Christians really know why Paul was imprisoned? Now, you know. Believe it or not, there is quite a bit of "shunning" against those of us who use the Name, even among Messianics who observe the appointed times. Paul's life, and many other Nazarenes' lives were taken for simply pronouncing the Name, and yet believers today shun and demonize those of us who seem to be making a "big deal" out of it. We can't help ourselves, the Name burns inside us. We would die for it too. If we are misguided, then those who have died over the Name have done so needlessly, including Paul and all the early Nazarene followers. 𐤉𐤄𐤅𐤔𐤏 revealed the Name to them, and He has done so to us as well. There are always 2 sides to most issues, but since the Name is the strong tower, that's the safer bet to go with. The Name turned the world upside down once, and here in the days of the final message, it is doing it again.

The Early Church Fathers

(Excerpts from: A History of AntiSemitism)

["For almost a century, the early believers in Yeshua the Messiah were culturally and ethnically the same as, and worshipped alongside, mainstream Judaism. The first believers in Messiah Yeshua were Jews. The Torah was of great importance to them and they kept its laws, keeping the Sabbath and performing circumcision. They did not follow 'another religion', but remained within the framework of Judaism. This Messianic movement spread largely among Jews to begin with, and for some time it remained as a **sect** within Judaism, mostly known as the sect of the Nazarenes (Acts 24:5). Thousands of Gentile 'converts' and 'God Fearers' joined themselves to the Nazarene sect. It is important to say something about the Nazarenes, as documentation of their existence and beliefs gives us much insight on how the early believers in Messiah thought and lived. The fourth century 'Church Father', Jerome, described the Nazarenes as *"those who accept Messiah in such a way that they do not cease to observe the Old Law"* (Jerome; On. Is. 8:14). Yet another fourth century Church Father, Epiphanius, gave a more detailed description of them: "*We shall now especially consider heretics who.. call themselves Nazarenes; they are mainly Jews and nothing else. They make use not only of the New Testament, but they also use in a way the Old Testament of the Jews; for they do not forbid the books of the Law, the Prophets, and the Writings... so that they are approved of by the Jews, from whom the Nazarenes do not differ in anything, and they profess all the dogmas pertaining to the prescriptions of the Law and to the customs of the Jews, except they believe in Messiah... They preach that there is but one God, and His Son Yeshua the Messiah. But they are very learned in the Hebrew language; for they, like the Jews, read the whole Law, then the Prophets...They differ from the Jews because they believe in Messiah, and from the Christians in that they are to this day bound to the Jewish rites, such as circumcision, the Sabbath, and other ceremonies. They have the Good news according to Matthew in its entirety in Hebrew. For it is clear that they still preserve this, in the Hebrew alphabet, as it was originally written*". (Epiphanius; Panarion 29; translated from the Greek). There is evidence that the Nazarene Sect continued to exist until at least the 13th century. The Catholic writings of Bonacursus entitled 'Against the Heretics', refers to the Nazarenes, who were also called 'Pasagini'. Bonacursus says: *"Let those who are not yet acquainted with them, please note how perverse their belief and doctrine are. First, they teach that we should obey the Law of Moses according to the letter - the Sabbath, and circumcision, and the legal precepts still being in force. Furthermore, to increase their error, they condemn and reject all the Church Fathers, and the whole Roman Church."*]

(Most spell the Name "Yeshua", which is Hebrew for "help", however "Yahusha" means "Yah is our Deliverer").

You will notice this quote states that the Nazarenes practiced "circumcision". Some may have; not understanding Acts 15, and other writings stating circumcision of the flesh is nothing. But, the Natsarim rejected Rome's change of the 7th day Shabbat to Sun-Day. The 4th Commandment actually **states** that the reason we are to keep the 7th day set-apart is because 𐤉𐤄𐤅𐤄 created the skies and Earth in 6 days, and He rested on the 7th. Thus, we honor Him as Creator by resting as He did (Heb. 4). There is no peace for the wicked. ***"But the wicked are like the tossing sea, which cannot rest"*** Yesha Yahu 57:20. Epiphanius also claims that the writings of "Matthew" were originally written in Hebrew.

Epiphanius, Bonacursus, Jerome, and later records up to the 13th century speak of these "Nazarenes", who were constantly castigated and repelled by the "new" revisionary doctrines, replacement theology, and supersessionism of the Universal Roman State religion. The gates of the grave have not prevailed. Benjamin Franklin wrote, *"History is the record of the winners."* History is the written record of events; the struggles people recorded through their eyes. Rarely do we read about history from the point of view of the losers, or the conquered. The "father of history", Herodotus, was objective in his report, but his "bias" still comes through. The Nazarenes almost vanished from recorded history, since they had to flee to the mountains to survive. Their outposts were discovered at times, forcing them to stay on the move. Some of them influenced the peoples around them, giving rise to little groups like the Anabaptists and Waldenses, who were persecuted by the Roman religion. Anyone who was not "Catholic" yet trusted in Rabbi 𐤉𐤄𐤅𐤔𐤏 was termed a "heretic", and exterminated, being a threat to the teachings of Catholicism. So, naturally Jerome, Bonacursus, and Epiphanius would call them "heretics". Now, we Nazarene Yisraelites are on the internet! The first settlers to America came to flee religious persecution. In early America, there were civil laws enacted which prohibited the celebration of "Christmas", because they knew it to be a Pagan festival counterfeited as a "holy" day (holiday). George Washington crossed the Delaware to attack the British on Christmas Day. George knew that because the

British celebrated on Christmas, they would be drunken and unprepared to defend themselves. But, as history will show, George was not a nice guy. When George was 25, he caused the French and Indian war by killing the French Ambassador. Then, George started *another* war with his own King over taxes on tea; taxes intended to help pay for the previous war! Our "history" is only written from the point of view of the winner. George was a Mason, and had his "apron" of righteousness to cling to. I'm not "judging" George, but these facts are easily researched for all to see. What will judge George? It will be the Living Word.

THE LIVING WORD

At Hebrews chapter 4, it is made very clear that those whom 𐤉𐤄𐤅𐤄 is angry with *will never enter His rest.* "THE WORD" of 𐤉𐤄𐤅𐤄 is His Torah, the instructions for how His wife/bride is to live. Those who hear THE WORD, yet do not profit from hearing it, are the ones who are not steadfast, but **disobedient**. The Yisraelites disobeyed in the wilderness, and wandered for 40 years until their bodies fell dead. ***"For who provoked Him when they had heard? Indeed, not all those who came out of Egypt with Mosheh? And with whom was He angry for 40 years? Was it not with those who sinned, whose bodies fell in the wilderness? And to whom did He swear that they should not enter His rest, but to those who were disobedient?"*** Heb. 3:16-18.

These "disobedient" did not ***believe***, therefore they did not ***obey***. Billions today "believe", but they believe the wrong thing; THE LIE. The enemy has sown "weeds" among the wheat, which are false teachings. He did it long ago. He said Shabbat was now "Sun-Day", and we can ignore the appointed times, because they are just "Old Testament Jewish Stuff". Shatan also taught the world that the Creator was so angry with Yisrael, that His New Covenant was with a new wife; THE GENTILES. This is called "Replacement Theology", and it is a lie.

The "sign" of 𐤉𐤄𐤅𐤄's Everlasting Covenant is His "rest": (Go read all of Exodus 31:12-18)

". . . . So the sons of Yisrael shall observe the Sabbath, to celebrate the Sabbath throughout their generations, as a perpetual covenant. It is a SIGN between Me and the sons of Israel FOREVER; for in six days 𐤉𐤄𐤅𐤄 made Shamayim and Eretz, but on the seventh day He ceased from labor, and was refreshed."

"And also I gave them My Sabbaths to be a SIGN between Me and them, that they might know that I am 𐤉𐤄𐤅𐤄 who sanctifies them." Ezek. 20:12.

"There remains therefore a Sabbath rest for the people of 𐤉𐤄𐤅𐤄. For the one who has entered His rest has himself also rested from his works, as 𐤉𐤄𐤅𐤄 did from His."

"Let us therefore be diligent to enter that rest, lest anyone fall through following the same example of disobedience."

"For THE WORD of 𐤉𐤄𐤅𐤄 is LIVING and active, and sharper than any two-edged sword, and piercing as far as the division of soul and spirit, of both joints and marrow, and ABLE TO JUDGE THE THOUGHTS AND INTENTIONS OF THE HEART." Heb. 4:9-12.

This "WORD" that is "living and active" is the Torah; it "judges" the thoughts and intentions of our hearts, and there is no way to hide how we feel about it from 𐤉𐤄𐤅𐤄. The Torah is ALIVE, because it came to life and walked this Earth as a man. It is now His Spirit living in His bride, and He has circumcised our hearts with this "LIVING WORD", enabling us to LOVE His Covenant Law. If we sin, it is not our spirits in agreement, but our flesh at war with our spirits.

PROTESTANT CONFESSIONS

This is from a tract published by the Bible Sabbath Assoc., 3316 Alberta Dr., Gillette,WY 82718, which is called *ROMAN CATHOLIC AND PROTESTANT CONFESSIONS ABOUT SUNDAY*, part 2, which I ran across re-printed by the *PETAH TIKVAH* (address in Resources section in the back of this book).

Protestant theologians and preachers from a wide spectrum of denominations have been quite candid in ADMITTING that there is no Biblical authority for observing Sunday as a Sabbath:

ANGLICAN / EPISCOPAL

Isaac Williams, *Plain Sermons on the Catechism,* vol. 1, pp. 334, 336:

"And where are we told in the Scriptures that we are to keep the first day at all? We are commanded to keep the seventh; but we are nowhere commanded to keep the first day . . . The reason we keep the first day of the week holy instead of the seventh is for the same reason that we observe many other things, not because the Bible, but because the church has enjoined it."

T. Enright, C.S.S.R., in a lecture at Hartford, Kansas, Feb. 18, 1884:

"I have repeatedly offered $1000 to anyone who can prove to me from the Bible alone that I am bound to keep Sunday holy. There is no such law in the Bible. It is a law of the Holy Catholic Church alone. The Bible says, 'Remember the Sabbath day to keep it holy'. The Catholic Church says: 'NO. By my divine power I abolish the Sabbath day, and command you to keep holy the first day of the week'. And lo! The entire civilized world bows down in a reverent obedience to the command of the holy Catholic Church."

Canon Eyton, *The Ten Commandments,* pp. 52, 63, 65:

"There is no word, no hint, in the New Testament about abstaining from work on Sunday . . . Into the rest of Sunday no divine law enters . . . The observance of Ash Wednesday or Lent stands exactly on the same footing as the observance of Sunday."

Bishop Seymour, *Why We Keep Sunday:*

"We have made the change from the seventh day to the first day, from Saturday to Sunday, on the authority of the one holy Catholic Church."

Dr. Edward T. Hiscox, a paper read before the New York ministers' conference, Nov. 13, 1893, reported in *New York Examiner,* Nov. 16, 1893:

"There was and is a commandment to keep holy the Sabbath day, but that Sabbath day was not Sunday. It will be said, however, and with some show of triumph, that the Sabbath was transferred from the seventh to the first day of the week. Where can the record of such a transaction be found? Not in the New Testament—absolutely not. To me it seems unaccountable that Jesus, during three years' intercourse with His disciples, often conversing with them upon the Sabbath question . . . Never alluded to any transference of the day; also, that during forty days of His resurrection life, no such thing was intimated. Of course, I quite well know that Sunday did come into use in early Christian history. . . But what a pity it comes branded with the mark of Paganism, and christened with the name of the sun god, adopted and sanctioned by the papal apostasy, and bequeathed as a sacred legacy to Protestantism!"

William Owen Carver, *The Lord's Day In Our Day:*
"There was never any formal or authoritative change from the Jewish seventh-day Sabbath to the Christian first-day observance."

Dr. R.W. Dale, *The Ten Commandments* (New York: Eaton & Mains), p. 127-129:
"It is quite clear that however rigidly or devotedly we may spend Sunday, we are not keeping the Sabbath . . . The Sabbath was founded on a specific Divine command. We can plead no such command for the obligation to observe Sunday . . . There is not a single sentence in the New Testament to suggest that we incur any penalty by violating the supposed sanctity of Sunday."

Timothy Dwight, *Theology; Explained and Defended* (1823), Ser. 107, vol. 3, p. 258:
The Christian Sabbath [Sunday] is not in the Scriptures, and was not by the primitive Church called the Sabbath."

DISCIPLES OF CHRIST

Alexander Campbell, *The Christian Baptist,* Feb. 2, 1824, vol. 1, no. 7, p. 164:
"'But', say some, 'it was changed from the seventh to the first day'. Where? When? And by whom? No man can tell. NO; it never was changed, nor could it be, unless creation was to be gone through again; for the reason assigned must be changed before the observance, or respect to the reason, can be changed! It is all old wives' fables to talk of the change of the Sabbath from the seventh to the first day. If it be changed, it was that august personage changed it who changes times and laws EX OFFICIO– I think his name is DOCTOR ANTI-CHRIST."

***First Day Observance,* pp. 17, 19:**
"The first day of the week is commonly called the Sabbath. This is a mistake. The Sabbath of the Bible was the day just proceeding the first day of the week. The first day of the week is never called the Sabbath anywhere in the entire Scriptures. It is also an error to talk about the change of the Sabbath from Saturday to Sunday. There is not in any place in the Bible any intimation of such a change."

LUTHERAN

***The Sunday Problem,* a study book of the United Lutheran Church (1923), p. 36:**
"We have seen how gradually the impression of the Jewish Sabbath faded from the mind of the Christian Church, and how completely the newer thought underlying the observance of the first day took possession of the church. We have seen that the Christians of the first three centuries never confused one with the other, but for a time celebrated both."

***Augsburg Confession of Faith.,* art. 28; written by Melanchthon, approved by Martin Luther, 1530; as published in *The Book of Concord of the Evangelical Lutheran Church,* Henry Jacobs, ed. (1911), p. 63:**
"They [Roman Catholics] refer to the Sabbath Day, as having been changed into the Lord's Day, contrary to the Decalogue, as it seems. Neither is there any example whereof they make more than concerning the changing of the Sabbath Day. Great, say they, is the power of the Church, since it has dispensed with one of the Ten Commandments!"

Dr. Augustus Neander, *The History of the Christian Religion and Church,* Henry John Rose, tr. (1843), p. 186:
"The festival of Sunday, like all other festivals, was always only a human ordinance, and it was far from the intentions of the apostles to establish a Divine Command in this respect, far from them, and from the early apostolic church, to transfer the laws of the Sabbath to Sunday."

John Theodore Mueller, *Sabbath or Sunday:*
"But they err in teaching that Sunday has taken the place of the Old Testament Sabbath and therefore must be kept as the seventh day had to be kept by the children of Israel . . . These churches err in their teaching, for Scripture has in no way ordained the first day of the week in place of the Sabbath. There is simply no law in the New Testament to that effect."

METHODIST

John Wesley, *The Works of the Rev. John Wesley, A.M.,* John Emory, ed. (New York: Eaton & Mains), Sermon 25, vol. 1, p. 221:
"But, the Moral Law contained in the Ten Commandments, and enforced by the prophets, he [Christ] did not take away. It was not the design of His coming to revoke any part of this. This is a law which never can be broken . . . Every part of this law must remain in force upon all mankind, and in all ages; as not depending either on time or place, or any other circumstances liable to change, but on the nature of God and the nature of man, and their unchangeable relation to each other."

DWIGHT L. MOODY

D.L. Moody, *Weighed and Wanting,* pp. 7, 48:
"The Sabbath was binding in Eden, and it has been in force ever since. This fourth commandment begins with the word 'remember', showing that the Sabbath already existed when God wrote the law on the tables of stone at Sinai. How can men claim that this one commandment has been done away with when they will admit that the other nine are still binding?"

PRESBYTERIAN

T.C. Blake, D.D., *Theology Condensed,* pp. 474:
"The Sabbath is a part of the Decalogue-the Ten Commandments. This alone forever settles the question as to the perpetuity of the institution. Until, therefore, it can be shown that the whole Moral Law has been repealed, the Sabbath will stand . . . The teaching of Christ confirms the perpetuity of the Sabbath."

What happened? By denying the "roots" of the faith, the engrafted Gentile assembly gradually became so anti-Torah, that there was no connection with 𐤉𐤄𐤅𐤄, and they became an instrument of death. When a few "reformers" began to crawl away from it, they were pursued to their death. The Christian assembly turned to fables and mythology:

"Preach the WORD; be ready in season and out of season. Reprove, rebuke, and exhort with great patience and instruction. For the time will come when they will not endure sound doctrine, but after their own lusts shall

they heap to themselves teachers to tickle their ears, and they shall turn away their ears from the Truth, and shall be turned aside to myths." 2Tim. 4:2,3. The "Word" is the Torah, and the "in season" - "out of season" refers to the annual appointed times like Passover, Shabuoth, and Sukkot (Tabernacles). False security is fostered in order to fleece the flock, and MANY will utter these words from Matt. 7:22,23:

"Many will say to Me in that day, 'Lord, Lord, have we not prophesied in your Name, and in Your Name done many wonderful works?' And then I will profess to them, 'I never knew you. Depart from Me, you who practice lawlessness.'"

What are we to do? ***"Come out of her, My people, so that you will not share in her sins, so that you will not receive any of her plagues; for her sins are piled up to Shamayim, and 𐤉𐤄𐤅𐤄 has remembered her crimes.*** Rev. 18:4. The "merchants" will mourn because no one will "buy" their lies anymore. Babylon, soon your doom will come. Armed with this knowledge, you can study on your own, and put the showmen preachers out of business by telling others who will listen. Support the orphans and widows, and especially your own family members in need (such as elderly parents). ***"The woman you saw is the great city that rules over the kings of the Earth."*** Rev. 17:18. The calendar and customs of the whole Earth are following the beast, seated in the ancient city of Rome. When your eyes are opened to this fact, you will be absolutely astonished. If you wonder what the "image" of the beast is, all you have to do is objectively open your eyes, to watch what it is that billions of people alive today bow down to. This is covered under **"QUESTIONS & ANSWERS"**, in the next section.

Something very curious happened when the detachment of soldiers came to arrest 𐤉𐤄𐤅𐤔𐤏 in the olive grove at Yahuchanon (John) 18:5,6:

"When 𐤉𐤄𐤅𐤔𐤏 said, 'I AM HE', they drew back and FELL TO THE GROUND." Many believe He spoke the <u>Name</u> of the Creator, and the power of the Name repelled them with a physical force. At 17:11,12, He prayed: ***"Qodesh Abba, protect them by the power of Your Name ~ the Name You gave Me ~ so that they may be one as We are one. While I was with them, I protected them and kept them safe by that Name you gave Me."*** He told us: ***"I tell you, you will not see Me again until you say, 'blessed is He who comes in the Name of 𐤉𐤄𐤅𐤄."*** ~ Luke 13:35. At Mattit Yahu 24:20, He said ***"Pray that your flight will not take place in winter or on <u>the Sabbath</u>."*** Very few, if any, Christians are praying for this, but Nazarenes are.

When all the changes that have been made are corrected, Scripture begins to make much more sense. It takes a great deal of dedication to the Truth for a person to step out from their family and preacher even after learning about the false deceptions. Most everyone who does will have no one around them at first who shares a love for the Name and the Torah. In fact, they will be bombarded with twisted quotes from Paul's writings that seem to annul the Sabbath or other appointed times. This situation is described in the Parable of the Sower at Luke 8, where the "seed" is stolen away, choked by weeds, or has no root. But, they must bear in mind the words of 2 Pet. 3:15-18, where it states that <u>Paul's writings</u> are twisted by unstable and ignorant men, leading to their destruction. We are each placed where we are as "salt"; so we are not intended to be "bunched up", but rather must reach the few around us who **will** listen to the Truth.

QUESTION from E-MAIL: You say in your book

EAGLES & CROSSES REPRESENTED THE SUN TO ANCIENT PAGANS — THIS MAKES THEM SYNONYMOUS. JUST STUDY THE DEVOTION IN THE FACE OF THE GENTLEMAN IN THE PICTURE AT LEFT. HE WOULD LIKE TO KNOW THE TRUTH, BUT IT WASN'T HANDED TO HIM LIKE IT WAS TO YOU. THERE ARE MANY OTHERS JUST LIKE HIM ALL AROUND EACH OF US. (THAT'S NOT A CHRISTIAN POW-WOW STICK JUST BECAUSE IT INVOLVES A CRUX).

Questions & Answers

ALWAYS LOOK TO SCRIPTURE, NOT TRADITION

that we should not give our tithe to help support our leaders (Rabbi). Well if that is their full-time job (teaching Yeshiva, leading Shabbat services, traveling, then how should they be supported? Furthermore we meet in a building that we are renting and somebody has to pay for the electric bill! Yes, we could meet in a house, but there are more than 500 of us. What's your view on this? We put our tithe in the box every week. I'm not sure how every penny is spent. Our leader says it's also from the Torah (I don't remember where) to publicize who pays their tithe and when each year. They print out a list with everyone's name on it declaring who gave their tithe and how often. What do you think about that? - [from e-mail]

ANSWER: ~ What your e-mail described was not a "tithe", but a social decision, which is fine, but it's not the purpose of the commanded tithe. The electric bill, and rent to house 500 people, are costs to run a school or club, and the payment being made is more like tuition, or club dues. The elders who teach are worthy of part of the tithe, in fact, a "double portion" (1 Tim. 5:17) of the meal fed to support the poor, widows, and fatherless children. Actually, no where in Scripture did any apostle take the whole tithe (10th part, ma'aser) for himself, to support him and his family! Paul said he supported not only himself with his own hands, but those who traveled with him. Sure, an elder is able to eat from his labors, but eat only, not pay mortgages, and personal support above and beyond staying with those he is teaching. The record at Acts 20:17-35 describes how Paul pleaded with the elders at Ephesus, which you should read very carefully, because it describes the situation we see today, which Paul wept over. Note carefully verses 20:32-35. He was speaking to the elders. Generosity to the poor gets Yahuah's attention (Acts 10:4). But, one should first see to the support of their own family in need, such as parents, or close relatives, rather than have them be a burden on the assembly of saints (1 Tim. 5:3-11). Here, there was a "list" mentioned (5:11) that one had to be on to receive support. I would emphasize 1 Tim 5:16, which says: "If any woman who is a believer has widows in her family, she should help them, AND NOT LET THE ASSEMBLY BE BURDENED WITH THEM, SO THAT THE ASSEMBLY CAN HELP THOSE WIDOWS WHO ARE REALLY IN NEED." We are all to progress in knowledge, and although we never become greater than the one who teaches us, we should become like them. I teach and work a job, like bro. Paul. We are to feed the sheep of Yahusha, not fleece them. If one man has a group of 100 people who regularly "tithe" 10% of their income to him, that one man gains an income that is TEN TIMES greater than that of any one of those who "tithe" to him. You see, this is the "business" of the merchants. They often attend ***seminaries****, which train them to be extremely successful at this, and they pay a percentage to their denomination. It mushrooms like an MLM, or pyramid organization. As long as one knows they are not paying a "tithe", but supports the costs of the group meeting, there's no problem. If there's 500 people, and each one gives 75 cents per week, that's $375 for a meeting place once a week. But, if 250 of them pay $20 each week, then that's $5000 a week. That's a big business, not the rental and electric bill. An elder is not to receive the whole tithe, but SHARE in eating with the poor among the assembly, if he doesn't work for a living like everyone else. I'm sure any man who is able to have the size income from an assembly as large as yours is, or even larger, would be very much against everything I teach on this subject. I could easily have 2000 or more attend a weekly meeting here in Louisville, and bilk them out of many thousands, but I have to teach the truth, and face my Rabbi one day. "In their greed, these teachers will exploit you with stories they have made up." ~ 2 Peter 2:3. In truth, we already pay quite a bit more than 10% to support the needy, just through Social Security, Medicaid, and various other public support mechanisms in place. There is no "tithe" to "spread the Gospel" in Scripture. Also, when we give, we are not to let our left hand know what our right hand is doing, so our Father who sees in secret will reward us. Our giving is to be "anonymous".

Reading all of Acts 4:32-35 shows that those in **need** received the proceeds, and there were no needy among the Nazarenes. "James" 1:27 says "*Religion that* 𐤄𐤅𐤄𐤉 our Father accepts as pure and faultless is this: to look after orphans and widows in their distress, and to keep oneself from being polluted by the world." 2Cor. 2:17 says "*Unlike so many, we do not peddle the Word of* 𐤄𐤅𐤄𐤉 *for profit*".

QUESTION: Christianity has always taught salvation is a free gift through faith, not works. Wasn't the "Law" done away with in the Messiah's atoning sacrifice, so we can now eat pigs, lobsters, blood,

*SEMINARY - MEANS "SEED PLOT"

and ignore Sabbaths?

ANSWER: What 𐤉𐤄𐤅𐤔𐤏's death accomplished was bringing an end to the *ceremonial law*, which required the shedding of blood for the forgiveness of sin. Our faith is in His atoning blood ~ we're covered! Animal sacrifices were not a permanent atonement, as the precious blood of 𐤉𐤄𐤅𐤔𐤏 is. Nor could animal blood change the inner man. Our "faith" is in 𐤉𐤄𐤅𐤔𐤏's shed blood covering our past sins, which is what all the animal sacrifices **pointed to**. Our life is in His resurrection, and His Spirit comes into us to dwell, circumcising our hearts with His MORAL Law. Allowing Him to write His Covenant Moral Law on our hearts is the New Covenant, promised at Yerme Yahu 31:31-34, and Heb. 8:10. This is commemorated each year at Shabuoth, called "Pentecost" (meaning *count* fifty). This is the 50th day after the Shabbat following Passover. This was when Yisrael was at Sinai in Midian, receiving the Torah Covenant, and took the marriage vows "I do". It is very fitting that the Spirit of 𐤉𐤄𐤅𐤔𐤏 came into the 120 Nazarenes on this day!

The model prayer, called "The Our Father", asks for 𐤉𐤄𐤅𐤄's "will" to be done on Earth, and His Kingdom to come. His "will" is His Covenant Laws, the Torah, or 10 Commandments (the marriage covenant). The eating of blood is even prohibited (Noahide law) at Acts 15:19-21, and it goes on to mention Shabbat, when Gentiles went to synagogue to learn more Torah. The "Sabbath" was changed to Sun-day by Constantine, in his attempt to "universalize" his Empire. At Mark 7, the text is twisted backwards with the ***addition*** of the words ("He thus declared all foods clean"). Our Mashiach was really saying that we sin because "evil" comes out of our hearts, it doesn't enter into our mouth from unwashed hands. Sin defiles us. The copyists added the words in *parenthesis*, to fit their lawless theology. (At Mark 7, the Pharisees were washing their hands because of a Kabbalistic superstition). Our "works" (actions) are evidence of our faith, as "James" says, "*You see that a person is justified by what he does, and not by faith alone.*" (2:24). Read all of James chapter 2. Of course "legalism" is always taught as a bad thing, but only Shatan would teach people **not** to obey ~ remember the deception of Adam's wife, Chuwah. No Scripture condemns anyone for obedience, but rather all Scripture teaches that we must obey.

"For not the hearers of the Law are righteous in the sight of Elohim, but the ***doers*** *of the Law shall be declared right."* (Rom. 2:13). The Spirit is only given to those who obey (Acts 5:32). Of course this will get you labeled as a "cult", but that's OK.

QUESTION: What is sin?

ANSWER: *"Everyone who sins breaks the Law; in fact, sin is Lawlessness".* (1 Yahuchanon 3:4). (The Gentilized name for Yahuchanon is "John".) Another way to translate the verse is *"Everyone practicing sin also practices Torahlessness; and sin is Torahlessness."* Paul answers it also: *"Is the Law sin? Let it not be! However, I did not know sin, except through the Law."* Rom. 7:7. Rabbi 𐤉𐤄𐤅𐤔𐤏 Himself said: *"Whoever then, breaks one of the least of these Commands, and teaches men so, shall be called least in the reign of* 𐤉𐤄𐤅𐤄 (the heavens); *but* ***whoever does*** *and* ***teaches them****, he shall be called great in the reign of* 𐤉𐤄𐤅𐤄*".* Mt. 5:19. The teachers of Torah today are thought to be cultists, or heretics, because great darkness has spread over the Earth, and the Torah is Light (see Prov. 6:23). The "Word" of 𐤉𐤄𐤅𐤄 is the Torah, His teachings: *"Your* ***Word*** *is a lamp to my feet, and a Light for my path."* Ps. 119:105. Psalm 1 begins, *"Blessed is the man who does not walk in the counsel of the wicked, or stand in the way of sinners, or sit in the seat of mockers; but his delight is in the Law* (Torah) *of* 𐤉𐤄𐤅𐤄*. On His Torah he meditates day and night."* Torah has a feminine ending in Hebrew, and is called "Wisdom" in Proverbs. This "woman", Wisdom, is supreme; therefore get wisdom. It will unlock the mystery of Revelation 13:18, and many other veiled secrets. Sin is lawlessness, living outside the Covenant. While the Commandments of the Creator were known and applied, the "vineyard" was green and fruitful because the "living waters" kept it alive. The symbol of the Torah is the Tree of Life, memorialized in the lampstand called a "menorah". Removing the "living waters", the vineyard has become dried up, and the dead branches will be burned in the fire. The "oil" that lights the lamps of the menorah is the Torah, the personality of 𐤉𐤄𐤅𐤄. The 10 virgins in the parable at Mt. 25:1 illustrate the difference between the "5 wise" and the "5 foolish". They all "slept", meaning they died. When the Bridegroom comes, He will call them out, but the lack of oil will impede the "5 foolish" virgins. Man-made rules have caused most to be deceived.

QUESTION: What is "The Gospel"?

ANSWER: Simply put, *"Repent, for the reign of* 𐤉𐤄𐤅𐤄 *draws near."* This "message", also called "testimony" is not popular, because it involves "repenting", or turning from sin. What we "turn back" to is the Covenant, or Torah of Yahuah. This is a "good report", and in Hebrew it is called "besorah". We must obey the Covenant, or Commands and teachings (Torah), but we cannot while in the "mind of the flesh". The carnal person "dies" at their immersion, calling on the Name of Yahusha, Who cleanses or washes the past Torah-breaking from them, and He comes into them, enabling them to "walk in the Spirit", because He changes their attitude about the Commands ~ they love the "Word" from that point. The writing of the Torah on our hearts is the New Covenant. That would be your next question.

QUESTION: Why are we here, and what is the meaning of life?

ANSWER: We were created to be companions to 𐤉𐤄𐤅𐤄, and rule the universe He created with Him. This really sounds like Mormonism, but it's not that at all. We will "inherit" the Earth, and 𐤉𐤄𐤅𐤔𐤏 will rule the universe from here. In the here-and-now, our purpose is to make "righteous offspring". That's not easy, believe me. Everything you see is passing away, and everything you can't see is eternal. We will become spatial beings, able to interact with the physical world as well as the unseen "space" or spirit energy, when the "children of 𐤉𐤄𐤅𐤄" are finally revealed. "Going to Heaven" is a Pagan myth; it's not an idea found in Scripture. (By the way, when you read the phrase *"Kingdom of Heaven"*, the word "heaven" was used to avoid saying the Name. It was probably changed by copyists.)

QUESTION: Where is sin?

ANSWER: Sin exists in the heart. Yirme Yahu 17:9 states: *"The heart is deceitful above all things and beyond cure. Who can understand it?"* The good news is at Ezek. 36:26, 27: "*I will give you a new heart, and put a new spirit in you; I will remove from you your heart of stone, and give you a heart of flesh. And I will put <u>My Spirit</u> in you and move you to follow My decrees and be careful to keep My Laws.*" When a person builds a thermonuclear bomb or landmine, a sin was committed. The idea itself was a sin if even the intention was there. 𐤉𐤄𐤅𐤄 doesn't make such things. Why? Because these things kill without selection! A gun or sword is not a sin to build, but their use can be. Automobiles and dynamite have killed, but they are not "sin". Sin is not outside us, it's in our hearts. 𐤉𐤄𐤅𐤔𐤏 told His students to arm themselves with a sword the night He was arrested, so a sword or gun is not the sin, but the use it is put to. The same logic applies to "images". If you bow down to a statue, picture, or object (like a national icon) for any reason, it is an abominable act, and the object also becomes an abomination, and must be destroyed. This happened to the serpent on the pole, Nehushtan, so it had to be destroyed (Num. 21:8,9, 2Kings 18:4). Also, food, money, gold, silver, or other valuables become defiled (in men's hearts) if they were offered to foreign elohim. But, the person must know this, or there is no problem. Paul explains this at 1Cor. 8. We know that foreign elohim are as nothing at all, but all people do not know this. The LOVE of money is the root of all kinds of evil, not the money itself.

QUESTION: Who is 𐤉𐤄𐤅𐤔𐤏?

ANSWER: He is the "Word of Life", and anyone who acknowledges the Son of 𐤉𐤄𐤅𐤄 has the Father. *"And this is the testimony: 𐤉𐤄𐤅𐤄 has given us eternal life, and this life is in His Son. He who has the Son has life; he who does not have the Son of 𐤉𐤄𐤅𐤄 does not have life."* (1John 5:11,12). The reason He appeared was to destroy the devil's work. *"We know we have come to know Him if we obey His Commands."* (1John 2:3). His indwelling <u>enables</u> us to do no sin. 𐤉𐤄𐤅𐤔𐤏 is the Mashiach, Who came in the flesh, *"Who, being in very nature 𐤉𐤄𐤅𐤄, did not consider equality with 𐤉𐤄𐤅𐤄 something to be grasped, but made Himself nothing, taking the very nature of a servant, being made in human likeness."* (Philippians 2:6,7). 𐤉𐤄𐤅𐤔𐤏 *"is the image of the invisible 𐤉𐤄𐤅𐤄, the firstborn over all creation. For by Him all things were created: things in Shamayim and on Earth, visible and invisible, whether thrones or powers or authorities; all things were created by Him and for Him . . . He is the beginning and firstborn from among the dead, so that in everything He might have the supremacy. For 𐤉𐤄𐤅𐤄 was pleased to have <u>all His fullness dwell in Him</u>, and through Him to reconcile to Himself all things on Earth or things in Shamayim, by making peace through His Blood, shed on the stake."* (Col. 1:15-20). He is the Spokesman Who made all the Covenants with Yisrael. He is the Ruach ha Qodesh, or "set-apart Spirit", the resurrection and the life. *"When he looks at Me, he sees the One Who sent Me."* (John 12:45). Philip said, *"'Rabbi, show us the Father, and that will be enough for us.' 𐤉𐤄𐤅𐤔𐤏 answered, 'Don't you know Me, Philip, even after I have been among you such a long time? Anyone who has seen Me has seen the Father.'"* (John 14:8). He is the living Word (Torah) ~ the personality of 𐤉𐤄𐤅𐤄, made flesh. The physical body of 𐤉𐤄𐤅𐤔𐤏 being the "Son", and the mind being 𐤉𐤄𐤅𐤄 is a better "grasp" for our limited abilities to comprehend. I guess that makes me a monotheistic modalist. But, so were all the prophets.

QUESTION: Is 𐤉𐤄𐤅𐤄 a "Trinity"?

ANSWER: The *Shema* (meaning "hear"):

"Hear, O Yisrael: 𐤉𐤄𐤅𐤄 our Elohim, 𐤉𐤄𐤅𐤄 is <u>one</u>! ***Love*** *𐤉𐤄𐤅𐤄 your Elohim with all your heart and with all your soul and with all your strength. These Commandments that I give you today are to be upon your hearts. Impress them on your children. Talk about them when you sit at home and when you walk along the road, when you lie down and when you get up. Tie them as symbols on your hands and bind them on your foreheads. Write them on the doorframes of your*

houses and on your gates." (Dt. 6:4-9). The words *"EhYah asher EhYah"* mean *"I will be Whom I will be".* Yahueh, Yahuah, Yahuwah, Yahweh, IAUE, IAOUE, etc., are transliterations from the Hebrew letters 𐤉𐤄𐤅𐤄 / יהוה. This Name means all three of the following: I was, I am, and I will be. *"'I am the alef and the tau', says the Sovereign* 𐤉𐤄𐤅𐤄, *'Who is, and Who was, and Who is to come, the Almighty (*Heb. *Shaddai*)'". (Rev. 1:8). The speaker was 𐤉𐤄𐤅𐤔𐤏, speaking to "John" (Yahuchanon) on the island of Patmos. Men who "interpret" the Writings with their own preconceived ideas can put a "spin" on them, making them seem to say things they don't say. They will admit that Mosheh and Daniel didn't think there was a "Trinity", but claim there was "progressive revelation" later on. If there were a "Trinity", then surely there would have been a great deal of explanation given in the Writings, because it goes against everything the Scriptures ever taught. You can't have monotheism, and trinitarianism! *"I am* 𐤉𐤄𐤅𐤄*; that is My Name!"* (Yesha Yahu 42:8). *"I am the First and I am the Last; apart from Me there is no Elohim."* (44:6). *"Is there any Elohim besides Me?"* (44:8). *"I am Elohim, and there is no other; I am Elohim, and there is none like Me."* (46:9). *"Before Me, no elohim was formed, nor will there be one after Me. I, even I, am* 𐤉𐤄𐤅𐤄*, and apart from Me there is no savior."* (43:11). He is infinite in power, space, and time. He is not a multiple personality, but can be anything He wills to be. Zechar Yah 12:10 reveals Who died at Golgotha: *"They will look upon Me, the One they have pierced, and they will mourn for Him as one mourns for an only child, and grieve bitterly for Him as one grieves for a first-born son."*

TRINITIES WORLD-WIDE Since Pagan religions were (and are) based on sex, the *father-mother-child* triad were common to them all. The four seasons were interpreted as manifesting a great cosmic cycle from impregnation (spring) to birth (winter, at the solstice). The power or control over the masses was in the hands of the very few who were "initiated" in the mysteries, and could tell when to plant, when to reap, and when to sacrifice their children to the deities. "deity" comes from the word "diva", and produces the words divine, deis, and day; it means ***to shine***.

Here are a few of the Trinities from the past:

Babylonian: Baal, **Semiramis**, **Tammuz**. (alt. Bel, Ishtar, Duzu). Ishtar was also known as Easter, Asherah, Astoreth, Astarte, Aphrodite, etc.

India: Brahma, **Shiva** (or Devaki), **Vishnu** (or Krishna). The family name of "Brahmans" may have stemmed from one of Abraham's descendants, due to the close spelling, so some say.

Egypt: Amon Ra, **Isis**, **Osiris** (or Horus). (Note: E.G.Y.P.T. is said to be short for *the Genie of Ptah.)* **I.H.S.** originally stood for *Isis, Horus, Seb.*

Greece: Zeus (or Apollo), **Demeter** (or Athena, Artemis), **Porsephene** (or Nike).

Rome (Roma)**: Deus** (form of Zeus, also known as *Zeus-Father,* or *Iu-piter, Jupiter*); **Venus** (or Astarte, Biblia, Charis); **Cupid** (or Bacchus, Nike).

Celtic: (also known as Druid, Wiccan, Norse, Gaelic); **Baal** (or Woden, Teutates, Heil); **Ceridwen** (or Freya, Frigga, Eostre); **Thor** (or Balder, Taranis, Dero). (alt. Esus, Taranis, Teutates).

Canaanite: (and Phoenician); **Baal** (or Moloch); **Asherah** (or Ishtar, Easter, Tanit); **Rompha**.

Chaldean: (and Zoroastrian); **Baal Mithras** (known as "wise-lord" *Ahura Mazda,* or *Ohrmazd*); **Astoreth**; **Haoma**.

Persian: Shamash, **Ishtar**, **Sin**.

Macedonian / Asian: Dagon (fish idol); **Cybele** (or Ceres); **Deoius** (or Janus).

Mithraic: (Chaldean fusion with Indo-Iranian); **Mithras** (or Marduk, called *Sol* by Romans); **Rashnu**; **Vohu Manah**.

Mandaean: Joshaman, **Abatar**, **Hibil Ziwa**.

Manichaean: Ohrmazd, **Maitreya** (New Age "Christ"); **Zurvan**.

In Japan, the Shinto religion has the phrase, ***"San Pao Fuh"***, which means *"one deity, three forms".* The Irish use one of their ancient Druid symbols, the trifolium clover leaf, as a symbol of their Celtic pride, but also as a secret symbol of their Trinity. The male and female symbols used in Biology are the secret Babylonian signs of Nimrod (Orion, Sagittarius ~ the mighty archer/hunter), and his wife/mother Semiramis (Great Mother, Magna Mater). All of these things and many more, were the "interpreted" mysteries of the Pagan religions, overseen by Wizards, sorcerers, warlocks, shamans, and priest-magicians who exploited the masses. (The "Magi" from Babylon were priests of Ahura-Mazda (Mithras), the sun deity. They arrived when the Mashiach was about two years old, and the gifts they bestowed enabled the family of Yosef, Miryam, and little Yahusha to live in Egypt until Herod died.)

Trinitarianism and Replacement Theology

Replacement theology, or *supersessionism, resulted from un-converted Pagans becoming part of the early assembly of believers.* The educated men were influencial and wealthy, and they swayed doctrines to conform to the mold of the Pagan mind, simply because it was the easiest thing to do. It also preserved their control over the masses. The Pagan mind was already skilled at "spiritualizing" everything through interpretation, and the early Church Fathers had all come from this mold. Augustine had been a Manichaean, which is a sun worshiper. Anti-Semitism (from the word *Shem*, a son of Noach) developed from the writing of the Church Fathers. By the 4th century, it had become conspicuous; the record bears witness to it in this letter of ***Faustus***, who wrote to Augustine:

"You have substituted your love feasts for the sacrifices of the Pagans; for their idols, your martyrs, whom you serve with the very same honors. You appease the shades of the dead with wine and feasts; you celebrate the solemn festivals of the Gentiles, their calends, and their solstices; and as to their ***manners****, those you have retained without any alteration. Nothing distinguishes you from the Pagans, except that you hold your assemblies apart from them."* The change-over to Paganism is right here on the record, witnessed by Faustus as it happened. Again during the 4th century, the learned ***M. Turretin*** wrote this into the record as he saw the changes occur:

"It was not so much the (Roman) *Empire that was brought over to the faith, as the faith that was brought over to the Empire; not the Pagans who were converted to Christianity, but Christianity that was converted to Paganism."*

In the year CE 439, the historian ***Socrates*** wrote:

"Although almost all assemblies throughout the world celebrate the sacred mysteries on the Sabbath of every week, yet the Christians of Alexandria and at Rome, on account of some ancient tradition, have ceased to do this."

In the year CE 440, the historian ***Sozomen*** wrote:

"The people of Constantinople and almost everywhere, assemble together on the Sabbath, as well as on the first day of the week."

The "love feasts" referred to by Faustus were the original commanded appointed times from Scripture, called ***Pesach, Shabuoth,*** and ***Sukkot*** (Passover, Pentecost, and Tabernacles, Lev. 23, Dt. 16). Today, those of us who observe these and the correct weekly Shabbaths are thought of as some kind of "cultists", or heretics. In reality, who are the real cultists and heretics? The APOSTASY is here, folks, and has been for a long, long time. They missed the big picture, and became overwhelmed by all the small Pagan details. They didn't want to be accused of substituting Pagan customs, so they "re-invented" them by revisionism over time.

Coming out of this Pagan background, it is no wonder Protestants carried out so many things from their "Mother", like Sun-day, altars, steeples, Easter, Christ-mass, trees and wreaths, the Trinity, and the fake name they use for the true Creator. It's also no wonder the "Jews" are so appalled by the Christian religion! Abandoning the Torah, and calling the Mashiach by a Greco-Roman Name might not be the best way to begin introducing the Savior to a Yahudi.

QUESTION: What about Paul's letters? Doesn't he clearly say that all days are special, and observing Sabbaths were "shadows"?

ANSWER: Paul's letters, especially Galatians, Romans, and Colossians have been used to "prove" certain things he was not saying at all. When Paul discusses the "Law", he is often speaking of the *Ceremonial Law* which dealt with *atonement*. When atonement for sin was made one time for all in Mashiach's death, the Ceremonial Law came to an end. The ***Moral Law***, which defines sin, will be in force for all eternity. Consider what Rabbi OWYƎƵ said at Mt. 5:17,18:

"Do not think that I came to destroy the Torah (Law) ***or the Nebi'im*** (Prophets). ***I did not come to destroy but to fulfill*** (fill full). ***For truly I say to you, till Shamayim and Eretz pass away, not one yod or tittle shall by any means pass from the Torah till all be done."***

The skies and Earth are still here, so the Moral Law is in force ~ every letter of it. Also, if you read Acts 6:13, and 7:53, the stoning of Stephen, there is concrete evidence that the "Law" is in force, AFTER the "crux", and the resurrection of Mashiach. Acts 1:12 states *"then they returned to Yerushaliyim, from the hill called the Mount of Olives, a Sabbath day's walk from the city."* This not only mentions a "Sabbath", but also mentions

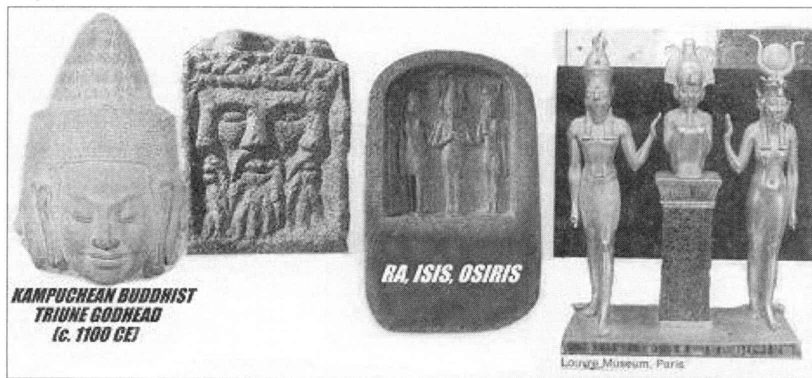

a maximum distance (1000 cubits) one can walk on a Shabbat. Even the day called "Pentecost" (Acts 2) is **Shabuoth**, the 50th day after the weekly Shabbat, following the weekly Shabbat after Passover, every year. See Lev. 23:15,16 to see that it is the day AFTER the seventh Shabbat. (To me, Shabuot/Pentecost/Feast of Weeks is always on the 1st day of the week, and there are some who disagree on this.) The "Fast" (Yom Kippur) is mentioned at Acts (27:9—the "Fast" being the 10th day of the 7th moon, in the autumn, when the storms at sea make traveling hazardous).

When Paul writes at Romans 14 about "fasting" and special days, he is addressing traditions of the Yahudim that arose, not Commandments. When the Temple was destroyed in 586 BCE, it became a custom to fast each year on the "9th of AV". The Temple was destroyed both times on this day! Ferdinand and Isabella's expulsion of the Yahudim from Spain occurred on this same day. At Col. 2:8, Paul says, *"See to it that no one makes you prey through philosophy* (commentary) *and empty deceit,* ***according to the traditions of men*** *. . ."* At Col. 2:21,22, Paul condemns ***asceticism*** (obsessive self-denial, austere living) because these are the commands and teachings of men.

Another place Paul's writings are used to negate Commandments is Col. 2:11-23. If you read the various *translations*, you will see huge differences in the texts, and even sentences that say the opposite of other translations. The text says, *"Let no one judge you . . .* ***FOR*** *the body of Mashiach."* The KJV shows the added word, "IS", to the phrase, *"but the body (is) of Christ."* At 2:16, it is being stressed that only the body of Mashiach should "judge" what you eat or drink, or regarding a religious festival, New Moon celebration, or a

Shabbat Day. Then at 2:17, he says these things are ***shadows*** of things to come. The NIV butchered the text, and men over the years have read into the text what they wanted to see.

QUESTION: Should we use crucifixes with, or without, the body of the Savior on them?

ANSWER: Many things thought, done, and said within the various denominations of Christendom can be traced to Constantine I. He set the pattern for Sun-day and Easter, and gave us the labarum emblem, a circle with a crux beneath it. This symbol, complete with the chi-rho letters in the circle, are on coins that date back to the 2nd century BCE. Tradition says that his aging mother, Helena, traveled to Yerushaliyim to find the actual wooden "cross" which the Savior hung on. It is claimed that she dug it up! Today, supposedly the pieces of this "discovery" are scattered all over the Earth. If brought together, there would be enough splinters to fill several railroad cars. Catholic "altars" contain 5 relics each, which the priest-craft kiss during their rituals. These relics are anything from human remains to clothing fragments of "saints", and often there is also a splinter of "cross wood" in the "altar". We have already seen that Pagans used the crux as their symbol of the sun, and the word in our translations came from the Latin Vulgate. Thanks to Constantine, the symbol of Christianity is the cross symbol. The 1965 *World Book Encyclopedia* vol. VII states:

"Cross forms were used as symbols, religious or otherwise, long before the Christian era in almost every part of the world . . . This symbol had a wide diffusion before the Christian era in Europe, Asia, and America, and is commonly thought to have been an emblem of the sun, or fire; and hence, of life."

The ancient symbol of life to the Egyptians was the ***crux ansata***, or ansate cross (ankh or anchor), and began to be embraced by Coptic Christians from their Pagan surroundings. The 1945 *Encyclopedia Americana* states,

"The symbol of the cross was used throughout the world since the later Stone Age; Greek pre-Christian crosses were the tau and swastika; ***the cross first became a symbol of Christianity during the reign of Constantine****."*

The swastika is four Greek *gamma* letters, and it is also seen prominently displayed on the entrances of Hindu and Buddhist temples, as an emblem of the *"wheel of Samsara"*. The 3rd Reich used it to identify itself with Christianity in Nordic caricature (runes), as all scholars agree. The use of halos, steeples, statues, candles, holy water, magic relics, spells, bells, amulets, necklaces, magic rings, scapulas, talismans, rosaries, and crosses enabled the designers of Christianity to appeal to masses of Pagans. The specimens pictured below illustrate pre-Christian religious

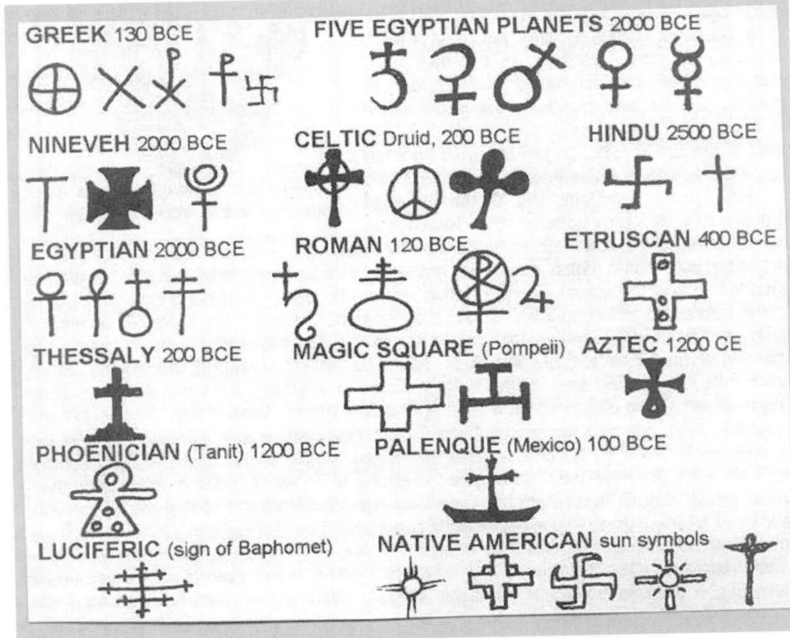

uses of the cross.

The 1945 *Encyclopedia Americana* continues:

"Prescott says that when the first Europeans arrived in Mexico, to their surprise, they found 'the cross, the sacred emblem of their own faith, raised as an object of worship in the temples of Anahuac'. The cross as a symbol dates back to an unknown antiquity. It was recognized in all countries throughout the world at all times. Before the present era the Buddhists, Brahmans and Druids utilized the device. In Eire Land, great monoliths beautifully carved into elaborate crosses are found everywhere. They date from the early Celtic period and they are freely decorated with Runic inscriptions. Constantine adopted the "labarum" as his standard. In CE 680 at the Council of Constantinople, the bleeding Lamb on the symbolic crucifix was forbidden, and the dying Savior's image on the cross was ordered to take its place, thus originating the present form of crucifix to be displayed to the public."

We find the word ***"TREE"*** used at 1Pet. 2:24:

"He Himself bore our sins in ***His body*** *on the tree, that we might die to sin and live to righteousness; for* <u>*by His wounds*</u> *you were healed."*

Here we see it was His ***body*** lifted up and wounded, not the object He hung on, that is the central point. Many teach that the palaeo-Hebrew letter "TAU" (see back of book—"X") was the "mark" placed on the servants spared at Ezekiel 9:4. Well, the Roman Catholics place an "ash crux" on their congregations' foreheads every "Ash Wednesday". If you reflect on the fact that the **mark** placed in the foreheads of the elect that protects them from harm at Rev. 7:3 is also called a "seal", the smoke and mirrors begin to clear up. There are 144,000 **sealed**. A seal is usually a Name, as seals in wax served as security checks. Again, at Rev. 14, this "seal" is identified as the <u>Name</u> of the Father in their foreheads: 𐤉𐤄𐤅𐤄, and the 144.000 are mentioned **again**. How likely is it that Yahuah would use a TAU (X) in one instance, and His Name in another?

Since the emblem of the **crux** has always been, and continues to be, a symbol to which the people of Earth <u>bow down</u> to, it is more likely that it, in what ever form it comes in, is the "**image of the beast**". Considering its source, this is the <u>only symbol</u> that makes sense, being a "blind-spot" of sorts for everyone. Add up what we know: it was used throughout all times and places by Pagans, and it was thrust upon the masses very early in Christianity's development. The adversary has used Christianity as an implement of death, and it's symbol is Pagan. 100 years ago, Alexander Hislop recorded more on this in his book, <u>*The Two Babylons*</u>. The fire worshippers raised a cross of candles in their temples, and this is done today by the Roman Catholics, in St. Peter's Cathedral. The Ku Klux Klan also use a fire cross, and when indoors, they use a cross of candles. The <u>emblem</u> of our Rabbi 𐤉𐤄𐤅𐤔𐤏 ~ the Light of the world, is a lampstand, called a MENORAH. So, I would think you would not want to go near a place displaying a crux, or wear one of any kind. Pagan priests wore them as talismans! Maybe "Dracula" is only afraid of it in the movies because it reminds him of the sun. Think about it. It's Shatan's symbol, and it's used in Black Masses! What agreement is there between light and darkness? When people are programmed with Pagan rituals and designs, and taught to ignore the Torah, Shatan effectively "disarms" them of the "sword of the Spirit", the thing that makes him flee. *"I have hidden Your WORD in my heart, that I might not sin against You."* Ps. 119:11. *"Have nothing to do with the fruitless deeds of darkness, but rather EXPOSE them."* Eph. 5:11. *"Put on the full armor of 𐤉𐤄𐤅𐤄, so that you can take your stand against the devil's schemes."* Eph. 6:10-17. The armor is the belt of Truth, breastplate of righteousness, shodding our feet in the message of peace, the shield of faith, helmet of salvation, and the sword of the Spirit, which is the Word of 𐤉𐤄𐤅𐤄. The Torah is the "seed" of the Kingdom.

THE MENORAH The actual word "menorah" was avoided by copyists, and we have inherited the word "lampstands". At Revelation 1:12, 𐤉𐤄𐤅𐤔𐤏 is clearly associated with the menorah, because He is standing in the <u>center</u> of "seven golden lampstands". At Revelation 1:20, the text says the menorah is the seven congregations, His **body**. At Revelation 2:5, He threatens to <u>remove</u> the menorah (Himself, the Light) from the congregation at Ephesus. So, the sign of the Son of man is a menorah, not a crux.

A menorah is essentially a **TREE**, with seven branches holding sources of light. It is the symbol of Yisrael, more so than any other. The 7 branches signify the 7 days of the week, the 7 annual appointed times, the 7 congregations mentioned at Rev. 1:20, and the 7 millennia. The 7th millennium will be a "rest", corresponding to the weekly "rest". In Yahudaism, the worship of Yah, the menorah is a symbol of the **TORAH**, and the Torah is called a "Tree of Life". At Proverbs 3:18, "Wisdom" (the Torah) is the "woman" we must embrace:

"She is a Tree of Life to those who take hold of her, and happy are all who hold her fast. Treasure My Commandments within you, make your ear attentive to Wisdom . . ."

The "Tree of Life" is mentioned in Genesis, Proverbs, and Revelation. Its leaves are to be used to heal the nations, and its fruit enable one to live forever. This is the Torah, which 𐤉𐤄𐤅𐤔𐤏 gave answer to the rich young man when asked how he might acquire eternal life. The Torah will go forth from Yerushaliyim, and it is also called *Living Waters*. When someone receives a LOVE for the Torah, they have received a precious gift, not a burden. Metaphorically, 𐤉𐤄𐤅𐤔𐤏 is the root, and we are the branches of the menorah, lighting the world with the Torah. The hatred of the Torah was put to death by 𐤉𐤄𐤅𐤔𐤏's execution, so that both the sons of the Covenant and engrafted Gentiles could be reconciled in one body to 𐤉𐤄𐤅𐤄. The Commandments weren't abolished, the hatred of them was. You will not be punished or lose the promise of eternal life by obeying the Torah. You WILL be unable to obey Torah without 𐤉𐤄𐤅𐤔𐤏, and for this you will be cast into the Lake of Fire. Shatan is NEVER going to tell you to obey the Torah, but he WILL tell you that you don't have to obey it. It's the wedding Covenant, which he is at war against. "Legalism" is not condemned in Scripture, lawlessness is. Shatan is in the business of religion. 𐤉𐤄𐤅𐤔𐤏 told us we cannot find the Kingdom by looking around for it, because it is within His people (Luke 17:20,21). In other words, you cannot go to it. It is within you, or it is not.

QUESTION: How long did Cain hate his brother?
ANSWER: As long as he was Abel.
QUESTION: What is greater than 𐤉𐤄𐤅𐤄, more evil than Shatan, the poor have it, the rich need it, and if you eat it, you will die?
ANSWER: (When asked this question, only 17% of Stanford University seniors knew the answer. Yet, 80% of kindergarten children had the answer right away.) To give you time to think, the answer will be given in the answer to the next question.
QUESTION: If a child is lost in the woods, and the rescue team wanted to hunt for him all night, what would you use to help?
ANSWER: **N**octurnal **o**perations, **t**hough **h**azardous, **i**nvolve **n**ight **g**oggles. (The answer you seek is the acrostic within the last sentence.)
QUESTION: Why is the penalty so severe for calling anyone a "fool" or an "idiot"?
ANSWER: The "lashon hara", or evil tongue, is any remark that puts down or belittles another person, and if said to their face, causes them to be harmed in a number of ways. If said behind their back, the harm is conveyed through others, ruining their reputation. The main insult, however, is directed toward their MAKER, and this puts the insulter in a very serious position. "*Set guard, O 𐤉𐤄𐤅𐤄, over my mouth; keep watch over the door of my lips*." ~ Ps. 141:3.
QUESTION: What is a cult?
ANSWER: One definition in Webster's Dictionary says it's *"a religion regarded as unorthodox or spurious* [and] *its body of adherents."* People who are not totally in line with "mainstream" Christianity in every way are often labeled a "cult". But, the word has only recently taken on a negative meaning, and it is defined as a "sect" also. Webster's also calls a cult *"a group of followers, sect."* Just reviewing the evidence provided in this book, it should be very apparent that the gross errors that came to overwhelm Christianity over the centuries makes it the most extravagant and over-blown "cult" one could possibly imagine. As I said, if you shoe-horned just a little bit more Paganism into it, it would pop. A considerable amount of "brain-washing" is certainly employed. But, without being persecuted, I would fear that I was not on the "narrow way". We must not seek the praise of men. Standing up for the Truth will cause men to shun us. The Light of Torah drives away those who will not repent. *"But everything exposed by the Light becomes visible, for it is Light that makes everything visible. This is why it is said; 'Wake up, O sleeper, rise from the dead, and Mashiach will shine on you.'"* ~ Eph. 5:13,14.
"Everyone who does evil hates the Light because their deeds are evil. Everyone who does evil hates the Light, and will not come into the Light FOR FEAR THAT HIS DEEDS WILL BE EXPOSED. But whoever lives by the Truth comes into the Light, so that it may be seen plainly that what he has done has been done through Elohim." ~ Yahuchanon 3:19-21.

Simply calling yourself a "Christian" is a generic reference, and could be applied to any follower of any "Christ". The Nazarene Mashiach, 𐤉𐤄𐤅𐤔𐤏, has followers who do not ***wish*** to sin, but they understand this is not what delivers them. ***"My dear children, I write this to you so that you will not sin. But if anybody does sin, we have one who speaks to the Father in our defense ~ Yahusha haMashiach, the Righteous One. He is our atoning sacrifice for our sins, and not only for ours but also for the sins of the whole world. We know we have come to know Him if we obey His Commands. The man who says 'I know Him', but does not do what He commands is a liar, and the Truth is not in him. But if anyone obey His Word, Elohim's love is truly made complete in him. Whoever claims to live in Him must walk as Yahusha did."*** 1Yoch. 2. Those who sin, of course, do not continue to sin, thinking they are living in "grace", because their spirit does not agree with sin. We will, at times, say or do things we shouldn't, but these things are not our "pattern" for living.
QUESTION: What does the word "nature" mean?
ANSWER: "Nature" is based on the Latin word, *NATURA*, and means *birth.* It is the root of the

word nativity. "Mother Nature" refers to the Earth Mother, also called *Regina Coeli* (Queen of Heaven). This is the root of all Paganism, and she was known as the SKY to the Egyptians, who called her NUT. Nut means *nurture* in Latin. Really, the sky was the time-clock used to determine when the fertilization cycle of events occurred. The calendar is the "stage" on which the Babylonian Pagan Mysteries are played-out on.

QUESTION: Why do people say "GOD bless you" when someone sneezes?

ANSWER: Pagans believed that when someone sneezed, their heart stopped, or at least skipped a few beats. Being that the sun was called "GOTT", the Celtic peoples would call on their highest deity to come to the aid of anyone sick, or leaving on a journey. When we say "good-bye", we are really saying "GOTT bless ye".

QUESTION: What is the "Gospel" of Yahusha ha Mashiach?

ANSWER: The word "Gospel" is two Celtic words, "GOD" + "SPELL". It came from the Greek word *evangelion*, and means "acceptable report" or "message". The Hebrew word is *BASAR*. The message brought by Yahusha, and carried by His cousin Yahuchanon, Paul, and all the students, was simply: *Repent, for the reign of Yahuah draws near.* This simple message was the core idea of what Paul spoke to the Greeks at Athens. At a meeting of the Areopagus, these Pagans wanted to know about what Paul was trying to say. (Read Acts 17:18-34.)

"In the past, Elohim overlooked such ignorance, but now He commands all people everywhere to REPENT. For He has set a day when He will judge the world with justice by the man He has appointed. He has given proof of this to all men by raising Him from the dead." - 17:30,31.

Here, Paul said it in a more elaborate way. The "Good News" also contains "Bad News", at least for those who do not understand and obey, because they will not REPENT. Their sinfulness must first be made apparent to them, then they must turn away from sinning, be immersed in the saving Name of 𐤏𐤔𐤅𐤄𐤉 for the forgiveness of their sins, then walk in the Commandments of freedom, having 𐤏𐤔𐤅𐤄𐤉 "circumcise" their hearts, and causing them to love the Torah. This is the New Covenant (Jer. 31, Heb. 8).

"But he is a Yahudi who is one inwardly; and circumcision is that of the heart, in the Spirit, not in the letter; whose praise is not from men, but from 𐤄𐤅𐤄𐤉*".* - Romans 2:29.

QUESTION: How can I prove to myself that the Name of our Creator was removed from the translations commonly used?

ANSWER: Check any encyclopedia under the Name "YAHWEH", and especially the preface and dictionary of your translations. You will see the Latin letters "YHWH". These stand for the Hebrew letters YOD, HAY, UAU, HAY. Also, the KJV slipped it in as the short form "JAH" at Psalm 68:4, but the letter "J" is less than 500 years old, being a YOD in Hebrew. ***"Everyone who <u>calls</u> on the Name of* 𐤄𐤅𐤄𐤉 *will be saved"*** ~ This text at Yah el (Joel) 2:32 is quoted at Acts 2:21 and Romans 10:13, and the Name is spoken of thousands of times as central to our salvation throughout Scripture. His people bear His Name, Daniel 9:19. He declares ***"This is My Name FOREVER, the Name by which I am to be remembered from generation to generation."*** (Ex. 3:15). You hear it in the phrase *hallelu YAH.* The Covenant Name is contained in the Name of our Redeemer, Yahusha. Husha or hushua means *save,* and you will recall the crowds shouted *"Husha nu"* (meaning *save us*) at John (Yahuchanon) 12:13. They also shouted *"baruch haba baShem* 𐤄𐤅𐤄𐤉", meaning *blessed is he who comes in the Name of Yahuah,* Yahuchanon 12:13 and Luke 19:38. This caused the Pharisees to scold our Rabbi because they were saying the Name aloud, which was to them "blasphemy". At Yahuchanon 17:6, He said: ***"I have <u>revealed</u> Your Name to those whom you gave Me out of the world."*** At Rev. 2:3, He says ***"You have endured hardships for My Name, and have not grown weary."*** We are "sealed" with the Father's Name (Rev. 14:1): ***"Then I looked, and before me was the Lamb, standing on Mount Tziyon, and with Him 144,000 who had His Father's Name written on their foreheads."*** (See also Rev. 7).

Malachi 3:16 says ***"Then those who feared* 𐤄𐤅𐤄𐤉 *talked with each other, and* 𐤄𐤅𐤄𐤉 *listened and heard. A scroll of remembrance was written in His presence concerning those who feared* 𐤄𐤅𐤄𐤉 *and honored His Name."***

To ***enter*** into His Covenant with Yisrael, and to have our sins removed and give ourselves to Him, we must be immersed in the Name above names, 𐤏𐤔𐤅𐤄𐤉. Without the Covenant, we are NOT counted in the citizenship of Israel, nor has there been any other covenant - see Eph. 2:8-13.

The following is a commentary on the Renewed Covenant written by Brick Parrish, the author of <u>Study Of Two House Restoration Of Israel</u>: (Article begins)

<u>*Is The Renewed Covenant Totally in Effect Today?*</u>

To answer this question, it is necessary to find out exactly what the Renewed Covenant is all about. The reason I use the term ***"renewed"*** is because in ancient Israel, previously existing covenants were amended in a principle known as "stacking". Only the parts of the Covenant that changed were affected. All other provisions of the covenant remained the same. This is the situation with the Renewed Covenant Yahusha made with us. The Covenant at Sinai was structured in a way that was familiar to Israel by following the outline of ancient Suzerainty treaties. In it was stated the parties to the covenant, the background, terms, conditions, duration and the witnesses.

The Covenant at Sinai was in reality, a marriage contract, or ***ketubah*** in Hebrew. Yahuah's proposal to Israel is found in Exo. 19:3-7 and the people's acceptance is in verse 8. The duration was to be ***forever,*** and the ***two witnesses*** were the "heaven and the earth." However, Israel disobeyed and broke the terms of the contract, so Yahuah divorced them.

Once a person divorced and remarried someone else, it is forbidden by Torah for him to remarry his original spouse. Israel committed spiritual adultery by going after the foreign gods of their neighbors, primarily Ba'al of the Canaanites. Israel in effect, married these false gods. Now, there was no way that Yahuah could remarry his former bride. Both the bride and the groom had to die and be reborn for this to happen.

We are all aware that Yahshua, which I believe to be Yahuah of the Tanakh (Old Testament), came to earth as a man, was born of a virgin, lived a sinless life, shed his blood and died on a crucifixion stake as payment for our sins. He was raised from the dead by Yahuah, the Father, on the third day and now has proposed to his bride, Israel. When we accept his proposal, the terms of the ***ketubah*** are set and upon our acceptance of them, we are then betrothed to him and are considered "born again". We become ***new creations***. However, the marriage process is not yet complete. We are only betrothed at this point. The marriage ***price*** has been paid for the bride, which was the shed blood of Yahuah's only begotten Son, Yahusha. This was the most precious price of all.

The next step in the betrothal process was for the prospective groom to go to ***prepare a place for his bride***, usually at his Father's house.

Joh 14:2 *In my Father's house are many mansions: if it were not so, I would have told you.* ***I go to prepare a place for you.***

Joh 14:3 *And if I go and prepare a place for you, I will come again, and receive you unto myself; that where I am, there ye may be also.*

We are not there yet. We are still in the betrothal stage and the provisions of the renewed covenant are not yet totally in effect.

Jer 31:31 *Behold, the days come, saith Yahuah, that I will make a new covenant with the house of Israel,* ***and*** *with the house of Judah*:*

The word translated "new" is "chadash" in Hebrew. The "*Etymological Dictionary of Biblical Hebrew*" by Matityahu Clark, gives the definition of this Hebrew word as "renewed". It is a renewed or expanded covenant with all the provisions of the old with some changes. These changes are spoken of in Hebrews chapters 7- 10 and deal primarily with changes to the Priesthood.

Another important thing to notice here is that the Renewed Covenant is made **ONLY** with the ***House of Israel*** and the ***House of Judah***. If you do not belong to either of these ***two*** groups of people, there is no sense worrying about it, ***it doesn't pertain to you***. The "Church" does not *replace* Israel, but must be *grafted into Israel* to have a part in this Renewed Covenant. This is done as explained in Romans 11.

Jer 31:32 *Not according to the covenant that I made with their fathers in the day that I took them by the hand to bring them out of the land of Egypt; which my covenant they brake, although I was an husband unto them, saith Yahuah:*

Jer 31:33 *But this shall be the covenant that I will make with the house of Israel;* ***After those days****, saith Yahuah, I will put my Torah in their inward parts, and write it in their hearts; and will be their Elohim, and they shall be my people.*

After ***what*** days? Chapters 30 and 31 are dealing with the re-gathering of all of Israel back into her land. The days spoken of here are the days when Israel is restored to her land. Those are the days when Yahuah will watch over them, to build, and to plant. (v.28)

Jer 31:34 *And they shall teach no more every man his neighbour, and every man his brother, saying, Know Yahuah: for they shall all know me, from the least of them unto the greatest of them, saith Yahuah: for I will forgive their iniquity, and I will remember their sin no more.*

I had long been puzzled as to why so few seemed to have the Torah written upon their hearts, because the majority of believers don't keep it today as many believe it has been abolished. So could it be that it means something different? Could it be speaking about the indwelling presence of the living Torah within our hearts

**HOUSE OF JUDAH: THE TRIBES YAHUDAH & BENYAMIN, OCCUPYING THE SOUTHERN LAND OF ISRAEL*

instead? If this is the case, do we now have all of the living Torah within our hearts that we're ever going to get? I will answer that in a moment.

Paul wrote to the Corinthians:

1 Cor. 13:9 *For we know in part, and we prophesy in part,*
1 Cor. 13:10 *but when that which is perfect is come, then that which is in part shall be done away.*
1 Cor. 13:11 *When I was a child, I spake as a child, I understood as a child, I thought as a child: but when I became a man, I put away childish things.*
1 Cor. 13:12 *For now we see through a glass, darkly; but then face to face: now I know in part; but then shall I know even as also I am known.*

Paul is writing about our not having a complete understanding of all these things, but when that perfection comes, we will all know Yahusha, the living Torah, from the least to the greatest of us and the fullness of these things will be revealed to us then. Then the Torah shall go forth out of Zion and the word of Yahuah will also go forth from Jerusalem to instruct the nations (Mic. 4:2; Isa. 2:3).

As I studied Jeremiah Chapters 30 and 31, as I previously mentioned, it became apparent that much of the Renewed Covenant spoken of in Jer. 31:33-40 is still a future event. These chapters were speaking about the restoration of all of Israel to her land. The Renewed Covenant is described as taking place afterwards. Other scriptures also bear this out.

Eze 11:17 *Therefore say, Thus saith Master Yahuah; I will even gather you from the people, and assemble you out of the countries where ye have been scattered, and I will give you the land of Israel.*

We will be re-gathered first.

Eze 11:18 *And they shall come thither, and they shall take away all the detestable things thereof and all the abominations thereof from thence.*
Eze 11:19 *And I will give them one heart, and I will put a new spirit within you; and I will take the stony heart out of their flesh, and will give them an heart of flesh:*
Eze 11:20 *That they may walk in my statutes, and keep mine ordinances, and do them: and they shall be my people, and I will be their Elohim.*

They are given a new heart and a new spirit to keep Yahuah's Commandments. A few chapters later the same illustration is made.

Eze 36:24 *For I will take you from among the heathen, and gather you out of all countries, and will bring you into your own land.*
Eze 36:25 *Then will I sprinkle clean water upon you, and ye shall be clean: from all your filthiness, and from all your idols, will I cleanse you.*
Eze 36:26 *A new heart also will I give you, and a new spirit will I put within you: and I will take away the stony heart out of your flesh, and I will give you an heart of flesh.*
Eze 36:27 *And I will put my spirit within you, and cause you to walk in my statutes, and ye shall keep my judgments, and do them.*

Do many people keep His Torah now? No! The non observance of His Feasts and Sabbaths are notable examples of willful disobedience of Torah.

Eze 36:28 *And ye shall dwell in the land that I gave to your fathers; and ye shall be my people, and I will be your Elohim.*

We are not back in the land yet and will not be until the bride groom returns for his bride and takes her to be with him forevermore. Yahudah is returning to the land now, but Israel has not yet returned and won't until Yahusha returns.

When Yahusha comes for his bride, which is Israel, the marriage ceremony will take place and the marriage will be consummated. I believe the third cup of the Passover ceremony, the cup of ***redemption***, was what Yahusha referred to when he said he would no more drink of the fruit of the vine until he could drink it anew with us in his kingdom. Yahusha instituted the Renewed Covenant with his blood, but it won't be ratified or consummated until we are with him in his kingdom and drink the cup of redemption with him there.

Another thing that leads me to believe the Renewed Covenant is not yet in full effect is that all parties have to agree to it. Most of the House of Yahudah does not at this time. They do not yet believe that Yahusha is the Messiah. But Scripture tells us that there will come a day before Yahusha returns when they will say ***"Baruch Haba B'shem Yahuah"*** or "blessed is he who comes in the name of Yahuah". This will happen when they are in dire straits, and no one can save them except Yahusha. They will cry out to Him, and Scripture indicates that when He does return, they will weep loudly when they recognize the nail scarred hands of their Savior (Zec. 12:10). When this siege of Judah and Jerusalem occurs, Ezekiel tells us in Eze. 4:3, that it will be a sign to the House of Israel. We will lift up our heads at that point because we will know our redemption draws nigh.

Yahusha will then rejoin the two "trees" of Ezekiel 37, the wild and the natural Olive trees, into the one Olive tree of Israel. Another clue we can see from Scripture that this will take place after Yahusha returns is looking carefully at the wording of Jer. 31:31 and compare with Jer. 31:33. This is also true of Heb. 8:8 and 8:10. Notice, verse 31 tells us that the renewed covenant is made with **both** houses of Israel and Judah and in verse 33, only the House of Israel is mentioned. Why? *It is because the **two** have been joined into one tree as per Eze. 37 and are now the **reunified** House of Israel, all 12 tribes.* Jerusalem shall not be plucked up, nor thrown down any more for ever. (Jer. 31:40). This alone indicates the Renewed Covenant is not fully in effect as Judah was thrown out of Jerusalem and the land in 70 A.D. They will one day dwell safely in the land of Israel as one unified kingdom under Yahusha, the Messiah, sitting and ruling upon the throne of David.

What about the New Testament references to the law being written upon our hearts? I believe this can be answered by the following scriptures:

2Co 1:22 *Who hath also sealed us, and given the earnest of the Spirit in our hearts.*

2Co 5:5 *Now he that hath wrought us for the selfsame thing is Elohim, who also hath given unto us the earnest of the Spirit.*

Eph 1:13 *In whom ye also trusted, after that ye heard the word of truth, the gospel of your salvation: in whom also after that ye believed, ye were sealed with that holy Spirit of promise,*

Eph 1:14 *Which is the earnest of our inheritance until the redemption of the purchased possession, unto the praise of his glory.*

Eph 4:30 *And grieve not the holy Spirit of Elohim, whereby ye are sealed unto the day of redemption.*

We have the ***"earnest"*** or down payment of the ***Spirit***, but not yet the fullness. Our present bodies could not withstand nor contain the fullness of the Ruach HaKodesh (Holy Spirit). As is stated in Ephesians 1:13-14, we have the down payment of our inheritance until our redemption. *We have just enough of this earnest to cause us to love the Torah and search out and hide in our hearts the things that please the Father.*

We have badly misunderstood the concept of the Renewed Covenant for many years. This is why it is so important to study the whole counsel of Scripture. There is nothing new in the Apostolic writings that is not found in the Tanakh (Old Testament). All the writers of the New Testament quoted and drew heavily from the Tanakh. Yahusha, himself, called our attention to the perpetuity of the covenant by reminding us that as long as the ***two witnesses*** (heaven and earth) existed, that one jot or one tittle would in no wise pass from the law until all had been fulfilled. See Deut. 4, 30 and 31 for more information as to why Yahusha referred to these ***two witnesses***.

To study only the "New Testament", one will not come away with a proper understanding of many of the precepts taught there. The Scriptures were written from a Hebrew mindset which is alien to the Greco/Roman thought patterns we try to apply to it. To ignore this is to do so at great peril to our eternal well being and standing in eternity.

By Brick Parrish* - Hunt, Texas (end of article)

Having read this, it makes you wonder how they can hand doctorate degrees to men that want to perpetuate a *belief* without a *covenant*, and who would spend the rest of their natural lives teaching people to ignore Yahuah's ***Torah***, saying things like *"that was just for the Jews"*.

They claim a Passover Lamb, but don't want a Passover. They reject the sign of the everlasting Covenant, *the Sabbath day*, which Yahuah ***blessed*** in the beginning and set it apart. What Yahuah has blessed ***stays*** blessed, ya'think?

Question: Why would a follower of Yahusha, the Mashiach of Israel, convert to any other walk than the Torah? Or in other words, why would any Yahudi need to change their religion in order to accept their own Messiah?
The answer is, they would not. Some bad teachings have twisted everything, and the bad seed has become an institution, based on lies.

**ORDER BRICK'S WORK, STUDY OF TWO HOUSE RESTORATION OF ISRAEL AT TORAHZONE.NET*

WORD SURVEY

Since ancient Babylon, the tongues (languages) of the nations have been babbling. The pure language, **HEBREW**, was undisturbed because Shem and his clan settled apart from his brothers' clans, the Babylonians. The babbling nations of today have in excess of 2,600 languages. They will be purged of their blasphemous terms, and one day call upon the Name of 𐤉𐤄𐤅𐤄. Zeph. 3:8,9: ***"I have decided to assemble the nations, to gather the kingdoms, and to pour out my wrath on them ~ all my fierce anger. The whole world will be consumed by the fire of my jealous anger. Then I will purify the speech of the peoples, that all of them may call upon the Name of 𐤉𐤄𐤅𐤄, and serve Him shoulder to shoulder."*** See? He knew the "wrong" wouldn't be using His Name.

ABBA Hebrew for male parent; this is what Rabbi 𐤉𐤄𐤅𐤔𐤏 also called His Father. ***ABINU*** is Hebrew-Aramaic for *our father.* The ending "u" is plural possessive.

ADONAI Hebrew, meaning *my sovereign.* The ending letter " i " (yod) makes it mean "my" ~ as expressed in *Eloi* (my mighty one), *rabbi* (my teacher), and *ani* (myself, me, my). Adonai was used in place of the Name.

AGNOSTIC Greek for *without knowledge;* A = against; GNOSTIC = knowledge.

APIS A "sacred" bull worshipped as Aton by the ancient Egyptians, having horns with a sun-disc between them. The Yisraelites made a golden calf, or apis, to worship the Creator, 𐤉𐤄𐤅𐤄 Elohim. He's on the record as being against images, and He was especially disturbed they used a previously Pagan image to represent Him. In fact, He hates to be worshipped in any Pagan way.

ARCHAEOLOGY From Greek, *ARKHAIOLOGIA, archaeo-* (ancient, beginning) + *logy-* (study, reason). It's the study of antiquity, customs, structures, etc.,.

ASCETICISM A severe, self-denying, austere way of life, supposed to permit union with the divine— a practice condemned as useless by Paul at Col. 2:21,22. Pagan monks and hermits often lived this way, most often celibate, and they still practice it. This was used by Catholicism, accompanied by "vows", to control literate men who copied and translated the Scriptures. In these monk factories, sentences from Scripture were divided, so the men could not make sense from them as they were copied and translated; a "vow of silence" was imposed so they could not discuss what they had worked on with others, so the sentences would remain incomplete in their minds.

ATHIEST Greek for one who subscribes to the belief there is no Creator, or spiritual being of any kind. *A-* (without), + *THEOS-* (deity, deus, elohim).

BAAL Hebrew for "LORD". This word was used as a proper name for the sun deity by the Canaanites, Phoenicians, and even the Druids. The familiar word *Beelzebub* is more accurately the Hebrew ***BAAL-ZEBUL***, meaning *LORD OF THE FLIES.* The names containing ***BEL*** are references to the Pagan deity, as in *Jezebel* and *Belshazzar.* Another name for Shatan (Satan) is *Belial.* So, to say "the LORD is my shepherd" doesn't relate to the Creator, but rather Shatan! Shatan "deleted" the true Name, and put in a generic term referring to himself. The main point is that the SUN was what the ancients related this term to, and we see it camouflaged in words like *bell, ball, and Cybele.*

BAPTISM From the Greek *baptizein,* to dip. Originally, it referred to dyeing fabric, but came to be used by Pagans for initiation ceremonies, using water or blood in sprinkling. The true Hebrew word is *TEVILA*, where a person is immersed in a body of water, called a *MIKVAH.* It also signifies repentance, and it is the most important event in one's life in the conversion of a Gentile, to become *engrafted into Yisrael.* It is a covenant sign to obey 𐤉𐤄𐤅𐤄, and identifies the convert with the death and burial of 𐤉𐤄𐤅𐤔𐤏, and is the death and burial of one's mind of the flesh. Rising up from the water of Tevila, a convert is identified with the resurrection, and walks in obedience, *enabled* to obey by the Spirit. It is the outward sign of or conversion, our ***circumcision***; and our entry-point as citizens of the nation of Israel.

BELLS The world's oldest bell was unearthed in Babylon. Bells are among the oldest items used in Pagan worship, and were one of several noise-makers used. They were employed to give worship to the sun, and were usually placed in or near the top of an obelisk or high-place. Orientals use gongs as well as the familiar bell shapes. They were brought into Christian worship along with "steeples" from Paganism. Augustus Caesar is on record as having dedicated an enormous bell, placed in the entrance tower to the temple of Jupiter.

BELIEF A mental act or habit of placing trust or confidence in an opinion, or the acceptance of something as true or real. To expect or suppose. When something believed-in is exposed as being false, a ***reaction*** is aroused. How an individual reacts depends on how well-equipped they are, and the degree to which they want to believe the falsehood. Dresden James wrote *"A truth's initial commotion is directly proportional to how deeply the lie was believed. It wasn't the world being round that agitated people, but that the world wasn't flat. When a well-packaged web of lies has been sold gradually to the masses over generations, the truth will seem utterly preposterous, and its speaker a raving lunatic".* The Smith Ministry in Abilene, Texas has stated, *"It isn't the fact that the Savior's Name is* Yahshua (OWY𐤄𐤉 - Yahusha, Yahusha) *that agitates people, but that His Name is not Jesus (Jhesus, Hey-Zeus, Yeh-Zus, Hesus)".* This means that people may think they have the facts, but all they really have are beliefs. If we are imputed "righteousness" by our belief alone, then why did Ya'akob (James) write *"show me your belief without deeds, and I will show you my belief by what I do. You believe that there is one Elohim—good! Even the demons believe that—and shudder . . . You see that a person is justified by what he does and* ***not by belief alone****."* We can believe "He knows my heart"~ but without LOVE, shown by our obedience, we have profited nothing. We can believe otherwise, but when we call Him "Jesus" or Hay-Zus, in Hebrew He hears "Yeh-horse", because the Hebrew word *SOOS* means "horse".

BIBLE This word was originally Phoenician, then passed into Greek, then Latin. It means *books* in Greek. It is no where to be found in the inspired text of Scripture ~ it's just put on the cover. If your Scriptures have maps in the back, check for a Phoenician port city called "BYBLOS". This city was named Byblos because the Phoenician fertility idol ***BIBLIA*** was worshipped there, in a temple dedicated in her honor. The city was later re-named *Gebal.* This port city exported papyrus, or the writing paper of the ancient world, so scrolls came to be called after the name of the city ~ which was named after an idol. It might not be wise to continue to call the Word of 𐤄𐤅𐤄𐤉 "The Bible" now that you realize this. He calls His Words to mankind the ***Torah*** (Teachings), ***Nebi'im*** (prophets), and ***Kethubim*** (writings). This is abbreviated to the acronym: T**a**N**a**K**h**. The Hebrew word for "scroll" is *megillah,* and His Words are called *debarim.* Remember Ex. 23:13.

BINDING and ***LOOSING*** At Mt. 16:19, Rabbi OWY𐤄𐤉 told His students whatever they would "bind" or "loose" would verified as true in Heaven. The idea of BIND means *to forbid,* and LOOSE means *to permit.* They had been fully trained in Torah by the Torah-Giver! He was going away, and his students would have to judge things as OK or not.

CATHEDRAL Latin, *cathedra,* for *throne.*

CEREAL Latin, *Cerealis,* the grain of Ceres, a Pagan deity.

CHARIS From Greek, *Kharisma,* a Pagan deity's name, *Charis,* wife of Hephaistos, the fire deity. "Charred" means burned. Other words produced from this are *charity, charisma, and charismatic.* The *"Three Graces"* or *Three Charities,* were a Pagan trinity known as the *Three Fates.* Their names were *Clotho* (our word "cloth", was the producer of the "thread of life"), *Lachesis* (carrying rods which she shook to determine the fate of mankind), and *Atropos* (who cuts the thread, determining the length of a person's life).

CHURCH The Old English word was *CIRICE*, and you will see it spelled *CHIRCHE* written above many old "church" entrances throughout England. This is from the West Germanic *KIRIKA*, which is based on the Greek deity's name, *CIRCE.* Circe was famous among Pagans for turning men into pigs, or other animals, using drugs. The original English translation from the Greek text by John Wycliffe (about CE 1380) used the word *congregation* for "ecclesia", the called-out body of believers. The original set-apart ones who studied and "did" the Word (Commandments) were called *qahal* in Hebrew, from which we get our word "call". The "saints" were the set-apart ones, known as *qodeshim.*

COMMANDMENTS The original Hebrew word is *MITZVAH*, both singular and plural. The Old English meaning is "edict". "Bar Mitzvah" means *son of the Commandments* (Torah), and "bat mitzvah" is the feminine. In the TaNaKh, there are 613 Commandments, but in the Brit Chadasha (NT) there are 1,089 technically specified. All of them are "summed up" in the 10 words, or Decalogue, called the 10 Commandments. These are further summarized into the "2 greatest Commandments", which Rabbi OWY𐤄𐤉 quoted to a lawyer who was testing Him: ***"Love 𐤄𐤅𐤄𐤉 your Elohim with all your heart and with all your soul and with all your mind"*** (Dt. 6:5), and ***"Love your neighbor as yourself"*** (Lev. 19:18, Mt. 22:37). OWY𐤄𐤉 warned us not to set aside any of the Commandments, ***"Whoever, then, breaks one of the least of the Commandments, and teaches men so, shall be called least in the Kingdom of Shamayim; but whoever does and teaches them, he shall be called great in the kingdom of Shamayim"*** ~ Mt. 5:19. "Shamayim" is skies, outer space, or "heaven", often used as a substitution for the Name of 𐤄𐤅𐤄𐤉. Our Rabbi restored the Name, but monks subsequently removed it again from the texts. We know this, because at Acts 7:57, the Sanhedrin covered their ears, and stoned Stephen to death ~ for saying the Name aloud. Shaul, later called Paul, was there giving approval for his death. 𐤉𐤄𐤅𐤔𐤏 told us to become **sons of light**, and the Torah is Light (see Pr. 6:23). Our eye must be filled with Light, or it is darkness (without Torah). The Commandments sum up how the wife (bride) of 𐤉𐤄𐤅𐤔𐤏 is to live, and is the Covenant. The "Ark" of the Covenant was the box which carried the Commandments, and now each of us who are of His bride are the "box", having them written on our hearts (the "New" Covenant). If we love Him, we will obey Him, and word comes from the Greek *clericos,* and went into the Latin as *clericus.* It means "literate", or having the ability to read and write. Probably, Peter couldn't read and write; so he had to enlist the help of Sila (1 Pet. 5:12) to record his words (illiterate, or *not clericus).* The words *cleric, clerk, and clergy all refer to a "man of letters".* Literate men could read "literature", and those who could read were given status, and therefore became known as "clergy". The Church of Rome divided their clergy from the "laity", by the distinction of being literate or not. They burned books and libraries in part to control literacy, and therefore power. Another reason to destroy records was so their revision of history could remain uncontested. People who threatened their control were exterminated by the Inquisition, implemented by the Jesuits and Dominicans.

CROSS (See QUESTIONS & ANSWERS) The word "cross" is derived from the Latin word, ***CRUX***, (stem, *cruc-*), perhaps originally Phoenician. The word "cross" came into the Latin translation when Jerome translated the Greek word ***stauros***. His real name was Eusebius Hieronymus Sophronius, and he did this during the years CE 391-403, calling his translation *The Latin Vulgate*. Catholicism considers this to be "inspired". The Greek word *stauros* means staff, stake, pole, or beam, corresponding to the Hebrew word ***NAS***, which the serpent Nehushtan was lifted up with in the desert (Yn. 3, Num. 21:9, 2 Kings 18:4). Many scholars strongly suspect this term and symbol were introduced from Paganism, because the use of the cross is so commonly found in Pagan religions world-wide. It usually symbolized the ***SUN*** (an eagle), which Constantine seemed to identify with "Christ". The 1934 Encyclopedia Britannica states:

"In every part of the world, crosses were used both as religious symbols or as ornaments long before the Christian era . . . It did not become the symbol of Christianity until 400 years later, during the time of Constantine."

IMAGE OF THE BEAST! If you think about it, what possible meaning could the words *"Take up your CROSS and follow Me"* have meant to a listener of Rabbi 𐤉𐤄𐤅𐤔𐤏 *BEFORE* His execution? All He was saying was *"Take up your STAFF* (a walking stick) *and follow Me."* These words meant to *walk* (Hebrew, *halak*, *halacha*) in His example, since He is the living model of Torah.

Images that we are programmed to embrace as "holy" need to be thoroughly researched, to see if they originated from Paganism or not. Catholics "genuflect" before a box with bread inside, before a crux with a statue figure of a dying person, supposed to represent our Rabbi. *"In the past, 𐤉𐤄𐤅𐤄 overlooked such ignorance, but now He commands all people everywhere to repent. For He has set a day when He will judge the world with justice by the Man He has appointed. He has given proof of this to all men by raising Him from the dead.*" Acts 17:30, 31. If you place no image before your eyes, you will not be found guilty of any wrong doing, but Scripture says FEW are going to make it (see Luke 13:24). *"Why do you also transgress the Command of Elohim because of your tradition?"* Mt. 15:3. *"But in vain do they worship Me, teaching as teachings the commands of MEN." v. 9.* The cross is really a solar eagle symbol.

ELOHIM Hebrew, enlarged from ***EL***, meaning *mighty-one.* Elohim being plural can also refer to the immensity rather than the "quantifying" aspect. The ending of many Hebrew names use the short form, as in *Micha**EL*** (who is like EL), *Rapha**EL*** (healing EL), *Yisra**EL*** (prince of EL), *Gabri**EL*** (warrior of EL), *Yishm**EL*** (EL hears), *Shemu**EL*** (Name of EL), *Immanu**EL*** (EL with us), *Yah**EL*** (Joel, Yah is EL). We see that 𐤉𐤄𐤅𐤔𐤏 referred to Psalm 22 as He continued to teach as He was dying on the stake, saying *"Eloi, Eloi, lama sabachthani?"* Eloi means *my mighty one.* EL is a pronoun, not a name. In translating this pronoun into various vernacular terms in Gentile languages, commonly they substituted the Pagans' principal deity's name, as was done in the English word "GOD" (GOTT, the sun). The Hebrew term ELAH became "Allah", but it is not a name.

EMUNAH Hebrew for fidelity, faithfulness, steadfastness. It is usually translated to our word "faith". This is a rabbi's foremost concern: that his pupils will remain steady and unswerving to their teachings of Torah. *"If you are* (unswerving) *in the small things, you will be* (unswerving) *in the greater things also."* The meaning points to obedience. The flesh must be disciplined, and by this practice, the one trained and walking in the "light" will remain steadfast. *"Your Word is a lamp to my feet, and a light for my path."* Ps. 119:105. *The righteous* (tzedek) *will live by his **EMUNAH**."* Hab. 2:4.

ERETZ Hebrew for Earth, soil, land. *Eretz Yisrael* means *Land of Yisrael.*

EUNUCH Greek, a castrated man, meaning *bed-watcher.* (*"Woman"* means *womb-man*).

EUROPA The Greek deity (mythology) who was abducted by Zeus disguised as a white bull, and taken to Crete. The continent of "Europe" is named for her.

GEMATRIA This is the use of letters as numbers, because Hebrew (and others) letters carried numerical values. The numerical values of each letter of a word are added up, so a word or name can be expressing a number. The Name of Yahuah has a value of 26. If you would like to calculate the number of the beast, first find the Hebrew letters, then add them together. **4th beast: Rome**

GETHSEMANE Two words in Hebrew, *gath + semane,* meaning OIL PRESS.

GOLGOTHA Hebrew for *place of the skull.* The Latin word "Calvary" means *cranium, skull, or bonehead.* Let's leave it the name Golgotha. "Japan" means *rising sun*, but we call it Japan.

GRACE Based on the Latin word, *gratia*, this word comes from the Hebrew word *chasid*, which means *unmerited loving kindness.* Preachers often give people false security by claiming we live in the *"Age of Grace",* but this is not supported by any Scriptural verse. Actually, the Creator has always been praised as the Elohim of forgiveness, and showed lovingkindness to all who would acknowledge sin and REPENT. We are of course under 𐤉𐤄𐤅𐤄's ***chasid*** by the once-for-all atoning death of His Son, but this is not a license to sin. Catholicism set up a "dispensational" method of "dispensing" grace through 7 "sacraments". This gave the "clergy" complete control over the "laity". First of all, the sacraments are a sham, only a trick used to mislead people. Second, we are *ALL* priests, and there is not a division in Scripture called "clergy" and "laity".

HANUKKAH **Amazing fact:** *if there had been no Hanukkah, there would never have been a Christianity.* Prior to 186 BCE, a ruthless Greek ruler named Antiochus Epiphanes was forcing Greek customs and religion on the nation of Yisrael, and outlawed the Torah. People were slaughtered, children were tortured to death in front of their parents, *forced to work on Shabbat,* eat swine flesh, and wear the little "beanie", a Greek hat of Hermes (scholar cap). The Temple was polluted with images of Zeus, swine was offered on the altar, and new brides were deflowered first by the Greek ruler. Only in extreme secrecy could the young study Torah. During such study, children would hide the Torah scroll and pull out a little "top" called a *dreidel* when they heard soldiers coming ~ thus they would appear to be playing an innocent game. A Hebrew family, the ***Maccabees***, succeeded in over-powering the Greek forces, and Antiochus was stricken with a fatal intestinal malady. He suffered a lingering, torturous death ~ his rotting body was such a foul stench that his own men could not bear to go near him!

<u>The Dedication</u> The word "Hanukkah" or Chanukkah is Hebrew, meaning ***dedication***.

What was dedicated (or re-dedicated) was the Temple, after a thorough cleansing after the Pagans were ejected. It took ***8 days*** to cleanse it. The ***Menorah***, or 7-branched lampstand, burned its lights for the 8 days of clean up, even though only enough oil was found to last for ONE day. Every year since this dedication, we remember the deliverance from the Pagan oppression which almost wiped out the observances of the Commandments, which the Yahudim have preserved as priests of the nations.

At Yahuchanon (John) 10:22, our Rabbi 𐤉𐤄𐤅𐤔𐤏 was walking in the Temple area during this festival called Hanukkah:

"Then came Hanukkah in Yerushaliyim. It was winter, and 𐤉𐤄𐤅𐤔𐤏 *was walking around inside the Temple area, in Shlomo's Colonnade."*

HEBREW This is what is called the Lashon Qodesh, or set-apart tongue, which will be restored during the 7th Millennium, Zeph. 3:9. The word comes from Abraham's great, great, great-grandfather, ***Eber***. It was the language our Rabbi spoke to Shaul when he was thrown to the ground, and at Acts 26 Paul explains to Agrippa that he heard a voice speaking to him in Hebrew. Actually, that's the only language Yahudim spoke to each other, except for those who were living in foreign lands. Aramaic is a dialect of Hebrew. Paul spoke many tongues.

HOLY This word became used instead of the Hebrew term *qodesh*, which means "set-apart". To a Pagan, "holy" related to the sun's glow, and relates to the word "halo", a glowing nimbus seen on statues and pictures. The Pagans called shrines "hallowed". The holy "halo" was to associate the statue of the glowing deity with the yellow sun. At Ps. 51:11, Dawid wrote *Ruach ha Qodesh* in Hebrew, which we see translated "Holy Spirit". Ruach means wind, or spirit. Even the gold ring used in marriage was inherited from Pagan priests who worshipped the unconquered sun. Ministers hold it up and say things about eternity and endless devotion. The Latin word *sacrare* means "dedicated", and is very close in meaning to qodesh, or holy.

J The letter "J", amazingly, didn't exist in any language until the 15th century, at which time printing styles differentiated the letter " i " when it was used at the beginning of a sentence, or the first letter in a proper name. They gave the " i " a little tail, and now we have a new letter. Since there was no letter in Greek or Latin like the Hebrew "yod" (𐤉), these languages opted for the i called "iota". The first letter in the Rabbi's Name is best transliterated as a " Y " in English.

JEHOVAH this is the formulation of the Creator's Name which was promoted by a man named *Petrus Galatinus* during the 15th century. Encyclopedias will explain this is a double error, since it is both a hybrid and a mongrel word. The four letters of the Name 𐤉𐤄𐤅𐤄 are YOD, HAY, UAU, HAY, and are read from right-to-left. In modern Hebrew, the Name is written: יהוה

Clement of Alexandria transliterated these letters into the Greek alphabet as **IAOUE**. The word is called the Tetragrammaton, which is Greek for "four letters". (Often seen as YHWH).

Since there is no letter " J " or " V " in ancient Hebrew, the Tetragrammaton YHUH was altered to JHVH, and the vowels were another mistake. The 10th century vowel pointing by the Masoretic copyists added little marks under the four letters, which were intended to "cue" a reader to pronounce "adonai" instead of pronouncing the Name. "Adonai" is Hebrew for *my lord.* ***The pronouncing of the Name was prohibited, and therefore considered unutterable.*** (This is a man-made law, and was central to the problem faced by our Rabbi and the apostles.) Our Mashiach was never called "Jesus", but rather "Yahusha" (yah-HOO'-sha). This is the **same name** as the successor of Mosheh, known by most as "Joshua", as can be proven in various literary sources, as well as the underlying Greek text at Acts 7 and Hebrews 4, where both names *Jesus* and *Joshua* have the Greek letters IESOUS as their basis. The Hebrew phrase, ***HALLELU-YAH*** means *praise you* (plural) *YAH.* Most don't realize they are saying the short form of the Name, and it is used in many prophets' names: *Yesha Yahu* (Isaiah), *Obad Yah* (Obediah), *Yirme Yahu* (Jeremiah), *Zechar Yah* (Zechariah), and others with an ending ~ **iah**.

JUBILEES This word comes from the original Hebrew *YOB-HEL*, and means "ram's horn" or *leading animal.* The late Greek word *iobelaios* was based on the Hebrew. The measurements of time in the Scriptural model are not "centuries", but rather "Jubilees", or groups of 50 years. The 10th day of the 7th moon of every 50th year being the time that all property is returned to the original owner or heirs according to primogeniture. A Jubilee also requires the release of all Hebrew slaves. The land is given a rest also. (Land is to rest every 7th year anyway). Since Adam died before he lived a complete "day" (a day is 1000 years to 𐤉𐤄𐤅𐤄), he lived 18 Jubilees plus 30 years, or 930 years (70 short of 1000). 20 Jubilees is 1000 years. The year of Jubilee is referred to in the inscription on the ***Liberty Bell*** at Independence Hall in Philadelphia, Pennsylvania: *"Proclaim liberty throughout the land to all its inhabitants"* ~ being words taken out of context from Lev. 25:10. The complete sentence says, *"And you shall set apart the* ***fiftieth year****, and proclaim release throughout all the land to all its inhabitants, it is a Jubilee* (Yob Hel) *to you."* The text at Genesis 6:3 says that mortals will be given 120 years, then 𐤉𐤄𐤅𐤄 would bring about a complete change because He will not contend with man (the ADAM) forever. The allotted time for man before the Messianic Age of rest will be 120 Jubilees (6000 years!). Then, fire will be brought upon the Earth, and the very **elements** themselves will burn (2Pet. 3:12). The Messianic Age will occur at the beginning of the "7th Day", as foreshadowed by the still unfulfilled prefigurements of the feasts of the 7th month's appointed times of Yom Teruah (now called Rosh Hashanah), Yom Kippur, and Sukkot. Our Mashiach was sacrificed approximately 80 Jubilees from Adam's beginning, and we are about 80 Jubilees away from the Noahic Flood right now. I wonder if these are related, since 𐤉𐤄𐤅𐤔𐤏 said *"The coming of the Son of man will be just like the days of Noach."* He is called the "second Adam".

KNACK People say, *"You've really got a knack for doing that".* A "Knack" was a spirit demon that was thought to possess a person like the 9 Muses, enabling them to have certain abilities.

KORAN The sacred text of Islam, believed to contain the revelations by Allah to Mohammed. It is also called <u>Alcoran</u>. The Arabic word *qur'an* means *reading* or *recitation.* It comes from the original Hebrew word, ***qura'a***, which means read or recite. ***QARA*** is the Hebrew for *"proclaim".* Israel's half-brothers, the Ishmaelites or Arabs, use lots of Hebrew words. The word "arab" is from *ereb*, which is Hebrew for *evening* or *darkening.*

KOSHER This is from a 3-letter Hebrew word, *kasher*, and means *approved, proper,* or *appropriate.* The consumption of "approved" animal flesh is stressed at Gen. 9:3,4, Lev. 3:17, 7:26, 27, 11:1 -47, 17:10-14, ***<u>and Acts 15:20 & 15:29</u>***. Acts 10 and Mark 7 are often used to "annul" the distinction of the clean and unclean. Those who permit themselves to be misled this way should read "Isaiah" 66:17. On the Day of 𐤉𐤄𐤅𐤄, those who "approve for themselves" to eat whatever they wish from the "garden" (farm), *"who eat swine's flesh, detestable things, and mice, shall* ***come to an end altogether****".* Your Writings, especially the KJV, will put the added words in parentheses from Mark 7:19. At Acts 10, Peter woke up and *"was greatly perplexed in mind as to what the vision which he had seen might be; behold the men* (3

Gentiles) *who had been sent by Cornelius . . . Appeared at the gate."* Acts 10:17. The "3 sheets" of unclean animals related to the <u>3 Gentiles</u> who were at his gate, whom Peter would otherwise never have gone with, or entered their residence without this vision. This is explained by Peter himself at Acts 11:18.

MARK OF THE BEAST Without the Torah to make one wise, this "mark" or sign cannot be determined. This calls for WISDOM. The Covenant, the Torah, which is the marriage Covenant with Yisrael, contains a "mark" or sign, called the sign of the Eternal Covenant. It is mutually exclusive with the beast's mark. All covenants made by 𐤉𐤄𐤅𐤄 have such a sign. Babylon, the Mother of Harlots, has established a sign, and it has remained the same within Catholicism, and her daughters which follow after her. This system is called a "beast" because dumb animals, or beasts, have no regard for 𐤉𐤄𐤅𐤄's appointments, processes, or invitations. The "feasts" of 𐤉𐤄𐤅𐤄 which He proclaims at Leviticus 23 and Deut. 16 are described in the parables, like Luke 14:15-24. The wife of 𐤉𐤄𐤅𐤄 carries the "sign" of the Sabbath, and Shatan is waging WAR against this woman and her offspring, and the <u>Covenant</u> (Rev. 12:17). This outward sign or "mark" of 𐤉𐤄𐤅𐤄 is how we ***acknowledge Him as Creator*** (Gen. 2:3, Ex. 20:11, Heb. 4:4). Exodus 31:13 declares that Shabbat (the weekly and annual appointments) are a sign between 𐤉𐤄𐤅𐤄 and His people FOREVER. Shabbat is celebrated *from evening* (twilight) *to evening.* Yesha Yahu (Isaiah) 66:23 speaks of a future time when, after the burning of the Earth, the people of all nations who serve 𐤉𐤄𐤅𐤄 will bow down *"from Shabbath to Shabbath".* Converts, like Cornelius, became engrafted to Yisrael, and rested on Shabbat. Gentiles in general are referred to as "dogs", or figuratively as "beasts" - like the Canaanite woman was at Mt. 15:26. The Babylonian "Sun-day" was imposed as a MARK under the penalty of death by Constantine I, and unknowingly the mark of the beast has been placed on everyone who follows after the beast. In the days of the "7th Angel" (Rev. 10:7), the mystery of these things is to be revealed, exposing Shatan, *"who leads the* ***whole world astray***" (Rev. 12:9). *"Then I saw another angel flying in mid-air, and he had the eternal message to proclaim to those who live on the Earth—to every nation, tribe, language and people. He said in a loud voice, 'Fear Elohim and give Him esteem, because the hour of His judgment has come. Worship Him* ***Who MADE the heavens, the Earth, the sea and the springs of water****."* ~ Rev. 14:7. The "sign" of this "worship" is <u>Shabbat</u>, and is seen prominently in *"those who obey Elohim's Commandments, and hold to the Testimony of 𐤉𐤄𐤅𐤔𐤏".* ~ Rev. 12:17. No lie is found in the mouths of His redeemed, those who have been sealed with the Father's Name. (Read all of Rev. 14).

MITRE This is a Pagan religious hat, originating in the worship of Dagon, the chief deity of the Philistines, a sea people. Its name, *mitre,* comes from the name *Mithras.* Popes, bishops, and cardinals wear them in the Church of Rome, and the Anglican Church uses them also.

MOABITE STONE This large stone over 3 feet high was discovered in 1868 CE, and was broken by Arabs in order to fetch more money for each piece. It contains the palaeo-Hebrew script, and the Name of 𐤉𐤄𐤅𐤄 is written on it.

MOSHEH This is the name distorted to "Moses", and it means <u>draw-out</u>. He was born during a time when all male children of Yisrael

The Oriental Institute, The University of Chicago

THE MOABITE STONE

This stone contains the Name of the Creator, and is written in palaeo-Hebrew!

The "monstrosity" (man-made from different parts) word "**Jehovah**" contains a <u>terrible</u> coincidental meaning in Hebrew. The word "hovah" in Hebrew is based on a word that means *ruin, calamity, destruction, and wickedness* according to Strong's concordance dictionary. Has the adversary done this to make our Creator's Name mean

"I am ruin, wickedness"?

were to be destroyed at birth in Egypt / Mitsraim. Pharaoh's daughter named him this Hebrew name because she *drew him out of the water.* He *drew out* the children of Yisrael from Egypt.

MITRE HATS
Dagon in Mesopotamian sculpture.
MITHRAS / DAGON
FISH HAT!
Proudly wearing the hat of Dagon, popes and bishops also display the symbol of Tammuz, mixing light & darkness.
Pope Paul VI wearing mitre.
Later Roman Flags bore letters standing for the Latin senate and people of Rome.
Holy Roman Empire Flag flew in what is now Germany from the 900's until 1806.
INQUISITION
"We wouldn't have to burn them - if they were just wrong . . . . we must silence them permanently for quite the opposite reason."
Over 600 years, Jesuits & Dominicans tortured and burned tens of millions of people - even whole families.

RABBI Hebrew for *my teacher.* 𐤉𐤄𐤅𐤔𐤏 was called Rabbi by His pupils and others at Mt. 26:25, 26:49, Mk. 9:5, 10:51, 11:21, 14:45, Yn. 1:38, 3:2, 3:26, 4:31, 6:25, 9:2, 11:8, 20:16, and many other places where the word "teacher" or "master" were translated. He's the ONLY one we call "rabbi", as He directed us at Mt. 23:8. We can only aspire to be "***assistant*** rabbi", or "***assistant*** pastor". There's only ***one*** Shepherd, and ***one*** flock.
Pastor is Latin for shepherd, a sheep-herder.

ROME The language of the Romans was called *Roma.* The Empire was called by the capital (head) of it, after an Etruscan myth of two orphaned boys name *Romulus and Remus.* This city is located in what is called Italy, where the pre-Roman civilization of Etruria used to be (5th century BCE).

TZITZIT Hebrew for *tassels.* At Num. 15:38, 39 and Deut. 22:12, we are commanded to wear tassels at the 4 corners of our garments, attached with a blue cord. The Throne of 𐤉𐤄𐤅𐤄 is on a sea of blue sapphire, and the color blue is to remind us of the Torah each time we see our tassels. 𐤉𐤄𐤅𐤔𐤏 wore them, and continues to; at Mt. 9:20 and 14:36, the text states that His tassels were touched by many people, and they were healed by doing so. He criticized the Pharisees for *lengthening* their tassels to make a show of outward righteousness. This is not a "talisman" like a Pagan would use. Pagans relied on objects to confer protection or powers over evil with runes, amulets, stones, tags, scapulas, necklaces, rings, and wands. This is idolatry. Wearing cruxes, medals, making magic signs, waving in the air, splashing water, or counting on a "rosary" is no different from VOODOO. They may as well twirl a chicken over their heads. Tzitzit are to remind us to obey the Torah always.

YARMULKE This is a Yiddish word for the kipa, or skullcap seen worn by the pope, and most orthodox Yahudim on the street, in the classroom, and in the synagogues. Mosheh would not know what it is. Alfred J. Kolatch, an orthodox author and "Rabbi", states: *The skullcap* ***has no religious significance in Jewish law.*** He goes on to say that it has no basis in Scriptural or Rabbinical law. To trace the use of the cap to its source, we find that it came into wider use only in the 17th century, where before that only a very few Yahudim used it. Did Rabbi 𐤉𐤄𐤅𐤔𐤏 wear a kipa? All researchers and historians say NO, and there is no evidence of its use in any data or archaeological finds at all. The pope of Rome and his cardinals wear them, but that is because it was originally a Greek hat of a scholar, called the "hat of Hermes" (Hermes is a Pagan idol, of course). You will recall the "cap and gown" of graduates from schools and universities employs this "hat of Hermes", topped with a square mason's board. A mason is a layer of bricks, and the mason's board holds the cement mix. These were scholars who graduated to different levels in their guilds; from apprentice to journeyman, then journeyman to master.

In ancient times, just prior to 186 BCE, the land of Yisrael was ruled by a Greek Seleucid, Antiochus Epiphanes IV. He was extremely cruel, and outlawed the Hebrew religion, forcing his Greek customs on them. In the record of 2 Maccabees, an apostate high priest (named "Jason" in translation, but really named Yeshua) helped this Greek ruler ***impose*** the Greek ways of living:

"And abrogating the lawful way of living, he

introduced new customs contrary to the Torah; for he willingly established a gymnasium right under the citadel (the Temple), *and he made the finest of the young men* ***wear the Greek hat***."

Paul writes at 1Cor. 11:7 that a man is not to have his head covered in the assembly, but a woman is required to, to keep from dishonoring one another's headship. OWYƎZ is the man's 'head', while a woman's 'head' is her husband. We are to follow the Torah, and not add to it in any way: *"Do not add to nor take away from it"*. Dt. 12:32.

Man-made customs, including all the camouflaged Paganism found in Christendom, are traditions that are forbidden in the worship of ƎYƎZ. They represent more than a "strange fire", but are like the **golden calf**. It is forbidden to worship Him <u>after the customs of the Pagans</u>. *"The one who says he abides in Him ought himself to walk* ***in the same manner as He walked***.*"* ~ 1 Yoch. 2:6. Walk in Light ~ the Torah.

<u>Human traditions</u> run unchecked from generation to generation. The word ***"Bible"*** is not found anywhere in the text of the Writings, yet people refer to oracles of Yahuah by this name of a Pagan deity, ***Biblia***. They will tell you it's a "translation" from the Greek word for "books", and stop there. If the word "Bible" isn't in the text, then what is it the text calls itself? Our Rabbi Yahusha referred to it as the Torah and the Prophets (Torah and the Nebi'im).

Now that you've come this far, you may realize almost everything about society is based on the Roman time system, and our lives are framed in a dragnet. Whether you're an atheist, agnostic, or believer, you live under the rule of a global system that originated in a Babylonian system of sun

BIBLOS, THE ORIGIN OF WORD "BIBLE"

THIS BIRD, A MYTHICAL PHOENIX, IS THE SYMBOL USED BY THE ADEPTS, 33rd DEGREE MASONS AND ABOVE.

IT IS ONE OF THE HIGHEST RANKING SYMBOLS THEY USE TODAY.

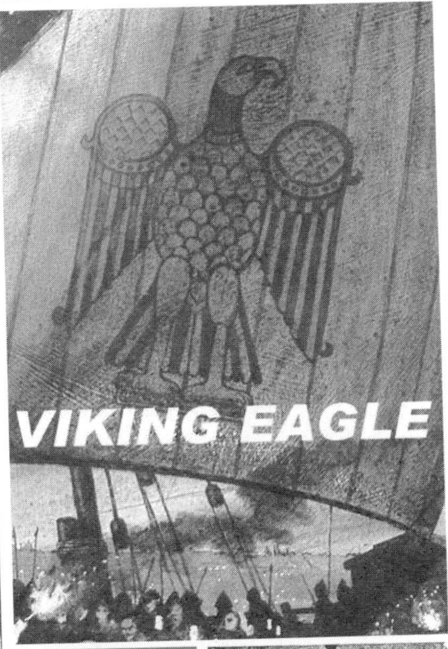

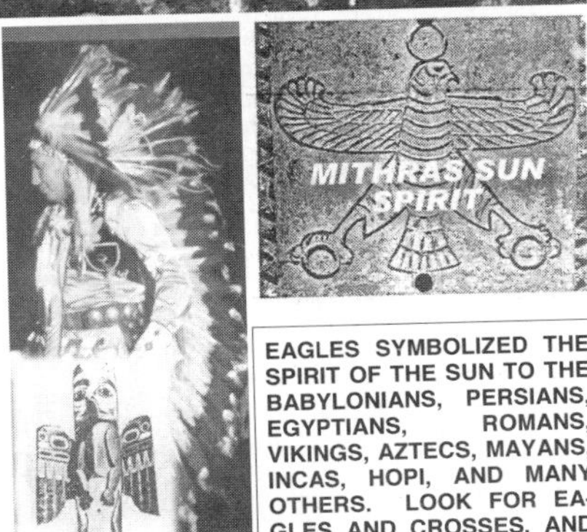

EAGLES SYMBOLIZED THE SPIRIT OF THE SUN TO THE BABYLONIANS, PERSIANS, EGYPTIANS, ROMANS, VIKINGS, AZTECS, MAYANS, INCAS, HOPI, AND MANY OTHERS. LOOK FOR EAGLES AND CROSSES, AND YOU'VE FOUND A LITTLE PIECE OF BABYLON.

ANY DIRECTION BUT
STRAIGHT

"They have left the straight way and wandered off to follow the way of Balaam" ~ 2Pet. 2:15
"Teach me Your way, O 𐤉𐤄𐤅𐤄, lead me in a straight path" ~ Ps. 27:11

worship. Fish are not smart, but they travel in groups, and move in perfect order. But have you ever watched sheep? They wander off, and become prey. We are very much like them. An evangelist on TV can hypnotize many of us to send money to him, and all he has to do is tickle the right emotions in us. The mega-churches use music and lighting to well-up emotions in their audiences. They use tried-and-true methods to pilfer your purse, with a rigid order of sequenced liturgies. People are surrounded by smiles, kindness, and gain a feeling of belonging to their special group. But, they learn very little. A showman merchant throws out the meaning of a Greek word here and there, leading people to believe he is very competent. They will often use the conversation between Peter and 𐤏𐤅𐤔𐤄𐤉 at Yahuchanon 21:15-19, and describe the Greek words for "love", paying great attention to the difference between eros, phileo, and agape "love". It never occurs to the listeners that the resurrected 𐤏𐤅𐤔𐤄𐤉 and Peter weren't speaking Greek, but the Hebrew dialect of Syraic Aramaic. It's all done to make the preacher look very knowledgeable. Actually, the reason Peter was asked ***3 times*** if he loved the Rabbi was because he had denied Him ***3 times***. Peter was instructed to ***feed*** His sheep, meaning teach them, not ***fleece*** them.

The serious offense against the man-made law of not speaking the Name of 𐤉𐤄𐤅𐤄 aloud made the Nazarenes easy prey. Shaul traveled far and wide to cities, and arrested Nazarenes in synagogues, bringing them back to "blaspheme" before the Sanhedrin, the elders of Yisrael. The assembly at Philadelphia, spoken of by 𐤏𐤅𐤔𐤄𐤉 at Rev. 3:7-13, remained steadfast in the Word, and His Name:

"I know that you have little strength, yet you have kept My Word, and have not denied My Name."

People will go to many extremes to show they are sincere and dedicated, yet even when confronted with the "straight" truth, it's more than they can bear to drop the nonsense they are programmed with. The praise and acceptance of men is more important to them than the changes required in abandoning Halloween, Christmas, Sun-day, and Easter. The largest group of Christians in the US is the Pentecostal sect, concentrated heavily in rural areas. Emotions and experiential "faith" seem to motivate them, and this makes it very simple for the showmen merchants to exploit them, cashing-in on their human nature. Yet Paul says ***"Tongues, then, are a sign, NOT FOR BELIEVERS, but for UNBELIEVERS; prophecy, however, is for believers, not for unbelievers. So, if the whole assembly comes together and everyone speaks in tongues, and some who do not understand or some unbeliever comes in, will they not say that you are out of your mind?"*** 1Cor. 14:22,23. He goes on to say that *prophecy* will convict us in our hearts of our sinfulness. "Prophecy" here really means *explaining what the Scriptures mean*, teaching us how to live. "Edify" means *educate.*

Our ears must be "tuned" to discern a lie. When people are not taught, but just undergo emotional experiences, they are trapped and stagnant. "Tongues" are known languages, and require interpreters for those who don't understand them. If everyone already speaks the same language, then foreign languages are unnecessary to use in an assembly. If you really want to sprinkle-in some "foreign" words, use the correct Name! Yet, I've heard Pentecostals say they use the name "Jesus" because *"it's His name in English".* With just a little research, you can find that Pagan deities were called ***ESUS, HESUS,*** and ***IEUSUS.*** Since DEMONS are behind the worship of false deities, then there is a demon named "JESUS". In Hebrew, "he-sus" means "the horse". They can manage to keep the word "Satan" relatively intact across the language barriers, and the word for the Yerushaliyim ***garbage pit*** unmolested, but the ***Name*** above all names they will not accept. This blindness is no doubt caused by programming to a large extent, but it is also possible they are not being sealed with the Name. Nazarene Messianics are coming out of the Paganized assemblies in large numbers today, beginning with their love for the Name. ***"Salvation is found in no one else, for there is no other name under heaven given to men by which we must be saved."*** ~ Acts 4:12.

PAGANISM IS VOMIT ~ 2Pet. 2:19-22

You now have more than enough evidence that proves that the calendar, customs, objects, symbols, and words used by popular religion overwhelmingly originated from Babylonian sun worship. Religion has become socialized, Gentilized, and sterilized of all Scriptural recognition. Every excuse under the sun is used to avoid actually living according to the directives given in the Torah. The Apostasy, as prophesied, is all around us. People have been tricked into following after the beast, and don't even know it. The religious merchants ***"promise them freedom, while they themselves are slaves of depravity— for a man is a slave to whatever has mastered him. If they have escaped the corruption of the world by knowing our Rabbi and Savior OWY3L ha Mashiach and are again entangled in it and overcome, they are worse off at the end than they were at the beginning. It would have been better for them not to have known THE WAY OF RIGHTEOUSNESS*** (Torah)***, than to have known it and then to turn their backs on the sacred command that was passed on to them. Of them the proverbs are true: A DOG RETURNS TO ITS VOMIT, and a pig that is washed goes back to her wallowing in the mud."*** ~ 2Pet. 2:19-22.

The religious merchants are experts in greed. Only a small handful of them can even recite the 10 Commandments, especially in order. The only thing we will carry beyond the grave will be the Torah. Without preparing by having this "oil", our lamps will go out, and we will not be ready when the Bridegroom calls *"Come out"*. Without this light to lead our way, and knowing His Name, we will be shut out from the Wedding Supper of the Lamb. This is not the popular message, so that, in itself, should testify that something is wrong. In fact, the Truth is so bizarre-sounding to most, those who follow it are labeled a "cult". The "familiar" and "popular" behavior of the majority provides a false security blanket. The odd thing is, Christendom is packed tight with so much Paganism, it would be difficult to imagine it containing more! This was done so slowly over time that the average person never questions anything. We need to question everything, and prove all things from Scripture. People who have preconceived notions of what the Scriptures are saying have to take sentences out of context, and "spin" them to mean what they are not saying. They say they KNOW why man is separated from his Creator, but they still make excuses for not doing what He requires, written over and over in His Word. They are messengers of Shatan, not 3Y3L, or they would warn you.

MYSTERY BABYLON
The Great Mother of Harlots and of the Abominations of the Earth:
IDENTIFIED.

BRIDE OF SHATAN: *EXPOSED!*

The goddess of the dawn, queen of heaven, abomination of desolation: ***Easter / Ishtar*** is her name. Astarte, Venus, were others.

The thought of the altar of Zeus being set up on the Temple Mount is unthinkable; but if the Olympic Games are ever held in Yerushaliyim, this could happen as part of a big "peace ceremony". Or, a "May Pole" could be utilized, which for all we know is an Asherah pole. Babylon is the origin of all false worship, and it is called a "harlot" because it draws us away from our Husband, and we pollute ourselves with its Paganism.

THE GREAT MOTHER

In ancient Babylon, the Pagans began to worship a trinity of father Sun, mother Earth, and the re-born "son", who was interpreted to also be the father, come back to life each winter solstice, beginning a "new year". The Sun was thought to be "dying" as it rose lower and lower on the horizon, until it "stopped" (sol-stice means "sun-stop"). By December 25th, it was evident that it had reached its stopping point, and in the ancient world this was the solstice. December 25th was celebrated by Pagans from all over the world, and has been the "birthday" of Nimrod, Baal, Moloch, Dagon, Hercules, Atlas, Mithras, Krishna, Zeus, Osiris, Tammuz, Horus, Apollo, Amon Ra, Bacchus, Ju-piter (Zeus-father), Hermes, Indra, and Buddha (Guatama Sidhartha was born on a different date, but as "Buddha", his birth is celebrated on Dec. 25). "Buddha" means *light-bringer,* just as the Latin word "Lucifer" means. This evidence only shows who is really lurking behind "Christmas", because there was a *Nativity of the Sun* already long established. But, since any "nativity" is a birth, the Pagans thought of it as the *Nativity of the Son*, followed by a "new year" in the dead of winter.

Nimrod established Babylon and Nineveh, in what is now Iraq. The making of bricks and building a tower in order to "make a name" for themselves became the Babylonians' nationalistic obsession. It was believed that the objects in the skies could be reached if one could build high enough. So, they constructed a "high place" on the highest ground they could find. Other than fire, the lights in the heavens were the only luminous objects around. The descendants of Ham and Yapheth wanted to communicate with these heavenly bodies. The principle deity (shining one) was the sun, worshipped for its life-giving warmth. The Babylonians had left the truth behind, and produced their own system of religion based upon **SEX**. The changes in the seasons were "interpreted" by the ancient Pagan mind in a sexual way. They pictured the Earth Mother Ishtar / Easter being "impregnated" in the spring near the Vernal (Venus) equinox. Then, ***nine moons later***, the Sun was said to be "re-born" at the winter solstice. Nimrod's mother, Semiramis, was probably the first "witch" ~ as a person who possessed secret knowledge and powers to manipulate the natural world (*wikkerie*). The "Great Mother", or Magna Mater, was a title given to her.

DEATH OF NIMROD

According to traditional accounts, Noah's son Shem had settled with his clan apart from his 2 brother's clans in Babylon. Nimrod was a descendant of Ham, and the abominations that he committed caused Shem to destroy him. To shock the Babylonians even further, Shem delivered Nimrod's body parts to the far reaches of his Pagan kingdom. This sent the Babylonians into shock, causing their activities to be "occult". Nimrod's mother began to comfort the people by telling them that she was pregnant with Tammuz, who was also "Nimrod", because he was the father of her child. And, she explained, Nimrod had gone into the heavens, and was now the Sun itself. People were led to believe that after death they too would go into the heavens. This is still the belief of many Christians, even though there is not a scrap of evidence contained in Scripture to support this belief (it's Babylonian). Actually, the "saints" (Hebrew: "qodeshim") will inherit the Earth, not heaven (see Ezek. 37:12, Isaiah 65:17, Mt. 5:5). The universe will be ruled from this Earth, restored to its Edenic state. The weeping for Tammuz became the Catholic "LENT".

MAGNA MATER

The Great Mother was translated as *Magna Mater* in Latin, and is this very same "sungoddess" or witch, Semiramis. To the Greeks, Zeus was the sun, and his mother was Lydia, shown riding a swan earlier in this book, with spikes on her head.

EAGLE BAAL-POLES
BAAL/MITHRAS CARRYING SUN ACROSS SKY ----
THE WHOLE WORLD SALUTES HIM TO MUSIC

"AWK ! ! ---- I'M EXPOSED!!"

"THE LONGER IT GOES ON, THE WEIRDER IT GETS."
---- RALPH DOUGLAS WHITE

WATCH-OUT FOR FLAGPOLES ---- MITHRAS IS NIMROD.

The Egyptians depict Isis holding Horus, who is somehow also Osiris, in art that looks **exactly** like the "Madonna and Child" art seen in Christendom. Shatan has been a very busy character, keeping us all in his control over the many thousands of years.

The Phoenicians called Semiramis ***Ishtar***. The Hebrews recorded her name as ***Asherah.*** She has been known throughout the world by many other names; Oster, Easter, Eastre, Eostre, Austron, Eostra, Astoreth, Ostara, Astarte, Artemis, Aphrodite, Tanit, Diana, Nana, Maia, Gaia, Devaki, Ceres, Cybele, Circe, Indrani, Venus, Isis, Frigga, Frey, Biblia, Usha, Eos, Aurora, Ausra, Ushastara, Stella, Aster, Nut (the sky), and others. Astarte, or Venus, was said to have fallen to Earth in a huge EGG ~ Ster; from the word *aster,* (e**Aster**), Latin *stella,* for ***STAR***. By diverting people from worshipping the true Creator, Shatan has designed traps to lure people to worship *him* through stealth. Most don't do it consciously. He removed the Name from our worship, so we won't know specifically who it is we honor: ***"They think the dreams they tell one another will make My people FORGET MY NAME, just as their fathers forgot My Name through Baal worship."*** This text from Yerme Yahu (Jer.) 23:27 is from a time that lying prophets were misleading the people by avoiding 𐤉𐤄𐤅𐤄's great Name. They had begun to just call Him "LORD" (Baal). Read YIrme Yahu 11.

The Magna Mater or "mother & child" worship doesn't mean Shatan is a "he" or "she", because he wasn't created as a male or female. But, he will accept any worship we can spare, as long as we don't do what 𐤉𐤄𐤅𐤄 asks of us. As the "Queen of Heaven" (YIrme Yahu 44:17) the Magna Mater is represented in sculpture with radiant sun-rays around her head. Carved images of her associated with "sacred pillars" rallied multitudes of Pagans to the seasonal observances, because these were the times their Pagan religion ordered grand sexual "services" to be conducted. Many of these people were "shrine prostitutes", both male and female, as can be determined from Gen. 38:21 (where Yahudah *thought* Tamar was a shrine prostitute). The "sacred pillars" were obelisks, like seen in Babylon, Egypt, Rome, London, and the "Washington Monument" in Washington, D.C. They are also the very same Pagan pillars seen on most Christian meeting places today ~ now they're called "steeples". The ancient mind interpreted these religious pillars as a male reproductive organ.

MYSTERY BABYLON: "Queen of Heaven"

The Great Earth Mother, and the religious customs inherited from Babylon, are richly entangled within our world-wide observances, though

WICCA - MEANS "TO BEND", AS IN BENDING EVENTS THROUGH CHANTS OR SPELLS TO DEMONIC SPIRITS

veiled to the average person on the street. Revelation 17 explains how this great prostitute will be brought down, and how she has deceived the nations ~ or caused them to be "intoxicated". Her title remains the same:

MYSTERY BABYLON
The Great Mother of Harlots
And of abominations of the Earth

This religious "system" sits on seven hills, called the Great City. Almost all scholars understand this is Rome, which is in fact built on seven hills from the early Etruscan period. The scholars confuse the issue by claiming this is only ancient PAGAN Rome, and draw a distinction there. This is done so as not to "offend" of course, and keep blinders on everyone. Let's consider if there is anything Pagan still there, shall we? Let me think. The "Great Mother" is what she was called? Well, the Church of Rome calls itself "Mother Church", which is literally "Mother Circe". Do they perform anything remotely Pagan? Yes, the name **Ishtar** became Astoreth, then Eastre, Oster, Astarte, and **Easter**. Easter was a Pagan spring observance brought into Christianity by Constantine I at Nicea in 325 CE. A Webster's Dictionary will tell you quite a lot about the word itself. If this is in fact the ***personal name*** of Mystery Babylon, the Great Mother, why is it the most celebrated observance of Christianity? The answer of course is, Constantine re-invented the meaning behind Easter in order to desolate Passover. He also established the practice of Sun-day, superseding the Scriptural day of rest, Shabbat, which is the "sign" that we worship the true Creator, *as* Creator. He claimed the resurrection as the reason for both Easter and Sun-day, and he got away with it!

EARTH MOTHER IN ROME

The statue of the Great Mother is in the Vatican Museum, and was called Artemis to the Greeks, and Diana to the Romans. "Di" means *to shine*. Diana means *bright one*. That's why she faces the rising sun; she's the dawn deity. The Statue of Liberty in New York Harbor even has seven sunrays, or horns, extending from her *TOWER* headpiece. Many statues of the Earth Mother throughout history have this tower emblem on her head, thus harkening back to Babylon. The torch is an old emblem of fire worship, and even the Greeks' lighting the altar of Zeus at Olympic Games owe this Pagan eccentricity to the ancient Babylonians. Child sacrifice was their real purpose for the torch and altar, and the Sun started the "sacred" flame for the offering.

COME OUT OF HER

WHO IS "SHE"? Asherah, Ishtar, etc.,.
WHAT IS THE "GOLDEN CUP" FILLED WITH ABOMINATIONS? (NOTE "ABOMINATIONS")

Well, what do we know already, and what is employed to lead or guide everyone astray?

MAINLY, IT'S THE BABYLONIAN

CALENDAR

The whole Pagan system is based on SEX. "She" is fertilized in the spring, and gives birth at the winter solstice, and the years are based on when the SUN is re-born. Take the calendar away, and the whole system falls apart! The Roman calendar is based on the same processes established in Babylon. If people live their lives by it, they will not recognize the "seasons" or appointed times that the lights in the sky were **put there** for us to know them (Gen. 1:14). The **calendar of Babylon** holds all the "abominations" together! This dragnet, or "gold cup" intoxicates the people of Earth, and they can't see clearly. The Pagan observances are "abominations", and they "desolate" the Scriptural observances, as Constantine intended.

THE ABOMINATION OF DESOLATION
HAS BEEN SET UP

I've been telling people for years that the Roman calendar is a "dragnet" that guides everyone into indirectly worshipping the sun, ordering their lives according to the old Babylonian mysteries. It fits when you consider the title "Mystery Babylon, the Mother of Harlots, and of the Abominations of the Earth". Since the calendar "regulates" when everyone does what, it has to be the dragnet that intoxicates us with the filth of the harlotries in the golden cup in the woman's hands. The woman in this case is Satan's bride, riding the beast. "Coming out" of her will indeed keep us from participating in her sins, as Rev. 18 describes. This "**Queen of Heaven**" and her daughters deceive the nations even today. Babylon masquerades today even as recorded at Yerme Yahu 44:17. Christianity assimilated her **ways** very early, and abandoned the true straight path of obedience to the Creator, Whose Name is 𐤉𐤄𐤅𐤄. As Peter put it, ***"a dog returns to its vomit . . . "*** ~ 2Pet. 2:22. Being called away from Paganism and idolatry, early Gentiles *fell back* into their old ways by mixing them together with the Messiah message. 𐤉𐤄𐤅𐤔𐤏 *commands us* saying ***"Come out of her, My people . . . "*** at Rev. 18:4. (Get ready for " **Y6K** ".)

"Formerly, when you did not know 𐤉𐤄𐤅𐤄, you were slaves to those who by nature are not elohim. But now that you know 𐤉𐤄𐤅𐤄 ~ or rather are known by 𐤉𐤄𐤅𐤄 ~ how is it that you are turning back to those weak and miserable principles? Do you wish to be enslaved by them all over again? You are observing special days and months and seasons and years! I fear for you, that somehow I have

THE EGYPTIAN SKY, OR QUEEN OF HEAVEN, WAS CALLED "NUT". THIS CLEARLY SHOWS IT IS A WOMAN, AND SEX WAS USED TO INTERPRET THE SEASONS AND PAGAN RITUALS.

COME OUT OF ASHERAH!

SHATAN MASQUERADES BEHIND BOTH MALE AND FEMALE DEITIES.

wasted my efforts on you." Gal. 4:8-11.

Being that the name of the Great Mother is in fact **EASTER**, you need to come out of the mother and her daughters, since they practice Easter, Sun-day, Christmas, and many other intoxicating filth from the golden cup in the Harlot's hand.

Alexander Hislop, in his work *The Two Babylons*, has written about this same topic over 100 years ago, explaining how this fusion occurred with Christianity long ago:

"To conciliate the Pagans to nominal Christianity, Rome, pursuing its usual policy, took measures to get Christian and Pagan festivals amalgamated, and by a complicated but skillful adjustment of the ***calendar****, it was found no difficult matter, in general, to get Paganism and Christianity ~ now far sunk in idolatry ~ in this as in so many other things, to shake hands."*

Ezekiel 8:12-17 discusses how 25 men (the 24 courses of priests + 1 high priest) ***"bowed down to the rising sun and put a branch to their nose."*** The Pagans used branches, wreaths, trees, and became really excited when a sprig of new growth sprang from a tree stump. To them this symbolized their slain Nimrod, and the new life of a branch growing from this stump symbolized Tammuz. In truth, this is how we came to be bringing trees into our homes at Christmas, carried over to the US by the Irish.

BRIDE OF SHATAN, CONSORT OF BAAL

The Great Mother, Easter, has been the main deception for mankind as recorded throughout Scripture. She was called ASHERAH, the "**Queen of Heaven**". Even the words "east" and "estrogen" refer to this abomination. "eAstrology", and "eAstronomy" contain her name as well. At Sinai, what happened was a wedding betrothal and Yisrael became 𐤉𐤄𐤅𐤄's WIFE, as He claims repeatedly. The Covenant was in two stone copies, one for each partner. The wife agreed to obey, and 𐤉𐤄𐤅𐤄 promised to provide. Yisrael was to show her love for 𐤉𐤄𐤅𐤄 by her obedience. Gentiles who convert and begin with the decision reached at Acts 15 engraft into Yisrael. Through belief, and obedience to 𐤉𐤄𐤅𐤔𐤏, they become part of the natural olive tree, Yisrael. Shatan's bride is deceived. They have not taken the name of the husband, but adhere to several Pagan titles such as GOD, LORD, and yes, even "CHRIST" (Kristos, Kris, Krishna, are only a few deities). They flounder aimlessly paying, observing Sun-day, Easter, and Christmas, and have no clue of their true origins. They call our Rabbi "Yeh-Zeus" (but He knows who they mean, right?). They blindly follow the traditions, forsaking the teaching (Torah) given for Yisrael as her marriage Covenant.

"You are servants to the one whom you obey ~ whether you are slaves to sin, which leads to death, or to obedience, which leads to righteousness . . . " Romans 6:16.

If you are obeying Shatan by keeping the traditions he's using to deceive the whole world, then you are embedded in Mystery Babylon, and are his bride, not 𐤉𐤄𐤅𐤔𐤏's. The abominations set up look and feel good, but they are the way of death, because they were not commanded by 𐤉𐤄𐤅𐤄. Their origins in Paganism should expose their Shatanic design. These counterfeit works and wonders were discussed by Paul:

"And then the lawless one will be revealed . . . The coming of the lawless one will be in accordance with the work of Shatan, displayed in all kinds of counterfeit miracles (great works)***, signs, and wonders, and in every sort of evil that deceives those who are perishing. They perish because they refused to love the Truth and so be saved. For this reason Elohim sends them a powerful delusion so that they will believe the lie, and so that all will be condemned who have not believed the Truth, but have delighted in lawlessness."*** ~ 2 Thess. 2:5-

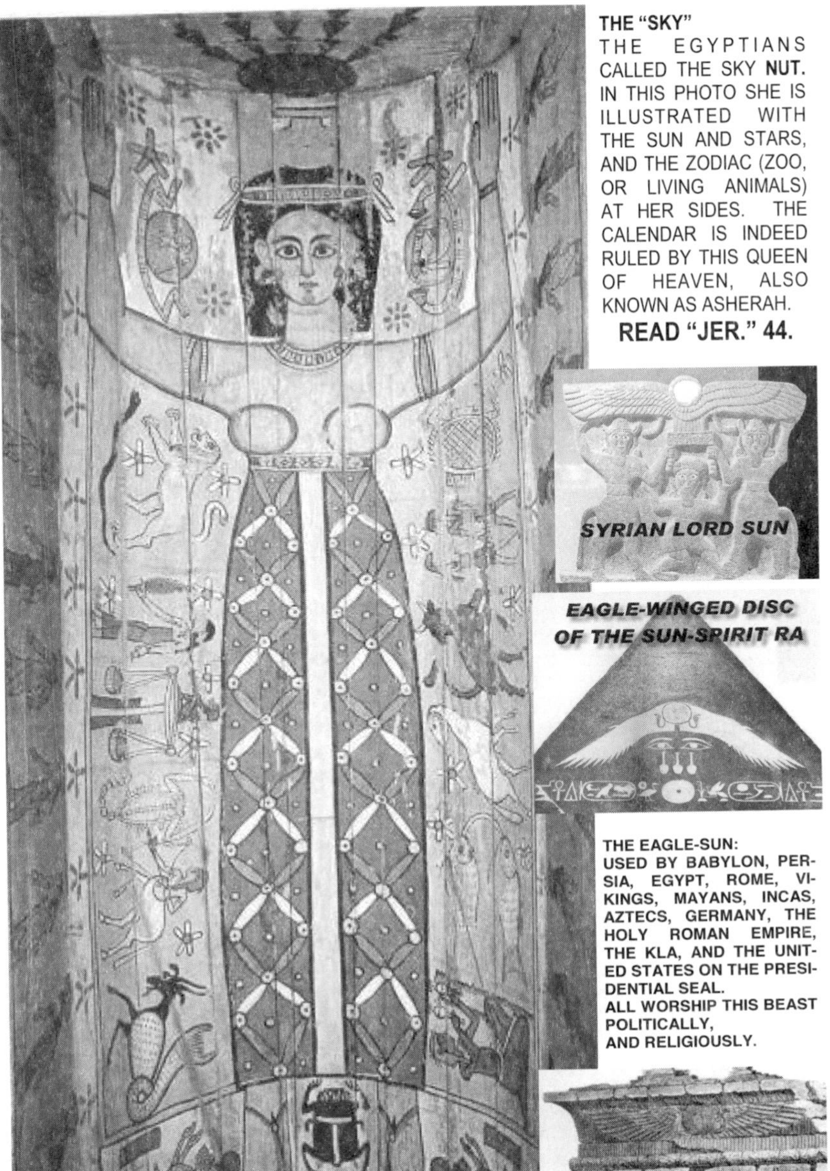

THE "SKY"
THE EGYPTIANS CALLED THE SKY **NUT.** IN THIS PHOTO SHE IS ILLUSTRATED WITH THE SUN AND STARS, AND THE ZODIAC (ZOO, OR LIVING ANIMALS) AT HER SIDES. THE CALENDAR IS INDEED RULED BY THIS QUEEN OF HEAVEN, ALSO KNOWN AS ASHERAH.

READ "JER." 44.

SYRIAN LORD SUN

EAGLE-WINGED DISC OF THE SUN-SPIRIT RA

THE EAGLE-SUN: USED BY BABYLON, PERSIA, EGYPT, ROME, VIKINGS, MAYANS, INCAS, AZTECS, GERMANY, THE HOLY ROMAN EMPIRE, THE KLA, AND THE UNITED STATES ON THE PRESIDENTIAL SEAL. ALL WORSHIP THIS BEAST POLITICALLY, AND RELIGIOUSLY.

12. Is "Sun-day" a delusion? Paul means these people will not obey the Commandments, and condemn "legalism", which the true bride obeys gladly. Those perishing *delight* in **not** obeying the law (Torah). "***Come out of her, My people.***" Do just a little research on *The Inquisition*, and find out what an "iron maiden" is ~ you will be very enlightened to see these things go completely against the "*love your enemies*" philosophy we were commanded to live by. You will recognize a tree by its fruit. In everyday life, you will find that if you pray for someone who is giving you a difficult time, there will be a change in their treatment of you. It actually works!

When we are not humble, we can walk around with a "chip" on our shoulder, and not even be aware of it. When we gossip or ridicule others who are poor, physically impaired, different from us because they're white, black, yellow, red, or some "ethnicity" (*ethnos* means "foreign"), ***we insult their Maker***. I've always tried to make it clear that when I teach or write about Pagan customs, I am not judging people at all, but rather the philosophies themselves. Invariably, some receive the information as an "unloving" criticism of people. In a popular magazine called BAR (*Biblical Archaeological Review*), a reader wrote in saying,

"I understand your position on reporting the facts, but I do not have to read such drivel."

The reader may as well have said,

"My mind's made up; DON'T CONFUSE ME WITH THE FACTS!" (author unknown).

It's easy to steer children down the path of error with Pagan programming. Growing older, many lose their belief because they see through a few things, and realize the shallowness of what they were taught. Others never have the opportunity to comprehend the basis of why the "world" does the things it does. They're "set in their ways". I'm not right about everything, and as I stated earlier, you may differ with me on some details. But, there is a "restoration" taking place, as prophesied at Acts 3:21. A French philosopher, Jean Paul Sartre, said,

"The more sand that has escaped from the hourglass of our life, the clearer we should see through it."

It's scary to think about, but the Scriptures we place our trust in are only translations made by fallible men. In many places they put into the text words and phrases that reflected their doctrinal understanding, and "monked" with it. This is why there are so many different versions. Even the Greek underlying the English has many versions, and no two sentences agree perfectly. This is evidence that the "New Testament" in Greek is only a translation itself!

Christianity today is so fully-packed with Paganism, that if you TRIED, you couldn't get any more in! But, if you took a shoe-horn and forced in a little more, it would POP. When we confront Christian ministers, evangelists, apologists, and so -called "men of GOD" with just a few of the issues brought up in this book, they become cold, and even hateful of us for being critical in our thinking. The bottom line is, their livelihoods are being threatened, because they are profiting from the ignorance of those who remain unaware of the truth.

"'Is not My Word like fire', declares 𐤉𐤄𐤅𐤄, 'and like a hammer that breaks a rock in pieces?'" ~ Yirme Yahu 23:29.

Too bad, but the Truth *will* be shouted from the rooftops! In the *Resources* section in the back, you can contact elder Jacob O. Meyer at the *Assemblies of Yahweh* for a book he has written on the topic of the Name. I know of no other work done on the subject that compares with it. If we can't learn the unadulterated Truth from institutionalized Christianity, then we have to turn to others. A Messianic Natsari from Australia (who recently moved to Tasmania) named John Steed is another elder who I list in the back. He has a wonderful web site with links to others in the Truth. The following is an article he published, re-printed as written:

NEPHILIM

WHEN GIANTS STALKED THE EARTH!

We are all well aware of the story of David and Golyath, how David as a young man killed Golyath who was a giant, around three metres tall. But rarely do we stop to consider how this giant came to be. Giants belong in stories for children like "Jack and the Beanstalk" don't they? Or do they? The idea that a race (or races) of giant semi-human beings once lived on Earth certainly sounds preposterous to most people. Certainly the scientists. When they uncover the skeletons of what appear to be 3-4m tall humans (as they do) they prefer to remain silent, instead speculating over a few bones of some deceased person! But the story of the giants, the Nephilim and the Repha'im, is clearly found in the Scriptures. It is also attested to by Josephus and other ancient Jewish literature. But surprisingly few people are aware of this.

You may, of course, question the spiritual value of knowing the story of the Nephilim ~ it lies in the fact that this forgotten facet of our history holds the answers to many questions that have been asked about the Scriptures. Just a few of the points it enlightens us on are:

1. Why the flood came.
2. Why Noach was chosen.
3. Why Israel was told to slaughter certain Kena'anite peoples ~ men, women and children.

Also it gives greater understanding of the following texts: 1Cor. 6:3, 11:10, & 2Kepha 2:4 ~ to name just a few. But, if nothing else, it like much in Scripture, is an important chapter of the history of sin's destructiveness which should be known by all. The story begins in 1 Mosh. (Gen.) 6:1,2:

"And it came to be, when the Adam began to increase on the face of the ground, and daughters were born to them, that the sons of the Elohim saw the daughters of the Adam,

that they were good. And they took wives for themselves of all whom they chose." (This is a very literal translation from Hebrew). Who were the "sons of the Elohim"? This expression is used only a few times in Scripture and always refers to a being which came into existence by the direct act of Yahueh. Adam himself is called such in Luke 3:38. Yahusha is such, and indeed He opens the way for us to become "sons of Elohim" by being "born again" (born *from above*) ~ Yoch. 1:12. But generally it is used in reference to heavenly beings ~ messengers or "angels" ~ as we see in Iyob (Job) 1:6 and 2:1. This usage is evident here in 1 Mosh. 6:1,2 as the "sons of the Elohim (Yahueh)" are shown in contrast to "the Adam" (mankind).

Some have objected to this concept ~ heavenly beings mating with human women ~ because of what Yahusha said in regard to those who are raised in the resurrection being "as messengers (angels)" and not marrying (Mark 12:25 and Luke 20:34-36). However it is not the meaning of this text in 1 Mosh. ~ That the heavenly beings marry, rather it shows that they departed from their proper role. Indeed other literature that we'll examine shortly supports Yahusha, and says that Yahueh did not intend for the messengers to take wives, but that this action on their part was rebellion against Yahueh. We may wonder how it is possible for heavenly beings to cross-breed with humans. We are not told how this was done, but in an age of in-vitro fertilization and genetic engineering, when human genes have been put into pigs, it should not be difficult for us to imagine how this could be done ~ as indeed it was!

We read further in 1 Mosh. 6:4 the following:

"The Nephilim were on the Earth in those days, and <u>also afterward</u>, when the sons of the Elohim came in to the daughters of the Adam and they bore children to them. Those were the mighty men who were of old, the men of name." Nephilim (Strong's #5303 from #5307 *"to fall"*) probably means "fallen ones" in reference to these heavenly beings who fell ~ physically and spiritually. Or alternatively it means "fellers" or "slayers" due to the fact that these beings brought slaughter to the Earth. This first occurrence is prior to the flood, and indeed as is mentioned in the chapter (v. 6) is the reason why the flood occurred. Mankind became so genetically mixed with the Nephilim that few of the pure race of Adam remained, and it probably would have become extinct if Yahueh had not intervened. We read in verse 9 of this chapter that Yahueh chose Noach because he was a "righteous man, <u>*perfect in his generations*</u> (descent, family history)". In other words, Noach and his family were of the pure race of Adam, able to carry the line into a new beginning.

Notice how in 1 Mosh. 6:4 it says that not only were the Nephilim on the Earth "in those days" but also "afterward", that is, after the flood. In 4 Mosh. (Numbers) 13:33 we strike the Nephilim for the second time in the report of the spies regarding the land of Kena'an ~

And we saw there the Nephilim, sons of Anak, of the Nephilim. And we were like grasshoppers in our own eyes, and so we were in their eyes."

This is the first direct reference to them being of large size (see previous verse also). Back in 1 Mosh. 6:4 we were only told that they were "mighty men . . . Men of name." Undoubtedly the actions and exploits of these Nephilim were the basis for the Pagan deities and mythology. These giants were also called Repha'im; we find this name used not only for the Anakim, but also the Emmim (5 Mosh. / Deut. 2:10,11, and Zamzumim (v. 20). Og, who you will remember was the giant of Bashan, was of the Repha'im (5 Mosh. 3:11). His bed was over 4m long! Indeed Bashan had formerly been a land of the Repha'im, the remnants of their giant-sized cities can still be found there today. They were there in the time of Abraham as we read in 1 Mosh. 14:5.

We are not told how this second outbreak of Nephilim came about. Those sons of Elohim who were responsible for the pre-flood outbreak had been imprisoned in the Earth to await the day of judgment as we read in 2 Kepha 2:4:

"For if Elohim did not spare the messengers who sinned, but sent them to Tartaros, and delivered them in chains of darkness, to be kept for judgment."

However, the Adversary undoubtedly had other heavenly beings at his service to corrupt the "seed of the women" ~ for this seems to have been the aim ~ to prevent the coming of the Messiah, the promised "seed" (1 Mosh. 3:15) by corrupting the genetic line. Yahueh Himself intervened by means of the flood in the first instance, and in the second He used the children of Abraham and Lot to destroy them (see 5 Mosh. 2:21-23). And He instructed Yisrael to completely destroy those peoples who had mixed with them (5 Mosh. 20:16,17). Of course it was David and his men who finally finished the job, killing the last of the giants ~ Golyath and his family (2 Shemu'el 21:15-22).

As mentioned earlier, ancient Jewish literature upholds these facts. Josephus the Jewish historian mentions it briefly ~ but I don't have his works at hand to quote them ~ check this for yourselves. The book of Jubilees 5:1-6 says the following:

"And it came to pass when the sons of men began to increase on the Earth, and daughters

were born to them that in the first year of the jubilee the angels of Elohim looked on them and saw that they were beautiful; and they took wives from as many of them as they chose. And they bore them sons: and they became giants . . . And against the angels He had sent on Earth His anger was so great that He uprooted them from their dominion and commanded us to imprison them in the depths of the Earth; and behold they are in prison there and separate".

The book of Enoch, which comes to us from the Ethiopian version of the Scriptures, and from which comes the quote in Yahudah / Jude 1:14,15, contains extensive material on this subject. Enoch, or more properly Chanok, was given a special mission to bear witness against these rebels and to record their actions to the end of time. Chanok records that these messengers were of the order called "Watchers" (see Dan. 4:13 & 23), so-called because their task was to watch over mankind ~ guardian angels. Chanok writes: ***"And it came to pass when the sons of men had increased, that in those days there were born to them fair and beautiful daughters. And the angels, the sons of heaven, saw them and desired them. And they said to one another, 'Come, let us choose for ourselves wives from the children of men, and let us beget for ourselves children.' And Semyaza who was their leader, said to them, "I hear that you may not wish this deed to be done, and that I may alone pay for this great sin.' And they all answered him and said, 'Let us swear an oath, and bind one another with curses not to alter this plan, but to carry out this plan effectively.' Then they all swore together and all bound one another with curses to it. And they were in all two hundred, and they came down on Ardis which is the summit of Mount Hermon."*** He then records a list of the names of the leaders of these two hundred, followed by:

"And they took wives for themselves, and every one chose for himself one each. They began to go into them and were promiscuous with them . . . And they became pregnant and bore large giants . . . These devoured all the toil of men, until men were unable to sustain them. And the giants turned against them in order to devour men. And they began to sin against birds, and against animals, and against reptiles, and against fish, and they devoured one anothers' flesh and drank blood from it. Then the Earth complained about the lawless ones." Further on he tells of Yahueh's judgment against them, this being first the sending of the flood ~ in the future ~ which Noach is informed of; then:

"Further Yahueh said to Raphael, 'Bind Azazel (who had taught mankind the making of weapons of war) ***by his hands and feet . . . And split open the desert which is in Deudael, and throw him there. And cover him with darkness; and let him stay there forever . . . That on the day of judgment he may be hurled into the fire.' And Yahueh said to Michael, 'Go inform Semyaza and the others with him . . . When all their sons kill each other, and when they see the destruction of their beloved ones, bind them for seventy generations under the hills of the Earth until the day of judgment . . . And in those days they will lead them to the abyss of fire.'"***

As mentioned previously, Yahueh also speaks of how the Watchers were not intended to have wives, He says to Chanok:

"And go, say to the Watchers of heaven who sent you to petition on their behalf, 'You ought to petition on behalf of men, not men on behalf of you. Why have you left the high and set-apart and eternal heaven, and lain with women . . . , and taken wives for yourselves, and done as the sons of the Earth and begotten giant sons . . . And for this reason I gave them (mankind) ***wives, namely that . . . Children might be born by them, that thus deeds might be done on the Earth. But you formerly were spiritual, living an eternal, immortal life for all the generations of the world. For this reason I did not arrange wives for you because the dwelling of the spiritual ones is in heaven.'"***

There is much more recorded in the book of Enoch on the subject of the sin of the Watchers, and Nephilim, including some interesting things regarding the source of evil spirits ~ but we will leave that for another time!

~ John Steed

"As the twig is bent, so grows the tree"
~ Alexander Pope

"I took a piece of plastic clay,
and idly fashioned it one day ~
"And as my fingers pressed it still,
It moved and yielded to my will ~
"I came again when days were past,
The bit of clay was hard at last ~
"The form I gave it still it bore,
And I could fashion it no more.

"I took the piece of living clay,
And gently pressed it day-by-day ~
"And molded with my power and art,
A young child's soft and yielding heart ~
"I came again when years had gone,
It was a man I looked upon ~
"He still that early impression bore,

And I could fashion him no more!
Author unknown

THE SEEDS OF THE KINGDOM

The Latin word "doctrine" means teaching, and the "teachings" are seeds. They are either sown by the Father, 𐤉𐤄𐤅𐤄, or an enemy. The evidence of what was sown is revealed by what grows. The true seed sown by the Father is His Commandments. This is illustrated by the parable of the Sower, at Mt. 13. Veiled hearts cannot understand the parables, as you will notice the footnotes in your Scriptures struggle to deal with the true meanings of texts that require spiritual discernment. (As most of them do!).

"The knowledge of the secrets of the Kingdom of heaven has been given to you, but not to them." Mt. 13:11.

Rabbi 𐤉𐤄𐤅𐤔𐤏 explained the meaning of the Sower, but even so, His explanation is not understandable to those whose hearts are veiled.

"Listen then, to what the parable of the Sower means: When anyone hears the message about the kingdom and does not understand it, the evil one comes and snatches away what was sown in his heart." The "birds" came and ate it up. This is Shatan saying, *"this Commandment was done away with"*, or *"that Commandment is only for Jews to obey"*. Thus, by trickery, the evil one explains we don't need a particular "seed".

"The one who received the seed that fell on rocky places is the man who hears the Word, and at once receives it with joy. But since he has no root, he lasts only a short time. When trouble or persecution comes because of the Word, he quickly falls away." This is like one of us who understands, but then his family, peers or preacher criticize him saying things like *"you've come in contact with some kind of cult"* or *"how can the whole world be wrong?"*. Then, they turn away from Truth.

"The one who received the seed that fell among the thorns is the man who hears the Word, but the worries of this life and the deceitfulness of wealth choke it, making it unfruitful." This is like one who works on the 7th day, and is intimidated by bosses or co-workers when he wishes to rest. They say, "*All it means is that we should take off one day in every 7*" or *"I can't afford to eat kosher, the meat is too expensive"*. But, you'll find that taking it day-by-day, week-by-week, it's easy to obey. The "Decalogue" (deca, *ten* ~ logue, *words*) will be around *forever.* They will cry *"legalism!!"* ~ and that's the persecution. We must listen to the guiding principles for Gentile beginners from the letter from the Yerushaliyim Council at Acts 15. Leviticus 11, 19, and 23 are still binding upon all believers, and easy to obey; but the enemy has stolen the true seed from most, and replaced it with the tares, or teachings of error. The teachings we live in are either our Father's Words, or they are the "tares" of the enemy, the one who changes the laws. The wife of Adam was deceived in this same way.

When you sincerely pray for Truth, you will receive it. When you cry for help, the eyes of Him who seeks to-and-fro for any who understand will immediately send you the Truth.

"How gracious He will be when you cry for help! As soon as He hears, He will answer you . . . Your teachers will be hidden no more; with your own eyes you will see them. Whether you turn to the right or to the left, your ears will hear a voice behind you, saying 'This is the way, walk in it.' Then you will defile your idols overlaid with silver and your images covered with gold; you will throw them away like a menstrual cloth and say to them 'Away with you!'". ~ Yesha Yahu 30:19-22. No matter how "precious" the Pagan observances were to you, you will become sickened by the whole calendar that spews out their Babylonian vomit. The cakes baked for the Queen of Heaven (birthday cakes), Christmas trees, Easter baskets, jack-o-lanterns, and the broad road of "Sun-day" will be like a menstrual cloth to you. People will ask you, *"Are you a 'Jew'?"* "Jew" means *Yahudi,* a worshipper of YAH. You are engrafted into Israel, in Mashiach. You are an "Israelite", of the sect of Messianic Natsarim. We are ALL priests, of the order of Melchizedek (King of Righteousness). You need not Earthly man's approval, or acceptance; rather, seek the approval of 𐤉𐤄𐤅𐤄, through His Son, 𐤉𐤄𐤅𐤔𐤏.

"<u>Do not learn the ways of the nations</u>, and do not be alarmed by the signs (Zodiac, ZOO, beasts, constellations, Pagan calendar observances) ***of shamayim -*** (the heavens)***, although the nations are alarmed by them. For the CUSTOMS of these peoples are worthless; for one cuts a <u>TREE</u> from the forest . . . They adorn it with silver and gold, they fasten it with nails and hammers so that it does not topple."*** ~ Yirme Yahu 10:2-4.

Again, remember there is <u>*no*</u> <u>*covenant*</u> with "Christians", but only with Yisrael. Psalm 147:19,20 says:

"He has revealed His Word to Ya'aqob, His Laws and Decrees to YISRAEL. He has done this for <u>no other nation</u>; They do not know His Laws."

The Torah is for all men to submit to. Wisdom cries out from the Scriptures. Our duty is to obey:

"Of the making of many scrolls there is no end,

and much study wearies the body. Now, ALL has been heard;
HERE IS THE CONCLUSION OF THE MATTER: Fear Elohim, and <u>keep His Commandments</u>, for THIS is the DUTY of ALL MEN. For Elohim will bring every deed into judgment, including every hidden thing, whether it is good or evil." ~ Ecclesiastes 12:12-14.

BEWARE THE DOCTRINES OF DEMONS

Following the Pagan calendar's prescribed events, people are unknowingly worshipping demons. Read all of 1 Timothy the first chance you get!

"The Spirit clearly says that in later times some will abandon the faith and follow deceiving spirits and <u>things</u> taught by demons." 4:1.

In this section, Paul explains men will forbid marriage, as was done by Catholicism. The food we eat that has been "consecrated" (meaning approved) by the Word (at Lev. 11) is all good to eat. This text is used to teach that lobsters, shrimp, crab, oysters, clams, swine, rabbit, etc., is now "clean" ~ but this is not what Paul is saying.

"All Scripture is Elohim-breathed and is useful for teaching, rebuking, correcting, and training in righteousness, so that the man of Elohim may be thoroughly equipped for every good work." 2 Tim. 3:16,17.

"Do not merely <u>listen</u> to the Word, and so deceive yourselves. Do what it says. Anyone who listens to the Word but does not do what it says is like a man who looks at his face in a mirror and, after looking at himself, goes away and immediately forgets what he looks like. But the man who looks intently into the PERFECT LAW that gives freedom (from sin)***, and continues to do this, not forgetting what he has heard, but doing it ~ he will be blessed in what he does."*** Ya'aqob (James) 1:22-25.

DING ! ! !
Oh-oh. . . . . .
There's that "eagle" again. And LOOK! He seems to have a dragon along for a friend. Does any of this "ring a bell"? The adversary leaves his signature, if you have the eyes to see it.

Bronze Bell from a Buddhist temple in Japan, used in religious rites.

When Galileo had refined his optics to the extent that he could see spots on the sun, orbiting moons circling the 5th planet, and had irrefutable proof of the Copernican Theory (sun-centered system), the RCC rewarded his efforts by arresting him. The Inquisitor Cardinal Bellarmine, who arrested Galileo, has a university named after him in Louisville, KY, USA. They almost burned Galileo at the stake, but he agreed to recant, and died under permanent house arrest. In CE 1989 they "re-instated" Galileo back into the Roman Mother Church. The search for truth is often met with violent opposition, and the Inquisition used violence to stamp out truth. They were not interested in truth, otherwise they would have pursued it, and used it to prove whatever it was they were promoting. Inquisitor Bellarmine might not have granted this book a "Nihil Obstat/Imprimatur" either.
I'd be killed, and so would anyone else who had ever been in contact with this book.

We have become numb and comfortable with the Paganism around us, but unaware of it or its consequences. The familiar illuminati image, with the "all-seeing-eye" of Nimrod, is on our US Dollar Bill. This same shining "Eye-in-the-Sky" held the people of Egypt in its spell as Horus. Because of Nimrod's idolatry, his uncle Shem killed him.

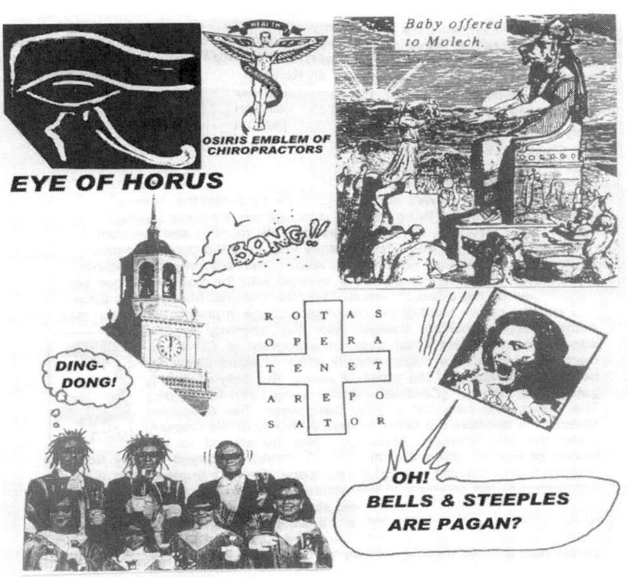

"There is no rest day or night for those who worship the beast and his image, or for anyone who receives the mark of his name." - Rev. 14:11. They will have NO Sabbath, which is the Covenant -sign of Creation, not the resurrection.

THE ISHMAEL SYNDROME:

"And the messenger of Yahuah said to her, 'see, you are conceiving and bearing a son, and shall call his name YISMAEL, because Yahuah has heard your affliction. '" (ISHMAEL means El hears) "'AND HE IS TO BE A WILD MAN, HIS HAND AGAINST EVERY ONE, AND EVERY-ONE'S HAND AGAINST HIM, AND DWELL OVER AGAINST ALL HIS BROTHERS.'"
GEN./ BERESHITH 16:11.12

This helps explain why there is so much trouble with Ishmael's descendants, and their spiritual descendants deriving from the Islamic threat and terrorism all over the civilized world today.

SUNS, EAGLES, CROSSES, BALLS, STEEPLES, AND BELLS . . . . .
JUST WHAT WE NEED!
COULD IT BE THAT THE IMAGE OF THE BEAST, THE EAGLE, IS WHAT CROSSES REALLY REPRESENT? THE "GREAT PROSTITUTE", OR FALSE RELIGION, HOLDS IT VERY DEAR. THE INHABITANTS OF EARTH WILL BE ASTONISHED!
READ REVELATION, CHAPTERS 13 THROUGH 18.

WHEN THE TRUTH IS UNCOVERED, THEY HIDE IT, LIKE THE GIANTS THE ARCHAEOLOGISTS DIG UP REGULARLY. THE NEPHILIM REALLY DID EXIST, BUT TO ADMIT IT WOULD CONFIRM THAT YAHUAH'S WORD IS ALL TRUE.

Some have hypothesized that Melchizedek was Shem. Nimrod's wife/mother, Semiramis, was perhaps the first noteworthy woman to be possessed by the adversary. She "deified" her dead husband Nimrod, and led the Babylonians to worship him as ***Baal***, the Sun. She became the Earth Mother, and was also known as the *"goddess of the dawn".* Towers or turrets were part of her crown all through the ages, based on the Babylonian "ziggurat", the tower of Babel. Diana (Artemis, Asherah) of Ephesus had a tower headpiece. The ***Statue of Liberty*** has both a tower headpiece, and rays. The more one studies history and Paganism, it becomes increasingly apparent that "Satan" has concealed himself as *female* just as often as male. The rising popularity of the ***"Mother Goddess"*** is simply another masquerade by which ha shatan diverts wor-

THE GREAT SEAL

ship toward "himself" — a sexless fallen cherub without a name.

The power *behind* powerful men all through history has been this nameless being we refer to as ha shatan, or Lucifer, the "light-bringer". Most all the popular customs over the Earth point back to ancient Babylon, and it's founder, Nimrod, the builder of towers. Masons celebrate Nimrod as their founder. Shem, the preserver of the ***Torah***, points the way for the "children of light". Nimrod, the tyrant who rebelled against 𐤉𐤄𐤅𐤄, has established a pattern of folly, and leads the world to continue the production of ignorant "children of darkness". The "sign" of this Nimrod / Sun God is "Sun-day", and this action is set against the recognition of the true Creator, Who set-apart the seventh day to commemorate His work (not Sun-day).

The "position" or "office" of the deceiver of men has moved across the Earth over time*. It began in Babylon, eventually found the throne of the king of Tyre (Ezek. 28:12-16), Pergamum (Rev. 2:13), Rome, Germany, and now resides in Washington mainly (although he can move about quite quickly around the entire Earth). He has always used the ***emblem of the eagle*** as his principal image. His rulership is not only over secular government, but all religious government as well. The Papacy has been one of his most deadly instruments. The "anti-Messiah" is one who stands "in place of" the Faithful and True Anointed One, and the title ***"Vicar of Christ"*** bestowed on the Pope has the meaning *"in-place-of"* Messiah. Daniel 11:37 describes this "office", *which will endure until the time of the end*, and this man of "celibacy" ***"will show no regard for the elohim of his fathers or for the DESIRE OF WOMEN".*** Looking at the towers and turrets around the Earth, it is apparent they are of some ancient significance. Could it be that the ***"elohim of fortresses"*** referred to in Daniel 11:38,39 is Nimrod, and these fortresses are the steeples, towers, turrets, and high places which our Father 𐤉𐤄𐤅𐤄 calls pillars of jealousy? Is Nimrod truly "the *Great Architect"* the Masons worship in their Masonic Temples? Behind Nimrod is ha Shatan, who is also Semiramis, Tammuz, Astarte, Asherah, Ashteroth, Ge, Gaia, Molech, Baal, Venus, Woden, Aphrodite, Cupid, Pluto, Jupiter, Mars, Mercury, Orion, Ninus, Zeus, Apollo, and Beelzebub. The names he/she goes by are without end. His/her image is on our currency, so no man may buy or sell without his image, seal, and value given in his name. "In GOD We Trust" is not exactly specific, is it? The GOD of this world exacts worship, honor, and obedience — and he is opposed to the Covenant, and hates those who live by it.

The United Nations' banner displays the whole Earth encircled by the ancient wreath/crown of Caesar. The General Assembly is eventually to be the legislative branch of the New World Order; the Security Council will act as the Judicial branch; NATO will be the executive branch. This beast's false prophet will be the papacy, who will use smooth words to convince the world to follow the leader of NATO, which will be a great peacemaker, but also the end-time anti-Messiah. He will anoint himself the leader and sovereign ruler of the Earth. From this position, he will move against those who do not conform to his proclaimed moons and "holy days". This is why we must be as "wise as serpents, but harmless as doves." The "peacemakers" are already fighting under the banner of the UN, and will ultimately move against the wife of 𐤉𐤄𐤅𐤄 — Tsiyon (Zion). **Israel** has a different calendar than Babylon. She is the bearer of the Covenant (marriage vows / Commandments), and is the wife of the Maker of the universe. The two witnesses will prophesy the end-time message of repentance to the whole Earth, and soon after that planet-wide destruction will threaten all life on Earth.

Nationalism began in ancient Babylon — the people sought to "make a name for themselves", so others would fear them. Control mechanisms began, national "laws" were instituted, and land was placed under dominion and ownership of powerful rulers. The nations themselves became more than just their populations; they took on a type of incorporeal persona, or life of their own. While individual men would live and die, the nation would go on. The men who were most corrupt, driven by greed, power, and lust, were usually the ones who rose to the top. So, today, and next year, where do our leaders come from? They are all struggling and fighting their way to the top of a pyramid of power, established by Nimrod back in Babylon. Babylon is the "head" of the kingdoms of the Earth. Men's kingdoms are really ruled by Shatan, who was once "the anointed cherub who

*** SATAN'S SEAT OR THRONE ..... EXAMPLE, REV. 2:13**

covers" (Ezek. 28:14), the "star of the morning, son of the dawn" (Yesha Yahu 14:12).

So, mankind's horrific history is not all his own doing, but rather his choices. Mankind has been led by a powerful entity that is filled with intense hatred. Fallen from the highest place of all, our nameless adversary once enjoyed being in the presence of the Throne of 𐤉𐤄𐤅𐤄. He was the most beautiful and powerful creature — above all the Watchers; and was loved dearly by 𐤉𐤄𐤅𐤄. When pride swelled inside him, it corrupted his judgment; he sought equality with 𐤉𐤄𐤅𐤄. This grew into a murderous rage, and there was WAR between the Sons of 𐤉𐤄𐤅𐤄 who followed him, and those who did not. This cherub set up a system of control on this planet, and each person born here unwittingly comes under his sovereignty.

Throughout time, a few of us have been chosen, and trained by the Spirit of Truth (𐤉𐤄𐤅𐤄) to leave a witness to the facts preserved in the writings of the prophets. We do not enter the pages of history, except in the instances that we become a threat, are discovered, and expunged. Of the increase of Yahusha's government there will be no end. This is not to say it will grow larger and larger visibly on the Earth, but that there will always be people awakened as others die — thus it still grows larger. As the time of the Gentiles grows shorter, so does the time for the fallen cherub.

THE SPIRIT WAS MOVING ON THE FACE OF THE WATERS

The "Spirit" is 𐤉𐤄𐤅𐤄 (Yahuah). Yahuah is Spirit, and cannot be seen. He put His "Spirit" on Mosheh, El Yahu (Elijah), El Yesha (Elisha); and Dawid pleaded "Do not take your Ruach ha Qodesh from me". Some perceive this "Spirit" is the personality of Yahuah; others claim it is his "power". Being Spirit, what does Yahuah want? He wants to look out through our eyes, completely possessing us. This involves a union that is analogous to a marriage. This is the purpose of all Creation, that Yahuah may be "all in all", and the Body of Yahusha is the pre-eminent focus of all Creation, with Yahusha as the Head. The Spirit of Yahuah made "covenants" with Abraham, Yitshaq, and Ya'akob, and the descendants of the 12 tribes / families of Yisrael, at Sinai -- the marriage of Yahuah to His Bride, Yisrael. Yahuah is ONE, He is not schizophrenic, nor multiple persons. He becomes the fulfillment of our needs, and takes on specific roles, as I can be a managing boss to my employees, a husband to my wife, a father to my sons, a friend to a neighbor, a brother to my brothers -- yet I'm just one man. Yahuah can manifest (show) Himself in diverse ways. Mosheh certainly didn't think He was a bush. The Shekinah Kabod was Yahuah, and He goes wherever His Name is honored. His "eyes" search back and forth across the Earth to find any who understand. The plural "Elohim" refers to His immensity; Yahuah is the El who swore oaths to Abraham, Yitshaq, and Ya'akob. The oaths are plural, not Yahuah. The titles Yahuah Rapha, Yahuah Yireh, Yahuah Nissi, etc., are "roles", they are not different names. Churchianity has come to accept the name "Jesus Christ" as if "Christ" were a last name. The Hebrew original was not "Christ", but Mashiach. This is a title also, meaning He is our "anointed" RULER. In Hebrew, it would be "Yahusha ha Mashiach". In this role, Yahuah is our salvation, and "Yahusha" means "Yahuah our Deliverer".

The New Covenant (Brit Chadasha) sealed in Yahusha's blood is the culmination of Yahuah's objective to redeem His chosen bride, the remnant. This New Covenant is: Yahusha WRITING His Torah on our hearts and minds, circumcising our hearts with His Commandments. This is referred to at Hebrews 8:8-12, Yerme Yahu 31:31-34, and Ezekiel 36:26,27. You will note that this Covenant is to be with the "House of Israel" and the "House of Yahudah" -- these are the two houses of the Northern and Southern Kingdoms. The 10 tribes of the House of Israel were scattered by the Assyrians into the nations.

Yahusha's mission, both 2000 years ago, and NOW, is to regather the "lost sheep of the *tribes* of Israel". He is doing this through His Natsarim, because many who thought they were "goyim" and following Nimrod's fossilized customs are returning to their Husband, and turning their backs on tradition. We announce the same "message" of the Kingdom, ***"Repent, for the Reign of Yahuah draws near."*** Repenting means to return, turn around. Yahusha came to restore the Torah to its fullness so that truth and justice could be restored. He told us to not even think He had come to destroy the Torah. This verifies that the "APOSTASY" (falling away) spoken of in 2 Thess. 2 has happened. It involves some definite "religious lawlessness" -- a delusion -- because those in the apostasy believe the LIE, and delight themselves with lawlessness. This "lawlessness" means they have not received the Spirit of Yahusha, Who circumcises our hearts with His Torah (Commandments) -- and they are not in the "New Covenant", but rather are deluded. Human customs ensnare millions of people, benefiting swindlers who "peddle" the Word of Yahuah for profit -- the rich merchants of Revelation 18.

Most perceive that the Scriptures teach we will "see" (GOD) and "Jesus" seated at His "right hand". Two seats? The first problem here is understanding the Hebraism "right hand". It means simply "authority", not literally on the right side of someone. These kinds of issues really don't matter salvationally. Remember, the thief on the stake who died next to Yahusha didn't have all his "dogma" worked out in every detail -- but he had enough LOVE, kindness, and sought justice; and accepted his penalty -- while the other thief was making a joke, and inviting Yahusha to do something to rescue them all. In fact, Yahusha WAS DOING something to rescue ALL OF MANKIND. So, in all our struggles attempting to understand these things, we must keep focused on love, joy, peace, patience, kindness, goodness, faithfulness, gentleness, and self control. We must have love for each other, and the Truth; even love our enemies.

Scripture also states that the Father is greater than the Son. Well, when we see Yahusha, we are seeing the Father; this is what Yahusha told brother Philip. Actually, Yahusha is all of the Father we will ever see, and He will be seated on the Throne Himself. Yahuah became a man. He took the form of sinful flesh, and died to atone once-and-for-all His bride. The Husband had to die, ending the Old Covenant / Marriage, so the Bride could re-marry; a bride is bound to her husband until he dies, and so, HE DID. The Old Covenant was imperfect, because it was written in stone, not the heart; it was also sealed in animal blood, and atonement required yearly offerings. Obedience was rewarded with blessing, disobedience with curses and death. The New Covenant involves the Torah circumcised on our hearts, so we walk in the Spirit, not the mind of the flesh -- which cannot and will not obey. Our immersion pictures this circumcision, the death of the mind of the flesh, and the resurrection to life of the mind of the Spirit. The Torah thus becomes our way of life, and wells up into unending rivers of LIVING WATER (the eternal Commandments of Life). If we have this seed (the Commandments) within us, we have the Truth, Life, and are children of Yahuah; children of LIGHT.

Constantine I decreed that the Venerable "Day of the Sun" was to be the empire's day of complete rest in 321 CE, thus fulfilling Dan. 7:25. This Universal (Catholic) Edict was imposed under penalty of death; and Shabbat (the 7th day, commemorating CREATION, Gen. 2:2, Ex. 20:8-11, Ex. 31:13-17, Ezek. 20:12, 44:24, Yesha Yahu 66:23, Hebrews 4:1-12) and it's observance were abandoned for the ways of Balaam, Nimrod, Shatan, etc.,. The ONE Who covenanted with Abraham, Yitshaq, Ya'akob and spoke with Mosheh in the burning shrub, was the same ONE Who became "the Son": Yahuah.

The Father is "greater" because He is infinite in size, time, and power; looking at the majesty of Yahusha is but a small glimpse, and for this reason Yahusha said ***"Abba is greater than I".*** Every knee will bow, and every tongue will confess that Yahusha is Yahuah, to the esteem of Elohim the Father". Didymus / Thomas fell down and confessed "my Adonai and my Elohim" to Yahusha. The "Captain of the Armies of Yisrael" allowed the man Yahusha / called Joshua to KNEEL before Him.

"And I will pour out on the House of Da'ud and on the inhabitants of Yerushaliyim the Spirit of unmerited lovingkindness and supplication, so that they will LOOK ON ME -- WHOM THEY HAVE PIERCED; and they will mourn for Him, as one mourns for an only son, and they will weep bitterly over Him, like the bitter weeping over a first-born." -- Zech. 12:10

This will reflect back to the execution of Yahusha, the Passover Lamb's purpose, and the covering of Adam and Chuwah in the bloody sheepskins put on them. It will also bring to mind the moment Yosef revealed himself to his brothers who sold him into slavery and he became the ruler of all Egypt. Those who looked on Yosef saw the authority of the Pharaoh, but yet it wasn't Pharaoh. Many of these things will become clearer through study, and this is why it is good that we are being forced to go to the Words of Yahuah. We must try hard to not go in with the intention of finding the passages that agree with our traditional mindset, but rather let the Truth come through to replace the errors we've been taught. There are not many who know Yahusha is Yahuah, but the overcomers are finding out. AT THE EASTERN GATE, WHEN YAHUSHA RETURNS, Scripture states: ***"And behold, the esteem of the Elohim of Israel was coming from the way of the east; and His voice was like the sound of many waters; and the earth shone with His esteem."*** -- Ezek. 43:2.

JUST BEFORE YAHUCHANON (John) TURNED TO SEE THE VOICE SPEAKING, HE HEARD:

"Behold, He is coming with the clouds, and every eye will see Him, even those who pierced Him; and all the tribes of the earth will mourn over Him. Even so, Amein. 'I AM THE ALEF AND THE TAU' says Adonai Elohim, 'WHO IS AND WHO WAS AND WHO IS TO COME, THE ALMIGHTY'". -- Rev. 1:7,8.

Then Yahuchanon turned, to see Yahusha speaking, amid a menorah (seven lampstands), His sign. The menorah represents the Torah, the Tree of Life, the oil of which gives LIGHT to the world (by metaphor, the Commandments). He is the Living Word, the Torah made flesh. The Hebrew word for the personal NAME of Yahuah literally means "I was, I am, I will be" ("I will be there" as translated by some). Look closely at the phrase in Rev. 1:8 above ***"Who is and Who was and Who is to come"***. Yahusha is describing the meaning of His Name. Those "sealed" with the Name of the Father (see Rev. 7, and 14:1) will

know His Name; these living saints will number 144,000, and no lie will be found in their mouths.

"You will not see Me again, until you say: 'Baruch haba baShem Yahuah'" (Blessed is the One Who comes in the Name of Yahuah)

Note that Yahusha is **not** saying we will not see Him again until we say "GOD", or Theos, or Lord. Alexander Hislop's work The Two Babylons mentions that Nimrod was widely known by many different names and titles. He traces all fire-worship back to him, and the custom of "purifying" oneself by offering one's children in fire. One of Nimrod's titles was "ADON", meaning LORD. This is simply the root of the Hebrew word *adonai*, which means "my lord". This eventually became *Aden, and "ODIN"* (Woden) in Norse mythology. So, we can see this is but one example of dozens that can show that Nimrod is very much still with us — he's hidden in the name for the 4th day of every week (Woden's Day). People who rationalize that the true Creator "knows our hearts," so we can continue in our Nimrod customs, are playing with not only their own welfare, but any others who may find comfort in large numbers. Remember, Yahusha told us that many would be taken by surprise, and His return would be just like the days of Noah. The majority were swept away, and only eight souls were preserved — because they had the courage to stand apart from the crowd.

A WINNOWING FORK IS SEPARATING US

Here in the US, as well as the UK, witchcraft and the occult have become the counter-culture of the young. The Pagan movements are seeking equal use of public facilities, especially those used by popular Christian sects. The gap between the worldly and spiritual is becoming well defined!

ALL-SEEING-EYE, AND EYE-IN-THE-SKY

The symbolism used on the US Dollar Bill is over 4.000 years old. The eye is seen in the meditation room at the United Nations. The new meanings we read into these symbols represent "revisionism". Those initiated in the occult understand the secret interpretation of the pyramid and eye point back to Nimrod of Babylon. The glowing eye is indeed a symbol of "deity", but a gross Pagan one; the "All-Seeing-Eye" is the same as the Egyptian's symbol of Horus, which was called the "Eye-In-The-Sky", referring to the Sun. Nimrod again. Nimrod was the first king on Earth, establishing Babylon and Nineveh. He was a "tower builder", and most believe his secular title was Sargon I, where "Sargon" means supreme ruler. Nimrod, the name, means "tyrant", equivalent to our idea of a dictator. (The word "deity" means "to shine", and is related to our words day, divine, and diva). Nimrod established human sacrifice, immoliating children through "purifying fire", the meaning of the name "Tammuz"!

The Masons were originally stone-masons. During the late Middle Ages, they organized into guilds, the proto-types of today's unions. By 1776, Adam Weishaupt of the Illuminati in Bavaria successfully melded his organization with the Masonic Lodges, which had evolved into a fraternal sect worshipping a mystic "Great Architect". This "architect" turns out to be Nimrod again, who was worshipped by the Babylonians as Baal (LORD), Moloch (KING), and Adon(LORD, SOVEREIGN) -- Adon later turned into the proper name "ODIN". Hislop's own words best describe this fire-worship started by Nimrod, for which Shem slew him:

"The name Moloch originally suggested nothing of cruelty or terror; but now the well-known rites associated with that name have made it for ages a synonym for all that is most revolting to the heart of humanity, and amply justify the description of Milton:

'First Moloch, horrid king,
Besmeared with blood of human sacrifice,
And parents' tears, though,
For the noise of drums and timbrels loud,
Their children's cries unheard, that
Passed through fire
To this grim idol.' (see page 206)

"In almost every land the bloody worship prevailed; 'horrid cruelty', hand in hand with abject superstition, filled not only the 'dark places of the Earth', but also regions that boasted of their enlightenment. Greece, Rome, Egypt, Phoenicia, Assyria, and our own land under the savage Druids, at one period or other in their history, worshipped the same god and in the same way." (Quoted from The Two Babylons, page 151).

The pyramid was sacred to many Pagan civilizations of history, being the top of an obelisk -- called a "pillar of jealousy" in Scripture, which the Israelites would not bow to. It was interpreted as a sun ray, but also as a male fertility symbol. It evolved into various religious towers, or "high places", such as steeples or turrets. They all trace back to the ziggurat of Babel. Poles and high structures were always a part of any Pagan temple, which Scripture refers to as an "image" in places. At Nimrod's death, the Babylonians worshipped him as the Sun -- which later was represented by the eagle, seen carrying the golden orb of the sun across the sky (hence our flag-pole ornaments). The eagle seen on the right side of the back of our dollar bill was first adopted by the Babylonians, and this very same pose can be seen by investigating "Ahura Mazda" (Persian/ Assyrian for "wise lord"). This was only a title, but it was still Nimrod -- they adopted the name "Mithras" for the Sun, and used the eagle as his symbol. The Zoroastrians (also fire-worshippers) had priests called "Magi" (magicians) which bore the emblem of their deity on their chests. They wore black garments, because they were constantly working with the ashes of the "sacred fire". Hence, religious garments of Pagans are black (Israel was told to wear only white linen by Yahuah). These Pagan priests made "holy water" by putting a lit torch of "sacred fire" into water. So, it will be found that every detail seen in Catholicism can be traced back to Chaldaen Paganism -- and much came into the daughters of this Mother of Harlots, most especially her CALENDAR.

So, on the US Dollar Bill, the eagle and the "eye" atop the pyramid are both really Nimrod, who was worshipped as the Sun. The Latin words ANNUIT COEPTIS NOVUS ORDO SECLORUM mean "announcing the birth of a new world order". The goal of the Babylonians was also to "make a name for themselves" (become feared as a nation, identified by their unity and power together to conquer). Nationalism was made with bricks, and the pyramid of power has had men in its grip ever since. They scramble to get to the top of it. The reason for all these cryptic symbols used by Franklin, Jefferson, and the other founding fathers is because these men were mostly Masons. The Masons revere Nimrod as their FOUNDER.

The number 13 is "unlucky" because of a Medieval superstition; the Catholics had interpreted that the "last supper" (a Passover Seder) was on an evening just before a "Fri-Day", and there were 13 men at this seder; actually the "preparation day" for the "Sabbath" was not for the "weekly" Sabbath, but rather the preparation day for the ***annual Sabbath*** of the 1st day of Matsah, called "Unleavened Bread". Six of the seven annual Sabbaths may fall on any day of the week, thus the "3 days AND 3 nights" works out as long as one doesn't try to interpret it the Catholic way, Fri-Day to Sun-Day. (The seventh-day Sabbath, now called "Satyr-Day", is a commemoration of CREATION, see Hebrews 4). Yahusha's resurrection was the fulfillment of the "First-fruits" offering, which is why He would not allow Miryam to touch Him when she saw him; He is the "wave-sheaf offering (see Lev. 23) come to life!

We've investigated why "Sun-Day" (the "Day of the Sun" to the sun / fire-worshippers) became the Christian Sabbath in the year 321 CE. Today, a Nazarene (sect of the Natsarim), or what might be called a "Messianic" movement has begun across planet Earth, restoring all things. The Inquisition murdered all of us they could find over the ages, but now we're on the internet. Nimrod, the "lawless one", is the antithesis of the Mashiach. Without the name, or the number of the name of the beast, no man can buy or sell. The real power given to this beast comes from a fallen cherub, called ha shatan; also known by the Latin word, "Lucifer", meaning "light bearer". He is nameless, yet goes by many names. Whose image and inscription is on our currency of exchange? Well, "IN GOD WE TRUST" takes on a strange meaning when you look up the origin of the word "GOD".

GOD (god):

"Common Teutonic word for personal object of religious worship, FORMERLY APPLICABLE TO SUPER-HUMAN BEINGS OF HEATHEN MYTH; on conversion of Teutonic races to Christianity, TERM WAS APPLIED TO SUPREME BEING."
(Encyclopedia Americana, 1945).

All of this points to the desperate struggle of a creature who is deceiving the whole world, and has successfully hood-winked the nations to conform to a pattern he instituted long ago in Babylon under Nimrod. Alexander Hislop put it into words over 100 years ago, that the papacy was disguised Nimrod worship. His book, The Two Babylons, you can order from us at www.torahzone.net.

The "renewed Covenant" promised at Yerme Yahu 31 has nothing to do with "sacraments" or dispensational "grace" — but rather is the Spirit of the Living Yahusha *writing His Commandments on our hearts*. Instead of beginning by debating whether or not we must obey a given Commandment, we must first ask "why" we are separated from our Creator. The answer is, our sin separates us from Him. We can only define what "sin" is by knowing the Commandments. In fact, sin is defined as the transgression of the Commandments. Without the Commandments to identify sin, there would be no sin. Having established the basic fact that the Commandments define sin, and that our ignoring these same teachings separated us from our Maker, and continue to do so, the next step is to accept the fact that we are, in fact, all sinners — we must be "convicted" of our sinfulness. Instead of just "believing" that all we must do is accept Yahusha's death as our justification for all past and FUTURE transgressions, we must **REPENT**, or turn away from sin. We cannot obey in our "mind of the flesh", but we need help; this is how the New Covenant brings us its most powerful promise: Mashiach IN US. Yahusha literally comes into us, and ENABLES us to actually **LOVE** His Torah, and SAVES us from sin. We can repent of the Paganism, the Popery, the Babylonian fire-worship customs of Nimrod, but without repenting of all the things the Commandments call sin, we will not receive the Spirit of Yahusha (Acts 5:32). Like I've always told my sons, *"You've got to really **want** it!"* (This applies to achieving something they want to accomplish; from getting a

A "Theological" Paradigm-Shift Is Coming!

Questions:

*Why would a follower of Yahusha, the Mashiach of Israel, convert to any other **walk** than the **Torah**?*

*Why would any Israelite need to change their religion in order to **accept their own Messiah**?*

Isn't Yahusha the "living Torah", and the Torah written on our hearts the renewed Covenant?

*Don't we **become** Israelites through the Torah/ Covenant?* (Eph. 2:8-13)

If Gentile converts don't need the Torah, then why were they instructed to learn the Torah at Acts 15:21?

"For Moses of old time hath in every city them that preach him, being read in the synagogues every Sabbath day." . . . And there's that ***Sabbath*** thing again. *Why not just go ahead and "do" the Word?* (Jas. 1:22)

Otherwise, what are we going to do with these texts:

"Blessed are those doing His Commands (TORAH) ***, so that the authority shall be theirs unto the tree of life and to enter through the gates into the city."*** REVELATION 22:14

"Great shalom have they which love thy TORAH: and nothing shall offend them." Ps 119:165

"Then the dragon was enraged at the woman and went off to make war against the rest of her offspring — those who obey Elohim's Commandments (TORAH) ***and hold to the testimony of Yahusha."*** Rev 12:17

"He who turns away his ear from listening to the TORAH,
Even his prayer is an abomination." Prov 28:9

IF YOU OBEY THE COMMANDMENTS OF YAHUAH BECAUSE YOU LOVE HIM, YOU WILL NOT BE A DISAPPOINTMENT TO HIM - ONLY TO MEN CONFORMED TO A "WALK" THAT YAHUAH IS NOT A PART OF.

higher grade, to playing a sport and scoring — Paul spoke of it using the example of a race — by running in such a way so as to WIN). Without the motivation, a person will just sit back and be an observer. Time is long passed for that, it's now time for the harvest workers to appear. Arise! Shine! For your LIGHT has come! The ideas we've summed up in this book can be further condensed into the following words of an unknown author (please take it as humor, yet truth):

"The **Circus** has the "can opener" (the Mashiach), and the **Frozen Chosen** have the can of beans (the Torah) -- all we need to do as Natsarim is show these 2 groups the New Covenant -- the Torah written on our hearts!" (Heb. 10, Yirme Yahu 31).

DEATH ROW Each one of us — no matter how healthy, free, or young — is on death row. None of us know the day or hour of our death, yet it hangs invisibly right before us all. Those who searched the occult for answers only met failure. Walt Disney had an obsession with the occult, and at the moment of his death, he arranged to be cryogenically frozen at that point — in the hope that one day medical science could revive him and extend his life. We live in bodies of DEATH; at some point we will die. Humans, when compared with the rest of the respirating animals, live longer than expected. We've learned how to extend our lives just a bit. If humans were to live lifespans predicted from the pattern of weight, heart and breath cycles for the rest of the animals, they would only live from 30 to 35 years. But, each of us only has so many breaths and heartbeats, then it's over. We must use our time here wisely.

Christianity, as we know it, is what Paul prophesied would happen after he was gone. Men would rise up and plunder the flock, and lead the Body into apostasy, and follow after myths. Worse still, they have become lawless, replacing the Commandments of Yahuah with traditions of men. Having said this, it may sound like I am condemning Christians -- but nothing could be further from the truth. Out of them, Yahuah is calling forth a remnant, that will lead the world as Israel was intended to originally, because they are finding out they ARE Israel. Yahuah has stated there is to be one "law" for the native born, and foreigner. His Torah is the wedding covenant, and the New Covenant in Yahusha's blood is written on our hearts, not like the old one in stone. Pagans did not know they were only worshipping "idols", the names they used meant just as much to them as they do to most Christians. So, if a Christian learns the true non-Pagan words, and certainly the personal Name of the One they claim to worship, how could it be they would still cling to the uncleanness and errors more so than the Truth? The answer is just as I stated: it's **programming**. Repenting is certainly difficult unless it has been given as a free gift (faithfulness). **Being "faithful" to the programming is not repenting** -- being faithful to the Truth requires real sacrifice. Friends, family, and other brothers and sisters in the old way can be powerful glue to keep change from occurring. This is what the parable of the Sower is all about. Rather than excusing and defending the long history of an apostate religion, we must plow ahead without looking back. It would be far more comfortable to remain within the structure of Christmas, Easter, and Sunday, but we must decide whom we will serve -- witchcraft and Satan, or the Creator Yahuah. That's why Satan is called a "deceiver"; he has people thinking they are serving Yahuah, but they are really obeying him. Looking at what Yahuah says He likes, then turning away and following the Pagan format is truly a strange way of showing it. Satan is masquerading. You can't peel away Yahuah's ways and find dirty Paganism underneath them, because He is not wearing a costume like Satan is.

YOUR FIRST STRUGGLE: OBEDIENCE

OBED — Hebrew for "servant". Who is a servant of 𐤉𐤄𐤅𐤄? The one who obeys. Like the rainbow He has set in the clouds as a "sign" of His Covenant with all living creatures to never destroy the Earth by water again, He has established a "sign" between Him and His bride, those who have chosen to obey His Voice, His Word.

Starting in Genesis, the 7th day was established as a sign which shows to Yahuah who we worship as CREATOR, since this 4th Commandment was given to commemorate creation. The Great Prostitute hates the "mark" of 𐤉𐤄𐤅𐤄, which is the "sign" of His Covenant. The Sabbath has nothing to do with the Resurrection, but people have been hypnotized to believe otherwise. The texts we usually hear used to "prove" the disciples changed the Sabbath to "Sun-day" to celebrate the Resurrection of Yahusha are examined here, because you will find great resistance to obeying the true Shabbat. Concerning the "Day of 𐤉𐤄𐤅𐤄" (translated "day of the LORD") at Rev. 1:10, many have been taught that this was "Sunday", yet it is really the future time of testing which Yahuchanon was writing about, as he said he was "in the spirit", a vision of the time of wrath was being shown to him. If he wanted us to know what day of the week it was, he would have said so, by saying "on the first day of the week" like other passages did.

Let's look at the texts about "SUN-DAY", which people seem to "see" in Acts 20, and 1 Corinthians. I can understand how strong the pressure is to not rock the boat, but it is only Tradition that has "interpreted" selected texts in order to attempt some Scriptural basis for a "Sunday" observance. You will notice that the "Sabbath" is referred to in Hebrews 4, and it remains for the people of Yahuah. Paul never stated that it was any other day, nor did Luke in his mentioning it in Acts. Acts 1:12 even mentions the "Sabbath's distance" of about 3/4 mile, and the NIV footnotes verify this. This was not a "Sunday". The best way to prove to yourself that Shabbath is the same day as it has always been is to just go through the entire book of Acts, and circle the word "Sabbath" every time it appears. Acts was written many years after the Resurrection. It was Constantine who instituted the "Sun-day Sabbath" change.

At Acts 20:7, Paul was preparing to leave the next morning, and the Sabbath had ended at sunset, and he and Luke (the writer) came together with a small group in a house, "on the first day of the week". Luke records "there were many lamps" in this upstairs room, because it was after dark, the beginning of the 1st day of the week -- and Paul went on speaking until midnight. Little Eutychus fell asleep and dropped out the window! It says they "broke bread", meaning they had a meal, like the meal Yahusha had with the two men on the road to Emmaus. (Yahusha was invited in, and "When He was at the table with them, He took bread, gave thanks, BROKE it, and began to give it to them" - Luke 24:30). "Breaking bread" is just eating.

At 1 Cor. 16:2, Paul was writing to the Corinthians to prepare for their gift to Yahuah's PEOPLE (the poor in Yerushaliyim), since he would be soon passing through on his way to Yerushaliyim. This was not a collection for Yahuah's "work", but rather it was for the poor, and it was only for that specific occasion! The "first day of the week" was (and still is) the first **work** day of every week, and so the people were to make this collection then, so everyone would do it in an orderly way - there is no "Scriptural" law of any kind to have this done at all times everywhere. The Corinthians may have met together at their synagogue on the 7th-day Sabbath (those who wished to), and then the funds for the poor were collected the following day, from the previous week's proceeds. This is not a big mystery, but it has been turned into a business by the ravenous wolves who plunder the flocks, and has been the tradition for well over 1,000 years under the authority of the Great Prostitute. Pesach (Passover) is the remembrance of our Passover Lamb, and Yahusha is metaphorically called the "Bread" of life, which came down from Shamayim. It is apparent that the wolves want to take 10% from their followers, and yet Paul wept for years over this, if you check what he told the elders at Acts 20:13-38. We take the emblems of bread & wine only ONCE every year, at Pesach, which is twilight as the 14th of the first moon begins Scripturally. Our "Roman" calendar is the "beast's", the golden cup filled with abominations in the prostitute's hand (man-made festivals, not Yahuah's).

At 1 Cor. 5:7-10, Paul says ***"For Mashiach, our Passover Lamb, has been slain. Therefore LET US KEEP THE FESTIVAL, not with the old yeast . . . but with bread made without yeast, the bread of sincerity and truth."*** Christendom has consistently framed Sabbaths and the festivals like Passover as "legalistic", and a "yoke" of bondage -- missing the meaning. It has turned previously Pagan observances into its own "legalism", and made man-made traditions replace the Torah observances, lived by and taught by the first Nazarenes. Christianity as it developed from Catholicism, later giving birth to her daughters the Reformers, HAS NEVER HAD a Passover, but instead invented their own "method", bent on plunder and deception, re-inventing previously Pagan observances (mixing the clean with the unclean, and darkness with light). If the blind lead the blind, BOTH will fall into a pit. If you are asking men who are blind to show you the way, what will be the end of it? Please just start by circling every occurrence in Acts where the word "Sabbath" occurs, and you will begin to see the **Truth**, and it will set you free. How "evil" would it have been if we had simply inherited the "tradition" of **obeying** the 4th Commandment as it is written? Even "Pentecost", called "Shabuoth", is one of the commanded festivals in Lev. 23, and commemorates the giving of the Torah at Sinai. The Nazarenes had the Torah written on their hearts, fulfilling the prophesied "New Covenant" described in Jer. 31:33, Ez. 36:26,27, Heb. 10:16. Satan has led away and deceived the whole world, and we have inherited the echoes of his sun-worship pattern, and not our Father's pattern. We are labeled "Judaizers" for obeying the Commandments, and rejecting human traditions.

Some of us are even now feeling the "chiseling" and refining of our hearts as we are being "hewn" by the Spirit of Yahusha. We are being ripped away from the common bedrock of tradition, and are encountering persecution. The "darkness" will not approach the "Light" for fear of exposure, and the enemies of the Torah flee from those who are likely to follow the example of Yahusha, by saying "IT IS WRITTEN . . . " If I may, I'd like to point out that it is really not the remnant which you have been seeking; you are the called-out remnant! We are the "Living Stones", and the Temple of 𐤉𐤄𐤅𐤄. Where ever two or more of us are gathered, He is in our midst—no building can ever be as set-apart as ourselves.

When I stopped searching for the "place", the "people", and the "organization", I turned to Him ~ and begged for the Truth. I found Him, and now work for Him. He is Wisdom, and by Wisdom all things were created! Daniel 11:33-35 describes the struggle with the Great Prostitute, but Daniel 12:10 is being fulfilled today. The Hebrew word for "wisdom" is CHOCHMAH. In Him resides all the depths of knowledge, and He will equip us for every work we are to accomplish while in our flesh. The Keys to the Kingdom of Yahuah have been given to us, and in our obedience to His Torah, we show our love for Him. With the wisdom of Torah, we can "bind & loose" (forbid & permit), so others can be guided by Truth. There will be many times your steadfastness will be tested, but remember to keep your eyes on Him, not the "winds" of human logic and tradition. Some will pull on you to believe diverse things regarding when an appointed day begins, or certain "rules" regarding Shabbaths, and Kabalistic "leavening" (puffed up knowledge), but remember all you need is written down in the inspired Word, which is useful for all teaching, rebuking, and correcting in righteousness. Practicing what it says will strengthen you like exercise strengthens muscles, and deeper understanding comes from observing the appointed times (Shabbath, Pesach, Shabuoth, Yom Teruah, Yom Kippur, and Sukkot). The adversary HATES the Covenant, and attacks Yahusha's bride. His servants you should avoid, because we have been warned to not cast our pearls before swine, or they will attack us! In all things, be filled with love, joy, peace, patience, kindness, goodness, faithfulness, gentleness, and self-control. If you treat others as you would have them treat you, you will achieve desirable results. One thing I've learned is, that when you are "debating" with someone who seeks to "prove" that staying where they are is the right thing to do, and they argue over the Name or Shabbaths, THEY ARE AT A CRITICAL POINT, and their "passion" reveals the struggle within them ~ they really WANT to be shown the Truth! Be patient and loving, and ask them if they love the Commandments . . . this will give them a perspective, and all the Scripture stored in their hearts will convict them of sin. This is the beginning! They must be convicted of their sinfulness - but all their lives they have been "programmed" to believe their sins are "covered", and never started in the right place. They started off out-of-step. Their sins are only "covered" when they "repent", and turn from sin! Yahusha enables them in their spirit to agree with the Torah, and they will pass from their mind-of-the-flesh into our realm, the mind-of-the-Spirit. They will never be able to go back, thinking that the Commandments are "done away". The Torah is Spiritual, and the mind-of-the-flesh cannot obey. Be patient with everyone who wants to learn the evidence and foundation of your faith. They are where we all were once; and as it happened for us, they can be used to carry the true message to many others.

No one is hopeless, if they are praying for the Truth. When it is shown that human traditions have become "religion", and partial truths have been **mixed** with lies and doctrines of demons, a rebellion will occur like no other has before, all over the Earth ~ and then Yahusha will return to rule over us. We are part of the restoration, the rebuilding of the Temple of Yahuah made without hands. This is the "Temple" that will come from the skies ~ it will be us. You have found the true Nazarenes. We are hated without a cause, like Yahusha; and we are in a war of Truth against lies, Light against Darkness.

✡ **THE STAR OF DAVID** (daleth-uau-daleth)

Many will indicate that this symbol was used by Pagans, but there is an origin to it that is overlooked. It isn't a "religious" symbol, yet is a Scriptural fulfillment. (The symbol of the Torah, Yahusha, is the menorah — a representation of the Tree of Life).

Yesha Yahu (Isaiah) 11:10-13 describes a "banner", which is a flag. "Ephraim", one of the 10 "lost" families of Israel, is mentioned, along with Yahudah, and Adonai Yahuah is said to reach out His hand A SECOND TIME to reclaim the remnant of His people who were "lost", dispersed over the Earth. On this "banner" is the "root of Yesse", and this word "root" means descendant, and this is none other than Da'ud! It's a king's SEAL, the literal name of Da'ud.

The "star" is really Da'ud's NAME, written in two palaeo-Hebrew letters, as a dalet and another dalet -- the beginning and ending of Da'ud's name. It stands as a banner, the flag of Israel, and is the symbol for ALL Israel, including the lost 10 families. Over time, Satanists began to use it, but only with a circle around it, since in conjuring up demons they believe they must stand in a circle of protection when doing so. (It's really nonsense, since candles and circles with symbols in them cannot protect anyone from demons). Many Christian teachers are actively promoting the notion that this "star" is demonic, and even elude to Acts 7:43, but they are mistaken. The "shrine of Molech and the star of your god Rephan" is the symbol used by Islam today, which is a moon and star, symbolizing ***child sacrifice*** to Molech. The moon symbol represents Semiramis / Diana / Artemis / Asherah / Ishtar / Easter; and the star is Tammuz, her child. (see page 206 for images of Molech).

Some will try to convince you that it is an evil talisman, able to be inhabited by demons. Try to educate them, but at all costs avoid being offensive. 1 Pet. 3:8-12 is a text that should guide us in love, and applies to many areas. But, if you have made up your mind already, try to accept those who don't agree with you on every point. There are so many things addressed in this book, it's most likely there will be differences of opinion — we don't all have the same knowledge; but we should be of the same MIND.

PAUL AND CIRCUMCISION

One of Paul's biggest challenges came from those Natsarim who *insisted* on *circumcising* Gentiles. Those who reject or misunderstand Paul sometimes force ritual circumcision on *new converts*. When Natsarim discuss these kinds of issues, I like to bear in mind that while there is an ideal and goal in all of Yahuah's wonderful teachings, our LOVE has to remain the foremost goal. Achieving absolute perfection *halachally* speaking, and not having love, we are doomed. Our love is the real test, and by the measure we judge, we will be judged -- if I am even 25% correct, it will be a miracle! The thief who died next to Yahusha certainly didn't have every detail of understanding we all strive for. But, specifically, circumcision is an eternal covenant. It is a covenant of land inheritance, but not eternal life. Our immersion (in the Name of Yahusha Who we covenant with) has become our circumcision, as Paul states it very clearly: ***"In Him you were also circumcised, in the putting off of the sinful nature, not with a circumcision done by the hands of men, but with the circumcision done by Mashiach, having been buried with Him in (baptism) and raised with Him through your faith in the power***

HALACHA: HEBREW, "WALK", REFERRING TO TORAH OBSERVANCE IN GENERAL

of Yahuah Who raised Him from the dead." Col. 2:11,12. Immersion represents our "circumcision" by the Sword of the Spirit, the Torah. The whole issue of the "council" recorded at Acts 15 regarding "Gentiles" turning to Yahuah involved the controversy of fleshly circumcision, and the decision reached remains unclear even to many Nazarenes today. Those who believe and are immersed will be saved -- Yahusha didn't include fleshly circumcision here, but can a Gentile become a "Yahudi" without a fleshly circumcision? Is the "sign" (oth) of the Eternal Covenant circumcision, or the Sabbath? The "sword" of the Spirit actually circumcises our hearts, so we can walk in the Spirit, obeying the Torah willingly, as an obedient bride. Eph. 2:11 onward discusses how a Gentile's citizenship in Israel is accomplished by Yahusha's blood, and the dividing wall is abolished between believing Gentiles and the "circumcised". Romans 3:28,29 states: ***"A man is NOT a Yahudi (Jew) if he is only one OUTWARDLY (circumcision), nor is circumcision merely outward and physical. No, a man is a Yahudi if he is one INWARDLY; and circumcision is circumcision of the heart, by the Spirit, not by the written code. Such a man's praise is not from men, but from Elohim."*** Romans 3:30 states that Yahuah "will justify the circumcised by faith and the uncircumcised through that same faith." But, Romans 4 goes into answering your question better than I or anyone ever could. I know this is and always has been an issue of controversy among Nazarenes, but I am not contentious over it -- but accept all who love Yahusha, and seek to follow Him, trusting in His salvation. This faith makes us children of Abraham, who was justified even before he was circumcised. All believers who have been circumcised by the sword of the Spirit in their hearts are children of Yahuah. I don't wish to be rebuked like Peter was, who would not sit with "Gentile" Nazarenes.

MANIFESTATION OF YAHUAH: YAHUSHA

"They will look upon ME, the one they have pierced, and they will mourn for Him as one mourns for an ONLY CHILD, and GRIEVE BITTERLY for Him as one grieves for a first-born Son." -- Zech. 12:10.

"The Son is the radiance of Elohim's esteem and the **exact representation** of His Being, sustaining all things by His powerful Word." -- Heb. 1:3.

Many words can be written to counter the above, but they will never change their meaning. The SECRET is withheld, being veiled to those who cannot accept that the HUSBAND had to die to end the Covenant. (Rom. 7:2, Heb. 9:15-17). If Yahusha were not Who He is, He could not possibly alter or amend any former covenant made by Yahuah.

"Even to this day when Mosheh is read, a veil covers their hearts. But whenever anyone turns to Yahuah, the veil is taken away. Now Yahuah <u>is the</u> <u>Spirit</u>, and where the Spirit of Yahuah is, there is freedom." -- 2Cor. 3:15-17.

"Who, being in very nature Elohim, did not consider equality with Elohim something to be grasped, but made Himself nothing, taking the very nature of a servant, being made in human likeness. And being found in appearance as a man, He humbled Himself and became obedient to death -- even death on ha'etz (the tree). Phil. 2:6-8. (Nas is "pole" or stake in Hebrew*).

"He is the image of the invisible ***Elohim***, the firstborn over all creation." -- Col. 1:15.

~ There is no creature able to take this attribute upon itself—certainly not Michael, one of the malakim. The veil has been removed for some of us, but remember that the thief who died next to Yahusha didn't have to know a great deal. Our defining attribute must be LOVE. Where there is contention and strife over what we believe, we don't exhibit love. If we who believe Yahusha is Yahuah are to be cast out as "idolaters", then we were misled by many, many Scriptures. He is Wonderful, Counselor, Everlasting Father, Mighty El, Sar Shalom, El Elyon, El Shaddai, Yahuah Tzedekenu, and Maker of all things seen and unseen. He appeared to Abraham. He walked with Enoch, Adam, spoke face-to-face with Mosheh, and wrestled with Ya'akob. And, He died for me, His pitiful servant. He did this for each of us, and wants to save each of us who will accept Him, by writing His Torah on our hearts. His resurrection is the central focus of all history, when death was swallowed up — and by faith in this, we all can have His life. He is the resurrection and the life.

DA'UD IS NOT IN "HEAVEN"??

Paul says to be absent from the body is to be present with Yahuah; after death, the very next thing you will know will be awakening and being with Yahusha. I may only differ with some on the passage of time, but we can easily see that Acts 2:34 clearly says: ***"For Da'ud did not ascend into the heavens . . . "*** and we also read that NO ONE ascended into the heavens -- EXCEPT the One Who descended. So, Da'ud is not yet with Yahusha, but *sleeps in the grave*, awaiting his resurrection. Daniel was told "many of those who sleep in the dust of the Earth will wake up . . ." (12:2). He was also told to ***"go his way to the end, and rest"***, and he would rise to "his lot" at the end of days.

I know that tradition interprets things in easily understandable ways, but really such unprovable details like this are not salvational issues. The

****NASA IS HEBREW FOR "LIFT UP", OR SEND, CAST, THROW***

thief who died next to Yahusha didn't have every single detail worked out, but Rabbi Yahusha assured him ***"I tell you TODAY, you will be with Me in paradise".*** See the comma? Many understand it this way, how Yahusha was simply emphasizing His decision when He said, "I tell you today, . . ." We have to be careful, and not snatch one sentence out of Scripture and build a case on ambiguity. Wisdom is to be found where there are many counselors, and two or more witnesses are necessary to provide evidence of truth.

Now that you have read so far into this little book, you might ask yourself if there have been enough "witnesses" brought forth to prove that human traditions have intentionally masked and altered the Truth. Many will not be convinced no matter *how much* evidence is presented, and to a large degree it is simply because they don't wish to repent — sin is fun for a season, but it will reap only death. The same amount of energy can be expended for doing what is right. We're all gambling with our own lives, and we must also realize that we are responsible for our children, and others who make contact with us. Your mission is to *GO, make disciples*, and immerse them in Yahusha's Name — this is not just for "leaders", but all of us. He will ask to see what you did with the 'talents' He left you with. When you have studied Scripture thoroughly, you will find that the CONGREGATION participates in every facet of getting people converted; we are ***ALL*** involved in teaching, immersing, correcting, and so on.

"... you are slaves (servants) ***of the one whom you OBEY ..."*** Romans 6:16

"... a foolish people has spurned your Name." Psalm 74:18

Dealing With Those Who Don't Understand

Please don't get ***discouraged*** by the enormous lack of love in many people's responses. Whether they are brash, new believers who have not yet "mellowed" and come into fuller knowledge, or they are deceived deceivers like anti-missionaries or Jesuits, it's hard to keep pace, or have peace in your heart, when all you get are arguments and debates constantly. Here I will briefly touch on the fact that there are 10 "lost tribes", and the anti-missionaries may be under the impression that there are only 2 or 3 tribes, now visibly called "Jews". Reading Ezekiel 36:17-38, and 37:1-28 (noting especially 36:27), they will find that the **TWO** HOUSES of ISRAEL (Yahudah, the southern kingdom, and Ephraim / Israel, the northern kingdom) will be UNITED as "one stick" in Yahuah's hand. We are about to witness the return of the ***10 lost tribes***, now embedded in the Gentiles; and see the return of Yahusha of Natsarith. When He reveals Himself to His brothers, it will be a day of great mourning, as it is described in Zech. 12, and one will be reminded of how it was when Yosef revealed himself to his brothers in Egypt, after being sold into slavery, imprisoned innocently by Potiphar, and rising to the highest position of the kingdom.

Not long ago, someone wrote to me from prison saying he was about to be released, but didn't think he could return to his wife and child because they were "Christian". Since learning the Truth, this individual was only interested in being with others like himself. So, I realized that to some degree, many others have these same tendencies -- so I've put a few paragraphs together to help straighten this confusion out.

Accepting Those Who Are Different

1 Cor. 9:19-23, (pilot text): Paul can be easily misunderstood, can't he? In this whole area of his letter, my "take" is that Paul is on a tangent, or line of thought, which pertains generally to his "right" to be called an emissary. He was under great stress, because other Nazarenes were questioning him constantly -- they didn't trust him completely. He seemed to be associating with people others turned their noses up at. Some even thought he 'believed' differently. He wanted only to say that he was under compulsion to spread the message of the Reign of Yahuah to all mankind, not for any boasting or reward. He tries to explain why it is that he speaks to anyone who will listen. He doesn't seem to see anyone as a lost cause, but all have the potential to win. He calls his journey a race -- and he encounters all types of people along the way. Some are beginning. Others are farther along in knowledge.

Even though Paul understood many things more deeply than other Nazarenes, like the meaning of the New Covenant (the Torah written on our hearts and minds), he knew we needed ***other*** basic advice; like how to get along with each other, and others who were not yet "all there".

Many nations are the seed of the Abrahamic Promise -- and the Spirit of Yahusha within us has a **goal** which many of us push into the background. He wants to *use us to reach the "lost" sheep of the tribes of Israel* -- the 10 "lost" tribes -- with the message of the Kingdom of Yahuah. How committed to this are we? Many place their highest goal on ***finding*** and ***meeting*** with others who believe like they do. Seeking others who use the same words, observe the same appointments, and a similar knowledge-level make the Kingdom of Yahuah more like an ***"Us versus Them"*** meeting. We can "see" the Kingdom of Yahuah, because we are of it; but ALL of us are *sent* to gather more to the wedding supper. We must have more workers for the harvest!

In 1 Cor. 9, Paul is telling us we must become

"like" the people around us -- that is, "infiltrate" them. This prisoner was dedicated to the Name, the appointed times, and so on; but he could not accept others who were different, even his own wife and child. I wrote to him about this. Even if it takes a lifetime, our place on this Earth is to help those who need us the most. It is NOT our mission to group together ***only*** with others who already follow and understand; we are ***SENT*** to help those being called-out.

I am sometimes criticized for the type of people I attract as my clientele -- the customers who come into my store are often adulterers, drug-addicts, alcoholics, thieves, liars, -- you know; REGULAR PEOPLE. But, I have been ***sent*** to them. From this number of sinful people, Yahusha is calling forth Children of Yahuah. I understand Paul, because I am sent to the same kind of people -- *all kinds*. I talk to observant Yahudim who don't know that Mashiach has come. They are "under the law", which according to Deut. 28-30 only promises blessings for obedience, and curses for disobedience. Paul sees this as very narrow with his eternal perpectives, given to him by the New Covenant. Paul has much to teach us all, but sadly few seem to understand him -- that's why Peter warned us in his letter about misinterpreting Paul "lawlessly". While we put forth our greatest efforts to *meet with the saved*, perhaps we should put forth as much effort to *reach the lost*. As seen today, the "2-tiered system" of pastor/flock is a remnant of centuries of human control. Often only one or two are ever heard speaking in assemblies. We must not remain stagnant, frozen pew-sitters. Most of us must become teachers ourselves, and become like our teacher. We need pastors, but this is not to say a pastor will rule over us for all our lives. Some of us must become pastors, evangelists, teachers, healers, givers, etc.,. these are "gifts" for the Body, and to the Body, which is served by all of us. This "Body" is Yahusha's Bride -- and many of them are waiting to hear from us. (The "givers" should carefully read 2 Cor. 8:3,4: ***"For I testify that according to their ability, and beyond their ability they gave of their own accord, begging us with much entreaty for the favor OF PARTICIPATING IN THE SUPPORT OF THE SAINTS."*** The idea continues in v. 14, ***"At this present time your abundance being a SUPPLY FOR THEIR WANT, that their abundance*** (one day) ***also may become a supply for your want, that there may be equality."*** This "support" was for those saints in dire NEED.)

At our meetings, we should let the Spirit of Yahusha speak to the group through ***whoever can give a teaching.*** You can plan a lecture topic, then the BODY of believers should ALL have the opportunity to speak, as Paul directed us. Note: 1 Cor. 14:26 states, ***"When you assemble, EACH ONE has a psalm, HAS A TEACHING, HAS A REVELATION, has a TONGUE, has an INTERPRETATION."*** This does not sound like one man dominating the group — the Spirit of Yahusha uses each one to speak to the Body!

I've found that the smaller the study group is, *the better.* Some things may come up that everyone needs to hear, but no one saw coming. The Spirit uses His Body to speak to us, so we should not imitate the Nicolaitans by just having one person's voice still everyone else's. It seems that many Natsarim ***focus*** on finding others to meet with, which is of course great; however our MAIN objective is to carry the message to the lost. Our meetings should encourage us, and we should gain instruction in how to accomplish our real goal -- *teaching others, and immersing them.* Remember, this is for ALL of us to do, not just a "leader".

The students of Yahusha took 3 1/2 years to get the basics. He left us so that He could live in all of us -- and we should listen to Him, and let Him use us to reach those who would otherwise never hear the Truth. We are sent to the lost -- so let's not turn our backs on those we were sent to. Let him use you to perfect and call-out His Bride. Take Paul's advice, and become "as" an unbeliever, in order to save some of them. As you get nearer to the "finish-line", you should be less critical of those you see just starting out across from you on the path.

"Be wise as serpents, but harmless as doves".
"If you abide in My Word, then you are truly disciples of Mine; and you shall know the Truth, and the Truth shall make you free." -- Yahuchanon 8:31,32.

The reason I did this research was to find out why there were so many hidden, mysterious things about religion, and to learn why Christian "faith" and Paganism were so closely aligned. It all seemed like such a paradox! My hope is you won't do as so many have, but stay where you were planted. Most who learn the Truth flee their surrounding friends, loved ones, and congregants, because they can't "relate" anymore. Some even wish to leave their spouse. But it is to these very people we are sent. The Truth will drive away the darkness, but if you shine it so as to blind them, they will have no part of you. You must just let an illuminating glow emanate, and then only when someone is interested in learning more. They only learn when they want to. It may take a lifetime for some, while others soak up the Truth like a sponge. Some will base what they choose to believe on a previous paradox they couldn't find any way of resolving, like where Cain could find a wife, or how the Great Deluge could have been global in scope. Within my own family, one of the dearest people to me was told that Constantine wrote the Scriptures, and this has caused a great barrier for any Truth to get through. I wonder how Constantine managed to stash those old scrolls in the hills of the Dead Sea, don't you? It was probably not an easy trick to get them into synagogues all over the world either. The point is, we all have to face people who need us, but we must be discerning, patient, and not judgmental. Believe it or not, you can live in the same house with someone who celebrates Halloween, Easter, and Christmas. It's your endurance that is put to the test, not theirs. Benjamin Franklin wrote, "you can catch more flies with honey than with vinegar."

Leaving Babylon is a spiritual journey, not a physical one. Behind Nimrod is Shatan, and all his lying wonders are deceiving the whole world. You may have a bath towel with a sun on it. If it has a face, it's Nimrod. The Orientals who honor the Dalai Lama or the "child of the sun" are also trapped in worshipping Nimrod. Nimrod is represented in many ways — eagles, gold balls, obelisks, steeples, cruxes, the Christmas Tree, Santa, the eye on the pyramid; and together with his mother, Semiramis, the whole world is caught up in witchcraft.

CARRYING MONEY ON SHABBAT?

Let's put on our thinking caps. Many of us have been taught conflicting things over the years, and **steered** into outcomes that benefited those who were doing the teaching. We know that the average Torah-observant person over the centuries would not carry something on Shabbat that required both hands, and walk around the town with it. Neither would they have a money bag hanging from their cloak-belt, jangling all over the place on Shabbat -- this would give the "appearance" of having just sold something, or the intention of going out to buy something. Even the giving of alms would cease on Shabbat. The beggars would have to take the day off from begging, no one would be carrying money anyway.

So, how is it that there are "collections" taken in to support the teachers (and calling them "tithes") on Shabbat? Going into an orthodox synagogue on a Shabbat might underscore my point here. If you asked the people there, *"When's the collection to be taken?",* you'd get some funny looks. It is not a custom, nor has it ever been, for observant Yahudim to carry even one coin with them on Shabbat. This illuminates the passage of 1 Cor. 16:1-5, where Paul writes concerning the "collections" for the set-apart ones (the saints — the poor Yahudim in Yerushaliyim like widows, and fatherless children):

(v. 2)***: "On the first day of the week, let each one of you set aside, storing up whatever he is prospered, SO THAT THERE ARE NO COLLECTIONS WHEN I COME."***

Contrary to popular interpretation, this "first day of the week" collection was not a permanent policy, but was just to be done up until Paul passed through on his way to Yerushaliyim. Nor was it because "Sun-day" was a "meeting day", or the "new Sabbath" of believers. It was an organized way to prepare for Paul's arrival, that's all, and was for THE POOR. It was done on the "first day of the week" because Paul knew they wouldn't be carrying money with them on Shabbat. Christians (led in the ways of the Chaldeans) have had the basket-passing method conducted in their assemblies for centuries, done on the man-made "Sabbath" called Sun-day, and everyone who drops something into the basket is basically shamed into it -- everyone is watching around them. Many "Messianic" groups do this also, or provide a box for it. This is not intended to judge individuals who have been doing this to the flock, but rather to point it out, de-program our habits, and restore a more scriptural method. It should be apparent that our "assembling together" shouldn't cost us anything. Teaching the Torah for pay is also not to be done. Teach harp, harmonica, architecture, geometry, or square-dancing if you want to support your family; not Torah.

You may have heard the excuses about the "Sabbath distance" (Acts 1:12), insisting that we MUST assemble even if the distance is greater than 1000 cubits. The saying is, "it is more important that we assemble, so we over-rule the Sabbath-distance to keep the Command to assemble." What Command? Lev. 23 declares convocations "in all our dwellings", not "drive hundreds of miles", or "go find an elder setting up a meeting". We should assemble whenever and wherever we can, sure; especially the 3 appointed times in a year (but a convocation can be just 2 people). Is it possible that the over-ruling of the Sabbath distance principle is taught so that those who have been gathering wealth from the flock can continue to do so? I'm not criticizing, I'm just asking.

If Exodus 35:3 says ***"You shall not kindle a fire in any of your dwellings on the Sabbath day"***, do we just go outside and do it? Of course not. We just obey the Commandment -- and this is

CONTINUED ON PAGE 146 . . . . .

"EGAD" A FORM OF SAYING "OH-GOD"

JUST LIKE DRESSING UP THE ORIGINAL JUPITER IMAGE IN "NEW CLOTHES" AS SHOWN EARLIER, OUR HABITS AND CUSTOMS HAVE BEEN "DRESSED UP" IN NEW MEANINGS TO CONCEAL THEIR PAGAN ORIGINS.

VOODOO!

FIDDLING WITH CROSSES, TREES, ASHES, ALTARS, WATER, ROSARIES, STATUES, CANDLES, WAVING IN THE AIR, KISSING RELICS, WEARING MEDALIONS, SACRAMENTS, AND TALKING TO BREAD WHILE KNEELING BEFORE IT DOES NOT HONOR THE LIVING ELOHIM, YAHUAH.

"Blessed rather are those who hear the Word of 𐤉𐤄𐤅𐤄 and OBEY IT." Luke 11:28
"He has also set eternity in the hearts of men, yet they cannot fathom what Elohim has done from beginning to end." - Ec. 3:11.

Wreaths, branches, boughs, and trees were originally used to worship the sun at the winter solstice, known as the *"re-birth"* of the unconquered sun. The tree was called ASHERAH. Nimrod of Babylon, slain by Shem, began to be worshipped as the sun, and trees represented his sexual prowess. The wreaths represented the womb that gives birth to the sun deity. These customs were absorbed or "inculturated" by Christendom. Tammuz' mother (Semiramis) was later worshipped as *Mother Nature,* under various names like Ishtar, Asherah, Easter, Ashtar, Astoreth, Asherah, Astarte, Artemis, Eastre, Nana, Nut, Frigga, Gaia, Maia, and many others. The hearth was the Pagan Roman family's place of worship, because fire was associated with the Sun, and thought to be sacred.
Most people don't think for themselves. They don't ask for evidence, look too closely, or ask questions. They just "believe" everything. *"The simple inherit folly, but the prudent are crowned with knowledge."* ~ Prov. 14:18. 14:15 says, *A simple man believes anything; but a prudent man gives thought to his steps."*

DANGER!

READING THIS BOOK COULD ALTER YOUR BELIEFS ABOUT THE CREATOR AND HIS PLAN FOR YOUR LIFE.

The fake name of the Mashiach, "JESUS", is a Greco-Romanism, and means absolutely nothing in Hebrew. If it were a "translation", then it could be "re-translated" back to Hebrew. When taken back to the Greek, it means *"hey-Zeus",* or "*hail Zeus".* The closest word to "sus" in Hebrew is "*soos",* and means *"horse". So "he-soos" means "the horse".* Zeus is depicted as a Centaur, and this half-man, half-horse is found in Babylonian Astrology in the constellation **Sagittarius**. Sus in Latin means PIG. In this book, you will discover the true Name by which we must be saved, which is: **Yahusha.**

Yahusha means:

"YAH is our salvation"

Many things have been concealed from us. In order to control people, those in authority tortured and executed millions of innocent people over many centuries. Now, in the fullness of time, all that was concealed and done in secret is laid bare in a logical framework.
The motive:

TO MISDIRECT WORSHIP TO THE ADVERSARY,
by way of the Pagan customs!

MASCOT: LATIN FOR <u>WITCH</u>

PAGANISM IS WITCHCRAFT, IDOLATRY, SATANISM, AND ANYTHING THAT OFFENDS THROUGH RELIGIOUS OR SECULAR CUSTOMS AND PRACTICES

decried as "Pharisaical". If we feel "others" are not observing the annual feast correctly, do we run to Yerushaliyim and cut the wave sheaf ourselves, wave it, and do what only the High Priest is to do? Of course not. If Exodus 16:29 says, "Let each one stay in his place, do not let anyone go out of his place on the seventh day", do we ignore this teaching and travel 60 miles? Of course "place" means immediate area, or village. But, if your "village" grows to the size of Los Angeles, can we rely on common sense?

The Body of Yahusha must endorse the decisions reached by the elders, and search out and prove all things. If we cease from carrying money on Shabbat, do you imagine this may be disagreeable to any of the pastors? A pastor who serves without pay is a true pastor, one who cannot be bought. Remember Balaam, the prophet for hire! Reading Acts 20:28-35 carefully may shed a great light on this plundering that has gone on unchecked for centuries. Speaking to the ELDERS of Ephesus (Acts 20:17), Paul says:

(v.20:28-35): ***"Therefore take heed to yourselves and to all the flock, among which the Set-apart Spirit has made you overseers*** (elders), ***to shepherd the assembly of Elohim which He has purchased with His own blood. For I know this, that after my departure SAVAGE WOLVES shall come in among you, not sparing the flock. Also from among yourselves men shall arise, speaking distorted teachings, to draw away the taught ones after themselves.***

"Therefore watch, remembering that for three years, night and day, I did not cease to warn each one with tears. And now, brothers, I commit you to Elohim and to the Word of His favor, which is able to build you up and give you an inheritance among all those having been set apart. I HAVE COVETED NO ONE'S SILVER OR GOLD OR GARMENTS. And you yourselves know that these hands supplied my needs, and for those who were with me. All this I did show you, by laboring like this, that YOU OUGHT TO HELP THE WEAK. And remember the words of the Master Yahusha, that He said, 'It is more blessed to give than to receive.'" *Have we ever heard these words used to make you feel we should give more to your pastor?*

It may not be a very popular message with those making a bundle of easy money from the Body, but the Body needs to know they can now help support the poor in their own families, and it will be a true "tithe". (For further study, see Acts 4:32-35, Romans 15:27, 1 Tim. 5:3-16, James 1:27, 2 Peter 2:3.)

We do many things because it became customary to do them, never knowing about the "law of first discovery". If something is done a certain way, and amended or changed later because there is a better way, fine. But, the original way shouldn't be hidden or covered up. The origin of the word "cop" is an innocent example of doing something, yet very few knowing why. In Chicago, Illinois during the early part of the 20th century, policemen wore uniforms with very large, prominent COPPER buttons. The slang term "coppers" developed from this uniform, and the word was shortened to "cops". When we go back to Scripture and explain the TRUE reasons for things, and not the invented interpretations, the messenger of the Truth is often labeled "heretic". Study on your own, and show the lies to everyone around you, but do it with LOVE. All knowledge without love is worthless. A pastor who works "full-time" traveling and teaching the poor wanted to know how he is to receive support. Well, we ***all*** aren't called to travel full-time, but brother Paul did it extensively for a while. He claimed he supported himself and those with him at Acts chapter 20, and was not a burden in the least on anyone else -- and speaking to these elders, he told them to imitate his example. So, how do we manage it?

The tithe, or ma'aser, was for the support of the Lewite priests. If we were to continue in that pattern, we'd be amiss in our duty if we couldn't prove we were descendants of the tribe of Lewi, and even more so if we didn't continue in all the duties they were obliged to perform. But, in the Brit Chadasha, we are all priests, under our Kohen Gadol, Yahusha. It is not the PERSONAL responsibility of just one individual to go, teach, and immerse others into the Name Yahusha, but **each one of us**. Our "assembling" is for one reason: "let all things (done in the assembly) be for edification." 1 Cor. 14:26. This means we are to have the ultimate goal of getting "built up" in knowledge, meaning educated. This costs nothing. If we choose to ***create circumstances*** that require a huge crowd of us to congregate into a hall and listen to ONE PERSON PREACH, this is a manmade situation. Mortgages, rents, utilities, and insurance costs are the result of circumstances we have control over, and we can make them disappear. 1 Cor. 14:26 also says that when we assemble, **EACH ONE** has a teaching, a prophecy, a message, a tongue, etc.,. -- This "lording over the laity" is evidence that Yahusha has been

GAGGED, because traditionally only one man gets to address His assembled Body. Try standing up in one of the Christian meetings, and telling everyone it's your turn to speak, and watch what happens to you. We've been led by the pattern of the **Nicolaitanes**, which goes all the way back to the Chaldean priests.

How each of us gets out there and spreads the message of the Reign of Yahuah, immersing others into the Name of Yahusha, should be facilitated by the specific GIFT we have been given by Yahusha's Spirit, not molded after a man-made technique. All people on Earth should be able to hear the message, and it should be carried to them for free as we allow Yahusha to do His wonderful work through all who believe and obey Him. He is working in many people from all walks of life.

We have to rely on the ability of the Message reaching others through the power of Yahusha's Spirit, by teaching the pure truth of the message, so it will be able to be CONVEYED THROUGH MANY OTHERS. We who know the Message of the Reign of Yahuah must live it and share it with any who will accept it. We share a **common responsibility**, and the "assistant pastors" who from time-to-time travel and visit distant places should be housed and fed by the brothers at their destination, but they must not be an undue burden, or over-stay their welcome. I know well the costs involved in printing, and keeping this kind of ministry paying its bills.

If we don't know what the "renewed Covenant" is, then we should learn what it is, and then go and teach it to those around us. It will spread on its own; like fire in dry grass, if we only teach it. People will believe it much more readily when its free, as it should be. We labor in the harvest not only with our money, but with our *personal efforts to reach those lost around us.* We don't necessarily have to travel to find them, but the message itself can span great distances. Stand still, and watch Yahuah win the battle. ***"Not by power -- not by might -- but by My Spirit"*** - declares Yahuah. We don't know where the wind comes from, nor where it will go, and the Spirit is like that -- and the Message will go wherever the Spirit goes.

From: ***Sunday Law Countdown***: South Dakota Latest State To Endorse Ten Commandments Version Change" (quoted text follows):

[" During the legislative process the South Dakota Senate has followed the state house's lead and approved a bill that would permit the commandments to be posted in public schools...The bill says the words of the Ten Commandments may be displayed along with other objects and documents of cultural, legal or historical significance...No word on whether South Dakota Governor Bill Janklow intends to sign it." Now, a very interesting thing happened with this bill during the legislative process. In the South Dakota bill HB 1261 introduced to the House 01.21.2000, **"the version of the Ten Commandments to be displayed was recorded in the Old Testament of the Bible"** (cited from the bill) - which would be the correct version, having both the Second Commandment intact and the Fourth Commandment about the Seventh-Day Sabbath with full text. BUT THEN SOMETHING HAPPENED. When the bill came to the State Affairs Committee, the bill text was totally changed and the reference to the Old Testament was deleted! Now why would such a thing happen? To permit display of the changed version of the Ten Commandment law of (God)? To avoid using the correct version which mentions the Seventh-Day Sabbath, thus giving honor to the Sabbath? (Added 02.25.2000) [CBN Now HB 1261 bill status HB 1261 bill text introduced HB 1261 bill text] enrolled Changed Ten Commandments now considered by Colorado legislature: From the bill SB114: **"Each school district shall post in every public school classroom and in the main entryway in every public school a durable and permanent copy of the Ten Commandments as specified in paragraph (b) of this subsection....The text here used is a compromise version developed by interfaith scholars..."** - and then follows a version of the Ten Commandments where the Second Commandment about the worshipping of images is left out, and the Fourth Commandment about the Sabbath day (now third) is heavily changed - **the portion of the Sabbath day being the seventh day is totally left out.** Thus the change made to this sacred Law of (God) by the Catholic Church is honored and support is given to the false Sabbath day, the heathen day of worship and feasting and celebration, SUNDAY - and the posting of this CATHOLIC INSPIRED DOCUMENT is now even in the process of becoming LAW, backed by RAW STATE POWER, in several states nationwide.

Its time to Wake Up America! This has been prophesied! (Added 02.16.2000) "] -- (quoted as sent by e-mail.)

If you read the full text of the 4th Commandment from Exodus 20, it becomes apparent that this "Sabbath" of rest doesn't honor the day, but rather the Creator, Yahuah. By entering into His rest, we show Him that we honor Him as our Creator, and so this weekly commemoration of the Creation sets us apart from all other people. We are Israel, and all those who join to us by engrafting will inherit great reward -- but we will suffer incredible hardships from the attacks of the evil one who hates us, and leads the whole world astray. A big clue is given to us:

"And the woman whom you saw is the great city, which reigns over the kings of the Earth." -- Rev. 17:18. Can you figure it out?

Keep in mind the text at Psalm 118:8: ***"It is better to take refuge in Yahuah than to trust in man."*** And yet trusting in man's religious designs is what is most commonly done. Psalm 118 contains this phrase 3 times: ***"In the Name of*** 𐤉𐤄𐤅𐤄 ***I will surely cut them off."*** And, it contains the phrase Yahusha told us we would say before we would see Him again: ***"Baruch haba baShem Yahuah"***

The " LIE " has become the thing that is believed by most in today's Christian denominations. It is taught that a person will still enter the Kingdom, and have a close relationship with 𐤉𐤄𐤅𐤄, <u>without having to obey His Covenant marriage vows</u>, because "they believe" that Yahusha's death paid for all their sins; past, present, and future! We're talking about DELIBERATE sins. Their ***consciences*** have become "seared", because even though they may be confronted with a specific marriage vow / Commandment, they will tell you it was "nailed to the cross". Once in the re-newed Covenant, a believing follower has no interest in sin, because they now walk in the mind of the Spirit. They have received a ***love for the Torah***. A repentant person turns away from what is offensive to their Maker, which includes Pagan customs; they don't return to their sin as a washed pig returns to a mud puddle.

"Do we then nullify the Law through faith? May it never be! On the contrary, <u>we establish the Law</u>." — Romans 3:31

What shall we say then? Are we to continue in sin that grace might increase? May it never be! <u>How shall we who died to sin still live in it?</u>" — Romans 6:1,2.

So, you stop celebrating birthdays, Christmas, Easter, and stay home and rest on Shabbat, teaching your children the WAY (Torah). Then, a close relative wants to bring a cake to your house for one of your children's birthdays, and celebrate with them (gross idolatry). This is where the rubber meets the road; do you love 𐤉𐤄𐤅𐤄 more than your parents, brothers, and sisters? They may remain unconverted in their hearts, and don't even begin to understand why you've changed so. They may blame this book; or claim you have become involved in a cult. Don't expect them to understand, because the unconverted human is hostile toward 𐤉𐤄𐤅𐤄 —

"For those who are according to the flesh set their mind on the things of the flesh, but those who are according to the Spirit, the things of the Spirit. (The Commandments are spiritual). ***For the mind set on the flesh is death, but the mind set on the Spirit is life and peace, BECAUSE THE MIND SET ON THE FLESH IS HOSTILE TOWARD ELOHIM; for it does not SUBJECT ITSELF TO THE LAW OF ELOHIM, <u>for it is not even able to do so;</u>***
And those who are in the flesh cannot please Elohim.

"However, you are NOT IN THE FLESH, but IN THE SPIRIT, <u>if indeed the Spirit of Elohim dwells in you.</u> But if anyone does not have the Spirit of Mashiach, he does not belong to Him.
(Note here, that the "Spirit of Elohim" is synonymous with the "Spirit of Mashiach" — so Yahusha IS ELOHIM, and He is the "Spirit"— and Yahuah is ONE Yahuah. There is no other elohim with Him).

And if Mashiach is IN YOU, though the body is dead because of sin, yet the spirit (of the individual) ***is alive because of righteousness. But if the Spirit of Him who raised Yahusha from the dead DWELLS IN YOU, He who raised Mashiach Yahusha from the dead will also give life to your mortal bodies through His Spirit who indwells you."***
Romans 8:5-11 (read context, because Paul is explaining how the New Covenant actually works in chapters 6, 7, and 8 of Romans).

Look at it like this; if I am trying to trick you, and I am really doing the bidding of the adversary, would I be trying to point you in the direction of obedience so that you will be condemned? Or, maybe it can be said that now obeying the Commandments will get us into trouble with He who gave these Commandments! I will tell you this: even if a servant obeys out of fear, not love, his master will not punish him. But, we have received love, not fear! Now, we can obey in the renewed Covenant, having Yahusha's Spirit within us, having His Torah written on our HEARTS. The same vows (Commandments) will stand forever and ever, because they reflect the personality of 𐤉𐤄𐤅𐤄. It is WE who have changed.

It is not widely known, but only Yahusha's BRIDE will be raised and live during the 1000 years after His return to rule Earth: ***"The rest of the dead did not come to life until the thousand years were completed. This is the first resurrection."*** (read Rev. 20:4-6). This will possibly occur at "midnight", due to the passages of the parables referring to "watching", a thief in the night, the returning master, two lying in a bed, and the Bridegroom coming at the midnight cry. Some believe it will be on the first day of Sukkot, or Yom Kippur (the **Fast**, Acts 27:9); making it obvious who those are who are "watching" (or observing) His appointments carefully. When He has finished sealing His 144,000 Natsarim with His Name, **watch out** — and this sealing is going on <u>right</u>

now. Repent, or perish. Inventing new reasons for Pagan customs and observances may conceal their character to most of mankind, but this is a wake-up call to those lost sheep who hear their Shepherd's voice beckoning them to return to His flock. His Voice sounds different than human tradition's teachings. If you are being called, your heart recognizes His voice, and you will follow it, and obey it. He told us at Hosea 2:16, 17 . . . ***That you will call Me Ishi*** (my Husband) ***and will no longer call Me Baali*** (my LORD), ***for I will remove the names of the Baals from her mouth, so that they will be mentioned by their names NO MORE."*** Many will someday know His Name, take His Name, and realize we're His WIFE; and stop the "my LORD" nonsense. How did He know? He dwells in infinity, and the future and the past are all before His eyes. The knowledge of the Truth has been kept from us, because the adversary has kept us from learning the Truth from his masquerading messengers of light. ***"My people are destroyed for LACK OF KNOWLEDGE. Because you have rejected knowledge*** (of His Torah, Word, Will), ***I also will reject you from being My priest. Since you have forgotten the Torah of your Elohim, I also will forget your children."*** Hos.4:6.

Ephraim, tribes of Yisrael, RETURN!! ***You are the prodigal son***. You have left your Father's House (the Torah), and gone to distant lands, and worshipped according to the Gentiles / Goyim. Now you are aware that you are sitting in a pig pen, eating (worshipping) with pigs; you yearn for the food (Torah) of your Father's House, don't you? RETURN!! Rise up, start on your journey home, to your Father. He will see you coming from afar off, and run to you. He will tell your older brother (Yahudah, the "Jews") who never left Him why He drew you home, and why He celebrated because of your return:

"But he answered and said to his Father, 'Look! For so many years I have been serving you, and I have never neglected a Command of yours; and yet you have never given me a kid, that I might be merry with my friends; but when this son of yours came (Ephraim, the lost tribes who return), ***who has devoured Your wealth with HARLOTS*** (false idols, Pagan customs), ***You killed the fattened calf for him.'***

"And He said to him, 'My child, you have always been with Me, and all that is Mine is yours. But we had to be merry and rejoice, for this brother of yours was DEAD, and is now ALIVE; and was LOST, and has been FOUND.'" — Luke 15:29-32. And you didn't suspect you'd ever see yourself written about in Scripture, did you?

Paul was overwhelmed with grief after his conversion, and lived with a pain he called a "thorn". Most likely this thorn was the daily knowledge that he had hunted down Natsarim and caused them to be put to death because they pronounced the Name. What else could be worse, bad eyesight? He then spent the rest of his life in the flesh spreading the Name and the message of the Reign of 𐤉𐤄𐤅𐤄.

SABBATH'S DISTANCE — is there one?

First, let me say that meeting together with other saints is very important, for edification; this little study brings up points on how we have been used in a power-play by ravenous wolves who have enslaved our minds with deceptions.

There is not a specific Shabbat "distance" in Torah as a Commandment to keep, however we **are** specifically told to "*stay in our place*" on Shabbat (Ex. 16:29). This means your "vicinity". Consider that we're not to ride on our animal, because the Commandment says to not make our animals work in any way. The providing of the manna in the wilderness was used **to teach Israel how to observe Shabbat**, which they had not done during their 430-year captivity in Egypt / Mitzraim. Manna is Hebrew, meaning *"what is it?"*

Concerning the gathering of **manna**, the camps of Israel had to walk some distance away to find enough to eat for the day; it wasn't just lying around a few feet from their tents / sukkot. Look closely at this passage:

"See, 𐤉𐤄𐤅𐤄 has given you the Sabbath; therefore He gives you bread for two days on the sixth day. REMAIN EVERY MAN IN HIS PLACE; LET NO MAN GO OUT OF HIS PLACE ON THE SEVENTH DAY." Ex. 16:29.

This text spells out the fact that there is no reason for us to have to GO anywhere on Shabbat. Neither is there any Command for everyone "gathering to hear the Torah" every week. Although the English word "convocation" is used in reference to weekly and certain annual Sabbaths, the *Hebrew* word is *"MIQRA"* (#4744, from #7121) and comes from the root word "QARA" (#7121), to call, ANNOUNCE, or **proclaim**. This **root** word has no use or meaning of "gathering together" whatsoever. It can mean cry, shout, dictate, or call. A "gathering" or "council" is the Hebrew word "SOD" (#5475). To assemble is the Hebrew word QABATS (#6908). The Hebrew word ***"YAAD"*** (#3259) is used at Numbers 10:3, and is specifically a summoned gathering -- a meeting together -- and this was for the leaders of the congregation to come together to prepare to set out. None of these words meaning "to meet together" are used in association with how to observe Shabbat. I thought this was odd, considering how we're programmed; but it started to make sense.

Of course Shabbat is a day to read Torah, but even this is not a *commanded* activity. However, common sense should prevail so that if we find ourselves needing to go on a long journey to be "with others", we've missed the point -- the command is to have a MIQRA QODESH, a set-apart proclaiming (to "rest" is what is to be proclaimed). It was Rabbi Yahusha's custom to go to the synagogue on Shabbat, or even go to the Temple on a daily basis. Within the walls of Yerushaliyim, the largest community in the land, one could easily go from one end of it to the other in hardly any time; certainly within a distance not considered to be a journey. His hometown was considerably smaller. Yahuah's Temple is to be a "house of prayer" -- and we are told to ***"pray without ceasing"***; this is because WE ARE THE TEMPLE OF Yahuah, Yahusha's Body. The physical Temple was symbolic for Yahusha, which makes His "play-on-words" even more interesting: ***"Destroy this Temple, and in 3 days I will raise it up."*** -- Yn. 2:19. We really don't have to go very far to be in His presence at all. Pastors call the buildings they have "services" in *the LORD's house*. A "church" is thought of as a building; see the programming?

We may be missing more than we know here, because if we go back and look at the Hebrew passages, the word "MIQRA", based on the word "QARA", may refer only to the DAY being "*proclaimed"* as set-apart, as a day of rest. So, a "set-apart convocation" might simply mean "QODESH PROCLAMATION", not "assembly" at all. We've forced the word "MIQRA" to mean only "assembly" -- but the Hebrew words for "assembly" are QAHAL, EDAH, KNESSET, SOD, or the summoned gathering, "YAAD". ***MOED*** is the Hebrew word for appointment, or set time. It can also mean a set-apart place. It is translated "assembly" twice out of over 200 uses. Translators bend words this way all the time. We never find the literal Hebrew words for "assembly" (QAHAL, KNESSET, EDAH, YAAD, or SOD) used in conjunction with the proper way to observe Shabbat. Maybe there is some reason. "Sabbath gathering" is actually not a *commanded* practice, but we've been programmed to think so by the translators who saw fit to tint certain passages. This was so they could make us drink their poisoned waters, and plunder us.

Concerning the fact that Luke wrote the words ***"Then they returned to Jerusalem from the mount called Olivet, which is near Jerusalem, A SABBATH DAY'S JOURNEY AWAY"*** (Acts 1:12), it could be based simply upon the "man-made" custom to only travel a maximum of 1000 cubits (roughly 500 yards). If a person ***didn't*** travel more than this distance on a Shabbat, no big deal. He's resting, so why not concede that 1000 cubits is reasonable and prudent to not exceed if possible? This distance is coincidentally the distance of the encampments of Israel from the tent of meeting in the wilderness (by traditional reckoning). It really was their "place", or "vicinity". Since we cannot find a solid **SECOND witness** from Scripture that would restrict our general movements on our day of rest, there is the possibility that one would not be in error for exceeding 1000 cubits, except that Luke did mention a "Sabbath's distance". But, consider that ***3 TIMES*** in Lev. 23 the phrase ***"in all your dwellings"*** is used in reference to how to observe various Sabbaths. It doesn't say "in all your gatherings". I've walked 1000 cubits on certain Sabbaths to attend baseball games my younger son played one summer. Getting there and back was a chore, especially in the hot sun! I know people today who drive 60 miles one-way each Shabbat to get to the assembly of their choice. This is almost like driving from Nazareth to Jerusalem in Israel. (OK, that may be 83 miles). Not to judge anyone, we're just discussing all this. Conservatively, I would rather teach someone to focus on RESTING primarily each Shabbat; and if I am wrong, I will be corrected in the resurrection of the saints. If, on the other hand, I teach everyone to travel to get to *an assembly* each Shabbat, I feel I will receive greater correction if I am wrong about that. I would rather see a person sleep all day on Shabbat, and get some serious rest! After all, the reason there was a double-portion of manna provided on the sixth day was to eliminate the gathering, *and the need to go anywhere* -- "Let no man go out of his place on the seventh day." If you have a small group that can get together each Shabbat where each of the people reside within a reasonably close proximity, that's marvelous! Like Yahusha said, two or more gathered together in His Name is all it takes to listen to Him speak through us; and *each one should be able to speak* (1 Cor. 14:26). Then there are the 3 annual "pilgrimage" festivals. Yahusha told the woman of Shomeron at the well, ***"Woman, believe Me, the hour is coming when you shall neither on this mountain, nor in Yerushaliyim, worship the Father."*** Yn. 4:21. For example, Scripture forbids sacrificing the Passover in any place other than the place He has established His Name, Yerushaliyim Dt. 16:5,6. We are ***commanded*** to *come up* to only Yerushaliyim for the place of worship in Scripture; but the day has come that all we can do is observe the festivals where ***we*** are; and these festivals are *shadows of things coming.* Today, believers pass each other on interstates going in opposite directions, to get to the assembly sites of their choice, *and this is acceptable.* Then they pour out their cash as an offering to those throwing the bash. Please don't read into this any condemnation; but if I report this in a neutral way, it just comes out sounding like a set-up every time. We all desire to get to the root of things, and want the Truth — even if it hurts.

The bottom line is, we have been led to believe that we must "assemble" *each and every* Shabbat, simply based on the word ***MIQRA*** -- and then we have been taught to "tithe" *to the men who have taught us to come to these assemblies*. It feels like a set-up to me, since there is **no example** in Scripture of an assembly on a Shabbat where *money was poured into baskets that were raked over the crowds.* I think the thrust of the Commandment is to rest, and to stay in our immediate vicinity. One could just as easily say that Hebrews 10:25 is only "**one witness**" in Scripture speaking of the "assembling together" of ourselves; and I'm **certainly** encouraging such assembling, although I'm simply pointing out that it is not commanded to do so *as we have inherited the pattern*.

I'd love to hear anyone's ideas on this topic, because I can't imagine anything in the Commandment that supercedes the Command to rest. Falling short of the Command would have more to do with NOT RESTING, than NOT ASSEMBLING, it would seem. Oops — I think my eyes rolled a little there. Hebrews 4:11 tells us to be diligent to enter His REST, not **diligent to scurry down the road to meet anyone.** The Command to "assemble" may be only an interpretation, but even if it is *accurate*, it's hard to picture the effort to assemble could negate the importance of resting. This will not be very popular with those engaged in looting the flock, will it? When Yahusha stood up to read in the synagogue, there were no collections made. People today who sell books and videos on Shabbat need to look at what they are really doing: buying and selling. No donations were ever made on Shabbat in Scripture, and they certainly aren't today in orthodox synagogues. If what I am teaching on this is true, and I believe it is, then the plundered should feel that the Truth has set them free; but the plunderers will be greatly disturbed. All the "good works" like "tithing" on Sun-day will be stubble, burned-up like hay; *it will do no good to pay a pastor to do what you were supposed to be doing, at no cost.* ***Why waste your money on what is not bread?*** (See Yesha Yahu 55, Micah 3:11; also, read Acts 20:17-38 carefully, where Paul met with the elders at Ephesus).

Think of how Yahusha drove out the men who had turned His Temple into a <u>house of merchandise</u>, and then picture in your mind ***the baskets of cash passing around in the assemblies.*** 𐤉𐤄𐤅𐤄 owns *quasars, galaxies, and can create universes out of nothing — does He really need our cash?* The offering to Him was to be received by the poor, Lewite, widow, and fatherless; and this should not be *intercepted* by anyone posturing themselves to receive it instead. ***"He who shows favour to the poor lends to 𐤉𐤄𐤅𐤄"*** — Pr. 19:17. Objectively, it would seem we have reconstructed some new form of artificially created house of merchandise all over again. This situation is the sustaining economic power-plant that gives life to the beast system in place; The great prostitute **lives luxuriously**, while spewing poisonous lies across the whole Earth. ***Come out of her, My people***; the great prostitute must pay for her sins -- drinking from her poisoned cup (false teachings) has made most of the world drunk (numb to Truth). *Please* wake up. Wormwood represents "poisoned water", which you will soon see. The Living Water, the Torah (and by association, the Spirit of Mashiach), has been tainted with deadly teachings mixed into it by *human traditions* and *interpretations* for centuries. By all means MEET TOGETHER when you can do so -- but watch out for the ravenous wolves who try to control the gatherings. They are the source of the poisoned waters, the wormwood, the lies.

Take away the money, and the pastors who remain are not masquerading — they seek a reward that thieves cannot steal.

ONLY A PROPHET?

"Take courage, My son, your sins are forgiven." — Mt. 9:2. Yahusha spoke these words to a paralyzed young man. What prophet was given the authority to forgive sins? Can Michael or Gabriel do this? Only Yahuah can.

To <u>*cover*</u> sins, the blood of animals was used as atonement (*kaphar*). This blood is *life*, given on the altar, and it was offered *in place of* the life of the person who sinned. Who was it that decided when sins were covered? Only Yahuah can forgive sins, and <u>He gave this authority to His Son</u>, Who came and spoke to us in the authority of Yahuah, not the authority of a prophet. Many don't yet know Who Yahusha really is. *All the Scriptures* are about Him. He is the Living Waters. The following is a very special article written by a sister in Arizona, named ***Mary Lou Frommert***, and she points out many Scriptures that show that Yahusha is the Living Waters that came down to us. She also explains "wormwood" using Scripture:

LIVING WATERS

Our Messiah Yahusha said He is the Living Waters springing up into everlasting life at Yn. 4:10-14. Yirme Yahu 17:13 states: ***"Those who depart from Me shall be written in the Earth, because they have forsaken Yahuah, the <u>fountain of living waters</u>."***

Yirme Yahu 2:13: ***"For My people have done two evils; they have forsaken Me, the fountain of living waters, to hew out for themselves cisterns; cracked cisterns, which do not hold water."***

Yn. 3:5: ***"Yahusha said, 'Truly, truly, I say to you, unless one is born of water and the Spirit, he is unable to enter into the reign of Elohim."***

We must be born of the Spirit and of His Water, His *Living Waters* — look at Ps. / Tehillim 1, and 36:8,9. It speaks of being filled with His Word. His Word is His *Water,* and we are washed clean by His Word. 1Cor. 10:4: ***"All drank the same spiritual drink. For they all drank of that spiritual Rock that followed, and the Rock was Messiah."*** Ibrim / Hebrews 10:22: ***"Let us draw near with a true heart in completeness of belief, having our hearts sprinkled from a wicked conscience and our bodies washed with clean water."*** We must let Him wash us with the *water* of His *Word*. Ephesians 5:26: ***"Husbands love your wives, as Messiah also did love the assembly and gave Himself for it, in order to set it apart and cleanse it with the washing of water by the Word."*** There it is; this is what our Messiah does for us His bride — Yn. 1:1,2: ***"In the beginning was the Word, and the Word was with Elohim, and the Word was Elohim. He was in the beginning with Elohim."***

Now I will show you what Yahuah has given me about His ***Word*** becoming ***Wormwood***. Wormwood is already here, and it has been here poisoning our spiritual waters from Yahusha.

Yirme Yahu 9:12b-15: ***"Why has the land perished, has it been burned up like a wilderness, with none passing through? And Yahuah says, 'Because they have forsaken My Torah which I set before them, and have not obeyed My voice, nor walked according to it, but they have walked according to the stubbornness of their own heart and after the Ba'als, which their fathers had taught them.' Therefore thus says Yahuah of hosts, the Elohim of Yisrael, 'See, I am making this people eat wormwood, and I shall make them drink poisoned water.'"***

Yirme Yahu 23:11 ***"'For both prophet and priest have become defiled. Even in My House I have found their evil', declares Yahuah. Therefore thus said Yahuah of hosts concerning the prophets, 'See, I am making them eat wormwood, and shall make them drink poisoned water.'"***

Amos 5:7: ***"O you who are turning right –ruling to wormwood, and have cast down righteousness to the Earth!"***

Rev. 8:10,11: ***"And the third messenger sounded, and a great star fell from the heaven, burning like a torch, and it fell on a third of the rivers and on the fountains of water, and the name of the star is called Wormwood. And a third of the waters became wormwood, and many men died from the waters, because they were made bitter."***

Daniel 8:9-12: ***"And from one of them came a little horn which became exceedingly great toward the south, and toward the east, and toward the Splendid Land. And it became great up to the host of the heavens. And it caused some of the host and some of the stars to fall to the Earth, and trampled them down. It even exalted itself as high as the Prince of the host. And it took that which is continual away from Him, and threw down the foundation of His set-apart place. And because of transgression, an army was given over to the horn to oppose that which is continual. And it threw the Truth down to the ground, and it acted and prospered."*** Now please look with your eyes open and see that Wormwood has been with us since the Truth of Yahuah's (and Yahusha's) true Name was cast down. When the Law — the Torah — was cast down, these were some of the stars that fell and were trampled down; *and we have drunk the poisoned waters of lies of Wormwood.* Many men have died drinking from the wrong spiritual waters. Everyone is waiting for our natural water to turn poisoned, and I'm sure they will soon; but let us also see that Wormwood is *already here*, and has been here for many, many years. Let each of us turn, repent, and seek Yahuah to show us His pure Waters; His Word, His Truth. Let us drink only pure Truth in these days of darkness all around us.

Here is a Truth Yahuah has shown me about our Messiah and His birth.

Yesha Yahu 7:14: ***"Therefore Yahuah Himself gives you a sign; Look, a virgin shall conceive and bear a Son and shall call His Name Immanuel."***

Luke 1:30-35: ***"The messenger said to her, 'Do not be afraid Miryam, for you have found favour with Elohim. And see, you shall conceive in your womb, and shall give birth to a Son, and call His Name Yahusha. He shall be great and shall be called the Son of the Most High. And Yahuah Elohim shall give Him the throne of His father Da'ud. And He shall reign over the house of Ya'aqob forever and there shall be no end to His reign.' And Miryam said to the messenger, 'How shall this be, since I do not know a man?' And the messenger answering, said to her 'The The Set-apart Spirit shall come upon you and the power of the Most High shall overshadow you. And for that reason, the Set-Apart One Born of you shall be called: Son of Elohim.'"***

(A child in a woman's womb carries the father's blood.)

Matt 1:25: ***"Yoseph knew Miryam not until she gave birth to her Son, the first born."***

1 Yohanan 5:6-8: ***"This is the one that came by water and blood. Yahusha Messiah, not only by water, but by water and blood. And it is the Spirit who bears witness because the Spirit is the Truth. Because there are three who bear witness: the Spirit and the water, and the blood. And the three are in agreement."***

Gen. 4:10: ***"The voice of your brother's blood cries out to Me from the ground."***

Gen. 2:24: ***"Husband and wife became one flesh."***

1 Cor. 6:15-20 talks about our bodies belonging to our Messiah and to flee fornication because it defiles our bodies. Remember in marriage a pure wife will bleed when they become one flesh, and this is why Miryam had to stay pure for the birth of her Son. This beautiful Messiah of ours had to come down out of His mother's pure womb through a pure passage untouched by a man. The first thing that happened was her water broke, and that had a voice; and then her blood flowed, which was pure and that had a voice; the Spirit bears witness of this in Luke 1:30-35 and Yohanan 5:6-8.

Yohanan 19:30: ***"So when Yahusha took the sour wine, He said, 'It has been accomplished!' And bowing His head, He gave up His spirit."***

V. 34: ***"But one of the soldiers pierced His side with a spear, and instantly blood and water came out."***

Our precious Messiah came into this world with the Spirit making Him in a pure womb, and with water and blood; the last thing He did was to leave this world giving us His Spirit, His Water, and His Blood. Let us walk in His Word; the pure water of His Word. Hungry and thirsty for His righteousness and truth, keeping our bodies and minds clean for Him as we are His Dwelling Place. I encourage you to walk pure and clean for your first love, Yahuah. Let us not be cracked cisterns that we have made, let us hold His sweet waters. Remember Yaaqob 3:11, ***"Does the fountain send forth the sweet and the bitter from the same opening?"*** Let us speak the truth, and live the truth Yahusha has called us to. His Spirit lives in us; His Blood washes away our sins. His Water is His Word we wash ourselves with each and every day. Let us not forsake our Living Waters — 𐤉𐤄𐤅𐤄. The Spirit, the Water, and the Blood bear witness, and we hear the Truth, and we are free. I leave you with these 3 Scriptures to wash with:

Yesha Yahu 30: 20, 21; 1 Yn. 2:12-17; Rev. 21:27. We are not written in the Earth as in Yirme Yahu 17:13, but we are written in the Lamb's Scroll of Life! Praise you, Father 𐤉𐤄𐤅𐤄, we hear Your Voice! May the favour of our Master Yahusha Messiah be with you.

Shalom — **Mary Lou Frommert**

Stunning prophetic Truth, I say. She mentioned that "stars" in Revelation represent certain *Commandments,* caused to fall by a "great horn" (power). Well, Rev. 8:10,11 quoted in her essay mentions a "great star" falling. This is indeed most likely the "Key of Knowledge", His personal Name! His Name was used in Scripture at least 7,000 times, but taken out completely for some reason. Which Commandment in the "big ten" has the most words? Which Commandment is mentioned throughout Scripture with the most fervor? Which Commandment is mentioned the most times? Overwhelmingly, it is the Sabbath. This single observance will announce to anyone in this world Who you serve. It will "mark" you in their eyes. Most will even say, *"are you Jewish?"* This "star" is indeed also great, and the "great horn" must be the BEAST. Yes, the beast is here, and will remain until the return of Yahusha.

Often, we can't see what we're involved in because we are so close to it all. You'd admit that there is a great deal in human customs that a person could simply not ever be involved in, and still be included in the assembly of the saints, or even the Bride itself, which is a much smaller number.

We have to start at the foundation. We believe in a Creator Being, Who is eternal, and exists outside of time: in *infinity*. He made all we see and perceive. He told us He is the LIVING WATERS, which metaphorically is His Spirit, but it is also what the Spirit brings to us: His Personality, or teachings, called Torah. All through time, sages have known that the Torah is the Living Waters, the Word of Yahuah. Yahusha is called the Living Waters, and the Word, made flesh.

Why don't we all see things the same? Because something polluted these Living Waters: WORMWOOD. Wormwood is "poisoned waters", and this is what has been taught, causing men to die (spiritually). The falling star called "Wormwood" took away the Name from us. I've been calling wormwood "Fossilized Customs". We don't have to debate about how many personalities Yahuah has, or how many heads, manifestations, and so on; we have to *begin* by teaching the message (gospel) of the coming kingdom,

"Repent, for the reign of Yahuah draws near." (See Mt. 4:17, Mk. 1:14, and other references).

This involves the fundamental process that involves the Torah, which CONVICTS EVERY MAN TO BE A SINNER. This will cause wise men to repent. The next step is to teach them how to covenant with their Maker, which is their *circumcision,* called "baptism". The NEW COVENANT cut in Yahusha's blood involves ***His*** "circumcising" their hearts with His Torah. There is no other New Covenant, but this one. Romans chapters 6 through 8 explain this. Yahuah is much more than a Trinity. Trinities are the pattern or paradigm embraced by every Pagan religion on Earth, from Babylonian times forward. Yahuah has manifested as a ROCK, a burning BUSH, a MESSENGER (to "Joshua" and Abram). He wrestled with Ya'aqob. He was in the Shekinah above the Ark of the Covenant (the box which held the marriage covenant with Israel). He spoke as a friend to both Abram and Mosheh at various times, and walked in the garden with Adam and his wife --- and yet each of these manifestations were about Yahusha. There is only one Elohim, and His last manifestation was the Son, Yahusha ha Mashiach of Natsareth (being the product of Yahuah's Spirit and the virginal human woman He chose).

The celebration of birthdays is strictly Pagan, and is only a custom that is preserved carefully because our flesh enjoys it so. Find the birthday celebrations in Scripture, and you will notice calamity surrounds each one. Iyyob (Job) lost all his children while they celebrated "each one on his day". Surely you can see that the candles, the making of a wish, and the cake (baked for the queen of heaven) is idolatry -- the Spirit will reveal this to you. The mark of the beast is very insidious. It is a mark, name, or number. It can be received by being led astray by the "first beast", which Scripture defines as Babylon. Revelation 13 through 18 will back this up, and as you know, Daniel prophesied FOUR beasts, each one based on the idolatry of the first. The last one will endure until the end (ROME). The highest sin, the grossest offense to 𐤉𐤄𐤅𐤄, is idolatry. Whose "mark" we bear identifies us as to whose servant we are. The MARK is not shown to those who lack wisdom ("My people are destroyed for a lack of knowledge"). The sign of the Everlasting Covenant (remember the marriage vows, the Ten Commandments) is the sign of the 7th day Sabbath of rest. This goes back to Creation, and shows Yahuah we are His people. It is our "mark", showing Yahuah we honor Him alone as Creator, by *commemorating* His work of creating, each 7th day. If we are His, Yahusha's Spirit is in us, and we show our love for our Husband by our obedience. And this is love: "THAT WE OBEY HIS COMMANDS".

Israel is more than just the "Jews" -- they are but one tribe of 12. 10 of the tribes are in the nations, and Yahusha was, and IS being sent to the "lost sheep of the TRIBES of Israel" — through us, today. The manna for 6 days was to RE-TRAIN Israel in the observance of Shabbat. Those being called from the nations are called "Ephraim" at Ez. 37, but are really 10 tribes. The parable of the "prodigal son" is about Ephraim, who is today mostly the Christians. The younger son (the lost 10 tribes) left the Father's House (His Torah). Upon drifting through the world of darkness, he came to his senses and realized he was living and eating (worshipping) among PIGS (Gentiles). He returned to his Father, and the OLDER brother (the tribe of Yahudah, the Jews) told the Father he had never left, and that he had always obeyed each Command of the Father. The Father explained that "this son of Mine" (the lost 10 tribes) was DEAD, and is now ALIVE". He was LOST, but is now FOUND.

Israelite, if you return to Yahuah, embrace the New Covenant as it is written (not as it is poisoned - the wormwood), you too will see the mark of the beast. It is the mark of the dogs, sorcerers, and all who practice a lie: the SOLAR mark of Babylon: SUN-DAY, established under the penalty of death by Constantine, and enforced by the Inquisition for centuries. They proclaimed Death to back-sliding "Judaizers" -- this is the martyring of the saints, which reaches all the way back to Babylon, the great prostitute who has made the whole world drink from the cup of her fornication (false teachings, wormwood, poisoned waters). It's Sun-day Israelite. I'm so glad you're interested in the Truth; I hope Yahusha writes His Torah on your heart, and you become a worker. We are labeled a cult because the world is so dark, and getting darker; but we are not. In the past, it was the term "heretic" that enabled Christians to justify burning most of us. The harvest is ripe, but you must first stop fighting against the Torah, and admit you love it. I love it, and so can you if you will ask for a love for it. Show Him you love Him.

CAN WE HEAR THE VOICE OF YAHUSHA?

In the renewed Covenant, we have both men and women. Those who belong to Yahusha have His Spirit dwelling ***in them***, and these individuals have experienced having the Covenant (Ten Words) "circumcised" on their hearts. They LOVE the Torah now, having been sealed in their foreheads with the Name of the Father (Yahuah), and immersed into the Name of Yahusha, for the forgiveness of their sins. They no longer **want** to sin. The "Sinai experience" of the giving of the Torah for us is in our hearts, and we obey willingly. We are the Temple, the living containers of the Covenant, as the Ark used to be. It was only a model, or form; we are the reality. It was a throne, or Mercy Seat; Yahusha is now enthroned in our hearts. Any Spirit-filled individual who meets with another one, or several together (2 or more), is in the presence of Yahusha in their midst. 1 Cor.

14:26 states that when we assemble together, EACH ONE has a teaching, prophecy, tongue, etc.,. It isn't to be just one man or woman "lording" over the people (nicolaitanism).

The "Spirit of prophecy" is the testimony of Yahusha. This phrase from Revelation 19:10 tells us that Yahusha speaks to us THROUGH one another. His voice is uttering prophetic messages to the assemblies all the time, but most of these prophetic utterances are ignored and those speaking them are sometimes disfellowshipped when this happens. An "evangelist" is a bearer of the message of the Kingdom, and they should be aware of what it is: "Repent, for the Reign of Yahuah draws near". It matters not whether the person is a man or woman, and all the esteem and honor goes to the Spirit of Yahusha dwelling in us -- He pours His Spirit upon both genders.

The Law Beside the Ark

You must test everything you hear, to make certain you are not just listening to "winds" -- and you know how they can blow all sorts of doctrines (teachings).

Christians have been taught for centuries that the "law" has been done away with, and that we now live under "grace". This has satisfied theologians and the laity (people) they have lorded-over very well, while none seem to have ever comprehended exactly WHAT the "New Covenant" actually is. The ceremonial laws, which were daily sacrifices pointing to Yahusha's one-time atoning death, were brought to a crashing halt, since they served as our temporary covering for sin. Daily, weekly, and annually ceremonial laws had to be performed, because they were impermanent. Yahusha's death ended the need for this ceremonial law. Even the Temple was removed in order to make it all come to an end. There was a change in priesthood also. We became the Temple; and the Torah (The Covenant Law, or Ten Words) was circumcised on our hearts by the giving of the Spirit of Truth. Yahusha fulfilled even the "drink offerings" by taking sour wine from a sponge as He hung dying, nailed to wood. Each ceremonial law was hostile to us, while the Commandments could never be hostile to us. There was a "law" OUTSIDE the Ark, while INSIDE the Ark was the Covenant itself. What was outside the Ark was impermanent, and passing away. Inside the Ark was the Covenant which is a lamp for our feet, and a light for our path. The ceremonial law was placed ***beside*** the Ark, not inside it.

Dt. 31:26 states:

"Take this book of the law and place it BESIDE the Ark of the Covenant of Yahuah your Elohim, that it may remain there as a WITNESS <u>AGAINST</u> you."

Comparing the above text with Col. 2:14, we can better comprehend which "law" was taken out of the way:

"Having cancelled-out the certificate of debt consisting of decrees <u>AGAINST</u> us which was hostile to us; and He has taken it out of the way, having nailed it to the stake."

So, we can see there really is a case for a "ceremonial law" that was cancelled-out. This is part of the central misunderstanding of Christianity, keeping people in bondage to sin, since they reject any idea of obedience to Torah. The true **renewed Covenant**, having the Torah written on our hearts, can be easily seen when the truth of this misunderstanding is dispelled. The "ceremonial" law was never referred to as "THE COVENANT", the "Ten Words" which are INSIDE the Ark <u>are the Covenant</u>. These were never "against" us, but are our wedding vows. It is a MARRIAGE COVENANT, between 𐤉𐤄𐤅𐤄 and the 12 tribes of Israel. Now, in the Brit Chadasha, this Covenant is written (circumcised) on our hearts, so that we LOVE them, and obey willingly. We are now the "Ark" of the Covenant, and represent ***living stones*** -- together we are built up as the ***Temple of*** 𐤉𐤄𐤅𐤄. We are the city, the "New Yerushaliyim", which will come from the skies "adorned as a bride". The third Temple is built, without hands, and will not be destroyed -- it is us. The Spirit of prophecy is the ***"testimony of Yahusha".*** He speaks to us through one another today. Where ever two or more are gathered in His Name, He is there; each individual has a prophecy or teaching. We can hear Yahusha speak.

"Indeed, He will speak to this people through stammering lips and a foreign tongue, He who said to them, 'here is rest, give rest to the weary', and 'here is repose' - but they would not listen." Is. 28 (see whole chapter).

MISTRANSLATIONS DECEIVE US

Reading only a single translation, believing it is saying what the author actually stated, puts us in a very dangerous position. Translators "translate" according to their own understandings and beliefs. Look carefully at this *NIV* translation:

Acts 20:6-8

"But we sailed from Philippi after the Feast of Unleavened Bread, and five days later joined the others at Troas, where we stayed seven days. On the <u>first</u> <u>day</u> of the <u>week</u> we came together to break bread. Paul spoke to the people and, because he intended to leave the next day, kept on talking until midnight. There were many lamps in the upstairs room where we were meeting."

CONTINUED ON PAGE 157 . . .

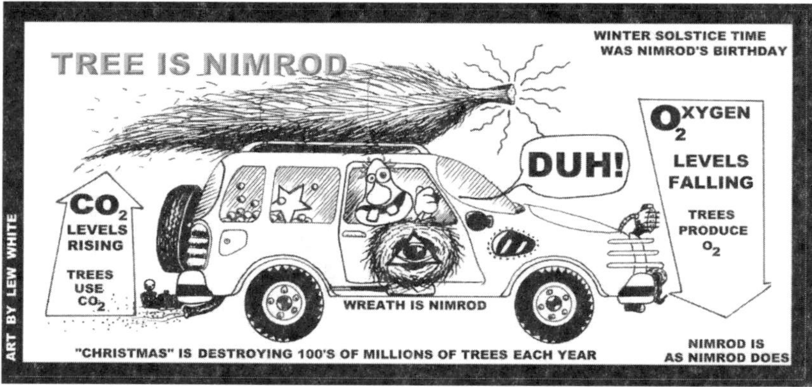

CANCER EPIDEMIC — Nobel Prize-winning German biochemist Dr. Otto Warburg, in researching into the cause of our world-wide cancer epidemic, has proof that it is largely caused by our increasingly oxygen deficient atmosphere. **Evergreens** produce *oxygen* and consume *carbon dioxide* all-year-round. High CO2 levels cause the green-house effect. If you **wanted** to cause the most damage possible, you couldn't improve on the course of action chosen: destroying evergreens by the 100's of millions each year. And, we are doing it *religiously* [pun intended]. There is no doubt that the adversary is using his scheme to destroy trees in order to cause the maximum damage, and human suffering as well. Imagine how he laughs at our stupidity as he watches the anguish he's caused; the loss of mothers, fathers, and children to the slow agonizing death of cancer. We're helping him to destroy the world, and ourselves along with it. With all our pompous sophistication and higher learning, we're *fabulously stupid* socially.

Do not learn the customs of the Gentiles, and do not be awed by the signs of the heavens, for the Gentiles are awed by them. For the prescribed customs of these peoples are worthless, for one cuts a tree from the forest, work for the hands of a craftsman with a cutting tool. They adorn it with silver and gold, they fasten it with hammers so that it does not topple." — Yirme Yahu 10:2-4.

The customs of the decorated tree in the home originated with Tammuz, led into the groves by his mother Semiramis, to place a gift on or ***beneath a tree*** of the forest. This custom was at the time of the sun's "birth" — the winter solstice, which in the ancient world was our December 25th. The tree was decorated with sexual symbols. The custom echoed through the cultures, until at last it found its way to the Celtic DRUIDS, who also worshipped the sun as Baal, among other names. Boniface influenced them to change from the oak tree to the evergreen tree during the 8th century.

We need much more oxygen. Air bubbles preserved in amber (ancient tree sap) contain a 38% oxygen content, indicating that oxygen levels in the ancient world were much, much higher. 50 years ago, our air contained 21% oxygen. In many urban areas now, it is as low as 12%. If it gets near 7%, we all die. No wonder we can't think — and our school children can't read. Our gas furnaces use the oxygen from inside our homes to combust the gas, *drastically reducing the precious-little oxygen inside.* We're literally causing our own cancers. Get a furnace that uses outside air for combustion, quickly; *and take vitamins each day.* We have to wise-up to what's going on. The way we live is harmful to life in many ways, but the decision to change is within the grasp of each of us. Read Yirme Yahu chap. 11, and you will see that we are all the victims of a ***conspiracy***. The conspiracy involves not obeying the Creator, and instead obeying the Pagan customs. I sincerely hope this book has been enriching to your knowledge, and lifted you up to a higher level so that you can see history with more clarity and truth.

IT HAD TO BE DARKENING AS HE DIED

Many of you have wondered why it was required that the Passover Lamb be slain at twilight, "between the evenings". And, if Yahusha is our Lamb, His death at 3 p.m. seems to be at a strange time of day (only to some), because it was not twilight. But it was. Even though it was a full moon and an eclipse would be impossible, ***darkness*** hung over the land for 3 hours — much longer than any eclipse could ever be. Yahuah *made* it happen correctly. It's wonderful to watch how He works.

The phrase ***"On the first day of the week"*** is *misleading* here. The Greek text literally says, ***"And on the first of the Sabbaths".*** Notice they *eliminated* the word ***"Sabbaths",*** and made it mean "week". The reference to ***"Unleavened Bread"*** is critical here; this refers to the feast of ***Matsah***, which Christianity ignores. Matsah is a 7 -day festival (often simply called *Passover week*, when we abstain from bread made with leaven). It is set according to the real moon (Lev. 23), and occurs in the springtime. The ***"count"*** to the next High Sabbath, Shabuoth (or Pentecost) is determined by counting "seven complete Sabbaths" *from the weekly Sabbath during the festival of Matsah.* ***"Seven complete Sabbaths"***, totaling 49 days, up until the ***"morrow after the seventh Sabbath"*** tells us when to observe the wedding anniversary (not a birthday), usually called Pentecost. ***Counting*** these ***weekly*** Sabbaths *between* Unleavened Bread (Matsah) and Shabuoth, we come to this ***"first of the Sabbaths"*** which Luke records for us above. Luke is really saying it was at the *time* of the first of Sabbaths, as we would say "*the weekend*", after Unleavened Bread.

Notice the ***"many lamps"*** in the upper room. It was NIGHT, and this meeting took place just as this "first Sabbath" had ended, and Shaul spoke to the group until midnight. They had a fellowship meal, which is what "breaking bread" means. The text is simply saying that it was at the "time" of the first of the Sabbaths, as you will notice Luke had just finished telling us ***"we sailed from Philippi after the Feast of Unleavened Bread, and five days later joined the others at Troas, where we stayed seven days."*** They stayed "seven days" and Luke was *with* Shaul when this meeting occurred *"on the first of the Sabbaths",* and the following day, Luke and Shaul ***departed together***.

If you casually read this area of text without knowing how they twisted the phrasing to fit the idea of "Sun-day" gatherings, you'd come away thinking that every "Sun-day" all the "Christians" came together to "break bread".

TRINITY?

Trinitarian teachings from Pagan origins came in among the many "gnostic" forms of the multiple christianities that developed, and their distorted teachings continue to this day.

Three "PERSONS" in "ONE GOD" is not found in Scripture, but is common to all the Pagans, having originated from Babel's Nimrod, Semiramis, and Tammuz. The concept of "PERSON" comes from Etruscan and Latin. It means **MASK**, or character, as in the ***role*** an actor takes on in a play.

We have inherited these outside ideas due to Gnosticism, the Greek word for "knowledge". It is mostly false knowledge we have inherited from our fathers. Our pursuit is love, not knowledge.

Gnostic teaching insists that one must have enlightenment for salvation.

ACTOR

HOLDING HIS "PERSONA"

(ROLE or CHARACTER)

Jer 30:1-31:1: ***" . . . The days are coming,' declares Yahuah, 'when I will bring my people Israel and Yahudah back from captivity and restore them to the land I gave their forefathers to possess,' says Yahuah." These are the words Yahuah spoke concerning Israel and Yahudah. This is what Yahuah says:***

'Cries of fear are heard--terror, not peace. Ask and see: Can a man bear children? Then why do I see every strong man with his hands on his stomach like a woman in labor, every face turned deathly pale? How awful that day will be! None will be like it. It will be a time of trouble for Jacob,but he will be saved out of it. In that day, declares Yahuah Almighty, I will break the yoke off their necks and will tear off their bonds; no longer will foreigners enslave them. Instead, they will serve Yahuah their Elohim and Da'ud their king, whom I will raise up for them. So do not fear, O Jacob my servant; do not be dismayed, O Israel, declares Yahuah. I will surely save you out of a distant place, your descendants from the land of their exile. Jacob will again have peace and security, and no one will make him afraid. I am with you and will save you, declares Yahuah. Though I completely destroy all the nations among which I scatter you, I will not completely destroy you.

" . . . This is what Yahuah says: I will restore the fortunes of Jacob's tents and have compassion on his dwellings; the city will be rebuilt on her ruins, and the palace will stand in its proper place. From them will come songs of thanksgiving and the sound of rejoicing. I will add to their numbers, and they will not be decreased; I will bring them honor, and they will not be disdained. Their children will be as in days of old, and their community will be established before Me; I will punish all who oppress them. Their leader will be one of their own; their ruler will arise from among them. I will bring him near and he will come close to Me, for who is he who will devote himself to be close to me?' declares Yahuah. So you will be my people, and I will be your Elohim.' See, the storm of Yahuah will burst out in wrath, a driving wind swirling down on the heads of the wicked. The fierce anger of Yahuah will not turn back until he fully accomplishes the purposes of His heart.

In days to come you will understand this."

The Mystery of Iniquity

(THE SECRET OF LAWLESSNESS)

RECEIVING A "LOVE FOR THE TRUTH" VS. RECEIVING A "STRONG DELUSION TO BELIEVE THE LIE"

Are the Commandments for Christians? If so, which ones? When ha shatan joined and corrupted "the Church" from within long ago, things became so twisted and confusing that even educated men couldn't make heads or tails of anything. The article below may help show the opposing perspectives as they exist today between the traditional viewpoints of "the law" and what Yahuah really expects. One perspective was sown by an enemy, the other was planted by Yahuah. Remember always that the only "law" we are no longer "under" is the ceremonial law of atonements, which was added due to transgressions. It was to come to an end, with Yahusha's perfect offering of Himself.

MYSTERY OF LAWLESSNESS

We are saved by "**chasid**", the unmerited loving kindness of Yahuah, through (by means of) His gift, our FAITH. The classic argument in favor of **lawlessness** is that we only have to believe, not obey. Ephesians 2:8-10 is one of Paul's most misunderstood passages, since it can be interpreted to mean that we not only **don't** have to obey, but if we do obey, we are somehow belittling Yahusha's blood covering our past sinful / law-breaking life, and trying to **save ourselves** by obedience.

That interpretation results from the way we LOOK at the Scriptures with an "eye filled with darkness".

Looking for excuses to disobey and using Scripture to "prove" such excuses is what Yahusha called having a "dark eye". In other words, the outcome is resting on how you "see" or interpret the texts. The result? Your whole body is filled with darkness, because you live in disobedience, and your conscience is "seared" -- incapable of convicting you of your sin, because you "**believe the lie**".

Our faith is Yahuah's gift to us. We are being saved by the unmerited kindness (grace) of Yahuah, THROUGH our faith, which is His gift to us, resulting in our future obedience. Our obedience isn't what saves us, but it is evidence of our faith, and evidence that we are being saved. Our wills are controlled by the **TORAH**, or "living Word" -- which is the **mind of the Spirit of Yahusha**. At 1 John, this Torah is referred to as the "Word" which you heard in the beginning. The "**Word**" of Yahuah is simply His Torah, the Covenant. And, it is an everlasting Covenant, because it defines how His wife is to behave. Acts 5:32 says that the Spirit (of Yahusha) is only given to those who obey Him. This is "receiving a love for the **TRUTH**", and since His "**WORD**", the **TORAH**, is what **TRUTH** is, **receiving a love for it** changes our wills, and the result is we walk in a mind of the Spirit. TORAH is the Hebrew word which specifically refers to the Covenant, or 10 Commandments at Exodus 20. It is also used to generally refer to the 5 books/scrolls of Mosheh (Moses). The Torah's effect on the world is LOVE for Yahuah and others. Rejecting it is hatred, and results in DEATH. Proverbs 1 through 4 calls Torah "her", and we see she is called "Wisdom". Proverbs 8 goes into how "Wisdom" is **crying out at the doorposts and gates**, where we are to WRITE the Commandments (see Deut. 6:4-9). The lie will sound very good: **"OBEDIENCE IS UNNECESSARY"** (This is the **opposite** of the New Covenant).

If we refuse to receive a *love for the Truth*, His Torah, then He sends us a strong delusion to believe the "**LIE**" -- that obedience is unnecessary. This is the ***secret of lawlessness***, called the mystery of iniquity. It's the same trick satan pulled on the woman in the garden of Eden. Simply believing Yahusha died for our sins so that we can continue to disobey and keep on sinning willfully is the very thing Hebrews 10:26-28 directly refutes, as well as the often quoted 10:16,17. First, the message of the Kingdom is: **REPENT** (stop sinning, and return, turn back to Torah) -- it is a mystery, veiled to those Yahuah does not call. This message is the one our Rabbi Yahusha said over and over, and it is what is called "**the gospel**". He enables us to love the Commandments by His supernatural power. This is a light yoke, but it comes with worldly costs attached -- persecution for righteousness' sake. His criticism of those of His religion in that time was only concerning the things that were ADDED by human tradition, He did not found or invent any NEW religion at all. Second, the **New Covenant** is having the Torah written on our HEARTS, as you will see if you read Jeremiah 31, Hebrews chapters 8 & 10. The same laws (or more accurately "teachings") are **written on our hearts** by Yahusha's Spirit, enabling us to LOVE them. This is what happened for the first time at "Pentecost". He said, "If you love Me, **keep My Commandments**". When we are convicted of our sinfulness, we are to repent of our sins, and obey. The Torah (10 Commandments) DEFINE what is a sin, 1 John 3:4. Please read 1 John 3:22-24, and see if anything harmonizes with what we're discussing here. Try to find in Scripture where "legalism" (according to Torah, not human traditions) is ever a *problem* for anyone's salvation. Human "legalism" is rampant -- look at "Sun-day", Easter, Christmas, and so on. These things are invented by men, and are not found anywhere in Scripture. Hanukkah is found (Yn. 19:22).

If you don't observe the *traditions*, you're considered strange. They are men's laws, or legalism. It's *lawlessness*, the ignoring of the **Torah**, that will condemn us; and this is what satan has been so successful in promoting. My words here are not enough to convince. You must look up the Scriptures I've quoted -- look also at James 1:23, and the entire chapter 2, where "faith" is perfected by "works". We *show* our faith by our obedience. This is *not* in conflict with Ephesians 2, because the "gift" is our faith, which enables us to do good works, such as observe the Torah. Read Eph. 2:8-13, carefully. The unconverted human who is still in the "mind of the flesh" interprets the Scriptures seeking out lawlessness from the dark point of view, and **will not submit to the Torah of Yahuah, nor can it do so**. But, the mind of the Spirit enables us to obey, because we AGREE with the Torah, and love it. I love the Commandments of Yahuah, and teach them. Yahusha told us that whosoever keeps and teaches them will be called great in the Kingdom, but whosoever annuls the least of them will be the least. Romans chapters 6 through 8 will explain the New Covenant to you.

The denominations each have their "seminaries" where they train young ministers according to their denomination's LIST OF EXCUSES for NOT OBEYING. Each denomination has their own peculiar list of excuses, and when these excuses are learned well enough by the seminary student, then they are granted their "ordination" to speak for the denomination. When you enter into the New Covenant fully, you will hear ANTI-MESSIAH each time you listen to such men. Seeing with eyes filled with LIGHT (Torah), you will be enabled to LOVE the Torah, and LOVE obeying. Your ears will be opened. Yahusha is near, ask Him to reveal the Truth to you -- and write His perfect Torah on your heart. Then, you will begin an incredible task He has prepared just for you to go and teach others all He has commanded, and immerse them into His Name, Yahusha. You will see your teachers (the Commandments), and hear a voice behind you, saying ***"This is the way, walk in it". - YeshaYahu 30:21***

You will love obeying. Your obedience is your way of showing Yahuah that you love Him. It is evidence of your salvation. The serpent is still lying to us from the tree! This time, let's not listen to the wrong voice. We can obey.

"AND THE DRAGON WAS ENRAGED WITH THE WOMAN, AND HE WENT TO FIGHT WITH THE REMNANT OF HER SEED, THOSE GUARDING THE COMMANDS OF ELOHIM AND POSSESSING THE WITNESS OF YAHUSHA MASHIACH."
REV. 12:17 (Also see 14:12)

NOTICE THE REMNANT *OBEYS* AND *BELIEVES*

Those who don't understand very deeply are often those we are sent to, but few usually show any signs of real brain activity related to the spiritual things we have to describe. The Words of life we carry are eternal, but they don't always drink from them, being not "thirsty". Hebrews 4:2 helps explain it:

"For indeed we have had good news preached to us, just as they also; but the WORD they heard did not profit them, BECAUSE IT WAS NOT UNITED BY FAITH IN THOSE WHO HEARD. For we who have believed enter that rest . . ." (This text specifically discusses the 7th day as a commemoration of Creation, honoring Yahuah).

WORD = TORAH, COMMANDMENTS

Also, Ephesians 2:8-10 explains how our own faith is Yahuah's gift, opening our minds to Truth. 2 Timothy 3:5 tells us that people in the last days will be "holding to a FORM of (Elohimliness), although they have denied its power (DYNAMIN, dunamis, dynamic -- intensity, force, mechanism, process, capability, ableness); and avoid such men as these."

This would mean that we should not "give up" until we see they deny the relevance, ability, and authority of the Torah, and they attempt to repel it. This condition of their heart will bring upon them the "strong delusion" because they did not receive a love for the Truth (Torah) which we see explained at 2 Thess. chapter 2.

The "apostasy" caused a falling-away from Truth long ago, and now the "mystery of iniquity (lawlessness)" is being revealed -- exposing the "lie" (the lie being, "you don't have to obey"). This

LIE, spoken to the first woman, is what Christianity is predicated on -- simply because they have not understood what the New Covenant is (having the Torah written on our hearts, being circumcised by the action of the Spirit of Yahusha in us). We become children of Yahuah through the Covenant made with Abraham only when we obey the Covenant, doing what Abraham did. His name, Abraham, means "father of nations", and so we may not descend from the tribe of Yahudah, but some other "lost" tribe or house of Israel. Even wild branches can be engrafted among the natural ones, so we must be accepting of all other Children of Yahuah who love the Covenant.

THE YEAST OF THE PHARISEES

We are going to see many Christians of every description coming out of their congregations in the coming years, as they move toward the Torah, learn the Name, and realize who they are in Yahusha. They will engraft into Israel, and know they are branches in the olive tree, and one of the "sticks" (ets, "trees") of Ezekiel 37*.

As you know, there is simultaneously a growing interest in the Talmud (oral law, Mishnah/Gemara) among Messianic Natsarim. The Talmud costs several thousand dollars for a complete set of its volumes. Many defend it's validity for study, since it does provide a great deal of insight into what certain things meant to those living long ago. I, for one, understand that it was over the "oral laws" that Rabbi Yahusha had many disputes with the Pharisees, although they were close in so many other ways. These "customs of the elders" which **added** to the Torah conflicted with the Torah, replaced it, and added burdens to the "light yoke".

So, we need to also be careful to note the "yeast" and puffing-up which we may observe in others as they grow in knowledge. The Talmud seems to be the best candidate among us for being this "yeast of the Pharisees", since from these early Pharisees (Prushim) all of Rabbinical Judaism sprang forth. The love of the "older brother", the nation of Yahudah, must be ever present with us, because anyone who does not love his brother does not have the love of Yahuah; but that doesn't mean we have to love the yeast / teachings of the Talmud also. The reason this is so much of an issue to me is because I visited 3 brothers whom I assisted in immersion over 15 years ago; they were studying the Talmud when I walked in, and the Torah was nowhere to be seen. I couldn't persuade them to see what was happening. If this goes on with others, then the Talmud will be spreading among us so fast it will cause division among us.

Rabbi Yahusha gave us the warning to beware of this ***yeast***, 'eh?. His students thought He was talking about ***bread***, and at first didn't understand what He meant. We all need to stay vigilant and not be deceived or misled by teachings from the Talmud. The prohibition of uttering the Name comes from the Talmud. It adds to the words of Torah. It's human error disguised as Truth. Oddly, most try to justify using the spelling "Yahweh" by citing the Jewish Encyclopedia, yet it is obvious this is just a shade away from the actual sound because the TALMUD prohibits the utterance of the Name, and the Jewish scholars revere Talmud. (I don't mean to be critical of those who believe "Yahweh" is the most correct sound! It's just that there should be 3 syllables, and the "litmus test" is another Hebrew word, YAHUDAH -- the same letters in the same order, with an added "dalet". The word YAHUDAH is the doorway to the actual sound.)

In my humble opinion, anything that adds to the Torah is leaven, and is dangerous. The oral law became the "Babylonian Talmud" and the "Jerusalem Talmud", made up of the Mishnah, and the Gemara. These Pharisaical sources were the seeds of Rabbinical Judaism.

When Yahusha told us, ***"Beware of the LEAVEN of the Pharisees"*** (Luke 12:1, Mk. 8:15, Mt. 16:6), He was describing the **ADDED human traditions called the "traditions of the elders",** as well as the many hidden mysticisms of the Zohar, Kabbala, and the Sefer Yetzirah (oral laws). The Torah specifically prohibits ADDING to Yahuah's Words, which the Talmud in fact does — "puffing-up" the Torah. All of Yahuah's Words were "READ ALOUD" in the hearing of the people, so that rules-out any "oral words" transmitted down to us. Mosheh "wrote down" all the Words of Yahuah. Those in certain "Messianic" circles have traditionally shunned pronouncing the Name aloud, to keep from "offending" their fellows who adhered to the ***Talmudic prohibition*** against the Name, and who used the traditional ***titles*** instead. Essentially, they are "no-namers", and the "memorial Name for all generations" (Ex. 3:13-15) is unknowable for them. They forsake the feelings of our Father Yahuah, in deference to pleasing their fellow man. This is the root of ***some*** of the division among us -- we are not ONE because we have not kept away from the ***leaven*** of the Pharisees, the ***Talmud***. Some of us have shunned the Name, which is to *keep us in unity, as one body*. We are *divided* over the Name; those who use it are sometimes dubbed "cultists" and heretics. "Rabbinical Judaism" stemmed directly from the *Pharisees*, and is just as filled with the errors of the Oral Law as ever. (The "Karaites" are the doctrinal descendants of the Sadducees, and don't hold to the "oral" traditions).

***SEE AMOS 9:9 ALSO; THE HOUSE OF ISRAEL (NORTHERN TRIBES). THE HOUSE OF YAHUDAH WAS THE SOUTH.**

The customs of the "fathers" (man-made human traditions from the oral law) were the hypocrisy which Yahusha kept throwing up to the Pharisees and Sadducees. Torah has outlawed it, but it persists. I will be attacked for having said this about the "oral law", but I must take a stand for Truth -- and let every man be proven a liar, and Yahuah's Word True.

The ***Talmud*** (Oral Law) has no bearing on Natsarim. Quoting from it should be done with words of warning. Among other things, it states that Miryam was a prostitute, and that Yahusha was the bastard son of a Roman soldier. We can read anything, but we must be discerning. Yahusha's words as recorded in the Brit Chadasha only make sense to those His Spirit indwells, and He will guide us into all that is True. When He told His pupils "beware of the leaven of the Pharisees", it was the "leaven" (puffing-up, adding) that was their main stumbling block -- and it's the oral traditions. Sure, there are many historical explanations found buried in Talmudic sources, but there are also dark mixtures of Kabbalistic influences as well. It speaks of when to stone "blasphemers". Pronouncing the Name is blasphemy to this work of hypocrisy, this idol to men's wisdom. Yahudim "mysticism" and other Babylonian / Chaldean syncretisms are blending into the Talmud, coming from the Zohar (Splendor), Bahir (Brilliance), and Sefer Yetzirah (Book of Creation). These influences gave rise to the customs like washing the fingertips before eating (to wash away evil spirits). The bottom line is, the Torah forbids studying other sources and mixing them into the worship of Him (see Duet. 12:28-32), which is also why we cannot observe Christmas, Easter, and other things like "Sun-Day".

Torah (Yahuah's Word, Teaching) instructs us not to "ADD" or take away from Torah, and the "leaven" of Talmud is exactly this, whether or not a pastor, rabbi, teacher, or leader sees it this way. All the Words of Yahuah were READ aloud in the hearing of the people -- there were no words that were "oral" -- this is only the TRADITIONAL mindset of flawed and misguided men. Torah knows nothing of the Talmud, and it makes no references to the other books I cited above. The Talmud is OK to own and read; but we have no time to use it as study material when Yahusha told us to beware of it. The only thing it is good for: understanding what went wrong with Yahudaism; and mainly, the Talmud (oral law) is what went wrong. This is the source that people get many ideas foreign to Scripture. The religion of Yahudaism (Judaism) followed along the lines of Pharisaical teachings, and the Talmud became the record book of their decisions over the centuries. There is the Yerushaliyim Talmud, and the Babylonian Talmud. If any group leader is insisting on spending any time on it as 'serious study' and not exposing the problems with it in spite of the dangers, this letter should be taken to the group (body), to make sure it is well understood what is happening among everyone. You can't mix clean water and poison together and drink it. Even Pagan religions had some truth in them! The Babylonians simply mixed truth and error together, as we see religions have continued to do down through the ages.

As we hear Yahusha's words ringing in our ears telling us to ***"Beware of the leaven of the Pharisees!",*** we should apply this to any human traditions that have become adopted by the leaders of our faith. We should contend for the TRUE and PURE faith, purging out the fossilized customs of our fore-fathers. Not adhering to the "traditions of the fathers" will bring us under severe persecution, and we will not be understood by the majority of those living in the flesh.

THE TEST ?

Always remember each Shabbat that the first week of Creation was a real week; otherwise it makes no sense that we rest for the last day (24 hours) of each one. A week foreshadows the "big picture", the millennia of 7000 years, within which we are now nearing the end of "day six". The MANNA (one of the items in the ARK) serves as a witness for us:

"I will rain bread from heaven for you; and the people shall go out and gather a day's portion every day, THAT I MAY TEST THEM, WHETHER OR NOT THEY WILL WALK IN MY INSTRUCTION." Ex./ Shemoth 16:4

(See Deut. 8:2,3 also)

". . . beware that you are not ensnared to follow them, after they are destroyed before you, AND THAT YOU DO NOT INQUIRE AFTER THEIR ELOHIM, SAYING 'HOW DO THESE NATIONS SERVE THEIR ELOHIM, THAT I MAY DO LIKEWISE?' YOU SHALL NOT BEHAVE THUS TOWARD YAHUAH YOUR ELOHIM, FOR EVERY ABOMINABLE ACT WHICH YAHUAH HATES THEY HAVE DONE FOR THEIR ELOHIM . . . WHATEVER I COMMAND YOU, YOU SHALL BE CAREFUL TO DO; YOU SHALL NOT ADD TO NOR TAKE AWAY FROM IT." Deut. 12:30-32.

CIRCUMCISION = IMMERSION

Question from Australia: I have a question for you, and hope you can help. Some of the new believers here are wondering about circumcision. I know that you say that it is of the heart and I agree with you. Norman Willis in his book that you recommend is teaching that it is for today. So, there is a little bit of confusion in my mind about this subject. If it is for today how does a man go about it, as surely it cannot be done just surgically; there would have to be some sort of ceremony. I know this is a difficult subject; sorry to dump this one on you.

Response: On physical circumcision, most understand the "perpetual" aspect of this covenant -sign as being the physical, man-made activity in the flesh. Norman is indeed one of those at the moment, as well as several others who come to mind. These men differ in their understanding of circumcision than I do, and both sides of this debate probably hope the other will come over to their view eventually. The writings of Shaul seem to solidify us both into our fixed opinions, just as the same sun which **melts** wax **hardens** clay. As you know, it is my view that the council of believers and elders at Acts 15 reviewed this issue concerning the Gentiles turning to Elohim. The ones who want to boast in one's flesh see the 4 "beginning" elements for Gentiles to observe at Acts 15, and assume they will hear Mosheh read in the synagogues and then have themselves circumcised eventually - in their flesh. Gal. 2:3,4 informs us:

"But not even Titus who was with me, though a Greek, was compelled to be circumcised. But as for the false brothers, sneakingly brought in, who sneaked in to spy out our freedom which we have in Mashiach Yahusha, in order to enslave us, to these we did not yield in subjection, not even for an hour, so that the truth of the Good News remains with you."

The condition of one's flesh is not going to count for anything, and it is not through human effort that we are called, chosen, and delivered. Our immersion into water is the "outward sign" of our circumcision of our heart. Romans 2:25-29 are verses so important to notice, since we can see that it is really the heart where our real decision must come from:

"For circumcision indeed profits if you practice the Torah, but if you are a transgressor of the Torah, your circumcision has become uncircumcision. So, if an uncircumcised one watches over the righteousnesses of the Torah, shall not his uncircumcision be reckoned as circumcision? And the uncircumcised by nature (physically), ***who perfects the Torah, shall judge you, who notwithstanding letter and circumcision, are a transgressor of the Torah! For he is not a Yahudi who is so outwardly, neither is circumcision that which is outward in the flesh*** (see that?). ***But a Yahudi is he who is so inwardly, and circumcision is that of the heart, in Spirit, not literally, whose praise is not from men, but from Elohim."*** (Explanation continues into Romans 3).

1 Cor. 7:19 and Col. 2:11 should give anyone pause who seeks to have their flesh circumcised, thinking Yahuah will count our flesh as anything. The whole book of Galatians is about this "law", addressed to the Gentiles there who put their hope in the wrong understanding of the New Covenant. Romans 4:11,12 show clearly that our faith is our justification, and even this is not of ourselves. Notice these words:

Col. 2:11-13: ***"In Him you were also circumcised with a circumcision NOT MADE WITH HANDS, in the putting off of the body of the sins of the flesh, by THE CIRCUMCISION OF MESSIAH, having been buried with Him in IMMERSION, in which you also were raised with Him through the belief in the working of Elohim, who raised Him from the dead. And you, being dead in your trespasses and the uncircumcision of your flesh, He has made alive together with Him, having forgiven you all trespasses."***

This act of immersion is clearly what represents our circumcision as the outward sign or act of our faith now, indicating the **circumcision of Messiah**. Men boasting in one anothers' flesh are missing the whole spiritual point. If we have received Yahusha's Spirit, we are His, and He has circumcised our hearts with our love for the Truth, a love for His Torah.

I was circumcised as a baby, and my boys were also. It is a health decision too, but I feel it is right to obey the physical command for our new-born children as we are believers. But, if an **uncircumcised adult** repents and turns to Torah, I would never recommend them to be physically obliged to do this, when the writings clearly express it is nothing. Our **immersion** acts as the outward covenant-sign of the circumcision of our heart. Shaul declared that those who disturbed the new Gentile believers with circumcision **of the flesh** should emasculate themselves (completely cut off everything) (Gal. 5:12). Biting and devouring one another over these things is very wrong, so I don't involve myself in these disputes, knowing the end will be controversy and division (which Yahuah hates). Those of the other opinion are working through these matters, and still have much to learn -- as do we all. As Ya'aqob says, we all stumble in many matters.

Col. 2:16 needs to be looked at in various translations; the easiest one to read the "added" words is the KJV, since they *italicize* the words they have added. The "Body of Mashiach" is all it should say, not "the Body (is) of Christ". Shaul (Paul) is referring to the food, drink, festivals (appointed High Sabbaths for instance), new moons, and Sabbaths as things which are "a shadow of of things to come". He is not saying they are **annulled** as the NIV footnotes will claim they are. For example, if you consider the book Luke wrote we call "Acts", the word "Sabbath" is used often; and this record to Theophilis was written in 28 chapters, 31 years after the resurrection and ascension of Yahusha. You'll notice situations describing "Gentiles" in the synagogues "on the Sabbath day", hearing the Torah and prophets read aloud, because the vast majority of attendees were in fact Gentile converts — much different from today.

The use of the word "shadow" implies that these things will become clearer realities in our understanding of them one day. The reality or substance determined from the "shadow" they are casting must be of extremely great importance, so it would be very unwise to dismiss them as "mere shadows" -- and Shaul said they represented shadows of "what is to come". They are here to teach us something; they are not here for us to cast them aside.

Galatians -- a book often referred to as "proof" that we are not obliged to obey the Commandments! Simply put, this book is speaking about one thing: **circumcision of the flesh**. Shaul opens and closes with it (2:3, 2:7, 2:8, 2:9, 2:12, 5:3, 5:6, 5:11, 6:12, 6:13, 6:15). This is so misunderstood -- "the law" of circumcision (of the flesh) is what Shaul is talking about; he is not in any way referring to the Covenant, the moral laws which define sin. We are circumcised by the Spirit of Yahusha in our hearts, and you should read more on this to explain it thoroughly by examining Romans 2:28, 29, 1 Cor. 7:19, Col. 2:11-13. Our "circumcision" is of and by the Spirit of Yahusha, not made with hands; **the outward act of obedience representing our circumcision is our immersion (baptism).** But, our circumcision is done to us by Yahusha, in our heart, when He writes His Commandments on our heart. This is the Re-newed Covenant. Our obedience to His Commandments is an outward sign that we love Him, but it also proves that we are being saved by Him -- it's evidence of our salvation, and His work in us. When we realize He is ***IN*** us, we can love His Commandments and obey them out of love. When we love Him enough to obey Him, He will write them on our hearts. Those who will not obey Him will not receive His Spirit (Acts 5:32). ***"He who turns away his ear from hearing the Torah, even his prayer is an abomination."*** Proverbs 28:9. ***"Listen to Me, you who know righteousness, a people in whose heart is My Torah; do not fear the reproach of men, nor be afraid of their revilings."*** Is. 51:7.

The following issue is something that has arisen since the 4th edition of Fossilized Customs that is of great importance to everyone being seduced by it.

This new wind of doctrine is extremely divisive, and is rapidly becoming a ***new custom*** within our generation. We must watch, and stand fast and hold the traditions which we were taught, and be without wrath and disputing.
(see 2 Thess. 2:15, 1 Tim. 2:8).

New Moons: Lunar Sabbaths?

The **new moons** are signals for us to tell time, and that is all they are. Sundials and clocks are round because the sun and moon are round. A very good question was asked of me about the pattern of 7 days we call a week:

"Can you find any Scripture that says there is an unending seven-day cycle from Creation? Is it safe to assume such without evidence?" *(name withheld)*

Answer: We already know about the 1st and 2nd chapter of Genesis (Bereshith), so we'll assume that isn't good enough proof, and look at a couple of other Scriptural situations where the cycle of 7 days are involved (a week of days). There are also cases where a "week of years" are mentioned. We'll even get the thrill of multiplying 7 x 7 to get the answer of 49 -- so pay close attention kids. We need to consider the Hebraic concept of the **week** as a unit, made up of seven days; and in some cases units of 7 years.

First, look in a concordance for the word "week" (Hebrew, ***SHABUA***, #7620). This word also means "7". The word ***Sabbaton*** is used 58 times in the Messianic writings, or Brit Chadasha, and translated as the 7th day of the week, or weekly Sabbath day. But, in 9 other cases, it is translated as "week", referring to the cycle or period of 7 days we are familiar with. Further, at Lev. 23:15,16 the weekly Sabbaths are used to count off 7 Sabbaths. It tells us to count 7 "completed Sabbaths", up until the "morrow after

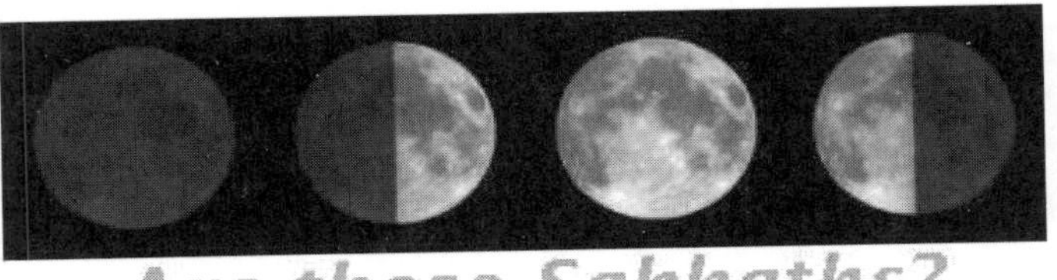

Are these Sabbaths?

IS THE WEEK DETERMINED BY THE MOON? IS SABBATH SHOWN BY THE PHASES? NO.

the *seventh Sabbath"*, you count 50 days. This instruction clearly numbers the ***total elapsed days involved***, so we know that "Shabuoth" falls on the 1st day of the week each year. ***Shabuoth*** (plural for *shabua*, week), is now called "Pentecost" (Greek, "count fifty"), and is our (Israel's) **Wedding Anniversary**. As Brian Allen recently pointed out, if the weekly Sabbath were governed by the moon, you'd run into trouble reconciling the "7 Sabbaths" within this 50 days, because you'd have 2 new moons falling within this period. The way I figure it, you'd have more than 7 Sabbaths within 50 days' time (in just 30 days, the lunar Sabbath folks calculate 6 Sabbaths, and so they reach their count to the day after their 7th Sabbath in only 37 days). A Shabua represents a complete week of seven days, from day 1 through Shabbath, the seventh day.

Sabbatical **years** are explained (7 cycles of 7 years each, ***sheba shabbathot shanah***, *seven Sabbaths of years* — seven times seven years, Lev. 25:8), and from them we can determine when the year of Jubilee arrives. Father Yahuah did not have to explain what a week (shabua) of 7 days was, until Israel had forgotten it; He used the **manna** to re-train them how to count the week again in the wilderness. If the week, and specifically the 7th day Sabbath (the completion of a week), could be ascertained at all from **something in the skies**, the manna would not have been necessary to train Israel.

A day without food tends to get your attention. One important thing to remember is that the moon phases in no way affects or rules over the **day/night pattern**, or the count of **the 7 days of creation**. The moon rules over the night, and the moedim, or annual High Sabbaths, the "appointed times". It can never effect the **7-day cycle of creation**. In Daniel, we see the "7 sevens", or 7 **weeks** of **years**. Again, at Lev. 25 we can apply this 7-year cycle for us to know when to let the land rest in the "Sabbatical years", and there is smooth rhythm of 7 x 7 years, making up 49 years, in the count to the "Jubilee year" following this "seven **weeks** of years", ***sheba shabua shanah***. If the 7 years (a **week of years**) establishes the model for the land to rest, we can be sure that our interpretation of the **week of days** is also sound. So, yes, it is safe to say there are Scriptures to back up the understanding of "***an unending seven-day cycle from Creation***"; the ***SHABUA.***

The Pagan Babylonians *did not* establish the 7-day week (*shabua*), nor did the Romans; it was Yahuah alone. Sabbath, the word, is not even a stone's throw from the Hebrew word for seven, *sheba,* or the word *shabua.* The "7 pillars" referred to at Ps. 75:3 and Prov. 9:1 in their context refer to the unmovable and unshakable foundation which Father Yahuah established for the 7 days of each week. The moon is brought in to determine the 7 annual High Sabbaths. The 7 millennia, or pattern of 7 periods of 1000-years each, is unaffected by the moon. The first 7 days (creation week) established a **repeating cycle of 7** in order that we **recall** creation, and honor the Creator each **7th day**.

Besides all this, if the Yahudim (Jews) and the 12 tribes of Israel dispersed all over the Earth think that the Sabbath Day each week is the same one the Pagans have been calling "Satyr Day" (or day of Satyrn), and it isn't REALLY the Sabbath, then why would Satan arrange to change the day of rest from the true 7th day of the week to Sun-Day (the 1st day of the week) for his deceived followers? (Under penalty of death, Constantine ordained the change of the Sabbath to his "Sun-Day" in the year 321 CE, in his "Edict of Milan"). Satan changed the day of rest for Mohammad's pupils in the 7th century to the **sixth** day of the week. **Why would Satan do that, if the 7th day was already wrong?** The real answer is, the 7th day of each week really is the **true Sabbath**, the commemoration of creation; and this honors the true Maker of Heaven and Earth, Yahuah - the ELOHIM OF ISRAEL. Even if the cycle of seven days had been changed at any point from some "lunar pattern", how could the whole Earth have adopted the flaw ***all at once***, without any echo of the previous "correct" pattern lurking about in some culture?

Also, remember that many remote cultures all over the Earth have retained in their **indigenous languages** the meaning, and often a close **sounding word** for the Hebrew word, "Sabbath" -- for their 7th day of each week (Shabbath, Sabbath, Sabo, Sabado, Subbata, Shubuta, etc.,.). The Sabbath is really the only day of the week that has a name -- the other days were only numbered, *until the Pagans decided to give homage to various deities by calling the days by the proper names of their false elohim* (i.e., Sun Day, Moon Day, Tyr's Day, Woden's Day, Thor's Day, Frigga's Day, Satyrn Day).

The *sun* rules over the *day*. A week of 7 days cycles over and over, and the moon is in no way able to interfere with it. The ***manna***, not the moon, was used to emphasize this "shabua" cycle to remind Israel. Days and months are not connected or geared together, but flow separately through time. The period of 7 days, which we call the **week** (Hebrew, ***SHABUA***, #7620), has been assaulted in recent years by the new teachings concerning new moons. This mostly is the result of deciding to believe something, then hunting down the texts that support that belief (eisegesis).

Once a person falls for the re-setting of the weekly pattern which they believe is caused by the moon, the **moon** becomes an all-consuming topic for them from that point on. They feel that they must convince everyone else to see the hidden secret they've discovered.

By **deduction**, or the *taking away* (discounting) of what is not discussed, we know there is only **one new moon day** which is a day of rest from work; the first day of the 7th moon. By simple ***deductive*** reasoning, we know that the other 11 **new moon days** are ***not*** rest days. The fact that men of Yahuah worked and traveled on new moon days is but one indication of this. The best method for study is by exegesis, not eisegesis.

We do not worship or serve the men who promote a floating weekly Sabbath involving the moon cycles, so we don't have to fear them or their teachings; but we should not be hateful to them in their deception either. There is not a single text from Scripture which suggests or implies that the 7th day Sabbath is regulated or connected to the moon or its phases; the only associations that can be made between new moon days and Sabbaths are imagined assumptions, and the mishandling of the Word of Father Yahuah. Bending, wrestling, and twisting the Scriptures is a grievous thing to do, and falling from our steadfastness can easily be the end result. We are not to judge the person, however as the Body of Mashiach we are to judge the teachings regarding food, drink, new moons, Sabbaths, and moedim.

It's natural to have differences of understanding, but we must not allow these to become roots of bitterness between one another. There are many points of contention today; the "new moon" re-setting the weekly Sabbath is one example. The controversy over who is to be the recipient of the tenth part of our increase is another point of difference, mostly argued by those who have been used to taking the tithe as teachers. Then there is the issue of whether the crescent moon sighting is the beginning, or the end, of the actual first day of the new moon. Like the Bereans, we need to test and examine if what we hear is really true.

TWO APPROACHES IN UNDERSTANDING SCRIPTURE

FIRST: We go to the Writings with an open, unbiased attitude, free of denominational slants or teachings, or previous impressions. This is called ***Exegesis*** (direct analysis or interpretation of Scripture). Allowing the Word to directly speak to us, we can form a solid foundation through personal study, guided by our Teacher, the Spirit of Yahusha. Listening to other men teach us what Scripture says is fine also, as long as we test everything we hear, being careful how we listen, as the assembly at Berea did (Acts 17:10,11).

SECOND: (the wrong approach) -- We go to the Writings to ***prove*** something we already believe, finding sentences which hint at the idea. This is called ***Eisegesis*** (analyzing from one's own ideas). In these cases the text is not **directly** describing or teaching the concept we are trying to prove, but rather the words are *extracted* and hunted-down, to "prove" what we believe. This is how men "twist" or "spin" the Words of Scripture, especially the letters of Shaul (Paul):

". . . as also our beloved brother Shaul wrote to you, according to the wisdom given to him, as also in all his letters, speaking in them concerning these matters, in which some are hard to understand, which those who are untaught and unstable TWIST (spin) ***to their own destruction, as they do also the other Scriptures. You, then, beloved ones, being forewarned, watch; lest you also fall from your own steadfastness, being led away with the delusion of the lawless."*** - 2 Kepha 3:15-17

Ha shatan, the adversary, hates the marriage Covenant, and Israel. This means the enemy of our beings hates the "sign" of our Covenant, the Sabbath. This being attacks Israel at every turn, and attempts to alter the Covenant, or make it seem unimportant. The "sign" of this Eternal (Everlasting) Covenant is the sign of the Sabbath, which is the **7th day of each week**. Today some have begun to believe that the Yahudim (tribe called "Jews" today) altered the original pattern for keeping track of the correct WEEKLY Sabbaths. They feel that the MOON was originally used to determine not only the ANNUAL High Sabbaths, but also the WEEKLY day of rest.

The 7-day pattern is found in **every corner** of our world, and the 7th day, which most English-speaking people call "Saturday", is widely known to be the Sabbath day which is found throughout Scripture. As I mentioned, many languages exist on our planet; and if you study the various names these languages have for this 7th day, you will find they closely relate cognatively to the Hebrew word for Sabbath, SHABATH (cease). So, even ***if*** the Yahudim ***attempted*** to change the pattern, it would become evident to everyone that they did so when the patterns are compared to one another. The pattern (shabua) of 7 weekdays is found across the entire planet without any conflict in its rhythm -- **none** of the cultures on Earth use a lunar-phase to determine or re-set their week each month. Their languages even identify within themselves the day of rest being the one called "Shabbath" in Hebrew. Their word for this day still bears a strong resemblance to the Hebrew original.

"My Sabbaths you are to guard, by all

means, for it is a <u>SIGN</u> (guarding His Sabbaths) ***between Me and you throughout your generations, to know that I, Yahuah, am setting you apart.*** (sign = mark, signal)

And you shall guard the Sabbath it is set-apart to you. Everyone who profanes it shall certainly be put to death, for anyone who does work on it, that being shall be cut off from among his people. Six days work is done, and on the seventh is a Sabbath of rest, set-apart to Yahuah. (Sabbath, *or Shabbath*, means "rest"). ***Everyone doing work on the Sabbath day shall certainly be put to death.***

"And the children of Yisra'el shall guard the Sabbath, to observe the Sabbath throughout their generations as an <u>everlasting</u> <u>covenant</u>. (Gentiles must engraft into Israel to partake of the Covenants, and the Sabbath is the sign of the Everlasting Covenant, the marriage between Yahuah and His wife, Israel).

"Between Me and the children of Yisra'el it is a <u>sign</u> forever. For in six days Yahuah made the heavens and the Earth, and on the seventh day He rested and was refreshed." Exodus (Shemoth) 31:13-17 (see also Ezek. 20:12-20)

Look at what Hebrews 4:4-16 says, <u>*referring to the above text*</u>:

"For somewhere (Ex. 31) ***He has said thus about the seventh day, 'And Elohim <u>rested</u> on <u>the seventh day</u> from all His works', and again, 'if they shall enter into My rest . . .'***

"Since then it remains for some to enter into it, and those who formerly received the Good News did not enter in because of disobedience, He again defines a certain day, "Today" . . . So, there remains a <u>Sabbath-keeping</u> for the people of Elohim. For the one having entered into His rest, has himself also rested from his works, <u>as</u> Elohim rested from His own. Let us therefore do our utmost to enter into that rest, lest anyone fall after the same example of disobedience." (Heb. 4:4-11)

The outward "sign" that we actually give worth-ship (obedience=worship) to the REAL Creator, ***"Who made heaven and the Earth, and sea, and fountains of water"*** (Rev. 14:4), is this "sign" of ***resting <u>as</u> He rested***, every seventh <u>day</u> - <u>*since*</u> <u>*creation*</u>. This message of the messenger sent forth ***"to announce to those dwelling on the Earth, even to every nation and tribe and tongue and people"*** is going forth from the Natsarim today:

"Fear Elohim and give esteem to him, because the hour of His judgment has come. And worship Him who made the heaven and the Earth, and sea, and fountains of water."

Again, it is important to discern how we have been deceived into believing we are giving worth-ship (worship, obedience) to the Creator of heaven and Earth, while having the "sign" of our worth-ship to Him ***removed*** by revisionism.

THE TEST OF THE MANNA

"And Yahuah said to Mosheh, 'See, I am raining bread (manna) ***from the heavens for you. And the people shall go out and gather a day's portion every day, in order to <u>try</u>*** (test) ***them, whether they walk in My Torah or not. And it shall be on the sixth day that they shall prepare what they bring in, and it shall be twice as much as they gather daily."*** (Ex. 16:4,5)

CRAFTY SCHEMES TO DIVIDE US

The elect can be deceived, and fall away from the Covenant, by crafty schemes and trickery.

". . . We should no longer be children, tossed and borne about by every wind of teaching, by the trickery of men, in cleverness, unto the craftiness of leading astray . . ." (Eph. 4:14).

Ephesians 4 reminds that while we grow toward a "unity" (oneness of belief and pattern for living), we have to be patient, humble, meek, and bearing with one another in LOVE. We will have to tolerate differences with patience, and not grow apart in bitterness. Yahusha said we would be known by the LOVE between us, not that we would all be exactly alike. The blind faith of those captured by the Mother of Harlots, Catholicism, may never be able to overcome the deceptions until they personally study and struggle to get at the Truth. We all must study.

The new teachings which are entangling the Natsarim today, come from **interpretations** of Scripture, which alter the patterns of the days, nights, and appointed times ruled by the **new moons**. Some interpret "day" (yom) and "night" (layelah) somewhat differently than others. Reading Genesis, some have come to believe that "creation" began with "<u>light</u>", therefore the 24-hour period begins at **sunrise**. In contrast, the **end** of the "day" which arrives at the moment the sun sets, beginning a new cycle of 24 hours, actually reflects the six creation days. At creation, it was first "**dark**", and Yahuah created water, Earth, and the rules of physics. Kepha (Peter) tells us that the Earth was formed out of water. **Darkness** was on the face of the deep. The first sentence of Genesis states:

"In the beginning Elohim created the heavens and the Earth. And the Earth came to be formless and empty, and darkness was on the face of the deep."

The evolutionist will say, "First, there was nothing. Then, it *exploded*. The elements were not yet existent, since all the energy (from nothing) was purely *kinetic* (active, non-material, radiation).

After the cooling effect from the expansion of space, and the propagation of the energy from this cosmic "big bang", the first elements coalesced together as Deuterium." *(I am not a proponent of the "big bang", nor string theory).*

So, even the blind theories and imaginations of non-believers are establishing the truth of the first several verses of Genesis to some extent. But many Natsarim believe creation began with LIGHT, therefore the periodic 24-hour night/day scheme is interpreted to be "day, then night" (light, then darkness), as opposed to "night, then day" (darkness, then light).

"And there came to be evening (darkening, Ereb) ***and there came to be morning*** (lightening, boker)***, the first day."*** (This suggests a 24-hour period).

By interpreting the order of occurrence differently, differences in patterns of behavior can be seen today among the Natsarim. This has the effect of making a Sabbath "day" only pertain to when the sun is up, and so "night" has no pertinence to the "Sabbath day". No man can "work" at night they will explain, from Yahusha's words at John/Yoh. 9:4. To these brothers, Sabbath begins at sunrise. Do we have the capacity to be different, yet have love? (Please don't do it because I do it, but study; I rest every week, beginning at sunset at the **end** of the sixth day (sunset), and there follows a twilight of nearly 30 minutes before night arrives (complete darkness). One of my favorite Scriptures to quote that establishes whether Shabbath begins at sunset or sunrise is Neh. 13:19 (also see context):

"And it came to be, at the gates of Yerushaliyim, as it began to be dark before the Sabbath, that I commanded the gates to be shut, and commanded that they should not be opened till after the Sabbath."

The interlinear Hebrew-English rendering of this text shows that before the Sabbath shadowed the gates of Yerushaliyim, they were commanded to be shut. Just as each "month" (new moon) BEGINS with a dark moon, so the beginning of each "day" begins at the darkening, *ereb*, the going-down of the sun. Beginnings seem to be a progression of darkness-to-light.

SABBATHS, NEW MOONS: ANY RELATIONSHIP?

Most Messianics who enter into the Lunar-Sabbath system are reading texts like Isaiah 66:23 and believe there is an equivalence between a weekly Sabbath and a New Moon day.

Let's analyze that carefully:

"And it shall be that from New Moon to New Moon, and from Sabbath to Sabbath, all flesh shall come to worship before Me, declares Yahuah."

They explain that the connective word, ***"and"***, makes both things the same (marrying them in likeness and oneness), not distinct. Is this really so? What this verse seems to be saying is that the SPAN "from" new moon TO new moon, and the SPAN "from" Sabbath to Sabbath, is when all flesh will worship -- it will be every day. Yahuah used these terms to gather all time into a kind of net to describe the fact that the span of time concerning His worship will have **no break** in it. Should we not worship every moment? Now, most do not; but those in the world-to-come will do so. "From new moon TO new moon" — and "from Sabbath TO Sabbath" ; can you see the interesting way this is expressed? Trying to force texts to say what they aren't actually saying is what Peter warns us of, and he called it "twisting" the Scriptures. The text does not say "ON new moons" or "ON Sabbaths", but FROM one TO the other.

Our Father has not put me on this Earth to judge my brother, because if I do this I also judge the Torah. The "manna" which Yahuah fed Israel for 40 years is very much related to the week, in that it made the arrival of each Shabbath very easily recognized. If the "hidden manna" really is about the moon, or the week and its relationship to Shabbath, then more are going to be lost than even I had realized. To me, it seems someone has brought in a corrupted "virus" of sorts among Yahusha's elect, confusing them. (I realize this can be taken either way, depending on which perspective one takes on the "lunar-setting Sabbath" issue). Yahuah used **manna**, not the moon, to teach us when the Sabbath day arrived each 7 days. (7=Shabua, week).

The use of the connective ***"and":***

When a statement is made in Scripture which involves a list of several things, and these are thought to not only *connect* the words together in the sentence, but that the "and" unites them — marries them in ***likeness and oneness*** — we are treading into very murky waters of interpretation. The "sun ***and*** the moon" are used with an "and" between them, but these two are not the same things. Good ***and*** evil, Qayin ***and*** Hebel, Adam ***and*** Chawah; These are **distinctions** between things and people, the ***"and"*** in no way makes them the same or equivalent. "*Sarah his wife* ***and*** *Lot his brother's son"* were not the same entities, but completely separate individuals in their persons. Dawid ***and*** Golyath were both people, but very different people. In the same way, *New Moons* ***and*** *Sabbaths* are distinct. If we are told the ***first day*** of the *seventh* moon is a Sabbath, this means by **deductive reasoning** that the other 11 new moons are ***not*** Sabbaths, unless they happen to coincide with the weekly pattern established during Creation Week. To reason from a general principle, using logic, we can arrive at what is factual truth by deduction. Deduction literally means that we arrive at our conclusion by *deducting, or taking away* what is known to not apply; and this principle is how we arrive at a conclusion by reasoning.

"My enemy's enemy is my friend".

This statement contains deductive reasoning.

"Whosoever is not against us is for us."

This is also an example of deductive reasoning. Sabbaths are days of rest from work, we would all agree. No one is in rebellion on that issue except those who deny they apply to us, or those who have changed the law. Shabbath is in fact the only day of the week which has its own name. Shabbath means "cease" or stop; and at the same time, it also means "**seventh**", as we see in several Hebrew words which derive from the root, such as Shabuoth (weeks). The Hebrew word for "seven" is SHEBA, #7651. I want to let the Word of Yahuah speak to us mostly on this, so I want to let you read the following text slowly, and go ahead and strain to make the moon seem to tell us when a Sabbath is, or relate to us how it "rules" the week in any way:

"And Elohim said, 'Let lights come to be in the expanse of the heaven to separate the day from the night, and let them be for signs and appointed times, and for days and years." Bereshith 1:14

Is there any indication that the moon resets the week each month? We all know that "signs and appointed times" are signals and "moedim", and we count the days of the moons which establish these moedim. But when we take a leap into applying it to also affecting the ***weekly*** pattern, suddenly the weeks are sliding around the Earth with the moon; and the bad math at the end of each month doesn't seem to indicate there's a problem. Can we find some text from Scripture that explains this bizarre anomaly? This is not asking too much. Does Scripture tell us anywhere we can find the weekly 7-day pattern in the sun or moon? It shouldn't be necessary to hunt it down, because if such a scheme were of the Truth, it would be seen everywhere we look in Scripture. If something becomes complicated or confusing, then something has gone terribly wrong. The following is NOT what Scripture states:

"And Elohim said, 'Let lights come to be in the expanse of the heaven to separate the day from the night, and let them be for signs and appointed times, and for days, (and weeks?) and years." No, it doesn't say the lights are for our weeks. The pattern of the week is not seen in the skies.

Now watch very closely; here's a few words which should show the ***distinction*** between a "new moon" and a "Sabbath":

"Why are you going to him today? It is neither New Moon nor the Sabbath." 2Kings 4:23. This is the text describing the events in Shunem, concerning the Shunammite woman, her son, and Elisha the prophet - her son had just died in her lap. But, this same text may cause some to make a Federal case out of it, declaring it to mean that all "new moon days" are also days of rest from work. They even go to the extent of allowing new moon days to recalculate the weekdays, without a single shred of evidence from Scripture for doing so.

"You are exhausted by your many counsels; let the astrologers, the stargazers, and those who prognosticate by the new moons stand up and save you from what is coming upon you." Isaiah / Yesha Yahu 47:13

In the above text, these moon-worshippers are equated with astrologers, stargazers, and witches. Both sun worshippers and moon worshippers will be devoured by fire, which they so fervently honor. The "lake of fire" will destroy the enemies of Yahuah, and His wrath at the end of days will consume them with fire. The **moon** was a deity among the Pagans, and it ruled their lives as we see it echoed in the horoscopes of Astrology today. Crystal gazing, Tarot card reading, and spellbinding (chants, enchantments to bewitch) are exploding in popularity all over the Earth today, reflected in the success of the adventures of *Harry Potter*. Moon dances and rain dances are performed at pow-wows, where incantations and dancing are used to invoke divine aid in hunting, battle, or against disease.

The elect can be drawn away from the **sign** of the Everlasting Covenant, and **deceived** into believing they have not been. Certain texts of Scripture ***seem*** to be telling us that each new moon is a Sabbath, but it doesn't actually state this in a resolute way - it's only arrived at by extrapolating (to broadly infer, or estimate from known information). **We read about directives to open gates and curtains, or to blow a shofar on a new moon; however there is only ONE new moon spoken of on which no work is to be done.** So, yes, there is one new moon out of the year that is, in fact, a Sabbath of rest prescribed by Torah. Can we bear with one another with love, enduring such a difference between ourselves? We have to. Colossians 2:16 tells us:

"Let no one therefore judge you in eating or in drinking, or in respect of a festival or a new moon or Sabbaths - which are a SHADOW of what is to come - for the body of Messiah." Even here, there is a distinction between new moons and Sabbaths. And, they are shadows of what is to come. A shadow is understood to mean a metaphor, or example of something else. It points to a coming reality, like a rough outline, and it is a semblance, and is insubstantial. If we condemn one another over an unreal, indistinct pattern we are wrong even if we're right. If we get it all perfect, and have all wisdom, and yet lack love, we have failed the big test.

"If I speak with the tongues of men and of messengers, but do not have love, I have become as sounding brass or a clanging cymbal.

"And if I prophesy, and know all secrets and all knowledge, and if I have all belief, so as to remove mountains, but do not have love, I am none at all.

"And if I give out all my possessions to feed the poor, and if I give my body to be burned, but do not have love, I am not profited at all.

"Love is patient, is kind, love does not envy, love does not boast, is not puffed up, does not behave indecently, does not seek its own, is not provoked, reckons not the evil, "does not rejoice over the unrighteousness, but rejoices in the Truth. It covers all, expects all, endures all.

"Love never fails. And whether there be prophecies, they shall be inactive; or tongues, they shall cease; or knowledge, it shall be inactive.

"For we know in part and we prophesy in part. But when that which is perfect has come, then that which is in part shall be inactive.

"When I was a child, I spoke as a child, I thought as a child, I reasoned as a child. But when I became a man, I did away with childish matters.

"For now we see in a mirror, dimly, but then face to face. Now I know in part, but then I shall know, as I also have been known.

"And now belief, expectation, and love remain - these three. But the greatest of these is love." 1 Cor. 13:1-13

Many articles have been written debunking the idea that the first day of **each** new moon is a Sabbath. Not only have many sincere Natsarim begun to believe each new moon is a Sabbath, but they also "re-set" the pattern of the **7-day week** <u>each</u> <u>new</u> <u>moon</u>. This reshuffles the 7-day week into a new beginning each month for these folks, and each new moon **begins** with the *seventh day rest, counting from nothing*.

The final few days of this pattern chop the last week of their month off with the abrupt arrival of a sudden "7th day Sabbath". It is not harmonious at all. The pulse of the first week of creation is lost to those who follow this pattern, and so they have become observers of some lunar-based Sabbath system. If the **weekly** Sabbath is set by the new moon, the arrangement of the week is under constant change. During the week of creation, the moon was brought forth on the 4th day, and is simply called the "lesser light" to rule over the night. It is also used to calculate the appointed times, or <u>annual</u> Sabbaths, referred to as "High Sabbaths". The greater light, the sun, is used to calculate day and night.

Ex. 16:1 tells us the Israelites were <u>traveling</u> on the 15th day of the 2nd moon.

How this will be weighed by Yahusha, the Righteous Judge of us all, is unknowable. He told us that stumbling blocks would come, but woe to those *<u>through</u>* *<u>whom</u>* they come. Those who ignore the Sabbath each week (the real one) are cut-off from Israel, and death is proclaimed as their judgment. If the **moon** were involved in such a vitally important operation as calculating the weekly Sabbath, it seems He would have mentioned it somewhere in His Torah. Even though the 29.5 days in each moon don't divide evenly by 7, this doesn't matter to them; the new moon comes and they re-set their week, and it BEGINS the new moon day as a Sabbath.

Even though the true Sabbath is supposed to be the 7th day of **each week**, they let the MOON tell them when that 7th day is — the previous week which the same moon "set" for them is interrupted with a sudden arrival of a new 7th day, the 1st day of the moon (the first day of the moon is the seventh day of their week). Careful, you could get cross-eyed thinking about this too long. The week is simply not in the sky, but set by the counting of **days**! The "greater light" determines these days, and all we have to do is count to 7, the number of completion. How could anyone possibly go for such a system? They read Scriptures which make them get panicky, and so hunt for other clues. A very strong urge comes from the following:

Amos 8:5 brings out a question,

"When does the new moon pass so that we <u>sell</u> <u>grain</u>, and the Sabbath so that we trade our <u>wheat</u>, to make the ephah small and the sheqel large, and to falsify the scales by deceit, to buy the poor for silver, and the needy for a pair of sandals, and sell the chaff of the wheat?"

The context of this verse in Amos shows that these are a list of things Yahuah finds ***displeasing*** to Him. The moon worship of that period had led many to observe strange customs, blending it together with His Torah. If we **add** to the Torah by reading something into the meanings of sentences like Amos 8:5, we can trouble ourselves. According to the **Torah**, resting on the new moon from work only applies to ONE of the new moons, and it ***is possible*** that this particular new moon spoken of in Amos 8:5 was the 7th new moon, the harvest time of some grain they wished to sell. I can abide the ***people*** who believe these things about the other new moons being Sabbaths, but I cannot abide this new wind of doctrine for these reasons:

Reason #1. **Torah doesn't know about it.**
The Shabbaths of Yahuah are listed at:
Leviticus / Wayyyiqra 23:1-44
Deuteronomy / Debarim 16:1-18

These are listed carefully, and only **ONE new moon** is designated as being distinguished from the other common new moons as a day of resting from labor. No indication is given that any other new moon is qodesh, or set-apart as a day of rest in any way. Further, there is **no hint** that the weekly Shabbath is related in any way to the **moon phases**. This is entirely a misreading of the text at Yesha Yahu (Is.) 66:23. If Father Yahuah wanted us to know that every new moon was a Sabbath, all He had to do was say so. By the act of telling us that the 7th new moon ***was*** a Sabbath, He told us by deduction that the other new moons were ***not*** days of rest, and therefore He distinguished the 7th new moon for us.

Reason #2. There are examples of work done on the first day of the moons:
At Genesis 8:13, Noach removed the covering of the ark he spent 100 years building. It was the 1st day of the moon.
At Num. 1:1, on the 1st day of the 2nd moon, a census was taken of all Yisra'el. How odd is that?
At Ezra 7:9, this prophet was **journeying** on two new moons.

Reason #3. The Sabbath is supposed to be the ***seventh*** day of each week, after 6 days' work; but if you re-start each new moon with this Sabbath rest, then it becomes the ***seventh day*** of a new week, without having a previous six work days for that week. The ***seventh day*** begins each of their months somehow, and makes the ***second*** day of each moon the ***first*** day of their week. With an operation like this going on, you would think that our Father would have given at least a couple of sentences explaining the relationship of the moon to the week. But, He's totally silent about this relationship. Again, these ideas don't come directly from Torah, but are ***inferred*** from phrases embedded in sentences. He knows how easily confused we can be, so by not mentioning something this important, it would have to mean He is hoping to trick us. I don't think He would do such a thing.

Reason #4. The moon circles the Earth in a period of approximately 29.5 days. For thousands of years, the same side of the moon has faced the Earth, perfectly synchronized with its orbital period and rate of rotation. Scientists cannot explain this circumstance, and mathematicians will tell you that it is almost infinitely improbable to ever develop this way on any planetary system in the universe. And yet, the planet we all happen to live on has this bizarre, unlikely situation. If our Creator can do this, then He could have just as easily made the week fit into the moon's orbit by division, and made the moon orbit in exactly 28 days. Then He could have also told us to watch for the new moons, and rest on each one. He could have also told us that each one of the new moons was also a 7th day of the week.

Reason #5. The **manna** was used to re-teach the Israelites when the seventh day was, not when the new moon arrived. During the captivity of the Israelites in Egypt, it is possible that no one on Earth had kept the record of days for the 7-day week. Israel had succumbed to the Pagan system, and lost it also. They had to be re-taught. This is why the 4th Commandment begins with the word "remember" - it had been forgotten. The manna was provided for 6 consecutive days without fail. There was no interruption in this cycle mentioned, nor did the new moon come into any references that pertained to the manna. A double-portion of manna coming before each new moon would surely have been a signal, and yet there is no record of this occurring. The new moons have no connection to the 7-day week.

Reason #6. The Yahudim (called Jews today) have kept the heartbeat of the 7-day week since they were among the Israelites being re-trained by the manna cycle in the wilderness. There is no record or any hint that a change in this pattern ever occurred. These are among the elect of Yahuah, and have preserved the Words of the Torah, prophets, and writings for us. They are also the direct recipients of the promises (Romans 9:4), and are of the lineage of Yahusha Himself. If I am going to trust any group to preserve this set-apart weekly cycle, I would lean heavily toward entrusting it to a group of orthodox "Jews" than a group / denomination that may shift on the sand of human counsel. Ephraim is the Scriptural term used for Gentile-dispersed descendants of Yosef, and the other lost tribes. A major problem with Ephraim is his arrogance, so the orthodox Yahudim will tell you.

"You are exhausted by your many counsels; let the astrologers, the stargazers, and those who prognosticate by the new moons stand up and save you from what is coming upon you." Isaiah / Yesha Yahu 47:13

We certainly are seeing many new winds of doctrine these days. There are even those who feel that the FULL MOON is the new moon, which would mean that when the Israelites came out of

Egypt, they had to travel in utter darkness. There is no end to the development of new winds of teaching. What is most important is that we listen to the advice of Ephesians 4, and not lose sight of our foundation.

Many now realize that the nicolaitans designed a crafty plot of control over civilization. From ancient cultures to the present, the authority over mankind has been a fusion or blend of religious and political purpose. One example is the obelisk described in the book of Daniel (3:18). Often the rulers were worshipped as the principle deity by the people, such as Pharaoh of Egypt or Caesar of Rome. It had begun this way under Nimrod, but after he was slain the Paganism became "occult" (hidden), and became shrouded in mystery. The true spiritual nature of what was being done was made to look innocent on the surface for the uninitiated.

After Yahusha, people who had his Spirit in them spread out in the Roman Empire. The old idolatry was being questioned and **exposed**, and began to falter. The Pagan religious cults began to feel the effects of the Truth. Something had to be done to save the order and control which those who ruled civilization had, and their religious Paganism was failing. Along came Constantine, a compromiser who could find the "middle ground". Keeping the previous Pagan priesthood and their **framework** intact, he brought together elders of the Natsarim from all over the Roman Empire to Nicaea in 325 CE (the first council of the Catholic Church). Upon hearing some of the matters being discussed, many elders fled for their lives. The elders who remained helped formulate what later became known as Catholicism, and they adopted the creed or constitution of the Roman Church, *The Nicene Creed*. This was to fight against what was called the Arian doctrine, thought to be a heresy at that time (research Arianism). The Pagan "leaven" would eventually leaven the whole lump. Shaul told the former Pagan Corinthians to purge-out the old leaven (errors, patterns), and be a new unleavened lump (1 Cor. 5:6-13). Yahusha also described this at Luke 13:21.

The former line of Caesars were of a family line, but Constantine was a break in that line; but he became the "father" of the Empire, assuming both political and religious control. The former Caesars (Czar, Kaisar) took titles such as "Pontifex Maximus" and Pope (father), and ruled over a body of Pagan priests called the ***Curia*** (Latin, *council).* The members of this body were called ***Cardinals***, from the Latin word *CARDO*, meaning *hinge.* The idea that they were a "hinge" (of a door) suggested that they assisting the high priest of Janus, who was "the door" to the Elysian fields, the Pagans' heaven.

These Pagan priests assisted the Caesar, who was this Pagan high priest of ***JANUS***. So the Pagan title of "Pope" was retained by the man who held the office of Pontifex Maximus (Latin, highest priest). This title literally translates **"bridge-builder"**, a reference to this man being the bridge to the after-life with the deities in the heavens.

With the **framework** remaining in place, the central control of the Pagan administration could go on, simply blending-in with the elements of the Messianic belief, but leaving out the elements essential to the obedience of Yahuah. The Pagan organization in place retained the office / title of Pope, the body of priests called Cardinals, and even the word Curia for council. The "Pope" was no longer thought of as the high priest of Janus, but to literally be the authority of "Christ" on Earth. **The former Pagan pattern was brought through perfectly intact**. Idolatry mixed with Truth became clothed in the former framework of sun-worship. The main objective was to anger our Creator by mixing the **patterns** of idolatry together with the Truth, so that it would become poisoned (wormwood). Darkness and Light would mix together, and be taught for centuries through a Pagan framework of priests, and a **calendar** based on idolatry. They didn't even have to put in a change of address; Rome remained the office of the 4th beast of Daniel, which will remain until the time of wrath.

MOON WORSHIPPERS ORIGINALLY:

"Allah" was the moon-deity of the Arabs before Muhammad brought his brand of religion to them. This term was adopted because of its "name recognition" among the population. You will often notice that the primary Islamic symbol is the **crescent moon**, placed above their places of worship in a similar way Christians use the cross. This name "Allah" (Arabs' former term for their moon deity) reflects the pattern of adopting familiar terms and symbols of former Pagans; the Celtic/Druidic sun-deity was worshipped under the proper name "GOTT", which was adopted into our English as "GOD". The Hebrew term is Elohim, but translators chose to use a more popular term with "name recognition". "English" is the language of the Angles, and the word England is derived from "Angle Land".

Author's Response to a Critic of Fossilized Customs

The following are the complete comments of a **congregational leader** in Texas who wrote to Rick Chaimberlin, who publishes Petah Tikvah -- a wonderful quarterly magazine I recommend to everyone. I address both Rick and our unhappy brother, point-by-point. I present this for you to read, since there are certain congregational leaders who seem to take opposition with many of the same topics discussed in Fossilized Customs. Even leaders can have trouble understanding that we are not all serving in the same capacity.

Dear brother Rick, (and congregational leader in Texas);

Lew: *If a member of the Body is found to be practicing or teaching error, he is to be confronted by the offended person privately first, and if this fails it is to be brought before the elders. If this fails to correct the man's error, it is brought before the whole assembly of saints, so that his shame is before all (Mt. 18:15-17). If I am a false witness to some, then I am in good company; Shaul was thought to be one because he witnessed that Elohim raised up Messiah (1 Cor. 15:15) -- a very unpopular idea to the establishment. To the establishment, men who expose error have usually and understandably been labeled rebels, or worse. As Shaul stated at Philippians 1:15-18, he rejoiced in the fact that Messiah was announced, whether in pretense, envy, strife, or selfish ambition -- so in the spirit of this concept I will not speak against anyone who is working in the harvest and giving of themselves in Yahusha's service. In the criticisms below I find no circumstances which effect one's salvation before* Yahuah, *regardless of which way one leans in belief. It would be my privilege to respond briefly to our brother's sincere concerns regarding what he finds offensive in my book Fossilized Customs, but I do not hope to win a debate at the expense of offending or shaming my brother:*

congregational leader: In the Oct-Dec 2003 issue of Petah Tikvah, on page 4, you have footnote 2, which makes mention of "Fossilized Customs" by Lew White. Let me make you aware of the dangerous material contained within this book.

congregational leader: 1. Lew White does not believe in the Tri-unity of the Godhead. He believes it's pagan in origin and based on pagan sexual practices (p. 91-93).

Lew: *If a person were to only have contact with the Scriptures, without any outside teachings or influences, it would be highly unlikely for them to develop a belief in a "Trinity" on their own. Too many texts reveal that Yahuah is ONE, not three.* ***Exegesis*** *(direct analysis or interpretation of Scripture) will often conflict with what a person has been taught or already believes as he brings them with him to the study -- prior beliefs must not be allowed to influence such analysis. When we approach Scripture with ideas we already believe and then hunt down the texts which support our belief, we find ourselves "proof-texting". In this case, if we read a text, the teaching we already believe is not directly being taught, but we can snatch or extract the necessary phrases in order to support our belief. This is not exegesis, but rather eisegesis.* ***Eisegesis*** *(analyzing from one's own ideas) is what we mostly see being done, where an explanation or analysis is based upon one's own ideas, which is often based on popular opinion. The "Trinity" entered the belief through what is called The Apostles' Creed, formulated as an integral part of the rite of baptism. A clearly divided and separate confession of Father, Son, and Holy Ghost, corresponding to the Divine Persons invoked in the formula of baptism was imposed by Catholicism, and this dogma has persisted strongly to the present. This Creed developed from a primitive teaching (c. 390), and is referred to in a letter addressed to Siricius by the Council of Milan (Migne, P.L., XVI, 1213), which supplies the earliest known instance of the combination Symbolum Apostolorum ("Creed of the Apostles"). Certainly any idea that it actually originated with the 12 Apostles is a myth. The actual inception of the doctrine of the Trinity seems to be best explained as coming from the Nicene Creed, formulated under the Emperor Constantine in 325 AD. All we need to do is find a text in the Scriptures which teaches anything about Yahuah being three distinct persons, and that belief in such a model is so paramount that our salvation hangs on it. He is neither trinity or "twin-ity", but if we would condemn one another over whether He is or isn't,* we are operating outside the bounds of what Scripture teaches us -- especially about judging one another. What I am guilty of (hopefully) is not judging people, but rather beliefs which entered the faith from outside. Constantine was marvelously talented at modifying and formulating things that appealed to what everyone already believed. He did not emphasize Scripture as our model and guide for doctrine. Fossilized Customs is not the only book which has been written which teaches that Yahuah is one.

Sir Isaac Newton and Alexander Hislop were non-trinitarians. "In the unity of that one Only God of the Babylonians, there were three persons, and to symbolize that doctrine of the Trinity, they employed, as the discoveries of Layard prove, the equilateral triangle, just as it is well known the Romish Church does at this day. In both cases such a comparison is most degrading to the King Eternal, and is fitted utterly to pervert the minds of those who contemplate it, as if there was or could be any similitude between such a figure and Him Who hath said, 'To whom will you liken (Elohim), and what likeness will you compare unto Him?'" The Two Babylons, pgs. 16,17.

congregational leader: 2. He does not believe in the tithe and states it is a social decision and not a biblical commandment (p. 89).

Lew: *Anyone who has read Fossilized Customs can see that it is Scriptural to tithe; the only controversy is who is to be the recipient of it. Yahusha was not supported by the tithe, but rather by those who were in the office of giving -- women of means (Luke 8:3, Mark 15:41) - it is important to support Yahusha's work in the world, by those who have the means. Miriam of Magdala was one of these women! The tithe is for the support of the widow, fatherless, lame, hungry, or any who are in temporary or permanent need of support. Giving to the poor is lending to Yahuah (Proverbs 19:17, Ya'aqob 1:27, Acts 10:4). There are many examples in Fossilized Customs supporting the tithe, but I also cite several Scriptures which expose how the sheep will be fleeced for gain (2 Cor. 2:17, 2 Kepha 2:3, Acts 20:32-35). We who labor in teaching are worthy of support, but only from those in the office of "helps" (1 Cor. 12:28). No where do we see any leader in Scripture teaching his students to give him 10% of their income. Certainly no Apostle ever took such plunder for personal use from any assembly they started. Performing a study of the phrase "ravenous wolves" might shed light on this subject better. If you have the means to support a leader who is working in the service of Yahusha's Body, PLEASE do so; but to call it the tithe is inappropriate. For this teaching, I am willing to be shamed for; but let Yahusha judge me. He is so much more forgiving than men are. Those who oppose this teaching may have much to lose financially, but it is so much more blessed to give than to receive. I know, because I must receive to do the work I do also. Without support, I would not be enabled to do the work I do. Another good word to study in this context is "nicolaitan" (no offense to my critic intended).*

congregational leader: 3. He believes ministers should not receive of tithes and offerings for their support. He believes ministers should get a job like everyone else and stop "bilking" the people out of their money.

Lew: *Did Kepha have a job? Andrew, Kepha, and Yohanan did quite a bit of fishing, and not for sport. Paul was a maker of tents, and he mourned for the occasions he was supported by assemblies when he needed to impose on them. He surely didn't confuse this support with the tithe; he carried offerings of food to the saints in Yerushaliyim when there was a famine (1 Cor. 16:3, Romans 15:26,27). The poor were foremost on the minds of these men (Galatians 2:10). We are to be supported as elders in the Body, and this is to do the work of the workman; we must not become a burden on every person to the extent of taking 10% from everyone's wages. Those with the means will have it put on their heart to invest in our work, and by doing so share in the rewards. The Gentiles who reaped spiritually from the people of Elohim were encouraged to share materially with them (Romans 15:26,27). Our brother's word "offerings" above was never a topic I taught against in the book. I still feel that we who serve the Body should work in an auxiliary capacity to earn a living, since we are not Levites and exempt from having a livelihood. Each one of the Body is of the priesthood of Melckizedek, and we are the living stones of the Temple of Yahuah.*

congregational leader: 4. He does not believe in gathering on the Sabbath, or in fact, ever needing to gather as Believers.

Lew: *We worship Yahuah by our obedience every day. Gathering on Shabbat (or after Shabbat, as we see done at Acts 20:7-12) is encouraged if possible in Fossilized Customs. But, we must study to see if it is* ***required*** *to assemble or not. Reading Exodus/Shemoth 16:29,30, we know we must not leave our "vicinity" on a Shabbat. Wherever 2 or more are gathered in Yahusha's Name, He is present. In the Sabbath assemblies 2000 years ago, a large amount of the attendees were Gentiles, so they could learn Torah. This has changed radically — there are no Gentiles attending synagogues, nor are the Christians reading the Torah in their assemblies. We are told to "observe" the Sabbath "in all your dwellings" (Lev. 23:3). This observance is primarily focused on resting - Sabbath was made for man's rest.*

We are commanded to assemble 3 times in a year (males over 20). On a typical weekly Shabbat, those who study may do so in their homes today with their families, where the basic focus or center of our life and walk begins. The family dwelling is the center, and the family structure is the model for teaching our offspring. We do not live to assemble; but we are to live to teach our children the Torah of Yahuah; it's no one else's responsibility. When we assemble as adults, it is for edification, and each one is to have a turn at ***teaching, prophesying, interpreting, revelations, singing, according to their gifts*** *(1 Cor. 14:26). If we never gather together, the Voice of Yahusha cannot speak to the Body -- the Spirit of prophecy is the testimony of Yahusha. He is in us, and teaches us through one another -- even the least of us. If we come together and only one speaks, then we have "gagged" Yahusha. Perhaps our brother misunderstood what I meant in the book; we are not "obliged" or commanded to assemble each and every Shabbat (as Catholicism has taught for centuries about their Sun-day worship services called the mass). If we choose to, we can sleep all day on Shabbat, and* *no wrong is done. Leaders who insist otherwise may have an agenda to push -- and their congregation should investigate what that may be. If a leader takes up a collection of money on the Sabbath, then they need to find where this behavior is seen in Scripture -- we should not be carrying money around at all on a Shabbat; even the beggars have to take this day off.* What does this text mean: *"**Six days work is done, but the seventh day is a Sabbath of rest, a set-apart miqra. You do no work, it is a Sabbath to Yahuah in all your dwellings.**" Please look up the Hebrew meaning of MIQRA, as it pertains to its root, QARA.*

congregational leader: 5. He believes in the "Two House / Covenant" theory, whereas, all Gentiles Believers are descended from the lost 10 tribes of Israel. This is the "Ephraimite Error."

Lew:** My error comes from Scriptural references which clearly contrast the terms **"house of Israel"** and **"house of Yahudah",** a division which developed after Da'ud's conflict with Abshalom. The Yahudim are indeed among the Elect of Yahuah, but there are "other sheep who are not of this fold". Please don't put me into a box by thinking I believe that England and America are the primary remnants of the 10 lost tribes. Amos 9:9 tells us **"For look, I am commanding, and I shall sift the house of Israel among the Gentiles, as one sifts with a sieve, yet not a grain falls to the ground."** Ya'aqob 1:1 is addressed **"to the twelve tribes who are in the dispersion, Greetings!"

*YirmeYahu 31 speaks of this "Ephraimite Error": **"For there shall be a day when the watchmen** (Natsarim) **cry on mount Ephraim, 'Arise, and let us go to Tsiyon, to Yahuah our Elohim."***

*The **"House of Yahudah"** (southern kingdom), and the **"House of Israel"** (northern 10 tribes), are called "two sticks", and even "sisters". We need to understand the end-time prophecies of the "**two sticks**" being made into **one** again, declared at Ezekiel 37, but if a person chooses to think these are Jews being re-gathered to Jews, then they are missing out on the understanding of the **secret of Elohim** which is being revealed just prior to the sounding of the 7th messenger (Rev. 10:7, Eph. 3:6). No harm done, but is this really an issue over which we have to become adversarial with one another? Shaul warned us to shun foolish controversies and genealogies - see 1 Tim. 1:4, and Titus 3:9. Something tells me this is not "foolish" at all, but prophetic fulfillment. But, I like knowing that the 12 gates into the New Yerushaliyim will be named for each of the 12 tribes, because Yahusha is finding each one of us -- and others also who are engrafting. The 12 tribes (Israel) are the priests to the nations.*

congregational leader: 6. He believes God has divorced Israel (p. 59) for her idolatry. Physical Israel no longer has a covenant with God unless they accept the New Covenant.

*Lew: Odd that you would bring this up! If you turn to YirmeYahu 3, you will read about the treachery which the northern "house" (Israel) did after Da'ud and Abshalom's conflict caused the division of the north and south. Yahuah even says that the house of Yahudah did not return to Him from her backsliding even after witnessing what He had brought on the north (Israel was carried away!). He pleads with the house of Yahudah, telling her that her sister (Israel of the north) would not return to Him, **"But she did not return. And her treacherous sister Yahudah saw it. And I saw that for all the causes for which backsliding Yisrael had committed adultery** (idolatry)**, I had put her away and given her a certificate of DIVORCE; yet her treacherous sister Yahudah did not fear; but went and committed whoring too."** YirmeYahu 3:7,8.*

congregational leader: 7. His use of "Paleo Hebrew" is outlandish and ridiculous, as there are many uncertainties about original character meaning and pronunciation. He believes that using "Paleo Hebrew" for God and Yeshua is the "only" correct way of representing them. He says the use of God is pagan and the use of Jesus/ Yeshua is incorrect.

***Lew:** Yahuah Elohim used palaeo-Hebrew to write the Torah in the stone tablets, so I stand on my choice of characters with Him. In fact, most of the prophets wrote in the archaic, primary Hebrew; it was only during the Babylonian Captivity that the Yahudim took the "Babylonian Hebrew" characters on -- Belshatstsar needed Daniel to read this "outlandish and ridiculous" script, because the Babylonians knew nothing of it. Mosheh, Abraham, Enoch, Da'ud, Shlomoh -- these men could not read modern Hebrew; they used that "outlandish and ridiculous" palaeo-Hebrew script. The Great Scroll of Isaiah (YeshaYahu) is a copy of the original, and it is on display in the Shrine of the Book Museum in Yerushaliyim -- the Name is preserved in its original "outlandish and ridiculous" palaeo-Hebrew script, while the rest of the text is in modern Hebrew. The original is the Qodesh script, and must never be referred to in a profane or disrespectful manner. The letters (22) of both scripts have the same meanings and sounds (with some exceptions). The words mean the same things too. Alef is "ox", Beth is "house", and so on. Being a "living language", changes have occurred in the Hebrew tongue. But the script we call the palaeo-Hebrew was taught to Enoch by a messenger of Yahuah (Book of Jubilees, source info). I have no axe to grind with the Aramaic* *whatsoever, but if we have to choose between them, I vote for the way my Father writes. We are babbling today, no doubt. Change is a form of corruption too. I can read both forms, both modern Babylonian/Aramaic as well as palaeo-Hebrew. I encourage everyone to draw closer to the original script, and for this I take a little heat once in a while.*

congregational leader: 8. His use of "Yahusha" is completely incorrect for representing Messiah.

Lew: *Y'shua is fine with me, since it was written on Ya'aqob's ossuary in this way. But, it should not be dangerous to know that Y'shua is short for something, just as "Larry" is short for Lawrence. Yahshua is another fine rendering. Yeshua might be alright, as long as it isn't attempting to modify the vowel for the sound of the Name, YAH. We mustn't argue over words, but grow in understanding why we are using them. If a person wants to dig into it a little, the Greek texts at Acts 7 and Hebrews 4 will reveal the fact that "Joshua" and "Jesus" have the same underlying Greek letters, and so scholars have deduced that the two men actually have identical spellings in Hebrew. Greek is an intermediate language, and we know our Rabbi did not have a Greek name, nor did He ever hear "Jesus" on His eardrums. "Joshua" is spelled yod-hay-uau-shin-ayin. If you notice the spelling of "Yahudah", the first three letters also match this Name as well as the first three letters in Yahuah, yod-hay-uau-hay. If the proper way to say yod-hay-uau-shin-ayin is not Yahusha, then I'm all ears to learn a better way.*

congregational leader: 9. His use of Ha-Shatan is an incorrect use of the Hebrew language.

Lew: *Shatan is word #7853, spelled shin-tet-nun, and means adversary or opponent. The prefix "ha" is simply an article equivalent to our word, "the". Is this something to get our hackles up over? Used as a pronoun, it is sometimes mistaken to be the same thing as a name; but in these cases it is merely a designation for a being who has, in fact, had his original name blotted out. The name this being had prior to its rebellion is easily researched; it is Azazel, meaning power of Elohim. Like us, this being has to go through time, so he doesn't exist in all time like Yahuah does. If the word were spelled shin-tau-nun, it would mean "to urinate". They sound the same -- so that may be poetic justice. Now we're having fun!*

congregational leader: 10. Throughout his book he has nothing good to say about anyone or anything, as he believes he is the only one who has the correct understanding.

Lew: *I didn't realize that the book was not only depressing, but also taken to be a monument to conceit as well. Please accept my apology if it was taken that way. But, I recall stating that I merely gathered facts from many sources, and put them together -- not to judge* ***people****, but rather* ***customs*** *which had unsavory origins. Sure, most of the investigation is a major bummer, but trashing nonsense and doctrines against the Truth are difficult to present with a gleeful outcome. The wonderful news is, lots of people can investigate on their own to find out if what I've uncovered is true or not. Then they can gain the understanding and see how it feels to have eaten the "red pill" (analogy to Matrix).* **"With much wisdom comes much sorrow; the more knowledge, the more grief."** *Eccl. 1:18. I will pray for you, brother, to be granted wisdom in greater measure, and I hold no bitterness against you for your position. In the future, you will find that using Scripture to correct and rebuke error will work much better than personal feelings and popular opinions (just a friendly tip).* **"Preach the Word . . ."** *2 Tim. 4:2.*

congregational leader: 11. The entire book is incoherent and rambles endlessly back and forth between subjects and concepts. The book has no set order, theme, or consistent message.

Lew: *The tapestry I chose to unravel is connected to many disciplines of knowledge, and what you said about the "rambling" back and forth is quite true -- but it is also true of the writings of brother Shaul. Reading FC is not for entertainment. Many who have read it tell me they begin to see more and more with their 2nd and 3rd reading. If it doesn't make sense to you, then read it again, and again, until the consistent message appears to you. Below, our brother rightly describes the contents of FC, calling them "abhorrent". I could not agree more. The deceptions that have been perpetrated upon all mankind are described more concisely by the messenger's words recorded by brother Yohanan:*

"Babel the great is fallen, is fallen, and has become a dwelling place of demons, a haunt for every unclean spirit, and a haunt for every unclean and hated bird, because all the nations have drunk of the wine of the wrath of her whoring, and the sovereigns of the earth have committed whoring with her, and the merchants of the earth have become rich through the power of her riotous living." *Rev. 18:2,3. If my worst sin is writing the book Fossilized Customs, exposing the deceptions and showing the Truth, then I am indeed relieved. The trouble is, I think I'm guilty of much worse -- I was doomed at one time without knowledge of Yahusha, and His love for me, and all His chosen ones.*

As I reflect back to when I could not understand ***Scripture****, I could have been guilty of having the same opinion of it, as you said of FC: "The entire* *book is incoherent and rambles endlessly back and forth between subjects and concepts. The book has no set order, theme, or consistent message".*

congregational leader: Rick, as a result of these things, I feel it is inappropriate to be promoting a man with such deviate and unscriptural ideas. I think it would be in proper order to print a retraction in your next issue and warn people against this man and his book. I have had to deal with this book numerous times, as a number of people have been led astray by it's abhorent contents.

Feel free to use any of this e-mail in either direct or indirect quote.

Lew: *(I concur, Rick; circulate this in any way you like.)*

Serpent Wisdom

THE FOLLOWING DATA IS DERIVED FROM THE RESEARCH OF ROBERT BOWIE JOHNSON JR, AUTHOR OF ***ATHENA AND KAIN, THE TRUE MEANING OF GREEK MYTH***. I RECOMMEND THAT YOU ORDER HIS BOOKS FROM SOLVING LIGHT BOOKS, IN ANNAPOLIS, MD. SEARCH FOR THEM ON GOOGLE.COM -- THE INFORMATION HERE WAS PUBLISHED IN AN ARTICLE BY ROBERT IN *TECHNICAL JOURNAL*, VOL. 17(3) ISSN 1036-2916, A SCHOLARLY BI-MONTHLY MAGAZINE OF ***ANSWERS IN GENESIS LTD.,*** CHRISTIAN SCIENTISTS WHO ARE CURRENTLY PIG-EATING SUN-DAY WORSHIPPERS, BUT THEY COULD CHANGE AT ANY TIME NOW. THIS ORGANIZATION IS BUILDING A CREATION MUSEUM NEAR CINCINNATI, OHIO. THEY ARE DOING SOMETHING VERY IMPORTANT, AND YOU CAN LEARN QUITE A BIT FROM THEM BY SUBSCRIBING TO THEIR CREATION MAGAZINE OR TECHNICAL JOURNAL. THEIR WEBSITE IS WWW.ANSWERSINGENESIS.COM

I've based the following on an article by Robert Bowie Johnson Jr., titled:

Chuwah (Eve), and her Greek counterfeit, Athena

When people get carried away with ideas that there are "bloodlines" of the adversary among our human population, or the "seed of Kain/Cain", they are getting way off-base with what reality actually is. First of all, the descendants of Kain all died in the Noahic Flood. The "way of Kain" re-surfaced after the Great Flood, but the "way of Kain" is not about genetics, and is rebellious Satanism in various forms. The "way of Kain" has the goal of re-gaining the "serpent wisdom". In the Greek mythology, Satanism mimicked the Scriptural account of the first man and woman in the garden of Eden. In the Greek mythology, real people were "deified", or transformed into mighty-ones. The adversary designed counterfeits for real people, and designed a counterfeit system of teaching, masquerading as righteousness (light).

In the Greek mythology, Adam equates with Ze-us, and Adam's wife, Chuwah, is identified with Ze-us' wife, Hera.

Abel had no off-spring; so Seth became the line of the "good", and Kain the line of the "bad", or rebellious. But, in the Greek Satanistic counterfeit mythology, Seth is the "bad guy" (called Ares), and his brother Kain is the "good guy" (called Hephaistos). Ze-us loves Hephaistos, and hates Ares. Ares is the Yahuah-believing son! The Greek religion is "Anthropomorphic", in that actual men are considered to be mighty-ones.

The Wisdom of the Serpent

In the Greek mythology, the real man, Nimrod, is named "Herakles" (Hercules), who desired the "wisdom of the serpent". The Greek mythology called Eden by the term "Garden of the Hesperides", in which was a tree with a serpent. The serpent's wisdom could only be obtained by eating from the fruit of this tree, which were "golden apples". This is where Christians get the "apple" idea -- really we don't know exactly what fruit Chuwah and Adam ate (it may have been a fig).

After the Great Flood, the "serpent wisdom" arose again within the Pagan religions around the Earth. The serpent had originally promised Chuwah that she would not die. To make good on this promise, a "new Chuwah" (Hera, the wife of Ze-us) took a new name later on which meant "deathlessness". The ancient Greek word for death is THANATOS. To put an "A" in front of this word changes it, and makes it mean the opposite. "A-THANATOS" means "deathlessness" -- and was shortened to "**Athena**". Athena is the counterfeit Chuwah, and Ze-us is the counterfeit Adam. Nimrod is counterfeited in "Hercules", who sought to find the "golden apples", in order to eat them and share them with his mother, A-thena, gaining the "serpent wisdom". This "mystery religion" actually turns the true facts on their head, and other Pagan formats do the same.

Yahuah does not hold one person accountable for another's transgressions. A child is not guilty of the transgressions of the parent. Each person stands or falls on their own before Yahuah. No matter how many books are written, or how many websites claim it, there is not an evil bloodline on Earth. This leads to racism, and "ethnic cleansing". Yahuah created the people, no one else. A child is innocent and pure until they become aware of right and wrong. The Torah teaches us love for Yahuah and our fellow human, and bloodlines are not involved in this education. All have sinned and fallen short of the esteem of Yahuah, but those who put their hope in Yahusha are our brothers and sisters -- even if their mom and dad were Pagans. All judgment is Yahusha's.

All the Pagan models follow a thread of fact, yet they conceal, confuse, and corrupt the original.

Mimicking and masquerading, the Pagan religions have mixed things together over time in such a way that trying to find the TRUE faith can be likened to a **shell game** for the casual observer. The Garden of the Hesperides is the counterfeit Eden in Greek mythology. Eden (means pleasant). The following picture is a photograph of the giant idol of Athena in the Parthenon in Nashville, Tennessee. Her right hand holds "Nike", the messenger of Ze-us.

The serpent rises up as a friend behind her shield — the one who had promised her deathlessness.

A Counterfeit

Natsarim and Nazirite ~

ARE THESE RELATED WORDS?

Natsar & Nazir -- A Crash Study

THE WORD ***"NATSAR"***

There is usually some initial confusion with the words Natsar and Nazir. The original Hebrew for "Nazarene" is based on the root "natsar", and means ***to watch*** -- this is because the ***area*** around the burg ***Natsareth*** was named for it, hence the word **"Gennetsaret"** *(vale of Netsar)* -- referring to the whole district. “Natsarith” as it is sometimes transliterated, was a community with a view. It was built on a hilltop. Natsarith’s root word, Natsar, points to the fact that the town was situated on high ground, and provided a ***panoramic view of the surroundings.*** It was an absolutely lovely place to grow up.

The "brow of the hill" which Yahusha's town-folk tried to throw Him over gave the name to the town itself. Natsareth (natsar, the root) hence means "watchtower", and Natsarenes are by extension "watchmen", but this also fulfills the prophecies of Yesh Yahu 11:1, and Zec. 6:12. In these places, the change in vowels forms the root "netser", meaning "branch"; it's a kind of synonym, like any word with two meanings, but the same spelling. "He shall be called a ***Natsarene***" (Mt. 2:23) refers to the verses above, but it is not a direct quote as we are led to believe. This synonym (word spelled the same) forms a play-on -words: "netser", meaning "branch", and "natsar", meaning "to watch". So, we can be called ***branches,*** and ***watchmen*** for this reason. Remember Yahusha said, "I am the vine, you are the branches" (Yahuchanon 15:5).

The original followers of Yahusha were known as "Natsarim", because you'll see ***"sect of the Nazarenes"*** written in your translations at Acts 24:5.

From the same chapter 31 of Yerme Yahu (Jeremiah) where the promised New Covenant is located, there are the words, ***"There will be a day when WATCHMEN will cry out on the hills of Ephraim"*** (31:6) -- referring to one of the ***10 lost tribes*** whom Yahusha was sent to, among these, some are "Natsarim" (like me); **and He is finishing that mission through His Natsarim today**. The word "watchmen" is from the same root, Natsar, from which we derive the words Natsareth, Gennetsaret, and Natsarim. Technically, we should not use a letter "z" in "Nazarene", because the letter is a tsadee, or "ts" sound -- and it confuses the word with nazir, which uses a zayin (z).

HOW CAN WE CALL OURSELVES "NATSARIM"? (see Acts 24:5)

Our "physical" (fleshly) origins count for nothing; we become children of Yahuah by our decision to obey Him, and this shows not only our love for Him, but also it is evidence to all around us Who we serve, and Whose children we are. ***If we are immersed into the Name of Yahusha, and pronounce our belief in His resurrection while trusting in His blood atonement, we are Natsarim.*** Very early, the term "Natsarim" became replaced with the gentile term "Christians". There is more to learn about this transition, and a matter for another study. "Jesus Christ" is a man-made fabrication; "Yahusha

Mashiach" is simply the order the phrase takes, because "Mashaich" is Yahusha's title, not His "last name". Mashiach refers to His being anointed, the Sovereign of Israel (all 12 tribes). Shaul and Da'ud were also "Mashiach" Yahuah's "anointed".

THE WORD ***"NAZIR"***

By contrast, the "vow" of the "**Nazirite**", is just based on an ancient tradition which became an institution at Num 6:1-21. The root of the word is "nazir", having distinctly different Hebrew letters: nazir = nun, zayin, yod, resh; natsar = nun, Tsadee, resh. The word ***nazir*** means "consecrated", similar to the word "qodesh". The oath or vow of the Nazirite is for a specific period of time, and can be taken by anyone provided they offer the prescribed offerings at Num. 6:1-21 -- but this is going to be very difficult without the Lewitical priesthood, Temple, Altar, and so on! It would also seem that Nazir (Nazirite) vows can be just annunciated by our lips, hence Yahusha's strong advice to be careful what we say, or vow! He recommends NOT to do it (for the average person). The person who takes a Nazirite vow is set-apart to Yahuah for the period specified. So, the words are completely dissimilar.

I hope this clears up some of the haze at least. Don't worry, it is quite normal to make this association between the two words, Natsarim and Nazirite. I didn't even open the Greek can-of-worms here, it only makes things more confusing. We can become a "Natsarene" because we follow Yahusha, the founder of our sect. Paul was a member of the sect of the Pharisees, but became a Natsarene also -- he still considered himself a Pharisee as well. Except for the "adding" (leavening) of the rules of the Pharisees, and their outward showing of hypocritical righteousness, Yahusha was very much in agreement with the general pattern of the Pharisees, apart from their "oral law".

WHO WERE THE "NAZARENES"?

They were the original Hebrew and Gentile converts who followed Yahusha, and so were called NATSARIM. You'll find that Shaul (Paul) was called a "ringleader" of the sect of the Natsarim at Acts 24:5. The true religion of the Messiah, His real Name, His mission, and what His followers' sect was called are facts being re-discovered today by thousands of diligent seekers. Born a Yahudi (Jew), He is of a different tribe than Shaul (Paul), who was a Benyamite. But, neither of them are Catholic, Baptist, Anabaptist, Amish, or lived as any sort of Christian today. Yahusha is the High Priest of the religion of Abraham, Yitshaq, and Ya'aqob; He obeys the 10 Commandments of the Elohim of Israel, Yahuah, and so do those who follow Him. Would He really tell you that the Sabbath was made for man, then change what day is the Sabbath? Is it possible His Name isn't "Jesus", and He's more like a Jewish Rabbi? Scholars know He never heard anyone call Him "Jesus", it's just tradition that allows this to continue, and it is the result of several intermediate languages' corruptions of His true Name.

Why does your translation of Scripture mention the Name "YHWH" in the preface, but substitute the English word "LORD" for it in the text? If the letter "J" is less than 500 years old, why use it in the Name "Jesus"? Isn't His real Name more like Y'shua, Yeshua, Yahusha, or Yahushua? To call Him "Yeh-soos" or "Yeh-zeus" may not be very good, considering "soos" is Hebrew for "horse", and of course you know who "zeus" is . . . . this Pagan name was used in many name-endings like Tarsus, Pegasus, Dionysus, Parnassus, etc., to honor Zeus phonetically. The Greek name endings like sus, sous, and seus were employed to give honor to "Zeus". "Sus" in Latin means "pig". The Latin Deus and Greek Zeus sounded the same, because D and Z were both joined in a "DZ" sound.

When the "anti-messiah" appears on the scene, don't you imagine ***most people*** will be expecting someone named "Jesus", because they were programmed this way? Our Creator is now sealing His people with His TRUE NAME in their foreheads. You will discover facts about the beast system, and that there is a correlation between Nimrod, Pharaoh, Caesar, Dalai Lama, and the Pope. Is the Pope the "false prophet"? Is Washington D.C. the new "Babylon"? Prove to yourself what name the anti-messiah will come in, so you can identify him when he appears.

Overcome the deception the whole world is in, but remember to stay balanced. Yahuah doesn't wish us to be ignorant, but if we use our knowledge for unloving outcomes and goals, we have failed. We are not to judge people, only Yahusha may do so; judging another's servant is not a wise thing to do. We are all learning at different rates, growing in wisdom and understanding, but at different places in the race.

THAT'S INTERESTING . . . . .

I have several encyclopedic dictionaries, and each has over 1900 pages; there's not one footnote in them. *Can they be trusted?*

I hope so, but like you reading this book, I'll be looking at other sources to check up on things. Sometimes people change and move closer to the Truth; other times, they move farther away from it. The weirder it is, the faster they go after it!

Anabaptist *A member of one of the radical movements of the Reformation that insisted that only adult baptism was valid and held that the Christians should not bear arms, use force, or hold government office. Name means "one who is re-baptized". Greek, ana = again + baptein = to dip.*

Mennonite *A member of a Protestant Christian sect opposed to baptism, taking oaths, holding public office, or performing military service. German Mennoit, after Menno Simons (1492-1559), religious reformer.*

Amish *An orthodox US Anabaptist sect that separated from the Mennonites in the late 17th century. German, amisch, after Jacob Amman, 17th century Swiss Mennonite bishop.*

OTHER FOUNDATIONS

"I fed you with milk and not with solid food, for until now you were not able to receive it, and even now you are still not able, for you are still fleshly. For since there is envy, and strife, and divisions among you, are you not fleshly and walking according to man? For when one says, "I am of Sha'ul," and another "I am of Apollos," are you not fleshly? What then is Apollos, and what is Sha'ul, but servants through whom you believed, as the Master assigned to each? I planted, Apollos watered, but Elohim was giving growth. So neither he who plants nor he who waters is any at all, but Elohim who gives the increase. And he who plants and he who waters are one, and each one shall receive his own reward according to his own labor. For we are fellow workers of Elohim, you are the field of Elohim, the building of Elohim.

According to the favor of Elohim which was given to me, as a wise master builder I have laid the foundation, and another builds on it. But each one should look how he builds on it.

For no one is able to lay any other foundation except that which is laid, which is Yahusha Mashiach.

And if anyone builds on this foundation with gold, silver, precious stones, wood, hay, straw, each one's work shall be revealed, for the day shall show it up, because it is revealed by fire. And the fire shall prove the work of each one, what sort it is. And if anyone's work remains, which he has built on, he shall receive a reward.

If anyone's work is burned, he shall suffer loss, but he himself shall be saved, but so as through fire." 1 Cor. 3:2-15

Let's grow up and not put each other into boxes. Denominations are not the work of Yahusha - they bear the fleshly work of men because they take the ***NOMEN*** (name) of men, and define divisions within the Body, based on men's rules. We should not be divided into classifications, but be built upon Yahusha, not the whims of men before us.

Some declare, *"We don't have to obey those laws / teachings, because we're not Jewish. We're under the New Covenant, as believers in Messiah, who obeyed the Law for us." Wow.* It sure sounds logical, and seems to be great rationalization. But, can we find a Scripture on it, telling us that because a Gentile believer wasn't raised correctly, they can ignore things like the Sabbath Day, or that they can eat blood, fat, bats, pigs, skunks, squirrels, rabbits, clams, oysters, turtles, and octopus? Why would a Gentile want to live against the Torah after coming to faith in Yahusha, then claim his birthright as a Gentile who can go on living as if he's dumber than a box of hammers?

There's an answer to this question: the lying teachers, masquerading as messengers of righteousness. Always err on the side of Torah when you can, and never promote ignoring Yahuah's teachings. He's the One Who said they were not difficult; Messiah's yoke is very light to bear. Try taking on the mark/sign of the eternal Covenant, and rest on the Sabbath Day. Then, come tell me how hard it was to obey.

Leviticus 23 (and Deut. 16) list the Sabbaths of Father Yahuah, which certainly those who worship the Elohim of Israel would be interested in. The annual High Sabbaths, or moedim (appointed times), are "shadows" of things to come. They model the redemption of Israel:

THE SEVEN SABBATHS OF THE YEAR: IT'S ABOUT LOVE

Deut. 16, Lev. 23: ***REDEMPTION*** is pictured (shadowed) in the seven annual Sabbaths, and collectively they are an "agricultural metaphor":

The *agricultural cycle* is used to "shadow" the redemption of Yahuah's BRIDE, which He calls "ISRAEL OF Yahuah". Each of the 7 annual Sabbaths conceal meanings which remain hidden from those who don't practice them, and even those who do practice them from a "fleshly" approach don't see the spiritual side of them. They are so important that the elements they portray play a part in whether or not we will enter into the world-to-come! The Mashiach is the Redeemer and active Character in them all.

PASSOVER The year **opens** with PESACH. We remember the protection and deliverance of all

Israel as they were rescued from the "bondage" of sin (Egypt) at this time of year, by the power of our Redeemer/Deliverer, Yahuah. The "door" (Yahusha, the Redeemer) is marked in a special way, indicating how our Redeemer/ Deliverer covers/atones for us by ***marking us as protected and selected*** — and our decision to obey is shown by our being "observant" of this shadow of things to come. He has knocked, and we invite Him inside our dwelling. We provide evidence of our conviction that we need Him as we acknowledge His protection and deliverance from sin -- the blood-marks on the lintel and 2 doorposts signify the ***wounds*** He bore for us at this time of year, and He told us to remember Him (and His death) by the emblems of bread and wine as we observe each Passover. It is His death we are to remember by observing Passover, until He comes. The First-born of Yahuah died to cover sin, while the former animal sacrifices could only remind the sinner of his sinfulness. CONVICTION OF SIN is our first step. Without the shedding of BLOOD, there is no remission (elimination) of sin.

UNLEAVENED BREAD Next, we prepare our "soil" — our lives are ***cleared as a farm field for planting***, by getting out the stones, boulders, and weeds — clearing our lives of the "sin" by our decision to repent. When we remove the "leavened" bread, we are seeing the "shadow" of the spiritual action taking place. Avoiding leaven for **seven days**, we are now prepared to receive what is to be sown. Something is coming into our soil to dwell and grow there - the TORAH (which is the personality of the Ruach, in the Name of Yahusha). The parable of the Sower shows how we are the different types of soil. Paul told us to "keep the feast" (1 Co. 5:8). The seven days picture the lifespan, Ps. 90:10, during which we attempt to clear out the sin, clutter, and nonsense in our lives. The 1st day of ***Matsah*** (Unleavened bread) is on the 15th of the moon, and is a day of rest, or annual High Shabbath, recalling the departure of Israel from ha shatan's kingdom, Egypt; the 7th day of the Feast of Matsah is also a High Shabbath, and corresponds to Israel crossing the yam suph (sea of reeds) on dry ground, when Pharaoh and his army was drowned. It also relates to our immersion/baptism, as did the flood of Noach's day; obeying by going into the waters begins our salvation by faith (1 Pet. 3:15-22). REPENTANCE (turning around) and away from sin is our second step).

SHABUOTH / PENTECOST

(the wedding anniversary) Having cleared our field and made ourselves ready for the good seed, WE ARE PLANTED with the "good seed" of the TORAH at Shabuoth. Mt. Sinai was an event: the marriage between Yahuah & ISRAEL. The "good seed" is the personality of Yahuah, the Torah. These teachings are the 10 Commandments, the wife's wedding vows. They grow in us during the growing season, summer. This is the time when we remember the giving of the Ten Commandments at Sinai in Midian, but now (in the New Covenant) they are written on the HEARTS and MINDS of Yahuah's Bride by the indwelling Spirit of Yahusha, Who circumcises His Commandments into us so we LOVE the Covenant. The same 10 Commands given in stone are now written on our tablets of flesh, fulfilling the "NEW" (or re-newed) Covenant promised at Yerme Yahu 31:31-34, Ezek. 36:26,27; Yerme Yahu 31 is quoted at Heb. Chapters 8 & 10. Our immersion pictures our **circumcision**, as a Bride washes after her period of uncleanness, when we make our personal COVENANT with Yahusha to obey Him as a Bride obeys a Husband. The first Natsarim received the Spirit of Yahusha at this time — We are His Temple now. The "Ark" of the Covenant was just a box made of gold — but we are so much more than it was. We contain the living Elohim, Maker of Heavens and Earth, and His Personality (the Torah) grows into our being as we practice obeying His Commandments — this is evidence that we are His (1 John 2:3-6). The third step is obedience, and begins with our immersion, accepting the Covenant (10 Commandments), and going to the water as our outward sign of becoming Yahusha's Bride, joining Israel, escaping the spirit of the world (mind of the flesh). Accepting the Covenant by immersion, we become Israel and His wife; we agree to obey our Husband, and He CIRCUMCISES our hearts with the Covenant, allowing us to LOVE the Torah, the Ten Commandments. Sinai happens to us personally, and our immersion is our circumcision by the Spirit of Yahusha in our hearts, the objective being love, evidenced by our obedience.

THE SEVENTH MONTH A final warning (Yom Teruah, day of the blowing of a shofar, shadowing the "last trump") comes at the **beginning of the seventh moon**. On the 10th day of this moon we are JUDGED at Yom Kaphar (the 10th day of the seventh month, called "the Fast" at Acts 27:9). The Judge of all flesh will one day look at each person, and decide whether or not they are of the wheat or the weeds, and separate them as with a winnowing fork. Some day, we will be HARVESTED (the feast of the harvest, called Tabernacles, or SUKKOT).

What should you see in your sukkah?

We are told to build a temporary dwelling and place branches freshly cut from trees of the brook upon it. This very clearly "shadows" our own bodies, our "tent". The seventy years of our life are pictured by the seven days, and we notice the branches slowly whither and die over the seven days of this feast.

These "shadows" of things-to-come will be understood better by practicing them. For now, we should observe the "times" appointed for us, and be mindful that it is not in the details of how "perfectly" we perform them, or of being critical of others as they observe them. Rather, we must ***understand what these "shadows" represent spiritually***, and grow in our appreciation and love for Yahuah — and love for those He has redeemed. As imperfect as we all are in our various levels of development, we are all very special to Him. We not only are commanded to love **one another**, but also our enemies. We are the living TEMPLE of Yahuah, and living waters (the TORAH) should flow from each of us. Remember to forgive, because no one is perfect except One: Yahusha ha Mashiach L'Natsareth. Those of the synagogue of Satan must leave it and begin to restore what has been lost, and return to their First Love. The Word (Torah, Yahusha) is living and active; it is a double-edged Sword, and able to discern between soul and spirit, joints and marrow, and to judge the thoughts and INTENTIONS OF THE HEART.

The Jesuit's Oath

The following oath is on record in Paris, among the "Society of Jesus", the Jesuits.

The Jesuits Oath:

"I, *A.B.* , now in the presence of Almighty God, the blessed Virgin Mary, the blessed Michael the archangel, the blessed St. John Baptist, the holy apostles St. Peter and St. Paul, and the saints and sacred hosts of heaven, and to you my ghostly father, do declare from my heart, without mental reservation, that his holiness Pope Urban is Christ's vicar general, and is the true and only head of the Catholic or universal church throughout the earth; and that by the virtue of the keys of binding and loosing given to his holiness by my Saviour Jesus Christ, he hath power to depose heretical kings, princes, states, commonwealths, and governments, all being illegal, without his sacred confirmation, and that they may safely be destroyed; therefore, to the utmost of my power I shall and will defend this doctrine, and his holiness's rights and customs against all usurpers of the heretical (or Protestant) authority whatsoever; especially against the now pretended authority and Church of England, and all adherents, in regard that they and she be usurpal and heretical, opposing the sacred mother Church of Rome. I do renounce and disown any allegiance as due to any heretical king, prince, or state, named Protestants, or obedience to any of their inferior magistrates or officers.

I do further declare, that the doctrine of the Church of England, of the Calvinists, Huguenots, and of other of the name Protestants, to be damnable, and they themselves are damned, and to be damned, that will not forsake the same. I do further declare, that I will help, assist, and advise all, or any of his holiness's agents in any place, wherever I shall be, in England, Scotland, and Ireland, or in any other territory or kingdom I shall come to; to do my utmost to extirpate the heretical Protestants' doctrine, and to destroy all their pretended powers, regal or otherwise.

I do further promise and declare, that notwithstanding I am dispensed with to assume any religion heretical for the propagating of the mother church's interest, to keep secret and private all her agents' counsels from time to time, as they intrust me, and not to divulge, directly or indirectly, by word, writing, or circumstances whatsoever; but to execute all that shall be proposed, given in charge, or discovered into me, by you my ghostly father, or by any of this sacred convent.

All which I, A. B., do swear by the blessed Trinity, and blessed sacrament, which I now am to receive, to perform, and on my part to keep inviolably; And do call all the heavenly and glorious host of heaven to witness these my real intentions to keep this my oath. In testimony hereof, I take this most holy and blessed sacrament of the eucharist; and witness the same further with my hand and seal in the face of this holy convent, this —— day of -— An. Dom., &c. —–" McGavins Protestant, Vol. ii. p. 256.

Source: Discourse in Commemoration of the Glorious Reformation of the Sixteenth Century, by S.S. Schmucker, D.D., reprinted from the original printing plates of 1838, Limited Edition, published by The Word Publications, 1984, P.O. Box 35695, Phoenix Arizona 85069, USA.

The Jesuit Extreme Oath of Induction

The Jesuit Extreme Oath of Induction as recorded in the Congressional Record of the U.S.A. (House Bill 1523, Contested election case of Eugene C. Bonniwell, against Thos. S. Butler, Feb. 15, 1913, pp. 3215-3216):

"I ______, now in the presence of Almighty God, the Blessed Virgin Mary, the Blessed Michael the Archangel, the Blessed St. John the Baptist, the Holy Apostles, Peter and Paul, and all the Saints, sacred hosts of Heaven, and to you, my ghostly Father, the Superior General of the Society of Jesus, founded by St. Ignatius Loyola, in the Pontification of Paul the Third, and continued to the present, do by the womb of the virgin, the matrix of God, and the rod of Jesus Christ, declare and swear that his holiness, the Pope, is Christ's Vice -regent, and is the true and only head of the Catholic or Universal Church throughout the earth; and that by the virtue of the keys of binding and loosing, given to his Holiness by my Savior, Jesus Christ, he hath power to depose heretical kings, princes, states, commonwealths and governments, all being illegal without his sacred confirmation, and that they may be safely destroyed.

I do further declare, that I will help and assist and advise all or any of his Holiness' agents in any place wherever I shall be, and do my utmost to extirpate the heretical Protestant or Liberal doctrines and to destroy all their pretended powers, legal or otherwise.

I do further promise and declare, that notwithstanding I am dispensed with to assume any religion heretical, for the propagating of the Mother Church's interest, to keep secret and private all her agents' counsels, from time to time as they may instruct me, and not to divulge directly or indirectly, by word, writing, or circumstances whatever; but to execute all that shall be proposed given in charge or discovered unto me, by you, my ghostly father. ...

I do further promise and declare, that I will have no opinion or will of my own, or any mental reservation whatever, even as a corpse or cadaver but unhesitatingly obey each and every command that I may receive from my superiors in the Militia of the Pope and Jesus Christ.

That I will go to any part of the world, whatsoever, without murmuring and will be submissive in all things whatsoever communicated to me. ... I do further promise and declare, that I will, when opportunity presents, make and wage relentless war, secretly or openly, against all heretics, Protestants and Liberals, as I am directed to do to extirpate and exterminate them from the face of the whole earth, and that I will spare neither sex, age nor condition, and that I will hang, waste, boil, flay, strangle and bury alive these infamous heretics; rip up the stomachs and wombs of their women and crush their infants heads against the wall, in order to annihilate forever their execrable race.

That when the same cannot be done openly, I will secretly use the poison cup, the strangulation cord, the steel of the poniard, or the leaden bullet, regardless of the honor, rank, dignity or authority of the person or persons whatsoever may be their condition in life, either public or private, as I at any time may be directed so to do by any agent of the Pope or superior of the Brotherhood of the Holy Faith of the Society of Jesus."

Now think. Do the words of these oaths reveal the love and heart of Yahusha ha Mashiach? In contrast, He told us to love our enemies, and pray for those who persecute us, not **"rip up the stomachs and wombs of their women and crush their infants heads against the wall, in order to annihilate forever their execrable race."**

It is obvious that an evil spirit has

conspired to usurp control over the whole Earth, by deceiving mankind over many centuries.

"Whatever is true, whatever is noble, whatever is right, whatever is pure, whatever is lovely, whatever is admirable—if anything is excellent or praiseworthy—think about such things," Philippians 4:8.

What's true? The Torah, or Word of Yahuah. What's the lie? That we only have to believe in "J-sus", and not obey Torah.

The "7 sacraments" are the primary tools used to deceive the nations. ***There are no sacraments, and therefore no need for the "priesthood" of Catholicism.*** The ultimate objective of the 4th beast is to rule the Earth from Yerushaliyim. Designs and plans for this are at least 1600 years in the making, if not much longer. In the photo at top-right, the Jesuit General, or "Black Pope", stands to the left of Kennedy. The army of the Jesuits have infiltrated every modern government, and slowly bring about the objectives of this modern-day Jezebel "Mother Church", with her teachings.

CHURCH AND STATE: JFK with Paul VI in 1963

Whose point of view should we consider as we learn the origins of our customs?

This discussion could take place between you and your parents, your brother or sister, or a close friend you love dearly. You tell them what you've learned about the origins of Christmas, that it's really Satan's "birthday", because this being was worshipped (obeyed) by diverting obedience away from the true Creator of the Universe. Observing Messiah's birthday is not a commanded activity, and in no way can our worship be man-made, or originate from a formerly Pagan custom. So, you've stopped observing Christmas, Easter, and Sun-Day worship services, but they want to remain a pig-eating Sun-Day worshipper regardless of what Scripture says. They haven't studied personally, and they think you've come in contact with some form of "cult".

You might say something like,

"If I understand your viewpoint about Christmas, it's OK for us to observe this formerly Pagan ritual birthday of the sun idol,

TEMPLE MOUNT TUMOR

THE DOMED BUILDING HERE WAS BUILT BY MUSLIMS. THEY BELIEVED IT TO BE THE 3RD TEMPLE. THE CITY OF YERUSHALIYIM IS CURRENTLY TRAMPLED UNDER FOOT BY FOREIGNERS TO TORAH. CHAPTERS 7, 8, & 9 OF DANIEL DESCRIBE THE WHOLE GAMUT OF HISTORY CONCERNING THIS CITY OF PEACE, UP UNTIL THE RETURN OF YAHUSHA.

because it's now revised in meaning, and applies itself to the worship of Yahusha, the Mashiach of Israel, and is no longer associated with its origins."

Researching the origins of birthdays, they come from Babylonian Astrology, not the guidelines of Scripture. (Research the word ***horoscope***, and find that it means *hour watcher*. This was one of the duties of the Chaldean priests of Babylon. They watched the skies at the hour of a birth). The person led by "tradition" is in the majority, and believes by simply **re-naming Saturnalia** "Christ's Mass", and reinterpreting the symbolic ideas surrounding this solstice festival, we can consider the Paganism purged and rejected, and the formerly Pagan-founded ritual is applied to the observance of the birth of Mashiach, which ***cleanses*** the idolatry completely. *Amazingly, it was just that simple to do this for every detail of Paganism* — this is why Scripture refers to this kind of devious, scheming, misleading behavior as: ***"masquerading", inheriting lies, strong delusion, washing a pig, returning to vomit, etc.,.***

Father Yahuah has a point of view concerning all the celebrations his children observe - do we take His feelings into consideration when we decide to follow men's traditions? If we only take the viewpoint of human tradition, and never question what we have inherited through human designs, we will never see things of the world from the viewpoint of Yahuah.

Concerning the lies and falsehood we have inherited, Jer. 16:19 tells us:

"In the day of distress the Gentiles shall come to You from the ends of the Earth and say, 'Our fathers have inherited only falsehood, futility, and there is no value in them.'"

The verses continue, and tell us that the folks that realize Who He really is, by His hand and might, they shall know that ***His NAME is Yahuah***. Not knowing the personal Name of the Creator, people today worship what they know not what, with great enthusiasm, fervor, and zeal; and are in great ignorance as they do so.

The prophet quoted above is telling us that the things the Gentiles have inherited (customs) are ***"only falsehood, futility, and there is no value in them."*** Surely this would not be speaking of technology, but rather the Pagan framework of world-wide celebrations held to be most dear to everyone, but abhorrent to **Father Yahuah.**

Most importantly, I would like to point out that we can interpret history differently, but Scripture is what we must use to **correct**, **rebuke**, and **train**. If we find a letter written in the 9th century by a mere man who wrote about someone like "Nicholas" who lived hundreds of years before and thousands of miles away, how does that relate to our obedience to Torah? The Catholics teach that Nicholas was a "saint", died on Dec. 6th, and was an elder (bishop). Yet, the same traditions tell us this lad died at the ripe old age of 17. Who cares if its all true, or entirely false? It is not related to anything *remotely* pertinent to our faith, or spiritual work while in our flesh. Revelation tells us that the dragon has ***deceived*** the whole world — how? **Eph. 5:11-13** clearly explains how we are to "expose" the darkness; **Jer. 10:2-5** shows the use of the tree in worship (it was a Pagan altar); **Ezek. 8:16, 17** exposes the sunrise services conducted at "Easter"; **Deut. 12:30,31** warns us to ***not learn*** the ways of the Pagans, nor worship Yahuah in those patterns; and **2 Pet. 2:22** clearly warns us to avoid returning to the former Paganism we are delivered from, which Peter likens to a "dog returning to its vomit". If we clean up a pig (a Pagan festival), **it's still what it is** in Yahuah's eyes. Patronizing or condoning traditions which clearly originated in Satanic patterns go against the Spirit we have been given, and the words of life we live by.

Idolatry is like adultery/harlotry in Yahuah's eyes, and Gentiles engrafting into Israel are to refrain from idolatry **(Acts 15)**. What I would hope to see accomplished by this debate is that Yahuah be True, even if all of us turn out to be liars, or deceived in our thinking. We all have to learn, then teach the Torah of Yahuah. Yahuah's children speak His Words. I am not offended if you believe Constantine had nothing to do with changing the Sabbath to Sunday, but I am convinced he did. That is simply a difference of opinion of what is fact. If possible, try to defend Christmas, Sunday, Easter, Holy Water, steeples, bells, wreaths, or the tree using Scripture - and you will be correcting with the highest of all authorities. If there are Scriptures which condone the adoption of ***formerly Pagan rituals*** as long as their purpose is revised, and in the end souls of men are saved through doing so, then we can all return to our "Mother", the Roman Catholic Curia and Pope rulership. The end would justify the means. The Roman—Eastern Orthodox schism can be healed again, and all the protestants can once again be re-united with the teachings and authority of Rome.

It is important to emphasize that I am not judging people, but the doctrines of demons which have replaced our Scriptural guidelines. As sheep, we can be deceived very easily without the leadership of our Shepherd. We need to ignore the voices calling to us, and listen only to His Voice. As Sheep, all we require to be deceived is to hear a good excuse, rationalization. If we are living in the mind of the flesh, our hearts are open to following after whatever the world wants to shovel, because we may be living with a mind set on the flesh, not the Spirit. We are the servants of the one whom we obey (Rom. 6:16); if we have been deceived by human traditions, and not searched-out the origins of what we do, and why we do them, we are like blind men. We must test all things. We are doubly deceived if we encounter the Truth, and reject a love for it when we hear it, **because then Yahuah sends forth the strong delusion that we believe the lie** (2 Thess. 2:5-12).

If Christmas, Sunday, and Easter are not delusions, but rather are found in Scripture, then bring the evidence forth*. Worshipping what we do not know can be zealous and sincere, but sincerely wrong and riddled with error. The deceived people don't know they are deceived, or they would not continue in error. Adopting ***Pagan methods*** to worship Yahuah is another golden calf (apis). Propping up a device or behavior rooted in a Pagan origin and diverted to the worship of Yahuah is an abomination — but only in His eyes, not ours (if we can't see it from His point-of-view). Even adding to His Word and performing something He never asked us to do for Him can lead to death, as we see in the example from the "strange fire" offered by Aharon's sons. But transforming a formerly Pagan pattern into a camouflaged man-made device has to be even worse. Many times, the root of our problem stems from simple ignorance . . . — and Yahuah's people are destroyed because of a lack of knowledge.

Why did Father Yahuah withhold, or allow the withholding of, the knowledge of His Name from the people of Earth? Israel, Father Yahuah's wife/bride, serves as the priesthood to the whole Earth, and the lips of a priest ought to preserve knowledge. Returning to Pagan practices, the Israelites grew apart from Yahuah more and more, as we see Christianity did through the adoption of Pagan elements over the centuries by "revisionism" (changing the reason behind the act).

If we are Yahuah's people, He says we will know His Name (Is. 52.6). If we are not engrafted into Israel, we are not His people, His chosen ones. There is no promise or covenant with anyone outside of Israel; Gentiles must ***engraft*** to partake of the promises and Covenant (Romans 11).

Through stammering lips and a foreign tongue, Israel will eventually learn and the battle for who they serve will turn **(Is. 28)**. He guides us into paths of righteousness "for His Name's sake" **(Ps. 23)**.

Jeremiah (YirmeYahu) 23:27 tells us that the association with Baal (LORD) worship caused the people to "forget" Yahuah's Name. Many of the prophets were persecuted for using the Name. Zeph. 3:9 tells us we will call on the Name eventually, after our lips are purified. **Ezk. 39** states Yahuah will make His Name known.

If you have access to an exhaustive concordance, you can do a wonderful study on the Name by looking at the many Scriptural references where the words ***Name, lips, and call*** are used by the translators. It is my opinion that Ya-

****Hanukkah is found in Scripture; Christmas isn't*** (see Yn. 10:22) huah removed His Name from the lips of people because they were headed "back to Egypt" by being drawn into Pagan practices. Literally, "making an alliance with Pharaoh" by adopting a Pagan element is the same as Satanism, so Yahuah would obviously remove His Name from those lips. As we draw closer to Him, Yahuah reveals Himself in ever-increasing measure. He has revealed Himself to us through His Son, **Yahusha ha'Mashiach of Natsarith**.

We all stumble in many matters; but we serve the same Mashiach. Our need to rush to point out perceived errors must be tempered with sincere love for one another, not motivated by selfish ambition. We have to accept correction with humility, but this correction needs to come from "the Word", as we are told at 2 Tim 4. Arguing over how we are to conduct ourselves with human reasoning is probably a dangerous and pointless endeavor. May we all serve Yahusha in ever-increasing unity of faith, resulting in obedience He finds acceptable. May His will (Torah) be done on Earth, as it is in Heaven.

"The Word" is the Torah of Yahuah.
Our receiving a love for it, and having it written on our hearts and minds, is the New Covenant -
Hebrews 10:16, 2 Cor. 3:3.
That explains why we love the Commandments — Yahusha wrote them on our hearts.

Our **immersion** into His Name is the outward sign that He has circumcised our hearts. (**Col. 2:11-13**)

Shouted from the rooftops

There are many things kept secret from men. Men also keep many secrets from each other. They even deceive themselves by ignoring what they know to be true. One of the best-kept secrets in the world doesn't involve crashed alien craft at Area 51, or any Top Secret plan of any government. What I am about to reveal to you is not even known by the men "at the top", because as you know, they aren't tuned-in to Yahuah's Word in a big way — and that goes for all rulers, whether political, ecclesiastical, or mercantile. The secret is simply this: those who are set up to rule over us are the ***lowest*** of men.

Daniel 4:17 does not lie:

"This matter is by the decree of the watchers, and the command by the word of the set-apart ones, so that the living know that the Most High is Ruler in the reign of men, and gives it to whomever He wishes, and sets over it the lowest of men."

Consider what this means the next time your conversation turns to the conditions in the world. It's sobering to realize that we have been duped into believing that ***we*** elect the men who rule over us.
It helps us to understand why the Amish, Anabaptists, and Mennonites have little, if any, participation in political affairs.

We have no king, but YAHUAH.

Strong Delusion:

You could be programmed to believe error!

For many centuries, Christians have "believed" specific things to be facts, yet their belief in some of them is unfounded by Scripture. Reality can be masked, or "misdirected", by the skilled suggestion of magicians, hypnotists, and other deceivers. The "power of suggestion" and the "placebo effect" were both popularized by the research of Dr. Franz Anton Mesmer (1734-1815). Dr. Mesmer ***studied*** the power of suggestion; he didn't discover it - it's been around since the Fall of mankind. Hypnosis was developed from his research on psychological suggestion. When people are exposed to errors mixed together with the truth, they can become "***mesmerized***", moving the line between what is real and what is not real in their belief system based upon opinions - subtly suggested/taught by trusted "teachers" they have made themselves subordinate to. To ***misdirect*** is to ***delude***. Certain beliefs are the direct result of the power of suggestion. We can be naturally fascinated by a teacher, and develop the response of aligning our beliefs to his repeated suggestions. The deceived deceivers bring up specific passages of Scripture, then "misdirect" (divert) your thought process to make you think of something other than what the text is actually saying. This is one example of "mesmerization".

A Diversion tactic: ACTS 20 "They" want you to notice one thing; the phrase ***"first day of the week"***, then hope you go numb to following the rest of the chapter. The Greek text actually says, ***"And on the first of the Sabbaths . . ."*** Acts 20:7-38 begins by describing this gathering of believers (Natsarim) in a home, an upper room, where they listened to Paul (Shaul) until midnight, *since Paul was departing the following morning*. This was at Troas, where they had arrived after ***"the days of unleavened bread"*** (7 days following Passover). Have you been taught about an appointed time called *"unleavened bread"*, or *Passover* as being a part of your annual activities as a Christian? Also, Notice ***"there were many lamps in the upper room".*** At the start of this gathering in the lamp-filled upper room, ***Sabbath had just ended***, and a few of the Natsarim had come together in this home, at night, and had a bite together (breaking bread). It was after sunset, the resting was over. It was officially the "first day of the week" when Sabbath ended at sunset. There was nothing going on here like a "Mass", or a "communion service". In fact, no one was "worshipping". The believers simply wanted to hear Paul (Shaul) before he left town. Next, they sailed on to Miletos, and called the ELDERS of Ephesos there, to hear an important matter. This whole section needs to be carefully studied, because WHAT SHAUL TAUGHT them is over-looked because of the distraction to make you think about how it was "the first day of the week", stated earlier in the chapter. Get past that, study this chapter closely, and READ THE WARNING Shaul gave to the elders he had called for. It will shake you to your roots, and probably wake-up many of you from a life-long slumber. You should be able to see the "diversion tactic" that has been used to block many people from seeing what Shaul wanted to warn us of. Another diversion tactic is used at 2 Pet. 3:14-18. They try to make you think about Shaul's letters being "Scriptures", to distract you from what is being said -- it's another warning to us. Our main job is to overcome the errors, so we can be effective in our service and reach the LOST with the Truth, the Word, the Torah of the Maker of Heaven and Earth. Our message to them is ***"Repent, for the reign of Yahuah draws near."*** Repentance means return to the Torah (Ten Words, the Covenant) -- but it has been turned into a misunderstanding, where "grace" and "being under law" are considered to be in conflict with each other. To partake of the New Covenant (Jer. 31, Heb. 8), we must receive a love for the Torah, allowing Yahusha to circumcise our hearts with a love for it.

"Therefore, go and make taught ones of all the nations, immersing them into the Name of the Father and of the Son and of the Set-apart Spirit, teaching them to guard all that I have commanded you." Mt. 28:19. How much of what He had commanded were they to teach "all the nations"? ***". . . all that I have commanded you."*** This is the work we all do, not just the "leaders" of our assemblies. Really, Yahusha is the only "leader" we have, and "pastors" are simply organizers. And not all pastors do things in the same way, nor is all pastoring the same. There are a variety of functions and members in Yahusha's Body, His living Temple. Our ministry (work) is different from most others, but no more or less vital to the health of the overall Body.

The answer is in Genesis, or what is called "Bereshith" in the original Hebrew; that we are to rest from all our work as Yahuah did on the seventh day of every week. It's given again as a directive in the book of Exodus, the 4th of the Ten

Commandments. ***The Sabbath is spoken of 9 times in the book of Acts.*** It is called "a sign" (oth) between Yahuah and Israel, the only sign of the "***everlasting*** Covenant" (Ex. 31:13-17, Ez. 20:12-20, directly referred to at Heb. 4). At **Hebrews 4**, we are told specifically that the "rest" involves the ***7th day of the week***, and that for the "people of Elohim" there remains a Sabbath-keeping. How could they get around that? Simple; by misdirecting the meaning, and deluding the listeners. They have even "suggested" picking a day out of every 7 to rest -- but when you pick the ***correct*** one, you're "legalistic". Well, that's better than being "***illegalistic***" I'd say.

If the Covenant is ***everlasting***, its sign is also: the weekly Sabbath. Our Messiah, Rabbi Yahusha, made the heavens and the Earth, and called them as witnesses to this Covenant, and as long as they endure, the Ten Commandments will stand, not just 9 of them. Not one letter can be altered. The Sabbath ***He kept*** is not the one Christianity recognizes, simply because Christianity is a religion ABOUT Him, and is not the same religion He teaches and adheres to Himself. Constantine changed the day of rest to his "SUN-day". Setting aside the Commandments of Yahuah in order to adhere to human traditions is very dangerous, as is worship in a way that is humanly invented. You must think outside of the box to get past some strong deceptions.

Many deceptive ideas and customs have been "hidden" in plain sight, openly practiced for all to see. Yet all the while those who promote these ideas have to constantly provide an explanation for them, like a "booster shot", to keep the masses under the spell of their "vaccination" against the real truth. Being under the spell of their excuses makes the listener "drunk", and numb to the truth when it does come along. The fact is, those who are "deluded" don't know they are. If they knew, they would not allow the delusion to continue. The truth comes with a price tag: giving up the comfort of feeling secure in one's beliefs about reality at any cost in order to attain the truth. It means we have to be prepared to "wake up" and become aware of our previous and/or existing delusions. The movie Matrix comes to mind immediately, since it portrays these circumstances clearly. Some of us are completely "awake", but walking around in a world with the majority of people "dreaming" a reality that's not really there at all. We want to share the truth with you, but you don't even realize that you're "dreaming" or living in a constructed matrix someone designed for you to remain deluded in.

2 Thess 2:7-12 is critical to understand that there is delusion, the working of error:

"For the mystery of lawlessness (the secret of "Torahlessness", living without law) ***is already at work; only he who now restrains*** (controls) ***will do so until he is taken out of the way. And then the lawless one will be revealed, whom the Master will consume with the breath of His mouth and destroy with the brightness of His coming. The coming of the lawless one is according to the working of Satan, with all power, signs, and lying wonders, and with all unrighteous deception among those who perish, because they did not receive the love of the truth, that they might be saved. And for this reason (Elohim) will send them strong delusion, that they should believe the lie, that they all may be condemned who did not believe the truth but had pleasure in unrighteousness."***

*The word "**delusion**" used here is translated from the Greek word, **PLANOS**, #4106 — and means a wrong opinion, errors in morals, a leading astray, a working of error.*

How can we tell if we are under a spell or hypnotic trance? Is it possible to test for such a condition in ourselves? The only ***sure test*** to find out if we are deluded is to do a ***personal topical study of Scripture***, and compare what we learn from this study with our "reality" as we have perceived it to be. We must be careful to let Scripture speak alone, without our bringing any former beliefs to the study we are undertaking. This will be very sobering to everyone who takes time to test themselves in this way.

If you are like 99% of sincere Christians, you honestly believe that "Sun -Day" is the "Christian Sabbath". At the same time, you may have been told that "Jewish" believers in the *same* Messiah may observe the usual "7th day" of the week Sabbath, because they were "BORN" as Jewish-folk. So, we immediately have re-built a ***dividing wall*** that had been removed by Messiah's death and resurrection (Eph. 2:14). Instead of ONE body, we have TWO bodies of Messiah, based on the ***distinction*** of being BORN as a Jewish person, or as a Gentile person. This surely cannot be -- it turns out to only be one of many "human traditions", brought about by a ***working of error*** (a delusion!).

As you slowly read the book of Acts, you will discover the truth of the matter - never has the 4th Commandment (the Sabbath) been "changed" by any doctrine ***originating in Scripture***. The first chapter of Acts will reveal this to you. A delusion (working of error) has hypnotically entranced most of the world in a deception practiced openly. Oh, but there's much, much more to be revealed. Are you prepared to fully awaken? The next level will cause you great pain, yet you will be so grateful for reaching it. You will meet with your pastor after you awaken, and he will show you a side of himself you never knew to exist.

He will seem to be "asleep" to you.

Topics that you should personally study to test yourself for being deluded:

The Sabbath - *has anyone changed which day is the Sabbath mentioned in the 10 Commandments? Sure they have - it was imposed by Roman emperor Constantine I. But can the change be found in Scripture? Well, yes; but it's a bad thing -- read Daniel 7:25. It may be that it is linked to the "mark of the beast"* (Rev. 13) *since "buying and selling" is NOT allowed to be done on the Sabbath Day. Those having the beast's mark (Sun-Day?) are allowed to buy and sell, but those having Yahuah's mark (the Sabbath) are not permitted to buy and sell -- but this is self imposed on these obedient folks, only pertaining to the day of rest. Scripture refers to those who disobey the Covenant (Torah) as dogs and beasts. The Commandments -- and those obedient to them out of love -- reveal who is of* Yahuah *and who is a servant of the deceiver of this world.*

(And this article is about delusion, deception, and error).

The Personal Name of our Creator - *has it been intentionally concealed and removed from the common translations, according to their own admission in the preface? Have you ever looked up the word "GOD" in a good encyclopedia to learn the origins of the word?*

Messiah's real Name - *Is there only one* (Acts 4:12), and *is it Yahusha or Jesus?*

The re-newed, or "New Covenant" - *What is it? Can we find it in the Scriptures?* (see Jer. 31, Ez. 36, Heb. 8).

Bible - *is this word found in the Scriptures, or ever used by Scripture to refer to itself? Or, is it a Pagan deity's name?* (investigate Biblia, Biblos).

To wet your appetite for more, here's a glimpse at some TRUTH:

This is what the <u>*Encyclopedia Americana*</u> (1945 Edition) says under the topic "**GOD**":

"**GOD** *(god): Common Teutonic word for personal object of religious worship, formerly applicable to super-human beings of heathen myth; on conversion of Teutonic races to Christianity, term was applied to Supreme Being."*

Rabbi Yahusha haMashiach informed us that the Scriptures bear witness of Him (Jn. 5:39). *He also told us He is the* ***Master of the Sabbath*** (Mk 2:28), *and to pray that our flight not be in winter or* ***on a Sabbath*** (Mt. 24:20 - an **END TIME** warning). *It is the sign of the everlasting Covenant* (Ex. 31, Ez. 20), *yet following human misdirection, we are easily deluded to believe it has been changed to Sun-Day. Human reasoning hypnotically explains our reality for us, while Scripture is completely silent about any change in Sabbath observance. Paul* (or Shaul), *the same fellow that most people quote to explain how they don't have to obey the Covenant* (Torah), *told us to "TEST" ourselves to see if we are in the true faith* (2Cor. 13:5). *I would ask no more of any of you. If Yahuah is going to severely punish the nations that fail to observe the feast of Booths* (Sukkoth) *during the Millennial Reign* (Zech. 14), *how much will He punish those who completely ignore* ***<u>ALL</u>*** *His Sabbaths? Another question to ask yourself is, would He punish anyone who stepped out of the line of "lemmings" and actually obeyed Him by resting on the 7th day of every week?*

Only the other lemmings will likely get upset over it.

When sent to "basic training", young men are re-programmed to ***suppress*** *their moral character, and to obey orders to KILL on demand. This "brain-washing" doesn't work on each individual, however the goal is to have enough affected that the objective is still achieved. When the principles of psychological suggestion are applied to religious control, the same effect is achieved -- repeated suggestions to suppress moral character (the conscience that warns us of being out-of-bounds) will brain-wash most of those exposed to it.*

TEST EVERYTHING YOU HAVE BEEN TAUGHT, INCLUDING THIS ARTICLE, WITH THE WORD OF YAHUAH -- HE DOES NOT CHANGE. **"SABBATH"** UNDERSTOOD HERE IS THE ACTUAL 7TH DAY OF THE WEEK, NOT THE CATHOLIC SABBATH CALLED "SUN-DAY" (THE CHANGE ENFORCED BY CONSTANTINE, EDICT OF CONSTANTINE, 321 CE). THE PROTESTANTS *INHERITED* THE DAY-OF-THE-SUN "SABBATH" FROM THE CATHOLICS. THOSE WHO BELIEVE **SUN-DAY** IS THE SABBATH MIGHT NEED TO INVESTIGATE THE USE OF THE WORD **"SABBATH"** IN THE BOOK OF ACTS, IF THEY'VE BEEN LED TO THINK THE APOSTLES CHANGED THE DAY OF REST. ACTS WAS WRITTEN BY LUKE ABOUT 31 YEARS AFTER THE RESURRECTION AND ASCENSION. ALSO, YAHUSHA (YAHSHUA) MADE THE ESCHATOLOGICAL STATEMENT, ***"PRAY THAT YOUR FLIGHT WILL NOT BE IN WINTER, OR ON THE SABBATH".*** *MT. 24:20* -- THIS WOULD HAVE BEEN A PERFECT OPPORTUNITY TO MENTION IT IF HE INTENDED TO CHANGE WHICH DAY IS THE SHABBAT, SO WE WOULD KNOW ABOUT IT NOW. TAKE NOTE: HE MENTIONED THE SABBATH IN THE CONTEXT OF DESCRIBING EVENTS IN THE ***END TIMES***. ALSO, THE CHURCH OF ROME FREELY ADMITS THERE IS NO SCRIPTURAL BASIS FOR THE CHANGE, BUT IT WAS THE CHURCH ITSELF THAT MADE THE SABBATH CHANGE (CONSTANTINE). CONSULT DANIEL 7:25 ALSO, BECAUSE IT PREDICTED THIS CHANGE OF LAW. IS SUNDAY THE SABBATH? THAT'LL BE EASY TO FIGURE OUT ONCE YOU MAKE A STUDY OF IT ON YOUR OWN.

This article needs to be read by every seminary student, teacher, theologian, truck driver, architect, electrician, accountant, salesperson, - - - every person alive. People's thoughts have been programmed to ignore Yahuah's Torah through mind-control techniques. Please do all you can to get it circulated so the Truth can set them free.

There has also been a long-term conscious effort in the fields of education and media to "steer" our culture toward Humanism. The "New World Order" ultimately seeks to eliminate all religion, the family, and private property. They promote atheism, socialism, and evolution. When lies are repeated over and over, they are eventually accepted as truth.

Do all you can to counter the lies with the Truth.

PERMISSION IS GRANTED TO SHARE ANYTHING IN THIS BOOK. THIS ARTICLE, ***STRONG DELUSION***, IS ABLE TO BE PRINTED FROM THE WEBSITE,

www.fossilizedcustoms.com

The Torah & Shaul

Paul believed in keeping the Law of **𐤉𐤄𐤅𐤄:**

Acts 24:14:

"But this I confess to you, that according to the Way which they call a sect, so I worship the Elohim of my fathers, believing all things which are written in the Law and in the Prophets. "

Acts 25:8:

"While he answered for himself, "Neither against the Law of the Yahudim, nor against the Temple, nor against Caesar have I offended in anything at all."

Acts 18:21:

"but took leave of them, saying, 'I must by all means

keep this coming feast in Jerusalem; but I will return again to you, Yahuah-willing.' And he sailed from Ephesus."

Romans 7:25: ***"I thank 𐤄𐤅𐤄𐤉 -- through Yahusha the Messiah our Master! So then, with the mind I myself serve the Law of 𐤄𐤅𐤄𐤉, but with the flesh the Law of sin."***

SHOULD WE PROCLAIM THE NAME?

YIRMEYAHU 20:9: ***"Whenever I said, 'Let me not mention Him, nor speak in His Name again,' it was in my heart like a burning fire shut up in my bones. And I became weary of holding it back, and was helpless."***

Ps. 118: ***"Blessed is He Who comes in the Name of 𐤄𐤅𐤄𐤉."***

Think of the way you live, and Who you serve, as more of a "**government**" than a "religion" - it will put a better perspective on things. There's authority, jurisdiction, behavior policy/process, and a governed Body. At some point, a judgment will fall on each person who rejects being ruled by Yahusha. May you escape the boxes built by men, freed by the **Truth** - the Covenant between the Creator of all things and human kind. The Covenant is the Truth; it's the Word of 𐤄𐤅𐤄𐤉.

THE BEAST & ANTIMESSIAH

Scripture gives us **4 beasts** to track. The first beast (Babylon, kingdom of Nimrod) gives "life" to the other beasts which follow. The "beast" (animals, dogs) is the entire Pagan system in ***rebellion*** against the Torah, the Covenant of Love between Yahuah and Israel.

There are 3 ways to get involved with the beast:

1. *Receiving the **NUMBER***
2. *Receiving the **NAME***
3. *Giving homage to the **IMAGE***

*The "**NUMBER**" may indicate the way we are programmed to measure TIME.* The word "measure" in Hebrew is *MENE,* and is equivalent to "number". So, the ***calendar*** may relate to this "numbering" in some way. The first beast is Nimrod's kingdom, Babylon, as we learn from the books of Genesis and Daniel. This head, the ***first beast***, actually received a "fatal wound" because Noach's son SHEM (*Name*) *slew Nimrod* (Rev. 13:12-14).

*The "**IMAGE**" is both concrete and figurative. The old image of the obelisk and the crux are combined in any "steeple". The "pattern" is seen in the practices, and taken together is witchcraft.*

The adversary has deceived, and is deceiving, the whole world. This being has programmed every facet of religious practice into everyone's lives, based on the ***pattern*** of worshipping Nimrod, his wife, and child. This has carried itself through cultures and other "beasts" which are men's kingdoms which ignore Yahuah's existence and Covenant. Rev. 13 tells us that in order to determine the number of the beast, one must have "**wisdom**", which is Torah. Without the Torah, people are "vomited-out" of the land they inhabit, receiving curses instead of blessings - by their own choices.

The pinnacle of power in men's kingdoms (behind which has always been ha shatan) has passed through the Sargon rulers, Persia's Shahs, the Pharaohs, Caesars/Khazars/Czars, Popes, and numerous tyrants of the recent past. The **framework** this beast system uses to impose itself on the world is the common calendar with its "measurements" inherited from the Pagan Romans. If this is taken away, the whole beast system falls in one day. Daniel's vision, given to him by Yahuah, illustrates the **4 beasts**. The 4th one is obviously Rome, which will remain until the time of the end.

We are watching the fulfillment of the parable of the Prodigal Son occurring right now. The older son represents the **house of Yahudah**, now called "Jews"; and the younger son represents all those who left the Covenant many generations ago and became "LOST" due to assimilation into the Gentiles (mostly the **house of Israel**). The lost tribes are all over the Earth; but this lost "son" comes to his senses and realizes (remembers) who he really is. If you look at Ezek. 37, Jer. 3, Jer. 31, Acts 15, and Eph. 3, you will see that there are 2 "houses" of Israel. These represent the 2 sons in the parable. One remained with the Father, held to the Covenant, and no longer remembers his younger brother. The **lost** brother has multiplied exceedingly among the Gentiles, but awakens to the fact that he is worshipping (eating) with PIGS (Pagans, unclean dogs who rebel against the Covenant). Reading the parable, you'll see that the Father has to explain to the older brother who the younger brother is. The lost younger brother "repents" and begins to obey the Father again, making the older brother jealous of the attention given to the younger brother over this. We are witnessing the events sealed in Scripture unfold before our eyes.

Shatan has programmed (molded) the entire world to be waiting for someone named "JESUS". Christian, Islam, Hindu, and New-Age Humanists are all waiting for the coming of this special deliverer. "Maitreya" means "Lord of Love", and to the Hierarchy/New World Order crowd this "messiah" will be the great teacher they have been waiting for. He is represented as the "laughing Buddha" in Eastern philosophy. Non-Christians and Christians alike will "*see what they want to see*" when he appears on the world stage. The diverse points of view among mankind will converge on this anti -messiah, and each observer will be blinded by their own bias:

"I wouldn't have seen it, if I hadn't believed it."

Our expectations can overwhelm us. Beliefs have to be **tested** to make sure they are facts that can be trusted in - like checking the rivets in the steel girders I referred to at the beginning of this little book. But let's take a closer look at how relevant "believing" is in itself.

Even SATAN is a *believer* (Ya'aqob/ James 2:19) ***. . . but this rebellious being will not serve and obey!***

*Our "worship" is really **obedience**, the doing of what Yahuah expects of us. If we neglect doing what He expects of us, but assume our **intentions** will serve the same results, then we didn't understand the Fall, the golden calf incident, nor why Qayin's (Cain's) offering was not pleasing to* Yahuah.

"If you do well, shall you not be accepted?" *(Gen. 4:7).*

Qayin made up his ***own mind*** how he was going to worship Yahuah, and what would be the offering. How is Christianity any different? All the Sun-day assemblies, Christmas trees, and Easter baskets in the world will not be acceptable to Yahuah, *unless He prescribed them as a form of worshipping Him.* So, our simple task is to find out ***what Yahuah expects***, then **"do well"** so that He will accept our worship of Him. Then, we can expect to hear, ***"Well done, good and faithful servant!"*** (Mt. 25:21). *Doing* "the Word" is ***obeying*** Him, not adding to it, or *taking away* from it, or mixing-in the Pagan culture of Rome as tradition has done.

Now, back to this name, "JESUS" that the world is expecting -
If the ***True Person*** - the REAL Messiah of Israel comes in the name "Yahusha", most of the population of this planet will have a serious conflict to resolve in their "programming". We're here to announce Him before He arrives, so that the "wise virgins" will have the oil they need. The unwise will not hear us on this topic. They are unprepared, and will remain so. The false Messiah (anti-messiah) may appear in the programmed name, "JESUS", and perform what Mt. 24:24 & Rev. 13:14 describe as "signs" — used to deceive even the ELECT (Israel). We will not fall for it, because he has sealed us with His True Name, Yahusha. To be sure, if the anti-messiah came in the Name "Yahusha", hardly any of the world would follow after him. So, it's obvious which name the anti-messiah will likely be using.

If we are alive to live through the days of this anti-messiah, we will witness him beguiling the world with anti-Torah instructions. Not being wise in the Word (Torah, instructions), most will be deceived by him. We who have entered into the re-newed Covenant will continue to obey the Commandments of Yahuah, and hold to the Testimony of Yahusha. This is because He has written (circumcised) a love for His Torah on our hearts. Being observers of Shabbat, we will stand out like a sore thumb; and in fact do already to the world. The NWO beast (revived/restored Rome/UN) may attack and kill many of us. Christian Rome persecuted both unbelievers and believers for a millennium, killing some 83 million over a 600-year period. The Inquisition was very real. We may again be labeled "Judaizers" (a term not found in Scripture).

The trap is set for most to willingly accept this **Maitreya "JESUS" anti-messiah**. I feel the **IMAGE** of the beast may possibly be the old Nimrod symbol of the sun, the EAGLE, in caricature. It's a **cross** emblem, honored by Pagans from around the world since the dawn of recorded history. This may even be the "**star of Rompha**" (Acts 7:43). Yet many think the seal of Da'ud (David, the double dalet seal of his name) is the "star" referred to in this text. What does the "star of Bethlehem" look like in many illustrations? A cross! Often, a point of light will "nazz" when you look at it through a screen, and it becomes a crux. The truth is arrived at by simple deduction;

"Once you have eliminated everything that is impossible, whatever is left, no matter how improbable, must be the truth." — Arthur C. Doyle

So, the **NAME** of this beast, received willingly by the unsuspecting world is likely: JESUS.

The **MARK** is likely some ***behavioral*** trait that is *practiced due to a belief*, and is actually a ***teaching of error*** "hidden" right out in the open for all to see (and hear): the diversion called ***Sun-day.*** The fact that no one can "*buy or sell*" without the "mark" of the beast is a ***riddle*** that can only be solved with "***wisdom***".

Wisdom is a *knowledge of the Torah of Yahuah. Walking in the Torah*, people will not "*buy and sell*" on <u>one</u> day of each week, but those that have the "mark" of the beast are *not restricted* by that one day at all. The *Torah* is what keeps us from buying and selling on Sabbath; *not the beast.* Yahuah blessed the Sabbath day. When Yahuah *blesses* something, it <u>*stays*</u> blessed. The Sabbath is <u>*the*</u> mark of Yahuah, a "sign" between Yahuah and His people forever. Receiving a document from the government, or a bank, that ***identifies*** us *is not against Torah*; so the fearful dread in many people over a "National I.D. card" is unfounded. Rev. 13 is a *riddle*, and it cannot be solved without our actions being founded on the Torah (wisdom). If we carefully examine and weigh what is forbidden and permitted, we'll conclude that a data card is ***not against Torah***, so it cannot be the "mark" of the beast. A "beast" is anyone living <u>*without*</u> the Torah.

The *mark* of the beast is *believing that we* <u>***are***</u> *permitted to buy and sell*, and this is because *we are without Torah*, and therefore "lawless". Our *lack of Torah* is why Yahusha will say "depart from Me". Many believe, but don't OBEY. They have been deceived by the beast religion, and walk (live) in darkness.

There is a "mystery of lawlessness", and we've been warned; but it's necessary to overcome the programming so that the Truth can set us free (from the programming of error). So, the beast "system" is here now, set like a trap, and has been spun like a spider's web, growing stronger and stronger over the last 1700 years through religious tyranny. The father of lies is behind this ***conspiracy***. Traditions laced with poisonous errors are the norm.

HOMOSEXUALITY -

arsenokoites: what it really means

QUESTION:

What does the Torah have to say about homosexuality?

ANSWER: Torah deals with the idea clearly, head-on:

"If a man lies with a man as one lies with a woman, both of them have done what is detestable. They must be put to death; their blood will be on their own heads." Leviticus/ Wayyiqra 20:13 Mm-Hmmm. . . death, eh?

The Christian translators opted to interpret a Greek word, ***ARSENOKOITES***, and used the word "effeminate" or the phrase "homosexual offenders". But when you see the <u>***literal***</u> meaning of the Greek, *it will leave no doubt in your mind.* The KJV 1 Cor 6:9-10:

"Know ye not that the unrighteous (Torah shunners) ***shall not inherit the kingdom of*** (*Elohim)? ***Be not deceived: neither fornicators, nor idolaters, nor adulterers, nor effeminate, nor abusers of themselves with mankind, nor thieves, nor covetous, nor drunkards, nor revilers, nor extortioners, shall inherit the***

IMAGE OF THE BEAST

IN THIS STAINED GLASS, YOU CAN SEE THE "STAR" OF BETHLEHEM - BUT IT'S REALLY THE PAGAN CRUX EMBLEM OF THE BABYLONIAN SUN DEITY, ***SHAMASH***. THEY HIDE IT OUT IN THE OPEN FOR ALL TO SEE. BELOW ARE A COUPLE OF MUSEUM PIECES DISPLAYING THE IMAGE OF SHAMASH, THE SUN; THE LOWER PHOTO IS AN INCENSE BURNER USED BY THE PAGAN PRIESTS.

kingdom of (Elohim)?" 1 Cor 6:9-10
The NIV: ***"Do you not know that the wicked will not inherit the kingdom of*** (*Elohim)***? Do not be deceived: Neither the sexually immoral nor idolaters nor adulterers nor male prostitutes nor homosexual offenders*** (these two words are where the Greek word "ARSENOKOITES" occurs) ***nor thieves nor the greedy nor drunkards nor slanderers nor swindlers will inherit the kingdom of*** (*Elohim)***."*** 1 Cor 6:9-10 *"Elohim" refers to Yahuah, but translators put in the word "GOD".
The word used at 1 Cor. 6:9,10 literally means "Male koites", the identical behavior of the *Sodomites*. Does anyone remember what happened to the city of *Sodom*, and ***why****?*
Translators soften this literal meaning by using *"effeminate"* or *"homosexual offenders"* to convey the idea.

The Greek word at 1 Cor. 6:9,10 is #733, **ARSENOKOITES**, partly based on #2845, KOITE (giving us our word coitus).

The first part of the word, ARSEN, means MALE - thus putting the two parts (ARSEN + KOITE) together, we see it is correctly defined as SODOMITES, the "S" ending in ARSENOKOITES makes the term masculine.

A gay pastor may fail to comprehend the meaning of the "sin of **Sodom**", which was destroyed as an ***example to us*** who would live in that way, and he would also be ignoring the clear warning given at 1 Cor. 6:9-11.

The translators did not bring the literal meaning across using either "sexual offender" or "effeminate". It is much more clear when you look up the Greek word itself, and put it into the context of the sentence. They clearly will NOT inherit the world-to-come, but be cast alive into the Yam Esh, the LAKE OF FIRE.

Men with *men*, or women with *animals* are both situations where it should be clear to everyone that something is wrong, and not normal. Many women have abandoned their *"natural function"* also, and turned away from child-bearing. Many who have put their professional lives ahead of making families fall into this thinking. Homosexuals, to make themselves *feel normal*, attempt to adopt children, and usurp the concept of marriage, calling on the legal systems to declare their union a marriage. They call heterosexuals BREEDERS, *as if this is an undesirable notion* -- where would humanity be without breeders exactly? Where would humanity be without homosexuals exactly? Humanity definitely needs one of these groups, and it appears that the BREEDERS get the prize here. No homo-fear or hate speech is involved here; only authentic, historical facts are presented. If anyone doesn't like the facts and wishes to

ignore them, that's their privilege, and they can accept full responsibility for their actions. Don't blame the messenger, even though in this case it may be one of those confounded BREEDERS.
All breeder wanna-be's desire to be accepted equally, without feeling different or accepting the consequences of their behavior. They need to ask themselves, ***"where did I come from?"***
The answer is, of course, ***<u>breeders</u>****!*

HOMOPHOBIC, OR <u>*HETEROPHOBIC*</u>?

When we are very young and impressionable, our inclinations are formed by the natural tendency to "fear the unknown". If we are unfamiliar with something, it takes courage and dedication to explore the foreign territory. When an impressionable young person begins to realize the existence of sexuality, the unknown elements of it are often overwhelming, and a certain level of FEAR (phobia) is instilled in them. Everyone recalls their first "date", as I do mine; and I'll tell you quite frankly that I was ***terrified***. When a person does not overcome their fear of the opposite sex, that fear remains with them. To accuse a heterosexual of being "homophobic" misdirects and distorts the issue, because the "homosexual" is the one that is ***<u>heterophobic</u>***. To be "homophobic" would imply that some men "fear" those of their own gender, or that some women "fear" those of their own gender. Let's use the correct terminology to describe the situation, and be courageous. Turning things on their head will never make them work out better.

Proverbs 10:17:

"He who heeds discipline shows the way to life, but whoever ignores correction leads others astray."

"Pharaoh" (or pharoh) means *lead shepherd* in the Hebrew language. In the Egyptian, "pharoh" is said to mean "great house", and his main ***<u>title</u>*** was "***good shepherd***" (that sounds familiar somehow). Satan (ha shatan) consistently seeks to usurp Yahusha's position; when this title is taken by any man, they place themselves along-side, or replace, the true Good Shepherd. If a man calls himself "pastor", then it is clear he wants to be put above the sheep, and usurp Yahusha's position over them. If a man allows others to call him their "pastor", he needs to repent immediately from this and humble himself. We are to *feed* Yahusha's sheep, not receive honor from them.

2 Peter 2:1-11:

"But there also came to be false prophets among the people, as also among you there shall be false teachers, who shall secretly bring in destructive heresies, and deny the Master who bought them, bringing swift destruction on themselves. And many shall follow their destructive <u>ways</u>, because of whom the way of truth shall be evil spoken of, and in greed, with fabricated words, they shall use you for gain. From of old their judgment does not linger, and their destruction does not slumber. For if Elohim did not spare the messengers who sinned, but sent them to Tartaros, and delivered them into chains of darkness, to be kept for judgment, and did not spare the world of old, but preserved Noah, a proclaimer of righteousness, and seven others, bringing in the flood on the world of the wicked, and having reduced to ashes the cities of Sedom and Amorah condemned them to destruction – having made them an example to those who afterward would live wickedly, and rescued righteous Lot, who was oppressed with the indecent behavior of the lawless (for day after day that righteous man, dwelling among them, tortured his righteous being by seeing and hearing their lawless works), then Yahuah knows how to rescue the reverent ones from trial and to keep the unrighteous unto the day of judgment, to be punished, and most of all those walking after the flesh in filthy lust and despising authority– bold, headstrong, speaking evil of esteemed ones, whereas messengers who are greater in strength and power do not bring a slanderous accusation against them before the Master."

Isa / YeshaYahu 8:9-16:

"Be broken, O peoples, and be shattered; and give ear, all remote places of the Earth.
'Gird yourselves, yet be shattered;
- gird yourselves, yet be shattered.
Devise a plan, but it will be thwarted;
state a proposal, but it will not stand,
for (Elohim) is with us.'
For thus Yahuah spoke to me with mighty power and instructed me not to walk in the way of this people, saying,
'You are not to say,
It is a conspiracy! - in regard to all that <u>this people</u> call a conspiracy;
and you are not to fear what <u>they</u> fear or be in dread of it.
It is Yahuah Shabuoth whom you should regard as qodesh.
And He shall be your fear,
And He shall be your dread.
Then He (Yahuah Shabuoth) ***shall become a miqdash (set-apart place);***
but to <u>both the houses of Israel</u>, a stone to strike and a rock to stumble over, and a snare and a trap for the inhabitants of Yerushalyim.
Many will stumble over <u>them</u> *(the existence of the <u>two houses</u> of Israel),*
then they will fall and be broken;

they will even be snared and caught.
Bind up the testimony, seal the Torah among my disciples.'"

We Natsarim (watchmen), all over the Earth, have been awakened by Yahusha. He is working through our efforts to awaken many more of the sleeping millions to the deceptions before they fall for the imposter that is to come. Yahusha warned us not to sleep, and this "sleep" is trusting in ***human*** traditions, interpretations, and expectations instead of Yahuah's Word. Obedience is love, and love is ***manifested*** by obedience. The Israelites were trained with the ***manna*** for 40 years in order to show them the pattern of the SHABUA (Hebrew, *week*), so that they would walk in Yahuah's SHABBAT. He even states that the *Sabbath was the "TEST"* (Ex. 16:4). The manna was all about the **7th day** of every week; and we have the True Manna from Shamayim (Yahusha in us) - and He is still the Master of the Shabbat. He is leading us into the promised land (His kingdom, government) - governed by Him, with His Life, the Torah (Living Water, Living Word), by having *received the gift of love for His Commandments*, which He has circumcised on our hearts.
His discerning wisdom placed within us will not allow us to become joined to the beast.

A man or *woman without Yahuah's Torah (instructions) is a *brute beast, and has no Covenant with Him.* The ideas in this book test and summarize how Scripture and the reality around us are in conflict, and explain how some of the deception of the world came about. At this moment somewhere in the world, a six-foot statue with rows of candles in front of it has *a deceived person KNEELING in front of it*. Can you be of any help in rescuing this person from their idolatry? The work is everywhere around each of us - it's not just the responsibility of our "assistant pastor" (remember, Yahusha is our only "Pastor", our Shepherd). The Spirit of Yahusha in you will prepare and enable you to go and teach, and assist others to enter into His Covenant of Love through immersion into His Name, Yahusha. Men's "ordinations" mean nothing - you must be ordained by Yahusha or you can do nothing.

The harvest is great. Pray to the Master of the harvest, and He ***will*** send workers. Scripture tells us that the "Gentiles" worship idols - so *we* are NOT Gentiles, but fellow citizens of Israel, through the Covenants (Eph. 2:8-13). If we claim to know Him, and ***do not keep His Commandments***, *we are deceiving ourselves*. (1Yn. 2:4).

We are now going to tread in the area of the 3rd Commandment, where the Name of Yahuah is to be honorable and never brought to naught, expunged, or *"circumlocuted"* (talked around):

Ex 20:7: ***"You do not take the Name of YAHUAH your Elohim in vain; for YAHUAH will not hold him guiltless that takes His Name in vain."***
dictionary definition for ***"vain":***
"ineffectual or unsuccessful; futile; a VAIN effort; without significance, value, or importance; baseless or worthless."

"Vain" is a *light* concept compared to the authentic idea conveyed by the *original Hebrew word*. The inspired Hebrew word which we translate the word ***"VAIN"*** from is: shin-uau-alef, **SHOAH**, #7724 and this is the definition of it in Hebrew:
Devastation, ruin, waste; DESTROY.
So, to destroy, omit, miss, obfuscate, circumlocute, substitute, shun, ignore, deny, change, replace, or treat lightly is what "SHOAH" means.

A Christian wrote:
"I stopped here because frankly, I had read enough. Look, God and Jesus both have many, many names in the Old and New Testament. God's true name is not "Elohim" or even "Yaweh". And God's native language is not Hebrew! Or even Aramaic. If God had first manifested himself to people in Mexico instead these "Nazarene Israel", people would be claiming his true name was "Señor". If God first appeared in Germany I guess we'd have to call Him "Gott". Good grief.
God is too big for any name, so to say that we need to use one particular set of names as if they are magic is farcical. I also don't see much problem with the source of some of these names either. If the words we are using are intended to say "king of all kings" or "Lord God almighty", that's what they mean. He also responds to "Abba father", an incredibly informal and intimate term that a child might use to refer to their father!
I don't think God cares about the words.
He is more intent on the heart and the intent."
(End of friend's opinion).
Our Christian friend feels the ***attributes*** and ***roles*** of Yahuah are "**names**", as the seminaries teach. Most of the reasoning in his response confirms that he is still firmly fixed in the "Christian" camp, which ***claims*** to obey the Torah, yet has eliminated what they call the "Jewish" laws. They still feel they obey, and refer to themselves as Gentiles. Gentiles are ***foreigners*** to the Covenants, so in this they are correct. To be joined to Yahuah requires that one enjoin to Him ***through the Covenants***, and then one becomes

****WOMAN: MEANS "WOMB-MAN". THE HEBREW WORD FOR WOMAN IS "ISHAH", AND "MAN" IS "ISH".***

a ***fellow citizen of Israel***. Yahusha is the ***Mediator*** of these Covenants, and *He writes a love for the Torah upon our hearts*, which is the "Renewed Covenant" with the "house of Israel" and the "house of Yahudah" (YirmeYahu/Jer 31, Heb. 8). Christians hear the word "Israel", and usually think "Jewish"; and they confuse us with "Rabbinical Judaism", which we most certainly are not.

"Names": To begin, ***where*** in Scripture do we find any reference to "**Names**" (plural) for Yahuah? A *name* is a distinctly personal, specific designation. As the term "Name" is used in Scripture, it refers exclusively to ***one word*** used at least 6,823 times: ***"YAHUAH".*** It is the personal, Proper Name which Yahuah points to repeatedly, and ***in this Name alone*** He makes each of His Covenants. It is identical to a "brand" or "trademark" really. A "pronoun" is used to ***generally*** identify a thing, a function or role, such as "father" or "it". A ***personal*** pronoun identifies a "specific" thing, using a ***particular*** term ascribed uniquely to that person or thing by a peculiar term, which we know as a "name". A boat is a *thing*. If we ***name*** the boat, we can specifically identify one boat from *all the other boats*. In this case, the term "GOD" is a prime example. *There are no "GODS"*, neither is this term applicable to the true, living Being we all know as the Creator of the universe. "Creator" is not a name either, but a pronoun that refers to the Being that did the creating.

GOD: *This is what the Encylopedia Americana (1945 Edition) says under the topic "GOD":*

"GOD (god): Common Teutonic word for personal object of religious worship, formerly applicable to super-human beings of heathen myth; on conversion of Teutonic races to Christianity, term was applied to Supreme Being."

Gen 4:26-5:1: ***"At that time men began to call on the Name of Yahuah."*** This statement alone unravels the debate in our favor. The text uses a singular form, SHEM (name), not "SHEMOTH" (names). It also presents the reader with that Name, *Yahuah*, which translators expunged (SHOAH, DESTROYED, REPLACED) for most of us.

Ex 3:13-15: ***"Mosheh said to Elohim, "Suppose I go to the Israelites and say to them, 'The Elohim of your fathers has sent me to you,' and they ask me, 'What is His Name?' Then what shall I tell them? Elohim said to Mosheh, 'ehYah asher ehYah'. This is what you are to say to the Israelites: 'ehYah has sent me to you.' Elohim also said to Mosheh, 'Say to the Israelites, YAHUAH, the Elohim of your fathers--the Elohim of Abraham, the Elohim of Isaac and the Elohim of Jacob--has sent me to you.' This is My Name forever, the Name by which I am to be remembered from generation to generation."***

Ex 5:2: ***"Pharaoh said, 'Who is YAHUAH, that I should obey Him and let Israel go? I do not know YAHUAH and I will not let Israel go.'"***

We are to be baptized in the *NAME* (not Names) - and we see at Acts 2 that singular Name is YAHUSHA, meaning "YAH is our salvation" (or Deliverer).

Mt. 10:22 tells us we will be "hated" because of *His Name***.** Yesha Yahu 52:6 tells us that *His people* shall *know His Name*. Ezek. 20:39 says there will come a day when His Name will no longer be profaned.

Ps. 118:26, quoted by Yahusha at Matt 23:39: ***"For I tell you, you will not see Me again until you say, 'Blessed is he who comes in the Name of Yahuah.'"***

Malachi 3:16-18: ***"Then those who feared Yahuah talked with one another, and Yahuah listened and heard. A scroll of remembrance was written in His presence concerning those who feared Yahuah and meditated upon His Name. 'They will be mine,' says Yahuah Shaddai, 'in the day when I make up my treasured possession. I will spare them, just as in compassion a man spares his son who serves him. And you will again see the distinction between the righteous and the wicked, between those who serve Elohim, and those who do not.'"***

Jer 20:9: ***"But if I say, "I will not remember Him, or speak anymore in His Name," Then in my heart it becomes like a burning fire shut up in my bones; And I am weary of holding it in, and I cannot endure it."***

HEBREW READS RIGHT-TO-LEFT

"ya - HOO - ah"

THESE SAME FOUR LETTERS ARE IN ANOTHER WORD:
THIS IS " YAHUDAH", HAVING THE ADDED LETTER "DALET":

IF WE ARE SAYING " YAHUDAH " CORRECTLY,
WE MUST HAVE " ya - HOO - ah " RIGHT ALSO!

THIS IS PALAEO-HEBREW FOR YAHUSHA:

Jer 23:26-27: ***"How long shall this be in the heart of the prophets that prophesy lies? yea, they are prophets of the deceit of their own heart; which think to cause My people to forget my Name by their dreams which they tell every man to his neighbour, as their fathers have forgotten my Name for Baal?"***

BAAL: definition: *LORD*

Ps 23:1 *"Yahuah* (or The LORD?) ***is my shepherd; I shall not want."*** *LORD = BAAL.*

Invoking His Covenant Name, Yahuah declared that the Yahudim would not utter His Name:

Jer 44:24-26: ***"Hear the word of Yahuah, all you people of Yahudah in Egypt. This is what Yahuah Shaddai, the Elohim of Israel, says: You and your wives have shown by your actions*** (making cakes, pouring drink offerings, and burning incense for ASHERAH) ***what you promised when you said, 'We will certainly carry out the vows we made to burn incense and pour out drink offerings to the Queen of Heaven*** (ASHERAH)***.' 'Go ahead then, do what you promised! Keep your vows! But hear the Word of Yahuah, all Yahudim living in Egypt: 'I swear by My great Name,' says Yahuah, 'that no one from Yahudah living anywhere in Egypt will ever again invoke My Name, or swear, 'As surely as the Sovereign Yahuah lives.'"***

Yahuah is saying that He removed His Name from their lips. But, at Zeph. 3:9, He will restore the pure language, and we will again CALL on His Name, and serve Him shoulder-to-shoulder. The customary adult beverage "toasts" to give honors to anything or anyone may be these "drink offerings" - to *"offer a toast"* may be a type of "boasting", or lifting up a glass to something other than Yahuah. It's worth avoiding this behavior.

If any man boasts, what should be the reason for his boasting?

Jer 9:24: ***"Let not the wise man boast of his wisdom or the strong man boast of his strength or the rich man boast of his riches, but let him who boasts boast about this: that he understands and knows Me, that I am Yahuah, Who exercises kindness, justice and righteousness on earth, for in these I delight,' declares Yahuah."***

Isa 42:5-9: ***"This is what Elohim Yahuah says-- He Who created the heavens and stretched them out, Who spread out the earth and all that comes out of it, Who gives breath to its people, and life to those who walk on it: 'I, Yahuah, have called you in righteousness; I will take hold of your hand. I will keep you and will make you to be a covenant for the people and a light for the Gentiles, to open eyes that are blind, to free captives from prison, and to release from the dungeon those who sit in darkness. "I am Yahuah; that is My Name! I will not give My esteem to another or My praise to idols. See, the former things have taken place, and new things I declare; before they spring into being I announce them to you."***

Our Christian friend stated above that His Name is NOT "Yaweh", intending to say His Name is NOT Yahuah; yet Yahuah stated that His Name in fact is Yahuah.

"Yeshua" Or ***"Yahusha"?***

"Joshua" isn't quite right; and "Yeshua" is still pretty far off, because Gabriel's explanation of the Name at Luke 1:21 describes the function (salvation) along with Who is providing that salvation.

The 1611 KJV was the first time in history that anyone on this planet set eyes on the name JE-

SUS in print. The Geneva translation had it spelled IESVS in 1599. **U,V, & W come from UAU**

"HE-SOOS" MEANS "**THE HORSE**" IN HEBREW, AND MEANS NOTHING AT ALL IN ANY LANGUAGE OTHER THAN GREEK, IN WHICH CASE IT REFERS TO ZEUS, AS DO OTHER GREEK WORDS SUCH AS:

TAR**SUS**, PARNAS**SUS**, DIONY**SUS**, THE GREEK DEITY OF HEALING, IEU**SUS**, PEGA**SUS**, AND OTHERS. THERE ARE DEITIES IN OTHER CULTURES THAT WE FIND, SUCH AS THE DRUID'S "ESUS", AND THE EGYPTIAN'S "ISIS" WHICH SEEM CLOSELY LINKED WITH THE TERM "JESUS", WHICH BECAME POPULARIZED BY THE SOCIETY OF JESUS, THE *JESUITS*. PROTESTANTISM PICKED UP THIS "JESUS" SPELLING FROM THE CATHOLIC INSTITUTION, NEVER DOUBTING ITS ORIGINS.

The elders of Israel were so steeped in the tradition of not saying the Name aloud, they conferred among themselves saying ***"But to stop this <u>thing</u> from spreading any further among the people*** (the Name)***, we must warn these men to speak no longer to anyone in this Name."*** Acts 4:17.

The Name 𐤉𐤄𐤅𐤔𐤏 contains the Name of 𐤉𐤄𐤅𐤄. Acts 4:7 begins their examination. Brought before the elders, Cephas and Yahuchanon are asked,

"By what <u>power</u> or by what <u>name</u> did you do this?".

*You will soon learn that the form "JESUS" is derived directly from **"YESHU"**, explained below. What "YESHU" means will change your thinking about this radically. In the Talmud, unbelieving Yahudim hatefully recorded the Name of the Mashiach of Yisrael as **"YESHU"**, often seen spelled today as **"Jeschu"**.*

Q: Where <u>did</u> we get the form "JESUS" from?

A: The Jesuits (They defend the form using the Greek and Latin, hoping you'll never discover what you are about to read):

The form **"YESHUA"** is from the ***acronym*** **"YESHU"**, a mutilation of Yahusha's Name used by unbelieving Yahudim during the late 1st and 2nd century CE. The *<u>letters</u>* in **"YESHU"** stand for the sentence, ***"may his name be blotted out"*** (from the scroll of life). This **"Yeshu"** acronym is the *real root* of the form "JESUS", after going through Greek, then Latin:

YESHU (remember, this is an acronym, meaning "may his name be blotted out", referring to the scroll of life). A rabbinic word-play, from the original Hebrew words:

<u>Ye</u>mach <u>Sh</u>mo <u>u</u>'Zikro

*NOTE: There's not actually a letter **"W"** in the Hebrew alef-beth; the letter shape **"V"** is the Latin shape for "U". The **"DOUBLE-U"** is recent. Our letter **"U"** is a perfect match with the sixth letter of the Hebrew alef-beth, now called a **WAW*** **(UAU).**

Acronyms are abbreviated messages, like "SCUBA" stands for "self contained underwater breathing apparatus".

YESU IESOU - Going into Greek, the letter "Y" became an IOTA because Greek has no "Y"; also, the sound of "SH" was lost, because Greek has no letters to make this sound. The letter combination "OU" is a diphthong, arising from the Greek attempt to transliterate the sound "OO" as in "woof". Our letter "U" and the Hebrew letter "UAU" does this easily. **JESU** is used also.

YESOUS IESOU took on an ending "S" to form IESOUS, since the Greek wanted to render the word masculine with the ending "S". Going to Latin, the diphthong "OU" became "U".

JESUS In the early 1530's, the letter "J" developed, causing a tail on proper names beginning with the letter " i ", and words used at the beginning of sentences. This "J" is really the letter "IOTA". Many European languages pronounce "J" as the letter " i ", or a "Y" sound. They even spell Yugoslavia this way: "Jugoslavia".

By the year 1611 the letter "J" was officially part of the English language and the King James Bible was printed along with pronunciation guides for all proper names like Jesus, Jew, Jeremiah, Jerusalem, Judah, and John. The name "Jesus" has been in use ever since.

THE <u>ALEF</u> <u>TAU</u> ENIGMA

In the inspired Hebrew texts of the first 5 scrolls of Scripture, ***scholars encounter an enigma.***

Two letters occur together, seemingly for no reason, that translators have not been able to explain. They are the two letters **"ALEF"** and **"TAU".** These are the first and last letters of the Hebrew "alef-beth" (alphabet).

It seems to occur near, and even ***next*** ***to*** the Name **YaHUaH** in the texts, making Yahusha's words at Revelation 1:11 a true "revelation" - By identifying Himself as the ALEF and the TAU, Yahusha is telling us that He is the very Being that spoke with Mosheh – *He is Yahuah.*

The translation received in the GREEK at Rev. 1:11 say "the **alpha** and the **omega**", as we read at Rev 1:7-8:

"Look, He is coming with the clouds, and every eye will see Him, even those who pierced Him; and all the peoples of the earth will mourn because of Him. So shall it be! Amn. ("AMN" is Hebrew to convey affirmation, used as we would say *"absolutely")*.

"I am the Alpha and the Omega," says Yahuah Elohim, "*who is*, and *who was*, and *who is to come*, the *Almighty*."

"ALMIGHTY" is the Hebrew term "SHADDAI", as seen in **"EL SHADDAI".**

Yahusha revealed to us that HE is the Being speaking to man in the text of the prophet Mosheh, and it is HE that is the mysterious "ALEF and the TAU", Who from the BEGINNING to the END has been speaking to His chosen ones. He then states that HE is El Shaddai, the Almighty. So Revelation 1:11 solves the enigma of the recurring letters "ALEF" and "TAU".

YAHUAH is a *unique* Hebrew word, #3068, based on the root **hay-uau-hay** #1933, ***HUAH***, often seen as **HAWAH** in Latin letters, meaning *to become*, or self-existence.

"who *is*, *was*, and *is to come*" is the ***definition*** of "YAHUAH", *existence* in all three tenses, *past, present,* and *future*.

"I will be there" is perhaps the most complete meaning of this unique Hebrew word, which is the Personal Name of the ETERNAL CREATOR. And, He has *no other Name*, as we find stated at Acts 4:12:

"Salvation is found in no one else, for there is no other name under heaven given among men by which we must be saved."

We respect everyone's attempts to pronounce the personal Name. The personal Name of our Creator as revealed at least 6,823 times in the TaNaKh is spelled: **YOD-HAY-UAU-HAY**

We prefer the literal sound of the letters as they appear comparatively in other Hebrew words, and the closest word using the identical letters in the same order as the Name happens to be:

YAHUDAH (the fourth son of Leah, and the name of the tribe / family from which springs all those who today call themselves "Jews", more accurately "YAHUDIM". This man's name, **YAHUDAH**, is spelled in Hebrew: YOD-HAY-UAU-DALETH-HAY - see chart on page 198.

Notice the following underlined letters, and imagine the sound of this word *without* the sound of the "D":

YOD-HAY-UAU-DALETH-HAY

Clement of Alexandria trans-lettered the Name from Hebrew into Greek using the following: **IAOUE**

People commonly use the Latin letters "YHWH" as an abbreviated form for the four letters, yod (Y), hay (H), uau (U), hay (H), although there is not really a letter "W" in Hebrew.

YaHUaH *is another way of rendering the four letters, and probably more accurate.* The shape of the original Hebrew can be used here only in the form of a picture, since most everyone would be looking at nonsense without the appropriate font installed on their system. The Hebrew words adonai, elohim, eloi, eloah, and others are pronouns as you know. Many people feel it is wrong to substitute formerly Pagan terms or names for Father Yahuah, of course (like GOD). I've never found any Scriptures using the term "haShem" to *replace* the Name Yahuah, yet we know it's in common use among many Messianics and orthodox Yahudim. There's no letter "V" in older Hebrew, but modern Hebrew uses such a letter (since the 17th century). "Jehovah" is a hybrid mongrelization of the Tetragrammaton Y.H.U.H., changed to JHVH, then the vowels of "adonai" are crammed in, to "CUE" the reader to *not* pronounce the Name, but instead say "adonai". *Remember the 3rd Commandment? (**SHOAH** = DESTROY).*

EL SHADDAI

Some teach that the patriarchs only knew Yahuah by the term "**El Shaddai**" -- due to the ***translation*** of Exodus 6:3 which commonly reads: ***"And I appeared unto Abraham, unto Isaac, and unto Jacob, by*** ("the Name of" are added words) ***God Almighty (El Shaddai), but by My Name, JEHOVAH, was I not known to them."*** *Ex. 6:3* KJV

Being known as "El Shaddai" conveys the meaning of "Elohim Almighty", yes, but it is not a proper noun - it is a description of *what* He is. Yahuah is not saying this was known to them as a NAME, but that He was KNOWN to them as *being* El Shaddai, the all-mighty Elohim. The translations miss a simple fact concerning this text: *it's a question!* Here is a better rendering of what Yahuah actually meant to say at Exodus 6:3

"And I appeared to Abraham, to Yitzchak, and to Ya'akob, as El Shaddai; and by My Name YAHUAH, WAS I NOT KNOWN TO THEM?"

The Scriptures we distribute corrects this text to read properly, and of course replaces the true Name to the text where it occurs in the original Hebrew. If you check to see if Abraham used the proper Name, YAHUAH, you'll see that he did. *So did all the other patriarchs.* So, if we read these men's own quoted words, seeing they *pronounced* it aloud, then the common translations of Ex. 6:3 convey an incorrect message to people. Y.H.U.H. stands for yod-hay-uau-hay.

Exodus 6:3 is a QUESTION, making the meaning of the sentence different from what most have been led to understand. Examining the conversations with these men it is easy to see they *knew* the Name. Men ***began to call on His Name*** very early, as we see at Genesis 4:26.

Hebrew has many similarities to our language, and in fact there are a large percentage of common English words that derive from Hebrew roots. The Hebrew root "AB" as we see in the name "ABRAM" or "ABRAHAM" is two letters (AB = alef + beth). **ABBA** equates to the Latin word for "PATER". The Hebrew word **ABRAM** literally means "exalted father", from the original words Abu Ramu. What about ***AVRAHAM?*** There is no letter "V" in the ancient Hebrew, but because Hebrew is a "living language", corruptions (changes) have occurred, so the modern Hebrew does have a letter sounding like a "V".

About the word *ABBA*; it's not a *name*, but a *pronoun*, just as FATHER isn't a name. It's like the word MOTHER; it's not a name. The Hebrew word for MOTHER is EMMA, which later became the Latin MATER, often shortened to "MA" by the hillbilly set. Yahuah refers to His "NAME" often in Scripture, and it's *always* associated with the same word: 𐤉𐤄𐤅𐤄 — yod-hay-uau-hay.

Yahusha revealed the FATHER to us, since Israel had not generally experienced Yahuah as FATHER, but more as El Shaddai. The translators of most editions of Scripture missed a subtle thing at Exodus 6:3. Yahuah did not say His "NAME" was El Shaddai, but that He appeared to them "as" Elohim Almighty (El, Elah, Elohim, & Eloah are all **pronouns**, *not proper names*).

Jesuit Influences: The Jesuits (*Society of Jesus*) designed the Roman calendar we use, modeled on the previous Pagan Julian calendar. They also use "GREEK" to explain our English transliteration for the Name above-all-names. Most are taught that the Name "JESUS" is a *translation*. If this were so, then it could be *"translated"* into some meaning into English, Greek, Latin, or Hebrew, no? No one can *"translate"* it back to Hebrew. To "translate" means to convey the MEANING of a word, not its SOUND. The "sound" of a word taken into another language is a *TRANSLITERATION.*

"TRANS-LETTERING" IS DIFFERENT FROM "TRANSLATING".

All scholars know that Yahusha never heard anyone say "Jesus" to Him 2000 years ago. It wasn't even invented until around 1530 CE, so how could anyone get "saved" in the name "Jesus" before it was invented? To try to make it mean something in Greek, the ending "sus" definitely refers to Zeus, as it does in many other Greek names such as Tarsus, Pegasus, Dionysus, and Parnassus. So, in Greek, the Name "JEsus" can mean "hail Zeus", or "son of Zeus". *It means nothing in Hebrew*, the language it supposedly came from . . . But, if you force it to mean anything, the closest it could come to any Hebrew word is "the horse", because "soos" is Hebrew for "horse". (HE-SOOS).

The word Yeshua (from the root ***yasha***) means "help" or "save", but the true Name "YAHUSHA" above means "YAH is our salvation". The association with Zeus with the "sus" ending is possibly an intended distortion, made by Pagan copyists of long ago. Zeus was sometimes depicted as a HORSE-MAN, or "centaur". The old Babylonian / Egyptian signs of the Zodiac/Zoo beasts in the skies included a centaur holding a bow and arrow, called Sagittarius - this is really Nimrod, the mighty hunter. He was known as Orion the hunter also. Satan (shatan) masquerades, changes, distorts, and misleads. Even "satan" came across rather close to its original: *shatan*.

And, like they say, the translators managed to get the name for the *Yerushaliyim garbage dump* correct also; but they just couldn't get the Name above all names right . . . . .

Joel 2:27-32: (Quoted by Kepha at Acts 2):

"Then you will know that *<u>I am in Israel</u>* -- that I am *<u>YAHUAH</u>* your Elohim, and that there is no other; never again will My people be shamed.

And afterward, I will pour out my Spirit on all people.

Your sons *<u>and</u>* daughters will prophesy, your old men will dream dreams, your young men will see visions.

Even on my servants, both men *<u>and</u>* women, I will pour out my Spirit in those days. I will show wonders in the heavens and on the earth, blood and fire and billows of smoke. The sun will be turned to darkness and the moon to blood before the coming of the great and dreadful day of YAHUAH.

***And everyone who <u>calls</u> on the <u>Name</u> of YAHUAH will be saved;* for on Mount Zion and in Jerusalem there will be deliverance, as YAHUAH has said, among the survivors whom YAHUAH calls."**

YOUR MISSION - SHOULD YOU CHOOSE TO ACCEPT IT:

We Natsarim are crying out on the "hills of Ephraim" to the nations (the 153 fish, Yn. 21:4-14), declaring the final warning, and obeying the "Great Commission", ***to teach all nations what Israel was to obey*** as we read at *Matt 28:19-20*:

"'Therefore go and make disciples of all nations, baptizing them in the Name of the Father and of the Son and of the Ruach ha'Qodesh, and teaching <u>them</u> to <u>obey</u> everything I have commanded <u>you</u>. And surely I am with you always, to the very end of the age.'"
As Natsarim Yisraelites, we are each commanded to act on this. We come in the Name of Yahuah; and <u>blessed</u> *is the one coming in the Name of Yahuah!*

Examine for a moment the photo (PAGE 203).
The scientific community ignores and regularly conceals monumental discoveries such as this, because it doesn't fit well into their world-view. Goliath of Gath, the Philistine, was such a Nephil, or *fallen one*, of giant size. The battle we face today is against TRUTH, and the giant organizations that have sown lies (bad seed, teachings) into the world for centuries are our target to expose. To this battle, we bring the ROCK of TORAH, the Living Word, which is the Testimony of Yahusha. ***In His Name*** the battle will be won, because the battle is His. The ***dogs*** we will face will resist the Truth, but some will be transformed by what we teach them, *and they will become Israel*, like us, through the Covenant. The following is one of my favorite texts, and contrasts the two "denominations" that exist on planet Earth: **Israel**, and the **dogs**. Yahuah is with ISRAEL, through His Covenants. He is not on the side of the ***anti-nomia*** ones, the lawless ones, that are not in a Covenant with Yahuah. The Mediator of the Re-newed Covenant is seeking the lost sheep through us, and the message of the Reign of Yahuah.

1 Sam 17:43-47 tells us:
"He said to Da'ud, 'Am I a dog, that you come at me with sticks?' And the Philistine cursed Da'ud by his elohim. 'Come here,' he said, 'and I'll give your flesh to the birds of the air and the beasts of the field!'"

"Da'ud said to the Philistine,
'You come against me with sword and spear

and javelin, but I come against you in the Name of YAHUAH Tsabuoth, the Elohim of the armies of Israel, whom you have defied. This day YAHUAH will hand you over to me, and I'll strike you down and cut off your head. Today I will give the carcasses of the Philistine army to the birds of the air and the beasts of the earth, and the whole world will know that there is an Elohim in Israel.

*"All those gathered here will know that it is not by sword or spear that YAHUAH *SAVES; for the battle is YAHUAH's, and He will give all of you into our hands."*

Dentists don't typically warn their patients to avoid candy, and Christian pastors don't typically read the Ten Commandments regularly (if ever) to their congregations; yet they instead program them to believe that obeying the Torah is a horrifying, "legalistic" thing to consider doing.

"Blessed are those doing His Commands, so that the authority shall be theirs unto the tree of life and to enter through the gates into the city." Rev 22:14

"Great shalom have they which love Your TORAH: and nothing shall offend them." Psalms 119:165

"Then the dragon was enraged at the woman and went off to make war against the rest of her offspring- those who obey Elohim's Commandments (TORAH) *and hold to the Testimony of Yahusha."* Rev 12:17

First-fruits = 144,000 of all the tribes of Israel.

You are responsible for what you know. Be found sowing the Truth when our Teacher returns.

Rev 19:1-8:

"After this I heard what sounded like the roar of a great multitude in heaven shouting:

'HalleluYah! Salvation and esteem and power belong to our Elohim, for true and just are His judgments.

He has condemned the great prostitute who corrupted the Earth by her adulteries.

He has avenged on her the blood of His servants.'

And again they shouted:

'HalleluYah! The smoke from her goes up for ever and ever.'"

**YAHUAH SAVES - THE WORDS USED IN THIS TEXT ARE LITERALLY: "YAHUSHA YAHUAH"*

HEBREW

LATIN SYMBOL	HEBREW NAME	PALAEO	MODERN	GEMATRIA	MEANING	GREEK NAME	GREEK
A	**alef**	𐤀	א	1	ox	**alpha**	**A**
B	**beth**	𐤁	ב	2	house	**beta**	**B**
G	**gimel**	𐤂	ג	3	camel	**gamma**	Γ
D	**daleth**	𐤃	ד	4	door	**delta**	Δ
H	**hay**	𐤄	ה	5	window	**hoi**	H
U	**uau**	𐤅	ו	6	hook	**upsilon**	**Y**
Z	**zayin**	𐤆	ז	7	weapon	**zeta**	**Z**
CH	**heth**	𐤇	ח	8	fence	**(h)eta**	**H**
T	**teth**	𐤈	ט	9	winding	**theta**	Θ
Y	**yod**	𐤉	י	10	hand	**iota**	I
K	**kaph**	𐤊	כ	20	bent hand	**kappa**	K
L	**lamed**	𐤋	ל	30	goad	**lambda**	Λ
M	**mem**	𐤌	מ	40	water	**mu**	M
N	**nun**	𐤍	נ	50	fish	**nu**	N
S	**samek**	𐤎	ס	60	prop	**xei**	Ξ
-	**ayin**	𐤏	ע	70	eye	**omega**	Ω
P	**pe**	𐤐	פ	80	mouth	**pei**	Π
TZ	**tsadee**	𐤑	צ	90	hook	**zeta**	**Z**
Q	**koph**	𐤒	ק	100	needle eye	**chi**	**X**
R	**resh**	𐤓	ר	200	head	**rho**	P
SH	**shin**	𐤔	ש	300	tooth	**sigma**	Σ
T	**tau**	𐤕	ת	400	mark	**tau**	T

MISSION STATEMENT

We are a Messianic ministry, promoting Scripture (the Torah of Father Yahuah) for study and understanding. We accept all the Scriptures as Yahuah-breathed, including "Genesis" through "Revelation". The translations have errors in them, but the original Hebrew, where it can be obtained, is the original text that remains perfect.

We are watchmen (Natsarim, Acts 24:5, Jer. 31:6), and consider all believers to be on the path to redemption through repentance, immersion, and obedience to the re-newed Covenant through the work of Rabbi Yahusha ha Mashiach, the Maker of Heaven and Earth.

We do not judge or separate people into denominations (even if they do), but steadfastly press on toward the perfecting of the saints.

Our goal, and the goal of all Scripture, is love. We teach the 10 Commandments as the Covenant of Love which they are called.

Our mission is to seek out the lost sheep of the **House of Israel** dispersed among the Gentiles, who are called and chosen to receive a love for the Truth. We hope this is your objective also, and that we can work together often to accomplish it as we are enabled to by the Spirit of Yahusha, our soon-coming King and Redeemer.

Messianic groups come in every shape and size, and vary greatly regarding beliefs. Scripture makes it clear that in Mashiach there is no distinction between Yahudi and Gentile, but those who live and think "in the flesh" make these distinctions all the time. When a leader of a group imposes his/her personal understandings on those in the group, as most do, exclusionary behavior is the result. The BODY (or group) is the mouthpiece through which the Voice of Yahusha speaks to us -- where ever 2 or more are gathered, He speaks to those present THROUGH the assembly. 1 Cor. 14:26 indicates that we all have to have a voice at addressing the assembly. In attending any Messianic group, be discerning of the good things you find, leaving the errors. The "lost" sheep of the ***house of Israel*** are not properly understood by most Messianic groups yet -- they tend to shun any reference to ideas that there are others who are not of the specific tribe of Yahudah that are called. But, even a former Pagan who has no bloodlines to Abraham can be gathered by the Spirit of Yahusha; upon entering the Covenant, they must be accepted as a native-born among the people of Yahuah, ***fellow citizens*** of ***Israel****** (Eph. 2:8-13). We are His "benai shalom", *children of peace*, **if** we are in a Covenant relationship with Him. This is the only way to become children of the ***household of Yahuah***. If anyone enters into the Covenant (by repenting, and immersion, calling on Yahusha's Name for forgiveness and salvation), they become like Ruth or Rehab, and are joined to Yahuah, becoming Israel; their former "self" is no longer living -- they are a *NEW* creation in Yahusha. When you sense this change within yourself, He is preparing you for the work you are to go and do, in serving Him and His body. I'm only here to serve the body in the role of a messenger of awakening -- I'm blowing a shofar, making people uncomfortable in their slumbering. The Body that is awakening is now being taught by the Spirit of Yahusha, GUIDING it into all Truth. You will plant more of the *same seed* that was planted and grows in you, and the fertile "soil" around you will sprout *others* of the same seed. This is the way the body is grown and nurtured by Yahusha. We will be hated because we seem "strict", because we don't compromise with error.

Sometime in the future, a "messiah" will appear on the scene to deceive the nations with power and great signs. Because he will be using the name "Jesus", most will believe and follow him. We were warned by Yahusha personally that this would occur. Translators have been deceived and have deceived most people into believing that our Savior is named "Jesus", and this programming has caused a raging battle over the true Name, revealed in this book.

ISRAEL currently consists of 2 "houses". One has *kept* Torah, and the other is *returning* to Torah from the pig pen. Only a remnant will do so, as we see YeshaYahu 11 tells us. Read it soon.

House of Yahudah & House of Israel

Father 𐤉𐤄𐤅𐤄 is the Elohim of all Israel. The "older brother" in the parable of the *Prodigal Son* can easily be understood to be the "House of Yahudah". The *prodigal* son is the lost tribes, Reuben, Ephraim, Naphtali, etc., and these are sifted among the nations (Amos 9:9), and are called Yahudah's "sister", the "House of Israel", also known as "Ephraim", the descendants of Yosef, or the "lost sheep". These 2 *houses*, **Yahudah** and Israel/**Ephraim**, are only "enemies" regarding the *belief* in Mashiach; but for the prophecies to be fulfilled, there is a blindness in part. These are the "two sticks" which will be re-united into *one stick* in Yahuah's hand one day soon in the future (Ez. 37). The older brother, ***Yahudah***, has preserved the "oracles of Yahuah", and are blessed of the Father; one day they too will come to understand, as we do, Jer. 30.

Ephraim and ***Yahudah*** currently strive against one another, but one day neither will vex the other (Is. 11:13). Ephraim still has the blessing of the first-born, and will be mightily blessed with a spiritual inheritance as they repent, and return to the Covenant.

* . . . NOT FELLOW CITIZENS OF CHRISTIANITY (SEE EPH. 2:8-13)

MOLOCH or Molech was the abomination of the Ammonites, the same as Chemosh of the Moabites. The image had the head of a bull with the arms and body of a ***seated man on a throne***. The ***lap*** area was a furnace. The out-stretched arms would receive a child, often unwanted and first-born, from which the child would be dropped into a white-hot furnace in the ***lap*** of the image. Parents today offer their children to this same demon when they take them to ***"sit on Santa's lap"***.
SHATAN is behind this, offering any wish of the child in exchange for the child's worship.

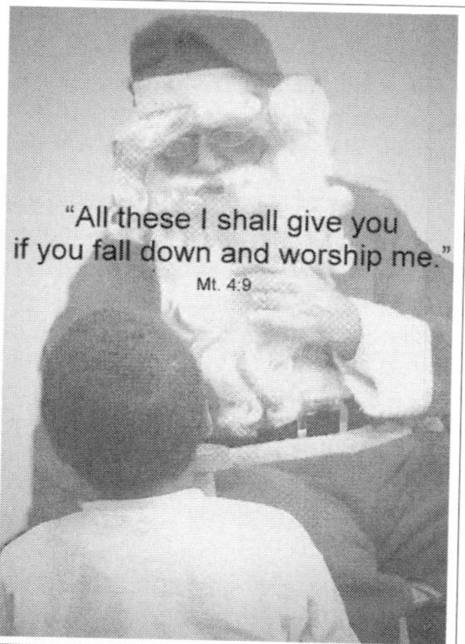

"All these I shall give you
if you fall down and worship me."
Mt. 4:9

HA SHATAN, THE FALLEN MESSENGER, DESIRES TO SIT ON HIS THRONE "IN THE NORTH":

Isa 14:12-14: ***"How you have fallen from the heavens, O Hělěl, son of the morning! You have been cut down to the ground, you who laid low the gentiles!***
"For you have said in your heart, 'Let me go up to the heavens, let me raise my THRONE above the stars of Ěl, and let me sit in the mount of meeting on the sides of the NORTH; let me go up above the heights of the clouds, let me be like the Most High.'"

The words above describe the aspirations of ha shatan. We clearly see that he desires to sit "enthroned", where his worshippers can come to him to make their requests. He wants to go up into the heavens and sit in the mount of meeting in "the north", no doubt riding in his sleigh pulled by flying horned beasts.
This is the modern ***form*** of MOLOCH,
and parents eagerly bring their children to him.
In the operation of this child sacrifice, the hands of the image holding the child were raised to the mouth (as if Moloch were eating) and the children fell into the fire where they were consumed by the flames. The people gathered before the Moloch were dancing on the sounds of flutes and tambourines to drown out the screams of the victims. Moloch's consort was Astoreth, the same as Asherah, so her symbol of the TREE is brought forth at the time of the year when the sun was "re-born". Moloch was the fire elohim, and was worshipped as the sun. The children sacrificed to him were believed to help keep the sun's fires burning brightly.

☜ LEFT:
POPE BENEDICT XVI SITS ENTHRONED
as "GOD on Earth",
"Vicar of Christ",
"Pontifex Maximus"

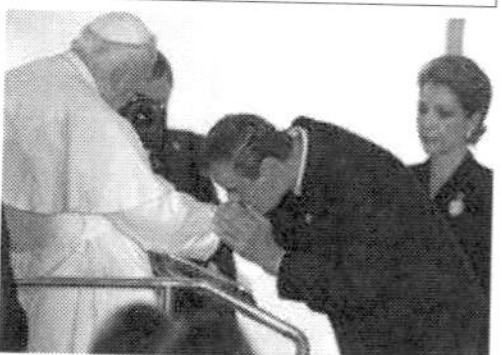

SANTA THRONE

THE AMMONITE FIRE-GOD MOLOCH.

MOLECH THRONE

CHILDREN BURNED ALIVE

FURNACE, HORNS

IN THE BELLY OF THE BEAST

BESORAH PROJECT

The final message to world is to be without guile, and done in the highest love (CHASID) and Truth by a select group of messengers sent to warn the world to repent.

The word that is sent forth is called the BESORAH, and prophecy describes it clearly. If it were not prophesied, I'd be at a loss to know what to call it. Up to now, the world has been calling it the "GOSPEL".

We've known that what has been hidden would one day be revealed. Teachings that are incorrect and incomplete will be made straight. Yahuah will be revealed, and what He expects of everyone.

I feel that what we are about to undertake is prophesied. He told us He would pour out His Spirit on all flesh, and men AND women would prophesy; and what they would prophesy would obviously be: **BESORAH**.

Carefully contemplate the **singular idea** expressed in these two texts, as they relate to the end times:

(KJV - so you'll see the old terms used):

"And this gospel of the kingdom will be preached in the whole world as a testimony to all nations, and then the end will come." Matt 24:14

"Therefore go and make disciples (talmidim, students) ***of all nations, baptizing them in the Name*** (Yahusha*) ***of the Father and of the Son and of the Holy Spirit, and teaching them*** (the nations) ***to obey everything*** (Torah) ***I have commanded you*** (Israel)***."*** Matt 28:19-20

These teachings concern the **Name**, and the **Torah**, being taught to "all nations" by the Natsarim, Israelite First-fruits folks that are His talmidim.

What is it (the message / report) ***called?***

The English world has put it down as "gospel of the kingdom". But it is really one HEBREW word, not "babbled" in any other language.

The word is:

BESORAH - This is what was prophesied to be announced to the whole world before the end.

Simple, eye-catching, and *speaking to those who will listen*. Everyone else will turn a deaf ear, as they are not called to it.

Yahusha didn't come babbling in a foreign language, but spoke to His prophets and Israel in **Hebrew**.

(For example, look at Acts 21:40, 22:2, 26:14).

You can see that this project **BESORAH** is inspired, and is happening because the **captivity** of Israel (among the Gentiles) is supposed to end in 2008, and the cry of the Natsarim is being heard on "the hills of Ephraim" (among the nations), since it is prophesied in YirmeYahu chapter 31 (details on page 214).

Look carefully at ***our cry***, as it was already written for us at Ps. 80.

IT IS A CRY OF RESTORATION

It contains echoes of the "priestly blessing", and refers to ***"the Son"*** that was resurrected, the ***"Man at Your right hand",*** and seems to be the plea of the returning prodigal son, after 2730 years! I'm repeating Psalm 80 in this book to give it emphasis, and I've underlined the words that show these are the lost tribes/sheep of Israel, scattered in 722 BCE. This is the ***cry of the Natsarim***, those who return to the Torah, and broadcast the **BESORAH**:

"Hear us, O Shepherd of Israel, You who lead YOSEF like a flock;

You who sit enthroned between the cherubim, shine forth before EPHRAIM, Benjamin and Manasseh.

Awaken Your might; come and save us.

Restore us, O Elohim; make your face shine upon us, that we may be saved.

O Yahuah El Shaddai, how long will Your anger smolder against the prayers of your people?

You have fed them with the bread of tears; You have made them drink tears by the bowlful.

You have made us a source of contention to our neighbors, and our enemies mock us.

Restore us, O El Almighty; make Your face shine upon us, that we may be saved.

You brought a vine out of Egypt; You drove out the nations and planted it.

You cleared the ground for it, and it took root and filled the land.

The mountains were covered with its shade, the mighty cedars with its branches.

It sent out its boughs to the Sea, its shoots as far as the River. Why have you broken down its walls so that all who pass by pick its grapes?

Boars from the forest ravage it and the creatures of the field feed on it.

Return to us, O El Shaddai! Look down from heaven and see! Watch over this vine, the root your right hand has planted, the Son You have raised up for Yourself.

Your vine is cut down, it is burned with fire; at your rebuke your people perish.

Let your hand rest on the Man at Your right hand, the Son of man you have raised up for yourself.

Then we will not turn away from you;

****FATHER/ABBA: YAHUSHA IS REFERRED TO AS "EVERLASTING FATHER" - SEE IS. 9:6***

revive us, and we will call on Your Name. Restore us, O Yahuah El Shaddai; make Your face shine upon us, that we may be saved." (Ps. 80)

The sign of authenticity that this is true:
Luke 7:37-38 (as seen in the KJV):
"And, behold, a woman in the city, which was a sinner, when she knew that (Yahusha) ***sat at meat in the Pharisee's house, brought an alabaster box of ointment,***
And stood at His feet behind him weeping, and began to wash His feet with tears, and did wipe them with the hairs of her head, and kissed His feet, and anointed them with the ointment."
Luke 7:44-47 ***"And He turned to the woman, and said unto Simon, Seest thou this woman? I entered into thine house, thou gavest Me no water for My feet: but she hath washed My feet with tears, and wiped them with the hairs of her head.***
Thou gavest Me no kiss: but this woman since the time I came in hath not ceased to kiss My feet.
My head with oil thou didst not anoint: but this woman hath anointed My feet with ointment.
Wherefore I say unto you, her sins, which are many, are forgiven; for she loved much: but to whom little is forgiven, the same loveth little."
Matt 26:7-13 (a different account of the event):
"There came unto Him a woman having an alabaster box of very precious ointment, and poured it on His head, as He sat at meat.
But when His disciples saw it, they had indignation, saying, To what purpose is this waste? For this ointment might have been sold for much, and given to the poor.
When (Yahusha) ***understood it, He said unto them, Why trouble ye the woman? for she hath wrought a good work upon me.***
For ye have the poor always with you; but Me ye have not always.
For in that she hath poured this ointment on My body, she did it for My burial.
Verily I say unto you, Wheresoever this gospel (BESORAH) ***shall be preached in the whole world, there shall also this, that this woman hath done, be told for a memorial of her."***
Matt 26:13 (as seen in the NIV):
"I tell you the truth, wherever this gospel (BESORAH) ***is preached throughout the world, what she has done will also be told, in memory of her."***

Telling you of this woman is the seal or validation that this is the BESORAH. If what you have read is an invalid message, then this report of the woman that anointed Yahusha would be missing. Her name was Miryam, also known as Miryam of Migdal; often called "the Magdalene". She was the sister of Martha and Elazar (or Lazarus), a family Yahusha was very close to in Bethany. Elazar was raised from the dead by Yahusha, and changed his name to "Yahuchanon", and you've known him as "John", the writer of the "fourth gospel", and the book called "Revelation". He also penned the letters called "1, 2, & 3 John". In the "fourth gospel", he is only known as ***"the disciple whom Yahusha loved"*** - note carefully the phrasing at Jn. 11:3, as compared with 13:23. Then, at the end of the book, this disciple identifies himself again as ***"the disciple whom Yahusha loved"***, explaining that he would be selected to remain ALIVE until Yahusha returns (Jn. 21:7-25). He was exiled to Patmos, because it was found to be impossible to kill him.
Probably, he ***will be*** one of the ***two witnesses***. Only "John" mentions the raising of "Lazarus", or the "two witnesses", and he is told by Yahusha that he would be a witness, to prophesy ***again***, and to whom at Rev 10:11:
"Then I was told, 'You must prophesy again about many peoples, nations, languages and kings.'" To remain alive, he would need help. ***Elazar*** means ***"Elohim helps".***

Now you have the BESORAH; be immersed into the Name of Yahusha for the forgiveness of sins, and teach all nations the ***Torah of Yahuah***, everything He commanded Israel to obey. You need no permission or license from men, only the anointing (ordination) of Yahusha. Be filled with the highest love (CHASID), and Truth (EMET), and walk in peace (SHALOM).
May Yahusha be with you always.

Birkat Kohanim:

"Yahuah bless and keep you.
Yahuah make His face shine upon you, and show favor to you.
Yahuah lift up His countenance upon you, and give you shalom." Num. 6:24-26

Hands shaping letter SHIN, for Shekhinah*:

**THE ORIGIN OF THE STAR TREK SALUTE - SHALOM ALEICHEM (PEACE BE WITH YOU)*

Resources

The Truth is the **Torah**, the **Word** of 𐤉𐤄𐤅𐤄. Torah means "teaching". Everything needed is there. To show yourself approved, study it. It's your sword, and your dedication to it will shield you. ***"To the Torah and the Testimony! If they do not speak according to this Word, they have no light of dawn."***~ Yesha Yahu (Isaiah) 8:20. ***"If you continue in My Word, then are you My disciples indeed; and you shall know the Truth, and the Truth shall make you free."*** Yn.8:32. Truth has stumbled in the street (Commandments).

NOTE: This author recommends the following for ***further study***, but use discernment — we all have disagreements on details, but we love each other.

Interlinear Hebrew-English Old Testament

This inter-linear can show you the word-for-word **Hebrew**-to-English if you order this item: it's called the Kohlenberger 4-volumes-in-1, available as stock # 6297 from Christian Book Distributors, CBD, POB 7000, Peabody, MA, 01961, USA. Phone 1-978-977-5000.

CBD's web site: http://www.christianbook.com (Beware of the NIV footnotes, and the fact that it doesn't *italicize* the added words).

This Hebrew-to-English Interlinear will show you the Hebrew Text letter-by-letter, **as inspired**; it is written in 'modern' Hebrew letters. The English words are below each Hebrew word! **CBD** also has *Exhaustive Concordances*, and these have wonderful Hebrew and Greek dictionaries to reference each word in English by number.

CBD carries Philo (#75931) and Josephus (#73868), as well as the *Jewish New Testament*, Greek Interlinears, and the "*Pseudepigrapha*", containing the books of Enoch, Jubilees, etc.,. In my research, I also used **Hendrickson's Interlinear Hebrew-Aramaic-Greek-English B-ble**, as well as many other resources.

OTHER RESOURCES USED FOR RESEARCH:

The Two Babylons, by Alexander Hislop

We also distribute ***The Two Babylons*** through our web site: **www.torahzone.net**

Oxford Dictionary of English Etymology.

American Heritage Illustrated Encyclopedic Dictionary.

Dictionary of Symbols, by J. E. Cirlot.

YOU CAN ORDER THE FOLLOWING FROM US:

Come Out Of Her My People, by Chris J. Koster. This is highly recommended. Available in the USA from Lew White, $12.95 S&H: ADD $7 + 10% of total order.

We use FedEx. www.torahzone.net

The Scriptures Restores the Name in Hebrew! can be ordered in the USA from Lew White.

$28 soft cover, or $38 hard cover.

S&H: ADD $7 + 10% of total order.

OUTSIDE USA, ADD $7 + 45% of total order for S&H, AND MUST BE PAID BY BANK CARD OR INTERNATIONAL MONEY ORDER.

Lew White's web sites:

www.fossilizedcustoms.com

www.torahzone.net

Distributing Scriptures, COOHMP, FC, tsitsith, menorahs, embroidered polo shirts, stickers, many messianic study materials and witnessing tools.

It is recommended that you download the FREE program to study all of Yahuah's Word from:

www.e-sword.net

There are many versions to add as modules, including The Scriptures, so you can compare the translations, and see the original Hebrew words. The Greek Received Text is included for the Messianic Writings (Matt.—Rev.).

The concordance words are based on the KJV (Strong's Concordance), but in most cases are very helpful for doing personal research.

Other Natsarim:

Frank Brown, elder - visit articles at: www.search-the-scriptures.org

www.eliyah.com

Because Christianity does not ***obey*** the Covenant, they ***have*** no covenant with Yahuah. Christians are made up of the "lost tribes" of Israel, but few realize it. We Natsarim strive to restore the lost tribes (house of Israel) to the Covenant through education, and thereby re-unit them to the house of Yahudah. We can then bring Yahusha to the house of Yahudah, and there will be one body - the house of Israel and the house of Yahudah will be one stick in Yahuah's hand (Ez. 37).

The Yahudim have not believed in their Mashiach because they cannot see any connection in the TaNaKh with the name "JESUS".

The Name is of vital importance, as Mosheh knew it would be (Ex. 3:13).

"Future generations will be told about 𐤉𐤄𐤅𐤄 ~ they will proclaim His righteousness (Torah) ***to a PEOPLE YET UNBORN — for He has done it."*** Ps. 22:30,31.

Christians call their religion Christianity, as if the Creator's religion/way has a ***Greek*** *name now. "Christianity" is not found in Scripture. The Torah of Yahuah is trampled in the streets, the Hebrew roots of the faith are severed. Eight of the Covenant Commandments are observed. The 3rd and 4th are commonly misunderstood. The Catholics only observe 7 of the 10, since they wiped-out the second Commandment, and made the 10th one into two Commandments. The 3rd Commandment tells us we are not to* ***destroy*** *(SHOAH) the Name of Yahuah. The 4th Commandment tells us to* ***rest on the 7th day of each week****, a day blessed by Yahuah, and set apart for all time during the first week of creation. The word "Sabbath" is used 61 times between MattitYahu and Revelation, 35% of its 170 occurrences in all of Scripture. It's apparent that the teachings of "Jezebel", the Canaanite/Phoenician mixture that polluted ancient Israel, are being practiced today all across the Earth.*

Misled by the teachings of Jezebel? The woman who rides the beast

"Nevertheless, I have this against you: You tolerate that woman Jezebel, who calls herself a prophetess. By her teaching she misleads My servants into sexual immorality* and the eating of food sacrificed to idols*. I have given her time to repent of her immorality, but she is unwilling. So I will cast her on a bed of suffering, and I will make those who commit adultery with her suffer intensely, unless they repent of her ways. I will strike her children dead. Then all the (assemblies) ***will know that I am He who searches hearts and minds, and I will repay each of you according to your deeds. Now I say to the rest of you in Thyatira, to you who do not hold to her teaching and have not learned Satan's so-called deep secrets* (I will not impose any other burden on you): Only hold on to what you have until I come. To him who overcomes and does My will to the end, I will give authority over the nations- He will rule them with an iron scepter; he will dash them to pieces like pottery- just as I have received authority from My Father. I will also give him the morning star. He who has an ear, let him hear what the Spirit says to the*** (assemblies)***."*** Rev 2:20-29 JEZEBEL GAVE ISRAEL THE **TREE (DATE PALM)**; **"Phoenicia" is Greek for "date palm".**

**Satan's so-called deep secrets, sexual immorality, and eating of food sacrificed to idols:*

*These secrets are the false sexual worship inherited from "**Jezebel**", her teachings of Baal/Asherah, including the use of Pagan images (trees, eggs, wreaths, rabbits, cruxes, statues, obelisks/steeples), objects ("holy" water, relics, garments, bells, rosaries, scapulars), and the superceding of Yahuah's Name and His appointed times with Pagan ones. Yahuah's reign draws near!*

CONE OF POWER

"In the Hermetic Order of the Golden Dawn this was described as a "vortex of energy" and was built up via circumambulation." — Llewellyn Encyclopedia

The cone of power is the name given to the union of witches' forces gathered around the circle, aimed at a common goal. In parts of ancient Syria, the cone was a symbol of Astarte (Asherah).

BIRTHDAY CELEBRATIONS

How much does YaHUaH like them?

The history of ***how birthdays came to be celebrated*** reveals everything we need to know about the custom.

Long ago, the average person never paid any attention whatsoever to the anniversary of their birth. The initial pattern that developed concerned the celebrating of the ***birthday of their deity***, once each year, at the winter solstice. This is the origin of Christmas, since the winter solstice was considered the "re-birth" or birthday of the solar deity. This alone marks the behavior as ***originating*** from the rebellion against YaHUaH, Who is the one and only Elohim of Heaven and Earth. Remember that YaHUaH commanded that we **not learn the ways** of the heathen (Dt. 12).

Later, people began to celebrate the annual birth of their king ***at the same time as their deity***, aligning their ruler with the same honors given to their deity. In their minds, their ruler became an anthropomorphic version of their deity. In the east, average people slowly began to celebrate their personal "birth day" once each year on what they believed to be "new year's day".

Eventually, people developed the custom of observing their personal birth day on the annual day they were actually born.

BIRTHDAY CAKE CUSTOM

Worldwide, baking ***cakes*** for the *"Queen of Heaven"* (Asherah) was entangled in birth day celebrations (Jer./YirmeYahu 7:18). This provokes YaHUaH's anger. By blowing-out candles and making a "secret wish", the celebrant performs IDOLATRY, because the "wish" is to their GENIE or JINN, a spell performed by Wiccans. The candles are part of the fire ritual; Pagans believed the solar presence to be fire. The rising smoke of the extinguished candles carried the "secret wish" into the skies. How do you think YaHUaH likes it when we teach our children to do these things, or propagate the custom of them? How about if we "think" of the "wish" being a prayer to YaHUaH? This is not going to be acceptable to YaHUaH, no matter how we wrap it in our minds. Worshipping YaHUaH in a Pagan format is the main problem we have today. We desperately need eye-salve to see better.
Fast forwarding to the present day, we know that witches esteem **Asherah** very highly. The most important day for any witch is the day of their birth. In Scripture, individuals recognizing birth days are Pagans, or those in rebellion. Look at the following verses describing the 7 sons and 3 daughters of Iyob, contrasted between the NIV and the KJV, then noting the literal meaning in the NAS version:
Job 1:4-5 (NIV): ***"His sons used to take turns holding feasts in their homes, and they would invite their three sisters to eat and drink with them. When a period of feasting had run its***

course, Job would send and have them purified. Early in the morning he would sacrifice a burnt offering for each of them, thinking, 'Perhaps my children have sinned and cursed (Elohim) in their hearts.' This was Job's regular custom."

Job 1:4 (KJV): ***"And his sons went and feasted in their houses, every one his day; and sent and called for their three sisters to eat and to drink with them."***

Job 1:4-5 (NAS): ***"And his sons used to go and hold a feast in the house of each one <u>on</u> his day, and they would send and invite their three sisters to eat and drink with them."***

It's hardly a mystery, and very simple for us to figure out what was going on here.
Also, you'll find that the only mention of birth-days being celebrated in all of Scripture involves men in rebellion against Yahuah:

Gen 40:20: ***"Now the third day was Pharaoh's birthday, and he gave a feast for all his officials."***

Mark 6:21: ***"On his birthday Herod gave a banquet for his high officials and military commanders and the leading men of Galilee."***

These texts are indications of practices seen in rebellious men, and I acknowledge that there is no direct Torah prohibition against a person observing their birthday. However, weighing the evidence together, any recognition of a person's birth day may offend Yahuah. If witches hold the day to be important (while Scripture is silent about the day of ones birth being important), and the historical development of birth day celebrations comes from Pagan origins, then we should have no participation whatsoever in them. We should not encourage it by sending cards or gifts. Many ask about this topic, since Scripture doesn't ***specifically*** condemn the observance of birthdays. But, Scripture doesn't ***specifically*** tell us not to observe "Sun day", Christmas, or Easter either. ***The fact that a behavior is Pagan in origin is our cue to not perform it.***

Deut 12:29-31: ***"But when you have driven them out and settled in their land, and after they have been destroyed before you, be careful not to be ensnared by inquiring about their elohim, saying, 'How do these nations serve their (elohim)? We will do the same.' You must not worship Yahuah your Elohim in their way, because in worshiping their elohim, they do all kinds of detestable things Yahuah hates."***
Deut 12:32 : ***"See that you do all I command you; do not add to it or take away from it."***

Our hearts are inclined to do what is right in our own eyes, especially when we're programmed by the popular culture around us. When we desire to know Yahuah's point-of-view, we see our error clearly.

THE RESTORATION

The statement I made on page 207 is regarding the "crying out" of the Natsarim on the "hills" (or mountains) of Ephraim, as we read of this in YirmeYahu 31. This is also directly related to Ps. 80, since this Psalm embodies the contents of our cry to Yahuah.

The final expulsion of the house of Yisrael (Ephraim) from Samaria by the Assyrians occurred in or around the year 722 BCE. Assyria had been hammering at them for the better part of 8 decades prior to this. Allow me to explain this in detail:
The prophecy given at Yehezqel 3 & 4 concerns the house of Yisrael, because Yehezqel is the ***watchman*** for the ***house of Yisrael*** (northern 10 tribes). In chapter 4, Yehezqel is told to lie on his left side for **390 days**, a day for a year, to bear the crookedness of the ***house of Yisrael***. This 390 years represents the time Yahuah gave them to ***repent*** - but they did not. Instead of remaining in captivity for 390 years, the **penalty** cited at Lev. 26 kicked in, **multiplying the captivity by a factor of 7, bringing it to 2730 years** (390 x 7 = 2730 years).

After 2730 years (722 BCE to 2008 CE), the lost tribes may begin a mass restoration to the Covenant of Yahuah, obeying it. The ***Restoration*** that we read about in the parable of the prodigal son (Luke 15) ***has begun***. These 2730 years may be the last opportunity for the lost tribes to return to the Covenant ***willingly***, and it will no doubt only be a remnant. There could be a "net" of time allotted, and after that the "door is closed", and a great tribulation (weeping & gnashing of teeth) will commence, closing on people like a trap. Some "trigger" will set into motion the times described at Mt. 24.

Ephraim is a term for the house of Yisrael, or descendants sons of Yosef. All 10 tribes may be referred to as Ephraim, because the ***dominant tribe*** is the name they are all known by (As Benyamin is included in the house of Yahudah). Ephraim was given the blessing of the **first-born**, so naturally the "older brother" (house of Yahudah) is jealous (as in the parable of the two brothers). Ephraim is returning to the Covenant now, and the time of restoration has begun. We are purging our idolatry, sun-pillars (steeples), idols (crosses, statues), and observing Yahuah's Sabbaths, the sign of the eternal Covenant.

Prov 12:15 : **"The way of a fool seems right to him, but a wise man listens to advice."**

Prov 14:12 : **"There is a way that seems right to a man, but in the end it leads to death."**

Being like sheep, easily led astray, those who seek to control us find it is very easy. Yahusha had a name for these "leaders", and He said He hates them. You'll recognize them when you see them:

NICOLAITANES, AND STRONGHOLDS

(also seen as "Nicolaitans" and "Nikolaites")

LORDING OVER (CONQUERING) ***THE PEOPLE*** with mind control (strongholds)

Definition from reference.com (encyclopedia):
"The meaning of the name, "victors over the people" or "rulers over the world" suggests to some of these authors that the Nicolaitanes were among those who maintained that there must be a religious hierarchy to control the spiritual development of the common people; it is believed they were trying to set themselves up as priests in a two-class system – one that would give them absolute control over the laity (common people), who would be completely dependent upon them for all spiritual knowledge, guidance, and access to (Yahuah)."
-- (Parenthetical term is my correction; author used "God" in sentence)

PRIME NICOLAITAN DOCTRINE: ***"Apostolic Succession"***

The Truth is, Yahuah has no headquarters on Earth.
There is no succession, kingdom, or government that can be "seen"; no "line" of apostolic authority.
Yahusha's ***Spirit*** guides us into all Truth, not an organization or denomination.
Those who have received His Spirit are now ***Israelites***, and are to teach the nations Torah:
Mat 28:19,20: ***"'Therefore, go and make taught ones of all the nations, immersing them in the Name of the Father and of the Son and of the Set-apart Spirit, teaching them to guard all that I have commanded you. And see, I am with you always, until the end of the age.' Amĕn."***

The *"two-class system"*, priests over people, is seen by many to be the reason for the destruction of the original assemblies of the original ***Natsarim***. Nicolaitanes seek to be recognized or distinguished from the "ordinary" folk, and often dress the part. Appearances are most important to them, and their behavior is an act to be seen by men. Hypocrisy and eye-service is condemned by Yahusha, as we certainly already realize. Nicolaitanes are playing a role, and expect that everyone should acknowledge their authority and status. They seek after titles and honors, and want their ideas obeyed without question.

These verses escape their attention:
Mat 23:8 ***"But you, do not be called 'Rabbi,' for One is your Teacher, the Messiah, and you are all brothers."***
Luk 17:20,21 ***"And having been asked by the Pharisees when the reign of Elohim would come, He answered them and said, "The reign of Elohim does not come with intent watching, nor shall they say, 'Look here!' or 'Look there!' For look, the reign of Elohim is in your midst!"***

Mt. 12:25: ***"And Yahusha knew their thoughts, and said to them, "Every reign divided against itself is laid waste, and every city or house divided against itself shall not stand."***

At Mt. 18:1: The talmidim/students pondered the question of who the greatest among them was.
At Mt. 20:21: The mother of the sons of Zabdai requested that they be seated on His right and left in the reign. The talmidim of Yahusha wanted to know which of them would be "in charge" after He departed.

At Rom. 16:17, we are told to keep our eye on those who cause divisions.

NICOLAITANES USE MENTAL STRONGHOLDS to control people's beliefs and thoughts.
Mental strongholds can be broken by simply *knowing they are there*.
The foremost "belief" they promote is that they (Nicolaitanes) are the enlightened, and boast that they

know Yahuah. *Everyone else must do as they say.* We have knowledge of Torah to overthrow them: 2Co 10:4-6: ***"For the weapons we fight with are not fleshly but mighty in Elohim for overthrowing strongholds, overthrowing reasonings and every high matter that exalts itself against the knowledge of Elohim, taking captive every thought to make it obedient to the Messiah, and being ready to punish all disobedience, when your obedience is complete."***
Luke 14 teaches us to take the "last place". Two key words used at 2Cor 10:4-6:

STRONGHOLDS: G3794 **OCHUROMA:** *argument, concept, thought;*
literally: a castle, stronghold, fortress
figuratively: anything on which one relies, such as the arguments and reasonings by which a disputant endeavors to fortify his opinion and defend it against his opponent. A mindset or viewpoint is a "stronghold", and may be true or false. If false, it needs to be overthrown with TRUTH.

IMAGINATIONS: (Greek) G3053 **LOGISMOS***: reasoning, imagination, computation*

Mat 23:12 ***"And whoever exalts himself shall be humbled, and whoever humbles himself shall be exalted."***
When someone hears you tell them the Truth, and their eyes glaze-over because their "stronghold" has them firmly bound, they might as well say,
"My mind is made up; **don't confuse me with the facts."** - unknown author

Examples of such ***factions*** *having long-standing doctrinal positions (old wine) would be:*

Rabbinical Judaism *(Pharisees, from Talmudic teachings of Rabbi Akiba);* ***Mormons*** *(Teachings of Joseph Smith, book of Mormon);* ***Catholics*** *(Constantine/Councils, "sacraments", rituals);* ***Islam,*** **SIKH** *(teachings of Muhammad's 5 pillars combined with Hinduism):*
SHAHADAH – no 'god' but Allah, and Muhammad is prophet
SALAH – pray at 5 fixed times daily
ZAKAH – alms giving
SAWM – fasting; ritual, repentant, ascetic
HAJJ – is a pilgrimage that occurs during the Islamic moon of Dhu al-Hijjah in the city of Mecca

Hindu, Buddhist *(reincarnation, Karma)*

Nicolaitanes are savage wolves:
Acts 20: ***"Therefore take heed to yourselves and to all the flock, among which the Set-apart Spirit has made you overseers, to shepherd the assembly of Elohim which He has purchased with His own blood.***
For I know this, that after my departure savage wolves shall come in among you, not sparing the flock. Also from among yourselves men shall arise, speaking distorted teachings, to draw away the taught ones after themselves."

Nicolaitanes are very concerned about control, and once they have power they seek to keep it.

Mar 9:33-35: ***"And they came to Kephar Nahum, and having come in the house He asked them,***

SUPREME RABBINICAL JUDAISM LEADER:
14 MILLION FOLLOWERS
Rabbi Yona Metzger, Chief Rabbi of Israel
Primary teachings: Talmud of Akiba + Torah, Prophets, Writings (TaNaKh)
"Rabbinical" Judaism is the unbroken line to the Pharisees of 2000 years ago, embracing the "Oral Law", or Talmud, first written down by "Rabbi" Akiba, who chose "Bar Kochba" as the "Jewish Messiah", and rebelled against Rome. Among their doctrines, a person must be under a "rabbi" for salvation. Coincidentally, all Pharisees held the title "rabbi", a word meaning "master" or literally "my teacher" (a word not found in the TaNaKh).

SUPREME MUSLIM: OVER 1 BILLION FOLLOWERS (highly diverse)
ISLAMIC IMAMS control the teachings of many sects, both "SHI'ITE" and "SUNNI". Sunni and Shia sects are rivals, in perpetual bloody conflict.
One Imam, Abdul Alim Musa, states that the United States will be "the Islamic State of North America" by 2050. Islam is the fastest-growing religion in the world, including the United States, France, and England.

YOU CAN SEE IT ON THE FACES OF THESE MEN; THEY'RE CLUELESS.

SUPREME SIKH LEADER: 23 MILLION FOLLOWERS ☞

Giani Joginder Singh Vedanti, India
No hair cutting (ever) – blend of ***Hinduism*** *and* ***Islam****.*
The average follower of this religion has no idea what they believe in, they only follow a strict set of customs handed-down as traditions they learn from their parents.

SUPREME LUTHERAN LEADER:

☜ *Mark S. Hanson* **65 MILLION FOLLOWERS**

3 "sacraments", trinity, crosses, strict liturgical process, hierarchical chain of command

SUPREME BUDDHIST: 376 MILLION FOLLOWERS ☞

Tenzin Gyatoso, 14th Dalai Lama of Tibet
Karma, reincarnation, Samsara, Nirvana, no deities, only "life force".
Objective: achieve nothingness, oblivion.
(Humanists love this man).

WHICH PRAYER BEADS CAME FIRST?

Pictured at right: ***Buddhist, Islamic, and Catholic*** Any thinking person realizes these things didn't just spring up spontaneously within these three religions. We know Yahusha didn't use "beads" when He taught us how to pray, and yet millions of people use them. Why? Their teachers are guiding them to do so. This is yet another Nicolaitane stronghold of false teaching.

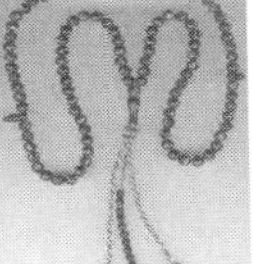

BUDDHIST (LEFT), **ISLAMIC** (CENTER), **& CATHOLIC "PRAYER BEADS"**

The ultimate goal of any Nicolaitane is to control "the laity", keeping them informed just enough to be frightened, and under their teachings (which of course are the only "true way" on Earth to get to the "GOD"). They often state or imply that they are the only ones who have it correct, and every other way is doomed. The foremost religions/sects are on display before you right here. What if none of them are even close? Their motivation is clear to all once they are exposed and the blinders fall from the eyes of those they are exploiting:

"'Woe to you, blind guides, who say, 'Whoever swears by the Dwelling Place, it does not matter, but whoever swears by the gold of the Dwelling Place, is bound by oath.'" Mat 23:16

A "**STARGATE**" IS OF NO USE.
— OR AN **E-METER** —
COUNTING OUR PRAYERS ON BEADS IS INSULTING TO HIM, IF ONLY BECAUSE IT'S PAGAN.

"What was it you disputed among yourselves on the way?" And they were silent, for on the way they had disputed with one another who was the greatest. And sitting down, He called the twelve and said to them, "If anyone wishes to be first, he shall be last of all and servant of all." To attempt to be "first" or "foremost" means we attempt to usurp the position of Yahusha.

Jeremiah / YirmeYahu 9:24: ***"'but let him who boasts boast of this; that he understands and knows Me, that I am Yahuah, doing kindness, right-ruling, and righteousness in the earth. For in these I delight,' declares Yahuah."***

STRONGHOLDS OF THOUGHT - *TEACHERS BOASTING OF THEIR WISDOM:*
Rabbis, Imams, Popes, Gurus, Lamas, Shamans, spiritual auditors, and straw men with titles:

LOS LUNAS COVENANT STONE:

an ancient artifact of Yisrael, *found in North America near Rio Grande*

The photograph at the bottom of this page shows the **Ten Commandments** written in the primary (palaeo) Hebrew script written on a large stone found in the 1800's at Los Lunas, New Mexico, near the Rio Grande. This stone carving could be 3000 years old, and it contains the Name "Yahuah". It was written in obedience to Dt. 6, as we are ***write them*** on our doorposts and on our ***gates*** — this stone was at the entrance to an ancient colony or settlement of Israelites that had navigated up the Rio Grande.

The style of the letter "yod" used on the stone indicates that the Israelites of the northern 10 tribes (Samaritans) were in North America.
It could have been inscribed on this stone as early as the ninth century BCE, during the reign of King Shlomo (Solomon), or as late as 146 BCE when the Carthaginians (Israelites) were conquered by Rome.

Many "diasporas" occurred, but we now know that Israel was mostly a ***sea empire***, and they were called "Phoenicians" *by the Greeks*.
Yes, the "Phoenicians" were *Israelites!*
They didn't call ***themselves*** "Phoenicians", Herodotus (5th century BCE) called them that.

The Israelites traveled the oceans of the world as they mined tin, copper, gold, and iron. Did you know that the distance from the western coast of Africa to South America is LESS than the length of the Mediterranean Sea?

Columbus didn't discover the Americas; Israelites were already living here, and many became what are now referred to as:
"Native Americans".

SUPREME HINDU: 900 MILLION FOLLOWERS

☜ *"Amma" Sri Mata Amritanandamayi in Amritapuri, India*
Practices sorcery for healing and divination, hundreds of deities.

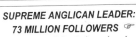

SUPREME ANGLICAN LEADER:
73 MILLION FOLLOWERS ☞

Rowan Williams, Archbishop of Canterbury, London
Same as Roman Catholic, only deny authority of the pope of Rome.
Approximately 5 million are seeking reuniting under authority of Pope of Rome. Sacramental "grace" is principal means of salvation.

☜ ***SUPREME EASTERN ORTHODOX: 240 MILLION FOLLOWERS***

His Holiness Aleksi II, Patriarch of Moscow
Same program of salvation as Rome (sacraments), and use "icons" (statues).

ROMAN CATHOLIC MAGISTERIUM: ☞
1 BILLION FOLLOWERS

His Holiness Pope Benedict XVI
Salvation through grace dispensed by 7 sacraments through appointed/ordained "priesthood".
They eliminated the 2nd Commandment, and made the 10th one into two Commandments.

NEW CATHOLIC CONVERT: ☞

Ex-prime minister of UK, Tony Blair, converts from Anglican Church to Roman Catholic, December 2007:

ROSARY (CHAPLET) PRAYER BEADS were adopted in 1090 CE (from Paganism), about the same time **"indulgences"** and **"celibacy"** were announced.

SCIENTOLOGY: 22 MILLION FOLLOWERS *L. Ron Hubbard - founded church 1954*
Hubbard discovered he could make more money in religion than in writing science fiction, so he designed a new set of beliefs: Dianetics; solves "engrams" (traumas) stored in soul (theta). Objective: To erase the engrams to a state of "clear" through the help of spiritual auditors and an electronic gizmo (E-meter, photo below).

A primitive type of "lie detector", the **E-meter** ☞

Part of the "teachings" include this historical gem:
"75 million years ago, there was an alien galactic ruler named Xenu who was in charge of 76 planets in our sector of the galaxy, including planet Earth." They teach that our problems are caused by the *spirits of space aliens inhabiting our bodies.* Tom Cruise converted to this belief in 1990, claiming that he was cured of his dyslexia by the teachings, and renounced his devout Catholic beliefs because of this sign / wonder (see Mt. 12:39). Like Tony Blair, Tom escaped from one "stronghold" only to be captured by another, because he did not have the Word of Yahuah sown in his heart by Yahusha. The billions and billions of people trapped in the various strongholds of Nicolaitanes can escape if they are exposed to the Truth. Yahusha warned us to beware of false teachers. What can you do to help? EXPOSE THEM TO TRUTH.

TOM CRUISE MAPOTHER, SCIENTOLOGIST

Detailed Transliteration study on the Name of the Messiah
yod-hay-uau-shin-ayin (The Name above all names)
THE MESSIAH'S NAME IS FOUND 219 TIMES IN THE TANAK.
The two Hebrew ***spellings*** used for the son of Nun (a leader of the tribe Ephraim) that we find in the concordance are numbered:

#1954: HAY-UAU-SHIN-AYIN, rendered in the KJV as "HOSHEA" (Dt. 32:44), and "OSHEA" (Num 13:16).
#3091: YOD-HAY-UAU-SHIN-AYIN, this spelling is found 216 times, rendered in the KJV as "JOSHUA".
In another two instances in all of Scripture it is spelled YOD-HAY-UAU-SHIN-UAU-AYIN, or "YAHUSHUA".

An interesting verse pertaining to the "name change" of this son of Nun is at Num 13:16:

"These[428] *are* the names[8034] of the men[376] which[834] Moses[4872] sent[7971] to spy out[8446 (853)] the land.[776] And Moses[4872] called[7121] Oshea[1954] the son[1121] of Nun[5126] Joshua.[3091]"

In the above verse you can see the concordance numbers embedded in the KJV English. The Hebrew root "yaSHA" means to deliver, and is the root of the name of the son of Nun, HUSHA (#1954). In two places, we see the letter UAU between the SHIN-AYIN at the end of the name. The only change Mosheh gave to his name was the addition of the letter YOD, causing the name HUSHA to become *YAHUSHA*, meaning *"YAH is our Deliverer".* The Mashiach and the son of Nun have identical spellings, #3091 above, as is evidenced by the fact that their spellings use the same Greek letters ***IESOUS*** (word #2424). Reference to the man called "JOSHUA" is found in only two places in the entire Brith Chadasha, ***Acts 7:45, and Hebrews 4:8:***

Act 7:45 **"Which[3739] also[2532] our[2257] fathers[3962] that came after[1237] brought in[1521] with[3326] Joshua[2424] into[1722] the[3588] possession[2697] of the[3588] Gentiles,[1484]. . ."**

Heb 4:8 **"For[1063] if[1487] Joshua[2424] had given them rest,[2664, 846] then would he not[3756 (302)] afterward[3326, 5023] have spoken[2980] of[4012] another[243] day.[2250]**

Many *"transliterations"* of Messiah's Name are used, among the most popular of them are YAHSHUA, Y'SHUA, YESHUA, YEHOSHUA, YAHUSHUA, and YAHUSHA. The fact is, His Name is identical to the Hebrew spelling of the man called "JOSHUA", whose name was originally spelled as above, only without the letter "YOD" at the beginning; Mosheh added the YOD to his name, which was originally HUSHA **(hay-uau-shin-ayin)**. Acts 7 and

Hebrews 4 use the same Greek letters for this man and our Mashiach.

The letter "W" (double-U) did not exist on Earth until the 13th century, so it is impossible for it to be used honestly in the Name *YAHUAH:* YOD-HAY-UAU-HAY (no letter W). In the Name *YAHUSHUA* -- SHUA, or "SHA" is the ROOT 'yaSHA", meaning *to deliver*. "SHUA" and "SHA" mean the same thing, to deliver. YAHUSHA: YOD-HAY-UAU-SHIN-AYIN (YAHUSHUA would be spelled YOD-HAY-UAU-SHIN-UAU-AYIN).
"YAHUSHA" and "YAHUSHUA" ***both*** mean "YAH – is our – Deliverer". (Alternately, "I AM – your – Deliverer").

There is a man named "Shua" in Scripture; 1 Chr 2:3, Shua, word #7770, and the letters are SHIN-UAU-AYIN. Another example is Malkiyshua (mal-kee-shu-ah); 1 Sa 31:2 is word #4444, and the ending of this man's name is also spelled SHIN-UAU-AYIN.
In 216 places out of 219, there is no letter UAU used between the SHIN-AYIN in the name for the successor of Moshe, but there is a UAU following the letter HAY, so "YAHUSHA" is the preferred way of rendering the Name in English letters. The letter UAU has been the most mysterious for many people for a very long time, and it renders the meaning of "our" or "your" to the word, in a plural sense. A YOD at the end of a word means "my", as in the word for "my teacher" (usually seen written "RABBI", because the Greek alphabet has no letter "Y").
Pronounce the *letter* UAU like this: *"OOO'-ah"*. This letter is commonly known as WAW, the 6th letter of the Hebrew "alef-beth".

Our Messiah's Name in Hebrew: יהושע

יהו The first part is not in question: *YAHU*

שע This requires our close attention; is the pronunciation - SHUA? Or is it simply *SHA?* BOTH DERIVE FROM "**YASHA**":
The root *yaSHA* means *"to deliver"* - **ישע**
Let's check out the correct Hebrew names of two prophets Isaiah and Elisha: (NOTE THE ROOT "**YASHA**"):

ישעיהו **YESHAYAHU** Strong's #3470 – *"Yah has delivered."*

ישע **YESHA** Strong's #3468 – *"Salvation, deliverance."*

שע Remove the י and we have – **SHA**

אלישע **ELIYSHA** Strong's #477 - *"El of deliverance."*

Therefore from the Hebrew we have יהושע = YAHUSHA
We have been ending His Name with **SHUA.**
How is this written in Hebrew and does it have a meaning?

שוע **SHUWA** Strong's #7768: *"Cry for help."*
Strong's #7769: *"Cry, riches."*

אלישוע **ELIYSHUA** Strong's no 474: *"El of riches."*

To get to the pronunciation *YAHUSHUA* we would have to insert a ו between the ע and the ש and spell His Name in Hebrew יהושוע with two ו .

"Yahushua" is seen twice out of 219 times in the TaNaK, so both "Yahushua" and "Yahusha" are acceptable transliterations.

YahuSHUA and YahuSHA - SHUA and SHA both contain the Hebrew root, yaSHA, meaning deliverance (salvation).

Both spellings, Yahushua and Yahusha, are endorsed by the inspired texts. Concerning the specific number of uses of the spelling Yahushua YOD-HAY-UAU-SHIN-UAU-AYIN (using 2 letter UAU's), There are exactly two instances in the TaNaK, referring to the successor of Mosheh (Joshua in the KJV). The two uses of this 6-lettered spelling are in fact found at Deut. 3:21 and Judg. 2:7. Even in these books, both variations in spelling are found. In these two books alone, this name was used with only *one* "UAU" in the following ratios:

Deuteronomy / Debarim: 7 to 1: seven times, the spelling was YOD-HAY-UAU-SHIN-AYIN (Yahusha), and 1 time YOD-HAY-UAU-SHIN-UAU-AYIN (Yahushua).

Judges: 5 to 1; five times, the spelling was the 5-letterYOD-HAY-UAU-SHIN-AYIN (Yahusha), and 1 time YOD-HAY-UAU-SHIN-UAU-AYIN (Yahushua).

Overall ratio: 216 to 3 (216 times, the spelling in the TaNaK was YOD-HAY-UAU-SHIN-AYIN, and twice it was YOD-HAY-UAU-SHIN-UAU-AYIN).

In one place, Neh. 8:17, the name is spelled YOD-SHIN-UAU-AYIN, *Y'shua*.

216 times found: Yahusha
2 times found: Yahushua
1 time found: Y'shua (Neh. 8:17)

Since these are used in Scripture, ***then all are acceptable***. All are equally correct, and have the same meaning; however one of the three forms is the more widely used in the inspired texts, and I am only pointing out to everyone that they should take a look at the facts. I feel that the more accurate would be the 5-lettered form used 216 times, but I have to accept that the spelling seen only twice is fine also. Even the spelling used once should be accepted as a shortened form.

A huge mistake to make is to think that the "vowel-pointing" of the 10th century CE Masoretes is without flaw. Anyone can make a blunder. We also know they had agendas, and one is with the Name Yahuah. Moreover, they were about ***2300 years*** removed in time from Mosheh, and many things they had to deal with were "best-guesses". We could not possibly know how William Shakepeare would pronounce certain words 400 years ago.

One spelling to examine closely is at ZecharYah 3. The Hebrew word #3091 used in these texts is **Yahusha**

(the KJV concordance numbers are imbedded to help with your further study):

Zec 3:1 **"And he showed**[7200] **me** [(853)] **Joshua**[3091] **the high**[1419] **priest**[3548] **standing**[5975] **before**[6440] **the angel**[4397] **of the LORD,**[3068] **and Satan**[7854] **standing**[5975] **at**[5921] **his right hand**[3225] **to resist**[7853] **him."**

(#3068 above should be rendered "**Yahuah**", not LORD)

Translators have obviously modified the texts with words from a wide variety of other languages between the Hebrew and English, such as the term "angel" seen above (which is not English, but Greek). The rendering "Joshua" is not very close to the better transliteration "Yahusha" either. But they completely obliterated the Name "Yahuah" when they substituted the letters LORD. This is where personal research into the Truth of the Name begins. If they will lie about the Name of the One we serve, then they will lie about anything. For certain, we must be "over-comers" to be found doing what our Mashiach expects of us until He comes. And there is much to overcome.

The translations cause misunderstandings for us, and here is another example:
Below we see how two translations render Mt. 26:17. The Greek text has a word which both versions overlook (G4413, PROTOS, which literally means "before" or "prior to"). "**Proto**" implies something that comes before, yet the translators overlooked the fact that when a person actually reads what they wrote, it makes no logical sense. They also added the words "on" and "day" to the KJV, enhancing the error. It isn't possible for the disciples to come to Yahusha on the first day of Matsah and ask Him ***"where do you wish us to prepare for You to eat the Passover?"*** — Passover would be over already:

Mat 26:17 ***"And on the first day of Unleavened Bread the taught ones came to (Yahusha) saying to Him, 'Where do You wish us to prepare for You to eat the Passover?'"***
(The Scriptures from ISR)

Mat 26:17 ***"Now[1161] the[3588] first[4413] day of the[3588] feast of unleavened bread[106] the[3588] disciples[3101] came[4334] to Jesus,[2424] saying[3004] unto him,[846] Where[4226] wilt[2309] thou that we prepare[2090] for thee[4671] to eat[5315] the[3588] passover?[3957]*** (KJV)

Recommendation for this verse:

"And before the feast of Matsah, the taught ones came to Yahusha saying to Him, 'Where do You wish us to prepare for You to eat the Passover?'"

A MESSAGE ADDRESSED TO ALL THE

SCATTERED TRIBES OF ISRAEL

FOR THEIR UNDERSTANDING IN THE LAST DAYS

Gen 49:1,2: ***"And Ya'aqob called his sons and said, 'Gather together, so that I declare to you what is to befall you in the last days: Gather together and hear, you sons of Ya'aqob, and listen to Yisrael your father.'"***

Before you can fully receive this information, a certain ***blindness*** will have to be lifted from your mind. The blindness that I'm referring to is the fact that the ***tribes*** (descendants) of Israel ***don't know who they are***, because they are "lost". Also, the word "Israel" must never refer to the land, or a government. It is a nation of ***people*** (the families/clans/tribes) who live in a Covenant with Yahuah. The "lost" tribes are their descendants living among the Gentiles, scattered upon the Earth. A remnant will awaken and understand here in the last days:

Rom 11:25-27: ***"For I do not wish you to be ignorant of this secret, brothers, lest you should be wise in your own estimation, that hardening in part has come over Yisrael, until the completeness of the Gentiles has come in. And so all Yisrael shall be saved, as it has been written, 'The Deliverer shall come out of Tsiyon, and He shall turn away wickedness from Ya'aqob, and this is My Covenant with them, when I take away their sins.'"***

The ***tribes*** of Israel are ***scattered*** across the face of the Earth, and are living as Gentiles, ***believing they are Gentiles.*** This is a *stronghold,* or false idea.

Any stronghold* is a false <u>belief</u> or <u>notion</u>. Strongholds can be broken by being *exposed by the* ***Truth***, *which sets us free. Once exposed by the Truth, the lies have no more power over us. The mind-control stops, and we can "see".*

2Co 10:4-6: "For the weapons we fight with are not fleshly but mighty in Elohim for overthrowing strongholds, overthrowing reasonings and every high matter that exalts itself against the knowledge of Elohim, taking captive every thought to make it obedient to the Messiah, and being ready to punish all disobedience, when your obedience is complete."

People are not conscious of the fact that they are "imprisoned" in many layers of contrived thoughts that are designed to keep them controlled, and in sin. They are mentally imprisoned by what they have ***accepted*** to be truth. As long as they continue to believe the lies to be truth, the fortresses that imprison them will hold them securely. Messiah Yahusha sets us free by guiding us into the Truth.

STRONGHOLD TEACHERS: NICOLAITANES Rabbis, Imams, Popes, Gurus, Lamas, Shamans, and men with titles

***Stronghold** is translated from the Greek word:
G3794 OCHUROMA:
figurative fortification: argument, concept, thought, reasoning, opinion, mindset, viewpoint.

▶ ***STRONGHOLD EXAMPLE: The word "ISRAEL" refers to only "Jews"***

*Not true. The word "Jew" is less than 500 years old, and refers to any descendant of one tribe/family, YAHUDAH. The first time the word "Yahudim" (Jews) is used in Scripture involved a **war** between the **house of Israel** and the **house of Yahudah*** (2Ki. 16:6). *To mislead us, the enemy of our beings (the dragon, ha shatan) has set before the nations his prophet (an office of authority), which has been established to oppose the "saints" (the elect, or the children of Israel - all 12 tribes). The term "Israel" has been misapplied to "Christians", a Gentile religious movement that developed without the Torah, but embraced the Messiah.*

The False Prophet of the Supreme Roman Catholic Magisterium:

Through *centuries* of *false teaching,* the nations have been lulled into thinking the original Covenant with Israel has ended, and that Yahuah has given up on the original 12 tribes. This ***"replacement theology"*** holds people in the belief that "Christianity" (specifically Catholicism's brand) has now become "Israel", that the "Jews" are synonymous with the old Israel, and that the *new* Israel (Christians) do not have to live according to the "Old Covenant" (Torah), the Ten Commandments. They say that Yahusha the Messiah has set them "free" from the "law". In these things, they misunderstand, and mislead ***the millions of living descendants of the tribes of Israel.*** The Messiah spoke of the coming deceptions:

This "mother church" is the "woman" who rides the beast REV. 17, 18, and thinks to change TIMES and TORAH - Daniel 7:25

This system, or beast, deceives the nations with a false method of salvation through contrived "sacraments" which they teach imparts "grace" to the common people through their "priesthood" hierarchy. The Eternal Covenant is said to be annulled or superseded, and they "celebrate" the death of Yahusha ha'Mashiach each time one of their deceived priestcraft officiates at a "mass".

RESEARCH THE TERM "NICOLAITANES" - THEY ARE *CONTROL FREAKS*

Mar 13:22: ***"For false messiahs and false prophets shall rise and show signs and wonders to lead astray, if possible, even the chosen ones."***

The *"elect"* or *"chosen ones"* are the descendants of the tribes of the man Ya'aqob, re-named "Israel", which means "ruler with El". Those chosen to inherit the Covenant were eventually to become an ***uncountable number***, and to become a ***"company of nations"*** (Gen. 35:11, 48:16), even to the ***"ends of the Earth***" (Dt. 33:17, Ps. 98:3, Is. 41:9, 43:6, 49:6). The Covenant stands forever.

Yahuah's Covenant with Israel will never end (Jer. 31:36,37). He took Israel to be His wife at Sinai. He clearly said that Israel would live in the land, *but only on the condition that she kept His Covenant.* While not in fellowship with Yahuah through that Covenant, Israel would be ***scattered***, *until they turned back to it <u>while</u> <u>among</u> the <u>nations</u> in the **latter days**.* This is confirmed by all the prophets.

Yahuah says we will obey in the latter days, *while among the Gentiles.* At Dt. 4, He reminds us of His Covenant once again (and repeats the Covenant at Dt. 5); and He tells us that we will again remember the Words of Torah* in the last

*TORAH: HEBREW FOR "INSTRUCTION", OFTEN USED TO REFER SPECIFICALLY TO THE COVENANT, OR BRITH. WE OBEY TORAH SINCE IT "DEFINES" SIN FOR US (SEE 1 JOHN 3:4). IF WE DO NOT OBEY TORAH, WE ARE BREAKERS OF THE COVENANT. WITHOUT TORAH, IT WOULD BE IMPOSSIBLE TO KNOW WHAT A SIN IS. IT IS OUR ALARM SYSTEM, SO WE MUST BE GUIDED BY IT.

days:

Deu 4:30: ***"In your distress, when all these words shall come upon you in the latter days, then you shall return to Yahuah your Elohim and shall obey His voice."***

Deu 30:1-20: ***"And it shall be, when all these Words come upon you, the blessing and the curse which I have set before you, and you shall bring them back to your heart among all the Gentiles where Yahuah your Elohim has driven you, and shall turn back to Yahuah your Elohim and obey His voice, according to all that I command you today, with all your heart and with all your being, you and your children, then Yahuah your Elohim shall turn back your captivity, and shall have compassion on you, and He shall turn back and gather you from all the peoples where Yahuah your Elohim has scattered you.***
If any of you are driven out to the farthest parts under the heavens, from there Yahuah your Elohim does gather you, and from there He does take you. For Yahuah turns back to rejoice over you for good as He rejoiced over your fathers, if you obey the Voice of Yahuah your Elohim, to guard His commands and His laws which are written in this Book of the Torah, if you turn back to Yahuah your Elohim with all your heart and with all your being. For this command which I am commanding you today, it is not too hard for you, nor is it far off. It is not in the heavens, to say,
'Who shall ascend into the heavens for us, and bring it to us, and cause us to hear it, so that we do it?' Nor is it beyond the sea, to say, 'Who shall go over the sea for us, and bring it to us, and cause us to hear it, so that we do it?' For the Word is very near you, in your mouth and in your heart – to do it. . . . (please read full context) ***. . .***
I have called the heavens and the Earth as witnesses today against you: I have set before you life and death, the blessing and the curse. Therefore you shall choose life, so that you live, both you and your seed,
to love Yahuah your Elohim, to obey His voice, and to cling to Him – for He is your life and the length of your days – to dwell in the land which Yahuah swore to your fathers, to Abrahim, to Yitsḥaq, and to Ya'aqob, to give them."

STOP: Read all the text at Jeremiah (YirmeYahu) chapter 31, taking note of what you have learned so far here. A bright light will dawn on you. Yahusha will return when the "fullness of the Gentiles" is *restored to the Covenant, since the Gentiles, as a whole, are the lost, scattered tribes, the descendants of Israel.* We must not attempt to *re-gather ourselves to the land before the proper time*, since our being *scattered* is the consequence of our not living according to the Covenant. Yahusha is the Mediator of the Cove-

Reminders:
NATSARIM: The original term for the followers of Yahusha of Natsarith, Acts 24:5
YAHUSHA is Hebrew for *"Yah is our deliverer", spelled yod-hay-uau-shin-ayin;*
The false name, "he-soos" means "the horse" in Hebrew.

nant, and He circumcises our hearts with a love for Torah. He takes away our hatred of the Covenant, as well as our sins against it. He is working through His ambassadors today, speaking to the remnant (first-fruits) He is calling back to the Covenant. The ***restoration*** is now underway. The ***re-gathering*** will occur at the ***end*** of the Great Tribulation, *when He returns to reign forever on the Earth.* ***He*** will then restore Israel into "one stick", and the "house of Israel" will be united under Him as ***one people*** (Ez. 37). For now, we are to be a light to the Gentiles, to awaken them to their idolatry and profanation of the Covenant, but also to their heritage: ***Yahuah and His Covenant.*** The "prodigal son" parable is about the lost tribes of Israel who left the Father's "household", His Torah/Covenant.

Here is the retelling of the Covenant for the tribes, given at Dt. 5:6-21:

(1): ***'I am Yahuah your Elohim who brought you out of the land of Mitsrayim, out of the house of bondage. You have no other mighty ones against My face.*** (2): ***You do not make for yourself a carved image, any likeness of which is in the heavens above, or which is in the earth beneath, or which is in the waters under the earth, you do not bow down to them nor serve them. For I, Yahuah your Elohim, am a jealous El, visiting the crookedness of the fathers upon the children to the third and fourth generations of those who hate Me, but showing kindness to thousands, to those who love Me and guard My commands.*** (3): ***You do not cast the Name of Yahuah your Elohim to ruin, for Yahuah does not leave him unpunished who casts His Name to ruin.*** (4): ***Guard the Sabbath day, to set it apart, as Yahuah your Elohim commanded you. Six days you labor, and shall do all your work, but the seventh day is a Sabbath of Yahuah your Elohim. You do not do any work – you, nor your son, nor your daughter, nor your male servant, nor your female servant, nor your ox, nor your donkey, nor any of your cattle, nor your stranger who is within your gates, so that your male servant and your female servant rest as you do. And you shall remember that you were a slave in the land of Mitsrayim, and that Yahuah your Elohim brought you out from there by a strong hand and by an outstretched arm. Therefore Yahuah your Elohim commanded you to observe the Sabbath day.*** (5): ***Respect your father and your mother, as Yahuah your Elohim has commanded you, so that your days are prolonged, and so that it is well with you on the soil which Yahuah your Elohim is giving you.*** (6): ***You do not murder.*** (7): ***You do not break wedlock.*** (8): ***You do not steal.*** (9): ***You do not bear false witness against your neighbor.*** (10): ***You do not covet your neighbor's wife, nor do you desire your neighbor's house, his field, nor his male servant, nor his female servant, his ox, nor his donkey, or whatever belongs to your neighbor."*** Yahuah has hidden the lost tribes of Israel among the Gentiles:

> Isa 49:2 ***"And He made my mouth like a sharp sword, in the shadow of His hand He hid me, and made me a polished shaft. In His quiver He hid me."*** Yahuah has ***multiplied*** Israel among the Gentiles for the last days.

STOP: Read all of (Isaiah) YeshaYahu 49. (Ezekiel) Yehezqel is all about the ***scattering*** and ***re-gathering Plan*** which Yahuah has for His people, to whom the Gentiles must "engraft" through the ***Covenants*** (Eph. 2:8-13, Romans 11). If you are alive, you are most likely a "lost" (cut-off) ***descendant*** of the tribes of Israel. When you repent and take up the Covenant again, through immersion into the Name of the Mashiach Yahusha of Natsarith, you become an Israelite, and a member of the ***Natsarim.*** The renewal of the Covenant is described at Heb. 8.

STOP: Now read all of Eph. 3, & Jer. 3 - and you will be enabled to know the ***secret of the ages.*** It was veiled to you until this time, but the veil is being lifted. Yahusha* was sent to **seek** and **save** that which was **lost**. If you accept His Covenant, He has done that for you, by writing His Covenant upon your heart.

TRIBES GATHERED AT THE RETURN OF YAHUSHA:
DAN, ASHER, NAPHTALI, MENASHAH,
EPHRAIM, REUBEN, YAHUDAH, LUI, BENYAMIN, SIMEON, ISSACHAR, ZEBULON, GAD (EZ. 48)

THOSE ISRAELITES IN THE LAND PRIOR TO THE REGATHERING ARE TO FLEE TO THE MOUNTAINS (NATIONS).
THE TRIBES OF ISRAEL WERE SCATTERED DUE TO THEIR UNFAITHFULNESS, BUT THE FAITHFULNESS OF YAHUAH TO HIS COVENANT IS UNWAVERING. HE PROMISED THAT THEY WOULD BE SCATTERED, AND IN THE LATTER DAYS OBEY HIS COVENANT WHILE STILL IN THEIR CAPTIVITY AMONG THE NATIONS. WHEN THE "FULLNESS OF THE GENTILES COMES IN" (TO THE COVENANT), YAHUSHA WILL RETURN AND REGATHER THEM FROM THE ENDS OF THE EARTH. THEY MUST NOT REGATHER THEMSELVES TO THE LAND PRIOR TO HIS RETURN, OTHERWISE THEY WILL BECOME PART OF THE GREAT "FEAST" OF YAHUAH FED TO THE BIRDS AND BEASTS AT THE END OF THE GREAT TRIBULATION (EZ. 39:17-29), JUST PRIOR TO YAHUSHA'S RETURN.

A reader wrote this question:
"Dear Lew, Fossilized Customs sparked our journey through the Hebraic roots of our faith - we have learned so much. It has changed our lives. My question for you is where are you at with the Hagadah and the seder plate?"

Lew's response: Some things we see done are "leavening" because they add to Torah and are expected (or required), and things are "human conventions" which remain optional. The house of Yahudah (both those who believe in Yahusha as well as those who don't) have many forms of behavior which are quite well-intended, long-lived traditions. There are some traditions which enhance Torah-observance by their presence, and others which are less so. Many traditions we tend to accept are not specifically commanded by Torah, yet they help in promoting the true faith. One example is the concept of the "synagogue", which grew in popularity even before the 2nd Temple was destroyed, and it made teaching foreigners more convenient because foreigners were not allowed to enter the inner areas of the Temple. Though not commanded, the synagogue made instruction of adult converts more efficient, as we find in the book of Acts there were many "Gentiles" listening to what was taught by attending structured readings of the TaNaK (Torah, Prophets, Writings).

To an extent, we can embrace some traditions as long as they don't become the end in themselves, and they are not used to promote a sense of "piety" when observed by others. Many things have no basis in Torah whatsoever, and are mostly for displaying outward piety. Men's approval or titles mean nothing to Yahusha, because He is watching for love and humility to bear fruit in us all. For our personal lives, we should accept or reject things based upon wisdom – knowledge guided by Torah. If anything is not required by Torah, we should not impose it on others. If we should be doing something, then we should study about it carefully in Torah, and teach our children how and why it is to be done. The Pharisees were those of a sect which called themselves "rabbis", and they also accepted Yahusha to be one of them (they called Him "Rabbi"). This sect evolved into the dominant framework of what is known today as "Rabbinical Judaism". This sect steers the Orthodox Yahudim, but it is not the "true faith" as many might perceive it to be; the problem with it is the Talmud. We are not to add nor take away from Torah. The seder plate and Haggadah (telling) can be fine, depending upon how much of their content is "added" or taken away from what is expected of us. The following are a bit more difficult to excuse:

Wearing of a kipa (skullcap, or yarmulke)
Wearing of a "prayer shawl" (as contrasted with just going into a small room alone to pray privately to our Father Yahuah)
Davening (rocking forward while praying) from Yiddish verb "daven", "pray".
(Praying is certainly fine, but rocking forward to be seen while doing so is a bit of a stretch)
Lighting two candles before Sabbath begins
Bestowing the title "rabbi", exaltations, or ordinations
(in the end, only Yahusha can exalt us)

What we teach our children and others needs to be well-founded in Torah, and less "chaff" that is worthless human tradition only for "show".
We have to be sensitive and not offend those who associate traditional behaviors like the above with devotion to Yahuah. Many believe it is pious to never pronounce the Name "Yahuah" - but all of these imposed thought processes are "strongholds" they need to overcome through more Torah study.

Yahuchanon (John) 8:31,32: ***"So Yahusha said to those Yahudim who believed Him, 'If you stay in My Word, you are truly My taught ones, and you shall know the Truth, and the Truth shall make you free.'"***
"Monkee see, monkee do" is a weak principle to base our behavior on.

Abiding in Yahusha's Word will enable us to know the Truth.

The following 4 pages addresses a widespread, on-going conflict among Natsarim.
There is a difference among us in observance of the annual festivals, and we all know about it. Those who choose to perpetuate the sighting of the "crescent moon" as the beginning-point of each month don't use Scripture, but rather a tradition they were taught. They start out describing the problem as being the "Hillel calendar error", then they say we have to set the new moons according to the "crescent" sighting (without any Scriptural evidence, because there is no crescent-sighting mentioned in Scripture). People tend to validate what they do based on what others have done in the past. What we practice should be based on reality, and the real moon is our timepiece. It's the elders who have been teaching the new Natsarim about the "sighted-crescent", and the math is wrong because they fail to start at zero, the dark moon. Scripture certainly doesn't teach us about a crescent-sighting (but the Koran and Hadith of Islam do). If the elders could break their own stronghold about this issue, then the sheep could be united - and the annual Sabbath days would be right where they should be.

Because there is no instruction to do so, the "sighted crescent" most have been taught to watch for is not the beginning of the first day, but rather the beginning of the second day. There is a Scriptural basis for using the "dark moon", because the full moon is evidence that we started correctly.

MOON PHASES

HOW TO TELL TIME USING THE MOON PHASES

The moon "renews" or begins again each time it passes ***directly in line with the sun.*** This position is "ZERO", and light builds up until it is "FULL", 15 days later.

The Moon orbits Earth every 29.5 days

IT'S NOT ***OUR*** POSITION ON THE EARTH AT SUNSET, BUT THE LOCATION OF THE MOON & SUN **RELATIVE TO THE WHOLE EARTH** THAT MATTERS.

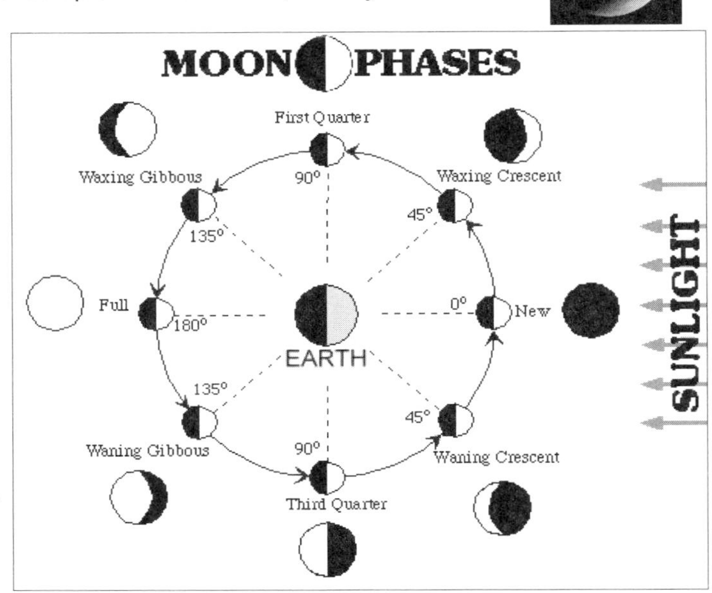

When I discovered the importance of the ***7 annual Sabbaths*** of Yahuah's year (Lev. 23, Dt. 16), at first I was influenced by older teachers who explained how to identify a "new" moon by ***watching for the sliver to appear in the western sky at sunset***. They teach this is the **signal** to watch for that begins the first day of the moon. For about 3 years, I counted to the feasts using this *"sighted crescent moon"* as the start-point. Each time, I discovered the "full" moon arrived when I had only counted to 14. By my count to 15 (the festival day), the moon had begun to shrink smaller (wane), and was missing the amount of light I had started with. Then I investigated for Scripture-based evidence that could validate what they were saying, and *found nothing to support it.* They claimed the Yahudim used to do it, but that's hardly validation because what some group may have practiced in the past doesn't make something correct. Certain "sects" of Israel were different in their practices, as we see several distinct groups mentioned in the Messianic Writings. The world-wide body of dispersed Yahudim that remain true to the Torah today have additional baggage (like Talmud), but they remain unchanging in their core principles, such as the 7-day week, the 7th day Sabbath, the annual mo'edim (appointments), and how they determine the beginning of each moon. In these practices, it's a good thing they have the bronze-foreheads they do, and when we test what they do with Scripture, the Truth will reveal itself to us. Yahuah may have considered that once they get the Torah in them, their stubborn streak will keep it there. Most of the Gentiles have Israelite blood in their veins, and are being called back to the Covenant in these last days by the Spirit of Yahusha. But, there are many pits to fall in as we ***"earnestly contend for the belief which was once for all delivered to the set-apart ones."*** SCRIPTURE MENTIONS ONLY 2 POSITIONS OF THE MOON WE ARE TO WATCH: THE "NEW" MOON, AND THE "FULL" MOON. THE MOON DOES NOT EFFECT THE 7-DAY WEEK AS SOME TEACH.

The pre-Islamic moon deity *Allah* is pictured at right with the ***crescent moon*** clearly seen in one of four views.

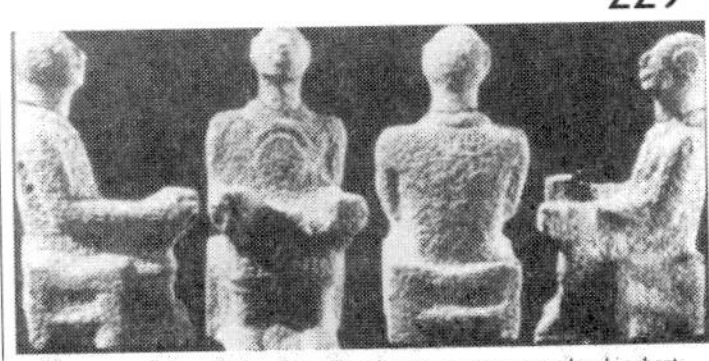

The moon-god from all four sides. Note the cresent moon carved on his chest.

From Yahuah's point-of-view, a day ends at sunset, and a new day begins (Gen. 1). He started creation with *complete darkness*, and light followed, even as a day begins at night and progresses until it is fully light, then wanes again toward night. The renewal of the moon follows this pattern. If we begin a new moon with zero-light, and watch the ***growth*** of light on the face of the moon each evening, we can become skilled at determining what day of the moon it is. If we follow the idea that "sighting" the ***crescent*** moon at sunset is the ***beginning*** of the "first day" of the month, then we ignore the fact that the light we are seeing as a *crescent* represents the amount of light that *had been building on it* when we could not see the moon disc in the brilliance of the sun, and it is really the beginning of the ***second day*** of the moon. We must begin our count with ***ZERO***, which is when the moon has reached its center-point ***between the Earth and the Sun***. If we call the second day of the moon the *first* day, then our count to the annual Sabbaths will be *one day off*. The full moon is consistently the 15th day of each moon, and the feast of Matsah as well as Sukkoth begin on the 15th day of the moon —when it is ***full*** (not waning). A text in Psalms describes the "Feast of Trumpets" and the festival of Sukkoth in the 7th moon. Consider this text, which describes "Yom Teruah", and demonstrates how the festival of Sukkoth begins on the ***full*** moon: (Ps. 81:3):

"Blow the shofar at the time of the new moon; at the full moon on our festival day."

The ***starting-point*** for a "new" moon continues to be a point of debate among various groups of Natsarim today. Many illustrations are provided like the one above, often promoting a "sliver" crescent-moon, sighted in the western sky after sunset as being the beginning of the first "day" of a moon. The sighting of the crescent sliver is declared to be the arrival of the first day of the moon. Most accept this explanation, and never question where this can be confirmed in the Writings of Scripture (Torah, the instruction). This activity is not found in Torah, but rather it is derived from the Koran and Hadith OF ISLAM. The ***crescent moon of Allah*** was the tribal symbol of Muhammad's family. The Arabic word for the crescent new-moon is ***Hilal***, the same word found in the Hebrew text of YeshaYahu (Isaiah) 14, which is translated as *"Lucifer"* in the KJV (see H#1966 in your concordance). ***Hilal*** is the Islamic term for the sighting of the ***crescent moon***, and is definitely associated with the pre -Islamic moon deity, ***Allah***.

The crescent moon is a very ancient symbol, revered by Persia, India, Egypt, Islam, and Masonry. At the higher levels of Freemasonry, the royal secret is revealed to the light-seekers: ***that they worship Lucifer*** under various names, one of which is Allah. Masons seek "the light".

In order for a person to become a ***Shriner***, he must go through all the degrees of Masonry, make blood-curdling oaths, worship all the various "gods" of Egypt, and make a blood-oath of *allegiance to Allah as his god, and Mohammed as his prophet*. The Shriner is then given a ***red fez*** with an Islamic sword and ***crescent*** jeweled on it. This originates from 7th century Arabia when the Moslems, under the leadership of Mohammed, slaughtered all Christians who would not bow down to Allah. Allah is the tribal deity -- "the moon god" -- of Mohammed. That is why every mosque today has a crescent moon on the top of its "dome". (FYI: A *dome* is a symbol of *Hermes* -the Greek deity of wisdom- revered by Masonry. The Hebrew word "**kipa**" -a yarmulke, means *dome*).

The bull (or ox) with a white ***crescent moon*** on his shoulder is the Egyptian ***Apis***. It was

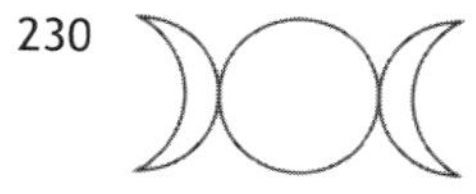

ABOVE SYMBOL:
al-Lat, al-Uzza and Manat
Allah's daughters

The crescent moon is associated with the Hindu deity ***Shiva***, seen here with it in his hair. On the left is the symbol of the triple moon goddess of Wicca, drawing from the 3 daughters of Allah The *waxing, full, and waning* forms represent the *maiden, mother*, and *crone* goddesses of the Arabs.

believed he would emerge from a river and rise into the air when the Egyptians gathered around him with music and chanting. ***Moon worship*** was the primary religious practice of the city known today as JERICHO: It is thought that the name is derived from the Canaanite name *Yareah*, meaning "moon". The moon was sometimes worshipped as a male, and other times as a female.

The pre-Islamic Arabian *moon-deity* was ***Allah***, the "greatest" deity of 360 idols in the Ka'aba, and the tribal deity of Muhammad. Mecca was the ***center*** of pre-Islamic Pagan worship. In the Koran, Allah swears by the moon in the verse at Surah 74:32. Before Islam, the Pagan Arabian moon deity Allah had 3 daughter goddesses, ***al-Lat, al-Uzza and Manat***, who were considered very powerful. Their names appeared in several verses of the earliest versions of the Koran, but the texts were later removed and labeled ***"Satanic verses".*** They were the *maiden, mother,* and *crone* goddesses of the Arabs. In 1988, Salman Rushdie published a book entitled ***Satanic Verses***, citing the verses of the Koran mentioning the 3 daughters of Allah that had been deleted. In response to this book, a *fatwa* (religious edict) was issued in 1989 by Ayatollah Khomeini (then Supreme leader of Iran), calling for the death of Salman Rushdie.

Wiccans honor the "Goddess", and the Crescent Moon is the primary symbol for "her". This deity has been worshipped under various names such as Diana, Artemis, Selene, and Libertas (the Latin name, Libertas, was adopted by Thomas Jefferson when he named the U.S. Capitol building the ***"temple of Libertas",*** and placed her statue atop the dome - he was a Mason, and simply had to honor the moon deity). Our Capital is dedicated to a Greco-Roman moon deity. If Shaul were to visit Washington DC, he could almost believe he was in Athens or Rome.

We have strongholds to overcome. A "stronghold" is a false belief or notion, and are overcome with Truth. The "sighting" of the crescent moon comes from every corner of ancient Pagan worship. In ancient Syria, the moon-deity *Sin* was represented by the crescent moon. In Ur, bread was baked in the form of a *crescent* to honor their moon-deity, *Nannar*, giving us the custom of *"crescent rolls"* (croissant). The word "**Mon**-day" comes from the Latin name for the second day, Dies **Lun**ae, *day of the moon.* Many languages reflect this custom: French: **Lun**di; Spanish: **Lun**es; German: **Mon**tag; Dutch: **Maan**dag; Italian: **Lun**edi. In Japanese, the days are named in order for the sun, moon, then five planets. Over the whole Earth, the cultures have adopted terms from the worship of the celestial objects; but one stiff-necked people have remained stubborn enough to never fully assimilate into whatever culture they have found themselves. They would be what we call "Jews", or the people descended from the tribe of Yahudah. If we examine when they observe the "renewed moon", we find they reckon from the dark moon. This way, the full moon (on the 15th) is always correct for the count to Matsah (in the first moon) and Sukkoth (in the seventh moon). We must begin the measuring of time from ZERO, which means zero light (darkness). As the first day of the moon is building, the moon is moving away from the conjunction point between Earth and the Sun, hidden in the brilliance of the Sun. The light reflected from the limb of the moon builds slowly until we can finally see the effects of the passed time on the moon just after sunset. The sighting of the crescent sliver declares the ***second*** day of the moon is beginning; it can't possibly be the beginning of the ***first*** day, it's already fully built. Prior to the renewed moon, a crescent of the moon can be seen in the ***eastern*** sky just before ***sunrise*** on the 29th day of every moon, which is often noticed by those awake in the early morning hours. When I was a paper boy in my youth, I often saw this waning crescent. A shepherd would also recognize this, and know that the "renewed moon" would be the following day:

1Sa 20:18 ***"So Yahonathan said to him, 'Tomorrow is the New Moon, and you shall be missed, because your seat shall be empty.'"***

Today we know where the moon is, and when the renewed moon arrives. Long ago, they knew how to count, and notice the waning crescent before sunrise. We can determine where the moon will be far into the future, even to predict when and where the shadow of the moon will fall (eclipses). We know where it is down to the inch. Recognizing the phases for what they are need not be a cause for division, and yet every annual Sabbath there are at least 3 divisions among the Natsarim as to how to reckon the renewed moon. The teachings we embrace are "strongholds" of thought, and we must overthrow the errors in teaching with Scripture.

2Co 10-6: ***"For the weapons we fight with are not fleshly but mighty in Elohim for overthrowing strongholds, overthrowing reasonings and every high matter that exalts itself against the knowledge of Elohim, taking captive every thought to make it obedient to the Messiah, and being ready to punish all disobedience, when your obedience is complete."***

Consider the "appointed times" we should be observing, as we have been enjoined to Yahuah as Israel through His Covenant (Lev. 23). The Sabbath (weekly), Passover, Unleavened bread,
Shabuoth (called "Pentecost"), and the appointments of the seventh moon, Yom Teruah, Yom Kippur, and Sukkoth (Tabernacles). Next, think of how these are Yahuah's ***redemption plan*** for Israel, and that Yahusha's work has, and will, be accomplishing that redemption through all of these ***"shadows".*** Reflect on the following correction of this verse we are all familiar with:
"Let no man therefore judge you in meat, or in drink, or in respect of a festival, or of the new moon, or of the Sabbath days which are a shadow of things to come for the body of Mashiach." (Col 2:16-17) Restoring this verse to its literal Hebrew roots, the meaning comes through clearly. The ***festivals*** are shadows, picturing how Yahusha is redeeming Israel.

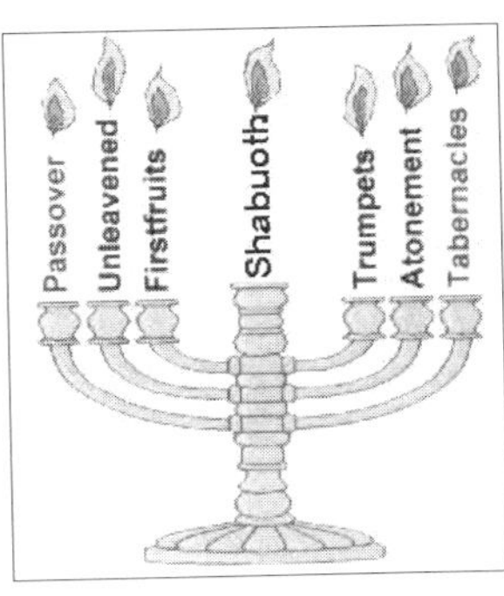

The crescent moon is a symbol for Shiva, seen at right with a crescent in his hair.
It is also symbolic for YOGA, considered to be a form of prayer to Hindus. "Crescent moon yoga" is very popular around the world, and the moon is used to regulate its worship in various yoga poses.

The idea of a "crescent moon" is not found in Scripture, yet many use a crescent to establish the festivals of Yahuah.

COME, I SHALL SHOW YOU

THE BRIDE; THE LAMB'S WIFE

If you are not the bride, ***but think you are,*** this is especially meant for you. Scripture identifies a "bride", which is the same as a "wife". Shaul (Paul) speaks of this bride, and so does the writer of Revelation, and the prophets of Yahuah. The "war in heaven" is still waging, and "the bride" will become a fortress on the day of redemption, also known as the return of Yahusha, at the end of the distress (great tribulation). After 1000 years (known as the Millennium), the war in heaven will end with all those in rebellion being cast alive into the lake of fire. **The bride** is discussed by one of the messengers that release the 7 last plagues:

"And one of the seven messengers who held the seven bowls filled with the seven last plagues came to me and spoke with me, saying, 'Come, I shall show you the bride, the Lamb's wife.'" Rev 21:9 (Please stop and read this chapter).

The bride is described as a "great city" coming from the skies, and "**her light**" was **like** a most precious stone, clear as crystal, and named the "New Yerushalayim". The 12 gates each bear a name for a tribe of **ISRAEL**, and there is a *qualification* stated concerning those who may enter her. ***People practicing error will be blocked from entering:***

"Blessed are those doing His commands, so that the authority shall be theirs unto the tree of life, and to enter through the gates into the city. But outside are the dogs and those who enchant with drugs, and those who whore, and the murderers, and the idolaters, and all who love and do falsehood." Rev 22:14,15

Clearly, we see there is unconditional *obedience* to the Commands of Yahuah required (not unconditional indulgence as many false prophets and teachers have stated). We are given our faith (belief, fidelity) as a gift, and that faith produces the "good works": obedience to the Torot (instructions) of Yahuah. If we practice idolatry, or worship Yahuah in a way He did not command worship, we must purge such things and learn what pleases Him. We are counted righteous by belief, and our belief is perfected and shown by our obedience (our obedience is the fruit of righteousness). We can identify a tree by the fruit we see on it. ***By the fruit we see in the bride, we can identify her.*** If we see what we think is the bride observing ChristMass, Easter (Ishtar), Sun-day, Lent, Ash Wednesday, Halloween (all of which stem directly from Pagan practices and times), is it remotely possible that we are deceived? *Where in Scripture was the bride instructed to practice any of these things?* "Houses of worship" using ***steeples*** (obelisks) and ***bells*** are of Pagan origins. If the "Christmas tree" didn't originate from Yahuah's Torah, *how did it get mixed-up with what people do?* It is not secular either; it is an **ASHERAH** (please verify this by personal research). Evidently, the bride currently has a few major "spots and wrinkles" which need to be wiped away.

(Google the words: ASHERAH, ORNAMENTS, TREE)

What we *do* is the *evidence* of our belief. Brother Ya'aqob (James) tells us:

"You see, then, that a man is declared right by works, and not by belief alone." Jas 2:24 He continues the idea in a later verse:
"For as the body without the spirit is dead, so also the belief is dead without the works." Jas 2:26

Shaul tells us that a person without belief (living solely in a perspective of the flesh) doesn't want anything to do with obeying:
"For those who live according to the flesh set their minds on the matters of the flesh, but those who live according to the Spirit, the matters of the Spirit. For the mind of the flesh is death, but the mind of the Spirit is life and peace. Because the mind of the flesh is hatred towards Elohim, for it does not subject itself to the Torah of Elohim, neither indeed is it able; those who are in the (mind of the) ***flesh are unable to please Elohim. But you are not in the flesh but in the Spirit, if indeed the Spirit of Elohim dwells in you. And if anyone does not have the Spirit of Messiah, this one is not His."*** Rom 8:5-9

The "mind of the flesh" is hatred toward Yahuah, BECAUSE it *does not* subject itself to *His Torah*. There are plenty of preachers who do not want anyone to submit to the Torah of Yahuah, ***and they tell us this quite often.***

THE BRIDE WAS HIDDEN, AS IN A FIELD, LONG AGO THE FIELD IS THE WORLD

As a result of *disobedience*, the bride (Israel, Yahuah's wife) *was scattered thoroughly among the nations*, driven from the land. This was the curse, *and it remains in effect*. The parable at Mt 13:44 speaks of a "treasure" (lost Israel, the bride) found by a man (Yahusha, the Pursuer of His bride), who bought the field (paid the ultimate price). The bride is now His property, but "she" remains hidden. Like Yusef in Egypt, Yahusha will one day reveal Himself to His brothers, to all the scattered tribes of Israel. The first work of Yahusha involved ***atonement***, but the second work is ***redemption***. He is sent to seek and deliver that which was lost, and will unite the ***house of Yahudah*** (the ruling tribe) and the ***house of Israel*** (also called Ephraim, first-born blessing tribe) into "one stick".
(See Ez 37:15-19).

Master, SAVE ME!!! Mt. 14:30

On Sea of Gallilee, also Lake of Gennesaret, Lake Kinneret or Sea of Tiberias

BLIND TO OUR MORTALITY

From Yahusha's point-of-view, *we are all sinking into oblivion, and the grave will consume us without His intervention. Our wanton dependence upon Him every instant is pushed aside in our daily lives, but Kepha experienced how fragile his life was for a few fleeting moments. Beyond the "surface" of this miracle lies the stark reality of our dependence, and that our susceptibility to death is overcome by belief in the authority of a single Person that has the power and will to rescue us.*

THE BRIDE WILL BE REVEALED ON THE DAY OF REDEMPTION

"For your Maker is your husband, Yahuah of hosts is His Name, and the Set-apart One of Yisrael is your Redeemer. He is called the Elohim of all the Earth." Is 54:5 (read the context)

Yahusha has chosen His bride, but He has not yet taken possession of her. The "wedding supper" is still ahead of us at a future festival of Sukkoth (the harvest festival we are to observe for 7 days in the fall, Lev 23, Dt 16. Notice in the following text the reference to a "booth"; "tents" (Hebrew, Sukkoth) will be the time of the return of Yahusha, at the harvesting of the Earth:

"And I, Yahuchanan, saw the set-apart city, new Yerushalayim, coming down out of the heaven from Elohim, prepared as a bride adorned for her husband. And I heard a loud voice from the heaven saying, 'See, the Booth of Elohim is with men, and He shall dwell with them, and they shall be His people, and Elohim Himself shall be with them and be their Elohim.'" Rev 21:2,3

Yahusha is preparing His wife so that she may be without spot or wrinkle. Again, from more texts we can see our redemption comes during the observances of the 7th month, after the last shofar, or "feast of trumpets":

1Th 4:13-18: ***"Now, brothers, we do not wish you to be ignorant concerning those who have fallen asleep, lest you be sad as others who have no expectation. For if we believe that Yahusha died and rose again, so also Elohim shall bring with Him those who sleep* in Yahusha. For this we say to you by the word of the Master, that we, the living who are left over at the coming of the Master shall in no way go before those who are asleep. Because the Master Himself shall come down from heaven with a shout, with the voice of a chief messenger,***

*SLEEP IS A EUPHEMISM FOR DEATH. THE DEAD ARE RAISED ON THE 1ST DAY OF THE SEVENTH MOON, ***YOM TERUAH*** - THE DAY OF THE SHOUT. WHEN WE ARE REDEEMED, WE WILL BE REBORN, AND IMMORTAL. UNTIL NOW, WE ARE NOT YET REBORN, ONLY "BEGOTTEN" FROM ABOVE.

and with the shofar of Elohim, and the dead in Messiah shall rise first. Then we, the living who are left over, shall be CAUGHT AWAY together with them in the clouds to meet the Master in the air – and so we shall always be with the Master. So encourage one another with these words."

"CAUGHT AWAY" in the above text is the *same Greek word* used at Acts 8:39 (*HARPAZO*, G726, *to seize*; Latin: *RAPTUS*, as in seizing property). Enabled by the Spirit of Yahusha, Philip was "teleported" to another location *instantly*; **as together, we will also at the coming of the Master.** For a clearer understanding, let's pretend that modern *"feminism"* never happened, and we're thinking like a person who lived long ago. To be Yahusha's "property", His *BRIDE*, we must examine how Scripture identifies those who live within the BONDS OF THE COVENANT* (of marriage) to Him. Every denomination on Earth sincerely believes they *are* the bride of the Mashiach, ahead of all others. While Yahusha is away to receive His Kingdom and prepare a place for His bride, those who await His return are partly wise, and partly foolish. At Mt 25:1-13, *"ten maidens"* seem to correspond to the *ten "lost" tribes of Israel.* Some have wisdom and have prepared themselves more than others. The "oil" that is discussed surely represents the guidance of Yahusha's Spirit, helping make the wise maidens aware of what is needed to prepare themselves for the abrupt arrival of the Bridegroom. Indeed, the wedding feast is an exclusive affair.

Yahuah says we will obey in the latter days, while among the Gentiles:

Deu 4:30: *"In your* **distress** (Great Trib), *when all these words shall come upon you* **in the latter days**, *then you shall return to Yahuah your Elohim and shall* **obey** *His voice."* (Read the full ***context*** of all the texts being quoted in this study!)

Deu 30:1-4: *"And it shall be,* **when all these words come upon you**, *the blessing and the curse which I have set before you, and you shall bring them back to your heart among all the Gentiles where Yahuah your Elohim drives you, and shall turn back to Yahuah your Elohim and* **obey** *His voice, according to all that I command you today, with all your heart and with all your being, you and your children,* **then Yahuah your Elohim shall turn back your captivity**, *and shall have compassion on you, and He shall turn*

*Gentiles ***engraft*** into Israel by entering into the same Covenant, at the point of their immersion.

RAPTURE: The Christian understanding of our redemption is partly correct, but it will occur at the END of the Great Trib, because our greatest work will be done during this period. We'll be *redeemed* at the same time we're *re-gathered.* The lost (those not sealed with the Name) will be helped greatly by our presence.
RAPTUS: In Catholic Canon law, this was a term commonly used for ***bride kidnapping***. "RAPTIO" was the confiscation or abduction of women. In Roman law the term covered many crimes of property, and women were considered property. The BRIDE of Yahusha will be seized by Him suddenly. A related term in Greek would be:
EK-STASIS (ECSTASY): A removal to elsewhere; to stand outside oneself. .... YAHUSHA, ***COME****!*

back and gather you from all the peoples where Yahuah your Elohim has scattered you. ***If any of you are driven out to the farthest parts under the heavens, from there Yahuah your Elohim does gather you, and from there He does take you."*** Ez 39:28,29: *"And they shall know that I am* <u>*Yahuah*</u> *their Elohim, Who* <u>*sent*</u> *them into exile among the Gentiles, and then* <u>*gathered*</u> *them back to their own land, and left none of them behind. 'And no longer do I hide My face from them, for I shall have poured out My Spirit on the* ***house of Israel****,' declares the Master Yahuah."* The One doing this is Yahusha, the Bridegroom, Who will end our captivity. Who is Yahusha married to? Is it "the church" as we have been told?

"THE BRIDE" REPRESENTS THE *"CHILDREN OF ISRAEL"*

The "church" (derived from a Pagan word, *Circe*) is really the KAHAL, or congregation of Israel. Israel is anyone who enjoins to the Covenant, "walking" according to the Torah. We who teach the Covenant are called ***fishers of men***, and ***hunters***:

"Therefore see, the days are coming, declares Yahuah, when it is no longer said, 'Yahuah lives who brought up the children of Yisrael from the land of Mitsrayim,' but, 'Yahuah lives who brought up the children of Yisrael from the land of the north and from all the lands where He had driven them.' For I shall bring them back into their land I gave to their fathers. 'See, I am sending for many fishermen', declares Yahuah, 'and they shall fish them. And after that I shall send for many hunters, and they shall hunt them from every mountain and every hill, and out of the holes of the rocks.'" Jer 16:14-16

THE BRIDE WILL BE RESTORED TO THE COVENANT IN THE "DAY OF DISTRESS" (GREAT TRIBULATION), AND REALIZE HER RELIGIOUS FILTH:

A SPIRITUAL FORTRESS

This Dwelling Place of Yahusha will be made up of His bride with 12 portals.

The ultimate camp of Israel, it will be unapproachable and safe from spiritual attack as well as physical attack.

"Then shall the righteous shine forth as the sun in the kingdom of their Father" (Matthew 13:43).
The diameter of the sun is 864,000 miles.
Thus New Jerusalem's walls, with an area of 864 million square furlongs, is the same as the sun's diameter of 864,000 miles multiplied by a thousand years.

SECOND TEMPLE (model)

A humanly-constructed Temple was allowed by Yahuah, and it served as a base for the *atonement phase* of Yahusha's work.

A man-made Temple for Yahuah to indwell is not in the plans, but rather one which is made up of *"living stones"*. Those stones will be those awakened from their graves (or those living at the time) after the great distress as described to Daniel.

"O Yahuah my strength and my stronghold and my refuge, in the day of distress the Gentiles shall come to You from the ends of the Earth and say, 'Our fathers have inherited only falsehood, futility, and there is no value in them.'" Jer 16:19.
(False terms like "GOD" and "LORD" will cease) Now notice Ps 80:14-19:

"Return, we beg You, O Elohim of hosts; look down from heaven, and see, and visit this vine, and the stock which Your right hand has planted, and the son whom You made strong for Yourself. It is burned with fire, it is cut down; they perish at the rebuke of Your face. Let Your hand be upon the One at Your right hand, Upon the Son of Adam whom You made strong for Yourself, and we shall not back-slide from You. Revive us, and let us call upon Your Name. Turn us back, O Yahuah Elohim of hosts, and cause Your face to shine, that we might be saved!"

The bride will eventually know her Husband, and take His Name on her lips. The bride has *always* been Israel, into which Gentiles must engraft (Is 56, Jer 3, Acts 15, Eph 3, Rom 11). Those who *bond* with Yahuah do so *through His Covenant*. Foreigners enter the Covenant by immersion in the Name of Yahusha, calling upon Him for deliverance through His blood offered for sin, and promising to obey Him, thus *becoming* His bride, taking their place in the commonwealth of Israel, as Eph 2:8-13 discusses. (Please stop and read Is 56). ***The Sabbath*** is mentioned because it is the "sign" of the Eternal Covenant (Ex 31:17, Ez 20:20), the *mark* of Yahuah.

THREE TEMPLES?

Everyone knows of the two Temples which were built on the Temple Mount, and we keep hearing about the re-building of the "third Temple". Schlomo (Solomon) built the first one, and the second was begun with the return of the Yahudim from Babylon under the leadership of NehemYah and Ezra. Herod the Great expanded it, so the second Temple is often referred to as "Herod's Temple". The first Temple was destroyed in 586 BCE with the invasion of Nebuchadnezzar's army from Babel. ***Every***

"Because you have guarded My Word of endurance, I also shall guard you from the hour of trial which shall come upon all the world, to try those who dwell on the Earth. See, I am coming speedily! Hold what you have that no one take your crown. He who overcomes, I shall make him a supporting post in the Dwelling Place of My Elohim, and he shall by no means go out. And I shall write on him the Name of My Elohim and the name of the city of My Elohim, the new Yerushalayim, which comes down out of the heaven from My Elohim, and My renewed Name." Rev 3:10-12

The prophet Daniel was told about the Great Tribulation, the first resurrection, and given a description of the "shining" of those who have "insight": ***"Now at that time Mikael shall stand up, the great head who is standing over the sons of your people. And there shall be a time of distress*** (Great Trib)***, such as never was since there was a nation, until that time. And at that time your people shall be delivered, every one who is found written in the book, and many of those who sleep in the dust of the Earth wake up, some to everlasting life, and some to reproaches, everlasting abhorrence. And those who have insight shall shine like the brightness of the expanse, and those who lead many to righteousness like the stars forever and ever."*** Dan 12:1-3

WE WILL HELP LEAD MANY TO RIGHTEOUSNESS **DURING** THE DISTRESS; THERE IS NO "PRE-TRIB" RAPTURE.

Kepha (Peter) speaks of us as living stones, and the reason for stumbling: ***"Drawing near to Him, a living Stone – rejected indeed by men, but chosen by Elohim and precious – you also, as living stones, are being built up, a spiritual house, a set-apart priesthood, to offer up spiritual slaughter offerings acceptable to Elohim through Yahusha Messiah. Because it is contained in the Scripture, 'See, I lay in Tsiyon a chief corner-stone, chosen, precious, and he who believes on Him shall by no means be put to shame.' This preciousness, then, is for you who believe; but to those who are disobedient, 'The stone which the builders rejected has become the chief corner-stone,' and 'A stone of stumbling and a rock that makes for falling,' who stumble because they are disobedient to the Word, to which they also were appointed."*** 1Pe 2:4-8 (The ***"Word"*** is the Covenant, or Ten Commandments).

"Let us be glad and rejoice and give Him praise, for the marriage of the Lamb has come, and His wife prepared herself." Rev 19:7

WE ARE DEDICATED TO THE WORK OF YAHUSHA IN RESTORING THE LOST TRIBES OF YISRAEL TO HIS COVENANT & UNITING THE TWO HOUSES OF YAHUDAH & ISRAEL INTO ONE - EZ 37

BORG CUBE - BASED ON FANTASY **NEW YERUSHALAYIM** - REAL!

FANTASY vs. REALITY

Even science-fiction writers draw from the words of Revelation. Their "antagonist" is portrayed as whatever threatens the perpetuation of ***human government***. The governments of men (led by ha shatan) will fight against the "threat" coming from the skies, because ha shatan's rule of Earth (through men) will be at its end. One of the most obvious parallels between science fantasy and prophecy is the appearance of the BORG CUBE and it's similarity to the New Yersushalayim. The **Borg Cube** has an "assimilation chamber", and a "hive mind", akin to bees or ants. Even this seems to reflect the "collective" mind of the Spirit, as we will all be "one" with Yahusha when He comes to reign. Resistance is futile, because resistance is rebellion against the King of kings. HUMAN GOVERNMENT WILL END.

stone was removed from the second Temple in 70 CE when the Roman army led by Titus laid-waste to Yerushalayim. In the fury of the battle, the fire melted the golden décor and the gold flowed into the crevices of the building stones. These 2 Temples served during the ***atonement*** phase of Yahusha's work. A THIRD Temple, ***built without the hands of men***, is coming from the skies and will endure for all eternity.

It is made up of "living stones", and it is the bride.

THE BRIDE IS DESCRIBED IN VARIOUS WAYS

Various terms and phrases are used to describe the same thing. All of these refer to ***the redeemed***. The foremost term used throughout Scripture is "ISRAEL". Those in the Covenant (and many descendants who are yet to be recalled to it) are referred to as:

The camp of the set-apart ones, the Beloved City, the Bride, living stones, the Great City, a spiritual house, a set-apart priesthood, sons of light, Dwelling Place, Hekel (Temple), etc.,.

The bride will literally be "living stones", making up the structure of the new city in their new ***immortal bodies***. Notice carefully what is declared to us in the message to the assembly of Philadelphia:

ALEF-TAU

The **first** and **last** letters of the Hebrew **Alef-Beth** are mysteriously placed near the Covenant Name (identity) of **Yahuah** throughout the Scriptures. It is an identity marker of the First and the Last, finally revealed by Yahusha ha'Mashiach as **Himself** at Rev. 1:8.

THE REVELATION OF YAHUSHA'S IDENTITY

The beast apparatus is the "world system", filled with deception for those who reject receiving a love for the Truth. For most of the past 2000 years, the influence of eastern mysticism and Gnostic "enlightenment" has dominated the western world. This ***Gnosticism*** has multiplied itself and is now seen *everywhere*, posing as the various forms of "religion", all posturing themselves to be the only "truth". At the core of them all is the worship of the "host of heaven" (Zodiac/ Astrology), originating in Babel's worship of *Nimrod, Semiramis, and Tammuz.* This is the premise of Alexander Hislop's book, ***The Two Babylons***. The false worship of the sun, moon, and constellations (Zodiac, zoo animals) manifests itself in the ***three heads***, and sometimes ***triple pairs of arms*** depicted in statues.

Beads, flowers, nimbuses (haloes), ashes (note forehead of image at right), and meditation positions are just a few of the aspects of Babel's false worship. The majority of the "church fathers" were originally followers of ***Manichaeism***, a religion founded by Mani (216-277CE).

Manichaeism was a major **Gnostic religion**, originating in Sassanid-era Babylonia.

Mani's Gnostic teachings about Yahusha became the pattern seen in many tenets of Christianity, adopted through the "church fathers". These pretenders are often referred to as "men of the cloth", wearing their special robes as we see with any other uniformed professional.

The people of Beroia (Acts 17) checked Scripture to **validate** everything they heard. Since the time of these "Bereans", **Gnostic** beliefs were adopted without research, and it was taught that the Creator is THREE, not ONE as the ***Shema*** states. This has been promoted so well that ***any who challenge that premise are regarded as heretics.*** For a moment, let's think ***outside that box*** (prison, stronghold), and go with the working premise that the Creator is **ONE**, as He claims He is.

BRAHMA

VISHNU

SHIVA

Since Yahusha declared that He and the Father are **one**, let's hypothetically take that statement at face value. If Yahuah entered into His physical world and ***appeared*** as one of us, that which we could see and touch of Him would be His "son", revealing Himself just as the opening words of Hebrews explain:

Heb 1:1-6: **"Elohim, having of old spoken in many portions and many ways to the fathers by the prophets, has in these last days spoken to us by the Son, whom He has appointed heir of all, through whom also He made the ages, Who being the brightness of the esteem and the exact representation of His substance, and sustaining all by the Word of His power, having made a cleansing of our sins through Himself, sat down at the right hand of the Greatness on high, having become so much better than the messengers, as He has inherited a more excellent Name than them. For to which of the messengers did He ever say, 'You are My**

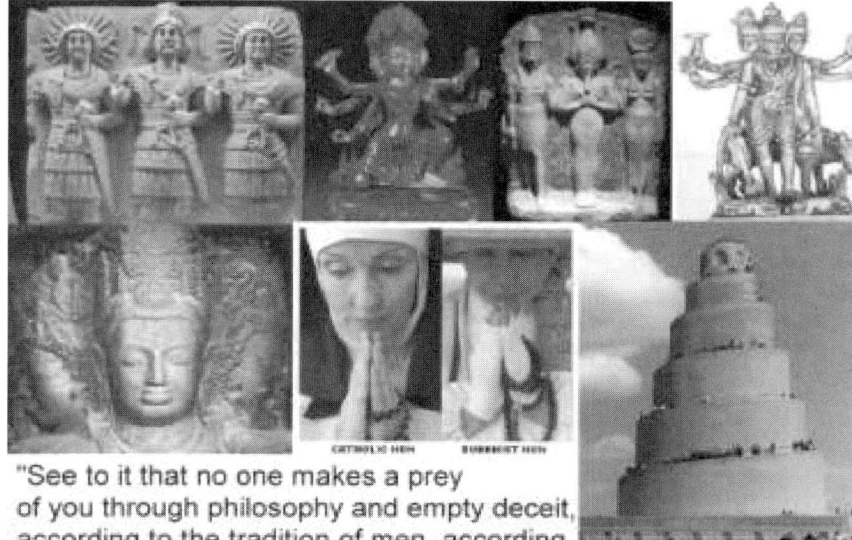

"See to it that no one makes a prey
of you through philosophy and empty deceit,
according to the tradition of men, according
to the elementary matters of the world,
and not according to Messiah." Col 2:8
STEEPLES, STUPAS, HALOES,
BEADS, TRINITIES, NAMASTE,
ASHES, HOLY WATER, IMAGES

Son, today I have brought You forth?' And again, 'I shall be to Him a Father, and He shall be to Me a Son?'
And when He again brings the first-born into the world, He says, 'Let all the messengers of Elohim do reverence to Him.'"

Yahusha's enemies understood ***exactly*** what He was saying, and they stated their understanding in the context of Yahusha's declaration that He is *one and **the same*** as the Father:

John / Yahuchanon 10:30-33:
"'I and My Father are one.'
Again the Yahudim picked up stones to stone Him. Yahusha answered them, 'Many good works I have shown you from My Father. Because of which of these works do you stone Me?'
The Yahudim answered Him, saying, 'We do not stone You for a good work, but for blasphemy, and because You, being a Man, make Yourself Elohim.'"

Joh 14:6-10: **"Yahusha said to him, 'I am the Way, and the Truth, and the Life. No one comes to the Father except through Me.**
If you had known Me, you would have known My Father too. From now on you know Him, and have seen.'
Philip said to Him, "Master, show us the Father, and it is enough for us."
Yahusha said to him,
'Have I been with you so long, and you have not known Me, Philip? He who has seen Me has seen the Father, and how do you say, 'Show us the Father'?
Do you not believe that I am in the Father, and the Father is in Me? The words that I speak to you I do not speak from Myself. But the Father who stays in Me does His works.'"

WHO IS EL SHADDAI?

The Hebrew term "**El Shaddai**" means "mighty-one almighty".
The term "**El**" indicates "mighty-one".
The term "**shaddai**" indicates "all sufficiency".

The **identity** of El Shaddai is revealed in two places:

Exo 6:2,3: **"And Elohim spoke to Mosheh and said to him, 'I am Yahuah.**
And I appeared to Abraham, to Yitshaq, and to Ya'aqob, as El Shaddai. And by My Name, Yahuah, was I not known to them?"

Rev 1:8: **"'I am the Aleph and the Tau, Be-**

ginning and End,' says Yahuah, 'Who is and Who was and Who is to come, the Almighty.'"

The "Almighty" (Shaddai) is revealed to be Yahusha, as well as the **literal meaning** of "Yahuah" in the statement
"Who <u>is</u> and Who <u>was</u> and Who <u>is to come</u>".

WHO IS YAHUSHA?

His identity has been hidden in countless controversial disputes, and it cannot be known unless it is revealed to you:
Luk 10:22-24: **"'All has been delivered to Me by My Father, and no one knows Who the Son is, except the Father, and Who the Father is, except the Son, and he to whom the Son wishes to reveal *Him*.'
And turning to His taught ones He said, separately, 'Blessed are the eyes that see what you see, for I say to you that many prophets and sovereigns have wished to see what you see, and have not seen it, and to hear what you hear, and have not heard it.'"**

Who the Son is, and Who the Father is, is ***unknown*** except to ***"he to whom the Son wishes to reveal"***. The greatest declaration of all, affirmed by Yahusha, is the Shema (Dt. 6:4), that Yahuah is <u>one</u>. Who is the Mashiach? Is there any deliverer or Redeemer, other than Yahuah?

Isa / YeshaYahu 49:26: **"'And I will feed them that oppress you with their own flesh; and they shall be drunken with their own blood, as with sweet wine: and all flesh shall know that I Yahuah *am* your Saviour and your Redeemer, the Mighty One of Ya'aqob.'"**

Isa / YeshaYahu 44:24: **Thus said Yahuah, your Redeemer, and He who formed you from the womb, 'I am Yahuah, doing all, stretching out the heavens *all alone*, spreading out the Earth, with *none beside Me* . . .'"**

Emmanuel, Prince of Peace, Everlasting Father, Mighty Elohim ~ these terms refer to ONE Being.
At Revelation chapter 1 quoted above, we find the One speaking calling Himself "the Almighty" (Shaddai). He further states He is the "***living One; and I was dead, and behold, I am alive forevermore***". Fascinating. Micah, the prophet, at 5:2 tells us that Bethlehem Ephrathah would have One "***go forth for Me to be Ruler in Israel. His goings forth are from long ago, from the days of eternity***." There is only <u>**one**</u> eternal Being, and He tells us there is no one beside Him, and identifies Himself as ***the first and the last*** (Yesha Yahu 41:4, 44:6).
"I, I am Yahuah, and besides Me there is no Savior." (Yesha Yahu 43:11).

Isa / YeshaYahu 44:8: **"Fear not, neither be afraid: have I not declared to you of old, and showed it? and you are my witnesses. Is there any Elohim besides me? yea, there is no Rock; I know not any."**

Yahusha is the **Rock** which the builders rejected . . . . there aren't TWO Rocks.

When Yahusha told Yahuchanon to record the Words to the assemblies, He revealed His identity as "El Shaddai", and included the answer to the mystery of the ages, Who the "Aleph-Tau" is. Ultimately, the **Father** reconciled the world's sin debt by taking that debt on to Himself by His Fullness dwelling in His Son, and shedding His Blood for our redemption. He is alive forevermore, the First-fruits of all Creation.
The Father ultimately receives the honor:
Php 2:9-11: **"Elohim, therefore, has highly exalted Him and given Him the Name which is above every name, that at the Name of Yahusha every knee should bow, of those in heaven, and of those on Earth, and of those under the earth, and every tongue should confess that Yahusha Messiah is Master, to the esteem of Elohim the Father."**

THE SCRIPTURES ARE <u>ABOUT</u> YAHUSHA
Jn 5:39: "You search the Scriptures, because you think you possess everlasting life in them. And these are the ones that bear witness of <u>Me</u>."

HIS NAME, "YAHUSHA", MEANS *"YAHUAH IS OUR DELIVERER"*

Jn 5:43 "I have come in My Father's Name and you do not receive Me, if another comes in his own name, him you would receive."

The only conclusion to draw from all that Scripture reveals to us concerning the

identity (including the Name of our Creator) is that Yahuah Himself is the Mashiach, the Melek (King) of Yisrael. ***This should not be a surprise since all Scripture states this.***

He is acting in the role of a SON, and as an actor might take up a *persona* (mask), Yahuah took the form of a servant, and came to be in the likeness of men.

Trinitarians call this approach *modalism.*

We call on Yahuah as Deliverer in the Name we are to be immersed in:

YAHUSHA

(This means "Yah is our Deliverer")

WHAT IS HIS NAME, IF YOU KNOW IT?

Pro 30:2-4:

"For I am more stupid than anyone, and do not have the understanding of a man. And I have not learned wisdom that I should know the knowledge of the Set-apart One.

Who has gone up to the heavens and come down? Who has gathered the wind in His fists? Who has bound the waters in a garment? Who established all the ends of the Earth? What is His Name, And what is His Son's Name, If you know it?"

The revelation of Yahusha's true identity is clearly connected to what we just read, and this text:

Jn 3:13: "And no one has gone up into the heaven except He Who came down from the heaven – the Son of Adam."

Php 2:6-8:

"Who, being in the form of Elohim, did not regard equality with Elohim a matter to be grasped, but emptied Himself, taking the form of a servant, and came to be in the likeness of men.

And having been found in fashion as a man, He humbled Himself and became obedient unto death, death even of a stake."

Yahusha is the "**Right Hand**" of Yahuah.
Yahusha is the power, the mighty Right Hand.
In the "***Day of Distress***", the nations will realize Who Yahusha is:

Jer / YirmeYahu 16:19-21:

"O Yahuah, my strength and my stronghold and my refuge, in the day of distress the gentiles shall come to You from the ends of The Earth and say, 'Our fathers have inherited only falsehood, futility, and there is no value in them.'

Would a man make mighty ones for himself, which are not mighty ones?

Therefore see, I am causing them to know, this time I cause them to know My hand and My might. And they shall know that

My Name is Yahuah!"

A "name" reveals the unique IDENTITY of a person or thing it is assigned to.

The *Aleph-Tau* reveals the identity of Who is speaking throughout Scripture.

Isa / YeshaYahu 52:5, 6:

"'And now, what have I here,' declares Yahuah, 'that My people are taken away for naught?

Those who rule over them make them wail,' declares Yahuah, 'and My Name is despised all day continually.

Therefore My people shall know My Name, *in that day,* for I am the One who is speaking. See, it is I.'"

"That day" has come, since we know His Name has been hidden, and we understand Who He is.

Those who "rule over" His people had been making them "wail" or "howl", because they were not speaking His Name, being deceived.

Psa 118:26: "Blessed is He who is coming in the Name of Yahuah! We shall bless you from the House of Yahuah."

And so we better understand the meaning of Yahusha's Words when He said:

Luk 13:35 "See, your House is left to you laid waste. And truly I say to you, you shall by no means see Me until *the time* comes when you say, 'Blessed is He who is coming in the Name of Yahuah!"

See Revelation 14:1

𐤉𐤄𐤅𐤔𐤏 is 𐤉𐤄𐤅𐤄

(YAHUSHA IS YAHUAH)

The ALEF-TAU, THE BEGINNING AND END

AFTER ALL, WHO CAN FORGIVE SINS?

DVD: MARRIAGE—What is it?
How it is done, and why it is so vital?
Our relationship with Yahuah through the covenant is a marriage. Marriage is the goal of Creation. Yahusha calls to His wife to return to Him.

DVD: Observances of Yahuah (Mo'edim)
Weekly and Annual Appointed Times given to us at Lev. 23 & DT. 16. ***Shadows of things to come.***
They reflect our response to His proposal, our acceptance of Him as our Husband.

DVD: WAR IN HEAVEN: A live seminar
"Who is the sovereign of esteem?"
How an **Identity Thief** has stolen the Identity of Yahuah, and installed himself on the throne of people's hearts through the False Name "**LORD**".

DVD: IMAGE OF THE BEAST
The magic symbol of the sun
Popular Symbols cherished by billions of people over the centuries have been worshipped, causing their defilement. A. Hislop and E. Bullinger during the 1800's revealed these things.

DVD: THE LAMB LEGACY:
The everlasting redemption provided by the **Blood of Yahuasha**. The Two-part work of redemption is reflected in the **two doves**, as well as the **two goats**. The first part involves death work, the second part involves life work. Yahusha is preparing His bride.

DVD: WORMWOOD:
Live seminar on Spiritual & Physical Wormwood. The words of Yahuah have been altered through centuries of institutionalized false teachings.

DVD: PERSECUTION –The price we pay for choosing to walk as Yahusha walked in this darkened world. We are told not to be shocked or overcome, but rather REJOICE, being strong and courageous because ***Yahusha is with us ALWAYS.***

Restoration of the lost tribes of Yisrael

When the prodigal son returns to the Covenant in the last days, Yahusha will return to re-gather them from the distant isles and lands where they are "captive". They are captives and need to come to their senses.

DVD: RETURN OF YAHUSHA

Direct evidence presented from Scripture on the timing of the so called "rapture" and the sudden return of Yahusha in the Day of Yahuah. Topics: Ten virgins, raising of the dead, sealing with the Name, day of darkness, harvest workers, reapers.

DVD: SYNCRETISM: THE ZODIAC STRONGHOLD

THE SOURCE OF ALL SORCERY

Worship of the host of heaven: MAZZAROTH
The old religion of Babel is a scheme of the devil, luring everyone in their pursuit of love.
Constellations/Astrology = IDOLATRY

DVD: The Real Final Solution

How do we cooperate with Yahusha in reuniting the Lost Tribes of Yisrael with the House of Yahudah? The divisions and battles over details can be overcome with humility and love. Jealousy and strife serves the Dragon. Yahusha's Will overcomes with love and peace.

DVD: Synagogue of Shatan

Is it people or doctrine?

Any place that teaches that Torah is evil must be the Synagogue of Shatan.

It is identified by its teachings. The "doctrines of demons" would naturally teach against Torah.

DVD: CHRISTMAS

The Spell of Satan's Birthday

A live seminar by Lew White into the true origin of Christmas and whose "Birthday" Dec. 25th really is. True identity of "Santa Claus" as inherited from the worship of Moloch. Why bring trees into homes and decorate them?

IS CHRISTMAS WITCHCRAFT?

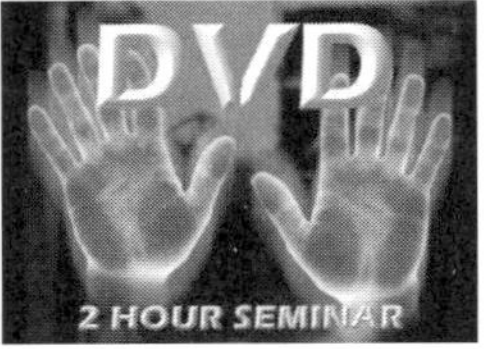

DVD: The Two Resurrections

2 hr presentation exploding the popularized **"rapture"** myth. The first resurrection: At Yahusha's Return, gathering the first-fruits (wise virgins). The second resurrection: 1000 years later, a general resurrection of both righteous and unrighteous.

DVD: White Robes live seminar

"Who are these dressed in white robes, and where did they come from?" Rev. 7:13

DVD: What is the Gospel?

It has *always* been Yisrael's COMMISSION to the nations, ***to go* and teach it.**

What is it?

DVD: THE NAME

The Key of Knowledge

An Intensive ***Hebrew letter study*** of the Name of **Yahuah** and the Name of the Mashiach, **Yahusha**. Mysteries of the Original Letters; the ALEF-TAU; the **BAAL-LORD** trick exposed!

DVD: EVOLUTION vs. Intelligent Design

A challenge for the atheist to ***listen*** — instead of speaking for a change.

Atheists have a deep-rooted need for *someone* to prove there is a Creator, and they have asked all but ONE to establish the fact.

Yahuah has words addressed to the atheist.

DVD: HUMAN TRADITIONS
— IN HIS FACE —
DO ALL RELIGIONS LEAD TO HEAVEN?
IS THAT EVEN WHERE WE ARE GOING?
ECUMENICAL MOVEMENT
INTERFAITH DIALOG, UNITED RELIGIONS (URI)

DVD: PHYSICAL EVIDENCE OF THE NAME
HIDDEN AROUND THE WORLD
ON SCROLLS, SEALS, STELAE, BULLAE, COINS, OSTRACONS

DVD: SABBATH BREACH
SUN-DAY STRONGHOLD ORIGINS
RESTORATION OF THE
SIGN OF EVERLASTING COVENANT

TORAH INSTITUTE IS ON THE INTERNET

LOOK FOR EXCITING DISCUSSIONS ON A VARIETY OF TOPICS WITH LEW WHITE AND MARK DAVIDSON

YISRAEL WAS A "SEA EMPIRE", AND LEFT "WAY-MARKS" IN MANY AREAS OF THE EARTH

THEIR **IDENTITY** HAS BEEN OBSCURED, BUT NOW THEIR DESCENDANTS ARE **AWAKENING AMONG THE NATIONS**

LEW & MARK DISCUSSING YISRAEL'S SEA EMPIRE

ORDERING GUIDE

MANY MORE ITEMS FOUND ON INTERNET:

TORAH-PROMOTING BOOKS AND VIDEOS

FOSSILIZED CUSTOMS 11TH EDITION (ILLUSTRATED)
(244 pgs) BY LEW WHITE; A MESSIANIC ISRAELITE BOOK EXPLAINING THE PAGAN ORIGINS OF CHRISTMAS, EASTER, SUN-DAY, THE CALENDAR, AND MUCH MORE. A UNIQUE OUTREACH TOOL THAT WILL ANSWER QUESTIONS YOU HAVEN'T EVEN THOUGHT TO ASK! IF YOU'D LIKE TO HAND SOMEONE SOMETHING (IN ADDITION TO THE SCRIPTURES) THAT CONTAINS EVERYTHING YOU'D LIKE TO TELL THEM, THIS WOULD BE THE BOOK. ***SIZE: 5.5" X 8.5"***
SEE TORAHZONE.NET FOR ALL PRICING

TORAH ZONE (140 pgs) BY LEW WHITE - *AN ANTHOLOGY OF ARTICLES*
A BOOK OF ARTICLES THAT COVER MANY MAJOR TOPICS FOR THOSE INTERESTED IN LEARNING ABOUT THE NARROW WAY, THE MEANING OF THE FESTIVALS OF YISRAEL, & THE EQUIPPING FOR TEACHING OTHERS.
SEE TORAHZONE.NET FOR ALL PRICING

THE RETURN OF YAHUSHA
(140 pgs) BY LEW WHITE; IS THE RAPTURE FOR REAL? WHO ARE THE ELECT? THIS BOOK DISCUSSES THE TWO WITNESSES, THE TRIBULATION, AN OVERVIEW OF THE FALL AND REDEMPTION, AND THE POSSIBILITY THAT ONE OF THE ORIGINAL APOSTLES *IS STILL ALIVE TODAY.* IN THIS BOOK THE ***SECRET OF ELOHIM*** IS REVEALED, FROM SCRIPTURE.
SEE TORAHZONE.NET FOR ALL PRICING

ORDERS BY PHONE: 502-261-9833

It occurred to me that the average **adult human brain** weighs about the same as a large cheese pizza. The difference between us and the average atheist is that we have **one ingredient** in our brain they don't have: **THE MIND OF MASHIACH.** So, to Yahuah, the atheist must not be much more than a cheese pizza with a vital ingredient missing. He is an eternal Spirit, and without Yahusha we might as well be a cheese pizza to him.

TORAH INSTITUTE
POB 436044
Louisville, KY 40253
PHONE: 502-261-9833

RESTORATION OF THE SCATTERED TRIBES OF YISRAEL TO THE COVENANT

FOSSILIZED CUSTOMS

THE PAGAN ORIGINS OF POPULAR CUSTOMS

ORDER ON-LINE FROM ANYWHERE: **torahzone.net**

YAHUSHA GAVE US A NEW COMMANDMENT:

"LOVE ONE ANOTHER AS I HAVE LOVED YOU"
Yahuchanon (John) 15:12